CURRENT
REVIEW OF
PAIN

CURRENT REVIEW OF PAIN

EDITOR: P. PRITHVI RAJ

MEDICAL DIRECTOR
NATIONAL PAIN INSTITUTE
ATLANTA, GEORGIA

1994

CURRENT MEDICINE

Managing Editor: .... Chris Baumle
Developmental Editor: .... Elizabeth Howard
Art Director: .... Paul Fennessy
Designer: .... Lisa Caro
Illustration Director: .... Larry Ward
Illustrators: ....Marie Dean, Wendy Jackelow,
      Wiesia Langenfeld, and Ann Saydlowski
Typesetting Director: .... Bill Donnelly
Production Manager: .... David Myers

ISBN: 1-878132-06-7
ISSN: 1069-5850

Printed in Korea by Sung in Printing Co., Ltd.

5 4 3 2 1

CONTRIBUTORS

CHARLES B. BERDE, MD, PHD
Pain Treatment Service
Children's Hospital
Harvard Medical School
Boston, Massachusetts

AARON CALODNEY, MD
Assistant Clinical Professor of Anesthesiology
University of Texas Health Science Center at Houston
Houston, Texas

AUGUSTO CARACENI, MD
Neurologist
Assistant, Division of Pain Therapy and Palliative Care
National Cancer Institute of Milan
Milan, Italy

MARK CHURCHER, MBBS
Honorary Consultant
Pain Relief Unit
Derriford Hospital
Plymouth, United Kingdom

SEYMOUR DIAMOND, MD
Director, Diamond Headache Clinic
Adjunct Professor of Pharmacology and Molecular Biology
The Chicago Medical School
Chicago, Illinois

RICHARD GREGG, MD
Director, University Pain Control Center
Cincinnati, Ohio

BENJAMIN W. JOHNSON, JR., MD
Vanderbilt Pain Control Center
Vanderbilt University Medical Center
Nashville, Tennessee

JENNIFER F. KELLY, PHD
National Pain Institute of Georgia
Atlanta, Georgia

TOM LORREN, LTP
Director, Restore Physical and Industrial Rehabilitation
Houston, Texas

DONALD C. MANNING, MD, PHD
Assistant Professor
Department of Anesthesiology
University of Virginia Health Sciences Center
Charlottesville, Virginia

JIANREN MAO, MD, PHD
Department of Anesthesiology
Medical College of Virginia
Richmond, Virginia

LAURENCE E. MATHER, PHD, FANZCA
Department of Anaesthesia and Pain Management
Professor of Anaesthesia and Analgesia (Research)
University of Sydney
Royal North Shore Hospital
St. Leonards NSW
Australia

DAVID J. MAYER, PHD
Department of Anesthesiology
Medical College of Virginia
Richmond, Virginia

RICHARD B. NORTH, MD
Associate Professor, Neurosurgery
Department of Neurosurgery
Johns Hopkins University School of Medicine
Baltimore, Maryland

WINSTON C.V. PARRIS, MD
Vanderbilt Pain Control Center
Vanderbilt University Medical Center
Nashville, Tennessee

DONALD D. PRICE, PHD
Department of Anesthesiology
Medical College of Virginia
Richmond, Virginia

P. PRITHVI RAJ, MBBS, FRCA, FACPM
Medical Director
National Pain Institute
Atlanta, Georgia

SRINIVASA N. RAJA, MD
Department of Anesthesiology
Johns Hopkins University Hospital
Baltimore, Maryland

RICHARD L. RAUCK, MD
Assistant Professor of Anesthesia
Director, Pain Control Center
Wake Forest University Medical Center
Winston-Salem, North Carolina

JOHN C. ROWLINGSON, MD
Professor of Anesthesiology
Director, Pain Management Center
University of Virginia School of Medicine
Charlottesville, Virginia

JERRY SCHWARZBACH, MD
Assistant Clinical Professor
University of Texas Health Science Center at Tyler
Tyler, Texas

PHILIP J. SIDDALL, MB, BS, PHD
Department of Anaesthesia and Pain Management
Senior Research Fellow, University of Sydney
Royal North Shore Hospital
St. Leonards NSW, Australia

SRIDHAR V. VASUDEVAN, MD
Clinical Professor of Physical Medicine and Rehabilitation
Medical College of Wisconsin
Brookfield, Wisconsin

VITTORIO VENTAFRIDDA, MD
Professor of Anesthesiology
Division of Pain Therapy and Palliative Care
National Cancer Institute of Milan
Milan, Italy

ROBERT T. WILDER, MD, PHD
Pain Treatment Service, Children's Hospital
Harvard Medical School
Boston, Massachusetts

ALON P. WINNIE, MD
Chairman, Department of Anesthesiology and Critical Care
Cook County Hospital
Professor of Anesthesiology
University of Illinois College of Medicine at Chicago
Chicago, Illinois

SETH M. ZEIDMAN, MD
Department of Neurosurgery
Johns Hopkins University School of Medicine
Baltimore, Maryland

CONTENTS

EDITORIAL: X
P. Prithvi Raj

CHAPTER 1: 1
NEURAL MECHANISMS
OF NORMAL AND ABNORMAL PAIN STATES
Donald D. Price, Jianren Mao, and David J. Mayer

CHAPTER 2: 17
CHARACTERISTICS, CLASSIFICATION, AND ASSESSMENT
OF ACUTE POSTOPERATIVE PAIN
P. Prithvi Raj

CHAPTER 3: 37
CLASSIFICATION AND ASSESSMENT OF CHRONIC PAIN
John C. Rowlingson

CHAPTER 4: 47
MANAGEMENT OF POSTOPERATIVE PAIN
Richard L. Rauck

CHAPTER 5: 61
REGIONAL APPROACHES
TO THE MANAGEMENT OF CHRONIC PAIN
Alon P. Winnie

CHAPTER 6: 79
SYSTEMIC APPROACHES TO THE MANAGEMENT
OF ACUTE AND CHRONIC PAIN
Philip J. Siddall and Laurence E. Mather

CHAPTER 7: 93
ACUTE PAIN IN CHILDREN
Robert T. Wilder and Charles B. Berde

CHAPTER 8: 103
GENERAL NEUROSURGICAL PROCEDURES
FOR MANAGEMENT OF CHRONIC PAIN
Seth M. Zeidman and Richard B. North

CHAPTER 9: 117
PSYCHOLOGICAL APPROACHES
TO THE MANAGEMENT OF CHRONIC PAIN

Jennifer F. Kelly

CHAPTER 10: 129
PHYSICAL REHABILITATION OF THE PAIN PATIENT

Sridhar V. Vasudevan

CHAPTER 11: 141
CHARACTERISTICS, PATHOGENESIS,
AND MANAGEMENT OF MYOFASCIAL PAIN SYNDROME

Aaron Calodney, Jerry Schwarzbach, and Tom Lorren

CHAPTER 12: 155
CANCER PAIN

Vittorio Ventafridda and Augusto Caraceni

CHAPTER 13: 179
MECHANISMS OF NEUROPATHIC PAIN

Benjamin W. Johnson and Winston C.V. Parris

CHAPTER 14: 195
DIAGNOSIS OF REFLEX SYMPATHETIC DYSTROPHY
AND THERAPEUTIC STRATEGIES BASED ON PATHOPHYSIOLOGY

Donald C. Manning, Mark Churcher, and Srinivasa N. Raja

CHAPTER 15: 209
MANAGEMENT OF PAIN CAUSED
BY ACUTE HERPES ZOSTER AND POSTHERPETIC NEURALGIA

P. Prithvi Raj

CHAPTER 16: 225
PHANTOM PAIN

Richard Gregg

CHAPTER 17: 231
MANAGEMENT OF CHRONIC HEADACHES

Seymour Diamond

Editorial *P. Prithvi Raj*

In the past year, many advances have been seen in some areas of pain management. Several questions still remain unanswered, however, and the outcome of treatment for many pain syndromes remains less than optimal. This edition of *Current Review of Pain* focuses on topics of continuing interest to pain specialists, with particular emphasis on developments that have occurred during the past year and on the personal experience of the contributing authors, with the hope of providing an in-depth summary of trends and current practices.

Recent findings about the neural mechanisms common to both normal and abnormal pain states, and the implications of this knowledge for new therapeutic approaches to the treatment of such chronic pain states, are the subject of a chapter by Drs. Donald Price, Jianren Mao, and David Mayer. Their discussion is based on the central concept that the presence of spatiotemporal characteristics in both normal and pathophysiologic pain suggests that pathophysiologic pain is caused by exaggerations or abnormal triggering of pre-existing neurophysiologic mechanisms—the same central neural mechanisms that are evoked by tissue injury. A review of the neural mechanisms associated with both pain states is linked to recent findings from animal studies that have suggested new treatment strategies. The authors provide a summary of possible excitatory central mechanisms of and pharmacologic interventions for postinjury neuropathic pain. Specifically, they suggest that chronic neuropathic pain that occurs after nerve injury may be related to an excitatory amino acid–mediated central excitatory cascade, which may be interrupted by local anesthesia or *N*-methyl-D-aspartate (NMDA) and non-NMDA antagonists and gangliosides. Excellent progress has been made to elucidate mechanisms in this area over the past few years, and we expect continued progress in the discovery of the mechanisms of complex pathophysiologic pain in the future.

Physical rehabilitation is part of the total interdisciplinary pain management program and should be used in conjunction with available surgical, pharmacologic, and psychological techniques for treating patients suffering from acute or chronic pain. Whereas physical modalities, manual therapy, and electrical stimulation often provide substantial relief for acute pain, therapeutic exercises provide a means for overall conditioning, thereby increasing the patient's physical activity and improving his or her general quality of life. The psychological aspects of these benefits, especially in patients with an incurable condition, cannot be overemphasized.

In my chapter on acute pain, I describe its characteristics. Acute pain consists of two major components—the sensory and the affective motivational components. Both of these components are regulated by neurotransmitters, the most important of which are substance P and calcitonin gene-related peptide. In addition to the neuropeptides, excitatory amino acids such as glutamate or aspartate also play a distinct role in nociceptive transmission. Excitatory amino acids are hypothesized to mediate fast nociceptive transmission, whereas neuropeptides are believed to mediate slow nociception.

One can classify pain as nociceptive, neuropathic, and psychogenic. The classification is useful in formulating a plan of treatment; however, each pain problem needs to be regarded as a unique entity requiring an individual plan.

Accurate pain measurement is of great importance in measuring the efficacy of analgesic therapy. In my chapter I point out that the visual analogue scale is a very useful pain assessment tool. The McGill Pain Questionnaire is another good tool that measures both quality and quantity of the patient's pain. This questionnaire distinguishes qualitative differences among various modes of pain therapy and provides information on the sensory, affective, and evaluative dimensions of pain.

Although the neurochemistry of pain is complex, opportunities exist for multiple sites of pain modulation. A comprehensive approach to ablate acute pain perception should include the use of nonsteroidal anti-inflammatory drugs, conduction blockade with local anesthetics and opioids, and the administration of anti-catabolic agents.

An issue that merits continued discussion is the need for a standardized classification system for chronic pain. Dr. John Rowlingson points out the need for such a taxonomy to make the pain specialist's task easier. The establishment of such a system is difficult presently because of the lack of an exact definition of pain, individual variations in patient responses, and the subjective nature of pain. Problems also arise in correct interpretation as a result of distortion through observer bias. There obviously is a need for more extensive research and better experimental models of chronic pain. Although the definition of pain by the International Association for the Study of Pain is a helpful starting point, no previously suggested organizational system has yet been proven adequate. The complex nature of chronic pain requires further elucidation of a taxonomy appropriate for universal application.

Whereas a systematic approach to assessment certainly assists in accurate diagnosis, the many factors influencing the differences in the patient's perception and presentation of pain make the development of a more universal, inclusive system extremely important for the advancement of the management of chronic pain. Energy and effort must continue to be directed toward the establishment of comprehensive taxonomic guidelines.

In his chapter, Dr. Richard Rauck points out the anesthesiologist's increasing assumption of responsibilities for the management of postoperative pain. This trend necessitates a new look at regional anesthetic techniques in the operating room, with the result that many procedures are being increasingly used. Whereas techniques such as epidural analgesia are commonly used, more work needs to be done in the following areas: development of local anesthetic agents with longer half-lives; effective liposomal encapsulation to allow increased convenient use of intercostal nerve blocks; research concerning the application and value of preemptive analgesia; development of new intraspinal opiates; study of the risks for respiratory depression and type and quality of analgesia resulting from the use of fentanyl; requirements for optimal respiratory monitoring during the use of intraspinal narcotics; and mechanisms of urinary retention in patients receiving epidural narcotics. Dr. Rauck's summary of currently used techniques sheds light on this evolving area of pain management.

Regional anesthetic nerve blocks for chronic pain have always been controversial as an efficacious means of treating chronic pain. However, these blocks have been efficacious in relieving severe and intolerable pain in patients with chronic pain. Dr. Alon Winnie summarizes current approaches for prevention of the development of chronic pain and use of neurolytic blocks for prolonged relief. As the author notes, sympathetic blocks are widely used in the treatment of acute herpes zoster and sympathetically maintained pain, along with intravenous blocks using guanethidine, bretylium, or ketorolac. Epidural injections of steroids are also widely used for the relief of radicular pain associated with herniated discs. Neurolytic blocks, *ie,* peripheral, intrathecal, epidural, and superior hypogastric plexus blocks and block of the ganglion impar, are recommended for the management of chronic malignant pain. These blocks remain controversial, however, for use in the treatment of nonmalignant pain.

Of particular interest is the description of Dr. Winnie's unguided technique for celiac plexus block. This technique makes use of a lateral position, only one needle, and much smaller volumes of phenol. According to the author this technique minimizes the dangers associated with improper needle placement or migration of the solution, minimizes adverse side effects, and reduces by half the possibility of complications. Also useful are the descriptions of modifications of celiac plexus block and superior hypogastric plexus block, as described by Dr. Steven Waldman [1,2].

Advances have been made recently in approaches to the systemic delivery of analgesics as well as in the development of new agents. The preoperative and perioperative use of analgesics and the development of pharmacokinetically designed computer-assisted infusion regimens, long-acting preparations, and drug modifications make analgesic delivery one of the most rapidly advancing areas of pain management. Many issues still remain, however. Choice of the appropriate analgesic agent and the best route of administration for the optimal therapeutic regimen is still difficult to make because pharmacokinetic and pharmacodynamic properties of analgesics vary among patients and there is a lack of well-established guidelines concerning the rate of absorption and bioavailability of drugs at different sites. Selection of agents for combination therapy requires extensive consideration of their pharmacodynamic properties.

The chapter by Drs. Philip Siddall and Laurence Mather provides a review of systemic analgesic management and highlights relevant issues of concern. As the authors remind us, despite improved techniques and pharmaceutical developments, systemic methods are still often not optimally used.

Now that it is widely accepted that infants and children do indeed perceive pain, there is certainly no excuse for inadequate pain management in this age group. Accurate measurement of pain in young children is still somewhat problematic even though several scales are now available to facilitate this assessment.

The chapter on acute pain in children by Drs. Robert Wilder and Charles Berde highlights the most commonly used treatment options, including behavioral techniques and the use of nonsteroidal anti-inflammatory drugs, opioids, and regional analgesia. Particularly helpful are the recommended dosages and troubleshooting recommendations. As the authors indicate, the importance of monitoring during acute pain management in children cannot be overemphasized.

The evolution of neurosurgical procedures and the recent development of new techniques has increased the number of pain states amenable to treatment and improved the outcome for patients undergoing treatment for chronic pain. Significant among these are improvements in neuroaugmentative procedures, which provide an important alternative to permanent ablative techniques. In their chapter, Drs. Seth Zeidman and

Richard North provide a succinct summary of anatomic, augmentative, and ablative procedures applicable for the treatment of chronic pain caused by cancer, failed back surgery, and trigeminal neuralgia. I concur with the opinion of the authors that training in pain management techniques should be part of the armamentarium of the neurosurgeon.

With the growing realization of the efficacy of a multidisciplinary approach to pain management, the role of psychological methods in dealing with pain has taken on added significance. Psychological components obviously influence the way every patient perceives and experiences pain, depending to a greater or lesser degree on the individual's psychological orientation and experience.

As Dr. Jennifer Kelly suggests, psychotherapeutic approaches such as electromyographic biofeedback, relaxation training, hypnosis, and cognitive and operant approaches provide useful adjuncts to other forms of treatment for a patient with chronic pain; however, for these approaches to be successful, the patient must actively participate. Instructing patients in methods to help alleviate discomfort and in redirecting attitudes, beliefs, and activities into more positive modes of functioning is certainly an important part of any comprehensive pain management program.

Dr. Sridhar Vasudevan points to the importance of keeping in mind both the "process" nature of rehabilitation, which actively involves patients and their families, and the use of a team approach involving several disciplines.

Skeletal muscle represents the largest organ of the body and almost half of body weight. Because of its contractile nature, this muscle is very susceptible to the stresses of daily activities and can develop trigger points causing pain and muscle spasm. Myofascial pain syndromes are extremely common and yet, because of the referred nature of the pain, are often unrecognized, delaying appropriate treatment and pain management.

As Drs. Aaron Calodney, Jerry Schwarzbach, and Tom Lorren suggest in their chapter on myofascial pain, accurate diagnosis is the most critical aspect of the management of this syndrome. It requires full patient compliance in the elimination of perpetuating factors and in adherence to a therapeutic exercise program. Education of the patient and aggressive management are of paramount importance and the management plan should be evaluated periodically for efficacy and the possible need for modification.

Cancer pain remains one of the most problematic areas of chronic pain management, and a large percentage of patients remain undertreated. Whereas this undertreatment can be attributed somewhat to a reluctance on the part of physicians to use controlled substances adequately, it can also be attributed, as Drs. Vittorio Ventafridda and Augusto Caraceni point out, to the highly individual nature of pain perception, which is influenced by the patient's past experiences and emotional state. Because experts estimate rising mortality rates for oncologic disease, cancer pain management continues to remain an area of importance.

As the authors indicate, several issues require further elucidation and investigation. There is a need for controlled efficacy studies comparing the continuous subcutaneous administration of opioids with the administration of spinal opioids, a need for the establishment of guidelines for the selection of epidural as opposed to intrathecal administration of opioids, and a need for further discussion of the efficacy of continuous infusion as opposed to intermittent boluses for spinal analgesia. Studies are needed to document the analgesic effects of tricyclic antidepressants in the treatment of cancer pain, to clarify the most efficacious treatment for opioid-resistant pain, and to compare the efficacy of technical approaches for celiac plexus block.

The need for a multidisciplinary approach toward treating the whole patient cannot be overemphasized. It is hoped that methods garnered from the growing palliative care movement will dramatically alleviate the management of pain for patients suffering from malignancies.

Several questions remain to be answered about the mechanisms of neuropathic pain, which undoubtedly accounts for the inconsistent success achieved in the management of patients with the neuropathic pain syndrome. Although we can only surmise about the mechanisms that may be responsible for the generation of neuropathic pain, I agree with Drs. Benjamin Johnson and Winston Parris that the effects of the higher centers of the brain and the highly individualized nature of the perception of pain necessitate a multidisciplinary approach. Their discussion summarizes potential mechanisms for the generation of neuropathic pain and discusses recent studies on this topic. The authors also review therapeutic strategies for managing neuropathic pain.

Reflex sympathetic dystrophy remains one of the most debilitating disorders a pain specialist has to treat. It continues to take a heavy toll in terms of suffering and rapid deterioration of quality of life for a large percentage of patients. The chapter on reflex sympathetic dystrophy by Drs. Donald Manning, Mark Churcher, and Srinvasa Raja clarifies many of the issues surrounding the terminology, pathophysiology, clinical manifestations, and management of this disorder, for which accurate diagnosis and prompt treatment are essential.

The treatment of herpes zoster remains an issue, with results from the prevention of postherpetic neuralgia poor. Distinguishing between herpes simplex and herpes zoster can be difficult. Although no single treatment has yet been found to be completely predictable in treating herpes zoster, antiviral agents are showing increasingly good results. Early treatment is an absolute necessity in an attempt to prevent development of postherpetic neuralgia.

As my discussion on this topic indicates, more needs to be learned about the mechanisms of herpes zoster and postherpetic neuralgia and their epidemiologic bases, and finding more consistently reliable methods of treatment remains an ongoing challenge. The intensity and intractability of the pain associated with postherpetic neuralgia—and the lack of an effective cure for this disorder—make accurate diagnosis and prompt, aggressive treatment of herpes zoster extremely important in the management of patients with this condition.

Phantom pain is yet another condition with only elusive success having been achieved in treatment. As for other pain syndromes, the treatment should be multidisciplinary and yet individualized for each patient. As Dr. Richard Gregg indicates, successful short-lived pain relief has been achieved in many patients with the use of calcitonin, transcutaneous electrical nerve stimulation, acupuncture, physical therapy, and medications; however, long-term positive results have been difficult to obtain. As the author suggests, the less invasive techniques should certainly be tried along with psychotherapeutic techniques, before more invasive procedures such as augmentations or ablative surgery are performed. The use of perioperative analgesia appears to offer a reduction in pain over the long term for many patients. Clearly, much work needs to be done in delineating the mechanism of and optimal management for phantom pain.

The management of chronic headache is another ongoing challenge frequently encountered by the pain specialist. In his chapter, Dr. Seymour Diamond summarizes the characteristics of pain and complaints associated with tension-type headaches caused by anxiety and depression as well as those associated with coexisting migraine and tension-type headaches. He also discusses options frequently used in the treatment of these disorders. Dr. Diamond concludes that diagnosis is essential for the initiation of appropriate therapy, that habit-forming medications should be avoided because of the chronic nature of these disorders, and that continuity of care is integral to successful treatment.

Improvements in modern techniques toward pain control continue to stimulate advances in acute, chronic, and cancer pain management. A greater understanding of physiologic and pharmacologic relationships to pain, as well as new technologies in drug delivery systems, have allowed many patients with acute and cancer pain to benefit from highly effective analgesia. Even though effective chronic pain relief is still not available and continues to be a significant problem, it is hoped that this book will increase the awareness of present shortcomings and the need for advances to be made in the future in this area. I also hope that the contents of this book will stimulate interest in practicing pain specialists to continue to search for methods of providing adequate pain relief for the thousands of patients suffering from pain.

REFERENCES

1. Lieberman RF, Waldman SD: Celiac plexus neurolysis with the modified transaortic approach. *Radiology* 1990, 175:274–276.

2. Waldman SD, Wilson WL, Kreps RD: Superior hypogastric block using a single needle and computer tomography guidance: description of a modified technique. *Reg Anes* 1991, 16:296–297.

Neural Mechanisms of Normal and Abnormal Pain States

DONALD D. PRICE, JIANREN MAO, AND DAVID J. MAYER

Pain is a normal consequence of tissue injury or intense stimuli that would produce tissue injury if maintained over time. After injury, the injury site and the region surrounding it become a source of ongoing "normal" pain. It is our usual experience that the pain from intense stimulation or injury diminishes as healing progresses, and it disappears when healing is complete. Another type of pain occurs as a consequence of dysfunction of the peripheral or central nervous system, usually as a result of damaged nerves or damaged regions of the spinal cord or brain. This latter type of pain is known as pathophysiologic pain.

In recent years, the relationships between normal and pathophysiologic pain have become a topic of intense interest and have led to possible new therapeutic approaches to the treatment of some types of chronic pain conditions. This chapter discusses these new findings and their implications. Neural mechanisms that subserve the transmission of nociceptive information, including the hyperalgesia and spontaneous pain that commonly follow tissue injury, are briefly reviewed. Evidence is presented indicating that some of these normal pain mechanisms become exaggerated or abnormally triggered in pathophysiologic pain states. Pathophysiologic pain related to injury of peripheral nerves is emphasized, although it is recognized that various forms of pathophysiologic pain also result from damage to various central nervous system pathways and regions. Finally, the relationships between this new understanding of neural mechanisms of both normal and pathophysiologic pain and new therapeutic directions for possible treatment of neuropathic pain are discussed.

NORMAL PAIN MECHANISMS

Three spatiotemporal characteristics of pain exist that are present during both normal and pathophysiologic pain [1,2]. The body area within which pain is perceived often increases as pain intensity increases, a phenomenon known as radiation. Radiation sometimes occurs even when the painful stimulus is punctate, and so it is likely to at least partly depend on the central spread of neural activity within the spinal cord or brain.

Pain also often outlasts the stimulus that evokes it and sometimes even the peripheral neural impulses that trigger it. Again, central mechanisms exist that produce maintained responses long after the arrival of the peripheral nociceptive input to the spinal cord.

Finally, repeated stimulation with the same nociceptive stimulus sometimes evokes a slow temporal summation of pain intensity, even though there is no progressive increase in the peripheral input provided by each successive nociceptive stimulus. The slow temporal summation has been shown to depend on central mechanisms.

All three of these spatiotemporal characteristics have been demonstrated for specific types of experimental pain and thus occur in normal pain-free human subjects. If that is the case, then their presence in pathologic chronic pain states may represent exaggerations or abnormal triggering of preexisting neurophysiologic mechanisms. Thus, it would be instructive to review the neural basis for these spatiotemporal characteristics.

Radiation

The spatial spread of painful sensations can be observed both in the case of experimental and clinical pain and, during intense pain, extends over dermatomes rostral and caudal to the focus of stimulation [1,3•]. Radiation is a predicted consequence of the way in which input from primary nociceptive afferents is transmitted to neurons of the dorsal horn and the way in which this input is dispersed over several spinal segments by means of propriospinal connections (Fig. 1-1) [2,4,5]. The intensity of painful stimulation at a given locus on the body is encoded by frequency of impulse discharge in primary nociceptive afferents and by the numbers of activated primary afferents. Unless the stimulus area increases, however, the progressive recruitment of primary afferent nociceptive neurons with increasing stimulus intensity is limited by the small receptive field sizes of primary nociceptive afferents [2,4] (< 1.0 cm^2). On the other hand, the spinal cord dorsal horn neurons on which primary nociceptive neurons synapse have a neuroanatomic-neurophysiologic mechanism for spatially dispersing the input arriving from primary nociceptive neurons (Fig. 1-1).

Part of the neuroanatomic basis for spatial dispersion of nociceptive input within the dorsal horn is that its deeper layers, laminae V–VI, contain neurons that extend propriospinal interconnections between several spinal cord segments, as is illustrated in Figure 1-1 [5]. These interconnections comprise the anatomic basis for progressive recruitment of dorsal horn neurons with increasingly painful stimulus intensities and for the spatial radiation of pain that is perceived in some types of experimental and clinical pain [6].

Nociceptive neurons of laminae V–VI, many of which are cells of origin of the spinothalamic or spinoreticular tracts, have physiologic characteristics that reflect their role in central spatial recruitment and radiation of pain. The most predominant type of nociceptive neuron in this region is the wide-dynamic-range (WDR) neuron. It is named as such because it responds differentially over a wide range of stimulus intensities ranging from very gentle to distinctly noxious levels and because it encodes painful stimulus intensities and very small differences in painful stimulus intensities with extreme accuracy [2,4]. These physiologic characteristics reflect, in part, the fact that various types of nonnociceptive as well as nociceptive primary afferents synaptically converge on these WDR neurons, as shown in Figure 1-2.

The receptive fields of WDR neurons reflect the direct convergence of these primary afferents and also the extensive propriospinal interconnections within this region (laminae V–VI) of the spinal gray matter. Thus,

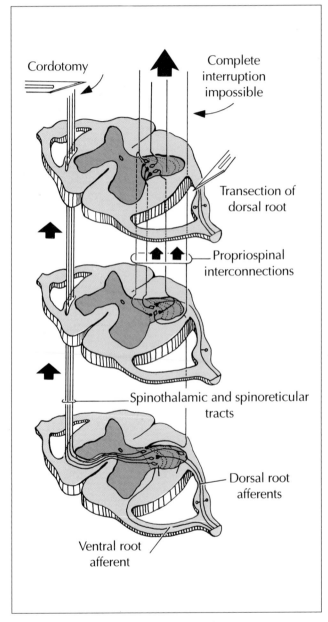

Figure 1-1 The anatomic role of propriospinal interconnections in ascending spinal pathways subserving pain. Dorsal horn neurons of laminae I and V form the origin of spinothalamic and spinoreticular pathways. Propriospinal neurons with ascending and descending interconnections provide some input to sensory projection neurons. This input could provide an alternate means of channeling nociceptive input to the brain, even after interruption of the spinothalamic tract.

as indicated schematically in Figure 1-3, WDR neurons usually have a small receptive field zone wherein gentle touch, firm pressure, and noxious pinch evoke progressively higher impulse frequencies [2,4,6]. These small zones are usually surrounded by much larger zones in which only intense and often painful stimuli are capable of evoking impulse discharge (Fig. 1-3). It is these large zones, which often extend across dermatomes, that reflect the propriospinal interconnections between several spinal segments. Given these receptive field characteristics of WDR neurons and the general somatotopic organization of these neurons within the spinal cord, a painful stimulus would be expected to activate more WDR neurons than a nonpainful stimulus.

Furthermore, there is increasing evidence that increasing stimulus intensity within the painful range (*eg*, 45°–51° C) progressively recruits more WDR neurons, and this recruitment occurs over an extensive rostral-caudal distance along the spinal cord [6,7•]. This rostral-caudal recruitment is likely to be related to radiation of pain that is seen clinically and can be demonstrated experimentally. The recruitment of increasing numbers of WDR neurons is likely to be a critically important factor in the actual encoding of perceived intensity of pain, since there is both earlier [6,8] and more recent [9•] evidence

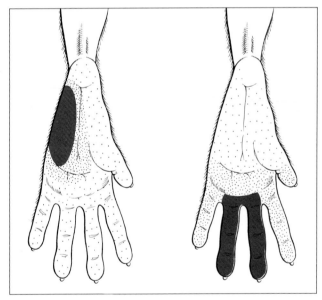

Figure 1-2 Typical receptive field organization of a wide-dynamic-range neuron based on actual receptive field maps of two different wide-dynamic-range spinothalamic tract neurons in an anesthetized monkey [6]. The central black portions are those in which stimuli ranging from very gentle to noxious levels evoke progressive increases in impulse discharge frequency. The more peripheral regions of the receptive fields are less sensitive, responding differentially only to pressure and pinch (*heavily stippled*) or to pinch only (*lightly stippled*).

that pain intensity is encoded by *both* the impulse frequencies and numbers of dorsal horn neurons activated.

After-responses and Slow Temporal Summation

Stimulation of nociceptive receptors, which are innervated by A-δ and C-primary afferent neurons, often leads to painful sensations that long outlast the activation of the receptors themselves and even the arrival of the slowest impulses in primary nociceptive afferent axons. At least part of the basis for these painful "aftersensations" are after-responses of WDR and nociceptive-specific neurons of the dorsal horn. Synchronous brief stimulation of A-δ and C-primary nociceptive afferents leads to prolonged impulse discharges in spinothalamic WDR and in some nociceptive-specific neurons that respond nearly exclusively to noxious stimuli [2,4]. Since these prolonged responses long outlast the responses of the primary nociceptive afferent neurons, they are dependent on long-duration central processes within the circuitry of the dorsal horn and on long-duration neurotransmitter action and effects of neuromodulator substances [10,11••,12•,13••].

A phenomenon that is similar to pain-related after-responses and may even involve the same mechanisms is that of slow temporal summation of second pain and its associated slow temporal summation of C-afferent–evoked responses within the dorsal horn of the spinal cord [2,3•,14]. This phenomenon has been studied in detail, both in electrophysiologic studies of the dorsal horn [6,13••,15,16] and in psychophysic studies of first and second pain [2,3•,14]. These phenomena are strikingly similar to slow temporal summation of pathophysiologic pain, observed in studies of postherpetic neuralgia [1], trigeminal neuralgia [17], and reflex sympathetic dystrophy [18•,19,20•]. When a single

brief nociceptive stimulus is applied to the hand or foot, the resultant experience is often that of a *first* pricking pain, followed 1.0 to 1.5 seconds later (depending on conduction distance) by a second burning, throbbing, or aching pain [2,14].

Several characteristics of second pain show remarkable parallels to the responses of spinothalamic tract neurons to similar synchronous stimulation of C-nociceptive afferents [2,6]. First, similar to the double pain phenomenon, synchronous stimulation of A-δ and C afferents reliably evokes a brief-latency, high-frequency impulse discharge followed by a long-latency (attributable to C-afferent conduction of impulses) discharge in the same spinothalamic tract neuron [6]. Second, both the second pain and the long-latency impulse discharge progressively increase in magnitude if the brief stimulus is repeated at or more often than once every 3 seconds (Fig. 1-4). Such slow temporal summation does not occur in the case of first pain or the brief-latency discharge of spinothalamic tract neurons. Finally, this slow temporal summation can only be evoked by C-nociceptive afferents and is never evoked by stimulation of A-β mechanoreceptive afferents in normal pain-free individuals [3••,6]. In fact, A-β input has an inhibitory influence on second pain and other types of pain in normal pain-free subjects, as is shown in Figure 1-5.

Both the perceived magnitude of second pain and the long-latency C-afferent–evoked impulse discharges of dorsal horn nociceptive neurons increase after blockade of impulses in A afferents (Fig. 1-5, for second pain). This enhancement is likely to be related to the reduction of the inhibitory influence of low-threshold A-β mechanoreceptive afferents and is highly relevant to some forms of pathophysiologic pain. These types of interactions are predicted consequences of the gate control theory of pain [21].

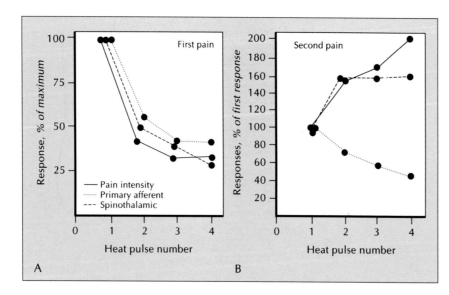

Figure 1-3 Repetitive heat pulses produce different effects on first and second pain. Repeating a 51° C heat pulse produced a progressive decrement in the neural responses of A-δ primary afferents and the brief-latency responses of spinothalamic tract neurons, as well as the judged intensity of first pain (*panel A*). However, these same stimulus conditions produced very different results for second pain (*panel B*). In this case, only the long-latency primary C-afferent activity decreased with repetitive stimulation. Long-latency responses of spinothalamic neurons and second pain progressively increased in magnitude. Apparently, a central dorsal horn neural mechanism exists for amplifying second pain with repetitive noxious stimuli.

Both prolonged impulse discharges evoked by A-δ and C-nociceptive afferents, and slow temporal summation evoked by impulses in C-polymodal nociceptive afferents have been recorded in neurons of layers I and II of the superficial dorsal horn and in neurons of the deep (layers V and VI) dorsal horn [2,6]. These neurons include spinothalamic tract and other sensory projection neurons as well as interneurons that directly receive synaptic connections from primary C-nociceptive afferents and transmit this information to spinothalamic tract neurons of layer I and possibly layer V. Thus, the neural mechanisms that produce prolonged discharges and C-afferent–induced temporal summation exist at the first synapse in nociceptive afferent pathways.

Neurotransmitter Mechanisms of Slow Temporal Summation, Expanded Receptive Fields, and Central Sensitization

As part of the inflammatory response to tissue injury, the inflamed area displays primary hyperalgesia, whereas secondary hyperalgesia occurs in much larger areas surrounding the inflamed tissue [22•,23]. Primary and secondary hyperalgesia are considered to be mediated by changes in both the peripheral nervous system and the spinal cord. Inflammation induces the release of chemical mediators such as histamine, prostaglandins, bradykinin, and substance P, and these mediators in turn produce reduced thresholds, exaggerated responses to suprathreshold nociceptive stimuli, and tonic impulse

discharges in otherwise silent nociceptors [22•]. Tonic input from nociceptive afferents, particularly C afferents, is thought to lead to central facilitation through the slow temporal summation mechanism described above [13••,22•]. The latter, in turn, leads to ongoing impulse discharges and expanded receptive fields of dorsal horn nociceptive neurons [22•,24]. Given the role of receptive field size in neuronal recruitment described above, expanded receptive fields would mean that a nociceptive stimulus would activate even more central neurons than would normally occur, leading to exaggerated pain and exaggerated spatial radiation of the painful sensation. Expanded receptive fields and sensitization of dorsal horn nociceptive neurons is likely to be at least part of the basis for secondary hyperalgesia, which is reflected by zones of skin or other tissue in which innocuous stimuli cause pain (allodynia) and in which mildly noxious stimuli cause exaggerated pain (hyperalgesia). C-afferent–evoked temporal summation and central facilitation appears integral to neural mechanisms underlying spontaneous pain and hyperalgesia that occurs after tissue injury. Therefore, neurotransmitter and intracellular mechanisms of this slow temporal summation have become areas of intense research interest in recent years.

Within the past several years, evidence has accumulated that indicates that prolonged after-responses and slow temporal summation of C-afferent–evoked responses of dorsal horn nociceptive neurons are mediat-

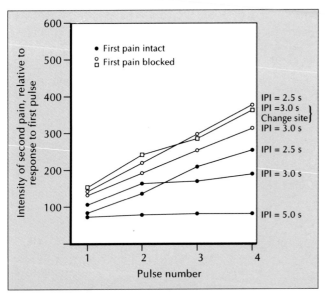

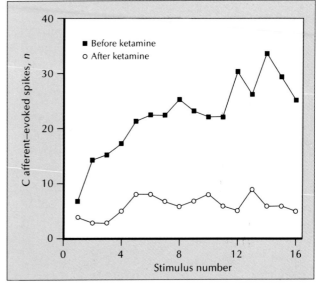

Figure 1-4 Relative intensity of second pain in response to trains of four heat pulses whose interpulse intervals (IPIs) were fixed at 5.0, 3.0, or 2.5 seconds, shown at *right. Open symbols* indicate the condition wherein first pain is selectively blocked. *Solid symbols* indicate the condition wherein first pain is intact. Summation occurs with IPIs of 3.0 and 2.5 seconds before and during blockade of first pain.

Figure 1-5 Slow temporal summation of C-afferent–induced impulse discharges is potently reduced by ketamine (2 mg/kg), an *N*-methyl-D-aspartate antagonist. The number of impulses discharged per C-afferent volley by a wide-dynamic-range neuron is plotted during a train of repetitive electrical nerve stimuli at C-afferent strength before and after systemic administration of ketamine.

ed by the co-release of glutamate and substance P and their respective activation of *N*-methyl-*D*-aspartate (NMDA) and neurokinin 1 and 2 receptors, leading to prolonged depolarizations [11••,12•,15,16]. Prolonged depolarization of dorsal horn neurons results from microiontophoresis of these agents [16,25] as well as from electrical stimulation of C afferents within dorsal roots or peripheral nerve *in vitro* spinal cord slice preparations [11••]. Furthermore, both substance P and NMDA receptor antagonists have been shown to powerfully block prolonged depolarizations evoked in dorsal horn neurons in *in vitro* preparations and to block the slow temporal summation evoked by electrical stimulation of C afferents in *in vitro* preparations [11••,12•,16]. The potent inhibition by ketamine, a noncompetitive NMDA antagonist, of C-afferent–evoked temporal summation of impulse discharges of a dorsal horn neuron is shown in Figure 1-6. Similar to this effect of an NMDA antagonist on slow temporal summation, substance P antagonists have been shown to selectively attenuate C-afferent but not A-afferent–evoked responses of dorsal horn neurons of the rat [10].

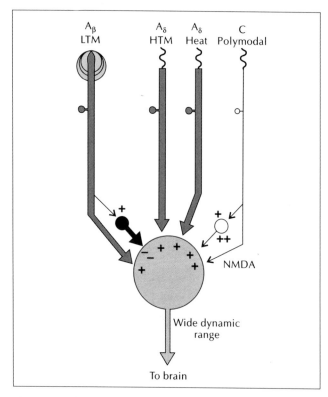

Figure 1-6 Normal nociceptive transmission mechanisms within the spinal dorsal horn. Sensory transmission neuron (*eg,* spinothalamic tract neuron) is designated by *large circle* and *arrow,* facilitatory interneuron by *small open circle* and *plus signs,* and inhibitory interneuron by *filled circle* and *minus signs.* HTM—high-threshold mechanoreceptive afferent; LTM—low-threshold mechanoreceptive afferent.

However, substance P activation of neurokinin receptors and glutamate activation of NMDA receptors may occur in concert to provide the necessary events for slow temporal summation of C-afferent–evoked depolarization and impulse discharges [11••]. The NMDA receptor remains inactive under physiologic concentrations of Mg^{2+} and even in the presence of released glutamate. In the presence of prolonged substance P–evoked depolarization, however, the depolarization could be of sufficient magnitude to remove the voltage-dependent Mg^{2+} block of the NMDA receptor, allowing the agonist action of glutamate to take effect on NMDA receptors.

C-nociceptive afferent–induced slow temporal summation leads to central sensitization of dorsal horn nociceptive neurons that is manifested as elevation in their spontaneous discharge frequencies, expansion of their receptive fields, and exaggerated responses to mechanical and thermal somatosensory stimuli. These neural mechanisms, in turn, are likely to be manifested behaviorally as allodynia and hyperalgesia. The expansion of receptive fields is likely to result in increased stimulus-evoked pain intensity and abnormally great spatial radiation of pain, if perceived pain intensity and radiation are functions of the number of central spinal neurons responding to a stimulus. Expanded receptive fields, increased spontaneous discharge, and increased impulse frequency responses are likely to operate in concert to cause these painful symptoms.

Inflammatory pains represent a normal pain condition under which the above mechanisms are manifested. For example, subcutaneous carrageenan injection into the hindpaw of a rat produces a hyperalgesic state evidenced by both thermal and mechanical hyperalgesia and some behaviors indicative of spontaneous pain [22•]. C-polymodal nociceptive afferents innervating the inflamed area evoked by carrageenan injection exhibit spontaneous activity [22•,24] and such activity is very likely to produce temporal summation and central facilitation within the dorsal horn. It is important to point out that C-polymodal nociceptive afferents do not normally exhibit spontaneous impulse discharges unless they have become sensitized by nociceptive stimuli [26].

A critical test of whether C-afferent–induced activation of NMDA receptors and temporal summation of C-evoked impulse discharges in spinal neurons is involved in such mechanisms of inflammatory pain is to attempt to antagonize the induced hyperalgesia by an NMDA antagonist. Yamamoto and coworkers [27••] carried out such a test in rats whose right hindpaws were injected with carrageenan. Using a radiant heat thermal test, the mean paw withdrawal latency for the carrageenan-injected paw was 5 to 6 seconds less than that of the untreated paw. Intrathecal (spinal) administration of MK-801, a noncompetitive NMDA antagonist, increased paw withdrawal latencies of the injected paw to the level of the untreated paw in a dose-dependent manner. Intrathecal MK-801 had no effect on the uninjected paw, indicating that this NMDA antagonist was not an analgesic in the conventional sense; it only eliminated the hyperalgesia.

In contrast, intrathecal morphine increased the paw withdrawal latencies of both the inflamed and normal hindpaws in parallel and did not change the difference in scores between the two hindpaws, a pattern of effects consistent with the known analgesic effects of morphine. When MK-801 and morphine were given together, an additive effect was observed between the antihyperalgesic effect of MK-801 and the conventional analgesic effect of morphine. This suggests that the combination of an NMDA antagonist and an opiate could be a powerful new approach to treating various types of pain, particularly inflammatory pain. Consistent with this behavioral study, intrathecal or systemic administration of the NMDA antagonist MK-801 has recently been found to reverse the expansion of receptive fields of spinal dorsal horn nociceptive neurons produced by carrageenan [28•].

Thus far, neural mechanisms subserving "normal" pain have been discussed and these are summarized in a diagram in Figure 1-2. This diagram indicates that different functional types of primary afferent neurons make synaptic contact with wide dynamic range neurons of the dorsal horn. Brief excitation is evoked in this central sensory transmission neuron by impulses in all of these types of primary afferent neurons. Excitation followed by inhibition is evoked by large, fast conduction A-β mechanoreceptive afferents and the A-β–evoked inhibition has figured prominently in major theories of pain mechanisms, particularly the gate control theory [21]. However, the multiple central actions of primary nociceptive afferents have been elucidated in much greater detail since the gate control theory. First, impulses in nociceptive afferents are now known to evoke both brief high-intensity excitation followed by a lower intensity prolonged impulse discharge [2]. However, continuous input over C-polymodal nociceptive afferents but not other types of nociceptive afferents additionally evokes slow temporal summation by activation of NMDA receptors and by release of neuromodulators such as substance P (Fig. 1-2). As discussed above, these latter mechanisms are the basis for centrally mediated hyperalgesia that occurs in persistent pain states such as inflammatory pain that follows tissue injury. This hyperalgesia is a normal consequence of injury and subsides with healing of the injured tissue.

PATHOPHYSIOLOGIC PAIN MECHANISMS

It has been known for a long time that injured tissue results in spontaneous pain, hyperalgesia, and allodynia; it has been known for over 20 years that injury-induced sensitization of primary afferent nociceptive neurons accompanies and is the peripheral cause of these phenomena [2,14,22•,26,29]. More recently, it has become evident that tissue injury is also normally followed by increased responsiveness of nociceptive neurons of the spinal cord [17,22•,30] and in other regions of the central nervous system [31,32•]. The following discussion reviews even more recent evidence that at least some types of pathophysiologic pains caused by nerve injury represent exaggerated or abnormally triggered expressions of the same central neural mechanisms that are evoked by tissue injury.

The Role of Damaged Peripheral Nerves in Persistent Pain

Similar to tissue injury itself, damaged nerves can become a source of ongoing input from primary nociceptive afferents, and there are multiple ways this can take place. Damaged peripheral nerves sometimes result in an abnormal sensitization of primary nociceptive afferents manifested as spontaneous impulse discharge, lowered thresholds, and exaggerated responses to suprathreshold nociceptive stimuli. This sensitization, however, is abnormal in the sense that it is divorced from its usual association with injured tissues.

One common way that sensitization of primary nociceptive afferents of injured nerves can take place is by acquiring an abnormal sensitivity to norepinephrine and hence to activity in sympathetic efferent neurons. For example, it has been shown that cutaneous C-nociceptive afferents that survive a partial nerve injury acquire noradrenergic sensitivity and are subsequently more easily sensitized by tissue injury [33••]. A more recent report indicates that selective damage to sympathetic efferents evokes the acquisition of sensitivity to noradrenaline in C-nociceptive afferents [34]. The regenerating sprouts of damaged nerves also acquire adrenergic sensitivity. Recent demonstrations of these specific mechanisms in animal models are consistent with the sympathetically maintained pains of reflex sympathetic dystrophy, causalgia, and possibly postherpetic neuralgia.

Besides the development of adrenergic sensitivity, there are other factors that can contribute to sensitization or continuous impulse discharges in primary afferent axons of damaged nerves. Transected nerves form sprouts that end in neuromas that develop exquisite sensitivity to mechanical stimuli. Ectopic discharges often arise from regenerating sprouts and neuromas and from dorsal root ganglion cells related to the damaged nerves [35–39]. Other possibilities include ephapses, wherein abnormal electrical connections and transfer of impulses occur between adjacent axons within damaged nerves, and extra "reflected" impulses in axons that are focally demyelinated [40••,41]. Clearly, there are multiple mechanisms possible whereby damaged nerves lead to tonic input over nociceptive as well as nonnociceptive afferents. Some of these depend on sympathetic efferent activity and some do not, relating to particular instances of sympathetically maintained and sympathetically independent pain, respectively.

Recent studies using animal models of neuropathic pain, as well as psychophysic studies of patients with neuropathic pain, provide evidence for the crucial role of tonic input from nociceptive afferents in maintaining the persistent pain and sensory abnormalities present in such diseases. This tonic input occurs in an animal model of neuropathic pain produced by loosely ligating the common sciatic nerve of the rat [42]. A progression of anatomical and functional changes occur in the nerve over the days following nerve ligation. First, the large A-β afferents cease to conduct impulses past the ligated region of the nerve and, second, spontaneous impulse discharges develop first in slow conducting A-δ afferents and then in C-polymodal nociceptive afferents [41,43•]. Many of these spontaneously active axons are likely to be nociceptive. That such spontaneous activity dynamically maintains the ongoing symptoms of hyperalgesia and spontaneous pain-related behaviors in these rats can be appreciated by the fact that local anesthetic block of the sciatic nerve reverses these symptoms for 24 hours after the block and hence even after the duration of action of the local anesthetic itself [44•,45••]. A similar interruption of pain symptoms in human neuropathic pain patients occurs with anesthetic block of the nerve related to the painful region and in some patients with anesthetic block of sympathetic efferents innervating the affected region [19,20•,37,46].

Central Pathophysiologic Pain Mechanisms Maintained by Tonic Primary Nociceptive Afferent Input

Because there are multiple ways that damaged peripheral nerves can become a source of tonic input from nociceptive as well as other types of primary afferents, and because similar tonic input occurs during inflammatory pain states, one might expect some general similarities between symptoms of inflammatory pain and neuropathic pain. Indeed, neuropathic pain may reflect dysfunctional expressions of the same processes that occur during persistent inflammatory pain. This idea is supported by the general observation that both inflammatory pain and neuropathic pain are characterized by the presence of hyperalgesia, allodynia, and ongoing "spontaneous" pain. However, recent psychophysic studies of neuropathic pain patients support this general observation and extend it by demonstrating the diversity of detailed sensory characteristics of neuropathic pain [19,20•]. Some of these sensory characteristics extend beyond those which are usually found in persistent inflammatory pain.

Studies of neuropathic pain patients and studies using animal models of neuropathic pain have both shown that these neuropathic conditions are characterized by zones of skin in which heat hyperalgesia is present and larger zones in which mechanical hyperalgesia is present. For example, the chronic constrictive nerve injury rat model of Bennett and Xie [42] shows heat hyperalgesia on the foot related to the injured nerve and mechanical hyperalgesia on both hindpaws [47]. Mechanical allodynia also occurs in skin territories outside those innervated by the injured sciatic nerve in this same model [48]. Zones of hyperalgesia and allodynia that extend well beyond the territory of the injured nerve clearly indicate the likelihood of altered central processing dynamically maintained by ongoing nociceptor input. Further evidence for this likelihood comes from experiments on patients who have one or more foci of unusually high sensitivity and areas of allodynic and hyperalgesic skin that are spatially remote from these small foci [49•]. Local anesthesia of these small foci was found to eliminate ongoing pain and allodynia and hyperalgesia in areas of skin spatially remote from the local injection of anesthetics.

The sensory symptoms that are maintained by tonic nociceptor input are diverse among neuropathic pain patients and at the same time their detailed analysis reveals important central mechanisms of these persistent pain states. Two recent studies have characterized three sensory abnormalities in patients with a diagnosis of reflex sympathetic dystrophy, the extent to which the three abnormalities were associated with each other, and the extent to which these three abnormalities are associated with the intensity of spontaneous pain [19,20•]. The three sensory abnormalities included heat-induced hyperalgesia, low-threshold A-β–mediated or high-threshold mechanical allodynia, and slow temporal summation of mechanical allodynia. These three sensory abnormalities occurred to widely varying extents among the 31 patients tested, although all patients perceived normally innocuous mechanical stimuli as painful.

For some of these patients, slow temporal summation of burning pain occurred when gentle mechanical stimuli or electrical stimulation of A-β afferents were applied at rates of once per three seconds, as shown in Figure 1-7. For other patients, slow temporal summation occurred only with more intense but normally nonpainful mechanical stimuli. Still other patients did not exhibit slow temporal summation with repetitive stimuli. Both mechanical allodynia and slow temporal summation of allodynia were completely or nearly completely reversed by anesthetic blockade of sympathetic ganglia in those patients with reflex sympathetic dystrophy tested, indicating that these sensory abnormalities were dynamically maintained by sympathetically driven nociceptor input.

Slow temporal summation of mechanical allodynia, particularly that induced by stimulation of A-β afferents, is abnormal because such types of stimuli do not evoke pain in pain-free subjects nor in these same pain patients when such stimuli are delivered to homologous contralateral pain-free zones. Abnormal slow temporal summation of mechanical allodynia may represent an exaggeration or abnormal triggering of physiologic mechanisms that already exist in normal pain-free individuals. Such mechanisms can be demonstrated in the latter by temporal summation of experimentally induced second pain (Fig. 1-4), as described earlier.

Thus, under some pathologic conditions after nerve injury, A-β input must somehow gain access to and trigger the same NMDA receptor–slow temporal summation mechanism that is normally activated by C-afferent stimulation. In other pathologic conditions, sensitized nociceptors themselves are likely to be the direct proximal cause of the slow temporal summation of mechanical allodynia.

Mechanical allodynia and slow temporal summation of allodynia may well be integrally related to the patients ongoing "spontaneous" pain. This relationship could occur if continuous input from A-β low-threshold afferents (evoked in the normal course of mechanical stimulation from walking, sitting or even contact with clothes) activated slow temporal summation of a type of burning, aching, or throbbing pain that built up slowly and dissipated slowly over time. This possibility was explicitly tested by comparing intensities of ongoing pain between patients who demonstrated slow temporal summation versus those who did not [20•]. The former had significantly higher intensities of ongoing pain (mean = 7.0 on visual analogue pain scale) than the latter (mean = 4.0 on visual analogue pain scale). Therefore, exaggerated or abnormally triggered mechanisms of slow temporal summation are likely to form at least part of the basis of persistent pain that sometimes follows nerve injury.

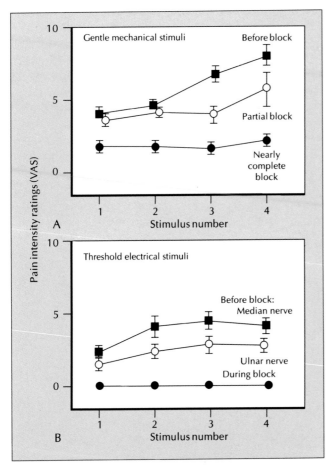

Figure 1-7 Pain intensity ratings of a patient with sympathetically maintained pain in response to trains of stimuli likely to activate A-β afferents. These ratings were made before and during successful sympathetic blocks. (*Panel A*) Slow temporal summation of burning pain in response to trains of very gentle mechanical stimuli, and its attenuation by sympathetic block. (*Panel B*) Slow temporal summation of pain in response to transcutaneous electrical stimulation of A-β afferents, and its attenuation by sympathetic block.

SPECIFIC NEURONAL AND INTRACELLULAR MECHANISMS OF NEUROPATHIC PAIN

There are two general mechanisms that may account for the pathologic pain states just described and they are not mutually exclusive. They are illustrated schematically in Figure 1-8. The essential abnormality of the first mechanism, indicated in Figure 1-8A, lies in the circuitry that controls the responses of WDR transmission neurons to A-β input, as proposed previously [20•]. The dorsal horn circuitry that generates A-β low-threshold–evoked inhibition (pre or postsynaptic or both) is deficient or absent, as is indicated by the loss of inhibitory interneuron function shown in Figure 1-8A. This absence is evident in neuropathic pain patients in whom high-frequency, low-intensity transcutaneous electrical nerve stimulation (HF-TENS) within the pathologic zone evokes not the usual reduction of pain but pain itself. The absence of A-β–evoked inhibition in the spinal dorsal horn of rats who are likely to have neuropathic pain has been verified in several ways, including the demonstration of a loss of A-β–evoked presynaptic inhibition [50•] as well as the demonstration of degeneration of small neurons in the substantia gelatinosa [51,52]. The loss of inhibitory mechanisms could occur as a result of tonic input from nociceptive afferents and excitotoxic release of glutamate which, in turn, results in dysfunction of small inhibitory interneurons (Fig. 1-8A). The loss of inhibition then could result in an exaggeration of the excitatory effects of A-β afferents and hence A-β allodynia.

The essential abnormality of the second mechanism involves development of ongoing impulse discharge in nociceptive afferents, particularly C-polymodal afferents, and an exaggeration of their central effects as a result of central sensitization, as is indicated in Figure 1-8B. Some of the details of this mechanism have already been described in the discussion of central mechanisms of hyperalgesia that occurs during inflammatory pain. If both of these general central mechanisms are not mutually exclusive, then either or both may coexist in the same patient and could partly explain the heterogeneity

of pain symptoms in neuropathic pain patients. There is even the possibility that both mechanisms contribute to the same symptom. For example, loss of A-β–mediated inhibitory mechanisms and excitotoxic-induced sensitization of WDR neurons by tonic input from nociceptors could work in concert to produce A-β allodynia.

Electrophysiologic recordings of spinothalamic neurons in animal models of neuropathic pain show important parallels to the sensory abnormalities described above for neuropathic pain patients. Recent studies by Palecek and coworkers [53••,54••] show that spinothalamic tract neurons of both rats and monkeys, particularly WDR neurons, increase their spontaneous activity and become hyperresponsive to innocuous brushing, noxious heating, and cooling of the skin as a result of an experimentally produced peripheral neuropathy. These changes are consistent with A-β allodynia, and thermal hyperalgesia and thermal allodynia in the case of cooling, all of which are observed to varying degrees in neuropathic pain patients. Consistent with these electrophysiologic studies of single neurons, metabolic mapping of elevated neural activity in the rat chronic constrictive injury model [55•,56•] shows that the largest increase in activity occurs in spinal cord laminae V–VI, a region of highest concentration of

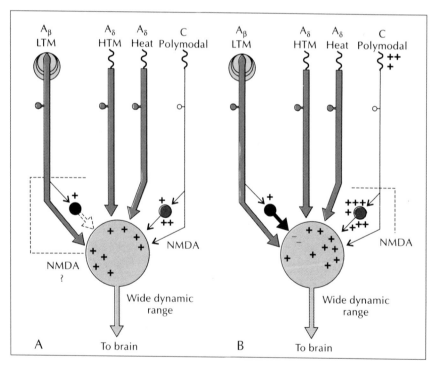

Figure 1-8 Pathophysiologic mechanisms of nociceptive transmission within the dorsal horn. The different types of neurons are designated in the same way as in Figure 1-6. (A) Loss of inhibitory mechanisms.
(B) Exaggeration or prolongation of neural plastic increases in excitability initiated by excitatory amino acid receptor activation (N-methyl-D-aspartate [NMDA] and metabotropic receptors) and their intracellular consequences. HTM—high-threshold mechanoreceptive afferent; LTM—low-threshold mechanoreceptive afferent.

WDR neurons [2,4]. The spatial distribution of this elevated activity extended over considerable rostral-caudal (L1–L5), dorsal-ventral (laminae I–VII), and medial-lateral distances, consistent with the idea that pathophysiologic pain involves spatial recruitment mechanisms that extend even beyond that which occurs in normal pain and with the extensive spatial radiation of pain sensation that occurs in neuropathic pain patients [1,57].

INDICATIONS FOR NEW DIRECTIONS IN PHARMACOLOGIC THERAPY FOR NEUROPATHIC PAIN

The idea expressed earlier that NMDA excitotoxic mechanisms are at least part of the basis for slow temporal summation and central sensitization that occurs in neuropathic pain has resulted in studies of behavioral and pharmacologic evaluations of pain-related behaviors in rats with chronic constrictive injury of the sciatic nerve [44•,45••,58•,59•,60,61•–63•]. Results of these studies indicate that thermal hyperalgesia and spontaneous pain behaviors are attenuated by preinjury and postinjury spinal cord (intrathecal) treatment with NMDA [45••,58•,61•–63•] or non-NMDA glutamate

antagonists [60] or with GM1 ganglioside [44•,59•,64••], an intracellular inhibitor of protein kinase C translocation and activation (Fig. 1-9) [64••]. Translocation of protein kinase C from the cytosol to the neuronal membrane and its consequent activation is an intracellular consequence of NMDA receptor activation and is a likely critical step in the long-term increases in neuronal excitability that occur in excitotoxic-induced central sensitization [64••]. In both the cases of NMDA receptor antagonist and ganglioside administration, the therapeutic effects outlast the treatments by several days, as is shown in Figure 1-9. Consistent with the above proposed mechanism of GM1 ganglioside, a subsequent study showed that dorsal horn levels of membrane-bound protein kinase C reliably increased in rats with painful neuropathy induced by chronic constrictive injury (CCI) of the sciatic nerve. This increase, which presumably occurred as a result of translocation [64••], covaried with postinjury neuropathic pain behaviors in CCI rats, and both membrane-bound protein kinase C and neuropathic pain behaviors were potently reversed by intrathecal administration of GM1 ganglioside. Because translocation of protein kinase C is known to be associated with NMDA receptor–mediated central nervous sys-

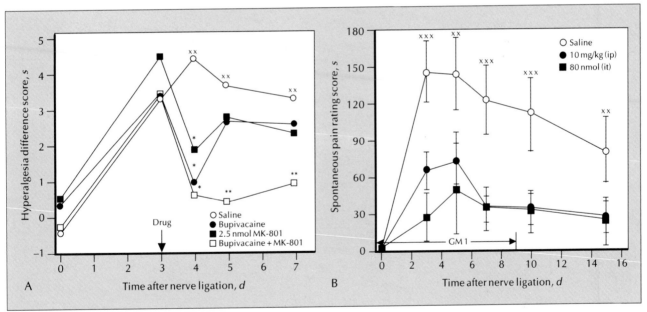

Figure 1-9 (*Panel A*) Intrathecal MK-801 and local nerve anesthesia synergistically reduce thermal hyperalgesia. *Double crosses* indicate *P* < 0.01 (ANOVA), as compared among different groups; *triple crosses* indicate *P* < 0.001 (ANOVA) comparing different groups. *Asterisk* indicates *P* < 0.05 (WD), as compared with the saline group. *Double asterisks* indicate *P* < 0.05 (WD), as compared with each of the three other groups. (*Panel B*) Effect of systemic and intrathecal GM1 treatment on spontaneous pain behaviors. *T-bars* indicate SEM. ip—intraperitoneal; it—intrathecal.

tem neuronal plasticity, mechanisms underlying postinjury neuropathic pain may be related to spinal cord hyperexcitability, resulting from excitatory amino acid–mediated central nervous system plastic changes.

The studies and the new concepts that they have generated suggest new treatment strategies for the clinical management of postinjury neuropathic pain syndromes. The possible excitatory central mechanisms of and pharmacologic interventions for postinjury neuropathic pain are summarized in Figure 1-10. Chronic neuropathic pain following nerve injury may be related to an excitatory amino acid–mediated central excitatory cascade. Features of this cascade include 1) ongoing abnormal peripheral input; 2) abnormal NMDA and non-NMDA receptor activation, which results in an

excessive increase in intracellular Ca^{2+}; and 3) a subsequent protein kinase C translocation from the cytoplasm to the neuronal membrane or protein kinase C activation, which may initiate substrate phosphorylation and consequent increases in synaptic efficacy and early gene expression (*eg*, C-*fos*). This cascade may be potentially interrupted by local nerve anesthesia, NMDA and non-NMDA antagonists, and gangliosides, which prevent or reduce protein kinase C translocation and activation. Clearly, the recent studies of neural mechanisms of neuropathic pain in animal models have led to the discovery of new therapeutic possibilities for treating these often intractable pain states. The combination of peripherally acting and centrally acting drugs may prove especially effective.

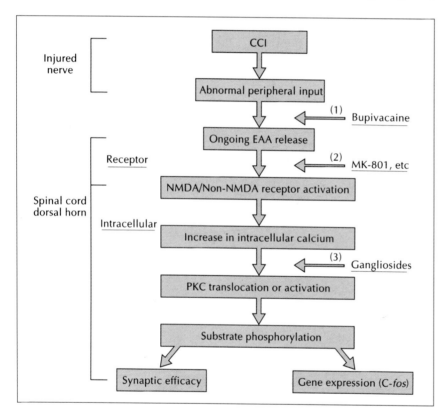

Figure 1-10 Possible excitatory central mechanisms of and pharmacologic interventions for postinjury neuropathic pain. Possible points for therapeutic intervention are indicated by (1), (2), and (3). CCI—chronic constrictive injury; EAA—excitatory amino acid; NMDA—*N*-methyl-D-asparate; PKC—protein kinase C.

REFERENCES AND RECOMMENDED READING

References of interest, published recently, have been highlighted as:
- Of special interest
- •• Of outstanding interest

1. Noordenbos W, ed: *Pain*. Amsterdam: Elsevier; 1959.

2. Price DD: Modulation of first and second pain by peripheral stimulation and by psychological set. *In Advances in Pain Research and Therapy*. Edited by Bonica JJ, Fessard DA. New York: Raven Press; 1976:427–432.

3.• Price DD, McHaffie JG, Stein BE: The psychophysical attributes of heat-induced pain and their relationships to neural mechanisms. *J Cognit Neurosci* 1992, 4:1–14.

Fundamental attributes of heat-induced pain have been characterized in psychophysical studies over the past 20 years. These include highly reliable thresholds for pain, relatively minimal adaptation to maintained nociceptive heat stimulation, slow temporal summation of heat-induced second pain but not first pain, spatial summation, and spatial radiation.

4. Willis WD, ed.: *The Pain System*. New York: Karger; 1985.

5. Yezierski RP, Culberson JL, Brown PB: Cells of origin of propriospinal connections to cat lumbosacral gray as determined with horseradish peroxidase. *Exp Neurol* 1980, 69:493–512.

6. Price DD, ed.: *Psychological and Neural Mechanisms of Pain*. New York: Raven Press; 1988.

7.• Coghill RC, Price DD, Hayes R, *et al.*: Spatial distribution of nociceptive processing in the rat spinal cord. *J Neurophysiol* 1991, 65:133–140.

The role of central spatial recruitment in spinal cord mechanisms of nociception was studied by a neural imaging method, the 2-deoxyglucose metabolic mapping method. Increasing levels of increasing nociceptive heat stimulation of rats' hindpaws produced increasing rostral-caudal spread of dorsal horn activity, particularly within the deep laminae (V–VI) of the dorsal horn.

8. Hayes RL, Price DD, Dubner R: Behavioral and physiological studies of sensory coding and modulation of trigeminal nociceptive input. In *Advances in Pain Research and Therapy*. Edited by Bonica JJ, Leibskind JC, Albe-Fessard DG. New York: Raven Press; 1979:219–243.

9.• Coghill RC, Mayer DJ, Price DD: Spinal cord coding of pain: the role of spatial recruitment and discharge frequency in nociception. *Pain* 1993, 53:295–309.

A study combining single neuron recording and 2-deoxyglucose neural imaging of rat dorsal horn neuronal responses to nonnoxious and noxious heat stimuli, as well as reports of human subjects to electrical stimulation of spinal pain–related pathways, shows that the encoding of pain intensity depends on two interrelated factors. These include the frequency of impulse discharge of spinal cord nociceptive neurons and the total number of recruited neurons.

10. Kellstein DE, Price DD, Hayes RL, *et al.*: Evidence that substance P selectively modulates C-fiber evoked discharges of dorsal horn nociceptive neurons. *Brain Res* 1990, 526:291–298.

11.•• Thompson SWN, Woolf CJ: Primary afferent-evoked prolonged potentials in the spinal cord and their central summation: role of the NMDA receptor. In *Proceedings of the VIth World Congress on Pain*. Edited by Bond MR, Carlton JE, Woolf CJ. Amsterdam: Elsevier; 1991:291–298.

The roles of long-duration synaptic potentials and synaptic mechanisms evoked by NMDA receptor activation and by substance P in temporal summation and hyperalgesia are explained. Such mechanisms are uniquely related to synaptic release of glutamate and substance P from C-polymodal nociceptive afferents onto nociceptive neurons of the spinal cord dorsal horn.

12.• Wilcox G: Excitatory neurotransmitters and pain. In *Proceedings of the VIth World Congress on Pain*. Edited by Bond MR, Charlton JE, Woolf CJ. Amsterdam: Elsevier; 1991:97–114.

The role of excitatory neurotransmitters in spinal cord mechanisms of pain is reviewed. A temporal model is presented that indicates the functional consequences of short-duration and long-duration synaptic events triggered by excitatory amino acids, neuropeptides, and inhibitory neurotransmitters.

13.•• Woolf CJ, Thompson SWN: The induction and maintenance of central sensitization is dependent on N-methyl-D-aspartic acid receptor activation; implications for the treatment of postinjury pain hypersensitivity states. *Pain* 1991, 44:293–299.

Mechanisms of induction and maintenance of central sensitization and behavioral hyperalgesia are elucidated in a series of electrophysiologic experiments in which temporal summation of the nociceptive flexion reflex is shown to be prevented by administration of NMDA antagonists. The implications of using NMDA antagonists to treat or prevent hyperalgesic states are discussed.

14. Price DD: Characteristics of second pain and flexion reflexes indicative of prolonged central summation. *Exp Neurol* 1972, 37:371–391.

15. Davies SN, Lodge D: Evidence for involvement of N-methyl-D-aspartate receptors in "windup" of class 2 neurons in the dorsal horn of the rat. *Brain Res* 1987, 424:402–406.

16. Dickenson AH, Sullivan AF: Evidence for a role of the NMDA receptor in the frequency dependent potentiation of deep rat dorsal horn nociceptive neurons following C fiber stimulation. *Neuropharmacology* 1987, 26:1235–1238.

17. Dubner R, Sharav Y, Gracely RH, *et al.*: Idiopathic trigeminal neuralgia: sensory features and pain mechanisms. *Pain* 1987, 31:23–33.

18.• Price DD: Characterizing central mechanisms of pathological pain states by sensory testing and neurophysiological analysis. In *Pain and Central Nervous System Disease: The Central Pain Syndromes*. Edited by Casey KL. New York: Raven Press; 1991:103–115.

Sensory tests for thermal hyperalgesia, mechanical allodynia, and temporal summation of mechanical allodynia are described. These tests reveal sensory abnormalities in human neuropathic pain patients that are indicative of exaggerated neural mechanisms known to exist in the spinal cord dorsal horn.

19.   Price DD, Bennett GJ, Rafii A: Psychophysical observations on patients with neuropathic pain relieved by a sympathetic block. *Pain* 1989, 36:209–218.

20.•   Price DD, Long S. Huitt C: Sensory testing of pathophysiological mechanisms of pain in patients with reflex sympathetic dystrophy. *Pain* 1992, 49:163–173.

Reflex sympathetic dystrophy patients are shown to be heterogenous with regard to several sensory abnormalities, including thermal hyperalgesia, mechanical allodynia, and temporal summation of mechanical allodynia. Of these abnormalities, that of temporal summation of mechanical allodynia is predictive of patients' level of ongoing spontaneous pain and may be causally related.

21.   Melzack R, Wall PD: Pain mechanisms: a new theory. *Science* 1965, 150:971–979.

22.•   Dubner R: Neuronal plasticity and pain following peripheral tissue inflammation or nerve injury. In *Proceedings of Vth World Congress on Pain: Pain Research and Clinical Management, vol. 5.* Edited by Bond M, Charlton E, Woolf CJ. Amsterdam: Elsevier; 1991:263–276.

NMDA receptor activation and consequent activation of a cascade of intracellular events are responsible for the long-term neuronal plastic changes that accompany hyperalgesia and allodynia in conditions of inflammatory pain and neuropathic pain. These neuronal plastic changes include expanded receptive fields and heightened responsiveness to both noxious and nonnoxious peripheral stimuli, all of which are paralleled by behavioral symptoms of hyperalgesia/allodynia.

23.   Hardy JD, Wolff HG, Goodell H, eds.: *Pain Sensations and Reactions.* Baltimore: Williams and Wilkins; 1952.

24.   Hylden JLK, Nahin RL, Traub RJ, *et al.*: Expansion of receptive fields of spinal lamina I projection neurons in rats with unilateral adjuvant-induced inflammation: the contribution of dorsal horn mechanisms. *Pain* 1989, 37:329–243.

25.   Urban L, Randic M: Slow excitatory transmission in rat dorsal horn: possible mediation by peptides. *Brain Res* 1984, 290:336–341.

26.   Campbell JN, Raja SN, Meyer RA: Painful sequelae of nerve injury. In *Pain Research and Clinical Management.* Edited by Dubner R, Gebhart GF, Bond MR. New York: Elsevier; 1988:135–143.

27.•• Yamamoto T, Shimoyama N, Mizuguchi T: The effect of morphine, MK 801, an NMDA antagonist, and CP-96,345, an NK1 antagonist, on the hyperesthesia evoked by carrageenan injection in the rat paw. *Anesthesiology* 1993, 78:124–133.

Morphine and MK-801, an NMDA antagonist, are shown to reduce behavioral indices of pain through independent mechanisms. Whereas morphine is shown to have a conventional analgesic effect, MK-801 reverses only the hyperalgesia produced by inflammation. When given in combination, these agents produce a much more powerful effect on nociceptive reflexes than either agent given alone. These results have important implications for the prevention and treatment of clinical pain.

28.•   Ren K, Hylden JL, Williams GM, *et al.*:The effects of a non-competitive NMDA receptor antagonist, MK-801, on behavioral hyperalgesia and dorsal horn neuronal activity in rats with unilateral inflammation. *Pain* 1992, 50:331–344.

Unilateral experimental inflammation (intradermal carageenan injection or Freund's adjuvant) produced hyperalgesia tested behaviorally in rats and expansion of receptive fields of dorsal horn nociceptive neurons tested in electrophysiologic experiments using rats. MK-801, a non-competitive NMDA antagonist, reduced both the behavioral hyperalgesia and the expansion of the receptive fields when given systemically. These results support the hypothesis that NMDA receptors are involved in dorsal horn neuronal plasticity and behavioral hyperalgesia that follows peripheral tissue inflammation.

29.   Campbell JN, Raja SN, Meyer RA, *et al.*: Myelinated afferents signal the hyperalgesia associated with nerve injury. *Pain* 1988, 32:89–94.

30.   Bennett GJ, Kajander KC, Sahara Y, *et al.*: Neurochemical and anatomical changes in the dorsal horn of rats with an experimental painful peripheral neuropathy. In *Proceedings of Sensory Information in the Superficial Dorsal Horn of the Spinal Cord.* Edited by Cervero F, Bennett GJ, Headley PM. New York: Plenum Press; 1989:463–471.

31.   Guilbaud G: Neuronal responsivity at supra-spinal levels (ventrobasal thalamus complex and SM1 cortex) in a rat model of mononeuropathy. In *Lesions of Primary Afferent Fibers as a Tool for Study of Clinical Pain.* Edited by Besson JM. Amsterdam: Excerpta, Medica; 1991:219–232.

32.•   Guilbaud G, Benoist JM, Jazat F, *et al.*: Neuronal responsiveness in the ventrobasal thalamic complex of rats with an experimental peripheral mononeuropathy. *J Neurophysiol* 1990, 64:1537–1554.

Neurons of the ventrobasal thalamic complex of rats with chronic constrictive injury of the sciatic nerve (Bennett model) are characterized by abnormally high levels of spontaneous impulse activity and hyperresponsiveness to innocuous and noxious stimuli. These characteristics reflect similar ones observed for neurons of the spinal cord dorsal horn in the same animal model (*See* Palecek and coworkers, *J Neurophysiol* 1992, 67:1562–1573).

33.•• Sato J, Perl ER: Adrenergic excitation of cutaneous pain receptors induced by peripheral nerve injury. *Science* 1991, 251:1608–1610.

Cutaneous C-nociceptive afferents that survive a partial nerve injury acquire noradrenergic sensitivity and are subsequently more easily sensitized by tissue injury.

34.   Bossut DF, Perl ER: Sympathectomy induces novel adrenergic excitation of cutaneous nociceptors. *Abstra Soc Neurosci* 1992, 18:287.

35.   Devor M, Govrin-Lippmann R: Spontaneous neural discharge in neuroma C-fibers in rat sciatic nerve. *Neurosci Lett Suppl* 1985, 22:S32.

36.   Ochoa JL, Torebjork HE: Paraesthesia from ectopic impulse generation in human sensory nerves. *Brain* 1980, 103:835–853.

37. Thomas PK: Clinical features and differential diagnosis of peripheral neuropathy. In *Peripheral Neuropathy*. Edited by Dyck PJ, Thomas PK, Lambert EH, Bunge R. Philadelphia: W.B. Saunders; 1984:1169–1190.

38. Wall PD, Devor M: Sensory afferent impulses originate from dorsal root ganglia as well as from the periphery in normal and nerve injured rats. *Pain* 1983, 17:321–340.

39. Wall PD, Waxman S, Basbaum AI: Ongoing activity in peripheral nerve: injury discharge. *Exp Neurol* 1974, 45:576–589.

40.•• Bennett GJ: Evidence from animal models on the pathogenesis of painful peripheral neuropathy, and its relevance for pharmacotherapy. In: *Towards a New Pharmacotherapy*. Edited by Basbaum AI, Besson JM. Chichester: John Wiley & Sons; 1991:365–379.

New models of neuropathic pain have been developed in rodents and primates. Chronic constrictive injury of the sciatic nerve in rats produces signs and symptoms strikingly similar to those seen in human neuropathic pain patients. Tight ligation of spinal nerves of primates also produces many of these symptoms. These animal models are leading to new pharmacologic therapies for treatment of difficult neuropathic pain diseases.

41. Calvin WH, Devor M, Howe J: Can neuralgias arise from minor demyelination? Spontaneous firing, mechanosensitivity, and afterdischarge from conducting axons. *Exp Neurol* 1982, 75:755–763.

42. Bennett GJ, Xie YK: A peripheral mononeuropathy in rat that produces disorders of pain sensation like those seen in man. *Pain* 1988, 33:87–107.

43.• Kajander KC, Bennett GJ: The onset of a painful peripheral neuropathy in rat: a partial and differential deafferentation and spontaneous discharge in A-β and A-δ primary afferent neurons. *J Neurophysiol* 1992, 68:734–744.

The time course of impulse conduction block in A-β afferents and increased spontaneous impulse discharge in A-δ afferents of the sciatic nerve was carefully determined in the Bennett and Xie model of painful neuropathy. The development of spontaneous discharge in A-δ afferents is likely to reflect a source of tonic nociceptive input that serves to maintain symptoms of hyperalgesia and spontaneous pain.

44.• Mao J, Price DD, Hayes RL, *et al.*: Intrathecal GM1 ganglioside and local nerve anesthesia reduce nociceptive behaviors in rats with experimental peripheral mononeuropathy. *Brain Res* 1992, 584:28–35.

Intrathecal GM1 ganglioside and local nerve anesthesia transiently reduced hyperalgesia and spontaneous pain-related behaviors of rats with experimental mononeuropathy. However, the combination of the two treatments extended the duration of therapeutic effect much longer (several days) than that of either of these treatments given alone.

45.•• Mao J, Price DD, Mayer DJ, *et al.*: Intrathecal MK 801 and local nerve anesthesia synergistically reduce nociceptive behaviors in rats with experimental peripheral mononeuropathy. *Brain Res* 1992, 576:254–262.

Intrathecal MK-801, a noncompetitive NMDA antagonist, and local nerve anesthesia both transiently reduced the hyperalgesia and spontaneous pain behaviors associated with a rat model of painful neuropathy (Bennett's model). However, when these two treatments were given together, the duration of therapeutic effect extended well beyond (several days) that produced by either treatment given alone.

46. Bonica JJ: Causalgia and other reflex sympathetic dystrophies. In *The Management of Pain*. Edited by Bonica JJ. Philadelphia: Lea & Febiger; 1990:220–256.

47. Attal N, Jazat F, Kayser V, *et al.*: Further evidence for 'pain-related' behaviors in a model of unilateral peripheral mononeuropathy. *Pain* 1990, 41:235–251.

48. Tal M, Bennett GJ: Mechano-hyperalgesia and -allodynia in the territory of the saphenous nerve in rats with an injured sciatic nerve. *Pain Suppl* 1993, in press.

49.• Gracely RH, Lynch SA, Bennett GJ: Painful neuropathy: altered central processing maintained dynamically by peripheral input. *Pain* 1992, 51:175–194.

A study of neuropathic pain patients reveals that isolated foci of tonic input from nociceptive afferents maintains symptoms of allodynia and hyperalgesia in skin regions that are remote from these foci. Local anesthesia of these foci eliminates the allodynia evoked from widespread and remote regions.

50.• Laird JMA, Bennett GJ: Dorsal root potentials and afferent input to the spinal cord in rats with an experimental peripheral neuropathy. *Brain Res* 1992, 548:181–190.

Evidence is provided that the development of pain-related symptoms in a rat model of painful neuropathy is accompanied by a loss of presynaptic inhibitory mechanisms. This evidence consists of demonstrating a reduction in the dorsal root potential evoked by A-β afferent input. This potential reflects the partial primary afferent depolarization that is considered to occur during presynaptic inhibition.

51. Sugimoto T, Bennett GJ, Kajander KC: Strychnine-enhanced transsynaptic degeneration of dorsal horn neurons in rats with an experimental painful peripheral neuropathy. *Neurosci Lett* 1989, 98:139–143.

52. Sugimoto T, Bennett GJ, Kajander KC: Transsynaptic degeneration in the superficial dorsal horn after sciatic nerve injury: effects of chronic constriction injury, transection, and strychnine. *Pain* 1990, 42:205–213.

53.•• Palecek J, Dougherty PM, Paleckova V, *et al.*: Responses of spinal thalamic tract neurons to mechanical and thermal stimuli in an experimental model of peripheral neuropathy. *J Neurophysiol* 1993, 68:1951–1966.

Enhanced responses to innocuous and noxious cutaneous stimuli as well as increased spontaneous activity were demonstrated for primate spinothalamic neurons in a model of peripheral neuropathic pain 2 weeks after ligation of the L7 spinal nerve.

54.•• Palecek J, Paleckova V, Dougherty PM, *et al.*: Responses of spinothalamic tract cells to mechanical and thermal stimulation of skin in rats with experimental peripheral neuropathy. *J Neurophysiol* 1992, 67:1562–1573.

Enhanced responses to innocuous and noxious cutaneous stimuli as well as increased spontaneous activity were demonstrated for spinothalamic neurons in a rat model of neuropathic pain (Bennett's model). These increased responses presumably underly the pain-related behaviors observed in this same animal model.

55.• Mao J, Coghill RC, Price DD, *et al.*: Spatial patterns of spinal cord [14C]-2-deoxyglucose metabolic activity in a rat model of painful peripheral mononeuropathy. *Pain* 1992, 50:89–100.

The 2-deoxyglucose metabolic mapping technique was used to determine the spatiotemporal distribution of increased neural activity within the spinal cord associated with a painful peripheral neuropathy (Bennett's model). The pattern of increased neural activity was characterized by considerable rostral-caudal, medial-lateral, and dorsal-ventral spread of increased neural activity with peak increases occurring in laminae V–VI of the fourth lumbar spinal segment. This pattern of activity is generally consistent with that produced by acute nociceptive stimulation and may partly account for the radiation of neuropathic pain and the spatial distributions of abnormal pain symptoms observed in human neuropathic pain patients.

56.• Price DD, Mao J, Coghill RC, *et al.*: Regional changes in spinal cord glucose metabolism in a rat model of painful neuropathy. *Brain Res* 1991, 564:314–318.

In the absence of any overt form of innocuous or noxious stimulation, elevations in neural activity are present in the spinal grey matter of rats with painful peripheral mononeuropathy (Bennett's model). These increases in neural activity provide some evidence for spontaneous pain in this model.

57. Livingston WH, ed.: *Pain Mechanisms: a Physiological Interpretation of Causalgia and its Related States*. New York: MacMillan; 1943.

58.• Davar G, Hama A, Deykin A, *et al.*: MK-801 blocks the development of thermal hyperalgesia in a rat model of experimental painful neuropathy. *Brain Res* 1991, 553:327–330.

This study is the first to show that an NMDA antagonist is effective in preventing the development of thermal hyperalgesia in the Bennett and Xie model of painful neuropathy.

59.• Mao J, Hayes RL, Price DD *et al.*: Post-injury treatment with GM1 ganglioside reduces nociceptive behaviors and spinal cord metabolic activity in rats with experimental peripheral mononeuropathy. *Brain Res* 1992, 584:18–27.

GM1 ganglioside has been shown to prevent the translocation of protein kinase C from the cytosol to the neuronal membrane. Thus, if such translocation is essential for the production of increased neuronal excitability that is causally related to neuropathic pain, then GM1 should reduce nociceptive behaviors and increased spinal cord activity associated with pain. Both were potently prevented by systemic administration of GM1 ganglioside.

60. Mao J, Price DD, Hayes RL, *et al.*: Differential roles of NMDA and non-NMDA receptor activation in induction and maintenance of thermal hyperalgesia in rats with painful peripheral mononeuropathy. *Brain Res* 1992, 598:271–278.

61.• Mao J, Price DD, Hayes RL, *et al.*: Intrathecal treatment with dextrorphan or ketamine potently reduces pain-related behaviors in a rat model of peripheral mononeuropathy. *Brain Res* 1993, 605:164–168.

The finding that nontoxic NMDA antagonists, such as ketamine or dextrorphan, reduce symptoms of painful neuropathy in an animal model is encouraging and supports the clinical use of these types of agents.

62.• Tal M, Bennett GJ: Dextrorphan relieves neuropathic heat-evoked hyperalgesia. *Neurosci Lett* 1993, in press.

Systemic dextrorphan reduced hyperalgesia and spontaneous pain behaviors in a rat model of painful neuropathy without producing significant motoric side effects. These effects were dose dependent over a range of 3 mg/kg to 30 mg/kg.

63.• Yamamoto T, Yaksh TL: Spinal pharmacology of thermal hyperalgesia induced by constriction injury of sciatic nerve: excitatory amino acid antagonists. *Pain* 1992, 49:121–128.

NMDA antagonists (MK-801, ketamine, and AP5) are shown to inhibit hyperalgesia produced in a rat model of neuropathic pain (Bennett's model) and to have no significant effects on flexion nociceptive reflexes in normal rats.

64.•• Mao J, Price DD, Mayer DJ, *et al.*: Pain-related increases in spinal cord membrane-bound protein kinase C following peripheral nerve injury. *Brain Res* 1992, 588:144–149.

Using a phorbol ester autoradiographic assay of membrane-bound protein kinase C, it was determined that the latter significantly increases in rats with painful peripheral mononeuropathy (Bennett's model). In a direct test of the hypothesis that translocated protein kinase C is essential for the expression of pain-related behaviors, GM1 ganglioside, which prevents protein kinase C translocation, potently reduced both membrane-bound protein kinase C and associated pain-related behaviors.

CHAPTER 2

Characteristics, Classification, and Assessment of Acute Postoperative Pain

P. PRITHVI RAJ

Even a brief review of the pertinent literature reveals a pervasive dissatisfaction with the adequacy of acute post-operative pain management [1]. The most conventional and time-honored approach, the intramuscular administration of a fixed dose of narcotic medication given on a fixed schedule or on an as-needed basis, has been rather roundly deplored. In addition, the extent of undertreatment continues to appear significant. It is not the therapeutic agents or techniques that are lacking, however. A variety of powerful drugs exist whose efficacy has been well established, and investigations into new routes and methods of administration have achieved some noteworthy successes. The problem is not that acute pain cannot effectively be managed in any individual case but that it is not effectively being managed in many cases.

CHARACTERISTICS OF ACUTE PAIN

Acute pain may be defined as the conscious awareness of tissue or emotional injury [2]. Its perception reflects activation of nociceptor afferent transmission to the spinal cord and relay via dorsal horn to higher centers. Pain perception consists of two major components. The sensory component, which describes the location and quality of the stimulus, is transmitted via myelinated A-δ fibers and relayed to the neothalamus and somatosensory cortex. This component quickly alerts

the organism, resulting in prompt withdrawal from the noxious stimulus. The affective-motivational component is slowly conducted via peripheral unmyelinated C fibers and establishes numerous synaptic contacts within brainstem and midbrain nuclei and the cortical limbic system. This component is primarily responsible for conditioned behavior and learned avoidance [2,3]. On a teleologic level such behavior serves to avoid further injury and promote wound healing; however, other affective responses, such as suffering, anxiety, and release of stress hormones and catecholamines, may be harmful if they persist.

Pathophysiologic changes associated with acute pain commonly include the following:

1. Neurohumoral alterations at the site and in regions adjacent to the injury
2. Alterations in synaptic function and nociceptive processing occurring within spinal cord dorsal horn
3. Neuroendocrine responses
4. Sympathoadrenal activation

INITIATION AND PROPAGATION OF NOCICEPTION

After a peripheral injury a complex cascade of events is initiated (Fig. 2-1). Several endogenous chemicals, including bradykinin, histamine, serotonin, products of

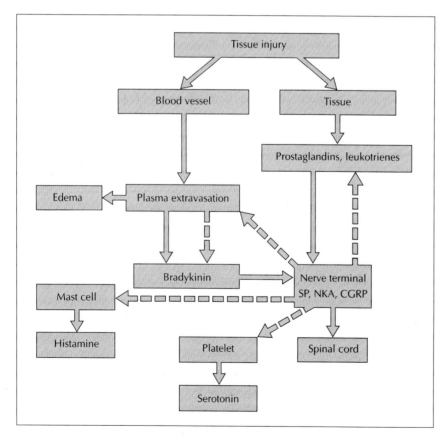

Figure 2-1 The peripheral activation of primary afferent fibers after tissue injury. *Solid lines* indicate initial responses; *dashed lines* indicate responses that occur after activation of the peripheral nociceptor. CGRP—calcitonin gene-related protein; NKA—neurokinin; SP—substance P. (*Adapted from* Sinatra and Hord [117]; with permission.)

the arachidonic acid cascade, and neuropeptides such as substance P, are released [4]. These chemicals activate receptors on the peripheral terminals of sensory afferents, which begins the process of nociceptive transmission. Many of the chemicals that are released after injury are those substances that are involved in the process of inflammation.

With the activation of the arachidonic acid cascade, there is the formation of prostaglandins and leukotrienes; these products are released from tissue and act to sensitize primary afferent terminals [5]. Prostaglandins such as PGE, and PGI_2 can act directly on the peripheral terminals of nociceptors [6]. The original injury also results in the enzymatic conversion of kininogen into bradykinin [7,8]. It is the action of the bradykinin in combination with prostaglandins that results in the activation of the receptors on the peripheral terminals of the primary afferent fibers. Prostaglandins [9] and leukotrienes [10] appear to act in concert with bradykinin to produce an enhanced activation of the primary afferent terminal. The activation of the peripheral terminal results in the release of mediators of nociceptive transmission within the dorsal horn of the spinal cord, the next step in the processing of nociceptive information.

The excitation of the primary afferent also produces an axon reflex that results in the peripheral release on neuropeptides such as substance P, neurokinin A, and calcitonin gene-related peptide (CGRP). The peripheral mediators are the same as those that are released centrally in the spinal cord. These neuropeptides act on blood vessels to produce plasma extravasation [11]. Substance P and neurokinin A have both been shown to produce plasma extravasation on their own but they also contribute to the effects of the other neurokinins [12]. Plasma extravasation is important in that it contributes to the production of edema and the continued release of additional vasoactive substances. Once activation has occurred, peripheral mediators can then act on other structures to release additional endogenous compounds, such as histamine [11], as well as to establish a feed-forward loop by which their release is continued. It is the continued release of these mediators that results in the spread of pain to surrounding areas (Fig. 2-1).

Bradykinin's effects in the periphery are specific and are mediated by B_2-bradykinin receptors, which are located on the terminals of primary afferent neurons [13,14]. In addition to producing pain, bradykinin has many other effects, including an increased vascular permeability, which results in plasma extravasation and the formation of edema. A synergy has been demonstrated between bradykinin and substance P in the production of plasma extravasation and pain [15]. Like substance P, bradykinin also acts on mast cells to promote the release of histamine [16]. Histamine in turn also pro-

duces plasma extravasation and excites the peripheral nerve terminal. In addition, the sympathetic nervous system also contributes to the peripheral activation of primary afferent fibers [17]. Thus, a complex system exists in the periphery by which many neurochemicals contribute to the enhancement of the transmission of nociceptive information.

Activation of the primary afferent nerve terminals begins the transmission of nociceptive information. It is the release of nociceptive neurotransmitters from these primary afferent fibers that activates the second-order dorsal horn neurons. The activation of these neurons results in spinal reflex responses as well as the activation of ascending tracts, which transmit nociceptive information to supraspinal sites (Fig. 2-2).

Consistent with a role in nociceptive transmission, substance P has been localized to small-diameter primary afferent fibers [18] that terminate in the area of the substantia gelatinosa. Numerous investigators have demonstrated the release of substance P from spinal cord *in vitro* as well as *in vivo*. Go and Yaksh [19] have extensively characterized the release of substance P into spinal cord superfusates. Substance P release is evoked after stimulation of the sciatic nerves at intensities that activate A-δ and C fibers but not after low-intensity stimulation. With the use of antibody-coated microprobes, the release of substance P after noxious stimulation has been localized to the superficial layers of the spinal cord [20]. The iontophoretic application of substance P onto dorsal horn neurons will produce a potent excitatory effect.

Substance P and CGRP coexist within sensory neurons [21–23]. The concurrent release of these two neuropeptides·has also been demonstrated [24,25]. The colocalization and simultaneous release of these two

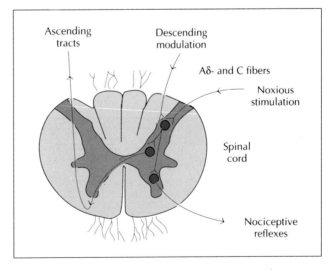

Figure 2-2 Schema of the processing of nociceptive information within the dorsal horn of the spinal cord. (*Adapted from* Sinatra and Hord [117]; with permission.)

neuropeptides is consistent with evidence that demonstrates an interaction between substance P and CGRP in nociceptive transmission [26,27]. Other neuropeptides such as bombesin and somatostatin have also been shown to produce an excitation of second-order nociceptive neurons [28].

In addition to the neuropeptides, excitatory amino acids (EAAs), such as glutamate or aspartate, also play a distinct role in nociceptive transmission [29–31]. It has been hypothesized that EAAs mediate fast nociceptive transmission, whereas neuropeptides are believed to mediate slow nociceptive transmission [31]. Considerable evidence supports an interaction between these two systems. Glutamate is colocalized with substance P in dorsal root ganglion cells [32] and in the central terminals of primary afferent fibers [33]. Both EAAs and substance P have been shown to be released into the spinal space after noxious stimuli [34,35]. Additionally, Murray and coworkers [36] have demonstrated that the intrathecal administration of antagonists for either EAAs or substance P receptors have been shown to be analgesic in a behavioral model of pain. The infusion of substance P into the spinal cord will also evoke the release of EAAs [32]. Thus, a role for substance P may be to promote the release of EAAs from the spinal cord, leading to enhanced synaptic transmission [37–39].

Clearly, multiple neurotransmitters contribute to the processing of nociceptive transmission within the dorsal horn of the spinal cord. It is not known if these neurotransmitters are differently released in response to specific types of nociceptive input. The activation of supraspinal sites is necessary for the perception of pain to occur. Because of the complexity of supraspinal organization, little is known about the neurotransmitters mediating nociceptive information within the brain.

MODULATION OF NOCICEPTION

At the spinal level, transmission may be modulated by either inhibiting the release of neurotransmitters from primary afferent fibers or inhibiting the activation of second-order dorsal horn neurons. The source of spinal modulation may either be intrinsic or descend from supraspinal sites.

Opioid Receptors

The dorsal horn of the spinal cord contains receptors for μ, δ, and κ opioid receptors. These receptors are located presynaptically as well as postsynaptically on second-order neurons. The localization of these receptors provides an anatomic basis for the ability of spinal opioids to modulate nociceptive transmission.

Inhibitory neuropeptides are also released into the spinal cord after nociceptive stimuli. Metenkephalin and larger enkephalin molecules are released into the spinal space after sciatic nerve stimulation. The release of dynorphin A into the areas of lamina I has been demonstrated from high-frequency stimulation [40]. The cell bodies for these endogenous opioids are contained within the spinal cord itself. The release of these molecules provides evidence for the endogenous substrates that have actions similar to those of morphine.

The inhibitor effects of morphine on the evoked release of substance P have been demonstrated *in vivo* [19,41]. An examination of receptor-selective agonists has revealed that both μ- and δ-opioid–receptor agonists produce inhibition of the evoked release of substance P [19,41,42]. Pohl and coworkers [43] have demonstrated the ability of μ and δ agonists to inhibit the evoked release of CGRP from dorsal spinal cord slices, but such ability has not yet been examined *in vivo*. Thus, it is likely that opioids may inhibit the release of multiple primary afferent neurotransmitters that are involved in pain transmission.

Evidence for a postsynaptic as well as a presynaptic action of spinal opioids has been reported. Opioid agonists will inhibit the firing of second-order dorsal horn neurons [44]. The intrathecal administration of opioid-receptor agonists will inhibit the nociceptive behavior produced by intrathecal administration of substance P. This provides presumptive evidence of a postsynaptic mechanism. It is likely that a combination of actions at both presynaptic and postsynaptic sites may occur. A presynaptic as well as a postsynaptic mechanism of action for systemically administered morphine has been proposed by Lombard and Benson [45].

Gamma-Aminobutyric Acid Receptors

The intrathecal administration of γ-aminobutyric acid (GABA) agonists yields antinociceptive effects [46,47]. The spinal administration of the GABA B—but not the GABA A–receptor agonists—has been shown to modulate nociceptive processing [47]. Although receptors for GABA have been located on primary afferent nerve terminals, unlike opioid and α_2 agonists, GABA has not been shown to inhibit the release of substance P [48]. Thus, the antinociceptive properties of GABA may serve to modulate segmentally the firing of second-order dorsal horn neurons. The use of the GABA B–receptor selective agonist baclofen as an analgesic may be associated with its ability to inhibit other spinal reflex pathways.

Adrenergic Receptors

The adrenergic system has also been shown to play a role in the modulation of nociceptive information [49,50].

The high concentrations of binding sites for α-adrenergic ligands are found in the substantia gelatinosa. α₂-Binding sites are concentrated in the dorsal horn. The ability of intrathecal norepinephrine to inhibit nociceptive behaviors produced by intrathecally administered substance P indicates that postsynaptic modulation contributes to the spinal antinociceptive actions of α-adrenergic drugs. Consistent with these data, the local application of α₂ agonists directly depresses the activity of dorsal horn neurons [51].

Noradrenergic agonists have been shown to inhibit the evoked release of substance P *in vitro* [48] and *in vivo* [19,52]. The α₂-receptor agonist ST-91 has been shown by Go and Yaksh [19] to inhibit the release of substance P evoked by sciatic nerve stimulation in the cat. The inhibition of substance P release produced by ST-91 was reversed by phentolamine or yohimbine administration. Consistent with a presynaptic location of receptors, a functional presynaptic effect of clonidine has been demonstrated on afferent fibers [53]. Dorsal root ganglionectomy has also been reported to decrease adrenergic binding in the spinal cord.

Adenosine Receptors

Adenosine receptors have been implicated in the modulation of nociceptive information [54]. Binding studies indicate that the adenosine receptors in the spinal cord may be located on intrinsic neurons and not on primary afferent fibers [55]. The antinociceptive effects of morphine have been shown to have an adenosine component [56,57]. The intrathecal administration of adenosine agonists produce a mild antinociception [58]; however, this effect is associated with motor dysfunction.

Many other agonists have been injected intrathecally to determine their role in nociceptive transmission [28,59]. Acetylcholine [60], neurotensin, serotonin, and somatostatin [61] have been shown to have spinal antinociceptive properties. However, care must be taken because the intrathecal administration of compounds can also result in motor dysfunction [58] or neurotoxicity [61].

By far the most well-characterized aspect of supraspinal excitation involves the engaging or activating of systems of descending inhibition (Fig. 2-3) [62–64]. The supraspinal sites involved in descending inhibition were discovered through activation of these areas by electrical stimulation and by demonstration of an inhibition of nociceptive reflexes or an inhibition in the firing of noxiously evoked dorsal horn neurons.

NEUROENDOCRINE RESPONSES

After extensive tissue injury, neurogenic stimuli affecting the hypothalamus, secretory target organs, or both, incite profound alterations in neuroendocrine responses [5,65]. These changes are characterized by an increased secretion of catabolic hormones (cortisol, glucagon, growth hormone, catecholamines) and an inhibition of anabolic mediators—in particular, insulin and testosterone [65–67]. Such alterations mediate the increased mobilization of substrate, hyperglycemia, and a negative nitrogen balance [65,67]. Associated metabolic changes including gluconeogenesis, glycogenolysis, proteolysis, and increased lipid turnover provide the injured organism with short-term benefits of enhanced energy production and availability; however, when amplified or prolonged, catabolic aspects of the stress response may adversely affect postsurgical outcome in the following ways: 1) excessive loss may lead to muscle wasting, fatigue, and prolonged convalescence; 2) impaired immunocompetence secondary to diminished immunoglobulin synthesis and impaired phagocytosis may result in decreased resistance to infection.

SYMPATHOADRENAL RESPONSES

After injury, nociceptive impulses stimulate sympathetic preganglionic neurons in the anterior lateral horn. These cells initiate a variety of stimulatory effects including increased cardiac inotropic and chronotropic activity, a pronounced increase in peripheral vascular resistance, and a redistribution of blood flow away from viscera to the heart and brain. Although such adaptive responses act to maintain blood pressure and cardiac output, a prolonged duration of heightened sympathetic activity may initiate many pathophysiologic changes, including altered regional perfusion, compromised function of key target organs, activation of the renin–angiotensin system, increased platelet activation, and reflex efferent hyperactivity.

Surgical trauma is promptly followed by increases in plasma epinephrine and norepinephrine concentrations [66]. The magnitude and duration of catecholamine release is directly related to the extent of surgical injury and patient age, with the highest plasma levels noted after more extensive procedures [66] and in younger persons. The earliest aspects of catecholamine response reflect pronounced but transient increases in adrenal medullary secretion, whereas later aspects represent continued release of norepinephrine from sympathetic nerve endings. Sympathetic tone and altered regional perfusion include the following:

1. An increased incidence of postsurgical hypertension that ranges from 5% after minor, uncomplicated procedures to approximately 50% in patients recovering from more extensive vascular surgery. Methods that limit the development of postoperative hypertension include regionally applied local anesthetics,

which blunt catecholamine release, and pretreatment with adrenergic antagonists, which block a receptor-mediated effect (Fig. 2-4).

2. Increased peripheral vascular resistance is associated with increases in contractility and myocardial oxygen consumption as the organism attempts to maintain or augment cardiac output. Increases in oxygen consumption, although usually well tolerated by healthy persons, may precipitate myocardial ischemia in patients with coronary artery disease. Enhanced sympathetic tone may be especially deleterious in patients recovering from peripheral vascular surgery, because elevations in arterial pressure may lead to the rupture of vascular anastomoses, and intense vasospasm may compromise graft patency.

3. Microcirculatory blood flow in injured tissues, in adjacent musculature, and in the viscera may be significantly diminished. Reductions in circulation have been associated with impaired wound healing, enhanced sensitization of nociceptors, increased muscle spasm, and visceral-somatic ischemia and acidosis.

4. Renal hypoperfusion results in activation of the renin-angiotensin-aldosterone axis. Angiotensin is a potent vasoconstrictor that, although capable of increasing renal perfusion, may further accentuate catecholamine release.

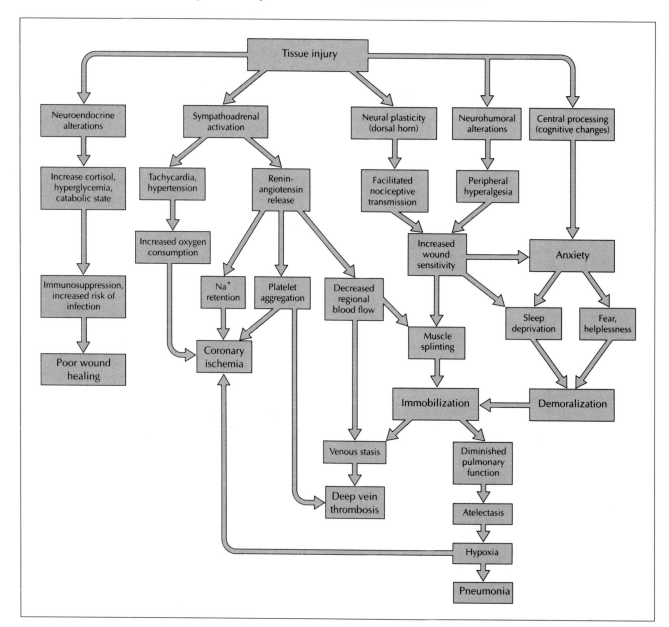

Figure 2-3 Pathophysiologic responses associated with surgical trauma and their impact upon key target organs. (*Adapted from* Sinatra and Hord [117]; with permission.)

CLINICAL EFFECTS OF PAIN ON VITAL ORGANS

Heart

In high-risk populations, perioperative ischemia is most likely to occur after surgery on postoperative days 1 to 3 [68]. Although a variety of factors may contribute to the development of postoperative ischemia including hypothermia, anemia, anxiety, and the need for tracheal intubation and suctioning, responses to poorly controlled pain play a prominent role [69–72]. In this activation, sympathoadrenal and neuroendocrine responses may have a major impact on myocardial oxygen supply and demand. Catecholamine-induced tachycardia, enhanced contractility, and increased afterload are well-characterized determinants of increased oxygen demand. Increased oxygen demand, together with hypervolemia, may precipitate ischemia and acute cardiac failure, especially in patients with poorly compensated coronary artery or valvular heart disease [68,72].

Myocardial oxygen supply may be diminished as a result of pulmonary dysfunction, particularly in atelectasis secondary to pain-induced hypoventilation, and pulmonary edema resulting from stress-induced hypervolemia [70]. Other causes of reduced oxygen supply include 1) coronary artery constriction secondary to high circulatory levels of catecholamines and increased coronary sympathetic tone [72,73]; 2) stress-induced increases in plasma viscosity and platelet-induced occlusion [74,75]; and 3) release of secretion after platelet aggregation, which may initiate coronary vasospasm [75].

Lung

Pulmonary function may be dramatically altered by surgically-induced pain. Atelectasis, pneumonia, and arterial hypoxemia are common postoperative complications whose incidence approaches 70% in patients recovering from upper abdominal surgery [70]. Such complications have been related to significant reductions in vital capacity (VC), functional residual capacity (FRC), and a reduced ability to cough and clear secretions (Fig. 2-5) [70]. VC is the first pulmonary parameter to change in the postoperative period. Significant reductions in VC are evident within the first 3 hours, and declines to 40% to 60% of preoperative values have been reported. Reductions in VC, FRC, and forced expiratory volume in 1 second (FEV_1) are greatest at 24 hours; thereafter, values gradually return to normal levels by postoperative day 7 [71].

The percentage reduction in VC is highest after upper abdominal surgery and lowest in patients recovering from extra-abdominal nonthoracic procedures. Other factors that influence the magnitude of VC reduction

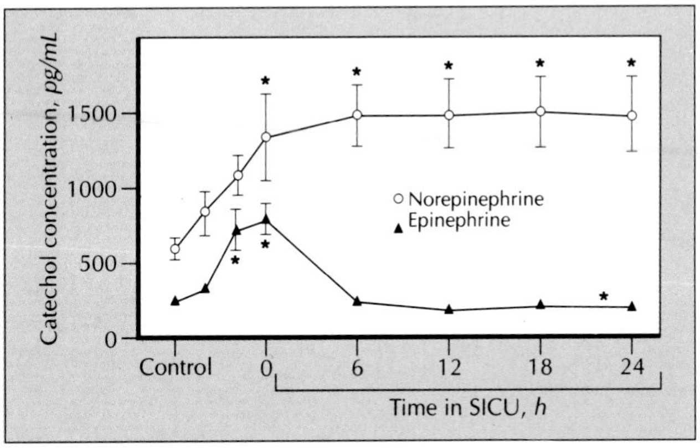

Figure 2-4 Plasma epinephrine and norepinephrine preoperatively, intraoperatively, and at 6, 12, 18, and 24 hours after aortic reconstructive surgery. Data represent mean ± SEM; *asterisk* indicates significant difference compared with preinduction value. SICU—surgical intensive care unit. (*From* Breslow [70]; with permission.)

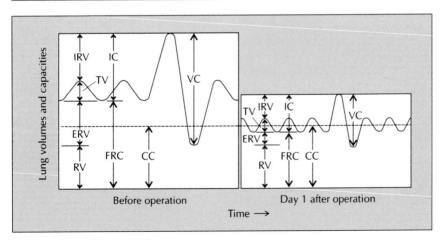

Figure 2-5 Postoperative reductions in lung volumes and capacities in upper abdominal surgery. CC—closing capacity; ERV—expiratory reserve volume; FRC—functional residual capacity; IC—inspiratory capacity; IRV—inspiratory reserve volume; RV—residual volume; TV—tidal volume; VC—vital capacity. (*From* Brown and Neal [113]; with permission.)

include duration of anesthesia, diaphragmatic injury [76], and history of chronic obstructive pulmonary disease.

Peripheral Vascular System

Inadequately controlled pain may predispose patients to the development of deep venous thromboses (DVT) and life-threatening complications of pulmonary embolism after surgery. Catecholamines and angiotensin released in response to surgical stress may result in platelet-fibrogen activation and the development of a hypercoagulable state. Severe pain is commonly associated with an impaired ability to ambulate and decreased venous flow [3,70]. Finally, surgical manipulation in and around the pelvis may damage venous conduits that return blood from the lower extremities. These factors make up Virchow's triad of hypercoagulability, venous stasis, and endothelial injury, which underlies the development of DVT.

CLINICAL CLASSIFICATION OF PAIN

Clinical pain can be classified as nociceptive (somatic and visceral), neuropathic, and psychogenic [77]. Shared characteristics and responsivity to various therapeutic interventions have been observed within each category, and hence this classification is useful when formulating an initial approach to treatment. However, despite similarities in mechanism and causation, each pain problem must still be regarded as a unique entity requiring an individualized plan that may need to be altered frequently. Factors that contribute to heterogenicity within a pathophysiologic group include the nature and severity of the insult; overall physical, emotional, and psychological condition; and interindividual differences in the response to drugs and other treatments. In many patients the cause of pain is the result of multiple, interacting mechanisms and components (sensory, affective, cognitive, and behavioral), the sum of which contributes to a complex pain syndrome that defies simple categorization.

Nociceptive Pain

SOMATIC PAIN

Somatic pain occurs as a result of activation of nociceptors in cutaneous and deep tissues. It is typically constant and well-localized, and is frequently characterized as aching, throbbing, or gnawing. Somatic pain tends to be opioid-sensitive and amenable, at least temporarily, to treatment involving the interruption of proximal pathways by chemical blockage or surgery.

VISCERAL PAIN

Visceral pain originates from injury to sympathetically innervated organs. When pain is caused by a lesion involving the abdominal or pelvic viscera, it is character-istically vague in distribution and quality, and is often described as deep, aching, dragging, squeezing, or pressure-like. When acute, it may be paroxysmal and colicky, and can be associated with nausea, vomiting, diaphoresis, and alterations in blood pressure and heart rate. Mechanisms of visceral pain include abnormal distention or mucosal irritation by algesic substances and other chemical stimuli, distention and traction or torsion on mesenteric attachments and vasculature, and necrosis [78]. The viscera are, however, insensitive to simple manipulation, cutting, and burning.

Visceral involvement often produces referred or "transferred" pain [78,79], a phenomenon of pain and hyperalgesia localized to superficial or deep tissues, often distant to the source of the pathologic condition. Several mechanisms have been proposed to explain the occurrence of referred pain, including the presence of dual innervation of multiple structures, chemical irritation by tumor-medicated algesic substances, and central convergence of afferent impulses [77]. Examples include back pain of pancreatic or retroperitoneal origin, abdominal wall pain and allodynia from peritoneal irritation, upper extremity pain of anginal origin, phrenic nerve–mediated shoulder pain of hepatic origin, and knee pain from metastatic lesions of the hip.

Neuropathic Pain

Neuropathic pain refers to pain syndromes associated with aberrant somatosensory processes induced by injury to some element of the nervous system (Fig. 2-6). The term *deafferentation pain* is used when the presumed site of aberrant processing is in the central nervous system. Subtypes include central pain, avulsion of a nerve plexus, and phantom pain [80]. Sympathetically maintained pain is another subtype, exemplified as reflex sympathetic dystrophy. This entity is associated with causalgic, dysesthetic pain, often accompanied by typical vasomotor and dystrophic changes. In the case of deafferentation, pain is usually localized to the area of sensory abnormality. When pain is of central origin, it tends to be located in the region that corresponds somatotopically to the lesion. Neuropathic pain is characteristically dysesthetic in nature. Dysesthesia refers to discomfort and altered sensations distinct from the ordinary, familiar sensations of pain. Dysesthetic pain is variously described as burning, tingling, numbing, pressing, squeezing, and itching, and is typically described as extremely unpleasant, often even intolerable.

Neuropathic pain may be constant, steady, and spontaneously maintained (*ie*, present independent of external stimuli). In addition to continuous pain, there may be a component of superimposed, intermittent, shock-like pain, most often characterized as shooting, lancinating, electrical, or jolting.

Associated findings, present in a variable proportion of patients, include, in roughly descending frequency, sensory loss, evoked pain, sympathetic dysfunction, and reflex abnormalities [80]. Evoked pain implies an altered sensory threshold and includes various similar phenomena recently defined by the International Association for the Study of Pain (IASP) [81]. The term *dysesthesia* includes evoked as well as spontaneous abnormal sensation. *Hyperalgesia* refers to increased response to a stimulus that is normally painful, and *allodynia* refers to pain caused by a stimulus that does not normally provoke pain. Similar phenomena that may be present include *hyperesthesia*, an increased sensitivity of stimulation, and *hyperpathia*, a painful syndrome characterized by an increased, often explosive, reaction to stimulus.

The development of neuropathic pain is idiosyncratic and unpredictable even among patients with similar lesions. No consistent predisposing factors have been demonstrated. Onset of pain may occur immediately after an injury or after a variable interval. When pain is delayed, it often follows a seemingly unrelated and sometimes trivial but stressful incident such as surgery, infection, or trauma.

Psychogenic Pain

Great controversy surrounds labeling a pain syndrome as wholly psychogenic in origin. That a patient's psychological state contributes significantly to complaints of pain and suffering is well recognized and forms part of the basis for the IASP's definition of pain as "...an unpleasant sensory and emotional experience associated with actual or potential tissue damage or described in terms as such" [81].

It is often difficult to ascertain the degree to which psychological disturbances are secondary to pain versus the degree to which they are the cause of pain. Regardless, symptoms and their associated distress are real to the patient, independent of whether there are psychological factors involved in their maintenance. The presence of anxiety or depression and their relative con-

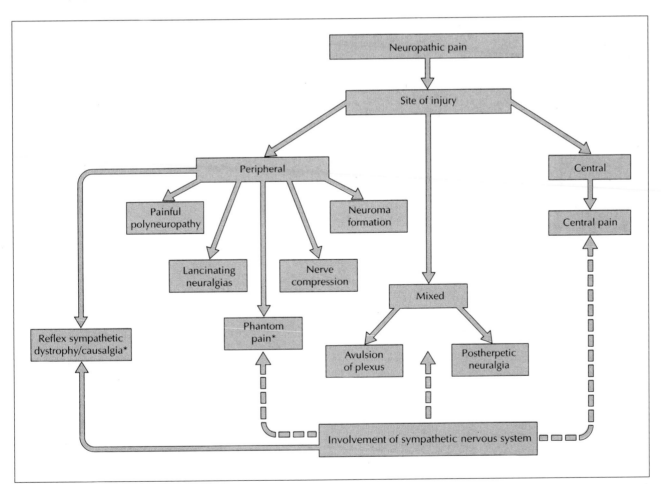

Figure 2-6 Classification of neuropathic pains by the site of neural injury. The dependence of the pain on sympathetic efferent activity has been reported for lesions at all locations, although it is far more prevalent with peripheral lesions and predominates in the sympathetically maintained pains, reflex sympathetic dystrophy, and causalgia. *Asterisk* indicates usually a peripheral lesion; *unbroken lines* indicate a direct response; *broken lines* indicate an indirect response. (*From* Portenoy [114]; with permission.)

tribution to complaints of pain should be carefully assessed so that appropriate supportive care and pharmacologic therapy can be instituted.

Anxiety

Anxiety is often the primary anticipatory emotional reaction to the acute pain experience. Research from experimental pain studies indicates that anxiety will increase the tendency to report stimulation as pain and will also increase physiologic arousal (such as heart rate) in response to acute painful stimuli [81,82]. Preoperative anxiety and fear may adversely influence the patient's physiologic status during surgery. One study demonstrated that anxious patients required an average of twice the dose of thiopental sodium for anesthetic induction and anxious patients had higher (20%) mean heart rates during surgery.

Preoperative anxiety and fear have also been associated with heightened postoperative pain, increased pain medication intake, and a more prolonged and complicated recovery [83,84]. In a sample of women undergoing outpatient elective laparoscopic surgery, anxious women reported higher levels of postoperative pain and discomfort and were more prone to complications from outpatient surgery [84]. In a sample of patients undergoing rectal cancer surgery, 68% of the group who were highly anxious experienced postoperative complications (such as pneumonia, bowel, and bladder problems) in comparison with patients with lower anxiety scores (only 17% had complications). Recently, a study of patients who had undergone orthopedic surgery and were using patient-controlled analgesia (PCA) showed that patients with higher anxiety reported higher levels of postoperative pain and made more frequent PCA demands during the postoperative period [85].

DEPRESSION

Depression is a less common response to acute pain and is more often observed in chronic pain. Depression may occur, however, in the acute pain situation, especially if the patient has chronic health problems (such as a patient with arthritis undergoing hip replacement), is anticipating future health problems (such as a patient with cancer undergoing surgery before chemotherapy and radiation therapy are started), or is undergoing repeated painful medical procedures.

ANGER, IRRITABILITY, AND FRUSTRATION

Anger, irritability, and frustration are also common in chronic pain but may be observed in acute pain situations as well. Patients experiencing acute pain and discomfort, or parents of children experiencing acute pain, may direct anger and frustration at the staff, for example, by demanding pain medication or complaining. Some preliminary evidence indicates that anger may increase the response to acute painful stimulation.

ASSESSMENT OF PAIN

Pain is a unique, highly subjective, multidimensional experience encompassing many sensory and affective components [86]. Sensory components characterize spatial and temporal elements of the stimulus, whereas affective or evaluative components underlie emotional reactivity to the painful experience.

The uniqueness of pain as it varies among individuals makes its objective measurement very difficult. Accurate measurement is of great importance, however, when one is attempting to assess the efficacy of analgesic therapy. Physicians and nurses involved with the daily care of patients in pain frequently misjudge pain intensity and the effectiveness of pain medications.

One reason why such assessments are inaccurate may be related to the use of observer scores [87–89]. Clinician and nurse observer pain scores are based on behavioral and autonomic signs, which have been shown to be unreliable indices of pain intensity [88,90–92]. Autonomic changes may result from the mere anticipation of pain or reflect unrelated patient anxiety. Behavioral signs are often colored by cultural responses, emotional status, and psychological variability. Whereas one patient may be stoic and express little or no signs of discomfort in response to a given stimulus, another will writhe in agony. In a recent study evaluating analgesic efficacy in burn patients, nurse observer scores were a frequent underestimation of pain intensity but an overestimation of the effectiveness of the pain medication [90]. Nurse observer scores were more accurate (49% concordance) when a patient's pain at rest was assessed than when pain during therapeutic procedures were evaluated (30% concordance) [87,90].

Several clinicians [93–95] have proposed that patient-controlled analgesia may be more accurate than observer assessments in the estimation of pain intensity because the patient has the capability to self-administer a greater or lesser amount of pain medication depending on the magnitude of a perceived pain stimulus. Unfortunately, many patients misuse PCA either because they do not fully appreciate the objective of such therapy or have difficulty understanding the operation of the pump.

VISUAL ANALOGUE SCALES

The Visual Analogue Scale (VAS) is a very useful pain assessment tool. It is an extremely simple, sensitive, and reproducible instrument that allows patients to express the severity of pain as a numerical value [96]. The VAS can be performed quickly, with minimal patient distraction, and can easily be adapted to individual situations. In addition to measuring the level of pain, it can also be used to measure other subjective variables such as nausea, pain relief, and patient satisfaction (Fig. 2-7).

The VAS is represented as a straight line, usually 10 cm in length. At either end of the line are two poles or "anchors" that are defined as the extreme limits of the sensation or response to be measured [97,98]. For example, the words "no pain" appear on the extreme left of this continuum, whereas "worst possible pain" is indicated on the extreme right (Fig. 2-7). Patients are instructed to draw a single line intersecting the VAS at a point that depicts their perceived level of pain at that particular moment. From this marking, a concrete measurement, in either millimeters or centimeters, can be obtained and used for analysis. Both vertical and horizontal scales have been used as measurements of pain, with good correlation; however, scores from the former tend to be slightly higher than those noted with the horizontal scales. Some VAS scales designate endpoints; however, adding these boundaries to the line may influence an individual score by forcing the patient to mark at a point further away from the extreme.

Although the VAS is easy to use, it is essential to ensure complete patient understanding. Even the simplest of concepts can be misunderstood, especially when people are placed in stressful situations. Whenever possible, it is advisable to instruct the patient in its use during preadmission or preoperatively to limit any confusion and thereby improve the reliability of the results. This form of measurement should be presented with minimal verbal and no finger-position cues, which can easily compromise accuracy. Accuracy can be further improved by having the scale presented by the same caretaker, using separate VAS scales for measuring resting pain scores and movement or wound-manipulation pain scores. The VAS scale should always be introduced with an appropriate statement standardized before the experiment, such as "Please mark on the line the intensity of pain you are experiencing at this moment." Standardization is of

great importance, because small changes in delivery have been shown to alter the performance of the scale. Visual analogue scales have been shown to be more sensitive than observer scores and simple descriptive pain scales [99]. However, sensitivity is reduced when distribution is not uniform. Because the VAS measures a variable at a specified moment, multiple evaluations must be performed to ascertain the patient's experience over a given period. On the other hand, tests performed too frequently may carry the risk of inaccuracy because either patients become uncooperative or they remember prior assessments and are influenced by those scores [86,100].

VERBAL PAIN SCALES

Another way of objectively assessing pain is achieved by having verbal and numerical cues superimposed on a VAS. This tool operates on the same concept as VAS in that patients are asked to rate pain intensity on a scale of 0 to 10, with 0 representing no pain and 10 representing the worst possible pain. Advantages to this method are that most people are familiar with the concept of increasing stimulation being related to increases in a numerical scale. It is generally accepted that the subjective experience of pain can be measured only by the power of speech. Rating scales that focus on intensity alone have been criticized because of their failure to reflect the multidimensional aspects of pain. Clinicians have long recognized the existence of qualitatively different aspects of pain, such as "throbbing headache," "crushing" chest pain, and "heartburn," to name only a few. To consider pain only in terms of overall intensity is analogous to seeing the world in shades of gray.

One of the first contributions to the assessment of pain by means of verbal descriptors was made in 1939, when a list of 44 words was compiled describing various qualities of pain. These adjectives were classified into groups characterizing 1) temporal components, ie, "palpating," "throbbing;" 2) spatial components, ie, "penetrating," "radiating;" 3) pressure, ie, "heavy," "pressing;" 4) affective coloration, ie, "ugly," "savage;"

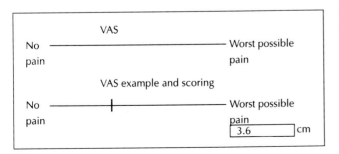

Figure 2-7 Visual Analogue Scale (VAS). (*Adapted from* Sinatra and Hord [117]; with permission.)

and 5) purely qualitative aspects, *ie*, "achy," "dull," and "piercing." It was from this original list that the McGill Pain Questionnaire (MPQ) was formed.

MCGILL PAIN QUESTIONNAIRE

The McGill Pain Questionnaire is a pain-assessment tool that measures both the subjective quality and the quantity of a patient's pain experience (Fig. 2-8). In the first part of the MPQ patients are presented with a list of 102 word descriptors that are separated into 20 subclasses. They are asked to select one word from each subclass that best describes their pain at that particular moment. Within each subclass, words are arranged in order from least painful to most painful (such as "flickering" to "pounding"). If there are no words within the subclass that accurately represent the patient's pain, none should be chosen. A high level of agreement regarding the intensity relationship between pain descriptors was noted among subjects from different socioeconomic, educational, and cultural backgrounds. Patients tended to be highly selective in their choice of words when the list was read by the examiner. There also exists a remarkable consistency with the constellation of symptoms for a particular pain syndrome.

Word descriptors fall into categories representing the three major dimensions of pain:

1. *Sensory*: how the senses perceive the pain
2. *Affective*: the emotional aspect of the pain experience
3. *Evaluative*: summation of the intensity of a patient's pain experience

Those components are addressed by various measurements. The pain rating index (PRI) is based on the total number of words selected either for all the categories combined or for those based on the individual scores of each category. Word descriptors implying the least pain are given a value of 1, the next given a 2, and so on, finishing with the words implying the most pain, represented by the number 5. The values of words chosen are

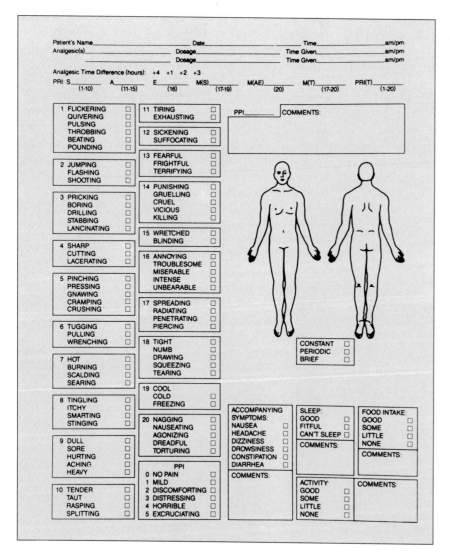

Figure 2-8 McGill Pain Questionnaire. (*Courtesy of* Dr. Ronald Melzack.)

then added for each of the major categories: sensory, affective, and evaluative.

The number of words chosen (NWC) index represents another pain-indexing scale in which the net change in the number of descriptors selected is calculated. Melzack and Torgerson [101] observed that significant changes in pain intensity or relief were not associated with decreases in the NWC. Patients experiencing improved analgesia tended to pick one word per subclass that had a lower intensity rather than drop that subclass altogether.

The present pain intensity (PPI) index is recorded as a number corresponding to pain descriptors denoting increases in the severity of pain. For example, 1 represents mild, whereas 5 indicates excruciating pain (Fig. 2-8). This assessment is similar to the numerical rating scale. As such, the PPI shares the disadvantage of being based on a single decision point. In turn, it may also be influenced by several psychological variables in addition to the patient's overall pain intensity.

The MPQ provides statistically significant information used for data analysis. This tool can distinguish qualitative differences among various modes of pain therapy and between different analgesics [86], attributable to the in-depth nature of the assessment. It also provides relative information regarding the sensory, affective, and evaluative dimensions of pain.

There are several disadvantages associated with MPQ testing. The first limitation is that it is too lengthy. Frequent pain assessments are not feasible because of time constraints involved. Patients tend to become frustrated and lose interest with long, frequently applied questionnaires, especially during the immediate postoperative period and at night.

ASSESSMENT OF PAIN IN CHILDREN

There are several methods that can be used to assess the pain of a child. The tool selected must take into consideration the child's age, cognitive ability, and communication skills [102].

Visual analogue scales can be used with children who are able to understand spatial differences and indicate their degree of pain on a relative scale. Although some authors indicate that a VAS can be used with preschool children, its practicality extends to those children older than 8 years of age.

The numerical rating score (NRS) is similar to the VAS, but it incorporates numbers along the continuum. The numbers 0 through 10 are spaced at intervals along the line. This method allows the child to relate to a concrete number corresponding to the intensity of the pain. NRS can be used with children who can count and have an understanding of the progression of numbers.

The Oucher Scale, sometimes referred to as the Faces Rating Scale, is based on the idea of a VAS [103]. This tool depicts six faces ranging from a sad, crying face to a happy face (Fig. 2-9). The child selects the face that best represents himself or herself at the time. These faces have a corresponding number indicating the degree of pain experienced. The sad and crying face, or the 5, represents the greatest pain, whereas the happy face is a 0—meaning no pain. This scale can be used for all verbal children, including adolescents.

Body outlines is a creative tool that allows children to express the location of pain by marking the affected area or areas on a diagram of the body (Fig. 2-10) [100]. Both anterior and posterior views of a child's body are presented to the patient, and they are instructed to color the areas that are hurting them at this time. Savedra and coworkers [98,100,104] combined three pain assessment methods to create a multidimensional tool to measure pain in children: body outline, pain-intensity scale, and a pain-word descriptor list. They found that a child's markings on a body outline corresponded with their surgical incision site in 94% of their patients (n = 47). They also found that children and adolescents completed this task most readily and without any difficulty. Although some difficulties did exist with the pain-intensity scale and the word list, they concluded that the children were able to use the multidimensional tool to report their pain after major surgeries.

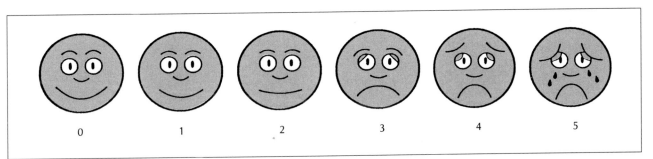

Figure 2-9 The Oucher Scale, the Yale Pain Management Service/face rating scale. (*From* Whaley and Wong [103]; with permission.)

Because coloring is a favorite pastime of many children, allowing children to use colors to demonstrate their pain intensity seems appropriate. Many associate the color blue to mean cold, whereas red is associated with hot. But what color is pain? Unfortunately, there is not a distinctive color that is uniform among children. This inadequacy limits the use of color selection. Colors predetermined by each individual child may be effective but this method is subject to controversy. Not only would this method be time consuming, but also children may change their minds or forget what was originally conveyed, thereby communicating erroneously.

CONCLUSIONS

The neurochemistry of acute pain is complex. Although much is known about the neurotransmitters that play a role in the processing of nociceptive information, much remains to be determined. In addition to the neurotransmitters described, many more certainly exist and have yet to be discovered. The functional significance of the interaction between multiple neurotransmitters has only begun to be determined and will certainly add to the complexity of the system.

Opportunities exist for multiple sites of pain modulation at each link in the pain-processing system. For example, morphine can exert its effects on multiple areas of the neuraxis including peripheral, spinal, and supraspinal sites. An increased knowledge of the physiologic and pharmacologic mechanisms of pain transmission will allow for the development of novel analgesic agents.

Several methods or agents may be combined in an effort to maximize analgesic effectiveness (Fig. 2-11) [74]. A comprehensive approach that could theoretically ablate aspects of acute pain perception and associated responses should include the following:

1. The use of nonsteroidal anti-inflammatory drugs, antihistamines, and serotonin antagonists, which are capable of attenuating nociceptor activation and the elaboration of hyperalgesia.

2. Conduction blockage of noxious transmission with dilute solutions of bupivacaine.

3. Dorsal horn modulation of nociceptive transmission with epidurally applied opioids and opioid–local anesthetic mixtures.

4. The administration of substrates such as glucose and branched-chain amino acids, and the systemic administration of glucocorticoids, which have been recommended to ablate the catabolic response.

The problem that needs to be addressed is whether the effort extended to prevent postoperative pain and ablate the stress response to acute injury results in improved outcome. Preliminary findings in high-risk patient pop-

ulations indicate that epidural analgesia may significantly reduce the incidence of major postsurgical morbidity and death [104–108]. These studies have been criticized, however, because of their small sample size and variability of anesthetic technique. Larger controlled studies are needed to confirm these findings.

Regional anesthesia with local anesthetics is presently the most effective, although not optimal, approach in the modification of the surgical stress response [109•].

Thoracic epidural anesthesia does not appear to offer cardiac protection for patients with coronary artery disease when applied intraoperatively only. With the recent knowledge of the importance of the postopera-

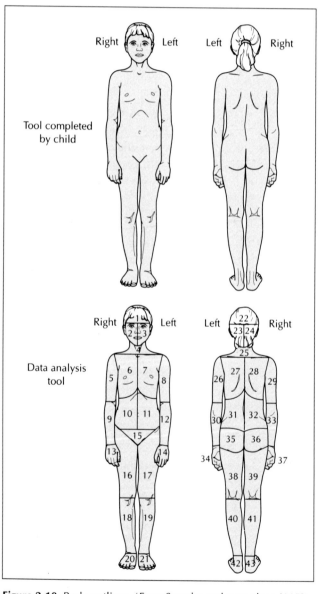

Figure 2-10 Body outlines. (*From* Savedra and coworkers [115]; with permission.)

tive management for cardiac outcome [105], it appears reasonable to perform further studies to determine whether postoperative pain relief with epidural or other regional techniques would reduce cardiac morbidity. Finnegan and coworkers [105] investigated whether thoracic epidural anesthesia added to light, balanced anesthesia is associated with a lower cardiac and pulmonary complication rate than general anesthesia alone. Three different postoperative pain regimens were used: subcutaneous morphine, epidural fentanyl, or epidural bupivacaine, equally distributed between the two anesthetic groups. Both cardiac and respiratory outcome were identical in the groups. Interestingly, a strong interdependency between respiratory and cardiac complications was observed. Thus, patients with respiratory complications had significantly elevated cardiac complication rates and vice versa.

These results confirm the inconclusive outcome data from two smaller clinical studies in which thoracic epidural anesthesia added to general anesthesia in major abdominal surgery was administered to moderate-risk and extreme high-risk cardiac patients [108,109•]. In the for-

mer study, epidural analgesia was prolonged into the postoperative period and excellent pain relief was documented compared to patients given systemic morphine. Nevertheless, cardiac outcome was not significantly better in patients with epidural anesthesia or analgesia [110••].

Further studies are needed to point out the benefits of regional anesthesia on pulmonary function in postoperative patients. A group of at-risk patients may benefit from the effects of regional anesthesia; however, further evidence is required to support this postulate (Fig. 2-12). Extradural opioids provide more frequent and pronounced episodes of hypoxemia than are observed with parenterally delivered opioids, which are accompanied by an insidious and unpredictable change in respiratory pattern. Bradyapnea and central and obstructive apnea would seem to be the cause of such hypoxemic episodes [110••].

Several clinical studies have shown that epidural analgesia with local anesthetics improves postoperative gastrointestinal functions, with normalized gastric emptying and reduced paralytic ileus time. In contrast, both epidural and systemic opioids have a negative effect on gastrointestinal propulsive motility and are combined

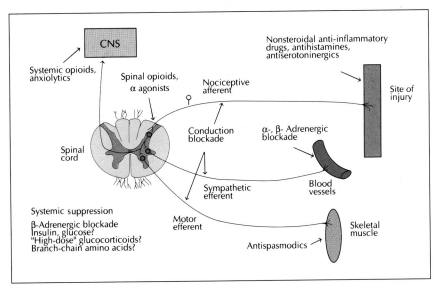

Figure 2-11 Agents and sites used to provide analgesia and attenuate the injury response. Postsurgical pain and the injury response may be attenuated at many levels including inhibition of nociceptor activation blockade of nociceptive afferent transmission, modulation of spinothalamic activity, and suppression of motor and sympathetic reflexes. Systemically administered adrenergic blockers and metabolic substrates have also been advocated to further suppress sympathoadrenal and neuroendocrine responses. CNS—central nervous system. (*Adapted from* Sinatra and Hord [117]; with permission.)

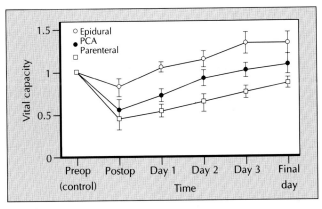

Figure 2-12 Changes in vital capacity relative to preoperative values in patients recovering from major surgical procedures and treated with either epidural morphine, patient-controlled analgesia (PCA), or intermittent opioid dosing (parenteral). (*From* Buckley and coworkers [116]; with permission.)

with a high incidence of nausea and vomiting, delaying commencement of enteral feeding [111•].

Neural blockade with neuraxial administration of local anesthetics or opioids has not yet established its efficacy and safety for postoperative pain treatment. In some situations, such as thoracoabdominal surgery, it has been documented to have superiority over alternative techniques. Further developments of "combined" therapy used in a preemptive way may contribute to prevention of chronic pain. Comparative clinical studies have shown that epidural and systemic opioids, but not epidural local anesthetics, delay postoperative gastric emptying [112].

REFERENCES AND RECOMMENDED READING

Papers of interest, published recently, have been highlighted as:
• Of special interest
•• Of outstanding interest

1. Mitchell RWD, Smith G: The control of acute postoperative pain. *Br J Anaesth* 1989, 63:147–158.

2. Bonica JJ: Definitions and taxonomy of pain. In *Management of Pain*. Edited by Bonica JJ. Philadelphia: Lea & Febiger; 1990:18–27.

3. Cousins MJ: Acute pain and the injury response: immediate and prolonged effects. *Reg Anaesth* 1989, 16:162–176.

4. Ohara H, Naminatsu A, Fukuhara K, *et al.*: Release of inflammatory mediators by noxious stimuli: effect of neurotrophin on the release. *Eur J Pharmacol* 1988, 157:93–99.

5. Cohen RH, Perl ER: Contributions of arachidonic acid derivatives and substance P to the sensitization of cutaneous nociceptors. *J Neurophysiol* 1990, 64:457–464.

6. Taiwo YO, Levine JD: Prostaglandin effects after elimination of indirect hyperalgesic mechanism in the skin of the rat. *Brain Res* 1988, 458:402–406.

7. Kaplan AP: The relationship of Hageman factor activation to the formation of bradykinin in humans: a historical perspective. *Prog Clin Biol Res* 1989, 297:311–323.

8. Kaplan AP, Silverberg M, Ghebrehiwet B, *et al.*: Pathways of kinin formation and role in allergic disease. *Clin Immunol Immunopathol* 1989, 50:S41–S51.

9. Taiwo YO, Levine JD: Characterization of the arachidonic acid metabolites mediating bradykinin and noradrenaline hyperalgesia. *Brain Res* 1988, 458:402–406.

10. Martin HA: Leukotriene BR induced decrease in mechanical and thermal thresholds of C-fiber mechanoreceptors in rat hairy skin. *Brain Res* 1990, 509:273–279.

11. Devillier P, Regioli D, Asseraf A, *et al.*: Histamine release and local responses of rat and human skin to substance P and other mammalian tachykinins. *Pharmacology* 1986, 32:320–347.

12. Louis SM, Jameson A, Russel NJW, *et al.*: The role of substance P and calcitonin gene-related peptide in neurogenic plasma extravasation and vasodilation in the rat. *Neuroscience* 1989, 32:581–586.

13. Dray A, Bettany J, Forster P, *et al.*: Activation of bradykinin receptor in peripheral nerve and spinal cord in the neonatal rat *in vitro. Br J Pharmacol* 1988, 95:1008–1010.

14. Steranka LR, Manning DC, Dehaas CJ, *et al.*: Bradykinin as a pain mediator; receptors are localized to sensory neurons, and antagonists have analgesic actions. *Proc Natl Acad Sci U S A* 1988, 85:3245–3249.

15. Shabata M, Uhkubo T, Takashi H, *et al.*: Interaction of bradykinin with substance P on vascular permeability and pain response. *Jpn J Pharmacol* 1986, 41:427–429.

16. Les PY, Pearce FL: Histamine secretion from mast cells stimulated with bradykinin. *Agents Actions* 1990, 30:67–69.

17. Levine JD, Taiwo YO, Collins SD, *et al.*: Noradrenaline hyperalgesia is mediated through interaction with sympathetic postganglionic neuron terminals rather than activation of primary afferent nociceptors. *Nature* 1986, 323:158–160.

18. Tuchscherer MM, Sybold VS: Immunohistochemical studies of substance P, cholecystokinin-octapeptide, and somatostatin dorsal root ganglia of the rat. *Neuroscience* 1985, 14:593–605.

19. Go VLW, Yaksh TL: Release of substance P from the cat spinal cord. *J Physiol* 1987, 391:141–167.

20. Duggan AW, Morton CR, Zhao ZG, *et al.*: Noxious heating of the skin releases immunoreactive substance P in the substantia gelatinosa of the cat: a study with antibody microprobes. *Brain Res* 1987, 403:345–349.

21. Lee Y, Takami K, Kawai Y, *et al.*: Distribution of calcitonin gene-related peptide in the rat peripheral nervous system with reference to its co-existence with substance P. *Neuroscience* 1985, 15:1227–1237.

22. Merighi A, Polak JM, Gibson SJ, *et al.*: Ultrastructural studies on calcitonin gene-related peptide-, tachykinins-, and somatostatin-immunoreactive neurons in rat dorsal root ganglia: evidence for the colocalization of different peptides in single secretory granules. *Cell Tissue Res* 1988, 254:101–109.

23. Skofitsch G, Jacobowitz DM: Calcitonin gene-related peptide coexists with substance P in capsaicin sensitive neurons and sensory ganglia of the rat. *Peptides* 1985, 6:747–754.

24. Morton CR, Hutchison WD: Release of sensory neuropeptides in the spinal cord: studies with calcitonin gene-related peptide and galanin. *Neuroscience* 1989, 31:807–815.

25. Saria A, Gamse R, Petermann J, *et al.*: Simultaneous release of several tachykinins and calcitonin gene-related peptide from rat spinal cord slices. *Neurosci Lett* 1986, 63:310–314.

26. Oku R, Satoh M, Fujii N, *et al.*: Calcitonin gene-related peptide promotes mechanical nociception by potentiating the release of substance P from the spinal dorsal horn in rats. *Brain Res* 1987, 403:350–354.

27. Woolf C, Wiesenfeld-Hallin Z: Substance P and calcitonin gene-related peptide synergistically modulate the gain of the nociceptive flexor withdrawal reflex in the rat. *Neurosci Lett* 1986, 55:226–230.

28. Yaksh TL, Aimone LD: The central pharmacology of pain transmission. In *Textbook of Pain*. Edited by Wall PD, Melzack R. New York: Churchill Livingstone; 1989:181–205.

29. Aanonsen LM, Wilcox GL: Nociceptive action of the excitatory amino acids in the mouse: effects of spinally administered opioids, phencyclidine and sigma agonists. *J Pharmacol Exp Ther* 1987, 243:9–19.

30. Raigorodsky G, Urca G: Involvement of N-methyl-D-aspartate receptors in nociception and motor control in the spinal cord of the mouse: behavioral, pharmacological and electrophysiological evidence. *Neuroscience* 1990, 36:601–610.

31. Schneider SP, Perl EP: Selective excitation of neurons in the mammalian spinal cord by aspartate and glutamate *in vitro*: correlation with location and excitatory input. *Brain Res* 1985, 360:339–343.

32. Battaglia G, Rustioni A: Co-existance of glutamate and substance P in dorsal root ganglion neurons of the rat and monkey. *J Comp Neurol* 1988, 277:302–312.

33. DeBiasi S, Rustioni A: Glutamate and substance P co-exist in the primary afferent terminals of the superficial laminae of spinal cord. *Proc Natl Acad Sci U S A* 1988, 85:7820–7824.

34. McCarson KE, Goldstein BD: Time course of the alteration of dorsal horn substance P levels following formalin blockage by naloxone. *Pain* 1990, 41:95–100.

35. Skilling SR, Smullin DH, Beitz AJ, *et al.*: Extracellular amino acid concentrations in the dorsal spinal cord of freely moving rats following veratridine and nociceptive stimulation. *J Neurochem* 1988, 51:127–132.

36. Murray CW, Cowan A, Larson AA: Neurokinin and NMDA antagonists (but not a kainic acid antagonist) are antinociceptive in the mouse formalin model. *Pain* 1991, 44:179–185.

37. Smullin DH, Skilling SR, Larson AA: Interaction between substance P, calcitonin gene-related peptide, taurine and excitatory amino acids in the spinal cord. *Pain* 1990, 42:93–101.

38. Kangrga I, Randic M: Tachykinins and calcitonin gene-related peptide enhance release of endogenous glutamate and aspartate from the rat spinal dorsal horn slice. *J Neurosci* 1990, 10:2026–2038.

39. Kangrga I, Larew JSA, Randic M: The effects of substance P and calcitonin gene-related peptide on the efflux of endogenous glutamate and aspartate from rat spinal dorsal horn *in vitro*. *Neurosci Lett* 1990, 108:155–160.

40. Hutchison WD, Morton CR, Terenius L: Dynorphin A: *in vivo* release in the spinal cord of the cat. *Brain Res* 1990, 532:299–306.

41. Aanonsen LM, Wilcox GL: Muscimol, gamma-aminobutyric acid A receptors and excitatory amino acids in the mouse spinal cord. *J Pharmacol Exp Ther* 1988, 248:1034–1038.

42. Hirota N, Kuraishi Y, Hino Y, *et al.*: Metenkephalin and morphine but not dynorphin inhibit the noxious stimuli-induced release of substance P from rabbit dorsal horn in situ. *Neuropharmacology* 1985, 24:567–570.

43. Pohl M, Lombard MC, Bourgoin S, *et al.*: Opioid control for the *in vitro* release of calcitonin gene-related peptide from primary afferent fibers projecting in the rat cervical cord. *Neuropeptides* 1989, 14:151–159.

44. Sabbe MB, Yaksh TL: Pharmacology of spinal opioids. *J Pain Symptom Management* 1990, 5:191–203.

45. Lombard M-C, Benson J-M: Attempts to gauge the relative importance of pre- and postsynaptic effects of morphine on the transmission of noxious message in the dorsal horn of the rat spinal cord. *Pain* 1989, 37:335–345.

46. Goodchild CS, Serrao JM: Intrathecal midazolam in the rat: evidence for spinally-mediated analgesia. *Br J Anaesth* 1987, 59:1563–1570.

47. Sawynok J: GABAergic mechanisms of analagesia: an update. *Pharmacol Biochem Behav* 1987, 26:463–474.

48. Pan I-H, Vasko MR: Morphine and norepinephrine but not 5-hydroxytryptamine and gamma-aminobutyric acid inhibit the potassium-stimulated release of substance P from rat spinal cord slices. *Brain Res* 1986, 376:268–279.

49. Fisher B, Zornow MH, Yaksh TL, *et al.*: Antinociceptive properties of intrathecal dexmedetomadline in rats. *Eur J Pharmacol* 1991, 192:221–225.

50. Yaksh TL: Pharmacology of spinal adrenergic systems which modulate spinal nociceptive processing. *Pharmacol Biochem Behav* 1985, 22:845–855.

51. Fleetwood-Walker SM, Mitchell R, Hope PJ, *et al.*: An alpha$_2$ receptor mediates the selective inhibition of noradrenaline of nociceptive responses of identified dorsal horn neurons. *Brain Res* 1985, 334:243–254.

52. Kuraishi Y, Hirota N, Sato Y, *et al.*: Noradrenergic inhibition of the release of substance P from the primary afferents in the rabbit spinal dorsal horn. *Brain Res* 1985, 359:177–182.

53. Calvillo O, Ghigone M: Presynaptic effect of clonidine on unmyelinated afferent fibers in the spinal cord in the cat. *Neurosci Lett* 1986, 64:335–339.

54. Sawynok J, Sweeney MI, White TD: Classification of adenosine receptors mediating antinociception in the rat spinal cord. *Br J Pharmacol* 1986, 88:923–930.

55. Choco JI, Green RD, Proudfit HK: Adenosine A1 and A2 receptors of the substantia gelatinosa are located predominantly on intrinsic neurons: an autoradiographic study. *J Pharmacol Exp Ther* 1988, 247:757–764.

56. DeLander GE, Hopkins CJ: Spinal adenosine modulates descending antinociceptive pathways stimulated by morphine. *J Pharmacol Exp Ther* 1986, 239:88–93.

57. Sweeney MI, White TD, Sawynok J: Involvement of adenosine in the spinal antinociceptive effects of morphine and noradrenaline. *J Pharmacol Exp Ther* 1987, 243:657–665.

58. Sosnowski M, Stevens CW, Yaksh TL: Assessment of the role of A1/A2 adenosine receptors mediating the purine antinociception, motor and autonomic function in the spinal cord. *J Pharmacol Exp Ther* 1989, 248:1269–1275.

59. Sosnowski M, Yaksh TL: Spinal administration of receptor selective drug as analgesics: new horizons. *J Pain Symptom Management* 1990, 5:204–213.

60. Yaksh TL, Dirksen R, Harty GL: Antinociceptive effects of intrathecally injected cholinomimetic drugs in the rat and cat. *Eur J Pharmacol* 1985, 78:81–88.

61. Gaumann DM, Grabow TS, Yaksh TL, *et al.*: Intrathecal somatostatin, somatostatin analogs, substance P analog and dynorphin A cause neurotoxicity in rats. *Neuroscience* 1990, 39:761–771.

62. Gebhart GF: Modulatory effects of descending systems on spinal dorsal horn neurons. In *Spinal Afferent Processing*. Edited by Yaksh TL. New York: Plenum Press; 1986:287–295.

63. Hammond DL: Control systems for nociceptive afferent processing. In *Spinal Afferent Processing*. Edited by Yaksh TL. New York: Plenum Press; 1986:363–390.

64. Mayer DI: Endogenous analgesia system: neural and behavioral mechanisms. In *Advances in Pain Research and Therapy*. vol. 3. Edited by Liebeskind JC, Albe-Fessard DG. New York: Raven Press; 1989:297–335.

65. Costello AH, Hargreave KM: Suppression of carrageenan-induced hyperalgesia, hyperthermia and edema by a bradykinin antagonist. *Eur J Pharmacol* 1989, 171:259–263.

66. Campbell JN, Raja SN, Cohen RH, *et al.*: Peripheral neural mechanisms of nociception. In *Textbook of Pain*. Edited by Wall PD, Melzack R. New York: Churchill Livingstone; 1989:22–45.

67. Cechetto DF, Saper CB: Neurochemical organization of the hypothalamic projection to the spinal cord in the rat. *J Comp Neurol* 1988, 272:579–604.

68. Christopherson R, Rock P, Parker S, *et al.*: Tachycardia occurs more frequently postoperatively than intraoperatively in patients at risk for perioperative myocardial ischemia. *Anesthesiology* 1989, 71:A950.

69. Beattie WS, Buckley DN, Forrest JB: Reduction of significant cardiac morbidity by epidural morphine in non-cardiac surgery. *Anesthesiology* 1990, 73:A71.

70. Breslow MJ: Neuroendocrine responses to surgery. In *Perioperative Management*. Edited by Breslow MJ, Miller CF, Rogers MC. St. Louis: Mosby Year Book; 1990:180–193.

71. Brown DL, Carpenter RL: Perioperative analgesia: a review of risks and benefits. *J Cardiothorac Anesth* 1990, 4:368–383.

72. Ellis JE, Busse JR, Foss JF, *et al.*: Postoperative management of myocardial ischemia. *Anesthesiol Clin* 1991, 9:609–635.

73. Blomberg S, Emanuelsson H, Kvist H, *et al.*: Effects of thoracic epidural anesthesia on coronary arteries and arterioles in patients with coronary artery disease. *Anesthesiology* 1990, 73:840–847.

74. Kehlet H: Modification of responses to surgery by neural blockade: clinical implications. In *Neural Blockade in Clinical Anesthesia and Management of Pain*. Edited by Cousins MJ, Bridenbaugh PO. Philadelphia: Lippincott; 1987:134–145.

75. Willerson JT, Golino P, Eidt J, *et al.*: Specific platelet mediators and unstable coronary artery lesions: experimental evidence and clinical implications. *Circulation* 1989, 80:198–205.

76. Sprung J, Cheng EY, Rodante JR: Mechanism producing respiratory insufficiency after abdominal surgery: pain vs. diaphragm dysfunction. *Anesth Analg* 1990, 70:S388.

77. Payne R: Cancer pain: anatomy, physiology and pharmacology. *Cancer* 1989, 63(suppl):2266.

78. Procacci P, Maresca M: Pathophysiology of visceral pain. In *Advances in Pain Research and Therapy*. vol 13. Edited by Lipton S, *et al.* New York: Raven Press; 1990.

79. Cervero F: Visceral pain. In *Proceedings of the VI World Congress on Pain*. Edited by Dubner R, Gebhart GF, Bond MR. Amsterdam: Elsevier; 1988:216.

80. Tasker RR, Dostrovsky JO: Deafferentation and central pain. In *Textbook of Pain*. 2nd ed. Edited by Wall PD, Melzack R. Edinburgh: Churchill Livingstone; 1989:154.

81. Merskey H: Classification of chronic pain: description of chronic pain syndromes and definition of pain terms. *Pain* 1986, 3(suppl):S1.

82. Cornwall A, Donderi DC: The effect of experimentally induced anxiety on the experience of pressure pain. *Pain* 1988, 35:105–113.

83. Jay SM, Elliott CH, Varni JW, *et al.*: Behavioral management of children's distress during painful medical procedures. *Behav Res Ther* 1985, 23:513–520.

84. Jamison RN, Parris WCV, Maxson WS: Psychological factors influencing recovery from outpatient surgery. *Behav Res Ther* 1987, 25:31–37.

85. Gil KM, Ginsberg B, Muir M, *et al.*: Patient-controlled analgesia in postoperative pain: the relation of psychological factors to pain and analgesic use. *Clin J Pain* 1990, 6:137–142.

86. Parker A: An analysis of casarean postoperative pain comparing meperidine, morphine and oxynorphone in PCA. Doctoral dissertation, Yale University School of Medicine, 1988.

87. Iafrati NS: Pain on the burn unit: patient vs nurse perceptions. *J Burn Care Rehabil* 1986, 7:413–416.

88. Jensen IB, Bradley LA, Linton SJ: Validation of an observation method of pain assessment in non-chronic back pain. *Pain* 1989, 39:267–274.

89. Seers K: Factors affecting pain assessment. *Professional Nurse* 1988, 3:201–206.

90. Choiniére M, Melzack R, Girard N, *et al.*: Comparisons between patients' and nurses' assessment of pain and medication efficacy in severe burn injuries. *Pain* 1990, 40:143–152.

91. Dalton JA: Nurses' perceptions of their pain assessment skills, pain management practices, and attitudes toward pain. *Oncol Nurs Forum* 1989, 16:225–231.

92. Ellis JA: Using pain scales to prevent undermedication. *Am J Maternal Child Nurs* 1988, 13:180–182.

93. Ferrante FM, Orav EJ, Rocco AG, *et al.*: A statistical model of pain in PCA and conventional IM opioid regimens. *Anesth Analg* 1988, 67:457–461.

94. Parker A, Sinatra RS, Harrison DM, *et al.*: A qualitative comparison of pain with the McGill Pain Questionnaire using meperidine, morphine, and oxymorphone in PCA. *Anesthesiology* 1987, 67:A239.

95. Sinatra RS, Sevarino FB, Chung JH, *et al.*: Comparison of epidurally administered sufentanil, morphine and sufentanil-morphine combination. *Anesth Analg* 1991, 72:522–527.

96. Bercker M, Hughes B: Using a tool for pain assessment. *Nurs Times* 1990, 86:50–52.

97. Holm K, Cohen F, Dudas S, *et al.*: Effect of personal pain experience on pain assessment. *Image, J Nurs Scholarship* 1989, 21:72–75.

98. Savedra M, Tesler M, Wilkie D, *et al.*: Pain location: validity and reliability of body outline markings by hospitalized children and adolescents. *Res Nurs Health* 1989, 12:307–314.

99. Chapman CR, Casey KL, Dubner R, *et al.*: Pain measurement: an overview. *Pain* 1985, 22:1–31.

100. Savedra MC, Tesler MD, Holzemer WL, *et al.*: Testing a tool to assess postoperative pediatric and adolescent pain. *Adv Pain Res Ther* 1990, 15:86–93.

101. Metzack R, Torgerson WS: On the language of pain. *Anesthesiology* 1971, 34:50–59.

102. Maunuksela EL, Olkkola KT, Korpela R: Measurement of pain in children with self-reporting and behavioral assessment. *Clin Pharmacol Ther* 1987, 42:137–141.

103. Whaley L, Wong D: *Nursing Care of Infants and Children.* 4th ed. St. Louis: Mosby-Year Book; 1991:1148.

104. Savedra M, Tesler M, Ward J, *et al.*: Children's preferences for pain intensity scales [abstract]. *Pain* 1987, 4:S234.

105. Finnegan RF, Thompson BW, MacDonald CM: Comparison of epidural and general anesthesia for lower extremity vascular surgery: postoperative graft flow rates. *Anesth Analg* 1989, 68:S85.

106. Hjortsø NC, Christensen NJ, Andersen T, *et al.*: Effects of extradural local anaesthetics and morphine on morbidity after abdominal surgery. *Acta Anaesthesiol Scand* 1985, 27:790–795.

107. Norris E, Parker S, Breslow M, *et al.*: The endocrine response to surgical stress: a comparison of epidural anesthesia/analgesia vs. general anesthesia/PCA. *Anesthesiology* 1991, 75:A696.

108. Mangano D, London MJ, Tubau JF, *et al.*: Association of perioperative myocardial ischemia with cardiac morbidity and mortality in men undergoing non-cardiac surgery. *N Engl J Med* 1990, 323:1781.

109.• Rigg J: Does regional block improve outcome after surgery? *Anaesth Intens Care Med* 1991, 19:404–411.

This paper examines the claim that the use of local anesthetics improves surgical outcome. The paper further attempts to examine the biological hypothesis on which the data was based and relevance of the clinical research methodology. The author recommends appropriate strategies in planning and execution of randomized trials to assess the efficacy of regional block in determining outcome after surgery.

110.•• Baron J, Barre E, Raimbault E, *et al.*: Thoracic epidural anaesthesia versus general anaesthesia for high risk surgical patients. *Anesthesiology* 1991, 75:611.

The authors studied the efficacy of thoracic epidural anesthesia in 173 patients undergoing abdominal aortic surgery. This was a randomized study and the purpose was to determine postoperative morbidity in comparison with the group who received balanced general anesthesia alone. Cardiovascular morbidity did not differ between the group with thoracic epidural anesthesia and the group with balanced general anesthesia. This is in contradiction to other studies that have shown less postoperative morbidity with thoracic epidural anesthesia.

111.• Wheatley R, Somerville ID, Sapsford DJ: Postoperative hypoxeamia: comparison of extradural IM and patient controlled opioid analgesia. *Br J Anaesth* 1990, 64:267–273.

In this study of 30 patients the authors analyzed the levels of arterial oxygen saturation (SaO_2) in three groups using either intravenous diamorphine with PCA, or extradural morphine or intramuscular morphine. Hypoxemia occurred in all three analgesia groups, but extradural diamorphine tended to cause longer periods. The authors believe that patients at risk of postoperative hypoxemia may be predicted by preoperative monitoring of SaO_2, however, extradural diamorphine boluses may cause postoperative hypoxemia even in patients with normal preoperative values.

112. Thorn SE, Wattwil M, Naslund I: Postoperative epidural morphine, but not epidural bupivacaine, delays gastric emptying on the first day after cholecystectomy. *Reg Anaesth* 1992, 17: in press.

113. Brown DL, Neal JM: Chronic obstructive pulmonary disease and perioperative analgesia. *Probl Anesth* 1988, 2:422–434.

114. Portenoy RK: Issues in the management of neuropathic pain. In *Towards a New Pharmacotherapy of Pain.* Edited by Basbaum AI, Besson JM. New York: John Wiley and Sons; 1991:393.

115. Savedra M, Tester M, Holzemer W, *et al.*: Testing a tool to assess postoperative pediatric and adolescent pain. *Adv Pain Res Ther* 1990, 15:86–93.

116. Buckley DN, Beattie S, Lindblad T, *et al.*: Epidural analgesia prevents loss of lung volume. *Anesthesiology* 1990, 73:A764.

117. Sinatra RS, Hord AS, eds. *Acute Pain Mechanisms and Management.* St. Louis: Mosby-Year Book; 1992.

CHAPTER 3

Classification and Assessment of Chronic Pain

JOHN C. ROWLINGSON

WHAT IS TAXONOMY?

The word *taxonomy* literally means the systematic classification of subjects into groups to reflect similarity, with generally broader groups residing over those that are more restricted. The process for establishing an orderly arrangement in the evaluation of chronic pain is an immense task and many systems have been proposed. Whatever system is created needs to have a wide enough application to cover both clinical practice and research and not just some bureaucratic regulations. It is reasonable to ask, "why do we need a taxonomy?" Clearly, there are problems we face with pain, which include the following:

1. We lack the universal acceptance of an exact definition of pain.

2. There is no scientific or mathematical way to easily measure or quantify pain. Pain is a subjective experience and, thus, the patient's personal report becomes the best assessment.

3. There are difficulties when we accept the patient's outward behavior as the significant indicator for the intensity of the pain, because there can be problems in interpretation as a result of distortion through observer bias.

4. The diverse meanings, the different expressions, and the spectrum of reactions to pain result in wide variability of patient response and in our clinical experience.

5. In the past there was minimal research and poor experimental models available, particularly for chronic pain. Now there is an explosion of research, but it is conducted in so many specialties that it is extremely hard to stay abreast of it all.

6. Poor communication among specialists delays the intellectual exchange of information, which is the basis not only for understanding the physiological and psychological aspects of pain but also its diagnosis and management.

7. There are problems with the teaching of what is known and what is being discovered, let alone the clinical application thereof.

WHAT IS PAIN?

The International Association for the Study of Pain (IASP) defines pain as "an unpleasant sensory and emotional experience associated with actual or potential tissue damage or described in terms of such damage" [1,2,3•]. It is important to emphasize from this definition that pain is always subjective, is always a sensation, is always unpleasant, and we are urged to evaluate both the physical and the nonphysical components of the experience called "pain." Pain is actually a construct or concept [2]. It is a function of the theoretical orientation one takes in regard to it. For instance, a neurosurgeon who sees pain as neuroanatomic or neurophysiologic events will not see the psychological aspects of pain as significant. On the other hand, the psychologist will understand pain to be an integration of physical, psychological, and social factors and apply to his patients emotional, environmental, and psychophysiologic questions in search of variations within these realms. Two qualified specialists, then, can come up with a very different impression of a patient with pain.

Chronic pain really means that the pain is not acute [3•]. This is pain that goes on and on despite good therapy and sometimes extraordinary treatment. Chronic pain can interfere with the patient's attitude about health and recovery, and his or her behaviors as well as lifestyle. Furthermore, these patients suffer. The emotional and psychosocial influence on pain was highlighted by Twycross [4] in 1980. He was assessing factors that affect the pain threshold (the point at which a given stimulus provokes the report of pain from a patient) in hospice patients in England. Twycross listed conditions such as discomfort, insomnia, fatigue, anxiety, fear, anger, and depression as factors that would tend to lower a patient's threshold. On the other hand, the threshold could be raised by relief of pain, restful sleep, relaxation, sympathy and understanding, elevation of mood, and diversion from the pain.

WHY IS PAIN SO DIFFICULT TO DESCRIBE?

When we try to comprehend why chronic pain is so complicated, we come up with the following comments:

1. Pain is clearly a multidimensional experience. It is neurophysiologic, biochemical, psychological, ethnocultural, religious, cognitive, affective, and environmental. Thus, its classification can be understandably complex and its management elusive.

2. Acute pain is not the same as chronic pain. When one applies acute pain evaluation and treatment principles to patients with chronic pain, satisfactory management may not result.

3. Lack of success in evaluation and treatment causes frustration and desperation in patients and healthcare professionals. We must be wary of decisions concerning treatment that are made out of desperation.

4. A comprehensive evaluation scheme is needed to yield the diagnosis of what is wrong with the patient and what is on his or her personal agenda. There then needs to be a taxonomy with which healthcare professionals can converse.

5. A comprehensive management program that will address all of the sources for the "pain" that are discovered in the evaluation is required. Creating this, explaining it thoroughly to the patient, and achieving compliance are time-consuming tasks for the healthcare professional.

6. Chronic pain results in physiologic, anatomic, and behavioral changes that persist even when the original pathologic condition is removed.

ORGANIZATIONAL SYSTEMS FROM THE PAST

Systems Based on Definitions

In the primitive past, the complaints of the patient were accepted as *the* diagnosis and the patient's problem was labeled as such. But what was pain to one person could be described quite differently by another. When the responsibility for diagnosis became the domain of the physician, the issue of classification of the disease was not solved owing to the opportunity for bias and variation in interpretation [5,6•]. The simplest system would use definitions and provide the following classification [3•]:

1. Acute pain
2. Chronic pain of nonmalignant origin
   a. Chronic medical illness with ongoing pain, acute or chronic
   b. Chronic pain with a specific diagnosis
   c. Chronic pain without a specific diagnosis
3. Cancer-related pain

Acute Versus Chronic Pain

When we begin to consider different types of pain, we can compare them. Table 3-1 characterizes the differences between acute and chronic pain based on clinical features. We appreciate that these two entities are different diseases, each distinguished by the knowledge base that is required for its evaluation and management, the clinical experience gained by healthcare professionals in their choice to deal with such patients, the extent of "body involvement" with pain and the time it takes for the chronic pain syndrome to develop, the responses of the nervous system to either the acute or the ongoing pain, the possibility that adverse behavioral consequences will develop, and the fact that all treatments done for acute pain may make chronic pain worse. Cancer pain will have features of both acute and chronic pain.

Cancer Pain

Foley [7] has long championed the classification of cancer-related pain problems by a system based on syndromes. This concept has recently been reaffirmed by Portenoy [8]. Cancer pain is broken down into the following categories:

1. Pain caused by the cancer process itself, *ie*, bony invasion or nerve compression or infiltration which is likely to present with acute pain features.
2. Pain arising from the treatment for the cancer process is likely to present as chronic pain. This might include pain that follows radical surgery, chemotherapy, or radiation therapy.

TABLE 3-1
CLINICAL FEATURES IN THE DIFFERENTIATION OF ACUTE AND CHRONIC PAIN

ACUTE PAIN	CHRONIC PAIN
Ample training and opportunity to treat	Less training and opportunity
Evaluation and treatment takes less time	Time-consuming evaluation process
Pain is a useful biologic signal	Pain is a disease affecting attitudes, lifestyles, and behavior
Pain plus anxiety	Pain plus frustration
Usually self-limiting; short treatment duration	Persists; long treatment duration
Individual problem	Pain involves more individuals than the patient
Priority of treatment options is clear	Different priority of treatment options
Patient's needs are in tune with treatment goals	Patient's needs are not necessarily to get better
Likelihood of successful treatment is high	Less likelihood of complete treatment success
Expectations of treatment are high	Need realistic expectations of treatment

---

3. It is quite possible, as per the contemporary definition of pain, that the patient will have "pain" that is not directly related to either the primary malignancy or to the treatment for it. Thus, such symptoms as bedsores, chronic infection, constipation, or concern that the patient's disease will drain the family's financial resources all become potential sources of "pain."

Chronic Pain

Feuerstein [2] delineated the components of an operational definition for chronic pain. In this categorization he found the following features would be important:

1. Pain sensation.
2. Pain behavior.
3. Functional status at work: this basically involves the traditional ergonomic considerations.
4. Functional status at home: this includes not just the physical environment but evaluation of the family interaction system based on roles that each member plays, the communications that occur, and the problem-solving skills that are available to individuals and within the family unit.
5. The emotional state of the patient: this plays a significant role in the initiation, exacerbation, and maintenance of chronic pain; again, pain is not all physical and this important component must be evaluated.
6. Somatic preoccupation: this reflects the undue focus the patient maintains on bodily symptoms, almost to the exclusion of the ability to function.

Feuerstein [2] also reminds us of the need for a classification system to address the modern-day issues of chronic pain:

1. Impairment, which is any loss or abnormality of psychological, physiologic, or anatomic structure or function. Functions that may be affected by chronic pain could include walking, standing, sitting, reaching, lifting, bending, attentional abilities, mood, and social interaction.
2. Functional limitation, which is any restriction or lack of ability to perform an activity in the manner or within the range considered normal for an individual that results from an impairment.
3. Disability, which is a disadvantage for a given individual, resulting from an impairment or a functional limitation, that limits or prevents the fulfillment of a role that is normal given the patient's age, sex, social, and cultural factors.

These issues were raised expressly concerning patients with low back pain in a recent article by Harper and coworkers [9]. There have to be ways by which medical specialists can communicate precisely with agencies whose involvement with patients depends on the degree of impairment, disability, and functional limitation. Thus, Harper and coworkers proposed a taxonomy that provides a diagnostic vocabulary for clinical and research use, aims to embellish the consistency and comparability of clinical observations, and purports to facilitate the understanding and management of dysfunction in patients with low back pain.

THE INTERNATIONAL ASSOCIATION FOR THE STUDY OF PAIN

Taxonomy and Classification of Pain

Single-axis classification systems, such as those mentioned previously that merely distinguish acute from chronic pain or describe cancer pain syndromes, generally become inadequate when descriptors and qualifiers are needed beyond the simple, primary designation for purposes of exacting exchange of information [5,6•]. The International Association for the Study of Pain (IASP) Subcommittee on Taxonomy created the first multiaxial system based on the region of the body involved in chronic pain, the organ systems affected, the temporal characteristics and pattern of the pain, its duration and intensity, and the source of pain [1,3•,5,6•].

Table 3-2 reveals the five-axis pain taxonomy. Axis 1, which deals with the regions in which the pain occurs, is shown in Table 3-3. Axis 2, which involves the systems of the body that are involved in the pain, is shown in Table 3-4. Axis 3 is one that relates the temporal characteristics of the pain with attention to the pattern of occurrence. These features are highlighted in Table 3-5. Table 3-6 reveals the statements of intensity (Axis 4) as provided by the patient, having to do with the time since onset of the pain. Table 3-7 demonstrates the components of Axis 5 which have to do with the source of the patient's pain.

THERE IS STILL A NEED TO KNOW MORE SPECIFICS

The advantages of the IASP five-region system are: this system was developed by a multidisciplinary association that was and is widely based in terms of both geography and expertise; the association publishes a respected and well-circulated journal so that the distribution of the taxonomic classification is very good; the system proposed uses criteria on five axes that are already used in medicine so that it should be relatively easy to adopt; and lastly, it is a starting point for a complex task [1,3•]. The system is acknowledged as being provisional yet it is a framework and a place to begin. Its use is hoped to improve communication in both the spoken word and written media for recording symptoms and complaints and to encourage the standardization of observations, reporting and relevance of research, exchange of information, and improvement in the management of pain throughout the world. It is clearly hard to be mutually exclusive and completely exhaustive

TABLE 3-2
OVERVIEW OF THE IASP FIVE-AXIS PAIN TAXONOMY

Axis I: Region

Axis II: System

Axis III: Temporal characteristics of pain: pattern of occurrence

Axis IV: Patient's statement of intensity: time since onset of pain

Axis V: Cause

IASP—International Association for the Study of Pain.

TABLE 3-3
IASP TAXONOMIC CLASSIFICATION OF PAIN: AXIS 1—REGIONS*†

Head, face, and mouth	000
Cervical region	100
Upper shoulder and upper limbs	200
Thoracic region	300
Abdominal region	400
Lower back, lumbar spine, sacrum, and coccyx	500
Lower limbs	600
Pelvic region	700
Anal, perineal, and genital region	800
More than three major sites	900

*From Merskey [1]; with permission.

†Record main site first; record two important regions separately. If there is more than one site of pain, separate coding will be necessary.

IASP—International Association for the Study of Pain.

TABLE 3-4
IASP TAXONOMIC CLASSIFICATION OF PAIN: AXIS II—SYSTEMS*

Nervous system (central, peripheral, and autonomic) and special senses; physical disturbance or dysfunction	00
Nervous system (psychological and social)	10
Respiratory and cardiovascular systems	20
Musculoskeletal system and connective tissue	30
Cutaneous and subcutaneous and associated glands (*eg*, breast, apocrine)	40
Gastrointestinal system	50
Genitourinary system	60
Other organs or viscera (*eg*, thyroid, lymphatic, hemopoietic)	70
More than one system	80

*From Merskey [1]; with permission.
IASP—International Association for the Study of Pain.

TABLE 3-5
IASP TAXONOMIC CLASSIFICATION OF PAIN: AXIS III—TEMPORAL CHARACTERISTICS OF PAIN: PATTERN OF OCCURRENCE[*]

Not recorded, not applicable, or not known	0
Single episode, limited duration (*eg*, ruptured aneurysm, sprained ankle)	1
Continuous or nearly continuous, nonfluctuating (*eg*, low back pain, some cases)	2
Continuous or nearly continuous, fluctuating severity (*eg*, ruptured intervertebral disc)	3
Recurring, irregularly (*eg*, headache, mixed type)	4
Recurring, regularly (*eg*, premenstrual pain)	5
Paroxysmal (*eg*, tic douloureux)	6
Sustained with superimposed paroxysms	7
Other combinations	8
None of the above	9

[*]*From* Merskey [1]; with permission.
IASP—International Association for the Study of Pain.

TABLE 3-6
IASP TAXONOMIC CLASSIFICATION OF PAIN: AXIS IV—PATIENT'S STATEMENT OF INTENSITY: TIME SINCE ONSET OF PAIN*

Not recorded, not applicable, or not known	0.0
Mild	
1 month or less	0.1
1 month to 6 months	0.2
More than 6 months	0.3
Medium	
1 month or less	0.4
1 month to 6 months	0.5
More than 6 months	0.6
Severe	
1 month or less	0.7
1 month to 6 months	0.8
More than 6 months	0.9

From Merskey [1]; with permission.
IASP—International Association for the Study of Pain.

TABLE 3-7
IASP TAXONOMIC CLASSIFICATION OF PAIN: AXIS V—CAUSE*

Genetic or congenital disorders (*eg*, congenital dislocation)	0.00
Trauma, operation, burns	0.01
Infective, parasitic	0.02
Inflammatory (no known infective agent), immune reactions	0.03
Neoplasm	0.04
Toxic, metabolic (*eg*, alcoholic neuropathy, anoxia, vascular, nutritional, endocrine, radiation)	0.05
Degenerative, mechanical	0.06
Dysfunctional (including psychophysiologic)	0.07
Unknown or other	0.08
Psychological origin (*eg*, conversion hysteria, depressive hallucination)	0.09

(Note: No physical cause should be held to be present nor any pathophysiologic mechanism.)

From Merskey [1]; with permission.
IASP—International Association for the Study of Pain.

with any system. The IASP system uses some natural breakouts as well as some that are artificial but convenient.

Ventafridda and Caraceni [10] criticized the IASP system for shedding little light on the classification issue and being only a listing of diseases and lesions that cause pain. They caution that we should be aware of using terms that deny the physical component of pain and would thereby influence treatment choices. Their orientation was that of cancer pain for which we still need descriptors for pain based on cancer's clinical and pathogenetic characteristics.

Procacci and Maresca [11] noted that, in trying to deal with international populations of patients, both linguistic and philological issues would need to be addressed as would the operative applicability of the taxonomy. There also would be epistemologic issues. One of their fundamental points was that the practitioner needs to be able to use the system. Their criticism was that the IASP system was too elaborate and difficult for the ordinary practitioner to use.

Turk and Rudy [12•] suggested that the lack of a universally accepted classification system has resulted in a lot of confusion and an inability of investigators as well as practitioners to compare observations and results of research. They noted that an infinite number of classification systems can be developed deductively, depending upon the rationale about common factors believed to discriminate among the diagnoses that are considered. Their primary purpose in presenting a study in 1990 was to test the generalizability of their so-called Multiaxial Assessment of Pain taxonomy by directly comparing its structure and profiles among several major but quite distinct groups of patients with chronic pain. They chose patients with chronic low back pain, those with temporomandibular joint dysfunction, and those with headache. In summary, their data suggest that the psychosocial and behavioral responses associated with chronic pain are common to a diverse sample of patients with pain despite the differences in demographic characteristics and medical diagnoses. They have proved the point that taxonomy is still an issue and that there is yet no universal system.

ASSESSMENT OF PAIN

Why is the Assessment of Pain Important?

Assessment is a process of evaluating something or somebody with the purpose of making decisions or forming an opinion. When used in reference to patients, this is not equivalent to just measuring a parameter such as the amount of pain. Assessment implies a broader-scale investigation into the patient's background, situation, and environment to provide a more global reference for the clinical

data being sought. Assessment of the patient with pain is important for at least the following reasons:

1. Pain has so many different meanings and expressions that we must identify accurately just what the patient means by complaints of "pain."
2. To diagnose the cause of the pain, we have to know what is really bothering the patient. This is not always what is obvious from observing his or her appearance.
3. Obtaining the diagnosis is paramount to providing appropriate therapy.
4. Once treatment has been provided, its effect must be repeatedly evaluated because this information is the basis on which the decision about continued or alternate therapy is made.

To assess patients who are complaining of pain, we need methods, techniques, and systems that will efficiently combine data from various clinical realms and that are relatively free from bias. This achievement is problematic because pain is a dynamic psychophysiologic event that is under the influence of many extraneous factors. Assessment tools must be reliable, sensitive, simple to use, and relate to a diversity of clinical situations.

That this assessment is important is the topic of many studies. Ferrell and coworkers [13] documented the vital role patient assessment has for nurses as a guide to their clinical decision-making and treatment of pain. Knowledge shared among the nurses, physicians, and patients was a key to making appropriate choices for pain management and addressing ethical decisions in patients with cancer-related pain. Gonzales and coworkers [14•] performed comprehensive assessments in referred patients who had cancer. Their stated goals were to identify the pain generators as well as to declare the patient's prognosis and define a realistic therapy program. Their evaluations revealed a previously undiagnosed cause for the pain in 64% of the patients. Their concluding statement that one needs an understanding of oncology, neurology, and medicine to assess patients with cancer reinforces the premise that assessment is a complicated process. Faries and coworkers [15] showed that the use of a systematic pain assessment tool by nurses correlated with improved pain management.

What Should we be Trying to Assess?

The answer to this question lies in the definition of pain, as mentioned in the first section of this chapter. We must attend to the pain's unpleasantness, its sensory aspects, the patient's emotional condition and reaction to the pain, and the associated tissue damage (whether real or only perceived). The dual nature of pain presented in the IASP definition provides a rough framework for answering the lead question.

PHYSIOLOGIC DATA

The concept that pain has a sensory component is the most well-accepted tenet of all. This concept implies that there is a physical source for the pain, and great attention has been devoted over the years to identifying the tissue damage and surmising the appropriate degree of pain related to it. Given the physical nature of pain, there should be physiologic parameters that aid in the assessment of the patient in distress secondary to pain. Thus, vital signs including blood pressure, heart rate, and respiratory rate are traditionally used as references to the amount of pain. This use is reasonable given that anxiety and stimulation of the sympathetic nervous system are commonly associated with acute pain events. Other variables that can be considered include the patient's appearance, posture, and muscle tone.

When patients have chronic pain, the physical assessment becomes more complex because the physiologic changes mentioned for acute pain do not linger into the chronic pain period. In addition, because the original injury that precipitated the chronic pain may have healed over time, there may be great confusion over the source of the pain. Furthermore, patients with chronic pain may have become inactive as a result of the pain and so may present with additional signs of physical deconditioning and frustration.

PSYCHOLOGICAL DATA

Because pain has a characteristic unpleasantness, emotions can so strongly influence the presentation of complaints and the perceived severity of the pain, and because the patient's behavior is routinely affected by pain, the psychological and behavioral aspects of the pain must be evaluated. Behavior is a form of communication, and observation is one technique for assessing this component of the patient's pain complaints. Arousal of negative emotions can increase the awareness of pain whereas positive emotions can decrease pain. Much insight into the patient's circumstances can be gained by interviewing the patient as well as noticing the ability to move, the facial expression (ie, grimacing, crying), the use of the limbs, the posturing, and so forth.

One of the newest areas for assessment is that dealing with the patient's attitudes toward, beliefs about, and expectations of the pain and its treatment. Strong and coworkers [16•] posit that the attitude a patient has will influence his or her behavior and that the patient's beliefs reflect what the pain means to him or her. Because these essential factors will influence compliance with therapy, the ability of the patient to cope with residual pain, as well as the overall treatment outcome, they must be understood.

ASSESSMENT OF THE PATIENT

History

It is obvious that a systematic approach to assessment is necessary to achieve the goals of diagnosis and an insightful appreciation for the patient's uniqueness. There is a constant struggle with any instrument used that it be reliable (which reflects trustworthiness and repeatability) and valid (the ability of a test to identify patients with the characteristic for which they are being screened).

An important first step in the assessment process is a review of the record. This review can provide an outline of the patient's story such that the actual interview time can be spent filling in details and allowing the patient time to tell what is significant to him or her. The records can reveal the history of the original injury, the mechanisms of injury, and the early management. The patient's chronic pain state will have evolved with the passage of time, and record review gives a perspective of how the physical aspects of the pain have intermingled with the development of the emotional tolerance for the situation. The record will also contain the details of the treatment course, which is often lengthy and confusing to the patient.

An effective technique for eliciting the essential and multiple components of the patient's history is the use of a questionnaire. This questionnaire can be filled out before the patient arrives for evaluation and provides crucial data in a format familiar to the staff. It can be used before formal evaluation to indicate the need for other necessary consultations that can be arranged for the day of assessment based on discoveries made in its review. The history of the pain's onset, characteristics, course over time, and response to treatment must be obtained. The responsible use of medications on a chronic basis and the compliance with all recommended therapy must be assessed. The patient's concurrent medical history is vital because other diseases can contribute to his or her chronic pain condition. Also, an appreciation for the psychosocial consequences of the pain will be gained by an analysis of the questionnaire.

The questionnaire may contain any number of assessment scales that are currently recommended. These tools are untilized by the patient to communicate the intensity of pain without necessarily relying on self-generated word descriptors [17••]. When using verbal scales, the patient is asked to pick a number between 0 and 10 or 0 and 100 that is representative of the current pain or a word along a continuum from "no pain" through "mild" or "moderate" pain to "terrible pain." Patients must be able to understand the premise of this concept for the responses to be valid. The most common technique used is the Visual Analogue Scale

(VAS). This is (usually) a 10-cm line drawn with the anchors of "no pain" and "worst pain imaginable" at the ends. It is simple, sensitive, quick, and provides reproducible results. The VAS is adaptable to many clinical situations and can be used for children older than the age of 8 years. As is true with the verbal scales, the patient needs to comprehend the underlying concept for the most accurate results to be obtained.

The McGill Pain Questionnaire is a traditional test that assesses the affective, evaluative, and sensory features of pain [18]. This questionnaire takes a long time for the patient to complete and demands a fair amount of education because the patient must understand the words provided and choose those that are descriptive of his or her pain. Its results can be influenced by repeat testing, past experience, and unrelated events. Drawings of a patient's pain on body figures are now a common evaluation mode. In general, the more widespread the drawing of pain, the more intense, frequent, and disruptive is the pain [19•]. Romano and coworkers [20] discuss the issue of chronic pain assessment and the comparison of some contemporary evaluation tests, including the Chronic Illness Problem Inventory, the Sickness Impact Profile, and the McGill Pain Questionnaire.

Physical Examination

The evaluation of the patient who is complaining of pain requires a physical examination of at least the painful area if not the related physiologic systems. Vital signs may give an indication of distress but do not necessarily correlate with the intensity nor the seriousness of the pain. Much can be learned from observing the patient's face (grimacing, crying, smiling while complaining bitterly) and body movements. The patient's ability to provide verbal responses also is indicative of the annoyance of the pain. A differential diagnosis for the complaints must be considered during the physical examination process so that all pertinent causes for the pain can be sought. It is crucial that all healthcare professionals acknowledge that infants and children feel pain. Craig and coworkers [21] are the latest researchers to have documented this reality by relating the stimulation from heel lancing in infants to behavioral and physiologic changes. Although indirect, these are the primary sources of information about pain in the nonverbal patient.

Attention to Psychosocial Factors

Because pain is a sensory and an emotional experience, attention must be paid to the powerful effect psychosocial circumstances can have on pain perception and the presentation of complaints [22••]. The growing availability of qualified specialists who have a genuine interest in patients with pain makes obtaining a formal psychological or psychiatric consultation a productive venture. We *must* appreciate how the pain has invaded the patient's life and contributed to changes in behavior, attitude, and lifestyle. The consequences of the pain will reinforce the illness behavior. It is crucial to identify what is on the patient's agenda regarding the pain and its management, because the patient's beliefs can strongly modify the cooperation with the evaluation protocol as well as the recommended therapy [16•].

Observation is a universal assessment tool that can have application in many clinical settings. We must acknowledge that data from this source are but one type of information used to form a clinical impression, a diagnosis, or a treatment plan. Waddell and Richardson [23] provide current comment on this issue by stating that under strict research conditions valid information can be obtained through observation, but that in routine clinical practice, the findings are subject to considerable observer error and bias.

Laboratory Testing

There is a tendency to rely on laboratory studies as the "ultimate" source of definitive data that will allow one to make a diagnosis. When specific, descriptive findings are returned, logical conclusions can be made. Problems arise when, as more commonly happens, the results are equivocal or require "clinical correlation." Even positive findings may not explain the patient's pain. One must be tactful in presenting the information that the laboratory test results are negative. This does not mean that there is no "real" pain nor that all the pain is based in emotions and nebulous psychosocial issues. Laboratory results are not necessarily the dominant component in the equation that leads to diagnosis.

CONCLUSIONS

Pain is a personal experience that is influenced by many extraneous factors and reveals itself through the patient's unique expressions, complaints, and behaviors. The patient must be assessed with a systematic protocol that is likely to encompass all of the possible sources for the complaints as well as the modifying circumstances. An abundance of assessment tools exist to aid the practitioner in formulating the clinical impression that will lead to a logical and appropriate treatment program. The specialty of pain medicine will mature when we have a standardized classification system into which the groupings of symptoms and diagnoses can be fit so that clinical and research communication can be facilitated.

REFERENCES AND RECOMMENDED READING

Papers of interest, published recently, have been highlighted as:
• Of special interest
•• Of outstanding interest

1. Merskey H: Classification of chronic pain: descriptions of chronic pain syndromes and definitions of pain terms. *Pain* 1986, DB(suppl 3):S1–S225.

2. Feuerstein M: Definitions of pain. In *Handbook of Chronic Pain Management.* Edited by Tollison CD. Baltimore: Williams & Wilkins; 1989:2–5.

3. • Bonica JJ: Definitions and taxonomy of pain. In *The Management of Pain.* Edited by Bonica JJ. Philadelphia: Lea & Febiger; 1990:18–27.
A good discussion of the impelling reasons why a classification system is needed, as well as a version of the IASP format.

4. Twycross RG: The relief of pain in far-advanced cancer. *Reg Anesth* 1980, 5:2–11.

5. Boyd DB: Taxonomy and classification of pain. In *Handbook of Chronic Pain Management.* Edited by Tollison CD. Baltimore: Williams & Wilkins; 1989:6–9.

6. • Longmire DR: Tutorial 7: The classification of pain and pain syndromes. *Pain Digest* 1992, 2:229–233.
A recent discussion of the evolution of taxonomy systems.

7. Foley KM: The treatment of cancer pain. *N Engl J Med* 1985, 313:84–95.

8. Portenoy RK: Cancer pain: pathophysiology and syndromes. *Lancet* 1992, 339:1026–1031.

9. Harper AC, Harper DA, Lambert LJ, *et al.*: Symptoms of impairment, disability and handicap in low back pain: a taxonomy. *Pain* 1992, 50:189–196.

10. Ventafridda V, Caraceni A: Cancer pain classification: a controversial issue. *Pain* 1991, 46:1–2.

11. Procacci P, Maresca M: Considerations on taxonomy of pain. *Pain* 1991, 45:332–333.

12. • Turk DC, Rudy TE: The robustness of an empirically derived taxonomy of chronic pain patients. *Pain* 1990, 43:27–35.
Expresses the need for a classification system to allow the comparison of observations and research.

13. Ferrell BR, McCaffery M, Grant M: Clinical decision-making and pain. *Cancer Nurs* 1991, 14:289–297.

14. • Gonzales GR, Elliott KJ, Portenoy RK, *et al.*: The impact of a comprehensive evaluation in the management of cancer pain. *Pain* 1991, 47:141–144.
A clinical demonstration of the benefit of a thorough assessment program.

15. Faries JE, Mills DS, Goldsmith KW, *et al.*: Systematic pain records and their impact on pain control. *Cancer Nurs* 1991, 14:306–313.

16. • Strong J, Ashton R, Chant D: The measurement of attitudes towards and beliefs about pain. *Pain* 1992, 48:227–236.
Attitudes are a very important piece of the database in assessment of pain.

17. •• Paige D, Cioffi AM: Pain assessment and measurement. In *Acute Pain Mechanisms and Management.* Edited by Sinatra RS, Hord AH, Ginsberg B, *et al.* St. Louis: Mosby-Year Book; 1992:70–77.
A very concise discussion of modern day evaluation techniques.

18. Holroyd KA, Holm JE, Keefe FJ, *et al.*: A multi-center evaluation of the McGill Pain Questionnaire: results from more than 1700 chronic pain patients. *Pain* 1992, 48:301–311.

19. • Toomey TC, Mann JD, Abashian S, *et al.*: Relationship of pain drawing scores to rating of pain description and function. *Clin J Pain* 1991, 7:269–274.
Emphasizes the significance of the patient's beliefs in the presentation of pain.

20. Romano JM, Turner JA, Jensen MP: The Chronic Illness Problem Inventory as a measure of dysfunction in chronic pain patients. *Pain* 1992, 49:71–75.

21. Craig KD, Whitfield MF, Grunau RVE, *et al.*: Pain in the preterm neonate: behavioral and physiological indices. *Pain* 1993, 52:287–299.

22. •• Turk DC, Melzack R, eds.: *Handbook of Pain Assessment.* New York: Guilford Press; 1992.
The most complete presentation of assessment by two experts in the field.

23. Waddell G, Richardson J: Observation of overt pain behavior by physicians during routine clinical examination of patients with low back pain. *J Psychomat Res* 1992, 36:77–87.

CHAPTER 4

Management of Postoperative Pain

RICHARD L. RAUCK

The application of regional techniques for acute pain management continues to evolve. Exceptional pain relief remains a primary goal. Improved morbidity and mortality outcomes have been demonstrated for some subsets of patients, and the practitioner using these techniques needs to know how to match a specific technique with an individual patient. One must be proficient in placement of each particular regional technique and understand the limitations of any given procedure. Which agent or combination of agents to use, and whether they should be administered by intermittent injection or continuous infusion must be considered. Risks and complications exist for any regional technique; these need to be understood, and vigilance maintained for their possible occurrence.

Regional anesthetic techniques have been well-used for many years in the operative setting and provide excellent surgical anesthesia. The use of these techniques has been largely ignored or underused in the postoperative setting. Only epidural analgesia has gained any widespread use, which can be directly related to the discovery of spinal opiate receptors. Standard operative regional techniques can be adapted to provide superb analgesia in the postoperative period. The use of catheters and infusions allow continuous analgesia without repeated instrumentation. As the anesthesiologist continues to evolve as the primary postoperative caregiver, this role should expand to include greater use of other anesthetic techniques.

INTERCOSTAL NERVE BLOCK

Blockade of the intercostal nerves (INB) can be performed for patients whose incisions are limited to the thoracic dermatomes. The quality of analgesia obtained for incisional pain by INB is unparalleled. Studies have demonstrated the effectiveness of repeated INB for postoperative analgesia [1]. Unfortunately, intermittent injection techniques are used less frequently today, a result of the high labor intensiveness involved by personnel skilled in these procedures. Many patients (eg, cholecystectomy patients) could still benefit from an initial set of intercostal blocks with subsequent intravenous analgesia. Catheter techniques for intercostal nerve blocks have been reported and used successfully (Fig. 4-1) [2]. If new local anesthetic agents are developed with longer half-lives, or effective liposomal encapsulation evolves, this technique will undoubtedly regain much popularity.

INTERPLEURAL ANALGESIA

Interpleural analgesia, initially described by Reistad in 1984 [3], offers an alternative approach to blockade of intercostal nerves. Most commonly, an epidural needle and catheter are used, with placement at the T7-8 level (Fig. 4-2). Recently, a specific interpleural tray has become commercially available. The needle should be inserted at the cephalad border of the rib margin approximately 8 to 12 cm from the midline. Placement at the cephalad border avoids the neuromuscular bundle of the intercostal nerve. The needle tip is directed midline to facilitate placement of the catheter in a medial direction. A loss of resistance technique is employed with a well-lubricated glass syringe filled with normal saline. Air-filled syringes have been alternatively reported but should be used circumspectly, because the air injected will proceed directly into the interpleural space. A loss of resistance at this level is quite pronounced and should not be confused with a more subtle loss of resistance seen on perforation of the intercostalis membrane.

Bupivacaine continues to be the most frequently used agent for interpleural analgesia. Concentrations employed range from 0.25% to 0.5% and depend on the degree of analgesia desired. Bupivacaine 0.25% rarely produces pin-

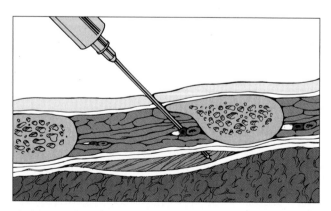

Figure 4-1 Intercostal catheter technique using an epidural style needle placed at the caudad border of the rib. A loss-of-resistance technique can be used. A catheter is threaded 5 to 10 cm within the space.

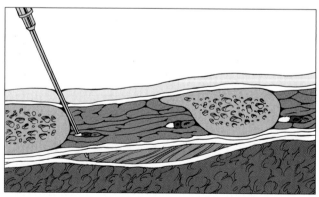

Figure 4-2 Interpleural catheter is positioned through an epidural style needle placed at the cephalad border of the appropriate rib. The T7-8 interspace is most commonly chosen; optimally, an interspace that approximates the painful dermatome should be used.

prick sensory analgesia, whereas 0.5% often does. Volumes of 20 to 30 mL have been advocated with each injection. Duration of analgesia ranges from 2 to 7 hours in most cases. Initial reports stated that continuous infusions through interpleural catheters were unsuccessful; however, recent articles have reported otherwise [4].

Regardless, the concurrent administration of low doses of systemic narcotics can effectively relieve any residual postoperative pain. The uptake of local anesthetics from the interpleural space into plasma occurs rapidly and can result in toxic plasma levels. This manifests clinically as seizures and has been reported with higher volumes of concentrated bupivacaine (0.5%) when injected by the interpleural route [5].

Pneumothorax resulting from this technique occurs less frequently than initially thought; however, one must exercise caution during placement of the needle to prevent the introduction of air into the pleural space. In those patients who will have a thoracotomy tube, placement of the interpleural catheter should be physically distant from the tube. Whenever possible, the tube should be clamped for 10 to 30 minutes after the local anesthetic injection.

BRACHIAL PLEXUS ANALGESIA

Brachial plexus blocks can provide 12 to 18 hours of postoperative analgesia. Often, patients benefit from autonomic blockade and regional analgesia beyond the initial 12- to 18-hour postoperative period. Repeated brachial plexus blocks cannot be advocated on a routine basis because of potential trauma to the neurovascular bundle. Catheters placed adjacent to the brachial plexus

have been used successfully. The two most frequently catheterized sites have involved the axillary and infraclavicular catheters (Figs. 4-3 and 4-4). The interscalene catheter has been employed but can be difficult to maintain in position because of the mobility of the neck. In most situations, the supraclavicular catheter has no clear advantage over the infraclavicular catheter, and the risk of pneumothorax with the necessarily larger needles used for catheter placement is increased with the supraclavicular technique.

The infraclavicular catheter can anesthetize all branches of the brachial plexus and can be easily immobilized against the skin to prevent dislodgment. A Becton and Dickinson Longdwel™ catheter (Rutherford, New Jersey) can be used with a nerve stimulator. Postoperative infusions of bupivacaine can be maintained for 2 to 7 days in most patients.

Axillary catheters have also been successfully employed. It can be more difficult to ensure block of the musculocutaneous nerve with this technique. Also, sterility of the axillary space and the immobilization of the arm may make it harder to prevent infection or dislodgment, respectively. An advantage to the axillary technique is ease of placement, and maintenance of a definitive sheath at this level allows the effective instillation of local anesthetic. Epidural needles can be placed into the brachial plexus sheath with a loss-of-resistance technique with subsequent catheters threaded through the needles; pediatric internal jugular kits involve threading a needle then a catheter over the wire. A 5 1/4-inch angiocath has also been advocated and used successfully.

Brachial plexus catheters will provide profound analgesia and surgeons need to be aware that anesthetized

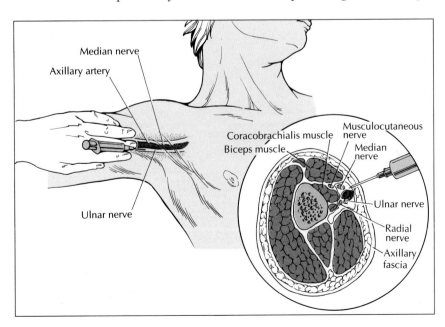

Figure 4-3 Axillary catheter technique for brachial plexus block using an epidural needle. A Hustead needle is preferred to the Tuohy because of a slightly sharper point. Paresthesias should be solicited and the artery avoided when possible. *Inset* shows needle in the neurovascular bundle close to the brachial artery. (*Adapted from Raj and coworkers [62]; with permission.*)

Median nerve

Axillary artery

Ulnar nerve

Coracobrachialis muscle
Biceps muscle

Musculocutaneous nerve
Median nerve
Ulnar nerve
Radial nerve
Axillary fascia

upper extremities result. Close vigilance of possible surgical complications (*eg*, compartment syndromes) must be maintained, because pain and numbness may not be reported by the patient. The anesthesiologist needs to be aware of the dosage limits of local anesthetics, which can be safely infused through these catheters [6].

The use of brachial plexus analgesia for postoperative care becomes more important in patients with preexisting pain problems. Patients with neuralgic pain problems, particularly patients with reflex sympathetic dystrophy, benefit greatly from dense neuraxial blockade. Optimally, these catheters should be inserted prior to surgery and maintained for 3 to 5 days after surgery. Decreasing or eliminating the barrage of nociceptive activity caused from surgery reduces the subsequent spinal cord wind-up, which can otherwise result in prolonged, unremitting pain. This reduction cannot be effectively or reliably achieved by systemic opiates. Likewise spinal cord opiates may decrease the pain and prevent sequelae but may not always be reliable. Peripheral, neuraxial blockade can most effectively reduce any nociceptive input to the spinal cord or higher central nervous system centers.

Any patient who has significant chronic pain prior to surgery should be considered for some regional postoperative analgesic technique. The benefit of preoperative analgesia was demonstrated in patients experiencing phantom limb pain. Those who received analgesia prior to surgery had decreased incidence of phantom pain postoperatively [7]. Knowledge of the value of preemptive analgesia is continuing to evolve and more research will be forthcoming concerning which patients will derive the most benefit and in what settings.

LOWER EXTREMITY BLOCKS

Lower extremity blocks for operative procedures have been successfully used for many years. At times the decreased morbidity from these blocks, when compared with either general anesthesia or neuraxial anesthesia, make them a desirable alternative. Their applicability for postoperative analgesia has been less clearly defined. Single shot blocks, such as a sciatic nerve block, can be beneficial for the initial 12- to 24-hour period. This may suffice in certain situations when the pain may be less extreme or other modalities can be subsequently administered. We have used this technique in patients who have had neuromas removed from a wide variety of locations on the sciatic nerve.

Unfortunately, the classic approach to blockade of the sciatic nerve at the sciatic notch is not amenable to placement of a catheter for prolonged periods. The catheters will usually migrate, a result of relatively large amounts of subcutaneous and muscular tissue between the skin and the sciatic notch.

For patients who can be expected to have prolonged, painful postoperative periods in the distribution of the distal sciatic (peroneal or tibial divisions), blockade at the level of the popliteal fossa can be easily performed with subsequent catheter placement (Fig. 4-5). Local

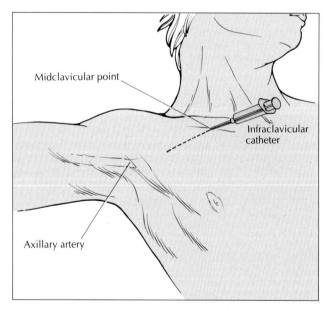

Figure 4-4 Technique of infraclavicular catheter positioning. Either an over-the-needle catheter (as shown) or through-the-needle catheter have been used. Paresthesias should be solicited or a nerve stimulator employed. (*Adapted from* Raj and coworkers [62]; with permission.)

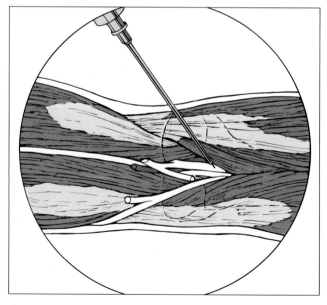

Figure 4-5 Lower extremity block using catheter placement on the sciatic nerve in the popliteal space. The needle is inserted 5 to 10 cm cephalad to the popliteal space, within the popliteal fossa. A catheter is threaded 5 to 15 cm into the space.

anesthetic infusions, bupivacaine 0.125% to 0.25%, can be delivered in volumes of 6 to 12 mL/h. These catheters can be managed for 5 to 7 days and longer in individual cases. When longer use is expected, the catheter can be inserted in a slightly more distal location (distal to the apex of the triangulated popliteal fossa) and threaded 5 to 10 cm cephalad.

Femoral catheters have also been employed for patients undergoing knee arthroscopy and other procedures involving the femoral nerve and occasionally the lateral femoral cutaneous (Fig. 4-6) or obturator nerve. Larger volumes of local anesthetic will be required when a 3-in-1 block is desired. Blockade of the knee joint will often require blockade of the sciatic nerve or instillation of local anesthetic solutions directly into the capsule itself.

EPIDURAL AND INTRATHECAL ANALGESIA

Postoperative epidural analgesia has been provided in the cervical, thoracic, lumbar, and caudal regions. Intrathecal postoperative analgesia has been provided by single injection of lumbar narcotics or by repeated injections of narcotics and local anesthetics or both through catheters.

Many different opiate compounds have been administered and include morphine sulfate (MSO_4), meperidine, hydromorphone, methadone, fentanyl, and sufentanil [8–12,13••]. Although other compounds such as the α_2-agonists are currently undergoing investigation, opiates remain the gold standard for intraspinal injec-

tion. In the following discussion, the term intraspinal will be used generically for both epidural and intrathecal administration.

Efficacy

Epidurally administered opiates must initially cross the dura mater before exerting their effect in the substantia gelatinosa (Rexed's laminae II–III). These agents are also subject to uptake into the rich epidural plexus of veins. Uptake and distribution into plasma after epidural administration resembles that seen after intramuscular injection. The portion of drug that is not taken into the vascular compartment is available to cross the dura. Hydrophilicity determines how much drug will cross the dura. Lipophilic agents such as fentanyl and sufentanil will cross the dura rapidly but also tend to retrace into the epidural space. Hydrophilic MSO_4 crosses the dura poorly but tends to stay subarachnoid once there.

The clinical effects of this characteristic are manifested in the intraspinal-to-systemic dose ratio and the ability of an opiate to truly provide analgesia via a spinally mediated mechanism versus redistribution into plasma with subsequent action supraspinally.

In comparison, MSO_4 has been shown in many studies to provide prolonged (12–16 h), excellent analgesia using a reduced dose [14,15•,16•]. If the dura mater is circumvented by placing the MSO_4 directly into the subarachnoid space, a minute dose (0.2–0.5 mg) can be used with similarly impressive duration [17]. The lipophilic agents do not enjoy these advantages. Doses

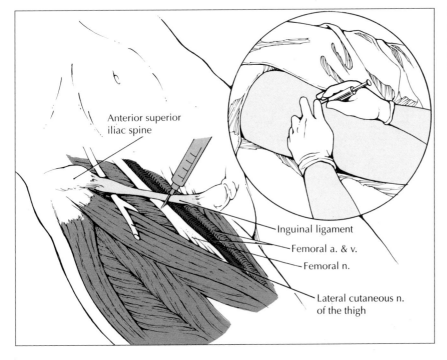

Figure 4-6 Lower extremity block using femoral catheter positioned along the femoral nerve. A nerve stimulator is most successful in correct subsequent placement of the catheter.

Anterior superior iliac spine

Inguinal ligament
Femoral a. & v.
Femoral n.
Lateral cutaneous n. of the thigh

similar to systemic doses must be administered to achieve analgesia [18,19••,20••,21•,22,23•,24••,25••]. This does not necessarily mean no spinal cord effect exists with these agents. The quality of analgesia may be theorized as enhanced by the intraspinal administration of these agents, a result of the opiate being present spinally in much higher concentrations and subsequently binding to the subarachnoid opiate receptor.

INTRASPINAL OPIATE AGENTS

The ideal intraspinal opiate would be hydrophilic in nature, have a high affinity for the opiate receptor, require occupation of a small percentage of receptors to provide analgesia, demonstrate a prolonged duration of analgesia, be free of side effects, and have no propensity to redistribute cephalad through cerebrospinal fluid (CSF) and cause delayed respiratory depression. An agent to match these characteristics does not presently exist. The intraspinal doses of commonly administered opiates are shown in Table 4-1.

Morphine sulphate was the initial intraspinal opiate injected and remains the prototypical available opiate. A major advantage is the hydrophilicity of MSO_4, which provides long analgesia and, if injected intrathecally, requires minute doses. Large series have all demonstrated the safety of intraspinal MSO_4 [14,15•]. In its preservative-free form, MSO_4 remains the only opiate that has FDA approval for epidural or intrathecal injection. Epidurally administered MSO_4 penetrates the dura poorly with an onset of action being 30 minutes and a peak effect not usually seen prior to 60 minutes. Thus, the injection of MSO_4 must be anticipated if adequate analgesia is to be achieved at the onset. With this understanding, MSO_4 has been administered routinely in the postoperative setting by intermittent injection and continuous infusion. Although MSO_4 has been used intraspinally by patient-controlled analgesia (PCA) tech-

nology, its characteristically delayed onset may make its use less than optimal by this route.

Hydromorphone

A recent comparative study has been performed with epidural morphine and hydromorphone [13••]. Hydromorphone compared favorably with morphine for analgesia after thoracotomy. No differences were seen in the analgesia when doses one fifth the morphine dose were administered with hydromorphone. This might be expected given that the hydrophilicity of hydromorphone is very similar to morphine. Both agents would be expected to traverse the dura poorly, yet provide long duration analgesia.

Meperidine

Meperidine has also been injected extensively and possesses the unique characteristic of having local anesthetic properties [26]. Its local anesthetic potency is sufficient when administered intrathecally to provide sensory anesthesia in some patients and surgical analgesia in most. The significance of its local anesthetic properties when injected epidurally is less clear. It does not produce sensory anesthesia in normal epidural doses; however, very low doses of local anesthetics such as bupivacaine are synergistic with opiates. The dual properties that meperidine possesses may provide synergism within the single compound.

Fentanyl

Fentanyl has achieved widespread popularity during the past 7 to 10 years [27,28•,29,30]. Its initial use stemmed from the hope that fentanyl might not show the same risk of respiratory depression that MSO_4 had been shown to have, but this question remains unanswered. The bulk of information presented would support the hypothesis that fentanyl does redistribute rostrally through the CSF less than the hydrophilic agent MSO_4,

TABLE 4-1
POSTOPERATIVE INTRASPINAL OPIATE DOSES

AGENT	SYSTEMIC DOSE	EPIDURAL DOSE	SUBARACHNOID DOSE	EPIDURAL INFUSION RATE
Morphine sulfate	5–10 mg	2–5 mg	0.2–0.5 mg	0.5 mg/h
Meperidine	50–100 mg	30–50 mg	10–20 mg	10–15 mg/h
Methadone	5–10 mg	3–6 mg	N/A	0.5 mg/h
Fentanyl	100–150 µg	100–200 µg	75–150 µg	70–100 µg/h
Sufentanil	25–50 µg	25–50 µg	25–50 µg	25–50 µg/h

and, as a result, may have fewer side effects associated with it [31]. Nonetheless, fentanyl does alter the carbon dioxide response curve, shifting it to the right in a manner similar to MSO_4 [32]. Like MSO_4, this property has rarely been a problem in the clinical setting.

The biggest unanswered question regarding fentanyl surrounds whether the analgesia obtained is a true spinal cord effect or a result of the drug being redistributed through plasma to supraspinal levels. Multiple conflicting studies have appeared during the past several years [19••,20••,21•,22,23•,24••,25••,27,28•,29,30]. The dose required to produce analgesia intraspinally is similar to that necessary by intravenous administration. Whether the quality of analgesia obtained is different has been more difficult to ascertain. An explanation may be that with initial injection there is a spinal cord effect, but with time either habituation or redistribution through plasma occurs to such an extent that the spinal cord effect is negligible.

A randomized, double-blind comparative study examined lumbar and intravenous fentanyl infusions for postthoracotomy pain relief [19••]. Good analgesia was obtained in both groups although those patients receiving lumbar epidural fentanyl received significantly larger infusion rates than the intravenous group ($P=0.0002$). Side effects were similar, and the authors concluded that lumbar epidural fentanyl infusions were equivalent to intravenous fentanyl infusions for postthoracotomy analgesia. The mechanism for analgesia after lumbar epidural administration appeared to be through systemic absorption.

If one accepts that fentanyl does not extensively travel cephalad through CSF, then one must place the spinal or epidural catheter at the dermatomal level appropriate for the surgical procedure. A lumbar epidural catheter will not provide analgesia by a spinal cord mechanism for thoracically mediated pain. This is in contradistinction to MSO_4, which has been shown to travel cephalad in sufficient quantity to provide analgesia at dermatomally distant sites from the catheter placement.

Many studies have contrasted epidural fentanyl with MSO_4 and other epidural agents [33•,34]. Some have demonstrated benefits of epidural fentanyl while many have shown little advantage over intravenous administration [19••,20••,21•]. A recent randomized comparison of intravenous versus lumbar and thoracic epidural fentanyl for thoracotomy pain demonstrated equivalent analgesia with the intravenous routes when compared with the epidural routes (Fig. 4-7) [20••]. Quantity of fentanyl required was also similar after all routes of administration. Side effects were slightly higher after with the intravenous route (greater incidence of nausea and more frequent boluses of fentanyl). Patients given thoracic epidural fentary had shorter hospital stays and sooner return to first bowel movement.

Whether the effect after intraspinal injection is spinally mediated or systemic, the rapidity of analgesic onset after fentanyl administration is so pronounced that there is use for the agent when patients are found to be acutely experiencing unacceptable pain. Patients in this setting are often not well served if they have to wait 30 to 60 minutes for the effects of an injection of intraspinal MSO_4. Fentanyl, in doses of 100 to 200 µg can provide quick analgesia while the longer lasting MSO_4 begins to set up.

Sufentanil

Sufentanil has also been used in the intraspinal canal [35]. The characteristics of the lipid-soluble fentanyl are magnified with sufentanil. Systemic doses are necessary and may be exceeded when used intraspinally [36,37]. Its theoretical advantage results from the strong affinity that sufentanil has for the spinal µ-receptor. Whereas MSO_4 requires 80% to 90% occupancy of the receptor to provide analgesia, sufentanil has to occupy less than 30%. This characteristic has relevance in the cancer population where tolerance and downregulation of the receptor is important but is probably unimportant in the acute postoperative setting.

TECHNIQUE OF DELIVERY

If opiates are to be injected by intermittent technique, the drugs can be administered either on a pretimed schedule or when the patient complains of pain. If medications are to be injected on a pretimed schedule, one must antici-

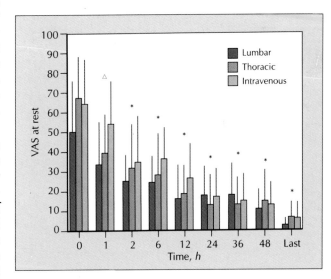

Figure 4-7 Evolution of pain at rest (mean ± SD), as measured by a 10-cm visual analogue scale (VAS), from the time just before starting the fentanyl infusion (0), until the day of discharge (last). Significant decrease in pain scores from baseline is observed after 1 hour in patients receiving thoracic epidural fentanyl (*triangle*), and after 2 hours in all groups (*asterisks*). (*From* Guinard and coworkers [20••]; with permission.)

pate the large interpatient variation in the analgesic half-life ($t_{1/2}$). For example, scheduling reinjection of MSO_4 every 12 hours would render a small percentage of patients inadequate pain relief prior to the scheduled reinjection, whereas others would not have required the subsequent injection for 6 to 12 hours past the scheduled time. Unnecessary pain or possible drug accumulation and side effects could result. The flexibility that is necessary to allow for interpatient variability has been most successful when trained nurses are allowed to inject epidural catheters during routine postoperative care. Unfortunately, many state nursing boards preclude registered nurses from reinjecting spinal catheters. If intraspinal opiates are injected only on demand, the qualitatively superior analgesia seen with intraspinal narcotics often regresses before a qualified person can respond to reinject. Patients suffer unacceptable pain before adequate analgesia is reestablished. This rollercoaster effect is less than optimal in postoperative management.

Continuous infusion of intraspinal narcotics prevents the regression of analgesia seen with intermittent injections by keeping patients in a steady state of continuous analgesia. If inadequate analgesia occurs, a change in the infusion rate can be ordered by the physician and performed by the nursing staff. Continuous infusions are particularly well suited for the lipophilic agents such as fentanyl and meperidine or local anesthetics. We have also had much experience in using continuous infusion with epidural morphine, showing excellent analgesia. Additional set-up is required using this technique, particularly volumetric pumps and tubing (Fig. 4-8). The largest risk inherent to the technique is inadvertent injection into the tubing by personnel mistaking the epidural line for an intravenous line. Drugs safe for the intravascular space could easily be catastrophic in the intraspinal canal. Our institution uses nitroglycerin tubing, which has no injection ports and makes this risk less likely to occur. Also, most volumetric pumps do not prevent patients from changing the rate of infusion themselves, behavior that would be expected to occur most frequently in patients with drug-seeking personalities. PCA pumps with locked drug chambers may provide a better alternative.

With the advances in PCA technology, studies have reported the efficacy of epidural opiates by this route of administration [38–40]. Fentanyl appears to be the logical agent, because its rapid onset meshes better with the principles of PCA dosing and would avoid the need for long lockout intervals [21•,23•]. However, Sjöstrom and coworkers [40] examined epidural morphine and meperidine given by PCA. Pain relief was excellent in both groups, although large interpatient variation existed in both groups. The plasma levels drawn for both drugs were significantly decreased compared with minimum analgesic concentrations after intramuscular administration. Further work will need to be performed in this area before specific recommendations can be made for routine clinical use.

PREEMPTIVE ANALGESIA

The role of providing analgesia prior to surgery and throughout the perioperative period has gained recent interest. In theory, preemptive analgesia would prevent spinal cord wind-up, a phenomenon that may explain some chronic pain states [41••,42]. Also, through prevention of peripheral nociceptive impulses, central neural sensitization can be avoided and less drug required throughout the postoperative period [43••].

Clinically, the phenomenon has been observed in several settings. Patients undergoing lower extremity amputations and receiving preoperative analgesia through epidural catheters had significantly less phantom limb and stump pain [7,44]. Other studies have shown similar decreases in analgesic requirements when pain relieving techniques have been provided preoperatively and postoperatively rather than just postoperatively [43••,45•].

Recent investigations support the theory of central neuroplasticity in the spinal cord [7,41••,42,43••, 44,45•]. Patients for thoracotomies were randomized to receive epidural infusions either before of after skin incision. Those patients who had their infusions begun prior to skin incision had significantly better pain scores and required significantly less patient-controlled morphine as rescue medication [41••].

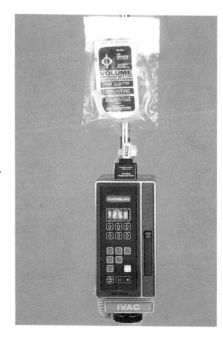

Figure 4-8 Tubing and pump set-up for continuous epidural infusion technique. Note that infusion tubing contains no side ports that would allow for erroneous or inadvertent injection into the epidural line. Also, a volumetric pump must be used because gravity controllers will not possess sufficient pressure for adequate infusion rates.

OUTCOME STUDIES

Several studies have examined the effect of epidural opiates on outcome in postsurgical patients. One of the initial studies to measure outcome criteria was performed by Rawal and coworkers [46], in which a group of morbidly obese patients receiving epidural narcotics postoperatively had shorter hospital stays, improved analgesia, and decreased morbidity [46].

The most frequently cited article concerning outcome measures in epidural patients has been the work of Yeager and coworkers [47] published in 1987. Twenty-eight patients received epidural analgesia, and 25 received intravenous narcotics. Morbidity, complication intensity, and mortality rates were all significantly less in the epidural group. Physician and hospital costs were significantly lower than in the group receiving epidural narcotics. One explanation for the beneficial effects of epidural anesthesia in high-risk surgical patients may relate to the effect of high thoracic epidural anesthesia on the diameter of normal and diseased epicardial arteries. Blomberg and coworkers [48] found thoracic epidural analgesia anesthesia to increase luminal diameter in stenotic segments from 1.35 ± 0.11 to 1.56 ± 0.13 mL but had no effect on nonstenotic segments. This effect could be quite significant in patients undergoing surgery who had poor cardiac reserve secondary to ischemic heart disease.

A recent study ($n = 173$) tried to compare the effects of thoracic epidural anesthesia in combination with light general anesthesia to "balanced" general anesthesia in high-risk surgical patients undergoing abdominal aortic reconstructive surgery [49•]. No difference in morbidity factors or mortality between groups was noticed. Postoperatively, patients in each group received either subcutaneous morphine sulfate, epidural fentanyl, or epidural bupivacaine. The effect of postoperative management on outcome was not addressed.

Risks of Epidural Analgesia

Risks initially identified with epidural narcotic analgesia included respiratory depression, urinary retention, pruritus, and nausea and vomiting.

Much has been published concerning the risk of respiratory depression from the administration of intraspinal opiates, reflecting the serious morbidity and mortality that can occur if respiratory depression goes unnoticed. Early respiratory depression results from the redistribution of narcotics from the epidural space into the vascular bed and subsequently to the respiratory center of the fourth ventricle. This occurs 20 to 45 minutes after an injection and mimics the effects that can be seen after an opiate is administered intramuscularly or subcutaneously. Early respiratory depression occurs much more frequently than delayed, late respiratory depression, but its consequences can be equally catastrophic if

patients are not observed closely. Undetected early respiratory depression is uncommon because most clinicians and nursing personnel know to monitor patients closely for 30 to 45 minutes after an opiate has been administered, regardless of the route utilized.

Delayed respiratory depression most commonly occurs 3 to 6 hours after administration but has been reported 18 hours after a single intraspinal injection. Delayed respiratory depression results from passive rostral flow within the CSF to the fourth ventricle. The risk of delayed respiratory depression increases manyfold if a concomitant dose of systemic narcotic is delivered. The clinician can easily forget that an intraspinal opiate injected 5 hours earlier will have peak ventricle levels at the same time that a systemic injection is made. This combination of epidural and intravenous administration was shown in Gustafsson and coworkers [50] survey to be the single greatest predictor of respiratory depression. Systemic opiates should never be administered while an intraspinal technique is being used.

Increasing age decreases the dose requirement of epidural narcotics. If a routine intraspinal opiate dose or infusion is administered to an elderly, frail individual, the risk of respiratory depression will be increased. Likewise, if during placement of an epidural catheter a dural puncture has occurred, the transfer kinetics of the agent passing from the epidural space to the subarachnoid space can be significantly altered. If a dural puncture occurs and a subsequent epidural catheter is successfully positioned, the initial dosage used should be extremely conservative, possibly reduced by a factor of 10, and the patient initially watched for any signs of respiratory depression. Doses can subsequently be cautiously increased if analgesia is incomplete.

The risks of respiratory depression from intraspinal narcotics have affected the management of patients receiving this technique, yet their risks may be no different than after systemic administration. A study by Miller and coworkers [51] reported 860 patients who received MSO_4 orally or systemically and found the instance of severe respiratory depression to be 0.9%, a number that compares favorably to the studies by the Ready, Gustafsson, and Rawal groups [15•,50,52].

No consensus of opinion exists on what degree of respiratory monitoring is necessary with the use of intraspinal narcotics. Unfortunately, a respiratory monitor that can be used on a regular nursing floor and is both reliable and predictive of a respiratory event has not been developed. In a 1986 survey of 73 centers by Mott and Eisele [53], they found that 67% of the centers kept intraspinally medicated patients in specialized care units. They found no difference in the incidence of respiratory depression: 0.4% overall but 0.6% in centers where patients were managed only in specialized units.

Measurement of mild respiratory depression in the clinical setting can be very difficult. A study by Wheatley and coworkers [54] compared the respiratory effects of intramuscular, intravenous PCA, and epidural analgesia following surgery. They defined respiratory depression as time spent with oxygen saturations below 94%. Although this definition is arbitrary and may have no meaningful clinical significance, the findings are relevant in a comparative study. Patients receiving epidural morphine spent significantly greater time with oxygen saturations <94% than either the PCA group or the intramuscular group.

We rely on hourly respiratory checks by our floor nurses and provide continuous inservicing. Standing orders provide guidelines for all potential emergencies. A patient is monitored in a specialized unit only if his surgical risk status and postoperative analgesic risk factors deem it appropriate.

Treatment of respiratory depression is simple and effective; naloxone will reverse the respiratory depression of all pure μ-opiate agonists. Routine cases will require naloxone in doses of 2 to 5 μg/kg/h to reverse the respiratory depression, but this must be titrated to effect and much higher doses may be necessary if an inadvertent overdose has occurred. Naloxone can be initially administered by a bolus injection but should always be followed by infusion when treating respiratory depression from intraspinal narcotics because its $t_{1/2}$ is much shorter than any of the narcotics.

Nausea and vomiting are associated with epidural narcotics, the extent of which may never be appreciated because many surgical patients experience nausea or vomiting from their surgical procedure. Estimates have ranged from 17% to 34% for MSO_4, whereas the lipid-soluble agents have been reported to have a decreased incidence of nausea and vomiting [14,55]. The emetic effect of epidural narcotics has been attributed to their effects on the chemoreceptors in the brain.

Treatment of intraspinally related nausea and vomiting can involve several regimens. An antiemetic such as cholopromazine can be included on standard order forms. Naloxone has also been reported effective in the treatment of nausea and vomiting, although many studies support the ineffectiveness of naloxone to reliably reverse nausea and vomiting [46]. Two studies have demonstrated marked effectiveness with scopolamine when applied as a patch the night before surgery [56,57]. Odanterisin may prove effective in refractory cases of nausea and vomiting.

The risk of urinary retention has often been understated and its significance unappreciated when compared with the life-threatening complications associated with respiratory depression. The incidence of urinary retention ranged from 22% to 50% in several studies and may

be less with the more lipid-soluble agents [58,59]. The morbidity associated with urinary retention and prolonged catheterization is far from insignificant and can preclude intraspinal analgesia as the optimal technique in otherwise healthy patients undergoing surgical procedures with only minimal postoperative pain.

The mechanisms of urinary retention have not been clearly elucidated in patients receiving epidural narcotics. Several studies have implicated a relaxation of the detrusor muscle and an increase in bladder capacity.

Treatment of urinary retention is often unsuccessful. Reports of naloxone to 0.8 mg have been described or infusions of 2 to 5 μg/kg/h prior to the administration of epidural narcotics. Our own clinical experience has often been less than encouraging [58].

Pruritus represents a commonly reported side effect of epidural narcotics. This can vary from a benign localized reaction to a diffuse, relentless problem that demands treatment. Ready and coworkers' study [15•] of 1106 patients and Stenseth and coworkers [14] report on 1085 patients revealed an incidence of 24% and 11%, respectively. This wide variation most likely reflects a difference in extent of questioning by investigators and a somewhat subjective determination of whether the pruritus was epidurally related or not.

Pruritus resulting from intraspinal narcotics can be managed successfully in most patients. Diphenhydramine reduces many localized reactions, whether of epidural origin or not, and can be listed on the standard orders. Naloxone can be administered in refractory cases and is almost universally effective in doses of 2 to 4 μg/kg/h.

Epidural narcotics, particularly MSO_4, have been reported to cause an increased incidence of recurrent herpes simplex infections in the obstetric population [60]. With the exception of a single case report, this has not been reported in other postoperative cases [61]. Why this association exists remains unclear.

Intrathecal Opiates

The use of intrathecal opiates in postoperative patients has been somewhat limited until recently because of unacceptable catheter technology. Single-dose injections have been administered at the time the subarachnoid block was placed, or in the case of some back operations, surgeons would elect to administer a dose during the surgical procedure. This technique could provide long-lasting analgesia (18–24 h in some patients) when MSO_4 was employed. The lipid-soluble agents do not have equally long analgesic profiles when administered intrathecally by single shot.

For operative procedures, when the duration of postoperative pain would not be expected to be prolonged and a subarachnoid technique is chosen for surgical anesthesia, single-dose subarachnoid opiates are an excellent choice and probably underused. Risks, potential complications, and monitoring should be no different than after epidural administration if equipotent doses are used.

The practitioner must be acutely aware of which opiates and preparations are suitable for intrathecal administration. Spinal cord toxicity issues vary greatly between epidural and intrathecal administration. A drug that is safe for epidural injection may be catastrophic if injected subarachnoid. The epidural space can be quite forgiving of some preservatives, whereas the subarachnoid space characteristically is not. In its preservative-free preparation, MSO_4 has been demonstrated safe for intrathecal administration. Fentanyl has been approved in Canada for subarachnoid use, and its extensive chemical use in the United States would support its safety. Although appropriate spinal cord toxicity studies have not been performed with meperidine, the clinical evidence supports its use in preservative-free forms.

Renewed interest has occurred with the technique of continuous spinal anesthesia. This initially occurred with the development of small bore catheters. These microcatheters ranged from 28 to 36 gauge and could be inserted through much smaller needles than previously used. This decreased the risk of spinal headaches; however, problems developed with these catheters with breakage and kinking with some prototypes. Also, the reported cases of cauda equina syndrome associated with these catheters have resulted in their removal from the market. Larger catheters remain available for use. It should be remembered that the cases of cauda equina syndrome most likely occurred secondary to excessively large spinal doses of drug being administered without an expected block. Regardless of the catheter size, it would appear prudent to change technique if a reasonable (1.5–2.0 times) spinal dose of drug is administered and the expected block is not obtained.

OTHER PERIPHERAL NERVE BLOCKS

Any peripheral somatic nerve can be blocked to provide postoperative analgesia. If a specific peripheral somatic nerve can be isolated as responsible for postoperative pain, a selective block may be appropriate. This can be done percutaneously in a preoperative or postoperative setting. Alternatively, this situation can arise when a surgeon is performing neural surgery (eg, neuroma excision). In these cases, the surgeon can often place the catheter under direct vision for postoperative analgesia. The subsequent infusion of low concentrations of bupivacaine (0.10%–0.25%) will provide excellent analgesia and can help stop the barrage of peripheral nociceptive afferent input, which can follow nerve surgery and theoretically avoid the susceptibility in some patients to the development of sympathetically maintained pain.

CONCLUSIONS

Regional techniques for acute pain management no longer means epidural analgesia. Alternative techniques exist that often suit the patient's needs better. For any given technique different agents are available, many of which can be combined, when appropriate, in synergistic fashion. In comparison with systemic routes of administration, these techniques provide excellent analgesia with small amounts of drugs. The future will yield new techniques, new technology to aid in the performance of regional analgesia, and new agents for administration. A final caveat remains that any reasonable technique has its own inherent risks, and the postoperative pain practitioner must act as the consultant to the surgeon in recommending a regional technique or systemic route for postoperative analgesia.

REFERENCES AND RECOMMENDED READING

Papers of interest, published recently, have been highlighted as:
• Of special interest
•• Of outstanding interest

1. Endberg C, Wiklund L: Pulmonary complications after upper abdominal surgery: their prevention by intercostal blocks. *Acta Anaesthesiol Scand* 1988, 32:1–9.

2. Murphy DF: Continuous intercostal nerve blockade for pain relief following cholecystectomy. *Br J Anaesth* 1986, 11:89–91.

3. Reistad F, Stromskag KE: Intrapleural catheter in the management of postoperative pain: a preliminary report. *Reg Anaesth* 1986, 11:89–91.

4. Brismar B, Pettersson N, Tokics L, *et al.*: Postoperative analgesia with intrapleural administration of bupivacaine-adrenalin. *Acta Anaesthsiol Scand* 1987, 31:515–520.

5. Laurito CE, Kirz LI, VadeBoncouer TR, *et al.*: Continuous infusion of interpleural bupivacaine maintains effective analgesia after cholecystectomy. *Anesth Analg* 1991, 72:516–521.

6. Raj PP, ed. *Practical Management of Pain, Second Edition.* St. Louis: Mosby-Year Book; 1992:690–694.

7. Mann RAM, Bisset WIK: Anaesthesia for lower limb amputation: a comparison of spinal analgesia and general anaesthesia in the elderly. *Anaesthesia* 1983, 38:1185–1191.

8. Rawal N, Sjostrand UH, Dahlstrom B: Postoperative pain relief by epidural morphine. *Anesth Analg* 1981, 60:726–731.

9. Donadoni R, Rolly G, Noorduin H, *et al.*: Epidural sufentanil for postoperative pain relief. *Anaesthesia* 1985, 40:634–638.

10. Chouchlov CN: On the fine structure of free nerve endings in human digital skin, oral cavity and rectum. *Anat Forsch* 1972, 86:273–288.

11. Rawal N, Sjostrand UH, Dahlstrom B, *et al.*: Epidural morphine for postoperative pain relief: a comparative study with intramuscular narcotic and intercostal nerve block. *Anesth Analg* 1982, 61:93–98.

12. Gustafsson LL, Johannisson J, Garle M: Extradural and parenteral pethidine as analgesia after total hip replacement: effects and kinetics: a controlled study. *Eur J Clin Pharmacol* 1986, 29:529–534.

13. •• Chaplan SR, Duncan SR, Brodsky JB, *et al.*: Morphine and hydromorphone epidural analgesia. *Anesthesiology* 1992, 77:1090–1094.

Authors performed comparative study of thoracic epidural morphine and hydromorphone for postthoracotomy pain. Results demonstrated equal analgesia and potency between the two agents; the only difference was that hydromorphone produced less pruritus.

14. Stenseth R, Sellevold O, Breivik H: Epidural morphine for postoperative pain: experience with 1085 patients. *Acta Anaesthesiol Scand* 1985, 29:148–156.

15. • Ready LB, Loper KA, Nessly M, *et al.*: Postoperative epidural morphine is safe on surgical wards. *Anesthesiology* 1991, in press.

Authors present a large series of patients treated postoperatively with epidural narcotics. Safety of intermittent injection of morphine, infusion of opiates and local anesthetics, and use of agents on routine surgical floors is presented.

16. • Weller R, Rosenblum M, Conard P, *et al.*: Comparison of epidural and patient-controlled intravenous morphine following joint replacement surgery. *Can J Anaesth* 1991, 38:582–586.

Equal analgesia was obtained with both techniques. However, patients required significantly less drug by the epidural route when compared with the intravenous route.

17. Wang JK, Nauss LA, Thomas JE: Pain relief by intrathecally applied morphine in man. *Anesthesiology* 1979, 50:149–151.

18. Loper KA, Ready LB, Downey M, *et al.*: Epidural and intravenous fentanyl infusions are clinically equivalent after knee surgery. *Anesth Analg* 1990, 70:72–75.

19. •• Sandler AN, Stringer D, Panos L, *et al.*: A randomized, double-blind comparison of lumbar epidural and intravenous fentanyl infusions for postthoracotomy pain relief. *Anesthesiology* 1992, 77:626–634.

Authors compared analgesia from lumbar epidural fentanyl with intravenous fentanyl and found no difference between groups for postthoracotomy pain. They concluded that no advantages existed with the lumbar administration of fentanyl over intravenous use.

20. •• Guinard JP, Mavrocordatos P, Chiolero R, *et al.*: A randomized comparison of intravenous versus lumbar and thoracic epidural to intravenous fentanyl administration. *Anesthesiology* 1992, 77:1088–1115.

Authors found no enhanced analgesia with epidural administration although more side effects were found with the intravenous route. The thoracic epidural route provided better analgesia in the early postoperative period. Thoracic epidural patients also had some better pulmonary function scores and had shorter hospital stays.

21. • Glass PSA, Estok P, Ginsberg B, *et al.*: Use of patient-controlled analgesia to compare the efficacy of epidural to intravenous fentanyl administration. *Anesth Analg* 1992, 74:343–351.

Patients were allowed to self-administer (PCA) intravenous or epidural fentanyl in a double-blind, randomized, crossover design. No differences in analgesia or amount of drug delivered were found with either route.

22. Ellis DJ, Millar WL, Reisner LS: A randomized double-blind comparison of epidural versus fentanyl infusion for analgesia after Cesarean section. *Anesthesiology* 1990, 72:981–986.

23. • Grant RP, Dolman JF, Harper JA, *et al.*: Patient-controlled lumbar epidural fentanyl compared with patient-controlled intravenous fentanyl for postthoracotomy pain. *Can J Anaesth* 1992, 39: 214–219.

Patients obtained good (equal) relief by either PCA lumbar epidural or PCA intravenous fentanyl for posthoracotomy pain. Less drug was required by the epidural route (1875±693 μg) when compared to the intravenous route (2573±890)(*P*<0.05).

24. •• Salomaki TE, Laitinen JO, Nuutinen LS: A randomized double-blind comparison of epidural versus intravenous fentanyl infusion for analgesia after thoracotomy. *Anesthesiology* 1991, 75:790–795.

Thoracic epidural analgesia provided equal analgesia with less medication required. Respiratory function was better and side effects fewer with the epidural group.

25. •• Coe A, Sarginson R, Smith MW, *et al.*: Pain following thoracotomy: a randomized, double-blind comparison of lumbar versus thoracic epidural fentanyl. *Anesthesia* 1991, 46:918–921.

Comparative study of thoracic versus lumbar epidural fentanyl for thoracotomy pain. No differences were observed in pain scores or side effects between groups. The infusion rate was approximately 60 μg/kg/h.

26. Glynn CJ, Mather LE, Cousins MJ, *et al.*: Peridural meperidine in humans: analgesic response, pharmacokinetics and transmission into CSF. *Anesthesiology* 1981, 55:520–526.

27. Welchew EA, Thornton JA: Continuous thoracic epidural fentanyl: a comparison of epidural fentanyl with intramuscular papaveretum for postoperative pain. *Anaesthesia* 1982, 37:309–316.

28. • Welchew EW, Breen DP: Patient-controlled on-demand epidural fentanyl. *Anaesthesia* 1991, 46:438–441.

Less than half the dose of patient-controlled epidural fentanyl was required to produce similar pain scores, sedation, and nausea as was required with systemic administration. A spinal cord effect of epidurally administered fentanyl was suggested.

29. Lomessy A, Magnin C, Viale JP, *et al.*: Clinical advantages of fentanyl given epidurally for postoperative analgesia. *Anesthesiology* 1984, 61:446–469.

30. Bailey PW, Smith BE: Continuous epidural infusion of fentanyl for postoperative analgesia. *Anaesthesia* 1980, 35:1002–1006.

31. Gourlay GK, Murphy TM, Plummer JL, *et al.*: Pharmacokinetics of fentanyl in lumbar and cervical CSF following lumbar epidural and intravenous administration. *Pain* 1989, 38:253–259.

32. Negre J, Gueneron JP, Ecoffey C, *et al.*: Ventilatory response to carbon dioxide after intramuscular and epidural fentanyl. *Anesth Analg* 1987, 66:707–710.

33. • Cohen SE, Subak LL, Brose WG, *et al.*: Analgesia after Cesarean delivery: patient evaluations and costs of five opioid techniques. *Reg Anesth* 1991, 16:141–149.

This study demonstrated enhanced analgesia with intraspinal opiates in comparison with PCA or intramuscular opiates. Analgesia was best with epidural morphine while epidural fentanyl did not decrease early postoperative pain. Side effects were less with PCA in comparison with epidural opiates.

34. Chrubasik J, Wust H, Schulte-Monting J, *et al.*: Relative analgesic potency of epidural fentanyl, alfentanil, and morphine in the treatment of postoperative pain. *Anesthesiology* 1988, 68:929–933.

35. Donadoni R, Rolly G, Noorduin H, *et al.*: Epidural sufentanil for postoperative pain relief. *Anesthesia* 1985, 40:634–638.

36. Whiting WC, Sandler AN, Lau LC, *et al.*: Analgesic and respiratory effects of epidural sufentanil in patients following thoracotomy. *Anesthesiology* 1988, 69:36–43.

37. Van der Auwera D, Verborgh C, Camu F: Analgesic and cardiorespiratory effects of epidural sufentanil and morphine in humans. *Anesth Analg* 1987, 66(suppl):999–1003.

38. Marlowe S, Engstrom R, White PF: Epidural patient-controlled analgesia (PCA): an alternative to continuous epidural infusions. *Pain* 1989, 37:97–101.

39. Eisenach JC, Grice SC, Dewan DM: Patient-controlled analgesia following Cesarean section: a comparison with epidural and intramuscular narcotics. *Anesthesiology* 1988, 68:444–448.

40. Sjöstrom S, Hartvig D, Tamsen A: Patient-controlled analgesia with extradural morphine or pethidine. *Br J Anaesth* 1988, 60:358–366.

41. •• Katz J, Kavanagh BP, Sandler AN, *et al.*: Preemptive analgesia: clinical evidence of neuroplasticity contributing to postoperative pain. *Anesthesiology* 1992, 77:439–446.

Epidural fentanyl administered to patients prior to skin incision for thoracotomy pain produced significantly lower pain scores and necessitated less rescue pain medication than in the group not receiving epidural opiates before incision. The authors concluded that preemptive analgesia may reduce central consequences of peripheral nociceptor activity.

42. Davies SN, Lodge D: Evidence for involvement of *N*-methylaspartate receptors in "wind-up" of class 2 neurons in the dorsal horn of the rat. *Brain Res* 1987, 424:404–406.

43. •• Ejlersen E, Bryde Anderson H, Eliasen K, *et al.*: A comparison between preincisional and postincisional lidocaine infiltration and postoperative pain. *Anesth Analg* 1992, 74:495–498.

Authors found that patients receiving local lidocaine infiltration prior to skin incision for inguinal herniography did better than those receiving injections after incision. The demand for analgesics occurred later and fewer patients required supplemental analgesics in the preincisional group.

44. Bach S, Noreng MF, Tjéllden NU: Phantom limb pain in amputees during the first 12 months following limb amputation, after preoperative lumbar epidural blockade. *Pain* 1988, 33:297–301.

45. • Jebeles JA, Reilly JS, Guitierrez JF, *et al.*: The effect of preincisional infiltration of tonsils with bupivacaine on the pain following tonsillectomy under general anesthesia. *Pain* 1991, 47:305–308.

The authors demonstrated the benefit of preincisional infiltration of bupivacaine for posttonsillectomy pain. Patients not receiving preincisional injection of bupivacaine had significantly higher pain scores and required more analgesic drugs postoperatively.

46. Rawal N, Sjostrand U, Christoffersson E, *et al.*: Comparison of intramuscular and epidural morphine for postoperative analgesia in the grossly obese: influence on postoperative amputation and pulmonary function. *Anesth Analg* 1984, 63:583–592.

47. Yeager MP, Glass DD, Neff RK, *et al.*: Epidural anesthesia and analgesia in high-risk surgical patients. *Anesthesiology* 1987, 66:729–736.

48. Blomberg S, Emanuelsson H, Kvist H, *et al.*: Effects of thoracic epidural anesthesia on coronary arteries and arterioles in patients with coronary artery disease. *Anesthesiology* 1990, 73:840–847.

49. • Baron J-F, Bertand M, Barré, *et al.*: Combined epidural and general anesthesia versus general anesthesia for abdominal aortic surgery. *Anesthesiology* 1991, 75:611–618.

Authors found no difference in patients receiving epidural and general anesthesia versus general anesthesia when the postoperative analgesia was controlled in both groups by epidural analgesia. Mortality, cardiovascular morbidity, and respiratory morbidity did not differ in this high-risk group of patients.

50. Gustafsson LL, Schildt B, Jacobsen KJ: Adverse effects of extradural and intrathecal opiates: report of a nationwide survey in Sweden. *Br J Anaesth* 1982, 54:479–486.

51. Miller RR, Greenblatt DJ, eds. *Drug Effects in Hospitalized Patients.* New York: John Wiley and Sons; 1976:151–152.

52. Rawal N, Arnér S, Gustafsson LL, *et al.*: Present state of extradural and intrathecal opioid analgesia in Sweden: a nationwide follow-up survey. *Br J Anaesth* 1987, 59:791–799.

53. Mott JM, Eisele JH: A survey of monitoring practices following spinal opiate administration [abstract]. *Anesth Analg* 1986, 65:S105.

54. Wheatley RG, Somerville ID, Sapsford DJ, *et al.*: Postoperative hypoxsemia: comparison of extradural, I.M., and patient-controlled opioid analgesia. *Br J Anaesth* 1990, 64:267–275.

55. Rawal N, Schott U, Tandon B: Influence of intravenous naloxone infusion on analgesia and untoward effects of epidural morphine [abstract]. *Anesth Analg* 1985, 64:270.

56. Kotelko DM, Rottman RL, Wright WC, *et al.*: Transdermal scopolamine decreases nausea and vomiting following Cesarean section in patients receiving epidural morphine. *Anesthesiology* 1989, 71:675–678.

57. Blomberg S, Emanuelsson H, Kvist H, *et al.*: Effects of thoracic epidural anesthesia on coronary arteries and arterioles in patients with coronary artery disease. *Anesthesiology* 1990, 73:840–847.

58. Rawal N, Mollefors K, Axelsson K, *et al.*: An experimental study of urodynamic effects of epidural morphine and of naloxone reversal. *Anesth Analg* 1983, 62:641–647.

59. Rawal N, Mollefors K, Axelsson K, *et al.*: Naloxone reversal of urinary retention after epidural morphine [letter]. *Lancet* 1981, 2:1411.

60. Gieraerts R, Navalgund A, Vaes L, *et al.*: Increased incidence of itching and herpes simplex in patients given epidural morphine after Cesarean section. *Anesth Analg* 1987, 66:1321–1324.

61. Cardan E: Herpes simplex after spinal morphine [letter]. *Anesthesiology* 1984, 39:938.

62. Raj PP, Pai U, Rawal N: Techniques of regional anesthesia in adults. In *Clinical Practice of Regional Anesthesia*. Edited by Raj PP. New York: Churchill Livingstone; 1991.

Regional Approaches to the Management of Chronic Pain

ALON P. WINNIE

DIFFERENTIAL NEURAL BLOCKADE

It is my opinion that the most unique and frequently rewarding tool that regional anesthesia can provide to physicians who treat patients with chronic pain (particularly those patients with pain of bizarre or unknown etiology) is differential neural blockade. Because regional anesthesia is an important part of an anesthesiologist's armamentarium, it is not uncommon for an anesthesiologist to establish a previously unexpected diagnosis as to the neural mechanism subserving a patient's pain when all of the usual diagnostic maneuvers and methods have failed. The anesthesiologist accomplishes this one of two ways: either pharmacologically, using differential spinals, differential epidurals, or differential plexus blocks; or anatomically, using sequential placebo injections, sympathetic blocks, and somatic blocks. Because the present discussion focuses on the role of regional anesthesia in the management rather than the diagnosis of pain, I will not describe these techniques in detail. Those interested in the details of this approach may find them elsewhere [1].

I would point out, however, that the efficacy of differential neural blockade in patients with pain of bizarre or unknown etiology is impressive as documented in an earlier report [2]. This report presents the results achieved with this approach in 100 consecutive patients referred to a pain control center by specialists who stated that all diagnostic attempts had failed to elucidate the cause of the referred patient's pain. Differential neural blockade indicated clearly that 92 of these patients had organic pain, of whom 74 had sympathetically mediated pain and 18 had pain mediated by A-δ and C fibers. Only 5% had "psychogenic pain," and 3% had "central pain." The significance of these findings is evidenced by the fact that most of these patients were treated successfully once the proper treatment was indicated by this diagnostic approach.

ACUTE PAIN TREATMENT TO PREVENT CHRONIC PAIN

Acute pain is not often treated in a pain control center, simply because acute pain is usually relieved by treating or removing the cause; and more frequently than not, most acute pain gets better if left alone or treated conservatively. There are, however, certain types of acute pain that *should* be referred to a pain control center *initially*, because these types of pain, if untreated or allowed to persist, become progressively worse. Once they become chronic they are difficult, if not impossible, to treat successfully. Such is the case with acute herpes zoster, reflex sympathetic dystrophy, and an acute herniated disc.

Acute Herpes Zoster

Acute herpes zoster, which ordinarily runs a course of 6 to 8 weeks, usually can be terminated by one or two sympathetic blocks performed at a level appropriate to the involved area. Although such a cure is dramatic and rewarding to the patient with painful "shingles," a more important fact is that the chances of a patient with herpes zoster subsequently developing postherpetic neuralgia are virtually nonexistent *if* the acute phase has been treated with sympathetic blocks. To prevent postherpetic neuralgia, however, the time of treatment is of critical importance: during the first 2 weeks following the vesicular stage of herpes zoster the success rate of sympathetic blocks is virtually 100%. After the spontaneous healing of the lesions, the success rate decreases rapidly, and after about 2 months sympathetic blocks become relatively ineffective in terminating acute herpes zoster, and more importantly, in preventing postherpetic neuralgia [3••].

The advent of acyclovir for the specific treatment of herpes zoster first appeared to represent a replacement for the nerve block therapy of this disease. However, it now has been shown that while acyclovir is effective in terminating the acute phase of herpes zoster in a high percentage of cases, it does not prevent (or even minimize) the development of postherpetic neuralgia [4]. It may even enhance the possibility in certain cases, because in those patients in whom acyclovir fails to terminate the acute phase of the disease, the course of acyclovir only serves to delay by several weeks the institution of sympathetic blocks. Because the effectiveness of sympathetic blocks in terminating the disease process is related to the time of therapy, the delay caused by the time required for a course of acyclovir could reduce the efficacy of the sympathetic blocks once they are administered.

Sympathetically Mediated Pain

Similarly, in sympathetically mediated pain (reflex sympathetic dystrophies, causalgias, and others) the performance of a sympathetic block, which establishes the diagnosis, actually begins the therapy. Early in the course of the disease, the treatment of sympathetically mediated pain simply consists of a series of sympathetic blocks with local anesthetic agents. In a typical course of therapy, each block provides a duration of relief that exceeds the duration of action of the local anesthetic and exceeds the duration of relief provided by the previous block. As long as the duration of relief continues to increase with each block, permanent relief with continued blocks is virtually assured. In an early review of our own experience, we found that over 95% of all patients with reflex sympathetic dystrophy did obtain permanent relief from such a series of sympathetic blocks *if treated early* [2].

As an alternative to repeated sympathetic blocks, Hannington-Kiff [5] introduced the technique of intravenous regional guanethidine. As compared with stellate ganglion blocks, this approach offered several theoretical advantages: the duration of a sympathetic local anesthetic block, even with bupivacaine, is only a few hours, whereas the intravenous regional block with guanethidine produces evidence of chemical sympathectomy for 3 to 5 days, meaning that a block is needed only every third day.

An advantage of intravenous regional guanethidine is that it does not require an injection in the neck, which some patients find unpleasant, whereas a series of stellate ganglion blocks does. On the other hand, patients with acute reflex sympathetic dystrophy may not allow the manipulation of the painful extremity required to exsanguinate it, nor the placement of a pneumatic tourniquet, insertion of a needle or catheter into a vein, or the injection of guanethidine. They might allow, or even prefer, an injection in the neck, because this is an area that is not involved in the pain syndrome being treated. Another advantage of intravenous regional guanethidine is that it may be used in anticoagulated patients, a clinical situation that is a relative contraindication to stellate ganglion block. The biggest obstacle to the use of intravenous regional guanethidine is that guanethidine is not available in the parenteral form in the United States. If used, it must be treated as an experimental drug. Therefore, its use must be approved by the institutional review board of the facility in which it is to be used, and forms must be filed with the Food and Drug Administration for each patient to whom the drug is administered. In addition, the patient must give informed consent for this procedure and must be aware that this is an experimental treatment of reflex sympathetic dystrophy.

Guanethidine has a biphasic action, initially releasing norepinephrine and then interfering with its reuptake at the synaptic cleft as well as inhibiting further release. Because sympathetic activity depends on norepinephrine release, chemical sympathectomy results from its blockade. In larger doses, this initial norepinephrine release may delay the maximal effect of the treatment until the day after the block. Also, as a practical matter,

5 to 10 mL of 1% lidocaine should be added to the guanethidine to prevent the transient but intense worsening of pain from the guanethidine-induced norepinephrine release. Blocks may be repeated after 3 days to maintain sympathectomy. It should be remembered that guanethidine has a high affinity for neural sites, and with serial blocks there is accumulation and prolongation of the sympathetic block.

Another agent that has been used for intravenous regional blocks is bretylium [6]. Bretylium produces a sympathectomy by being taken up by and concentrated in adrenergic nerve terminals, and with the initial uptake of bretylium, as with guanethidine, there is some displacement and release of norepinephrine. Until recently, the literature contained contradictory results with intravenous regional bretylium: Whereas Ford and coworkers [6] reported sustained relief after a series of intravenous regional bretylium treatments in four patients, subsequently, Hanowell and coworkers [7] and Manchikanti [8] reported only transient relief in four patients in each of their reports. However, more recently the efficacy of bretylium was established by Hord and coworkers [9••], who carried out a controlled, double-blind study comparing bretylium 1.5 mg/kg in 40 mL of lidocaine 0.5% with 40 mL of lidocaine 0.5% alone in 12 patients with reflex sympathetic dystrophy. The intravenous regional bretylium provided pain relief of 30% or more for a mean duration of 20.0 (±17.5) days (range 3–69 d), whereas the lidocaine alone provided similar relief for a mean duration of only 2.7 (±3.7) days (range 0–12 d), a difference that was both clinically and statistically significant.

Obviously, a more desirable form of treatment would be one that provides permanent, or at least long-lasting, relief, so intravenous regional sympatholytics may not ultimately play a significant role in the management of sympathetically mediated pain. Nonetheless, the experience gained with intravenous regional guanethidine and bretylium has led to the hypothesis that in sympathetically mediated pain α_1-adrenoreceptors become expressed on primary afferent nociceptors such that the release of norepinephrine by the postganglionic sympathetic terminals leads to the activation of the nociceptors and pain. This hypothesis then led to the phentolamine test for sympathetically mediated pain as a substitute for diagnostic sympathetic blocks [10•], and indeed this line of thought led several investigators to explore the use of oral phenoxybenzamine [11] and prazosin [12] for sympathetic pain.

The most recent and innovative application of this "anesthetic technique" (IVRA) to sympathetically mediated pain is the use of intravenous regional ketorolac:

according to Robert's theory [13] as to the mechanism of sympathetically mediated pain (Fig. 5-1), A-fiber mechanoreceptors are activated by sympathetic efferent activity in the periphery, resulting in the presynaptic release of norepinephrine. Norepinephrine in turn activates cyclooxygenase, which induces the release of prostaglandins, and these peptides sensitize both chemical receptors and mechanoreceptors. Theoretically, ketorolac, by inhibiting cyclooxygenase, should reduce prostaglandin synthesis and thus reduce pain. Putting this theory to the test (although admittedly a preliminary study), Vanos and coworkers [14•] recently showed that 60 mg of ketorolac administered by the intravenous regional technique produced significant and prolonged relief in seven patients with refractory sympathetic pain.

Acute Herniated Nucleus Pulposus

When Mixter and Barr [15] demonstrated the relationship between disc protrusion and radicular pain, they believed that the signs and symptoms of sciatica were due to the mechanical compression of the nerve root by the protruded disc, and this mechanical explanation of sciatica prompted surgeons to consider laminectomy to be curative. Surgical results, however, were not always satisfactory, and surgery frequently resulted in significant complications.

Olsson [16] experimentally produced cervical disc protrusion in dogs and found that the size of the disc and the amount of compression were less important in the production of the symptomatology than the accompanying inflammation. The etiologic role of inflammation in sciatica is supported by the observation during lumbar laminectomy under local anesthesia that inflamed spinal nerves adjacent to a prolapsed disc are very sensitive to minor manipulations, whereas nerves that are not inflamed can be manipulated with very little discomfort [17]. Inflammation of nerve roots in patients with low back pain has been demonstrated myelographically [18] and visually [19] at the time of surgery and has been confirmed by histologic examination of biopsy specimens taken from nerve roots during surgery [20–22]. Indeed,

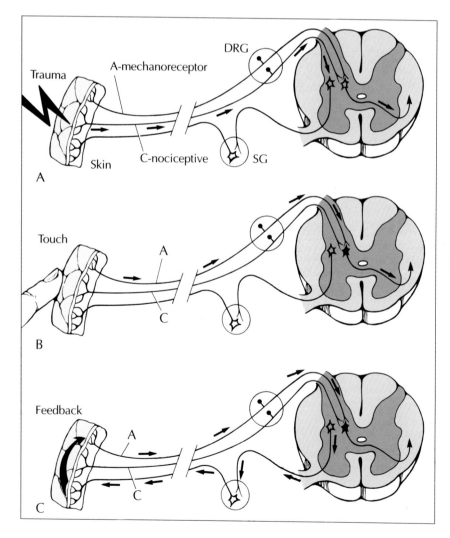

Figure 5-1 Physiologic model developed by Roberts [34]. (A) Immediate response to trauma. Action potentials in C-nociceptors propagate through the dorsal root ganglia (DRG) to the spinal cord, where they activate and sensitize wide-dynamic-range (WDR) neurons, whose axons are sent to higher centers. (B) The WDR neurons remain sensitized and now respond to activity in large-diameter A-mechanoreceptors, which are activated by light touch. This state produces allodynia. (C) The same sensitized WDR neurons respond again to A-mechanoreceptor activity, but this activity is initiated by sympathetic efferent actions on the sensory receptors in the absence of cutaneous stimulation. This phase represents sympathetically maintained pain. (*Adapted from* Roberts [34]; with permission.)

improvement in clinical symptoms has been shown to coincide with the resolution or diminution of nerve root edema in the presence of a persistent herniated intervertebral disc [18].

Once it was established that sciatica is the result of an inflammatory process involving a specific nerve root, it was a logical step to utilize corticosteroids in the vicinity of the inflamed nerve root to counteract the inflammation. Applying the technical skills acquired in providing regional anesthesia for surgery and obstetrics, anesthesiologists began to apply this information clinically by treating discogenic pain with intrathecal and epidural steroids [23]. Though the success rate was similar with both approaches, because of the increasingly litigious state of medicine, intrathecal steroid injections gave way to epidural injections, even though there have been no complications reported in the literature following intrathecal steroid injection provided that 1) reasonable dosages were administered; 2) the number of injections was reasonable; and 3) the patient was free of central nervous system disease, *ie*, multiple sclerosis.

Today, the epidural injection of steroids represents one of the most widely used therapeutic modalities in most pain control centers—at least in those centers managed, coordinated, or directed by anesthesiologists. The reported success rates have varied tremendously, both because of the variation between reports as to the indications for this treatment and as to the time of its administration. Nonetheless, it would appear that if administered early after herniation of a disc (when the pain is mainly caused by inflammation of nerve roots), epidural steroids approach 100% success, and then with the passage of time (as the inflammatory response gives way to scarring and mechanical compression), the success rate decreases progressively [24,25]. This obvious relationship between the time of treatment and success provides clinical evidence that epidural steroids produce their therapeutic benefit through their anti-inflammatory effect.

NEUROLYTIC BLOCKS FOR CHRONIC PAIN

Neurolytic blocks represent the most obvious extrapolation of regional block techniques from surgical anesthesia to pain management. Surgical anesthesia is provided by the action of local anesthetics that temporarily and reversibly block nerve conduction to a part of the body to allow surgery without pain; whereas neurolytic agents block nerve conduction permanently and irreversibly to relieve chronic pain.

Neurolytic Solutions

The solutions that we use for neurolytic blocks are as follows: for subarachnoid blocks, absolute alcohol is used when a hypobaric solution is desired, and 6% phenol in glycerine is used when a hyperbaric solution is desired. For peripheral nerve blocks, absolute alcohol is used for blocking the cranial nerves, whereas 6% to 12% aqueous phenol is used to block all other peripheral nerves. The reason that phenol is preferred to alcohol for peripheral nerve blocks is that the incidence of neuritis is significantly less with phenol than with alcohol.

Because of the "permanence" of the complications of neurolytic blocks, should they occur, these blocks should be used only after consulting a dermatome chart to determine precisely which nerve or nerves should be blocked (Fig. 5-2). In some cases, myotome and sclero-

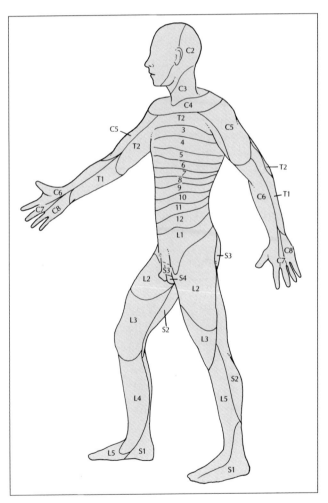

Figure 5-2 A side view of the dermatomes. (*From* Foerster [35]; with permission.)

tome charts (Fig. 5-3) should also be consulted, because occasionally an area of muscle or bone receives innervation that is different than that of the innervation of the skin overlying it. Finally, a prognostic local anesthetic block should be carried out prior to the performance of any neurolytic block to allow patients to experience the numbness that will replace their pain. Most patients will prefer numbness to pain, but the occasional patient will find it intolerable, and this should be determined *prior* to the decision to perform a neurolytic block.

Peripheral Neurolytic Blocks

Virtually all peripheral nerves are mixed nerves, so when carrying out a peripheral neurolytic block, one must assume that it will produce both a motor and sensory block. In actual practice, phenol frequently does not produce a motor block when applied to peripheral nerves, but one can not guarantee the patient that motor function will be spared. On the other hand, for pain other than that involving the extremities, one may not be concerned about the production of a motor deficit, *eg*, intercostal nerves.

Intrathecal Neurolytic Blocks

The only neurolytic procedure that allows sensory block to be carried out without motor block is intrathecal chemical dorsal rhizotomy (more appropriately called rhizolysis). Because it is the most precise way to block one to three dermatomes without motor dysfunction, it is particularly valuable for pain in an extremity due to malignancy when preservation of motor function is important. The technique can be carried out using one of two techniques—a hypobaric technique, using absolute alcohol, or a hyperbaric technique, using phenol in glycerine. In our experience, alcohol has most frequently been the agent of choice for the simple reason that most patients in pain cannot lie on the painful side, as is required to use hyperbaric phenol. When hypobaric absolute alcohol is to be used, the patient is placed in the lateral spinal position with the painful side up and is then rolled anteriorly about 45° (to place the dorsal root uppermost) (Fig. 5-4). He or she is then propped up with pillows and stabilized with straps so that he or she can remain in this position for a significant period of time.

In carrying out a neurolytic subarachnoid block, the dorsal root must be blocked where it leaves the spinal cord. Therefore, an intrathecal chemical rhizotomy

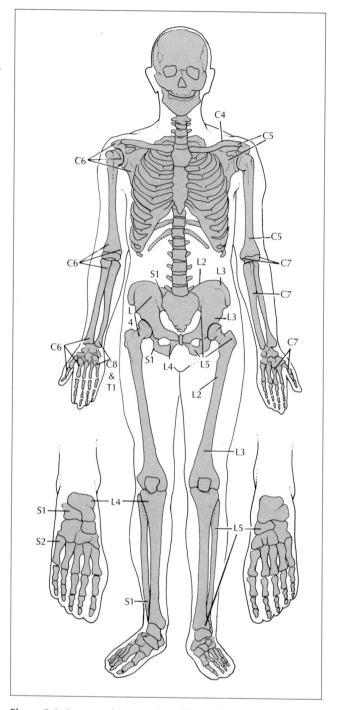

Figure 5-3 Segmental innervation of the skeleton, anterior view. (*Adapted from* Dejerine [36]; with permission.)

should never be undertaken without consulting a chart that indicates the bony vertebral level at which a particular nerve leaves the spinal cord, which is invariably at a higher level than the level at which the nerve leaves the vertebral column (Fig. 5-5). When the appropriate level of entry has been determined, a needle is inserted into the spinal canal at this level, but a test dose of local anesthetic should *not* be used, as no local anesthetic can be made as hypobaric as absolute alcohol. Instead, the patient is told that he or she will experience localized burning for a fraction of a second following the injection of a minute amount of alcohol and that he or she must determine whether that burning occurs *at* the level of the pain, *above* the level of the pain, or *below* the level of the pain.

Thus, the burning produced by the first two or three 0.1-mL increments of absolute alcohol (injected with a tuberculin syringe) indicates whether the needle is placed at the appropriate level. If burning occurs at the level of the patient's pain, a total 0.7 mL of absolute alcohol is injected in 0.1-mL increments. If the burning occurs above the site of the patient's pain, a second or even a third needle must be inserted at a lower level until the burning produced by the alcohol corresponds to the distribution of the patient's pain. (The 0.1 mL of alcohol injected at an inappropriate dermatome will cause insignificant problems.) Similarly, if the burning occurred below the patient's pain, then a second or third needle must be inserted at a higher level until the injection of 0.1-mL increments of absolute alcohol produces burning in the distribution of the patient's pain, after which the entire 0.7 mL (given in 0.1-mL increments) will produce the desired anesthesia.

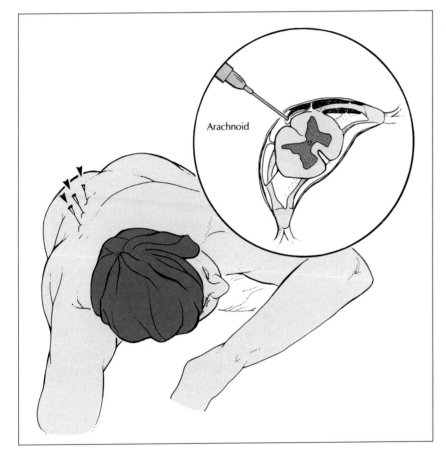

Arachnoid

Figure 5-4 Demonstration of the layering of hypobaric absolute alcohol injected intrathecally with the patient tilted forward and the painful side up. The hypobaricity of the alcohol and the positioning of the patient allow the solution to rise and bathe the dorsal root. (*From* Raj and Denson [37]; with permission.)

Prior to injecting intrathecal alcohol, spinal fluid should not be aspirated into the syringe, for it will form a white coagulum; in addition, if the needle is placed a little too low or too high, the alcohol cannot be "floated" to

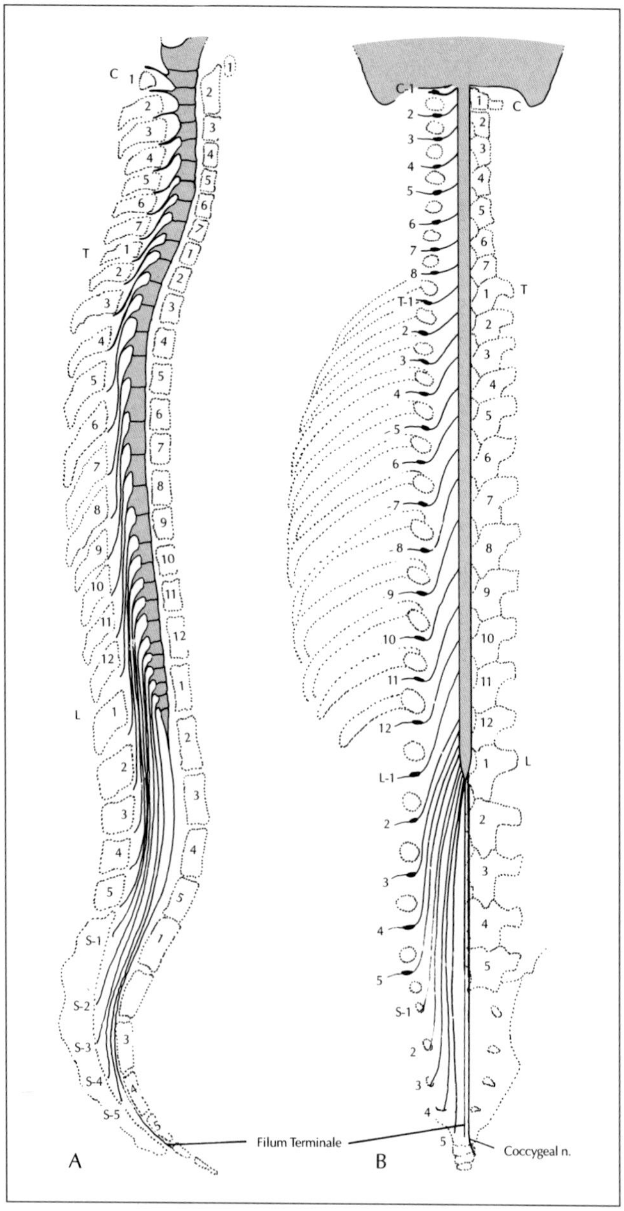

Figure 5-5 The relation of the spinal column and the spinal cord, nerve roots, and the formed nerves. (A) Lateral view. (B) Posterior view. Note the direction of the spinal rootlets and roots in the various segments. The size of the spinal cord in relation to the spinal canal is exaggerated in *B* for the sake of clarity of the numbers of the spinal cord segments and their relationship to the vertebrae. (*From* Bonica [38]; with permission.)

a higher or lower level (as a hypobaric local anesthetic can), as the alcohol "fixes" too quickly. Thus, a separate needle must be placed at each nerve root to be blocked.

Alternatively, phenol in glycerine can be used intrathecally. This neurolytic solution is less widely used, since as stated earlier, with this hyperbaric technique the patient must lie on the painful side, and most patients with pain of malignant origin have a problem doing this. However, if appropriate, the technique is similar to that followed using alcohol except that the patient is positioned with the dorsal root lowermost and with the head of the table slightly elevated (Fig. 5-6).

After the completion of the subarachnoid injection of either alcohol or phenol in glycerine, 0.2 to 0.3 mL of air is injected to flush the alcohol or phenol out of the needle prior to the removal of each needle, and the patient is then kept in the same position for approximately 30 minutes. Although alcohol fixes "quite rapidly," for medicolegal reasons it is prudent to carry out this latter maneuver to satisfy the "standard" as stated in most textbooks. However, if the patient is unable to remain in the "injection position," a compromise would be to allow the patient to lie on their stomach following alcohol neurolysis or on their back following phenol for the required half hour following the injection.

Epidural Neurolytic Blocks

Indications for epidural neurolysis include pain in the shoulder or upper extremities, pain in the thoracic wall or pleural cavity, or pain in the upper abdominal wall. The theoretical advantages of epidural over intrathecal neurolysis are that the positioning of the patient is not as critical; neurolysis can be carried out over a large number of dermatomes; and neurolysis can be carried out over a period of 2 to 3 days by repeated intermittent injections of phenol through an epidural catheter.

With the patient in a lateral position and with the painful side down, an epidural catheter is inserted as close to the targeted nerve roots as possible. After negative aspiration, 5 mL of 1% lidocaine is injected, followed by 2- to 3-mL increments every 15 minutes until there is evidence of decreased pinprick sensation over the entire painful area. If the pain (using a visual analogue scale) is decreased more than 75% and if this is satisfactory to the patient, the lidocaine block is allowed to wear off completely. Then, 15% phenol in 15% glycerol (75% of the lidocaine volume necessary to block the painful dermatomes) is injected through the epidural catheter. After 15 minutes, the presence of pinprick sensation over the area of pain is examined; if absent, no further injection is necessary. If not, phenol in increments of 1 to 2 mL is injected every 30 minutes until sensory block is demonstrated over the painful area. The catheter is left in place and the patient is observed for the next 12 hours for narcotic use and pain levels. If the pain relief is not complete, then the injection is repeated the following day. Success rates with this procedure have not been adequately documented, although anecdotal reports of success rates ranging from 33% to 90% have been reported [26,27].

Celiac Plexus Block

The celiac plexus usually lies in loose areolar tissue anterior to the bodies of the twelfth thoracic and first lumbar vertebrae. Celiac plexus block, therefore, employs a technique similar to that of lumbar paravertebral sympathetic block but at a slightly higher level. Traditional, unguided techniques were carried out with the patient in the prone position utilizing two needles through which a large volume (50 mL) of 50% alcohol was injected (Fig. 5-7).

The author's unguided technique is carried out in the lateral position, using a single needle and much smaller

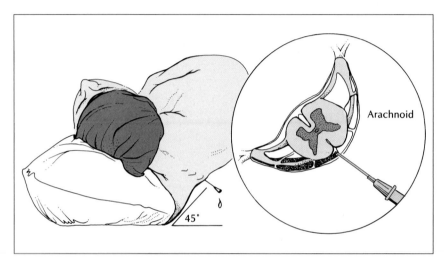

Figure 5-6 Demonstration of the layering of hyperbaric phenol injected intrathecally with the patient tilted 45° backwards with the painful side down. The hyperbaricity of the phenol and the positioning of the patient allow the solution to bathe primarily the dorsal root. (*From* Raj and Denson [37]; with permission.)

Arachnoid

45°

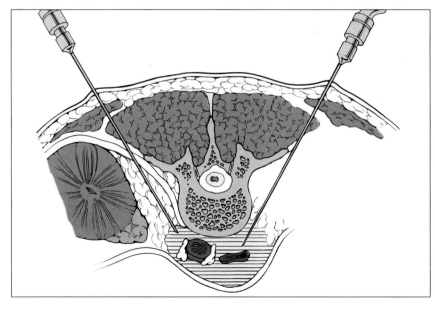

Figure 5-7 Final needle position in the traditional, unguided, two-needle technique of celiac plexus block with relationship to the surrounding anatomic structures. (*Adapted from* Thompson and Moore [39]; with permission.)

volumes (5 to 10 mL) of 6% phenol (Fig. 5-8). The patient is placed in the lateral decubitus position, the spinous process of the first lumbar vertebra (L-1) is identified and marked, and a circle about one half inch in diameter is drawn at the point where the lateral edge of the paravertebral muscles intersects the lower margin of the twelfth rib. After preparing the skin, a wheal is raised in the center of this circle through which a 5-inch, 22-gauge needle is inserted and directed toward the body of L-1. Ordinarily, because the point of insertion with this technique is further lateral than with other techniques, the transverse process is not contacted, and the body of the vertebra is encountered upon the first insertion of the needle. The needle is then withdrawn and reintroduced progressively more anteriorly until it "walks off" the anterolateral surface of the vertebral body, at which point it is then advanced an additional 1 to 2 cm so that it lies in the loose areolar tissue anterior to the vertebral body. After aspirating carefully for blood (or spinal fluid) in three or four quadrants, incremental injections of 2 to 3 mL of 2% lidocaine or mepivacaine are injected until pain relief is produced. After pain relief is achieved, sufficient time must be allowed prior to injection of a neurolytic solution for the local anesthetic to produce motor or sensory block, which would indicate improper needle placement. However, if after 10 to 15 minutes the patient continues to have pain relief without sensory or motor blockade, a volume of 6% phenol equal to the volume of local anes-

thetic solution required to produce pain relief is injected in increments with repeated, intermittent attempts to aspirate throughout the injection. Following the injection of the phenol, 1 mL of air is injected to clear the needle, and then the needle is withdrawn.

With the onset of the celiac plexus block, generalized splanchnic vasodilatation may result in hypotension. Usually this is minimal in young healthy subjects, but in older patients who cannot compensate by vasoconstriction of the unaffected vessels, the hypotension may be severe and prolonged, particularly when a neurolytic agent is used. In either case, a patient who has just received a celiac plexus block should be returned to the upright position very slowly and incrementally and may require the administration of intravenous fluids, vasopressors, or both. Thus, neurolytic blocks should not be carried out on an out-patient basis, as these patients may faint upon resuming the upright position after leaving the hospital.

The safety of the author's unguided technique lies in the use of a test dose and small volumes of phenol rather than large volumes of alcohol. The test dose of a solution of local anesthetic, having a concentration above the critical motor threshold, should alert the operator to improper placement of the needle or migration of the solution, and this will prohibit injection of the neurolytic solution. Furthermore, the use of 6% phenol instead of 50% alcohol will minimize the adverse sequelae of such an injection, should any occur, without reducing the incidence of effective pain relief. In addition, the use of the lateral position will tend to allow the kidney to fall away from the course of the needle and occupy a position that is more anteromedial than that which it occupies in the prone position, in which the kidneys are pushed posteriorly into the path of the needle by the abdominal viscera. Finally, the use of a single injection (as opposed to two) reduces the possibility of a technical complication by 50%, and only rarely in our experience has a second injection on the opposite side been required to provide complete pain relief.

There have been several modifications in celiac plexus block techniques introduced over the past few years, and many anesthesiologists now carry out the procedure under some form of radiograph control. A large number of them perform the technique using fluoroscopy, and with this technique advancement of the needle anterior to the upper border of the L-1 vertebral body is accomplished under direct fluoroscopic guidance. Once the needle is properly placed, aspiration is carried out, and if negative, a small amount of local anesthetic is injected to ensure that the needle is not in the diaphragm (in which case, the patient coughs immediately or complains of shoulder pain). Dye is then injected under fluoroscopic control to make sure the spread of the solution remains anterior to the verte-

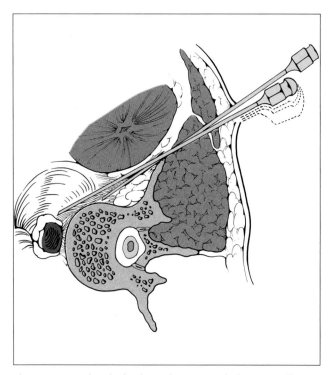

Figure 5-8 Landmarks for the author's unguided, one-needle technique of celiac plexus block.

bral bodies, and, if the spread of dye is in the appropriate plane, 20 to 25 mL of local anesthetic is injected as a diagnostic and prognostic block (Fig. 5-9). If pain relief ensues, 50 mL of 50% alcohol is injected. Those who use this technique feel that the demonstration of the spread of the injected dye by fluoroscopy provides absolute proof that the injection is not being made into the epidural or intrathecal spaces. However, even when fluoroscopic control is used, the author believes that the fact that the injection of local anesthetic produces pain relief but not motor or sensory block is a better index of safety and efficacy than just fluoroscopic documentation of the spread of dye.

More recently, computed tomography (CT) guidance has been advocated for celiac plexus block, and a single needle transaortic technique has been introduced by Lieberman and Waldman (Fig. 5-10A) [28]. The patient is placed prone in the CT gantry, and a scout film is taken to identify the T-12–L-1 interspace.

Because the celiac plexus is wrapped around the anterior surface of the aorta, a 13-cm Hinck needle is inserted through a skin wheal 2 inches from the midline, and the needle is advanced until the free flow of arterial blood indicates penetration of the posterior wall of the aorta. At this point a syringe containing preservative-free saline is attached, the needle is advanced through the anterior wall of the aorta using a loss-of-resistance technique, and 6 mL of local anesthetic mixed with renograffin is injected. If the CT scan shows proper placement of the needle (the tip has not been advanced into the peritoneal space) (Fig. 5-10B) and if pain relief has been produced by the local anesthetic, 12 mL of neurolytic solution is injected. The needle is then flushed with 1 mL of preservative-free saline and removed. This technique assures, perhaps more than any other, antecrural rather than retrocrural spread of the neurolytic solution and thus minimizes the risk of unwanted sensory or motor blockade.

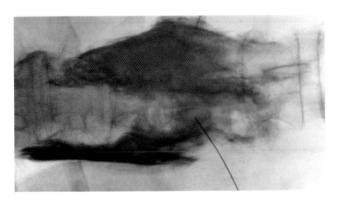

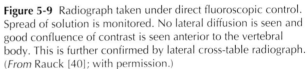

Figure 5-9 Radiograph taken under direct fluoroscopic control. Spread of solution is monitored. No lateral diffusion is seen and good confluence of contrast is seen anterior to the vertebral body. This is further confirmed by lateral cross-table radiograph. (*From* Rauck [40]; with permission.)

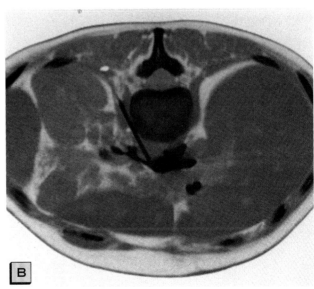

Figure 5-10 (A) Transaortic approach to celiac plexus nerve. Cross-sectional diagram at the L-1 vertebral level: the patient lies prone, and the skin entry site is below the 12th rib. Ao—aorta; CG—celiac ganglia; IVC—inferior vena cava; LC—left crus; PV—portal vein; RC—right crus; SV—splenic vein. (B) Spread of contrast material anterior to crura indicates correct needle position for alcohol injection. (*From* Lieberman and Waldman [28]; with permission.)

Superior Hypogastric Plexus Block

Although celiac plexus block successfully alleviates upper abdominal visceral pain, pain of lower abdominal or pelvic origin can be managed by a similar block of the superior hypogastric plexus. In 1990, Plancarte and coworkers [29] described a two-needle technique very much like the traditional technique of celiac plexus block, except that it was carried out at the level of the body of the first sacral rather than the first lumbar vertebra (Fig. 5-11A and B).

Waldman and coworkers [30••] simplified the technique by using a single injection and CT control. With the patient prone in the CT gantry, a CT scout film is taken to identify the L-4–5 interspace. A 13-cm, 20-gauge Hinck needle is inserted through a skin wheal raised 6 centimeters lateral to the L-4–5 interspace and directed 30° mesiad and 30° caudad, placing the tip of the needle anterior to the body of L-5. A glass 5-mL syringe filled with preservative-free saline is attached, and the needle is advanced with constant pressure applied to the syringe. When a "pop" and loss of resistance indicates penetration of the anterior fascia of the psoas major muscle, after careful aspiration, 2 to 3 mL of isohexol-140 is injected, and a CT scan is taken to confirm proper retroperitoneal placement of the needle (Fig. 5-12). Ten milliliters of local anesthetic is then injected, and if adequate pain relief is obtained without undesirable side effects and without sensory or motor blockade, 10 mL of the neurolytic solution is injected. Usually the dye, the local anesthetic, and the neurolytic solution spread to include the contralateral side; so usually a second needle need not be placed.

Block of the Ganglion Impar

Plancarte and coworkers [31] recently introduced blockade of the ganglion impar (ganglion of Walther) as a means of managing intractable perineal pain of sympathetic origin. The patient is positioned in the lateral decubitus position, and a skin wheal is raised in the midline at the superior

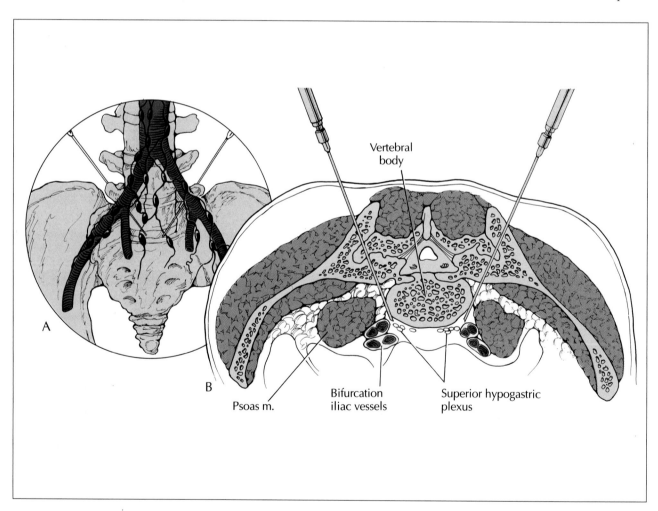

Figure 5-11 (A) Anterior view of pelvis illustrating location of superior hypogastric plexus and correct bilateral needle placement. (B) Cross-sectional schematic view illustrating bilateral hypogastric plexus block and needles' relationship to fifth lumbar vertebra, psoas muscle, and iliac vessels. (*From* Plancarte and coworkers [41]; with permission.)

aspect of the intergluteal crease, over the anococcygeal ligament but just above the anus. A 22-gauge 3-1/2 spinal needle is bent about 1 inch from its hub to form a 25° to 30° angle to facilitate positioning of the needle tip anterior to the concavity of the sacrum and coccyx. The needle is then inserted through the skin wheal with its concavity oriented posteriorly. Then under fluoroscopic guidance, it is directed anterior to the coccyx, approximating the anterior surface of the bone, until its tip is observed to have reached the sacrococcygeal junction (Fig. 5-13).

Retroperitoneal location of the needle is verified by observing the spread of 2 mL of water-soluble contrast medium (Fig. 5-14), which typically assumes a smooth contour between the sacrococcygeal region and the air-filled rectal "bubble." If the solution remains retroperitoneal, 4 mL of local anesthetic is injected, and if this produces pain relief, 4 to 10 mL of 10% phenol is injected for therapeutic neurolytic blockade.

NEUROLYTIC BLOCKS FOR NONMALIGNANT PAIN

Stellate Ganglion Block

For the diagnosis and management of early reflex sympathetic dystrophy, the author is beginning to rely more on differential and therapeutic brachial plexus block,

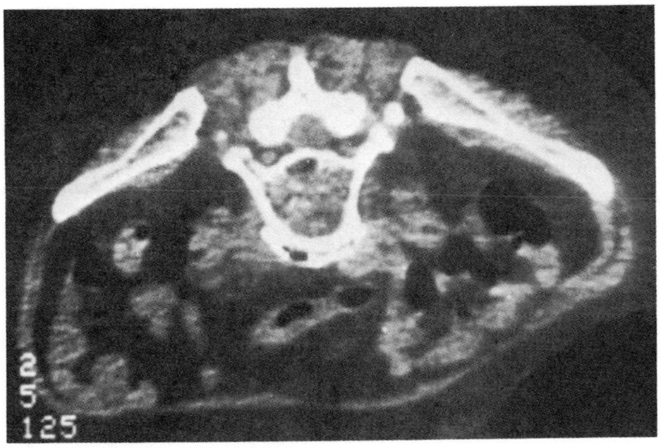

Figure 5-12 Computed tomography after the injection of air and contrast medium bilaterally at the level of the hypogastric plexus. Note retroperitoneal location of contrast medium. (*From* Plancarte and coworkers [41]; with permission.)

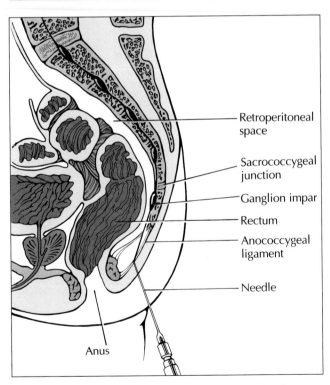

Retroperitoneal space

Sacrococcygeal junction

Ganglion impar

Rectum

Anococcygeal ligament

Needle

Anus

Figure 5-13 Lateral view demonstrating correct needle placement for blockade of ganglion impar, and anatomic relations. (*From* Plancarte and coworkers [41]; with permission.)

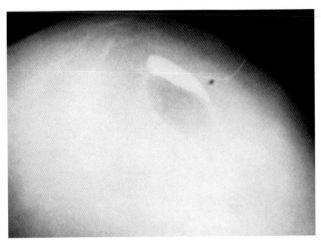

Figure 5-14 Lateral radiograph demonstrating correct placement of bent 22-gauge needle for block of the ganglion impar. Note smooth contours of contrast medium in retroperitoneum between sacrococcygeal region and rectal bubble. (*From* Plancarte and coworkers [41]; with permission.)

since a recent study has indicated a higher rate of success (diagnostically and therapeutically) with this technique than with stellate ganglion block [32••]. However, for a neurolytic block for sympathetically mediated upper extremity pain, there is no alternative to a stellate gan-

glion block. While a stellate ganglion block is a simple and straightforward technique (Fig. 5-15), if the needle is misplaced, very dangerous and life-threatening complications can occur, especially when neurolytic solutions are used. Using the classic paratracheal technique, if the

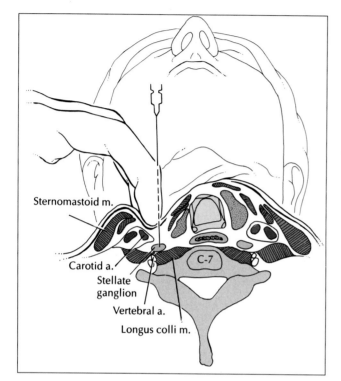

Figure 5-15 Cross-sectional schematic demonstrating technique of stellate ganglion block at the C7 level. Technique is similar when block is performed at the C6 level (*see text*). Note that the pressure exerted by the nondominant hand both retracts the carotid artery laterally and minimizes the distance between the skin and transverse process. (*From* Plancarte and coworkers [41]; with permission.)

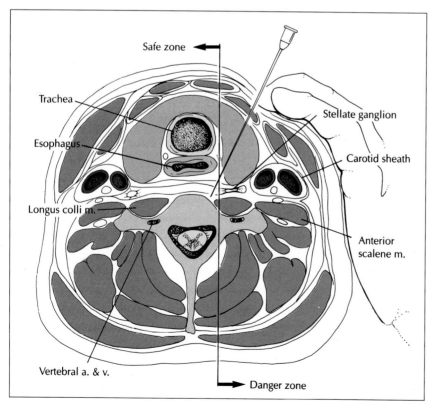

Figure 5-16 Racz's technique for neurolytic stellate ganglion block. Note that the standard approach has been modified by the introduction of a mesiad inclination to the needle, which is placed at the C7 level. The needle tip is intended to reach the vertebral body medial to the indention of the longus colli muscle. An imaginary line separates the "safety zone" from the "danger zone," where complications related to injection near the vertebral artery, exiting spinal nerve root, and epidural space may be less likely to occur. (*From* Racz and Holubec [33]; with permission.)

needle is misplaced, very dangerous and life-threatening complications can occur, especially when neurolytic solutions are used. Using the classic paratracheal technique, if the process fails to encounter the pedicle or transverse process of C6, an injection could block one or more cervical nerves, could enter the vertebral artery or vein(s), or could even enter the epidural or subarachnoid spaces; a needle placed below this level could enter the pleura and produce a pneumothorax.

Racz and Holubec [33] have described a minor modification to minimize the incidence of these complications (Fig. 5-16). However, whatever technique is used, prior to the injection of a neurolytic substance, an injection of local anesthetic mixed with radioopaque dye should be made with fluoroscopy or CT scan to confirm that the injection is in the correct plane. Then, if the local anesthetic produces the desired relief without undesirable side effects, 6 to 8 mL of the neurolytic solution is injected.

Lumbar Sympathetic Block

As with pain in the upper extremity, diagnostic and therapeutic blocks for early reflex sympathetic dystrophy are being carried out increasingly with sympathetic epidural blocks rather than with lumbar paravertebral sympathetic blocks, because the former technique has recently been shown to produce more complete sympathetic denervation of the lower extremity than the latter. However, for sympathetic neurolysis, lumbar paravertebral sympathetic block is, again, the only alternative.

With this technique (Fig. 5-17), the needle is inserted through a skin wheal raised about 3 inches lateral to the midpoint of the spinous process of L-2 and directed mesiad toward the body of the vertebra. If the transverse process is encountered, the needle is reinserted more caudally until the body is contacted, at which time the needle is reinserted several times slightly more anteriorly until it "walks off" the anterolateral border of the vertebral body. Radiopaque dye mixed with 6 to 8 mL of local anesthetic is injected, and if fluoroscopy or CT scan confirms proper spread of the solution (Fig. 5-18), and if the expected pain relief ensues without sensory or motor block, 8 to 10 mL of the neurolytic solution are injected.

MISCELLANEOUS THERAPEUTIC MODALITIES

A physician with a firm grasp of neuroanatomy and training in the techniques of regional anesthesia will be able to use other therapeutic modalities, such as radiofrequency lesioning and cryoanalgesia, trigger point

and facet joint injections, transsphenoidal pituitary adenolysis, and implantation of narcotic delivery systems and dorsal column stimulators, to name a few. However, the present discussion focuses on those modalities whereby regional anesthesia techniques *per se* provide unique tools useful in the management of chronic pain.

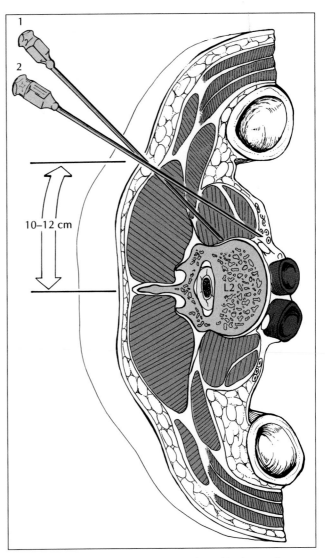

Figure 5-17 Technique of lumbar sympathetic block. (1) A line is drawn through the center of the spinous processes; this will lie below the transverse process of that vertebra. Needle insertion is at the lateral margin of the erector spinae muscle (approximately 10–12 cm from midline). If it is desired to check the depth of the transverse process, the needle must be angled cephalad. Otherwise, the needle is inserted approximately 45° toward the vertebral body until this structure is located. The needle is then angled more steeply until it slips just past the vertebral body and through the psoas fascia. (2) A single needle can be used instead of two or three needles; however, an increased volume must be injected. (*From Löfström and coworkers [42]; with permission.*)

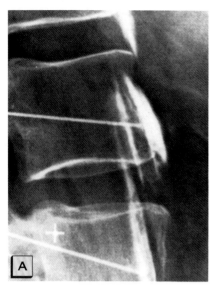

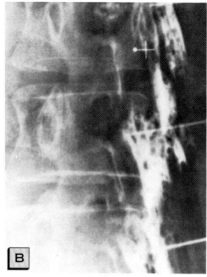

Figure 5-18 (A) Lateral view. Complete coverage of L2 and L4 vertebral body levels with injection of only 1 mL of 10% phenol in an aqueous radiographic contrast material (Conray 420) at each level. (B) Anteroposterior view to show spread of solution following line of psoas muscle. Note limitation of lateral spread to reduce risk of genitofemoral nerve involvement. (*From* Löfström and coworkers [42]; with permission.)

REFERENCES AND RECOMMENDED READING

Papers of interest, published recently, have been highlighted as:
• Of special interest
•• Of outstanding interest

1.   Winnie AP: Differential neural blockade: clinical utility and current concepts. In *Anesthesiology and Pain Management*. Edited by Stanley TH, Ashburn MA, Fine PG. Boston: Kluwer Academic Publishers; 1991:131–152.

2.   Winnie AP, Collins VJ: The Pain Clinic I: differential neural blockade in pain syndromes of questionable etiology. *Med Clin North Am* 1968, 52:123–129.

3.   •• Winnie AP, Hartwell PW: The relationship between the time of treatment of acute herpes zoster with sympathetic blockade and the prevention of postherpetic neuralgia: clinical support for a new theory of the mechanism by which sympathetic blockade provides therapeutic benefit. *Reg Anesth*, 1993, 18:277–282.

This article for the first time quantitates the therapeutic window of sympathetic blocks in preventing the development of postherpetic neuralgia following acute herpes zoster. The authors also postulate the mechanism by which sympathetic blocks exert this therapeutic effect.

4.   McKendrick MD, McGill JI, Wood MJ: Lack of effect of acyclovir on postherpetic neuralgia. *BMJ* 1989, 298:431.

5.   Hannington-Kiff JE: Intravenous regional sympathetic block with guanethidine. *Lancet* 1974, 1:1019–1020.

6.   Ford SR, Forrest WH, Jr, Eltherington L: The treatment of reflex sympathetic dystrophy with intravenous regional bretylium. *Anesthesiology* 1988, 68:137–140.

7.   Hanowell LH, Kanefield JK, Soriano SG, III: A recommendation for reduced lidocaine dosage during intravenous regional bretylium treatment for reflex sympathetic dystrophy. *Anesthesiology* 1989, 71:811–812.

8.   Manchikanti L: Role of intravenous regional bretylium in reflex sympathetic dystrophy. *Anesthesiology* 1990, 73:585–586.

9.   •• Hord AH, Rooks MD, Stephens BO, *et al.*: Intravenous regional bretylium and lidocaine for treatment of reflex sympathetic dystrophy: a randomized, double-blind study. *Anesth Analg* 1992, 74:818–821.

This is the first study to delineate and document in a prospective, double-blind, controlled fashion the therapeutic efficacy of intravenous regional sympatholytic agents. It also demonstrates the limited duration of relief provided by this modality.

10. • Raja SN, Treede RD, Davis KD, *et al.*: Systemic α-adrenergic blockade with phentolamine: a diagnostic test for sympathetically maintained pain. *Anesthesiology* 1991, 74:691–698.

This paper verifies the concept that sympathetically maintained pain involves α_1-adrenoreceptors and may lead to a treatment regimen involving the systemic administration of specific blocking agents.

11. Ghostine SY, Comair YG, Turner DM, *et al.*: Phenoxybenzamine in the treatment of causalgia. *J Neurosurg* 1984, 60:1263–1268.

12. Abram SE, Lightfoot RW, Jr: Treatment of long-standing causalgia with prazosin. *Reg Anesth* 1981, 6:79–81.

13. Roberts WJ: A hypothesis on the physiologic basis for causalgia and related pains. *Pain* 1986, 24:297–311.

14. • Vanos DN, Ramamurthy S, Hoffman J: Intravenous regional block using ketorolac: preliminary results in the treatment of reflex sympathetic dystrophy. *Anesth Analg* 1992, 74:139–141.

This preliminary study indicates that there are multiple biochemical sites at which the peripheral biochemical feedback loop can be interrupted to prevent the development of allodynia in sympathetically maintained pain.

15. Mixter WJ, Barr JS: Rupture of intervertebral disc with involvement of the spinal canal. *N Engl J Med* 1934, 211:210–215.

16. Olsson SE: The dynamic factor in spinal cord compression: a study on dogs with special reference to cervical disc protrusion. *J Neurosurg* 1958, 15:308–321.

17. Murphy RW: Nerve roots and spinal nerves in degenerative disc disease. *Clin Orthop* 1977, 129:46–60.

18. Berg A: Clinical and myelographic studies of conservatively treated cases of lumbar intervertebral disc. *Acta Chir Scand* 1953, 104:124–129.

19. Roaf J: Some observations regarding 905 patients operated upon for protruded lumbar intervertebral disc. *Am J Surg* 1959, 97:388–399.

20. Lindahl O, Rexed B: Histologic changes in spinal nerve roots of operated cases of sciatica. *Acta Orthop Scand* 1950, 20:215–225.

21. Irsigler FJ: Nikroskopische befunde in den ruckenmark-swurzeln beim lumbalen und lumbosakrolen (dorsolateralen) diskusprolaps. *Acta Neurochir* (Wien) 1951, 1:478–516.

22. Marshall LL, Trethwie ER: Chemical irritation of nerve-root in disc prolapse. *Lancet* 1973, 2:230.

23. Winnie AP, Hartman JT, Meyers ML, Jr, *et al.*: Pain clinic II: intradural and extradural corticosteroids for sciatica. *Anesth Analg* 1972, 51:990–1003.

24. Brown FW: Management of diskogenic pain using epidural and intrathecal steroids. *Clin Orthop* 1977, 129:72–78.

25. Ryan MD, Taylor KF: Management of lumbar nerve-root pain by intrathecal and epidural injections of depot methylprednisolone acetate. *Med J Aust* 1981, 2:532–534.

26. Ferrer-Brechner T: Epidural and intrathecal phenol neurolysis for cancer pain: review of rationale and techniques. *Anesth Rev* 1981, 8:14–20.

27. Korevaar VC, Kline MT, Donnelly CC: Thoracic epidural neurolysis using alcohol. *Pain Suppl* 1987, 4:S133.

28. Lieberman R, Waldman SD: Celiac plexus neurolysis with the modified transaortic approach. *Radiology* 1990, 175:274–276.

29. Plancarte B, Amescua C, Patt RP, *et al.*: Superior hypogastric plexus block for pelvic cancer pain. *Anesthesiology* 1990, 73:236–239.

30. •• Waldman SD, Wilson WL, Kreps RD: Superior hypogastric block using a single needle and computed tomography guidance: description of a modified technique. *Reg Anesth* 1991, 16:286–287.

This paper simplifies the first neurolytic technique for controlling lower abdominal and pelvic pain.

31. Plancarte R, Amescua C, Patt RB, *et al.*: Presacral blockade of the ganglion of Walther (ganglion impar). *Anesthesiology* 1990, 73:A751.

32. •• Durrani Z, Winnie AP: Diagnostic and therapeutic brachial plexus block for RSD unresponsive to stellate ganglion block. *Reg Anesth* 1991, 15(1S):51.

This study indicates that occasionally stellate ganglion blocks fail to relieve reflex sympathetic dystrophy of the upper extremity, whereas perivascular blocks are capable of doing so. The authors also postulate the anatomic basis for this difference between the two techniques in providing *complete* sympathetic denervation of the upper extremity.

33. Racz GB, Holubec JT: Stellate ganglion phenol neurolysis. In *Techniques of Neurolysis*. Edited by Racz GB. Boston: Kluwer; 1989:137.

34. Roberts WJ: An hypothesis on the physiological basis for causalgia and related pains. *Pain* 1986, 24:297–311.

35. Foerster: Innervation of the skin and muscle. In *Peripheral Nerve Injuries*. Edited by Haymaker W, Woodhall B. Philadelphia: Saunders; 1956:175.

36. Dejerine: Innervation of the skeleton. In *Peripheral Nerve Injuries*. Edited by Haymaker W, Woodhall B. Philadelphia: Saunders; 1956:186.

37. Raj PP, Denson DD: Neurolytic agents. In *Clinical Practice of Regional Anesthesia*. Edited by Raj PP. New York: Churchill Livingstone; 1991.

38. Bonica JJ: Applied anatomy relevant to pain. In *The Management of Pain, Second Edition*. Edited by Bonica JJ. Philadelphia and London: Lea & Febiger; 1990:135.

39. Thompson GE, Moore DC: Celiac plexus, intercostal, and minor peripheral blockade. In *Neural Blockade in Clinical Anesthesia & Management of Pain*. Edited by Cousins MJ, Bridenbaugh PO. Philadelphia: Lippincott; 1980:396.

40. Rauck R: Sympathetic nerve blocks. In *Practical Management of Pain, Second Edition*. Edited by Raj PP. St. Louis: Mosby-Year Book; 1992:798.

41. Plancarte R, Velazquez R, Patt RB: Neurolytic blocks of the sympathetic axis. In *Cancer Pain*. Edited by Patt RB. Philadelphia: Lippincott; 1993:384–420.

42. Löfström JB, Lloyd JW, Cousins MJ: Sympathetic neural blockade of upper and lower extremity. In *Neural Blockade in Clinical Anesthesia and Management of Pain, Second Edition*. Edited by Cousins MJ, Bridenbaugh PO. Philadelphia: Lippincott; 1988:461–500.

CHAPTER 6

Systemic Approaches to the Management of Acute and Chronic Pain

PHILIP J. SIDDALL AND LAURENCE E. MATHER

Systemic approaches remain the mainstay of most management strategies in the treatment of chronic and acute pain. Recent years have seen the development of new techniques that use regional, surgical, or psychological approaches for pain management; however, there have also been interesting developments with the introduction of new agents coupled with novel methods of delivery for agents that have been used for many years. This chapter will present a review of analgesic and other agents commonly used in the systemic management of both acute and chronic pain, currently available methods of administration, and issues involved in the use of these agents in the clinical setting.

AGENTS USED IN THE MANAGEMENT OF PAIN

Nonopioid Analgesics

The first line of management in the systemic treatment of pain usually falls to the nonopioid analgesics, principally acetaminophen (paracetamol in the UK and elsewhere), aspirin, and other nonsteroidal anti-inflammatory drugs (NSAIDs). The use of aspirin is widespread, and it is effective for mild to moderate pain such as headaches and musculoskeletal pain. Acetaminophen has an advantage over aspirin in that it does not harm the mucosa of the gastrointestinal tract and does not affect platelet function; by the same token, however, it does not provide significant anti-inflammatory activity.

Nonsteroidal anti-inflammatory drugs act to inhibit the synthesis and release of prostaglandins at the site of trauma or inflammation. This results in a reduction in the hyperalgesia produced by sensitization of nociceptors produced by prostaglandins following tissue injury. The mechanisms of action of acetaminophen are still subject to some uncertainty, but current teaching is that it inhibits prostaglandin synthesis centrally more than peripherally.

Although NSAIDs have been used for many years in the management of acute and chronic musculoskeletal pain, attention has focused on their use in acute postoperative pain only recently. Diclofenac [1,2•,3,4], naproxen [5], and ketorolac [6] have been used in the perioperative period with subsequent reductions in postoperative pain, reduced analgesic intake, and reduced length of hospital stay. Recent studies using ketorolac suggest that this drug is as effective as morphine in the relief of mild to moderate postoperative pain (Fig. 6-1) [6]. It can be noted from this figure that a plateau effect is observed following administration of increasing doses of ketorolac. A maximal level of analgesia is obtained with 30 mg ketorolac, with no advantage in administering 90 mg. This suggests that 30 mg is an adequate intramuscular dose. As with other drugs in this group, however, there is a risk of gastrointestinal bleeding, and therefore, its use so far has been restricted to the acute postoperative period. Because NSAIDs have a different mechanism of action to opioids, they are often used in combination. This produces effective analgesia and reduces the requirement for opioid intake, thereby reducing the associated risks of opioid use (Fig. 6-2) [7]. This also demonstrates that continuous infusion of ketorolac at the same dose rate as intermittent bolus administration results in a further reduction in morphine consumption.

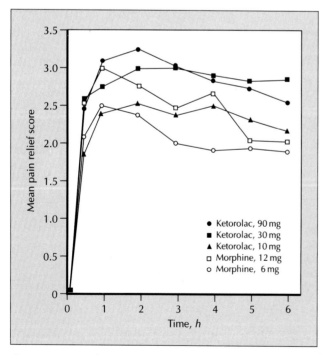

Figure 6-1 Time course of mean pain relief scores for five treatment groups receiving different concentrations of either ketorolac or morphine. (*From* O'Hara and coworkers [6]; with permission.)

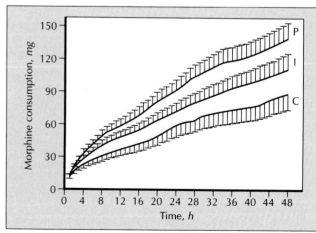

Figure 6-2 Cumulative morphine consumption of patients receiving placebo (P), intermittent (I), or continuous (C) ketorolac for 48 hours after upper abdominal surgery. *Data line* indicates mean; *T-bars*, SEM. (*From* Burns and coworkers [7]; with permission.)

The use of combination therapy is widespread in community practice; typically, an NSAID (often aspirin or ibuprofen) or acetaminophen is combined with an opioid, such as codeine. With the use of combination preparations, however, there is often little consideration given to the different pharmacokinetic properties of the individual components that make up the drug. If these preparations contain ingredients with mismatched pharmacokinetics then the treatment can become unbalanced, particularly if based on multidose regimens. For example, if an opioid with a relatively long half-life such as dextropropoxyphene (half-life approximately 10–20 h) is combined with a drug having a relatively short half-life such as acetaminophen (half-life approximately 1–3 h) and, if the combination is then given at 4- or 6-hour intervals, dextropropoxyphene and its metabolite norpropoxyphene (half-life approximately 20–25 h) will accumulate relative to acetaminophen in the body. This increases the possibility of side effects derived from this ingredient (Fig. 6-3) [8,9].

Opioid Analgesics

Opioid analgesics are most commonly used in the management of severe acute pain and chronic cancer-related pain. Morphine is the most frequently used drug in this class. For chronic pain management, oral administration is favored, for which morphine is available as elixir, immediate release tablet, and controlled release tablet. Either the elixir or immediate release tablet is used to titrate the dose required for effective analgesia. Dosage intervals of 2 to 6 hours are usually found necessary. Once the correct dosage rate is obtained, the patient can then be switched to the equivalent in a controlled release form. This usually increases the dosage interval up to approximately 12 hours. While being more convenient

to use, however, the dosage rate is more difficult to adjust with the long-acting preparation.

Although opioids are often effective as pain relieving agents, they have the well-known disadvantages of constipation, nausea, vomiting, sedation, respiratory depression, tolerance, and dependence, even if these have been overrated in some situations. It has been demonstrated that respiratory depression following opioid administration at the appropriate dose level is minimal in those patients who have pain [10]. Similarly, tolerance is not a clinical problem when treating opioid-sensitive pain at an appropriate dose [11••]. Several agents that have an agonist-antagonist action also may be used in pain management: these include pentazocine, nalbuphine, butorphanol, as well as the partial agonist, buprenorphine.

With the recently developed synthetic opioid, tramadol, it has been demonstrated that doses sufficient to produce acceptable postoperative analgesia produce less respiratory depression than morphine [12•,13•]. This may provide another avenue of treatment particularly where respiratory depression may be a concern.

Analgesic Adjuvants

Analgesic adjuvants may be used in association with the analgesic agents. These drugs are not regarded as having analgesic properties in their own right, but are often used in association with other analgesics to enhance their analgesic properties. They include the antidepressants, anticonvulsants, psychotropics, relaxants, and antihistamines. Antidepressants are often helpful in relieving chronic pain in a variety of conditions [14•]. These include both tricyclic antidepressants and monoamine oxidase inhibitors. They are thought to have a direct action in reducing pain quite apart from their mood-altering action [15]. Several mechanisms of action have

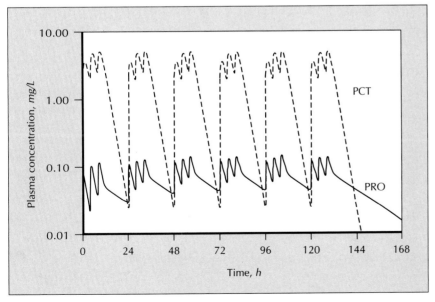

Figure 6-3 A computer-derived simulation of the plasma concentration–time profiles of dextropropoxyphene (PRO) and acetaminophen (paracetamol, PCT) as might be used in a well known proprietary combination. The dose regimen simulated is commonly suggested in Australia of 2 tablets each containing 32.5 mg dextropropoxyphene and 325 mg acetaminophen taken every 4 hours with not more than 6 tablets/24 h. The pharmacokinetic data were derived from Gram and coworkers [8] and Clements and Prescott [9], modified by an estimated lag time of oral absorption of 20 minutes, and a half-life of absorption of 40 minutes.

been proposed. It has been suggested that tricyclic antidepressants may have an analgesic effect by blocking the reuptake of serotonin and norepinephrine (noradrenaline). However, recent evidence would suggest that it is blockade of norepinephrine rather than serotonin reuptake that is most likely responsible for analgesia [16••]. Alternatively, their anticholinergic action may reduce spontaneous firing of central neurons responsible for pain sensation particularly following deafferentation [17•,18]. Anticonvulsants are also useful in the management of pain especially for the lancinating pain associated with deafferentation. This effect is also thought to be due to dampening of abnormal central nervous activity, which follows nerve damage [19].

Anticonvulsants include carbamazepine, sodium valproate, and clonazepam. Although the evidence for their effectiveness as analgesic agents is not conclusive, phenothiazines are often used in the management of pain. Antihistamines are included in some proprietary pain relieving compounds and are thought to assist in pain relief, perhaps through their sedative or calmative action. There is also evidence from both clinical and animal studies that antihistamines have analgesic properties of their own [20,21]. Steroids can relieve nerve and bone pain by reducing inflammation and edema [22]. They also work by reducing neuronal excitability, possibly by a direct action on cell membranes [23].

α-Adrenoceptor agonists, such as clonidine and dexmedetomidine, are used either alone or in combination with opioid analgesics. There is evidence that they produce an enhancement of opioid analgesia and therefore may be more effective in conjunction with opioid analgesics. Gordon and coworkers [24] found that clonidine by itself produced little relief of dental postoperative pain but produced a significant increase in the analgesia produced by pentazocine analgesia. Similarly, it has been demonstrated in animal studies that dexmedetomidine, or its stereoisomeric form medetomidine, suppresses nociceptive responses [25].

Systemic Use of Local Anesthetic Agents

Systemic injection of local anesthetic agents has been reported to produce relief of pain in a variety of conditions of neuropathic and central pain syndromes [26•]. It is postulated that local anesthetics such as lidocaine (lignocaine), flecainide, and mexiletine act to "stabilize" neuronal membranes and make them less responsive to excitation. Some forms of neuropathic pain and paresthesia are believed to be due to ectopic discharge from ends and dorsal root ganglia of injured axons. Therefore, these agents are being used increasingly in these types of pain. Systemic administration of lidocaine has demonstrated a selective action to block ectopic impulse initiation rather than impulse propagation following nerve injury [27••]. This provides a "therapeutic window" in which systemic local anesthetics will block abnormal neural discharge and associated neuropathic sensory symptoms with little or no effect on normal sensory, motor, and cardiovascular function. Mexiletine has been demonstrated to be effective in the management of neuropathic pain states, such as diabetic neuropathy and thalamic pain [28,29,30•], where it is effective when administered orally.

ROUTES OF ADMINISTRATION

The agents described above are all variously used in the management of acute and chronic pain. However, effective pain management can depend not only on appropriate choice of agent, but also on an appropriate route of administration. Inappropriate selection will result in a pharmacokinetic profile of less than optimal delivery to the intended site of an appropriate dose of the chosen agent and therefore to ineffective relief of pain. For administration of analgesic agents, it is important to balance simplicity, esthetic appeal, and efficacy, keeping in mind that both the degree of invasion of the patient and the compliance of the patient may vary greatly between methods.

Analgesic drug delivery systems can be broadly divided into two types: direct (ie, the drug is placed in the region of the receptors directly and reaches the receptors by bulk flow or diffusion), and indirect (ie, the drug is supplied to the blood for distribution to the receptors) (Fig. 6-4). Whereas direct methods are usually employed in the administration of regional anesthesia, such as intrathecal and epidural administration, systemic techniques of pharmacologic pain management usually rely on indirect methods. These include methods such as the intravenous, intramuscular, oral, and subcutaneous routes that have been used for some time and are routinely used in providing analgesia. However, recent advances have seen the development or rediscovery of other methods of drug delivery that offer substantial and exciting advantages over the more traditional routes.

Most routes allow rate-controlled or patient-controlled techniques, thereby facilitating the matching of drug supply with patient demand. Most of these are also "needleless" techniques, thereby enhancing their usefulness, particularly suitable for the very young or the debilitated. It must always be remembered that even with the most advanced methods of drug delivery, there is no substitute for appropriate observation of patients during treatment. Only this will provide the right environment for safe and effective treatment of pain.

If the desired effect is to be achieved, a drug must be present in an appropriate concentration at its site of action. Therefore, the purpose in delivering any agent is to supply drug into the blood and to keep the resultant blood-drug concentrations within a therapeutic window. When the concentrations decrease below the lower

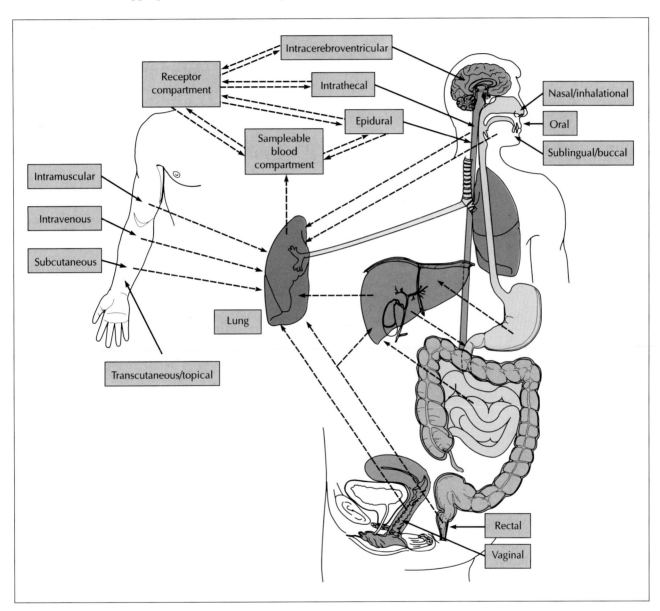

Figure 6-4 Various methods and routes of administration for the delivery of analgesic agents.

boundary, there is not the expectation of efficacy. If the concentrations exceed the upper boundary, there is the expectation of toxicity. This can be influenced by several factors such as drug concentration and duration of action. These principles are illustrated simply in Figure 6-5.

Pharmacodynamic and pharmacokinetic factors must always be considered in optimizing patient treatment. It has been demonstrated that the "minimum effective analgesic concentration," *ie*, "the lowest (blood) concentration of opioid agonist consistent with the patient's report of complete analgesia" [31] may vary at least fourfold among patients. Variation between patients caused by ingestion of food, acute or chronic pathology, and drug interactions may all affect clearance of the drug, the amount of drug available to the blood, the rate of drug absorption, and may affect the magnitude and time course of blood-drug

concentrations. Even in the same patient, variation can occur, and dose revisions may be necessary with the development of tolerance or pathology.

A variety of methods of drug delivery is available to the pain practitioner. The importance of this range is twofold. First, some patients will not be suitable candidates for drug treatment with one or other of the conventional methods, *eg*, oral administration in the patient with nausea and vomiting. Second, the variety of compounds now available or under development may require novel methods of administration to take best advantage of their pharmaceutical properties. For example, molecules that are chemically unstable, in solution for injection or in acid of the stomach, could be inhaled as dry particles.

The response to a particular drug when given systemically may vary enormously because of a variety of factors.

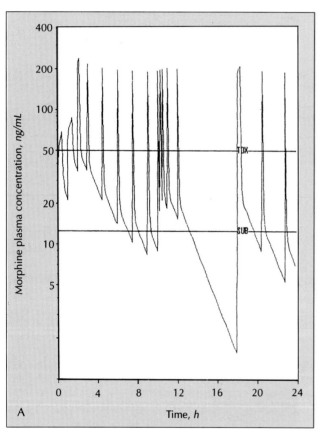

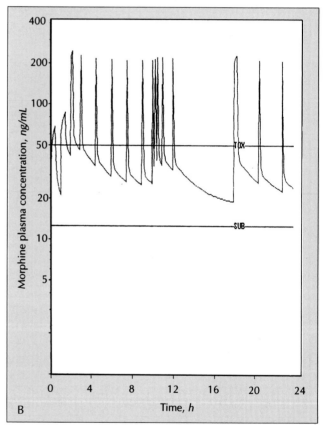

Figure 6-5 Computer-simulated arterial plasma concentrations of morphine following bolus patient-controlled analgesia (PCA) (A) and bolus PCA with background infusion (B). A lockout interval of 5 minutes and incremental doses of 1 mg were set. The lines labeled subeffective (SUB) and potentially toxic (TOX) indicate the approximate "therapeutic window." (This is a very "rubbery" scale and is quite variable between patients; transitory arterial concentrations above the upper boundary are usually without serious consequence.) In both cases a loading infusion of morphine sulphate 5 mg was provided from 0 to 30 minutes and from 60 to 90 minutes while the patient was in the recovery room. The patient was allowed to make a series of demands on

returning to the ward at around 3 hours, followed by occasional demands until a series of demands before settling for the night at around 14 hours. At around 18 hours the patient woke in pain and needed a series of demands to "catch up." The total morphine consumption after loading was 20 mg over 24 hours. The same simulation was reproduced in *B* except that a background infusion of 1 mg/h was added. The difference in maintaining the "trough" plasma concentrations above the lower boundary is clear. This, however, is at greater potential risk as one of the inherent safety features of PCA is thereby suspended. Furthermore, it has been found that patients' demands are not usually reduced by the amount of the added infusion.

Genetic factors are believed to underlie both the response to drugs and the clearance rates of drugs that undergo biotransformation for termination of activity. This can result in differences in function of enzyme systems in the body, which are involved in drug metabolism, resulting in different levels of metabolites and thus response to administration of the same level of drug.

If a drug is administered extravascularly, the rate of absorption needs to be considered. This is determined principally by the perfusion (ie, flow/volume) at the site of administration and absorption and by the physicochemical properties of the drug. It is clear that the absorption rate is enhanced by a high perfusion of the site of administration and by a high lipid solubility of the drug.

A number of pharmaceutical and pharmacologic factors may further modify the rate of absorption from a particular site. For example, absorption may be faster from injection of a smaller volume of a more concentrated solution than from a larger volume of a more diluted solution, but such effects may be opposed by the greater tonicity and viscosity of a more concentrated solution. The release of histamine by morphine, for example, may cause vasodilatation and local edema, both of which may affect the absorption rate but in opposite directions. Because drugs are more readily absorbed in the nonionized (lipid-soluble) form, alteration of local pH to increase the fraction of drug in the nonionized form may enhance the rate of absorption. Local acid-base balance may be critical for drugs administered by the gastrointestinal tract, eg, sublingually, buccally, or rectally, to maintain a sufficient fraction of the dose in the nonionized form to promote absorption. Drugs in their nonionized (or neutral) forms are, in general, poorly water soluble. Hence, if a drug exceeds its limiting solubility at a particular pH and precipitates, its absorption may be limited by the rate of its redissolving in its microenvironment. Although such factors have been addressed in principle, there is little practical information to guide the pain therapist.

The important consideration is the extent of absorption or systemic bioavailability of the drug administered. Bioavailability involves the continued product of the fraction of dose presenting for absorption multiplied by that passing across the capillary membrane successively multiplied by that escaping local destruction in the gut, the liver, and the lungs, as appropriate. Although this is most commonly evaluated in the context of enteral administration, it should not be taken for granted that parenteral administration provides complete bioavailability.

Oral

The oral route of administration is the simplest and most frequently used route of administration of analgesic agents. Whereas the oral route is simple, the bioavailability of some analgesics is low and often unpredictable when taken orally. This means that the oral route is also potentially the most complex. First-pass metabolism by the liver removes from the circulation significant proportions of the dose, transforming agents into metabolites, which may range in pharmacodynamic activity profiles from little to much compared with their parent drugs or may actually have adverse effects, especially upon accumulation. Well-studied examples include the formation from morphine of morphine-6-glucuronide, which may augment the actions of morphine and of morphine-3-glucuronide, which may block the actions of morphine, the formation from meperidine (pethidine) of normeperidine (norpethidine), which has central nervous system excitatory activity, and the formation from dextropropoxyphene of norpropoxyphene, which may have cardiac arrhythmogenic activity. Of course the same metabolites are generally formed from parenteral as from oral administration, but the concentrations are usually lower because the doses used are usually smaller.

Different formulations of agents are now available to increase ease of use or to produce a more stable blood concentration of the drug. For example, several sustained-release tablet preparations of morphine have been developed commercially, which can be administered as a twice daily dose with effective pain relief [32]. Although these are useful in the management of cancer and chronic non-cancer pain, they do not appear useful in the management of acute postoperative pain [33,34].

Intramuscular

The intramuscular route is commonly used for administration of opioid analgesic agents, particularly in the postoperative situation. The recent impact of ketorolac derives, in part, from its presentation of an injectable dose form. Despite this, there are several disadvantages to using this route. There is discomfort associated with injection, and the drug itself can cause local tissue irritation. Absorption is unpredictable and uneven, making it difficult to provide the correct blood level required for optimum analgesia without side effects. This means that the minimum effective analgesic blood drug concentration may be reached for only a fraction of the time between doses [35,36].

Subcutaneous

Although subcutaneous administration of opioids dates back many decades, it has only recently been rediscovered as a useful method and may be used either by intermittent injection (including use with patient-controlled analgesia [PCA] apparatus) or by continuous infusion using a subcutaneous scalp vein needle. There is some evidence that the subcutaneous route offers excellent analgesia with less side effects than when given intramuscularly and may be preferred by patients to the peripheral intravenous route [22]. It is also technically simple and cost-effective [37].

This approach allows continuous infusion of opioid analgesics in patients who are unable to take drugs by mouth or have persistent vomiting. It is a potentially important method of administration for morphine, which has been found useful for management of postoperative pain [38] as well as cancer-related pain [39]. There is a difference in relative potency of opioids when given by oral and parenteral routes according to the relative oral bioavailability (and the activity of metabolites, although this is not normally taken into consideration because of the paucity of relevant data). For morphine, for example, one half to one quarter the dose used orally is required when given by the subcutaneous route. In general, prolonged subcutaneous infusions require the infusion site to be changed every 4 to 7 days, but this might be as short as 1 day in some patients because of local drug intolerance.

Intravenous

Intravenous drug administration avoids the uncertainties associated with administration by the subcutaneous and intramuscular routes and allows greater control over the rate of drug delivery and thus the blood concentration of the drug. Virtually all opioids can be given intravenously if appropriate pharmaceutical preparations are available and venous access can be obtained. However, this route is also limited by the need for aseptic techniques, the skill required to institute and maintain venous access, and rapid changes in plasma concentrations.

Controlled-rate infusions can be used to achieve and then maintain steady-state blood concentration of the drug that is optimal for analgesic efficacy. These systems are effective but there is no evidence that this method results in reduced drug doses. The main problem with continuous infusion is the poor predictability of individual dose requirements. Therefore, it is difficult to predict the optimal dose to produce effective analgesia without overdosing (as also applies to other routes). With infusion methods this difficulty imposed by not knowing individual pharmacokinetics and pharmacodynamics necessitates patient observation and readjustment of the dosage regimen. Recently, systems have been developed to try to produce blood drug concentrations within the boundaries indicated for a particular population of patients. This method may be based upon simple translation of pharmacokinetic parameters into a dosage regimen [40] or may use a complex computer-controlled infusion method that tries to take into account drug pharmacokinetics for the population at large as well as individual characteristics of the patient receiving the infusion [41].

A significant development in intravenous administration of analgesics has been the use of PCA systems [42••]. These are computer-controlled pump-driven systems, which enable patients to control the amount and timing of doses of analgesic agents they receive.

Such devices allow the patient some degree of individual control over their analgesic requirements and, thereby, maximize the probability of successful treatment. It also avoids the problems of unpredictability and variability associated with administration via the intramuscular route.

Although it does have these advantages, PCA still requires informed prescribing. The rationale for the choice of agent, the incremental dose, and the lockout interval between doses is still somewhat arbitrary [43–45]. In fact, the concern over the potential for patients to overdose themselves still makes some clinicians set the incremental dose or lockout interval conservatively. The incremental dose should be large enough to provide an analgesic effect but small enough to produce a tolerable respiratory effect. The lockout interval should be set to a long enough period to appreciate the effect of a dose before the next, but short enough so that the effectiveness of the technique is not hampered.

The use of a background infusion to prevent the need for "catch-up" demands is controversial. Where it has been studied, a background infusion has resulted in more medication being used and, by inference, loss of inherent safety of the technique [46,47]. It has been found that self-administration dose rates of morphine are similar whether or not there is a background infusion and therefore the use of a background infusion results in a higher total consumption with the same degree of pain relief (Fig. 6-6) [48]. Overall, PCA helps to reduce the incidence of inadequate analgesia on the one hand and excessive sedation on the other hand. Computer-assisted infusion technology, which infuses the drug continuously at a program-driven rate,

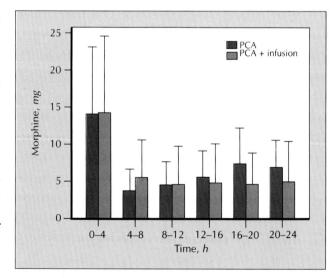

Figure 6-6 Mean self-administered dose rates of morphine for two groups receiving patient-controlled analgesia (PCA) or PCA and infusion in the 24 hours following surgery. *T-bars* indicate standard deviation. (*From* Russell and coworkers [48]; with permission.)

reduces the fluctuations that are produced by bolus PCA, in principle maintaining drug plasma concentrations more accurately at the optimal level (Fig. 6-6).

Patient-controlled analgesia methods may be used with routes other than intravenous [43]. Recent studies have highlighted the advantages of alternative routes such as epidural administration for use of opioids, and this is dealt with more fully elsewhere in this edition. However, it has also been demonstrated that, particularly in the case of a highly lipophilic drug such as fentanyl where there is significant systemic absorption, there is little difference in analgesic efficacy of epidural versus intravenous fentanyl 60 minutes following administration [49], although there is good evidence that the average epidural dose will be less, perhaps by one half, for similar pain control [50••].

Inhalational

The inhalational route is usually restricted to anesthetic agents but, particularly in the obstetric situation, is routinely used for analgesic administration. Several other agents have been investigated such as nebulized morphine [51,52] and fentanyl [53,54], but this method, as yet tested, does not appear to offer significant advantages over other forms of administration.

Transdermal

Transdermal application and transdermal administration of agents, such as fentanyl and clonidine [55•], have now been used for some time. These systems deliver a sustained release of drugs and are well tolerated by patients. The route also has the advantage of by-passing the gastrointestinal system and first-pass hepatosplanchnic metabolism. Commercial devices use a rate-controlling membrane that produces a predictable drug plasma concentration by releasing a drug at a rate that is less than the skin is capable of absorbing. This means that the transdermal system rather than the patient's skin is responsible for the rate of drug delivery across the skin. Thus, the dose is determined by the area of the product applied.

Despite the obvious advantages of the transdermal route of administration, it also has several limitations. In the case of fentanyl, which is currently the only analgesic agent being used by this route, there is some variability in pharmacokinetics, slow onset and offset times, and a high incidence of patient nausea and vomiting. Pharmacokinetic studies have shown that the skin provides a depot for fentanyl, and, consequently, there is a lag of some 36 to 48 hours before a steady-state concentration is reached in the blood and a similar lag before concentrations decline after the preparation has been removed [56]. Therefore, it seems particularly suitable for chronic treatment where patients are unable to receive analgesic agents by mouth or injection and where sustained blood concentrations of the drug are required. Whether less lipophilic opioid analgesic agents such as hydromorphone would also be suitable is interesting speculation, but the larger masses of drug required for clinical analgesia and the potential problem of local irritation would need thorough evaluation before clinical use. The advantages and disadvantages of the transdermal route are listed in Table 6-1.

Iontophoresis is a method that may overcome some of the shortcomings associated with transdermal application of drugs. Recent studies that have used this technique indicate that this provides a more controlled rate of drug absorption and, therefore, may prove to be a more readily controllable method of administration [57].

TABLE 6-1
ADVANTAGES AND DISADVANTAGES OF THE TRANSDERMAL ROUTE OF ADMINISTRATION

ADVANTAGES

Bypasses the gastrointestinal system and avoids first-pass hepatosplanchnic drug metabolism

Ease of use, noninvasiveness, and skin fixation lead to improved compliance

System membrane controls rate of skin permeation of drug

Sustained steady-state drug concentrations even with drugs with a short half-life

DISADVANTAGES

Onset and offset times following application and removal can be slow because of depot effect in the skin

Can produce skin irritation

Transmucosal

The mucosal membranes of the mouth, nose, and tongue have all been used for the application of analgesic agents. They allow rapid systemic absorption due to the inherent properties of the mucosa and avoid the systemic bioavailability problem of hepatosplanchnic first-pass metabolism. Several agents have been tested using a transmucosal route. Buprenorphine has been used for some time by the sublingual method in the management of both acute [58,59] and chronic pain [60]. A fentanyl lollipop has been developed, which is used for premedication of both adults and children. Both routes are useful when swallowing is difficult or when the parenteral route is not suitable. This does provide sedation within a reasonably short time (20–40 min) but is also associated with a fairly high incidence of facial pruritus, nausea, and vomiting. However, the drug bioavailability from sublingual and buccal preparations will depend on the relative amounts absorbed through the mucosa and swallowed and, therefore, does result in some variability.

The nasal cavity and its septum, like the buccal and sublingual routes, also presents a relatively large surface area of well-perfused mucosal lining that can be used for the absorption of drugs. It offers the advantages of bypassing the gastrointestinal tract and is a relatively non-invasive method of administration. Drugs can be instilled either in droplet form or as a dose-measured swab. Several agents have been used via the nasal route. These include sufentanil and midazolam. Morphine has also been used by aerosol in patients receiving oxygen by mask following surgery [61]. These are particularly useful in the pediatric situation.

Rectal

A variety of agents have been used or trialed using the rectal route of administration either alone or in combination with other routes and forms of analgesia [62]. It is a convenient alternative route of administration particularly where the parenteral route may be unsuitable, such as in children or debilitated patients [63]. An important advantage of the rectal route of administration is that it is independent of gastric motility; however, drug bioavailability is very sensitive to the position of the preparation in the rectum. Placement too high in the rectum results in greater first-pass elimination, because the upper portion of rectal venous drainage is connected with the portal system. On the other hand, the lower portion is connected with the general circulation resulting in greater bioavailability, but if it is placed too low may be expelled. The bioavailability of morphine and other analgesic preparations via the rectal route has been compared with the oral route and compares favorably in most cases [64].

CLINICAL APPLICATION

Clinical practice seems not to have found much need for routes of administration beyond the traditional ones: the indirect routes, intravenous, intramuscular, and oral administration must still account for the vast majority of doses of analgesic agents administered. Whether this is a matter of old traditions dying hard or a genuine lack of application of the innovation is difficult to ascertain. It is clear, however, that pain management is still suboptimal and that clinical practitioners should concentrate on optimal use of even the traditional routes.

Whatever the drug and method of delivery chosen it must always be remembered that individual patients may differ markedly in their requirements for analgesic medication. Analgesia is not suited to predetermined dosage regimens, which usually fail to take into account the varying circumstances and needs of the patient. Even patient-controlled systems require readjustment, and observation of patients is required during treatment. Individualized dosage regimens therefore remain elusive. It is important that consideration is given to the particular characteristics of the patient that will affect the effectiveness of the agent being administered. Furthermore, the needs and expectations of the patient must also be considered. Particularly where administration is in the hands of the patient, the most suitable drug will be completely ineffective if there is no compliance.

Acute Versus Chronic Pain

For acute pain management there are two fundamental choices in the methods of analgesic drug delivery: many repeated doses of an agent with a higher clearance or fewer repeated doses of an agent with a lower clearance. The implied intention of both is the same—to maintain the same mean blood-drug concentration for as long as needed. From a patient's point of view, there can be relevant differences. Opioid analgesic agents tend to have steep blood concentration—analgesic effect relationships [65,66]. The repeated use of a higher clearance agent may mean periods of fluctuating analgesia as the blood-drug concentrations rise and fall during each dosage interval, and this may be exacerbated if the patient is left waiting for the medication and compounded by any unpleasantness that accompanies it. The alternative use of a lower clearance and longer-acting agent may avoid these problems, but if side effects occur, these too may be long-lasting. If the dose is administered intravenously, the repeated doses with higher clearance agents can often be replaced by continuous intravenous infusions. Then, should adverse effects occur, cessation of infusion will mean that no more drug will be admitted to the circulation, and blood concentrations will start to decrease immediately. This contrasts with drug administration by an absorption method where absorption will continue relentlessly, irrespective of adverse effects. For routine chronic therapy, more use is made of oral than intravenous methods so that knowledge of absorption rates and bioavailability is required in addition to the fundamental pharmacologic properties of the analgesic agent.

Benign Versus Cancer Pain

There are many similarities in the treatment of benign, noncancer pain and cancer pain. Usually as prescribed by the World Health Organization ladder, there is use of simple analgesics followed by the addition of "weak" opioids if pain continues, and followed by the addition of "strong" opioids if pain is not controlled. These drugs are used in conjunction with adjuvant drugs to provide more effective relief.

There has been much discussion recently concerning the use of strong opioids in the management of chronic noncancer pain [67,68•]. It is now accepted that the risks of dependence and respiratory depression in the treatment of cancer pain are almost nonexistent [11••,69]. Even when there is a risk, it is considered that the need for the patient to have a pain-free existence is paramount. However, many now consider that strong opioids should also be considered for the "nonresponder" pain patients without cancer. There is increasing use of opioids for the management of chronic pain of nonmalignant origin. However, this should only be done after careful consideration and trial of other options preferably within the context of a multidisciplinary clinic. It was also believed that certain types of pain, such as neuropathic pain, were not responsive to opioids; however, recent evidence suggests that this lack of response is not absolute, but response will be obtained with a sufficient dose [70].

Preoperative Versus Postoperative Analgesia

There is increasing evidence that opioid or NSAID premedication may be important in reducing the amount of pain experienced postoperatively and thus reduce the need for analgesic agents. This is important in reducing the intake of opioid analgesics with the associated side effects, reducing the functional and metabolic sequelae of the recuperating patient with pain, and reducing the incidence of ongoing pain syndromes. Kiss and Kilian [71•] have shown that operative pretreatment with meperidine (pethidine) and triflupromazine results in less demand for analgesics postoperatively compared with a similar group pretreated with flunitrazepam. Similarly, use of ketorolac in the intraoperative period has been shown to decrease analgesic requirements in the postoperative period as effectively as morphine but with less postoperative nausea and vomiting [72].

THE FUTURE—TARGETED DRUG DELIVERY?

Pharmaceutical Manipulation

As alluded to previously, dosing methods can be improved to obtain therapeutic advantage that is not simply dose-related but may be due to improved control over the blood-drug concentrations, eg, with pharmacokinetically designed computer-assisted infusion regimens and through the provision of long-acting preparations of morphine. It is tempting to propose that improved pain relief by PCA is due to more than simple control over the time course of blood-drug concentrations. Other gains may be made through chemical modifications to the drug itself or to the pharmaceutical presentation of the drug to alter its uptake into particular regions of the body.

The brain is the accepted principal site of action of opioid analgesics administered systemically; the blood-brain barrier has evolved to keep out unwanted foreign substances, particularly those with polar hydrophilic characteristics. Morphine, it is traditionally taught, does not pass through into the brain readily because of its hydrophilicity. To improve the brain uptake of morphine, lipidic esters of morphine have been prepared by coupling lipidic amino acids to the phenolic hydroxyl group. These have been found to be active in experimental animals when administered by intravenous and by oral routes [73]. Whether such derivatives are likely to offer significant improvements over lipophilic morphinoid or other opioids already available is not yet known.

Formulation changes made to analgesic agents for spinal administration by liposome encapsulation have also been tested in experimental animals. Liposome encapsulated spinal alfentanil has been found to have the same latency of onset and the same intensity of analgesic effect but with longer duration of action than aqueous alfentanil and without generating pharmacologically active blood-drug concentrations [74]. An analogous change has been made by cyclodextrin complexation to decrease the relative lipophilicity of substances and increase their hydrophilicity. This manipulation has been shown to prolong the residence in cerebrospinal fluid of morphine and fentanyl derivatives administered intrathecally, thus prolonging their spinal actions and diminishing their supraspinal actions [75].

Regionally Targeted Drug Delivery

A present, targeted drug delivery is practiced only through the direct drug delivery methods discussed

This chapter examines differences in the way we approach pain in children as compared with pain in adults. Three major areas are highlighted: the perception of pain by infants and children, the ability to determine when children are experiencing pain and how much pain they have, and differences in drugs and dosages for pediatric patients.

PHYSIOLOGIC COST OF PAIN

As recently as 20 years ago, it was believed that the prevention and treatment of pain in children, particularly infants, was unimportant and even unnecessary. The rationale cited was twofold—that neonates and infants, because of poor myelinization of peripheral nerves, do not experience pain as adults do, and that, even if they do perceive pain, they won't remember it later anyway, so it doesn't matter. A classic example of this belief is the Liverpool technique for neonatal anesthesia. This consisted of nitrous oxide and muscle relaxant without supplemental potent inhaled agents or narcotics.

This view has recently come under attack on both humanitarian and physiologic grounds. Anand and coworkers [1–4] suggest improved outcome of patients undergoing cardiac surgery when high-dose narcotic anesthesia and sufentanyl postoperative analgesia replaced techniques providing less complete control of the surgical stress response. These studies, occurring at a time of increased awareness of the need for pain management in adult patients, have led to improvements in anesthesia and pain management for pediatric patients.

MEASUREMENT OF ACUTE PAIN IN CHILDREN

One of the fundamental problems in pain management is determining the degree of pain experienced by patients. This problem is even more difficult in the pediatric population. While adults are usually able to articulate their pain complaints, this may be less true of children. Toddlers may lack an adequate frame of reference on which to base a comparison with their current pain. This will make any pain they are currently experiencing the "worst possible pain," limiting the value of a visual analogue scale (VAS). The problem is further compounded for infants and other children who are unable to speak at all. Several specialized pain scales have been developed to address this problem in various age groups.

Self-Reporting Scales

VISUAL ANALOGUE SCALE

The prototypical pain scale is the VAS. This consists of a plain line 10 cm in length. It may be labeled "no pain" on one end and "worst possible pain" on the other. Patients are instructed to mark a point on the line corresponding to the intensity of their pain. The score can then be easily read off the line with a ruler. The visual analogue has been shown to correlate with pain intensity but is best used to measure differences in pain intensity in a single subject over time rather than to make comparisons among subjects. Younger children are ineffective at using the VAS, however, so specialized self-reporting scales have been developed for toddlers and young school-age children.

FACES SCALES

The Oucher is a pain scale described by Beyer [5]. It consists of a series of pictures of children, ranging from calm and happy to agitated. It has been used in children as young as age 3 with success, although use in children younger than age 5 requires skill on the part of the practitioner. Another advantage of the Oucher is its availability with pictures of black and Hispanic children, which increases the ability of these children to identify with the faces on the scale. It has been verified as correlating well with other types of self-reporting scales [6], although a later study found a nonlinear correlation between the faces and the numeric value obtained using a VAS when children were able to use both scales effectively.

Based on the lack of linearity between the faces, McGrath [7] developed a scale of drawn faces that has been correlated with an independent VAS. The scores assigned to the faces are thus nonlinear numerically but are shown in rank order.

OTHER SELF-REPORTING SCALES

Other self-reporting scales that have been described as useful in children are the analogue chromatic continuous scale (ACCS) [8] and the poker chip tool [9]. The former, also known as the "pain slide rule" consists of a 10-cm ruler, one side of which is a color gradient. The gradient ranges from white at the end labeled "no pain" and continues through light red to an intense solid red at the end labeled "most pain." The back is ruled for easy scoring. This system has been used successfully in children as young as 3 years of age [6].

Behavioral and Physiologic Pain Scales

For children unable to verbally report their pain intensity in a meaningful and consistent fashion, behavioral pain scales have been derived. These depend on observable parameters such as vital signs and behavior. A consistent problem with these scales is that there may be many causes for the observed changes besides pain. For example, crying inconsolably may be caused by pain but also by hunger, frustration from restraints, or anxiety. Because of this, behavioral scales tend to score too high a value for pain associated with acute procedures. On the other hand, these scales may underestimate tonic pain, and the child will often stay quiet to avoid provoking pain with movement. The Children's Hospital of Eastern Ontario Pain Scale (CHEOPS) has been shown not to correlate well with self-report scales [8].

The objective pain scale, described by Broadman and coworkers [10] at Children's National Medical Center in Washington, DC, has been compared with self-reporting scales [11]. It uses a combination of physiologic and behavioral parameters in an attempt to increase the specificity greater than that obtained using either technique alone (Table 7-1). The ability to calm the child with food, rocking, or verbal reassurance needs to be considered when evaluating children with this scale. The scale is easy to learn and use, requiring only a brief observation period and a blood pressure measurement. Other attempts to use infants' behavioral parameters include using specialized techniques such as analyzing facial expressions [12] or pitch of cry. Although these may prove to be useful and specific approaches to measuring pediatric pain, these techniques have not been independently verified.

TREATMENT OF ACUTE PAIN IN CHILDREN
Behavioral Treatments of Acute Pain

Many children will respond well to behavioral approaches to the management of acute pain, including such techniques as guided imagery and distraction. Young infants will often respond to being held and rocked by a parent. McGrath and DeVeber [13], Kuttner [14], Zeltzer and LeBaron [15], and Olness [16], have shown that older children are able to undergo even painful procedures such as bone marrow aspiration or lumbar puncture without sedative or analgesic drugs if guided imagery is administered by trained personnel. For this to be successful, the child should ideally be trained in the technique prior to the first procedure and have an experienced coach working with him or her during the procedure. If the child has already had a painful, frightening experience with previous procedures, trying imagery and distraction is more difficult because the child will be too afraid to cooperate. This technique, although requiring greater effort than sedating the child with medications, can be very rewarding and safer for the child. Age is not a major factor in determining which

TABLE 7-1
THE OBJECTIVE PAIN SCALE

PARAMETER	SCORE		
	0	1	2
Blood pressure	Normal	≥ 20% over preop	≥ 30% over preop
Crying	No	Easily consolable	Inconsolable
Movement	None	Restless	Thrashing
Agitation	Asleep/calm	Mild	Hysterical
Verbal	Asleep/none	Reports mild pain	Reports moderate to severe pain

From Broadman and coworkers [10]; with permission.

children will be successful with this technique. Many younger children with good imaginations are excellent candidates for imagery and relaxation.

Acetaminophen

Acetaminophen is a widely used antipyretic and analgesic with a high therapeutic ratio. Standard recommended doses are probably too low for optimal analgesic effect. Based on pharmacokinetic and pharmacodynamic studies, acetaminophen should be given in doses up to 15 mg/kg every 4 hours by mouth [17] or 20 mg/kg by rectum [18]. The latter dose is recommended because of the poor degree of absorption of acetaminophen by the rectal route. For mild to moderate pain, acetaminophen may be adequate by itself. For severe pain, acetaminophen should be added to a regimen of narcotics, as it will give additional analgesia and decrease narcotic requirements.

Nonsteroidal Anti-inflammatory Drugs

Nonsteroidal anti-inflammatory drugs (NSAIDs) have been underused until recently in the treatment of acute pain in the United States. Maunuksela and coworkers [19–22] have demonstrated the safety and efficacy of rectal ibuprofen and intravenous indomethacin for postoperative pain control. Intravenous indomethacin, however, has not been approved for this purpose in the United States, nor has there been a readily available form of rectal ibuprofen. With the advent of ketorolac, a parenteral NSAID released in the United States in 1990, this has been rapidly changing. Ketorolac permits use of NSAIDs in patients unable to take oral medications. Some studies suggest an analgesic efficacy similar to that of morphine sulfate 0.1 mg/kg intramuscularly [23•]. Based on single-dose pharmacodynamic studies in children [24] and extrapolation from multiple-dose pharmacokinetic studies in adults, it is reasonable to recommend dosing ketorolac 0.9 to 1.0 mg/kg as a loading dose followed by 0.5 mg/kg every 6 hours thereafter. Parenteral ketorolac is only approved for short-term use. It is usually feasible to change to enteral NSAIDs after 2 to 3 days, however, so this is not generally a limitation. Ibuprofen, now available as a flavored elixir (Pediaprofen; McNeil, Fort Washington, Pennsylvania), is useful for this purpose. In children younger than 8 years of age, the recommended dose is 8 to 10 mg/kg given orally four times per day. It is well tolerated by most children.

It must be kept in mind that ketorolac has the same side effect profile as other NSAIDs. Despite the fact that ketorolac is given intravenously or intramuscularly, it may cause gastric irritation. This is particularly important to consider in patients with other predisposing factors, such as burns or multiple trauma. These patients should be given prophylaxis against gastric ulcers if ketorolac or other NSAIDs are used. Renal compromise

and any bleeding diathesis are also contraindications to the use of NSAIDs. Although ketorolac has been shown not to increase intraoperative blood loss from healthy patients in a variety of procedures, it will have a measurable effect on platelet function. When intraoperative or postoperative bleeding is a concern, it is prudent to avoid ketorolac until bleeding concerns have subsided.

Opioids

PHARMACOLOGY OF OPIOIDS IN INFANTS AND CHILDREN

At birth, neonates have poorly developed hepatic enzymes and are unable to metabolize opioids as rapidly as adults [25]. These enzymes mature rapidly, however, such that by 6 months of age the pharmacokinetics are similar to that of an adult [25,26]. Although early work by Way and coworkers [27] suggested that neonates are more susceptible to respiratory depression from morphine, more recent work suggests that infants behave similarly to adults in this regard [28].

INTERMITTENT BOLUSES

It is not unusual in the pediatric population to have patients for whom it is difficult to anticipate their analgesic requirements. A common example of this is children with myelomeningocele who present for postoperative analgesia after urologic or lower extremity orthopedic procedures. The dermatomal level of the procedure may be near their sensory level. In addition, these children often have a Type I Arnold-Chiari malformation that makes them uniquely sensitive to the respiratory depressant effects of narcotics. Although patient-controlled analgesia (PCA) using small boluses (0.010–0.015 mg/kg) may be useful for older children, it is often inappropriate for children younger than 7 years of age. A continuous infusion is inappropriate in this situation, given a possibility of no pain and increased sensitivity to narcotics.

Intermittent boluses of narcotics, given on demand, represent the most sensible compromise. Intramuscular narcotics should, as a rule, be avoided in children. They will lead to underreporting of pain, increased complications from oversedation after the injection, and greater periods of inadequate pain control [11]. Small doses of intravenous narcotics are useful. Adequate pain control may be achieved with intravenous morphine 0.030 to 0.100 mg/kg given every 1 to 2 hours as needed. This approach is often overly labor-intensive for a busy postsurgical nursing ward, however. A useful alternative is intravenous methadone. Because of its longer elimination half-life, methadone may be given every 4 to 6 hours, yet still maintaining the patient in the therapeutic range. One approach to this medication is to load the patient in the recovery room until she or he is comfortable using 0.050 mg/kg boluses every 10 minutes. Thereafter, a "reverse PRN" sliding scale is used to maintain comfort. The patient is given methadone every 4 hours after a pain evaluation by a nurse using either an objective pain scale or a self-reporting scale, as appropriate. Suggested methadone doses are given in Table 7-2.

OPIOID INFUSIONS

Continuous opioid infusions are useful for providing constant plasma concentrations and a steady level of analgesia. A typical infusion for postoperative pain would be morphine sulfate starting at about 25 µg/kg/h for children older than 6 months of age. The final dosage range is from 10 to 40 µg/kg/h or occasionally higher [29]. When using any drug infusion, it is necessary to keep in mind that steady state drug levels will not be reached for 3 to 5 half-lives after starting the infusion. Given morphine's 4-hour elimination half-life, this would mean at least 12 hours of suboptimal pain relief. The solution is to adequately load the patient before starting the infusion. This is normally done in the postoperative recovery area or may be done by a physician in attendance on a medical floor. Morphine should be titrated 30 to 50 µg/kg every 5 to 10 minutes until the patient is comfortable. Starting the infusion at this point will generally maintain the patient in the therapeutic range. If the initial infusion rate proves to be inadequate, an additional bolus of 50 mg/kg should be given when the infusion rate is increased.

Because infants younger than 3 to 6 months do not metabolize morphine and other narcotics as quickly as older infants and adults, it is appropriate to start these patients at lower infusion rates. A starting rate of 0.015 mg/kg/h will provide safe, adequate analgesia for most infants, although individual variation in metabolic rates, pain thresholds, and stimulus intensity will require adjustments in some patients. Continuous monitoring of respiratory rate and oxygen saturation for children younger than 6 months is prudent, given the lower rates of metabolism and increased sensitivity to the respiratory depressant effects of narcotics.

PATIENT-CONTROLLED ANALGESIA

Patient-controlled analgesia has been used successfully for children and adolescents in many centers. It has been demonstrated that children as young as 7 years of age are not only capable of using PCA effectively, but also obtain better pain control and greater patient satisfaction using PCA than can be achieved with intramuscular injections. In the study of orthopedic patients, a continuous background infusion of opiates further improved pain scores and patient satisfaction without increasing side effects. More recent studies of PCA have questioned both the improvement in pain control and the safety of using background opiate infusions. Currently, fewer background opiate infusions are being used at Children's Hospital in Boston than previously. This is because of concern for patient safety, as well as the advent of ketorolac as an adjunctive analgesic (see previous text). With the addition of an NSAID, most patients can achieve acceptable pain control without the use of a background infusion.

Patient selection is very important to obtain the best results using PCA in the pediatric population. Children younger than 7 years will often not use the pump effectively despite appropriate preoperative teaching. For many 6-year-old children and occasional bright 5-year-olds, PCA is worth trying, as some of these children will be able to use it effectively. However, it is important to monitor the ability of these children in order to obtain effective pain relief with this technique, and to be prepared to rapidly switch to another modality of pain control if PCA proves ineffective. Other patients who may be unable to use PCA include children with developmental delay and, occasionally, children who are physically unable to push the PCA button because of cerebral palsy or bilateral

TABLE 7-2
METHADONE DOSES

LOADING DOSE		0.1–0.3 mg/kg given in a monitored setting
NO PAIN	Pain score = 0	0 mg
MILD PAIN	Pain score = 1, 2, 3	0.025 mg/kg q 4 h
MODERATE PAIN	Pain score = 4, 5, 6	0.050 mg/kg q 4 h
SEVERE PAIN	Pain score = 7, 8, 9, 10	0.075 mg/kg q 4 h

hand surgery even when they might have a good understanding of how to use PCA.

Some centers have used parent-controlled analgesia for these younger children. This defeats one of the basic safety principles of PCA, however, which is that a sedated patient will not push the button and is therefore unlikely to produce respiratory depression. Only the patient should be allowed to press the PCA button except in very unusual circumstances. When a young patient has chronic pain from cancer or acquired immunodeficiency syndrome, the parents may be instructed how to assess their child's pain and sedation levels and administer PCA narcotics. In general, this should be reserved for those patients who will need intravenous narcotics for pain control while outside the hospital. The patient will be given a PCA pump while hospitalized so the parents can be trained in its use and dosing parameters can be adjusted.

Regional Analgesia

Regional anesthetic techniques have come to play an important role in postoperative pain management. These may be conveniently considered in two groups: single injection techniques, which may be used to provide 4 to 12 hours of pain relief after minor surgical procedures, and continuous catheter techniques, which may be used to provide pain control for several days.

SINGLE INJECTION REGIONAL ANESTHETIC TECHNIQUES

The single injection techniques are extremely useful for minor surgical procedures, especially those performed on an outpatient basis. The physician performing these blocks should be familiar with appropriate dosing of local anesthetics in different age patients as well as the changing anatomy with maturation of the pediatric patient. Several common blocks are discussed briefly.

Single injection caudals may be appropriate for many procedures on the groin, lower extremities, and perineum [30]. Its wide applicability, ease of placement, and long record of safety have made the single shot caudal a commonly used block. If placed at the start of the procedure, it may actually hasten turnover time because the lighter plane of general anesthesia required will allow faster wake-up. The caudal canal is easily located by making an equilateral triangle with the apex caudad using the posterior, superior iliac spines as the other two vertices. In the child the sacral cornua are easily palpated. The needle is placed between the sacral cornua at a 60° angle to the skin. A distinct pop will be felt as the needle pierces the sacrococcygeal ligament. The needle should then be laid parallel to the skin and advanced 2 to 3 mm. The needle should advance easily, without resistance if it is in the epidural space. It should not be advanced more than the recommended 2 to 3 mm, however, to avoid puncturing

the dural sac, which extends further caudad in children than in adults. After aspiration to assure that the tip of the needle is not in a vessel or the subarachnoid space, bupivacaine 1/8% to 1/4% may be given in doses up to 1 mL/kg in divided doses. It is important to aspirate four to five times during the injection to assure that the tip of the needle is not in a vein.

Peripheral nerve blocks, including the dorsal penile block and ilioinguinal nerve blocks may have an advantage over the single shot caudal for specific procedures. Although the single injection caudal will generally only provide four to six hours of pain relief, peripheral nerve blocks, particularly plexus blocks, may last significantly longer. They may also be associated with fewer side effects; there will be no numbness or motor block of the lower extremities and no problems with urinary retention as has been reported with a low incidence using single shot caudals. Both these blocks are easily learned. The penile block is useful for operations on the distal two thirds of the penis including circumcision and many hypospadias repairs [31]. Several alternative techniques are available including ring block of the penis and the dorsal penile block. The latter is performed by injecting local anesthetic just distal to the symphysis pubis. This is done either perpendicularly in the midline or about 1 cm laterally with the needle directed mediad. After penetrating the skin, a distinct pop will be felt as the needle penetrates Buck's fascia. Care should be taken to stop at this point to avoid injuring or injecting into the corpus cavernosum. A hematoma deep to Buck's fascia is the concern associated with this technique. Although rare, an expanding hematoma beneath the unyielding fascia may cause a compartment syndrome, which can compromise viability of the penis. Ilioinguinal-iliohypogastric nerve blocks may either be performed preoperatively or intraoperatively. The former, which has the advantage of providing preemptive analgesia, is placed by injecting local anesthetic at a point 1 cm inferior to and 1 cm medial to the anterior superior iliac spine. The ilioinguinal nerve lies between the transversalis and anterior oblique fascial plane. The iliohypogastric lies between the anterior and posterior oblique fasciae. Local anesthetic is placed in a fanwise pattern between each fascial plane. Intraoperative placement of the block by the surgeon may have the advantage that the nerves are readily visualized within the herniorrhaphy incision allowing accurate deposition of the local anesthetic. When the block is not placed until the end of the procedure, the advantage of using only a light plane of general anesthesia is lost, however, as is the possible benefit of preventing windup in the spinal cord by blocking nociceptive input during the procedure.

One additional nerve block worth attention is the fascia iliaca block first reported by Dalens in 1989 [32].

Similar in effect to the three-in-one block of Winnie, it provides blockade of the femoral, lateral femoral cutaneous, and obturator nerves. The fascia iliaca block can be performed in the anesthetized patient with a greater success rate, however [32]. In addition, because the block needle is not placed near any major vascular structure or nerve, it is safer than the three-in-one block as well. Using this block we have obtained 12 to 24 hours of analgesia with high success rates.

Figure 7-1 demonstrates the technique for placing the fascia iliaca block. Briefly, the inguinal ligament is located from the anterior superior iliac spine to the symphysis pubis and marked on the skin. It is divided into thirds. At the junction of the lateral third and medial two thirds, a perpendicular line is drawn 0.5 cm caudad. A short beveled 1.5-inch needle is introduced perpendicular to the skin. As the needle is advanced, two distinct pops are felt as the needle transverses the fascia lata and the fascia iliaca. There is also a loss of resistance to injection of local anesthetic as each fascial layer is penetrated. At this point, the position of the needle is fixed and pressure is applied caudad to the needle to force the local anesthetic solution cephalad. Bupivacaine 0.25% is injected using 0.8 mL/kg to a maximum of 40 mL. For all unilateral procedures on the hip and anterior thigh, this provides an excellent nerve block.

Continuous Catheter Techniques

To obtain several days of pain relief from neural blocks, a catheter is required for continuous infusion of local anesthetics or narcotics. The most common are catheters placed into the epidural space from the caudal, lumbar, or thoracic approaches. The caudal approach is an excellent alternative in infants. The landmarks are easily defined, and the loss of resistance obtained when piercing the sacrococcygeal ligament is easily appreciated. It has also been shown that in infants other than prematures it is possible to advance an epidural catheter cephalad as high as the upper thoracic spine without having the catheter deviate through foramina or loop on itself [33–35]. Despite concerns about soilage of these catheters, a higher incidence of infection has not been documented for caudal as opposed to epidural catheters. Meticulous care must be used in skin preparation and dressing the catheters with occlusive dressings, however, and the physician should have an extremely low threshold to remove the catheter if soilage of the site does occur.

For procedures on the lower thoracic, lumbar, and sacral dermatomes, the lumbar approach to the epidural space is often most appropriate. In experienced hands, a catheter can be safely placed into the lumbar epidural space in children of all ages. The use of small needles and catheters such as the 19-gauge needle and 23-gauge catheter manufactured by Portex (London, United Kingdom) aid the practitioner in accurate placement. It is important to remember that the epidural space is quite shallow in infants. It is reached only 1.5 to 2 cm below the skin in the neonate as opposed to greater than 4 cm in the adult. When locating the epidural space in children it is important to use saline for loss of resistance. Two cases of paradoxical air embolus have occurred during epidural placement using air for loss of resistance. Although this technique is advocated for adults, it is important to remember that many children have a patent foramen ovale. All children should be treated as though they are at risk for this complication, contraindicating the use of air for loss of resistance. Lumbar epidural catheters in infants and small children should only be placed by physicians familiar with the procedure or by those who are expert at epidural catheters in adults and have a good appreciation for the differences in anatomy between adults and children.

For upper abdominal and thoracic surgery, the tip of the epidural catheter should ideally be in the thoracic epidural space. The steep angle of the posterior processes and the presence of the spinal cord immediately deep to the epidural space make thoracic epidural catheter placement theoretically more risky than lumbar catheter placement, although we are unaware of any cases of neurologic injury due to thoracic epidural placement in children. In the older, cooperative child, a thoracic epidural catheter will often be placed with the patient awake so that he or she may in theory complain of pain if the needle enters the spinal cord. (This has never happened in our experience.) Awake placement is impractical for infants and small children, however. If these patients require a thoracic epidural, many clinicians prefer instead to advance the catheter cephalad from the caudal approach. A small

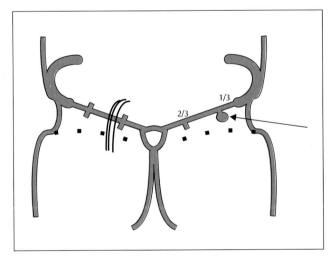

Figure 7-1 Technique for placement of fascia iliaca block. *Arrow* indicates line drawn 0.5 cm caudad to inguinal ligament, and a needle introduced at right angle to skin. Two "pops" are felt as needle is advanced.

volume of contrast dye (0.5–1 mL) injected through the catheter before a chest radiograph will confirm appropriate position of the catheter tip.

Appropriate dosing of epidural catheters is extremely important for safe use of this technique. Recently two reports of local anesthetic–induced convulsions following chronic administration of bupivacaine have appeared [36,37•]. An accompanying editorial suggested via meta-analysis of the available literature a safe upper limit for bupivacaine infusions of 0.4 mg/kg/h [38••]. A guide for dosing of epidural catheters is suggested in Table 7-3. The maximum suggested dose of bupivacaine solution will thus be 0.4 mL/kg/h. Note that narcotics are suggested at all levels in all patients with the exception of premature infants less than 60 weeks estimated gestation age in whom one is trying to avoid the potential for apnea. This is because bupivacaine is more likely to cause toxicity at doses high enough to provide analgesia than is epidural fentanyl. However, children younger than 6 months and all patients with hydrophilic opiates (morphine or hydromorphone) should be monitored continuously with electronic monitors in addition to hourly checks by a nurse.

MONITORING CHILDREN RECEIVING ACUTE PAIN MANAGEMENT

Most patients receiving acute pain management can be appropriately cared for on a regular nursing ward if appropriate guidelines are followed. The most important aspect of caring for these patients is to ensure the availability of adequate personnel. Patients receiving intravenous or neuraxial narcotics should be cared for by a service that always has a physician available to manage complications. This physician should have a good understanding of the risks and complications of each of the techniques used and be trained in appropriate resuscitative techniques. This training will include the pharmacokinetics and pharmacodynamics of narcotics and local anesthetics administered by a variety of routes in children of various ages.

The single most important monitor of patients receiving acute pain management is frequent observation by a trained nurse or physician. Hourly observation, including assessment of respiratory rate and depth and evaluation of the patient's degree of sedation, has been shown to be effective in preventing severe respiratory depression [39]. This is more effective than either cardiorespiratory monitors or pulse oximeters. Not only are both subject to frequent false alarms in the awake, active patient, they may also fail to pick up respiratory depression in its early stages. Many patients will initially develop a rapid shallow respiratory pattern, which is counted as normal by the cardiorespiratory monitor. This pattern may nonetheless produce inadequate ventilation with carbon dioxide retention and later respiratory failure. Pulse oximetry is also a late sign of respiratory failure. The sigmoidal shape of the oxygen saturation curve requires that the arterial partial pressure of oxygen fall to less than 65 mm Hg before significant desaturation occurs. When supplemental oxygen is being administered, the patient must be virtually apneic before this will occur. These monitors are useful as supplements to hourly observation by a nurse in the high-risk patient but should never be considered as an adequate substitute.

TABLE 7-3
DOSING OF EPIDURAL CATHETERS

SURGICAL DERMATOMES/ CATHETER SITE	LUMBAR OR SACRAL	LOW THORACIC	HIGH THORACIC
Lumbar or sacral	Bupivacaine 0.1% with fentanyl 0.002 mg/mL	Bupivacaine 0.1% with morphine or hydromorphone 0.01 mg/mL	Morphine or hydromorphone only
Low thoracic	Not done	Bupivacaine 0.1% with fentanyl	Bupivacaine 0.1% with fentanyl
High thoracic	Not done	Not done	Bupivacaine 0.1% with fentanyl 0.002 mg/mL

REFERENCES AND RECOMMENDED READING

Papers of interest, published recently, have been highlighted as:
• Of special interest
•• Of outstanding interest

1. Anand KJS, Aynsley-Green A: Does the newborn infant require potent anesthesia during surgery? Answers from a randomized trial of halothane anesthesia. *Adv Pain Res Ther* 1985, 10:329–335.

2. Anand KJS, Hickey PR: Pain and its effects on the human neonate and fetus. *N Engl J Med* 1987, 317:1321–1329.

3. Anand KJS, Sippell WG, Aynsley-Green A: A randomised trial of fentanyl anaesthesia in preterm neonates undergoing surgery: effects on the stress response. *Lancet* 1987, 1:243–248.

4. Anand KJ, Hickey PR: Halothane-morphine compared with high-dose sufentanil for anesthesia and postoperative analgesia in neonatal cardiac surgery. *N Engl J Med* 1992, 326:1–9.

5. Beyer JE: *The Oucher: A User's Manual and Technical Report.* Evanston, IL: The Hospital Play Equipment; 1984.

6. Beyer JE, McGrath PJ, Berde CB: Discordance between self-report and behavioral pain measures in children aged 3–7 years after surgery. *J Pain Symptom Manage* 1990, 5:350–356.

7. McGrath PA: An assessment of children's pain: a review of behavioral, physiological and direct scaling techniques. *Pain* 1987, 31:147–176.

8. Grossi E, Borghi C, Cerchiari EL, *et al.*: Analogue chromatic continuous scale [ACCS]: a new method for pain assessment. *Clin Exp Rheumatol* 1983, 1:337–340.

9. Hester NO, Foster R, Kristensen K: Measurement of pain in children: generalizability and validity of the pain ladder and the poker-chip tool. In *Advances in Pain Research and Therapy: Pediatric Pain.* Edited by Tyler DC, Krane EJ. New York: Raven Press; 1990:79–84.

10. Broadman LM, Rice LJ, Hannallah RS: Testing the validity of an objective pain scale for infants and children. *Anesthesiology* 1988, 69:A770.

11. Berde CB, Lehn BM, Yee JD, *et al.*: Patient-controlled analgesia in children and adolescents: a randomized, prospective comparison with intramuscular administration of morphine for postoperative analgesia. *J Pediatr* 1991, 118:460–466.

12. Grunau RV, Craig KD: Pain expression in neonates: facial action and cry. *Pain* 1987, 28:395–410.

13. McGrath PA, DeVeber LL: The management of acute pain evoked by medical procedures in children with cancer. *J Pain Symptom Manage* 1986, 1:145–150.

14. Kuttner L: Management of young children's acute pain and anxiety during invasive medical procedures. *Pediatrician* 1989, 16:39–44.

15. Zeltzer L, LeBaron S: Hypnotic and nonhypnotic techniques for reduction of pain and anxiety during painful procedures in children and adolescents with cancer. *J Pediatr* 1982, 101:1032–1035.

16. Olness K: Hypnotherapy: a cyberphysiological strategy in pain management. *Pediatr Clin North Am* 1989, 36:873–884.

17. Temple AR: Pediatric dosing of acetaminophen. *Pediatr Pharmacol* 1983, 3:321–327.

18. Gaudreault P, Guay J, Nicol O, *et al.*: Pharmacokinetics and clinical efficacy of intrarectal solution of acetaminophen. *Can J Anaesth* 1988, 35:149–152.

19. Maunuksela EL, Olkkola KT, Korpela R: Intravenous indomethacin as postoperative analgesic in children: acute effects on blood pressure, heart rate, body temperature and bleeding. *Ann Clin Res* 1987, 19:359–363.

20. Maunuksela EL, Ryhanen P, Janhunen L: Efficacy of rectal ibuprofen in controlling postoperative pain in children. *Can J Anaesth* 1992, 39:226–230.

21. Olkkola KT, Maunuksela EL, Korpela R: Pharmacokinetics of postoperative intravenous indomethacin in children. *Pharmacol Toxicol* 1989, 65:157–160.

22. Maunuksela, EL, Olkkola KT, Korpela R: Does prophylactic intravenous infusion of indomethacin improve the management of postoperative pain in children? *Can J Anaesth* 1988, 35:123–127.

23.• Wheatley RG, Somerville ID, Sapsford DJ, *et al.*: Double-blind comparison of the morphine sparing effect of continuous and intermittent i.m. administration of ketorolac. *Br J Anaesth* 1991, 67:235–238.

This study suggests that ketorolac has an analgesic efficacy similar to that of 0.1 mg/kg intramuscularly of morphine sulfate.

24. Watcha MF, Jones MB, Lagueruela RG, *et al.*: Comparison of ketorolac and morphine as adjuvants during pediatric surgery. *Anesthesiology* 1992, 76:368–372.

25. Olkkola KT, Maunuksela EL, Korpela R, *et al.*: Kinetics and dynamics of postoperative intravenous morphine in children. *Clin Pharmacol Ther* 1988, 44:128–136.

26. McRorie TI, Lynn AM, Nespeca MK, *et al.*: The maturation of morphine clearance and metabolism [erratum appears in *Am J Dis Child* 1992, 146:1305]. *Am J Dis Child* 1992, 146:972–976.

27. Way W, Costley E, Way E: Respiratory sensitivity of the newborn infant to meperidine and morphine. *Clin Pharmacol Ther* 1965, 6:454–461.

28. Lynn A, Opheim KE: Morphine intravenous infusions and effects of $PaCO_2$ in infants and toddlers following cardiac surgery. *J Pain Symptom Manage* 1991, 6:207.

29. Lynn AM, Opheim KE, Tyler DC: Morphine infusion after pediatric cardiac surgery. *Crit Care Med* 1984, 12:863–866.

30. McClain B: *Pediatric Caudal Anesthesia.* Augusta, Georgia: Medical College of Georgia; 1990.

31. Dalens B, Vanneuville G, Dechelotte P: Penile block via the subpubic space in 100 children. *Anesth Analg* 1989, 69:41–45.

32. Dalens B, Vanneuville G, Tanguy A: Comparison of the fascia iliaca compartment block with the 3-in-1 block in children. *Anesth Analg* 1989, 69:705–713.

33. Rasch DK, Webster DE, Pollard TG, *et al.*: Lumbar and thoracic epidural analgesia via the caudal approach for postoperative pain relief in infants and children. *Can J Anaesth* 1990, 37:359–362.

34. Schulte SO: Uber den Einsatz von Leitungsblockaden bei Kindern. *Anaesthesiol Reanim* 1990, 15:43–54.

35. van Niekerk J, Bax VB, Geurts JW, *et al.*: Epidurography in premature infants. *Anaesthesia* 1990, 45:722–725.

36. McCloskey JJ, Haun SE, Deshpande JK: Bupivacaine toxicity secondary to continuous caudal epidural infusion in children. *Anesth Analg* 1992, 75:287–290.

37.• Agarwal R, Gutlove DP, Lockhart CH: Seizures occurring in pediatric patients receiving continuous infusion of bupivacaine. *Anesth Analg* 1992, 55:284–286.

Reports local anesthetic–induced convulsions following chronic administration of bupivacaine.

38.•• Berde CB: Convulsions associated with pediatric regional anesthesia [editorial; comment]. *Anesth Analg* 1992, 75:164–166.

This editorial accompanying Argarwal [37] suggested a safe upper limit for bupivacaine infusions of 0.4 mg/kg/h.

39. Ready LB, Oden R, Chadwick HS, *et al.*: Development of an anesthesiology-based postoperative pain management service. *Anesthesiology* 1988, 68:100–106.

General Neurosurgical Procedures for Management of Chronic Pain

SETH M. ZEIDMAN AND RICHARD B. NORTH

Pain is the most frequent reason patients consult physicians in general and neurosurgeons in particular. Relief of intractable pain has been an objective of neurosurgery since its inception. Chronic pain is defined as pain that persists or recurs after the usual course of an acute disease or beyond a reasonable time for an injury to heal. Chronic pain can be divided into two general categories: malignancy-associated and nonmalignant. An extensive array of procedures have been developed for relieving these entities, ranging from relatively trivial peripheral procedures to major intracranial surgical interventions. The art and science of pain management has been refined considerably in recent years, allowing treatment of many complex pain entities with minimal morbidity. Mastery of these techniques should be a part of general neurosurgical practice.

Neurosurgical procedures for relief of intractable pain fall into three general categories: anatomic procedures, which are directed at the structural lesion producing pain; augmentative procedures, which reversibly modulate the pain using electrical or pharmaceutical agents; and ablative procedures, which destroy portions of the nervous system while blocking pain transmission pathways.

Examples of these procedures are described in Table 8-1. Some procedures have wide application and are adaptable to general neurosurgical practice; others are infrequently indicated or highly specialized, or both. Examples of the former will be discussed here; the latter are the subject of another chapter. Three common conditions—cancer pain, failed back surgery syndrome, and trigeminal neuralgia—illustrate the evolution of therapies for chronic or intractable pain.

NEUROSURGICAL PROCEDURES FOR INTRACTABLE PAIN

General Indications

1. The etiology of pain should be clearcut and ideally should provide an objective basis for pain (eg, spinal metastasis, arachnoid fibrosis).
2. All feasible alternative therapies should be exhausted or unacceptable (eg, medical analgesic therapy, physical, or behavioral therapy).
3. Psychological issues should be addressed (no major psychiatric or personality disorder, issues of secondary gain, serious drug habituation problems, or other abnormal illness behavior).
4. Demonstration of temporary relief of pain by a method analogous to the proposed treatment should precede a permanent procedure when feasible. Augmentative procedures such as spinal cord stimulation and intraspinal narcotics may be tested directly, with percutaneous temporary electrodes or catheters. Anatomic procedures such as spinal stabilization may be tested temporarily with bracing. Ablative procedures may be tested by temporary, reversible local anesthetic blocks, which may have limited positive predictive value but are assumed to be accurate when negative.

The preferred protocol of procedures starts with anatomic (corrective) procedures, when appropriate in terms of the risk-to-benefit ratio and life expectancy. Augmentative procedures, which are reversible, are considered prior to attempting ablative procedures. The potential benefits and risks of each approach vary by diagnosis (Table 8-2).

TABLE 8-1

NEUROSURGICAL PROCEDURES FOR MANAGEMENT OF CHRONIC PAIN

ANATOMIC*	ABLATIVE‡
Decompression	Open
Stabilization	Neurotomy
Reconstruction	Sympathectomy
	Ganglionectomy
AUGMENTATIVE†	Rhizotomy
Electrical	DREZ
stimulation	Cordotomy
Transcutaneous	Myelotomy
Implanted devices	Tractotomy
Peripheral nerve	Percutaneous radiofrequency
Spinal cord	Neurotomy (eg, facet)
Intracerebral	Rhizotomy (eg, trigeminal)
Chemical	Cordotomy
Infusion systems	Cingulumotomy
Spinal epidural	Percutaneous chemical
Spinal	Lytic subarachnoid block
subarachnoid	Celiac alcohol block
Intraventricular	Stereotaxic hypophysectomy

*Directed at the structural cause.
†Modulate pain transmission by electrical or chemical means.
‡Block pain transmission by destroying pain pathways.
DREZ—dorsal root entry zone.

CANCER PAIN

Anatomic Procedures

Patients with intractable pain caused by metastatic cancer who have failed radiotherapy and analgesic therapy may be candidates for palliative surgical resection if life expectancy is sufficient to warrant the risk and expense. Metastatic involvement of the spine, which may preclude neuroaugmentative procedures including intraspinal drug delivery, exemplifies this situation. Performance of an anatomic, corrective procedure may have additional benefits, including prevention of neurologic sequelae, which influences the choice of treatment. Patients with spinal metastases often require more than a simple decompressive laminectomy; fortunately, anterior stabilization or instrumentation procedures are increasingly a part of general neurosurgical practice [1].

Augmentative Procedures

Metastatic lesions, not directly involving the nervous system but producing nociceptive pain, commonly respond to intraspinal narcotics even when systemic narcotics are ineffective [2]. Spinal epidural drug delivery offers an order of magnitude dose advantage and subarachnoid delivery two orders of magnitude over systemic administration, minimizing central side effects.

Before implanting a permanent drug delivery system, individual patient response to epidural or subarachnoid infusion should be determined.

A variety of catheter and drug-delivery systems are available. The simplest is an epidural catheter with a percutaneous extension. This may be appropriate when life expectancy is limited. The risk of catheter occlusion by fibrosis is low during a brief interval, as is the cumulative risk of infection. Implantation cost is minimal; however, when expected survival exceeds several months, the maintenance costs of such a system, including ongoing nursing care and increasing drug doses, will exceed those of an implanted pump and subarachnoid catheter. Despite the higher initial costs of the implantable pump, it can be more cost effective.

Recent innovations in implantable pump designs include battery-powered programmable devices, allowing noninvasive adjustment of infusion rate (and therefore dosage) and complex infusion profiles (eg, bolus administration, circadian variation). Battery longevity limits the lifetime of these devices. Less expensive passive devices with fixed infusion rates are available but are inflexible and require refill with new drug concentrations to change dose. They do not have, however, any life-limiting components necessitating periodic replacement.

TABLE 8-2
NEUROSURGICAL PROCEDURES FOR INTRACTABLE PAIN FOR GENERAL PRACTICE

	ANATOMIC	ABLATIVE	AUGMENTATIVE
CANCER PAIN	Debulking Decompression	Rhizotomy Cordotomy Myelotomy	(Intrathecal narcotics)
FAILED BACK SURGERY SYNDROME	Decompression Stabilization	Radiofrequency facet Denervation	Spinal cord stimulation
TRIGEMINAL NEURALGIA	Microvascular decompression Balloon Rhizolysis	Radiofrequency Glycerol Stimulation	(Thalamic or trigeminal)

Parentheses indicate procedures that are not recommended for general practice.

Development of tolerance or progression of disease leading to recurrent intractable pain necessitates alternative therapeutic agents, including local anesthetics, which may be substituted or combined with spinal narcotics. Intraventricular infusion of narcotics via a standard ventricular catheter coupled to an Ommaya reservoir (Heyer-Schulte, Deerfield, Illinois) or implanted infusion pump can often alleviate the pain of head and neck malignancies refractory to spinal narcotics [3,4].

Electrical stimulation may be effective with neurogenic or deafferentation pain caused by tumor infiltration or side effects of radiation and chemotherapy. Spinal cord stimulation is applicable to radicular or segmental pain problems. Thalamic stimulation has not been reported widely for the relief of cancer pain.

Periaqueductal or periventricular gray stimulation can relieve the pain of many malignant conditions (Fig. 8-1). In series in which the pain etiology is more than specified, periaqueductal/periventricular gray stimulation provides more than 50% pain relief in 80% of patients who use the system chronically after responding to a brief trial of stimulation [5–10]. Deep brain stimulation may be indicated in patients with diffuse, bilateral, or midline pain who cannot tolerate general anesthesia and refuse destructive procedures. This technique is still in development.

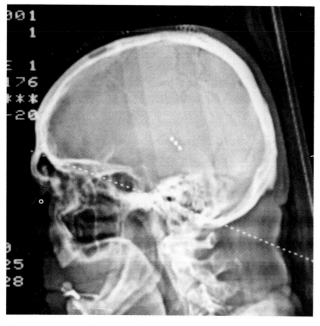

Figure 8-1 Deep brain stimulation. Scout computed tomography view of deep brain electrode array in place.

Ablative Procedures

When the neurologic sequelae are acceptable and life expectancy is limited, ablative procedures may be appropriate for managing cancer pain (*eg*, sacral rhizolysis in an incontinent patient). Percutaneous neurotomy or rhizotomy using radiofrequency, cryogenic, or chemical techniques is the simplest approach. Rhizotomy can relieve pain in the territory of the destroyed nerves in up to 100% of patients but is only useful for well-circumscribed pain problems. For more diffuse pain topographies, an anterolateral cordotomy addresses contralateral pain problems beginning several segments caudal to the procedure.

Percutaneous radiofrequency cordotomy by the lateral approach is most easily performed at C1–2 and is among the most useful procedures for patients with unilateral pain below the C5 dermatomal level. Open high thoracic cordotomy usually provides excellent analgesia for at least a year in patients with unilateral cancer pain below mid-thoracic levels. Bilateral cordotomy may be appropriate for midline or bilateral pain but carries a high risk of respiratory depression if performed at C1–2. Bilateral upper thoracic cordotomy avoids respiratory compromise but risks creation of a neurogenic bladder.

Midline (commissural) myelotomy is an alternative to bilateral upper thoracic cordotomy and addresses midline or bilateral pain in the pelvis, perineum, or both lower extremities with a single procedure, but requires an extensive longitudinal, intradural exposure [11]. Midline myelotomy is relatively safe and effective in properly selected patients, but postoperative motor weakness and bladder and bowel incontinence are common.

Stereotactic mesencephalotomy is useful for relieving cancer pain involving the face, head, neck, upper extremities, and trunk with minimal morbidity or mortality. When a high analgesic level is desired, the procedure can be performed bilaterally or on the side opposite a previous C1–2 cordotomy without producing respiratory depression.

In combined series, stereotactic thalamotomy for cancer pain with lesioning of the somatosensory relay nuclei (VPM/VPL), the centromedian/parafascicularis complex, or the pulvinar yields 54% to 100% satisfactory pain relief for patients. The use of computed tomography or magnetic resonance imaging guidance allows single-stage procedures under local anesthesia. These procedures, however, have significant morbidity with neurological complications including hemiparesis and dysesthesias in up to one-third of patients. Selective stereotactic radiosurgical lesioning of the centromedian nucleus or pulvinar can be performed without sensory loss or operative morbidity [12].

Recurrence of pain following ablative procedures, which may occur on the basis of deafferentation, limits their role in patients with longer life expectancies (greater than 6 months). Postcordotomy dysesthesias can be more difficult to relieve than the original pain.

The dorsal root entry zone (DREZ) lesion is the only operation specifically designed to treat central and deafferentation pain (Fig. 8-2). The DREZ operation entails a series of lesions directed at the substantia gelatinosa Rolandi and the surrounding fiber tracts. Rossitch and coworkers [13] reported five patients in whom nucleus caudalis DREZ lesioning was effective for the treatment of intractable facial pain caused by cancer. At long-term follow-up (mean = 14.4 mo), three patients reported sustained pain relief and an improved level of function. The remaining patients noted decreased pain postoperatively,

with persistent functional limitation because of pain. Patients with typical deafferentation pain, without accompanying hyperesthesias or previous neuroablative procedures, had the highest probability of a successful outcome.

Increasing use of high-dose systemic, intraspinal, and even intraventricular narcotics diminishes the role of ablative procedures in the treatment of cancer pain. Some neurosurgeons have not been exposed to large numbers of ablative procedures, limiting their application in general neurosurgical practice.

FAILED BACK SURGERY SYNDROME

Anatomic Procedures

Persistent or recurrent pain after lumbosacral spine surgery may indicate the need for reoperation to correct the presumed cause. North and coworkers [14•] assessed their overall experience with reoperation by disinterested third-party interview, and found a rate of "success" of approximately one-third with significant morbidity. Refinements in diagnostic imaging, including gadolinium-enhanced magnetic resonance imaging and three-dimensional computed tomography improve preoperative diagnosis of conditions, including epidural fibrosis, lateral recess, and foraminal stenosis. Whether this translates into improved results of reoperation is undetermined. Some cases of persistent pain result from established nerve injury and are refractory to anatomic correction. Others are failures of selection for the primary procedure [15] and are generally refractory to any intervention.

Augmentative Procedures

Spinal cord stimulation offers substantial advantages over ablative procedures such as cordotomy; it is less invasive and reversible. Early devices required laminectomy for electrode placement and were problematic when the appropriate level for implantation in an individual patient was not known, resulting in conflicting claims of efficacy. Percutaneous techniques developed for temporary electrode placement established the feasibility of pain relief and permitted mapping of the epidural space for the optimal electrode position and overlapping of pain by stimulation paresthesias—a necessary condition for pain relief. These methods were then adapted to placement of permanent electrodes, eliminating the need for laminectomy. Electrode arrays and programmable implants allow noninvasive selection of anode and cathode positions permitting addi-

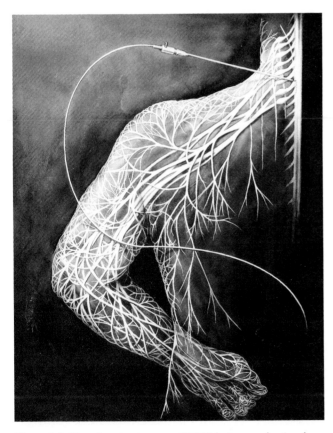

Figure 8-2 Dorsal root entry zone (DREZ) lesion production for the relief of deafferentation pain.

tional flexibility (Figs. 8-3 and 8-4). These devices are more reliable, making electrode position revision generally unnecessary. Clinical results with contemporary devices have improved, reducing the rate of clinical failures (patient no longer using device as primary method of pain control) (Figs. 8-5 and 8-6) [16,17••]. A representative selection of contemporary electrodes for spinal cord stimulation is shown in Figure 8-4.

Spinal cord stimulation is typically reserved for patients who have exhausted traditional surgical therapy, ie, multiple operative procedures. Arachnoid fibrosis ("arachnoiditis") is common in this population. North and coworkers [16,18••] observed better results with spinal cord stimulation for patients with the failed back surgery syndrome using the same outcome measures as for reoperation in their retrospective review. Because patients with spinal cord stimulation often have more impressive disease (viz., arachnoid fibrosis), this comparison is all the more remarkable, but the selection criteria for the two procedures differ in other ways. Only a prospective, randomized study will allow a valid comparison.

Spinal cord stimulation is more easily applied to radicular, neuropathic pain than to axial, nociceptive low back pain, because overlap of radicular pain by stimulation paresthesias is more easily achieved. Targeting the low back requires psychophysical testing and comparisons of amplitude thresholds over the range from initial perception to discomfort or motor recruitment [19]. Radicular paresthesias are elicited at virtually all settings and electrode positions and are superfluous. The goal of the procedure is stimulation coverage of the low back while minimizing radicular paresthesias. This may require two-dimensional electrode arrays for control of the physiologic midline, with a resultant greater burden of adjustment to the device for optimal effect. Automated equipment, allowing direct patient interaction and psychophysical threshold data, is under development [20]. Although treatment of radicular pain by spinal cord stimulation is adaptable to general neurosurgical practice, consistent treatment of axial low back pain is very difficult to achieve [19] and awaits further developments.

Intraspinal narcotic therapy has been reported in small series of failed back-surgery syndrome patients with encouraging results [21]. None have extended follow-up or disinterested third-party assessment, making comparison with other therapies difficult. Chronic subarachnoid narcotic infusion in patients with arachnoiditis, with a demonstrated propensity to react adversely, is problematic [22].

Deep brain stimulation is an effective, reversible, nondestructive technique for selected patients with intractable nociceptive or central deafferentation pain states including the failed back surgery syndrome. In some patients with low back or lower extremity pain refractory to peripheral nerve or spinal cord stimulation it has been quite effective. The periaqueductal/periventricular gray area was the most effective stimulation site [9]. Although severe complications are rare, greater risks are associated with deep brain stimulation than other neuromodulatory modalities. However, it remains an experimental technique, not yet adaptable to general neurosurgical practice.

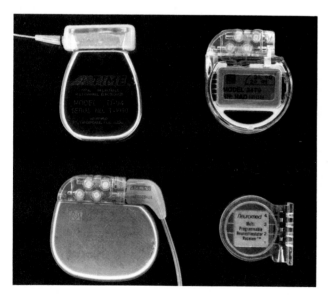

Figure 8-3 A representative selection of contemporary spinal cord stimulator receivers.

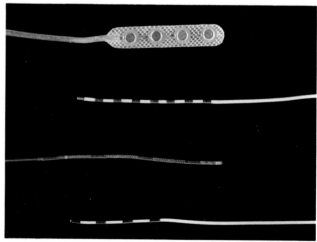

Figure 8-4 A representative selection of contemporary spinal cord stimulation electrode arrays.

ABLATIVE PROCEDURES

Rhizotomy and Dorsal Root Ganglionectomy

Chronic, intractable, lumbosacral radicular pain occasionally responds to dorsal rhizotomy, but the series with the longest follow-up have shown the lowest yield [23,24]. Identification of ventral root afferents with cell bodies in the dorsal root ganglia [25] provides an anatomical basis for persistent pain after rhizotomy. Inclusion of dorsal root ganglionectomy has been postulated to interrupt these ventral root afferents in addition to those interrupted by rhizotomy, resulting in improved clinical results.

North and coworkers [26] reviewed their experience of dorsal root ganglionectomy with 13 patients with failed back-surgery syndrome and a monoradicular pain syndrome confirmed by diagnostic root blockade. Follow-up disinterested third party interviews were conducted to assess outcome with a mean of 5.5 years after ganglionectomy. Treatment "success" (>50% sustained pain relief and patient satisfaction) was noted in two patients (15%) at 2 years and in none at 5.5 years after surgery. A minority of the patients reported improvement in activities of daily living or a decrease in analgesic intake. Loss of sensory and motor function was common.

Dorsal root ganglionectomy has minimal efficacy and may reduce the effectiveness of supplementary neuroaugmentative procedures. Destroying primary afferents removes presynaptic opiate receptors, which constitute half of the spinal cord receptors, and eliminates primary afferents ascending in the dorsal columns, which could compromise the results of spinal cord stimulation if the mechanism of pain relief involves "dorsal column" stimulation [27]. Only one of the six patients undergoing dorsal root ganglionectomy received pain relief with

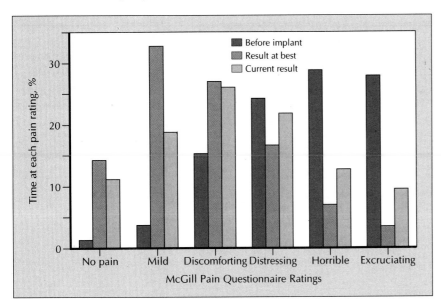

Figure 8-5 Histogram of the average rating, by patient receiving permanent implants, of the percentage of time spent at each level on a standard six-point McGill Pain Questionnaire verbal pain rating scale. (*From* North and coworkers [17••]; with permission.)

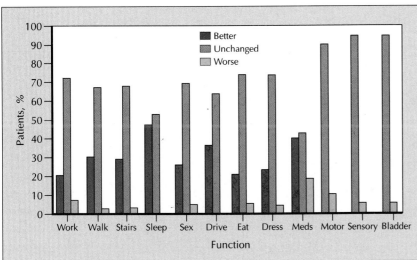

Figure 8-6 Histogram of changes in patients; ratings of their ability to perform various activities of daily living in terms of impairment due to pain, of ongoing medication use, and of reported neurologic symptoms. The results of facet denervation compare favorably with those we have reported for reoperation on the lumbosacral spine, and for dorsal root ganglionectomy, using the same outcome measures shown here. Improvement was reported by a substantial fraction of patients in most activities of daily living; loss of function was rare. A majority of patients reported reduction in or elimination of analgesic intake. A very small number reported progressive neurologic symptoms that were not associated with or attributed directly to the procedure. There were, in fact, no reported complications from the procedure. (*From* North and coworkers [17••]; with permission.)

spinal cord stimulation, a percentage far below the usual in the particularly favorable subgroup of patients with monoradicular pain.

Diagnostic nerve blocks do not reliably predict the results of ablative or decompressive procedures. Nerve blockade distal to a painful root or peripheral nerve lesions may provide temporary relief [28,29]. These nonspecific results relate in some cases to the systemic effects of lidocaine (which can relieve, for example, post-ganglionectomy dysesthesias) [30].

Radiofrequency Facet Denervation

Percutaneous radiofrequency lumbar facet denervations have been used for treating intractable, mechanical low back pain for over two decades. High success rates have been reported in selected patients in most series, but there has been limited long-term follow-up, objective outcome assessment, and analysis of prognostic factors. North and coworkers [16] recently reviewed their experience with 82 patients who underwent diagnostic medial branch posterior primary ramus blocks with diagnostic lumbar facet blocks and percutaneous radiofrequency denervations over a 7-year period, and they assessed long-term outcome by disinterested third-party interview. Forty-two patients (51%) reported ≥50% pain relief and proceeded to permanent denervation. Of these

patients 45% reported ≥50% pain relief 2 years after the procedure or at last follow-up (mean, 3 y). Forty patients underwent temporary blocks, with 13% reporting ≥50% pain relief (*ie*, spontaneous improvement or placebo effect) at follow-up. This was a statistically significant difference, favoring the patients undergoing denervation. There was no significant difference in the rate of response between the 56 patients who had undergone prior lumbosacral spine surgery and the 26 who had not. There were no complications from the procedure.

Percutaneous lumbar facet denervations are a worthwhile procedure with minimal morbidity and should be considered for use in general neurosurgical practice; however, comparisons or meta-analyses of the literature are difficult (Table 8-3). They compare favorably with other interventions, such as reoperation for failed back-surgery syndrome [14•,18••]. "Diagnostic" temporary blocks have limited positive prognostic value but have negative prognostic value in selecting patients for this procedure.

TRIGEMINAL NEURALGIA
Anatomic Procedures

Vascular compression of the trigeminal nerve root entry zone has been described as an anatomic basis for trigemi-

TABLE 8-3
VARIATIONS IN PATIENT SELECTION, TECHNIQUES, AND OUTCOME ASSESSMENT OF RADIOFREQUENCY LUMBAR FACET DENERVATIONS*

STUDY (AUTHOR, YEAR)	TEMPORARY BLOCKS, N	RF DENERVATIONS, N	PATIENTS WITH PRIOR SURGERY
Andersen, 1987	>200	47	55%
Burton, 1976	NA	126	Few
Ignelzi, 1980	61	41	NA
Lora, 1976	>119	119	Most
McCulloch, 1976	Some	82	11%
Mehta, 1979	NA	162	NA
Ogsbury, 1977	70	37	NA
Oudenhoven, 1979	NA	337	NA
Pawl, 1974	50	33	NA
Rashbaum, 1983	NA	>100	NA
Schaerer, 1978	NA	71	24%
Shealy, 1976	NA	380	NA
Sluitjter, 1981	NA	60	NA

(Table continued on page 111)

nal neuralgia and the rationale for microvascular decompression (MVD) [31]. A compressive blood vessel is not identified in up to a third of these procedures, and the operation culminates in selective posterior fossa trigeminal rhizotomy [32]. The incidence of symptomatic microvascular compression remains poorly defined, because patients responding to surgery may be responding to nerve manipulation. In some circumstances—eg, multiple sclerosis, in which there is a significant increase in the incidence of trigeminal neuralgia—there is presumably no associated increased incidence of microvascular compression [33].

The overall results reported for microvascular decompression compare favorably with other procedures for trigeminal neuralgia; but the morbidity and mortality are higher [34,35]. This may limit application of the procedure in older patients, for whom the risk is greater, but may also limit application in the young, for whom the stakes are greater. Microvascular decompression may be deferred in favor of a lower morbidity, percutaneous procedure. Concern has been expressed, by supporters of early MVD, that patients who fail percutaneous procedures and then go on to MVD have inferior results [32]. This may reflect a cause-effect relationship or a selection bias.

Microvascular decompression is indicated as a primary operative treatment in patients with trigeminal neuralgia refractory to medical therapy. Mortality and morbidity rates are low in the hands of neurosurgeons with ample experience with microsurgery in the cerebellopontine angle.

Augmentative Procedures

Electrical stimulation of the trigeminal nerve and ganglion via implanted electrodes may be effective for refractory cases of facial neuralgia, including peripheral trigeminal nerve injuries. This procedure is investigational in the United States. Classic trigeminal neuralgia, on the other hand, is adequately addressed by percutaneous and microsurgical procedures.

Anesthesia dolorosa, which can develop as a complication of retrogasserian rhizotomy, is relieved in fewer than 25% of patients by further ablative surgery at the brainstem or thalamic level, but may be treated by implantation of deep brain stimulating electrodes. However, long-term pain relief with thalamic or periaqueductal/periventricular gray deep brain stimulation has only been reported in less than 25% of patients. Like trigeminal stimulation, this is also investigational in the United States.

Ablative Procedures

Trigeminal neuralgia is unusual among nonmalignant pain syndromes in that ablative procedures are so successful. These procedures are selective and minimally destructive; complete ablation of the trigeminal nerve is undesirable and is regarded as a complication. Not only are corneal and facial anesthesia unacceptable, but there is an association with anesthesia dolorosa, a deafferentation pain syndrome.

TABLE 8-3
(CONTINUED FROM PAGE 110)

STUDY (AUTHOR, YEAR)	FOLLOW-UP RANGE, MO	FOLLOW-UP MEAN, MO	PATIENTS WITH PAIN RELIEF ≥ 50%, %
Andersen, 1987	up to 42	8	17
Burton, 1976	NA	36	42 "excellent"
Ignelzi, 1980	6–30	19	41
Lora, 1976	6–30	NA	39
McCulloch, 1976	6–20	8	50
Mehta, 1979	NA	12	28 "good"
Ogsbury, 1977	Minimum 6	NA	35
Oudenhoven, 1979	NA	26	83 "good-excellent"
Pawl, 1974	7–13	NA	42
Rashbaum, 1983	up to 36	NA	68
Schaerer, 1978	4–24	13.7	35
Shealy, 1976	6–37	27	82 "significant"
Sluitjter, 1981	NA	12	58 "substantial"

*From North and coworkers [16]; with permission.
NA—not available; Rf—radiofrequency.

Three percutaneous ablative techniques commonly used for trigeminal neuralgia are available.

Radiofrequency retrogasserian rhizolysis is a selective ablative procedure producing graded anesthesia in the trigger zone or the painful division of the trigeminal nerve. First division (V1) involvement is problematic because of the risk of producing corneal anesthesia and subsequent keratitis. Many patients lack a well-circumscribed trigger zone.

Localization of the appropriate division of the trigeminal nerve by percutaneous electrode placement has been improved by development of specialized, curved electrode tips, which allow selective coagulation of only those divisions involved in the patient's pain.

Radiofrequency rhizolysis requires detailed sensory testing for physiological confirmation of electrode position within the ganglion, necessitating patient attention and cooperation and precluding deep sedation. The anesthetic management of patients during this procedure is more technically demanding than other percutaneous procedures, involving repeated administration of short-acting agents. Radiofrequency lesion production can be quite painful, producing cardiac decompensation and uncontrolled hypertension severe enough to produce intracerebral hemorrhage, mandating deep sedation during lesioning.

Several large series have reported immediate postoperative pain relief in 95% of patients with a recurrence rate of 16% over 4 to 12 years [34,36]. The published experience with radiofrequency retrogasserian rhizolysis is extensive, with results comparing favorably with other percutaneous procedures [11]. The procedure is more technically demanding than other percutaneous procedures for both the neurosurgeon and the anesthesiologist.

Retrogasserian glycerol rhizolysis has been developed over the past decade, following its serendipitous discovery by Hakanson [37]. It is an anatomically guided procedure, with the goal of needle placement in the trigeminal cistern, as reflected by cerebrospinal fluid return or trigeminal cisternography [38,39]. Techniques to specifically lesion particular divisions of the trigeminal nerve have been described but are not critical to success, in contrast with radiofrequency lesioning. There is no need for detailed sensory testing to establish a graded endpoint. Limited sensory testing excludes corneal anesthesia, allowing liberal use of local anesthetic agents and deeper sedation.

The long-term results of glycerol rhizolysis assessed by disinterested third-party interview [40], reveals that good results last a median of 2 years [40,41]. Patients with classic trigeminal neuralgia, including response to carbamazepine, have even better results (Table 8-4) [38,40,42].

Glycerol injection is only weakly neurolytic, but deficits can occur as complications of the procedure. Intraneural injection can produce profound sensory loss. A small fraction of patients develop corneal anesthesia, facial sensory loss, and facial dysesthesias [35,40–43].

Balloon microcompression is anatomically guided [36,43–45], allowing deeper sedation. The larger needle required by the Fogarty-type balloon (14 vs. 20 gauge for

TABLE 8-4
VARIABLE REPORTED SUCCESS RATES, OUTCOME MEASURES, AND FOLLOW-UP FOR PERCUTANEOUS RETROGASSERIAN GLYCEROL RHIZOTOMY

STUDY (AUTHOR, YEAR)	TOTAL CASES, N	FOLLOW-UP PERIOD, MO	INITIAL SUCCESS RATE WITH MEDICATION
Arias, 1986	100	6–36	0.90
Beck and coworkers, 1986	58	2–40	0.72
Burchiel, 1988	60	3–44	0.80
Dieckmann and coworkers, 1987	319	1–24	0.91
Fraioli and coworkers, 1989	32	60 (mean)	0.83
Håkanson, 1981	75	2–48	0.85
Lunsford and Bennett, 1984	112	4–24	0.67
Sweet and coworkers, 1981	27	short	0.88
Waltz and coworkers, 1985	71	1–32	0.59
Young, 1988	162	6–67	0.78

(Table continued on page 113)

glycerol injection) and the severe pain associated with compression of the trigeminal ganglion necessitate deep sedation or general anesthesia. Long-term results are comparable with other percutaneous procedures.

CONCLUSIONS

Management of chronic, intractable pain has become more sophisticated, particularly with development of improved neuroaugmentative and ablative procedures. Employment of these techniques occurs with increasing frequency and earlier in the treatment sequence, broadening the population eligible for neurosurgical treatment. The "management morbidity" of an overall subject population, not just the surgical candidates, should be taken into account when making treatment decisions.

Weighing the potential benefits and the risks of alternative neurosurgical procedures and placing greater emphasis on neuroaugmentative rather than ablative procedures improves the yield and reduces management morbidity for chronic, intractable pain.

TABLE 8-4
(CONTINUED FROM PAGE 112)

STUDY (AUTHOR, YEAR)	INITIAL SUCCESS RATE WITHOUT MEDICATION	RECURRENCE RATE	OVERALL SUCCESS RATE
Arias, 1986	-	0.10	0.80
Beck and coworkers, 1986	0.79	0.24	0.76
Burchiel, 1988	NA	0.47	18 mo half-life
Dieckmann and coworkers, 1987	0.96	0.10	0.90
Fraioli and coworkers, 1989	NA	0.57	0.44
Håkanson, 1981	0.86	0.18	0.83
Lunsford and Bennett, 1984	0.90	0.18	NA
Sweet and coworkers, 1981	NA	NA	NA
Waltz and coworkers, 1985	0.75	0.14	0.72
Young, 1988	0.86	0.14	0.82

From North and coworkers [40]; with permission.

REFERENCES AND RECOMMENDED READING

References of interest, published recently, have been highlighted as:
• Of special interest
•• Of outstanding interest

1. Sundaresan N, Krol G, Digiacinto GV, *et al.*: Metastatic tumors of the spine. In *Tumors of the Spine: Diagnosis and Clinical Management*. Edited by Sundaresan N, Schmidek HH, Schiller AL, Rosenthal DT. Philadelphia: W.B. Saunders; 1990:279–304.

2. Onofrio BM, Yaksh TL: Long-term pain relief produced by intrathecal morphine infusion in 53 patients. *J Neurosurg* 1990, 72:200–209.

3. Lobato RD, Madrid JL, Fatela LV, *et al.*: Intraventricular morphine administration for control of pain in terminal cancer patients. *J Neurosurg* 1983, 59:627–633.

4. Obbens EA, Hill CS, Leavens ME, *et al.*: Intraventricular morphine administration for control of chronic cancer pain. *Pain* 1987, 28:61–68.

5. Levy RM, Lamb S, Adams JE: Treatment of chronic pain by deep brain stimulation: long term follow-up and review of the literature. *Neurosurgery* 1987, 21:885–893.

6. Hosobuchi Y: Chronic brain stimulation for the treatment of intractable pain. *Res Clin Stud Headache* 1978, 5:122–126.

7. Hosobuchi Y: The current status of analgesic brain stimulation. *Acta Neurochir Suppl (Wien)* 1980, 30:219–217.

8. Hosobuchi Y: Combined electrical stimulation of the periaqueductal gray matter and sensory thalamus. *Appl Neurophysiol* 1983, 46:112–115.

9. Hosobuchi Y: Subcortical electrical stimulation for control of intractable pain in humans: report of 122 cases (1970–1984). *J Neurosurg* 1986, 64:543–553.

10. Young RF, Kroening R, Fulton W, *et al.*: Electrical stimulation of the brain in treatment of chronic pain: experience over 5 years. *J Neurosurg* 1985, 62:389–396.

11. Gybels JM, Sweet WH, eds. *Neurosurgical Treatment of Pain.* Basel: Karger; 1989.

12. Steiner L, Forster D, Leksell L, *et al.*: Gamma thalamotomy in intractable pain. *Acta Neurochir (Wien)* 1980, 52:173–184.

13. Rossitch E Jr, Zeidman SM, Nashold BSJ: Nucleus caudalis DREZ for facial pain due to cancer. *Br J Neurosurg* 1989, 3(1):45–49.

14. • North RB, Campbell JN, James CS, *et al.*: Failed back surgery syndrome: five-year follow-up in 102 patients undergoing reoperation. *Neurosurgery* 1991, 28:685– 690.

The authors report 5-year mean follow-up for a series of 102 patients with failed back surgery syndrome who underwent reoperation for lumbosacral decompression or stabilization between 1979 and 1983. Patient characteristics and modes of treatment were assessed as predictors of long-term outcome. Favorable outcome was associated with a history of good results from previous operations, the absence of epidural scar requiring surgical lysis, employment before surgery, and predominance of radicular (as opposed to axial) pain.

15. Long DM, Filtzer DL, Bendebba M, *et al.*: Clinical features of the failed-back syndrome. *J Neurosurg* 1988, 69:61–71.

16. North RB, Kidd DH, Zahurak M, *et al.*: Spinal cord stimulation for chronic, intractable pain: superiority of "multichannel" devices. *Pain* 1991, 44:119–130.

17. •• North RB, Kidd DH, Zahurak M, *et al.*: Spinal cord stimulation for chronic, intractable pain: two decades' experience. *Neurosurgery* 1993, 32:384–395.

The authors review their experience in 320 consecutive patients treated with spinal cord stimulation between 1972 and 1990. Technical details of treatment as well as patient characteristics were assessed as predictors of clinical outcome and of hardware reliability. Their analysis of technical and clinical prognostic factors may be useful to the clinician selecting patients for this procedure.

18. •• North RB, Ewend MG, Lawton MT, *et al.*: Failed back surgery syndrome: five-year follow-up after spinal cord stimulator implantation. *Neurosurgery* 1991, 28:692–699.

North and coworkers review their experience with spinal cord stimulation for treating "failed back surgery syndrome," and assess patient and treatment characteristics as predictors of long-term outcome. Statistical analysis showed significant advantages for female patients and for those with programmable multicontact implanted devices.

19. Law JD: Targeting a spinal stimulator to treat the "failed back surgery syndrome". *Appl Neurophys* 1987, 50:437–438.

20. North RB, Fowler KR, Nigrin DA, *et al.*: Automated "pain drawing" analysis by computer-controlled, patient interactive neurological stimulation system. *Pain* 1992, 50:51–58.

21. Auld AW, Maki-Jokela A, Murdoch DM: Intraspinal narcotic analgesia in the treatment of chronic pain. *Spine* 1985, 10:777–781.

22. North RB, Cutchis P, Epstein JA, *et al.*: Spinal cord compression complicating subarachnoid morphine administration: case report and laboratory experience. *Neurosurgery* 1991, 29:778–784.

23. Loeser JD: Dorsal rhizotomy for the relief of chronic pain. *J Neurosurg* 1972, 36:745–754.

24. Onofrio BM, Campa HK: Evaluation of rhizotomy: review of 12 years' experience. *J Neurosurg* 1972, 36:751–755.

25. Coggeshall RE, Applebaum ML, Fazen M, *et al.*: Unmyelinated axons in human ventral roots, a possible explanation for the failure of dorsal rhizotomy to relieve pain. *Brain* 1975, 98:157–166.

26. North RB, Kidd DH, Campbell JN, *et al.*: Dorsal root ganglionectomy for failed back surgery syndrome: a five-year follow-up study. *J Neurosurg* 1991, 74:236–242.

27. Campbell JN, Davis KD, Meyer RA, *et al.*: The mechanism by which dorsal column stimulation affects pain: evidence for a new hypothesis. *Pain* 1990, 5:S228.

28. Kibler RW, Nathan PW: Relief of pain and paresthesiae by nerve block distal to a lesion. *J Neurol Neurosurg Psychiat* 1960, 23:91–98.

29. Xavier AV, McDanal J, Kissin I: Relief of sciatic radicular pain by sciatic nerve block. *Anesth Analg* 1988, 67:1177–1180.

30. Tabu A: Suppression of post-ganglionectomy dysesthesia by systemic lidocaine. Presented to the American Pain Society, Washington, DC, 1986. *Neurosurgical Treatment of Persistent Pain.* New York: Karger; 1989:123.

31. Jannetta PJ: Microsurgical approach to the trigeminal nerve for tic doloreux. *Prog Neurol Surg* 1976, 7:180–200.

32. Bederson JB, Wilson CB: Evaluation of microvascular decompression and partial sensory rhizotomy in 252 cases of trigeminal neuralgia. *J Neurosurg* 1989, 71:359–367.

33. Adams CBT: Microvascular compression: An alternative view and hypothesis. *J Neurosurg* 1989, 70:1–12.

34. Burchiel KJ, Steege TD, Howe JF, *et al.*: Comparison of percutaneous radiofrequency gangliolysis and microvascular decompression for the surgical management of tic doloreux. *Neurosurgery* 1981, 9:111–119.

35. Young RF: Glycerol rhizolysis for treatment of trigeminal neuralgia. *J Neurosurg* 1988, 69:39–45.

36. Fraioli B, Vincenzo E, Benjamino G, *et al.*: Treatment of trigeminal neuralgia by thermocoagulation glycerolization and percutaneous compression of the Gasserian ganglion and/or retrogasserian rootlets: long-term results and therapeutic protocol. *Neurosurgery* 1989, 24:239–245.

37. Hakanson S: Trigeminal neuralgia treated by the injection of glycerol into the trigeminal cistern. *Neurosurgery* 1981, 9:638–646.

38. Arias MJ: Percutaneous retrogasserian glycerol rhizotomy for trigeminal neuralgia. *J Neurosurg* 1986, 65:32–36.

39. Lunsford LD, Bennett MH: Percutaneous retrogasserian glycerol rhizotomy for tic douloureux: Part I. Technique and results in 112 patients. *Neurosurgery* 1984, 14:424–430.

40. North RB, Kidd DH, Piantadosi S, *et al.*: Percutaneous retrogasserian glycerol rhizotomy: predictors of success and failure in treatment of trigeminal neuralgia. *J Neurosurg* 1990, 72:851–856.

41. Burchiel KJ: Percutaneous retrogasserian glycerol rhizolysis in the management of trigeminal neuralgia. *J Neurosurg* 1988, 69:361–366.

42. Sweet WH, Poletti CE: Problems with retrogasserian glycerol in the treatment of trigeminal neuralgia. *Appl Neurophysiol* 1985, 48:252–257.

43. Fujimaki T, Fukushima T, Miyazaki S: Percutaneous retrogasserian glycerol injection in the management of trigeminal neuralgia: long-term follow-up results. *J Neurosurg* 1990, 73:212–216.

44. Brown JA, Preul MC: Percutaneous trigeminal compression for trigeminal neuralgia: experience in 22 patients and review of the literature. *J Neurosurg* 1989, 70:900–904.

45. Mullan S, Lichtor T: Percutaneous microcompression of the trigeminal ganglion for trigeminal neuralgia. *J Neurosurg* 1983, 59:1007–1012.

Psychological Approaches to the Management of Chronic Pain

JENNIFER F. KELLY

This chapter discusses the various psychological approaches for the management of chronic pain. Effective use of psychological techniques has been associated with improved functioning in patients with chronic pain . The improvements observed include decreased pain perception, decreased psychological distress, and the use of more appropriate coping strategies. Additionally, decreased clinic visits have been observed in patients receiving psychological intervention. This translates to decreased health care costs [1•,2]. One of the main goals of the psychological approach is to teach patients techniques to manage the condition themselves.

Pearce [3] categorized the psychological interventions in terms of the component of the pain experience that it is to target, *ie*, physiologic, subjective, or behavioral (Table 9-1). Biofeedback and relaxation training are used to treat the physiologic component of the pain. For example, a patient would use electromyographic (EMG) biofeedback to treat muscle contraction headache. Hypnosis and "pain-directed" cognitive methods focus on sensations and feelings of distress and discomfort, whereas contingency management, or operant approaches, target the behavioral component of the pain experience, such as wincing or taking pills. Patients could be treated with a combination of the various methods simultaneously, depending on the nature of their pain problem.

BIOFEEDBACK

Biofeedback is now a widely accepted approach in the management of chronic pain, primarily because of its noninvasive nature, as its effectiveness relies mostly on the patient's internal resources. Biofeedback uses electronic equipment to reveal involuntary physiologic events so that patients can learn to bring them under voluntary control (Fig. 9-1) [4]. It has been successfully employed to treat a variety of pain syndromes, including muscle contraction and migraine headache, low back pain, myofascial pain syndrome, reflex sympathetic dystrophy, and arthritis [5].

The rationale for using biofeedback in treating chronic pain are as follows:

1. To modify the specific physiologic process that is thought to underlie the pain disorder. For example, EMG biofeedback is used to treat muscle-contraction headache. A reduction in muscle tension achieved through biofeedback training should result in a corresponding decrease in muscle contraction headache. This rationale is not supported by many researchers, mainly because there are some pain syndromes in which the etiology is not clear [6,7].

2. To facilitate the relaxation response. A reduction in autonomic arousal is expected to lead to a corresponding reduction in pain. Stress and tension are known to exacerbate pain; therefore, relaxation should be associated with its relief.

3. To help the patient develop self-regulation. In using biofeedback, patients become more aware of their own contribution to the pain experience as well as their ability to influence the pain. For biofeedback to be effective, patients must take responsibility for coping with the pain. With the technique, they also learn that their pain may be under internal, as op-

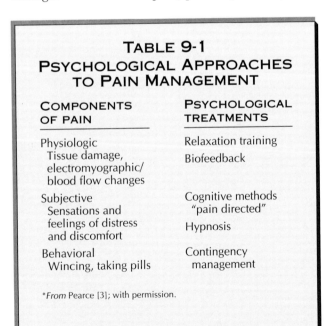

TABLE 9-1
PSYCHOLOGICAL APPROACHES TO PAIN MANAGEMENT

COMPONENTS OF PAIN	PSYCHOLOGICAL TREATMENTS
Physiologic Tissue damage, electromyographic/blood flow changes	Relaxation training Biofeedback
Subjective Sensations and feelings of distress and discomfort	Cognitive methods "pain directed" Hypnosis
Behavioral Wincing, taking pills	Contingency management

*From Pearce [3]; with permission.

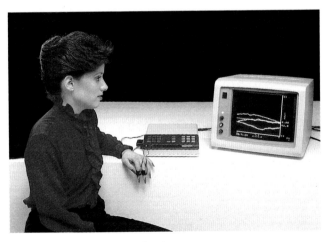

Figure 9-1 Set-up of biofeedback session.

posed to external, control. The patient's view of the pain should change, which can result in greater acceptance of personal responsibility for managing the pain. The internal focus can also facilitate patients in developing a more optimistic outlook for the future. The patient's affective state may improve and participation in the treatment process can increase [6,8].

The most common forms of biofeedback used with the chronic pain population continue to remain EMG biofeedback and skin temperature or thermal biofeedback. Alpha biofeedback has been investigated as a treatment for chronic pain, but it is not commonly used at pain management centers.

Electromyographic biofeedback provides a measure of the electrical discharge in the muscle fibers, which indicates relaxation or contraction of the muscles. The effective use of EMG biofeedback should result in reduction in muscle tension, which in turn produces a decrease in pain experienced [6]. The pain syndromes that EMG biofeedback has been successfully used to treat include muscle contraction headache, temporomandibular joint pain, myofascial pain syndrome, and fibromyalgia.

A potential problem with EMG feedback is that the EMG readout may not provide an accurate measure of the muscle tension and pain that the patient is actually experiencing. In these cases, the pain could be the result of deep muscle tension that is not easily measured by EMG surface electrodes or the pain may originate at a site different from where it is experienced [6,9]. Also, studies have not consistently shown a positive correlation between reported pain relief and reduction in EMG. It is, therefore, possible for a patient to be successfully trained in EMG biofeedback, yet not have a reduction in pain [10]. In some cases there may be a delay between reduction of EMG and the corresponding reduction of pain [11].

The basis for the use of skin temperature, or thermal biofeedback in treating chronic pain is that activity in the sympathetic nervous system may result in vasoconstriction of peripheral arterioles and that reduced sympathetic nervous system activity is associated with vasodilation. The goal of skin temperature biofeedback is to teach patients to increase the skin temperature in their extremity, usually their finger, thereby increasing vasodilation and reducing sympathetic nervous system activity. Additionally, an increase in skin temperature is associated with a full relaxation response [6,12]. Pain syndromes that skin temperature biofeedback has been used to treat include reflex sympathetic dystrophy and migraine headaches; however, the exact physiologic

mechanism by which it works with the syndromes remains unclear [7,13].

Studies evaluating the effectiveness of skin temperature biofeedback in treating migraine headache have yielded mixed results [12,14,15]. The analysis of studies evaluating its effectiveness is frequently complicated by the use of additional techniques, such as autogenic training. It seems that the use of skin temperature biofeedback is effective in treating selected cases of migraine. Its usefulness may be related to the nonspecific factors in biofeedback therapy, such as relaxation and patients' perceived control over the pain [16].

Electroencephalogram (EEG) biofeedback is used to assist patients in producing alpha brain activity (8–13 Hz). This is a relaxed state, which is incompatible with pain [17]. Early studies examining the use of this form of biofeedback in reducing pain yielded positive findings; however, they were not well controlled [18,19]. These studies did prompt further investigation of the procedure in the management of pain, but they have not provided sufficient support for its use for pain control.

RELAXATION TRAINING

The main purpose of the various relaxation techniques in pain management is to elicit the relaxation response. Relaxation is thought to reduce pain by reducing arousal. Studies have shown that physiologic changes consistent with decreased sympathetic nervous system activity often accompany the relaxation response [20–22]. The changes observed include decreases in oxygen consumption, reduction in heart rate, and a marked decrease in arterial blood lactate concentration. Relaxation facilitates one's ability to use suggestion and imagination to provide relief of pain. Focused concentration helps the patients learn ways of disrupting preoccupying thoughts, especially those related to pain [23].

Relaxation has also been used to teach patients body awareness. Patients experiencing pain, especially myofascial pain, frequently tense their muscles in response to pain or in anticipation of pain, thereby exacerbating the pain. By becoming more aware of the physical sensations in their bodies, patients can learn to reliably decrease the muscle tension and thereby cope with the pain more effectively.

There are various forms of relaxation approaches available to use with patients with chronic pain. Progressive muscle relaxation is the most common approach used. This technique involves tensing and relaxing the major muscle groups so that patients can learn to relax the tense muscles that contribute to pain.

When the patients have consistently achieved success with progressive muscle relaxation, a shorter version of the technique can be substituted. The eventual goal is reduction of tension by recall, thus eliminating the need to actively tense muscle groups. As patients become more advanced with using the technique, they can incorporate visual imagery and autogenic phrases to elicit relaxation [7].

Relaxation training has been used to treat a wide variety of painful disorders, with much success. The syndromes include muscle contraction headache, migraine headache, temporomandibular joint pain, chronic back pain, and myofascial pain syndrome.

COMPARISON BETWEEN BIOFEEDBACK AND RELAXATION TRAINING

Studies have compared the relative effectiveness of biofeedback and relaxation training in treating chronic pain. The majority of research indicates that relaxation and biofeedback training are equally effective in the management of pain [24]. However, the two approaches can be useful to the patients in different ways (Fig. 9-2). Biofeedback provides patients with an overt indicator of the relationship between behaviors and cognitions and changes in physiologic processes. With this feedback, the patients can develop control over the specific physiologic mechanism that contributes to pain [25••]. Biofeedback provides patients with objective data on the progress during the treatment sessions. Additionally, patients seem to like the instrumentation and technology associated with the biofeedback unit. The main advantages of using relaxation training are its practicality and cost effectiveness [26].

In many settings, biofeedback and relaxation are used as conjunctive treatments. The relaxation training provides the technique to alter physiologic processes and the biofeedback is used to shape the patient's relaxation response. The biofeedback can help pinpoint the source of training problems as well as open up new intervention tactics. By providing objective data to the patients, the instrumentation and measurement techniques can serve to place the techniques in a "scientific" explanatory framework. In the treatment sessions, the patients should be encouraged to verbalize the control strategies, attend to sensations experienced during the training sessions, and use conditioned verbal cues to promote generalization of techniques learned to daily life. The patient should not develop excessive reliance on the machine.

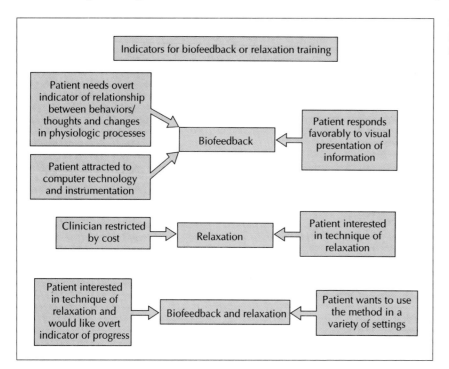

Figure 9-2 Indicators for use of biofeedback or relaxation training techniques in managing chronic pain.

BIOFEEDBACK AND RELAXATION TRAINING TREATMENT PROTOCOL

This protocol is part of a multidisciplinary treatment program that uses interventions from other specialties, such as anesthesiology, physical therapy, and occupational therapy (Table 9-2).

Session 1: Collection of Baseline Data and Explanation of Biofeedback

The purposes of session 1 are to explain the process of biofeedback and how it can be of use with patients in helping them cope with their chronic pain and to collect initial baseline data. Progress made in future sessions will be compared with measures obtained in the baseline session. In this session, patients can ask questions regarding the nature of biofeedback. Depending on the nature of the pain complaint, either EMG or skin temperature is monitored. The specific site for the placement of the EMG electrodes is dependent on the pain complaint, but they are usually placed on the frontalis or neck and shoulder area. The skin temperature probes are placed on the index finger of both hands.

Sessions 2 through 6: Relaxation-assisted Biofeedback Training

In sessions two through six, patients are instructed in the use of relaxation techniques—progressive muscle relaxation in the second and third sessions, followed by autogenic relaxation in the fourth and fifth sessions. The first 15 minutes of each session is an introductory period during which time is spent discussing any of the patients' concerns and presenting the goals for the session. Following this, patients participate in 30 minutes of relaxation-assisted biofeedback training. The last 15 minutes is spent discussing the training session and any

problems encountered. Progressive muscle relaxation techniques are implemented to teach the patients general body awareness. With the techniques the patients are required to tense and then relax the muscle groups. Additionally, they learn controlled-breathing techniques. They are taught ways of determining the difference between tension and relaxation of the muscles. After the patients have developed mastery over the techniques, usually in about three sessions, they then progress to using the autogenic relaxation techniques.

During the session the patient is provided with visual or auditory feedback. Occasionally, both skin temperature and EMG feedback are provided (Fig. 9-3). At the end of each session, the patient is given data on the EMG and skin temperature readings obtained during the session. The mean, as well as the low and high reading, for each minute of the training period is measured.

To facilitate their training in the clinic, the patients are provided with relaxation tapes and are encouraged to use them at least once daily and when they experience severe levels of pain and tension.

Sessions 7 and 8: Further Development of Skills

As the patients obtain an adequate degree of self-control with the relaxation and biofeedback training, there should be focus on further development and improvement of the skills in the seventh and eighth sessions. They should also use the skills learned for self-regulation. Instead of practicing the structured progressive muscle or autogenic relaxation, patients can use simple phrases to facilitate the relaxation response and for self-regulation. During these sessions there should be focus on incorporating these skills into daily routines, such as using the simple phrases when engaged in daily activities. Patients will become more comfortable using these techniques as they recognize the benefit of using them in daily situations.

HYPNOSIS

The mechanism by which patients with pain are able to achieve dramatic pain relief with hypnosis is not well understood. Studies have indicated that the hypnotic analgesia received is not mediated by the endorphin system (Finer and Terenius, Paper presented at the Meeting of the Third World Conference on Pain of the International Association for the Study of Pain, Edinburgh, Scotland, 1981) [27]. However, there has been research support for the theory that cognitions play

---

TABLE 9-2
BIOFEEDBACK AND RELAXATION TRAINING PROTOCOL

Session 1	Collection of baseline data and explanation of biofeedback training
Sessions 2–6	Relaxation-assisted biofeedback training
Sessions 7–8	Further development of skills

an important role in hypnosis and hypnotic analgesia [28]. Hypnosis focuses on the subjective aspect of the pain experience, such as feelings of distress and discomfort.

Hypnosis can provide an analgesic experience for many patients, but the technique in and of itself is not expected to cure chronic pain. It provides a sensation of peacefulness and comfort, and short-term relief of pain can be experienced. For lasting benefit to occur, however, hypnosis should be part of a broader psychotherapeutic regimen [29]. It is more effective in managing pain of organic etiology than in managing psychogenic, or functional, pain. This is because persistent psychogenic pain often has complicating factors that need to be addressed, such as secondary gain [30]. Using hypnosis to treat disorders with secondary gain could potentially result in symptom substitution [31].

Generally, the effectiveness of hypnosis depends on two factors—the patient's imagination and the ability of

the clinician to capitalize on that imagination. Hypnotic responsiveness varies considerably among individuals, and hypnotizability can be modified by various means, such as through operant training and biofeedback [32,33]. What appears to be most important is the specific technique that is used with the individual, as it has been shown that subjects with low responsiveness on susceptibility tests often respond favorably when different approaches are introduced.

Various hypnotic methods are available to achieve hypnotic pain control, and they include the following (Table 9-3) [29,34].

1. Altering the perception of the pain. This blocks the patient's awareness of pain. Analgesia or anesthesia is created by suggesting that the pain is diminishing, changing, or that the area is becoming numb.

I have successfully used this technique on numerous occasions with patients with chronic pain. In one

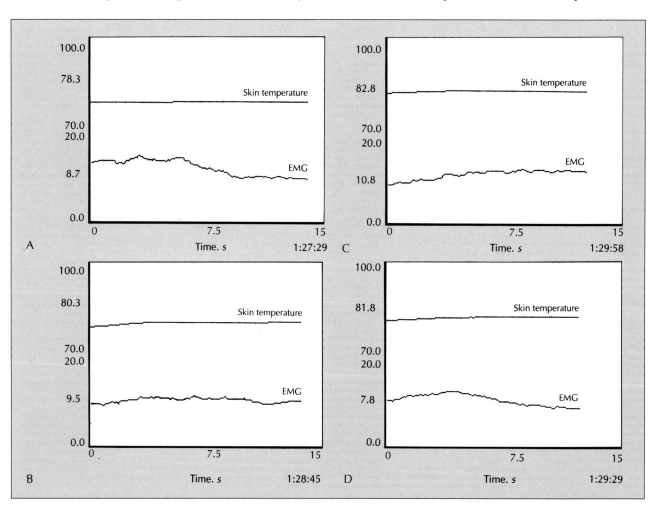

Figure 9-3 (*Panels A–D*) Mean skin temperature and electromyographic (EMG) readings for four consecutive 15-second intervals of a relaxation-assisted biofeedback training session. *Lower right hand corner* of each panel shows time.

case the technique was used with a patient suffering with reflex sympathetic dystrophy of the upper extremity. She would not participate in any form of exercise because of the severe pain experienced. Because she would not exercise, her functioning would not improve. The procedures used with her have been described by Bassman [35]. The goal was to allow her to experience enough hypnotic analgesia so that she would allow her hand to be manipulated. While in a hypnotic trance, she was to visualize three objects on a table: a soft velvet glove with a smooth silk lining; a new brightly colored pail, filled with a sparkling, blue liquid; and a large, open jar of hand cream that was filled with a pleasant and aromatic perfume. She was told that each of the objects contained a potent anesthesia, such that the part of the body coming in contact with it would become numb. She was to select one of the objects to place the affected hand in and the hand would become numb. She was also to use the unaffected extremity to rub the anesthetic solution all over the hand and arm of the affected extremity. She consistently experienced hypnotic analgesia using this technique and allowed her hand to be manipulated.

2. Substitute the painful sensation with a different or less painful sensation. Some patients are able to use this technique more effectively if the substituted feeling is not totally pleasant. For example, they can substitute stabbing pain with a pinch-like sensation.

3. Move the pain to another area of the body. The new location of the pain should be an area of lesser psychological vulnerability. For example, a writer who has pain in the dominant hand can be given hypnotic suggestions that the pain is moving to the tip of the small finger. The eventual goal is for the pain to be moved outside the body.

4. Dissociation of awareness of the pain. This technique is useful for patients when they do not need to be functional, such as when they are undergoing medical or dental procedures, or in the latter stages of a terminal illness. Patients are taught to experience themselves in another state, place, or time, such as in a vivid daydream.

5. Alter the meaning of the pain. With this technique the patient is given suggestions that the pain is becoming less meaningful and debilitating.

6. Distortion of time. Patients are taught ways to distort time so that the amount of time experiencing a painful sensation, such as spasms, is altered. The patient can be taught to perceive the time when a painful sensation occurs as rapidly passing.

An eventual goal of using hypnosis with patients suffering from pain is to teach them self-hypnosis. In this way, they can use the hypnotic techniques themselves for self-regulation of the pain.

COGNITIVE APPROACHES

The basic premise with the cognitive approaches is that expectations, attitudes, and beliefs affect the manner in which patients cope with pain (Fig. 9-4). Changes in negative cognitions can result in better pain control [36]. It is believed that behavior and affect result from the way in which a person construes the world [37]. Inadequate coping mechanisms seen in patients with chronic pain are related to errors in cognition. Patients who tend to misinterpret their experience of pain are usually more severely disabled [38,39]. The goal of the intervention is to cor-

TABLE 9-3
METHODS FOR ACHIEVING PAIN RELIEF THROUGH HYPNOSIS

Alter the perception of pain

Substitute the painful sensation

Move the pain to another location

Dissociation

Alter the meaning of the pain

Time distortion

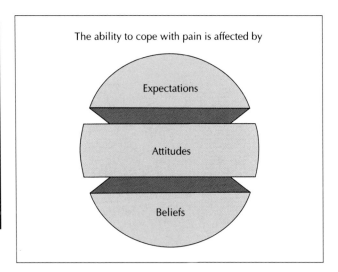

Figure 9-4 Psychologic factors affecting the ability to manage pain.

rect faulty thought processes that contribute to prolonged suffering and disability, and maladaptive beliefs are replaced with more adaptive ones [40].

Studies conducted provide support for the use of cognitive approaches in treating chronic pain [41•,42••]. The cognitive approaches have been associated with the following benefits [43]:

1. Patients have the necessary coping skills to deal with the pain more effectively.

2. Patients live more satisfying lives despite the presence of physical discomfort.

3. Patients have decreased reliance on the health care system and a reduction in dependence on analgesic medications. A message emphasized to the patients is that they are not helpless in dealing with their pain and it should not control their lives.

There are a wide variety of therapeutic techniques under the cognitive model, but they have common elements. The interventions are structured, action-oriented, and are usually time-limited. The approaches can be taught in individual or group sessions [37].

Turk and coworkers [37] describe three phases of the intervention process (Table 9-4):

1. Patients are taught how thoughts and feelings influence pain.

2. Patients are taught specific methods for coping with pain. The methods taught include relabeling painful sensations, attention diversion, reinterpreting pain sensations, relaxation, and imagery. Four steps are

involved in this teaching process: preparing for minor painful sensations; confronting more severe pain; coping with feelings that tend to exacerbate pain, such as anxiety or frustration; and learning to provide self-reinforcement for successfully coping with pain.

3. Generalization of the skills to situations outside the clinical setting are facilitated by initially practicing them in the office setting and then having the patient use the techniques in outside situations such as the work or home environment. The therapist should exercise flexibility with the approach and allow patients to proceed at their own pace.

The cognitive approach of Ciccone and Grzesiak [40] is based on rational-emotive therapy and focuses on changing specific errors in thinking. The premise on which this approach rests is that the extent to which the patient with chronic pain becomes disabled is directly related to that person's perception and subsequent evaluation of the pain. The cognitive errors that are responsible for eliciting the patient's symptoms should be corrected with the intervention. Verbally challenging patients to defend their irrational beliefs is a way of accomplishing this. For this approach to be effective, the patient has to be willing to accept cognitive change, as treatment offered without a patient's consent may adversely affect the therapeutic relationship and therefore make it difficult for other changes to occur.

Brown and Nicassio [44] evaluated the relative effectiveness of active and passive coping strategies. Active coping strategies require the patient to engage in some action, such as exercising, to cope with the pain. Patients using passive coping strategies either withdraw or give up control to an external agent. Examples of passive coping strategies include resting or taking medications. The authors observed that rheumatoid arthritis patients using active coping strategies had better psychological and physical functioning, and passive coping was associated with depression for patients who reported high pain levels. Additionally, longitudinal research indicated that the use of active and passive strategies during the pain experience predicted long-term (6 month) depression and disability. Use of the active strategies was associated with better long-term adjustments.

Parker and coworkers [45] used the Ways of Coping Scale to assess the relationship between coping and psychological adjustment in male patients with rheumatoid arthritis. Cognitive restructuring, such as thoughts about people worse off than they, was associated with lower levels of depression. Wishful thinking and self-blame were associated with higher levels of depression.

TABLE 9-4
STAGES OF INTERVENTION USED IN THE COGNITIVE APPROACH TO PAIN MANAGEMENT

Patients are taught how thoughts and feelings influence pain

Patients are taught specific methods for coping with pain:

  –Prepare patient for minor painful sensations

  –Have patient confront severe pain

  –Teach patients to cope with feelings that exacerbate pain

  –Teach patients to provide self-reinforcement for coping with episodes of pain

Generalization of skills

OPERANT APPROACHES

The operant approach in the management of chronic pain is based on the assumption that the patient's behavior is governed by its consequences in that the environmental consequences of a behavior determine whether or not it will reoccur (Fig. 9-5). If the reinforcers are positive, then there is an increased likelihood that the behavior will reoccur, while negative reinforcement decreases the likelihood. The goal of the operant approach, or contingency management, is to replace learned maladaptive behaviors with behaviors that are incompatible with the sick role [46]. Environmental contingencies are changed so that appropriate "healthy" behaviors are reinforced and pain behaviors are not rewarded. For this to occur, the targeted behaviors and possible reinforcers need to be identified, and there should be a manipulation of the reinforcers. Family members and health care providers are instructed to reinforce appropriate behaviors, while ignoring pain behaviors, such as complaining of pain, using narcotics, and remaining inactive. Other forms of intervention, such as marital counseling, family therapy, and vocational planning, can be incorporated in the treatment.

GROUP THERAPY

An important component of a pain management program is group therapy. The two main purposes for group intervention are to provide psychological support and to disseminate information. The use of group therapy is time efficient for the psychologist, who generally has many patients to treat. Its format allows multiple ideas to be presented, shared, and discussed. The members of the group provide support, encouragement, and can serve as a reality check for other group members [47•].

In the group setting, patients can obtain information regarding the psychosocial influences on their pain experience. Among the educational topics that I discuss in the group setting are vicious pain cycles (*eg*, pain-depression cycle, pain-narcotics cycle, and pain-stress cycle), effective coping strategies, acceptance of the pain, and compliance issues.

CONCLUSIONS

In summary, there is much support in the literature for the use of the previously mentioned approaches in managing chronic pain. For the approaches to be successful, the patients must accept responsibility for successful management of the pain. The interventions are most beneficial when they are incorporated into a comprehensive pain management program.

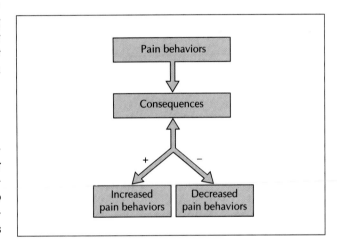

Figure 9-5 Environmental consequences of a behavior can determine whether or not it will reoccur; replacement of maladaptive pain behaviors with appropriate ones can aid the patient in managing chronic pain.

REFERENCES AND RECOMMENDED READING

Papers of interest, published recently, have been highlighted as:
• Of special interest
•• Of outstanding interest

1. • Caudill M, Schnable R, Zuttermeister P, *et al.*: Decreased clinic use by chronic pain patients: response to behavioral medicine intervention. *Clin J Pain* 1993, 7(4):305–310.
Effective use of psychological techniques has been associated with decreased pain perception, decreased psychological distress, the use of more appropriate coping strategies, and decreased clinic visits. This translates to decreased health care costs.

2. Schneider C: Cost effectiveness of biofeedback and behavioral medicine treatments: a review of the literature. *Biofeedback Self Regul* 1987, 12(2):71–92.

3. Pearce S: A review of cognitive-behavioural methods for the treatment of chronic pain. *J Psychosom Res* 1983, 27(5):431–440.

4. Basmajian JV, ed: *Biofeedback: Principles and Practice for Clinicians.* Baltimore: Williams and Wilkins; 1983.

5. Jessup BA: Biofeedback. In *Textbook of Pain.* Edited by Wall PD, Melzack R. New York: Churchill Livingstone; 1984.

6. Schuman M: Biofeedback in the management of chronic pain. In *Psychological Approaches to the Management of Pain.* Edited by Barber J, Adrian C. New York: Brunner/Mazel; 1982.

7. Grzesiak RC, Ciccone DS: Relaxation, biofeedback, and hypnosis in the management of pain. In *Persistent Pain: Psychosocial Assessment and Intervention.* Edited by Lynch NT, Vasudevan SV. Boston: Kluwer Academic Publishers; 1988.

8. Ciccone DS, Grzesiak RC: Cognitive dimensions of chronic pain. *Soc Sci Med* 1984, 19:1339–1345.

9. Linton SJ: Behavioral remediation of chronic pain: a status report. *Pain* 1986, 24:125–141.

10. Peck CL, Kraft GH: Electromyographic feedback for pain related to muscle tension. *Arch Surg* 1977, 112:889–895.

11. Philips C: The modification of tension headache pain utilizing EMG feedback. *Behav Res Ther* 1977, 15:119–129.

12. Chapman SL: A review and clinical perspective on the use of EMG and thermal biofeedback for chronic headaches. *Pain* 1986, 27:1–43.

13. Nigl AJ, ed.: *Biofeedback and Behavioral Strategies in Pain Treatment.* New York: S.P. Medical and Scientific Books; 1984.

14. Sargent JD, Green EE, Walters DE: Psychosomatic self-regulation of migraine and tension headaches. *Semin Psychiatry* 1973, 5:415–428.

15. Turin A, Johnson WG: Biofeedback therapy for migraine headaches. *Arch Gen Psychiatry* 1976, 33:577–579.

16. Turk DC, Meichenbaum DH, Berman WH: Application of biofeedback for the regulation of pain: a critical review. *Psychol Bull* 1979, 86:1322–1338.

17. Pelletier KR, Peper E: Developing a biofeedback model: alpha EEG feedback as a means for pain control. *Int J Clin Exp Hypn* 1977, 25:361–371.

18. Coger R, Werbach M: Attention, anxiety, and the effects of learned enhancement of EEG in chronic pain: pilot study in biofeedback. *Pain: Research and Treatment.* Edited by Crue BL. New York: Academic Press; 1975.

19. Gannon L, Sternbach RA: Alpha enhancement as a treatment for pain: a case study. *J Behav Ther Exp Psychiatry* 1971, 2:209–213.

20. Benson H, Pomeranz B, Kutz I: The relaxation response and pain. In *Textbook of Pain.* Edited by Wall PD, Melzack R. New York: Churchill Livingstone; 1984.

21. Levander VL, Benson H, Wheeler RC, *et al.*: Increased forearm blood flow during a wakeful hypometabolic state. *Fed Proc* 1972, 31:405.

22. Wallace RK, Benson H: The physiology of meditation. *Sci Am* 1972, 226:84–90.

23. Sachs LB: Teaching hypnosis for the self-control of pain. In *Psychological Approaches to the Management of Pain.* Edited by Barber J, Adrian C. New York: Brunner/Mazel; 1982.

24. Blanchard EB, Andrasik F, Ahles TA, *et al.*: Migraine and tension headache: a meta-analytic review. *Behav Ther* 1980, 11:613–631.

25. •• Cott A, Parkinson W, Fabich M, *et al.*: Long-term efficacy of combined relaxation: biofeedback treatments for chronic headache. *Pain* 1992, 51:49–56.
This article discusses the differences between biofeedback and relaxation training in treating headaches, as well as the efficacy of the techniques. There is discussion of the appropriateness of combining the techniques.

26. Schneider CJ: Cost effectiveness of biofeedback and behavioral medicine treatments: a review of the literature. *Biofeedback Self Regul* 1987, 12:71–91.

27. Hilgard ER, Hilgard JR, eds.: *Hypnosis in the Relief of Pain.* Los Altos, CA: William Kaufmann; 1975.

28. Hilgard ER: The alleviation of pain by hypnosis. *Pain* 1975, 1:213–231.

29. Barber J: Incorporating hypnosis in the management of chronic pain. In *Psychological Approaches to the Management of Pain.* Edited by Barber J, Adrian C. New York: Brunner/Mazel; 1982.

30. Orne MT: Hypnotic methods for managing pain. In *Advances in Pain Research and Therapy.* Edited by Bonica JJ, Albe-Fessard GG. New York: Raven Press; 1983.

31. Orne MT, Dinges DF: Hypnosis. In *Textbook of Pain.* Edited by Wall PD, Melzack R. New York: Churchill Livingstone; 1984.

32. Sachs L: Construing hypnosis as modifiable behavior. In *Psychology of Private Events.* Edited by Jacobs AB, Sachs LB. New York: Academic Press; 1971.

33. London P, Cooper LM, Engstrom DR: Increasing hypnotic susceptibility by brain wave feedback. *J Abnorm Psychol* 1974, 83:554–560.

34. Barber J, Gitelson J: Cancer pain: psychological management using hypnosis. *Cancer* 1980, 30:130–136.

35. Bassman SW: The effects of indirect hypnosis, relaxation and homework on the primary and secondary psychological symptoms of women with muscle-contraction headaches. Doctoral dissertation, University of Cincinnati, 1982.

36. Brownell KD: Behavioral medicine. *Ann Rev Behav Ther* 1984, 9:180–210.

37. Turk DC, Meichenbaum D, Genest M, eds.: *Pain and Behavioral Medicine: A Cognitive-Behavioral Perspective.* New York: The Guilford Press; 1983.

38. Lefebvre MF: Cognitive distortion and cognitive errors in depressed psychiatric and low back pain patients. *J Consult Clin Psychol* 1986, 54:222–226.

39. Smith TW, Follick MJ, Ahern DK, *et al.*: Cognitive distortion and disability in chronic low back pain. *Cog Ther Res* 1986, 10:201–210.

40. Ciccone DS, Grzesiak RC: Cognitive therapy: an overview of theory and practice. In *Persistent Pain: Psychosocial Assessment and Intervention.* Edited by Lynch N, Vasudevan S. Boston: Kluwer Academic Publishers; 1988.

41. • Nicholas MK, Wilson PH, Goyen J: Comparison of cognitive-behavioral group treatment and an alternative non-psychological treatment for chronic low back pain. *Pain* 1992, 48:339–347.

The authors examined the efficacy of cognitive-behavioral techniques, including relaxation training, in patients with chronic pain compared with physical therapy. The methods section contains useful information on specific coping strategies that can be taught to patients.

42. •• Manne SL, Zautra AJ: Coping with arthritis: Current status and critique. *Arthritis Rheum* 1992, 35(11):1273–1619.

This article presents studies examining coping strategies in rheumatoid arthritis patients and useful information on passive and active coping strategies.

43. Turk DC, Meichenbaum D: A cognitive-behavioral approach to pain management. In *Textbook of Pain*. Edited by Wall PD, Melzack R. New York: Churchill Livingstone; 1984.

44. Brown GK, Nicassio PM: The development of a questionnaire for the assessment of acute and passive coping strategies in chronic pain patients. *Pain* 1987, 31:53–65.

45. Parker J, McRae C, Smarr K, *et al.*: Coping strategies of rheumatoid arthritis patients. *J Rheumatol* 1988, 15:1376–1383.

46. Sternbach RA: Behaviour therapy. In *Textbook of Pain*. Edited by Wall PD, Melzack R. New York: Churchill Livingstone; 1984.

47. • Umlauf RL: Psychological interventions for chronic pain following spinal cord injury. *Clin J Pain* 1992, 8:111–118.

This article presents information on the use of peer groups and group therapy techniques in working with patients with chronic pain.

Physical Rehabilitation of the Pain Patient

SRIDHAR V. VASUDEVAN

One of the leading causes for visits to physicians and other health care providers is the symptom of pain. Pain, regardless of its source, produces physical impairments and limitation of function. The use of physical agents in the treatment of pain and other disorders dates back thousands of years. Their use, however, has been empirically based until the explosion of research in the advances of pain mechanisms over the past three decades, which has provided a rationale for the use of physical agents in the optimal rehabilitation of individuals with pain.

Rehabilitation is a treatment process that is goal-oriented and provided through an interdisciplinary team. It is directed at preventing and reversing impairments when possible, but always focuses on the goal of maximizing the individual's function. Rehabilitation not only involves medical management but addresses the physical, psychological, social, vocational, and recreational aspects of the individual and assists individuals and their families in the assumption of their usual roles.

PHYSICAL REHABILITATION

Physical rehabilitation focuses on the use of physical modalities such as heat, cold, and electricity, as well as hands-on manual techniques such as manipulation, mobilization, massage, and traction. It also involves the appropriate balance between rest to the injured part, prevention of reinjury through appropriate orthotic devices (braces and splints), and specific exercise programs.

Despite the long history of the availability and use of physical rehabilitation approaches, traditional medicine in western societies has generally deemphasized physical approaches and focused on pharmacologic and surgical interventions for pain problems. However, many Third World countries have relied on physical approaches for the management of pain problems because they are easily available, inexpensive, noninvasive, associated with less morbidity, and foster independent functioning.

The treatment of pain-producing conditions can be traditionally considered under four major approaches: surgical, pharmacologic, psychological, and physical. With the advance in technology, surgical intervention has vastly improved, as well as the ability to be more precise in the diagnosis of pain-producing conditions. With the advent of the neurochemical basis of pain, inflammation, and neural modulation, pharmacologic approaches have become the primary approach in managing patients with symptoms of pain. The past two decades have seen great emphasis on the psychological dimensions of pain and the need to incorporate psychological principles in the treatment of patients not only with chronic and persistent pain but also with acute pain.

It is, however, important for the primary-care physician, as well as the specialist who cares for individuals

with pain, to recognize the rationale for the physical approaches and to incorporate them in the optimal rehabilitation of individuals who present with pain. It should also be emphasized that rehabilitation is a "process" that requires active participation of patients (and their families) working toward specific goals, as well as the integrated and coordinated functioning of several professionals working as a team. The application of the physical methods described in this chapter should not be used in isolation but in conjunction with medical and psychological treatment focusing on the appropriate treatment of pathologic conditions, prevention and correction of physical impairments, and eventual improvement in function. Unlike the traditional concept in which rehabilitation was perceived as the treatment process after preventive and acute management, rehabilitation should be integrated into the overall management of any patient with pain-related dysfunction and disability.

All physicians, whether in primary care or medical or surgical specialties, should become knowledgeable regarding the availability of physical methods for controlling pain and the rationale behind the use of these approaches. Physical rehabilitation approaches should become an integral part of aggressive, nonsurgical conservative treatment in patients with acute as well as chronic pain from musculoskeletal and neurologic disorders [1••].

The physical methods of pain control can be administered in a variety of settings: physician's office, free-standing pain clinic, hospital setting, pain rehabilitation center, or at home. Even when the underlying disease process may not be "curable," physical methods provide a way to decrease symptoms, improve function, and decrease disability. The value of incorporating aggressive rehabilitation techniques to improve function has been recently highlighted and emphasized [2••,3].

Physical Modalities

Physical modalities include superficial heat, (thermotherapy), deep heat (diathermy), cold (cryotherapy), and electrical current (electrotherapy). These have been beneficial for pain relief even when the underlying disorders were untreatable [1••]. In certain acute conditions, temperature modalities assist in early healing, prevent further inflammation, and reduce pain by their direct action on nerves [4–7].

THERAPEUTIC HEAT

Heat has been used extensively as an effective agent in relieving pain. Superficial heat can be provided by means of hot packs, hot water bottles, hot moist compresses, electric heating pads, or chemical and gel packs. It can also be provided through immersion in water (hydrotherapy) via whirlpool, Hubbard tank, heated pool, and so forth. All these modalities convey heat by the physical properties of conduction or convection. Superficial heat elevates the temperature of the tissues and provides the greatest effect at 0.5 cm from the surface of the skin.

Diathermy (deep heat) is a method by which some form of energy is converted into heat through sophisticated devices. Short-wave diathermy uses high-frequency electrical current (Fig. 10-1). Microwave diathermy uses electromagnetic radiation. Ultrasound was introduced for medical use in the United States in the late 1940s. In this process, acoustic vibration of high frequency is converted into heat. These deep-heating modalities increase the temperature at depths of 3 to 5 cm. Diathermy, especially in the form of ultrasound, is preferred in the treatment of many painful disorders, especially those arising from soft tissues, tendons, and ligaments, because they can penetrate deep structures without increasing temperature to the overlying skin [8].

The physiologic effects of heat include pain relief, increase in extensibility of collagen tissues, reduction of muscle spasm, as well as other effects. One of the mechanisms by which pain may be relieved is by relaxation of the muscle, which may be in spasm. The exact mechanism of muscle relaxation is still uncertain. It may be that there is a selective decrease in the excitation of nociceptive nerve endings that may secondarily reduce muscle tone. Increased muscle temperature has been shown to decrease spindle sensitivity [5]. Since heating of the skin can relax the underlying muscle [9], superficial heating devices are indicated when the pain is due to muscle spasm.

Heat has been shown to increase blood flow to the underlying muscles [5,7]. This mechanism of increased blood flow by heat seems to play a role in producing pain relief in muscle.

Heat also increases the extensibility of collagen tissues. Thus, heat is an important adjunct in the stretching of soft tissues such as muscles and tendons as well as a preventer of muscle injury when doing stretching and strengthening exercises [7]. Deep-heating modalities, such as ultrasound, are very useful in the treatment of tight, periarticular tissues such as those seen in adhesive capsulitis (frozen shoulder). Tight hamstrings, heelcords, or postsurgical scarring can be softened with the use of deep heat followed by stretching exercises. The reduction of joint stiffness is the result of the effect of deep heat on collagen tissue and muscle spasm. Because of the direct physiologic effects of heat, including alteration of pain threshold and increased extensibility of collagen, thermal agents are ideally suited for use during the initial phase of treatment in preparation for many active exercises and manual procedures.

Superficial heating modalities can be provided through devices such as the hydrocollator pack, which uses conductive heating, hydrotherapy, such as whirlpools that use convective heating, and through the use of infrared lamps (sun lamps), which provide radiant heating.

The hydrocollator pack is one example of the superficial heating modality. It is frequently used in most physical therapy departments and can also be used at home by the patient. The pack is applied to the painful area and left to drip dry for 20 minutes under layers of terry cloth towel. The proper technique to provide the appropriate regulated heat dosage is to vary the thickness of the terry cloth layers and to layer them on top of the painful area rather than have the person lay on the terry cloth layer (hydrocollator pack) [5,7].

The use of paraffin wax is another approach to the provision of superficial heat to selected parts. Paraffin wax is kept in a thermostatically controlled container and is useful for specific body parts such as the hands, fingers, or feet. The common technique is to provide a thick coating of paraffin which is solidified by dipping the affected portion of the body repeatedly into the paraffin wax. The paraffin-soaked area is then wrapped appropriately for 20 minutes. Note that not all parts of the body can be dipped in paraffin wax [1].

Fluidotherapy is a recent addition to the types of superficial heating devices. The device consists of a bed of finely divided solid or ground cellulose particles. By changing the air flow temperature blown through these particles, the cellulose can be thermostatically controlled to provide the expected physiologic response. Usually,

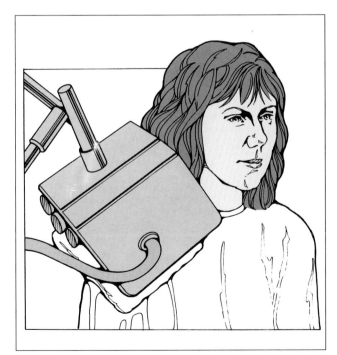

Figure 10-1 Short-wave diathermy application with induction coil (drum applicator). (*Adapted from* Lehmann and DeLateur [44]; with permission.)

this technique is applied for 20 to 30 minutes and is useful for body parts such as the hands and wrist. A major advantage of fluidotherapy is prevention of edema by avoidance of the dependency position that is assumed with many hydrotherapy techniques.

Hydrotherapy is the most common type of heating modality used. It can be provided in the form of a heated whirlpool, Hubbard tank, walking tank, or a heated swimming pool. Thus, a single part of the body, such as a lower or an upper extremity, can be submerged in a whirlpool bath, or the entire body can be submerged in a Hubbard tank or heated swimming pool. A major advantage of hydrotherapy is the buoyancy, which minimizes the stress to the joints during exercises. Swimming pools and walking tanks also allow the performance of non–weight-bearing exercises for the benefit of lower extremities and eliminate the gravitational stressors on the lower extremities and spine.

Thus, superficial heating modalities frequently serve as techniques for preparation before exercise, whether it be stretching or strengthening, provide pain relief and muscle relaxation, and can be taught to the patient to be used at home without the need to depend on personnel or expensive equipment.

The deep-heating modalities are useful when the intention is to treat muscles and deeper structures such as joints and ligaments. Microwave and shortwave diathermy are contraindicated in the presence of metal because they selectively absorb the heat and can produce damage to these tissues surrounding the metal. Microwave diathermy also selectively heats tissues with high water content such as muscles and is contraindicated over joints with effusion or cavities with fluids. Both shortwave and microwave diathermy are contraindicated in the presence of pacemakers [5,7,8].

Ultrasound is the method of choice when deep-heating modalities are considered. In addition to the temperature effects, ultrasound produces several nonthermal effects as well. One of these effects is increasing the extensibility of collagen tissue, which makes it specifically useful in treating trigger points, tight tendons, and capsular structures. Ultrasound can also be provided under water. Another major advantage is that ultrasound can be judiciously used in the presence of metal implants. Diathermy is generally contraindicated over areas of active malignancy [5,7,8]. Where pain is directly related to cancer, superficial heat should be used as a method of pain relief if a heating modality is desired.

COLD THERAPY

Cold therapy includes the use of ice packs, commercially prepared chemical gel packs, and cold baths. Ice massage is a specific technique that uses cold application. Use of vapocoolant spray is another technique of cold therapy.

The effectiveness of cold treatment, like that of heating modalities, can probably be explained by the gate control theory of pain, which was proposed by Melzack and Wall [10]. Recent studies have indicated that pain relief from cold and heat modalities can also occur through modulation by neurotransmitters [11].

Cold packs are applied usually for 15 minutes, and they are helpful because they conform to body contours and can produce comfortable and safe pain relief. They should be adequately wrapped with a layer of towel or other cloth to prevent skin irritation. Cold therapy can produce a longer effect of pain relief than can heat, provided the muscle is actually cooled [8]. Cold therapy is contraindicated for any medical condition in which vasoconstriction increases symptoms, such as certain connective tissue diseases, Raynaud's syndrome, and so forth [5]. In the specific technique of ice massage, the skin is rubbed with a block of ice (Fig. 10-2). This technique is based on the counterirritant theory, which has three stages: first, the patient experiences a coolness lasting 1 to 2 minutes, then a burning sensation lasting another 1 to 2 minutes, and finally numbness [8]. Patients have to go through all three phases prior to assessing the results. Ice massage is particularly useful in treating small areas such as trigger points and tendons and bursae, and can precede massage and stretching programs.

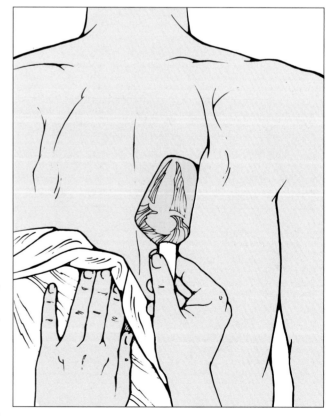

Figure 10-2 Use of ice stick in ice massage. (*Adapted from* Condon [45]; with permission.)

The use of ethylchloride and fluorimethane, both vapocoolant sprays, has been popularized in the treatment of myofascial trigger points. While the muscle is kept at a passive stretch, the trigger point and the referral zone are sprayed in unidirectional parallel sweeps [12].

Cold is the treatment of choice in acute injuries because of its effect of decreasing the inflammatory response and subsequent swelling. Cold reduces the metabolism of underlying tissues, reduces nerve conduction velocity, and, by its direct effect on muscle spindle activity, reduces resultant muscle spasm [8].

Cold is the treatment of choice in the first 24 to 72 hours after an acute injury. Severe adverse effects of cold application are rare. Some patients have a hypersensitivity syndrome to cold caused by a reaction to the histamine-like substances that may be released [5].

To summarize, both heat and cold modalities help in decreasing pain through various physiologic mechanisms. Temperature modalities are an easily available, nonpharmacologic approach to the treatment of patients with pain. In selecting a modality, one should consider one that could be transferred to a home program. Superficial heating and some of the cold modalities lend themselves to such carryover.

MANUAL THERAPY

Manual therapy includes techniques that involve a "hands-on" approach to the patient in handling tissues. These techniques include massage, mobilization, and manipulation.

Common techniques of massage include stroking, friction, and kneading [13]. Therapeutic massage involves handling of tissues by trained personnel to achieve a specific purpose. Stroking massage (Fig. 10-3) is gently handling the superficial tissues in a direction from periphery toward the center and is useful in decreasing edema and swelling.

Friction and kneading massage involve handling of tissues vigorously to break down intramuscular adhesions and prepare muscles and soft tissues for stretching [13,14]. Classic massage includes stroking and friction massage and these techniques are useful in reducing edema, stiffness, and pain, as well as in preparing the muscles for appropriate stretching and strengthening exercises [14].

Mobilization includes techniques in which a trained physical or occupational therapist uses hands and fingers to handle tissues, including muscles and fascia. Myofacial release is a method of soft-tissue mobilization that focus-

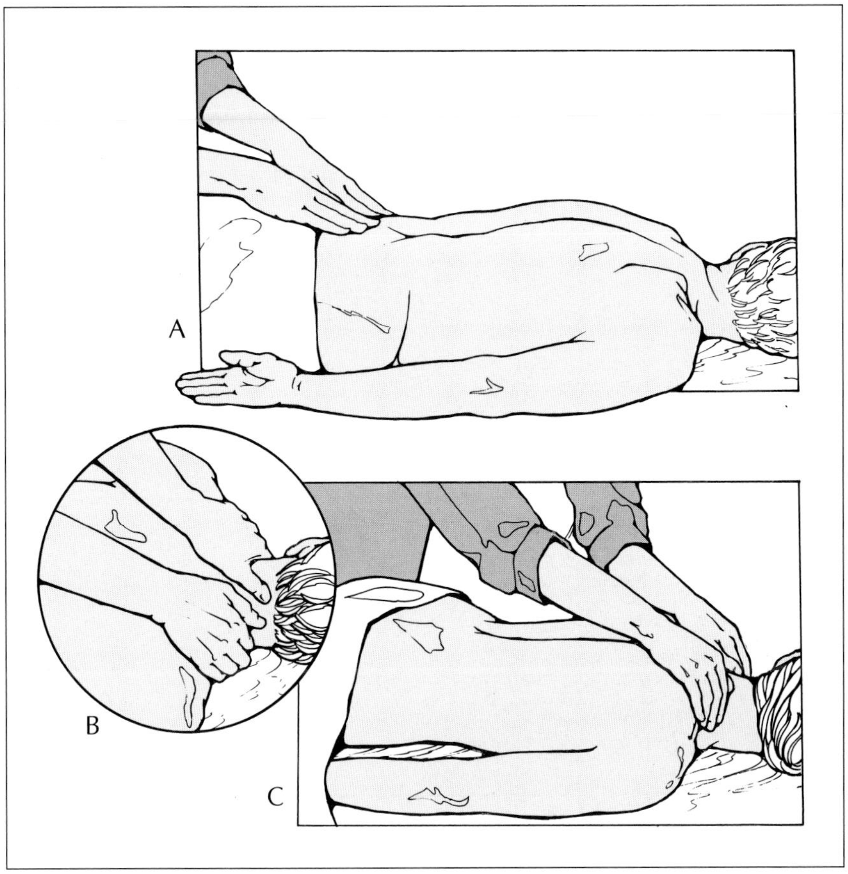

Figure 10-3 Deep palmar stroking. (A) The fingers of both hands start the deep stroke at the lower border of the sacrum; the thumbs are crossed for reinforcement and the hands stroke upward on each side of the spinous processes with firm pressure. (B) The hands separate at the neck and stroke over the top of the shoulder, as the thumbs stroke up to the first cervical vertebra on both sides of the spinous processes. (C) The hands then stroke back, drawing the muscles back also, until the fingertips are at the top of the shoulder. (*Adapted from* Wood and Becker [46]; with permission.)

es on the fascial component of musculoskeletal pain and dysfunction. Fascia is defined as a "three dimensional web of connective tissue surrounding and infusing every structure of our body, all the way down to the cellular level" [15]. Normally, fascia is slightly mobile, but it may shorten and tighten as a result of inflammation or poor posture secondary to pain. These fascial restrictions may generate enormous pressure on underlying structures. Fascia are richly innervated but poorly vascularized, leading to pain and poor healing [16].

Myofascial release techniques involve stretching along the lines of fibers of the restricted muscle until resistance before the stretch is felt. This stretch is held in position until the soft tissue is felt to relax or "release" [17].

Manipulation is a skilled passive movement to a spinal segment either within or beyond its active range of motion [18]. Various medical professionals including osteopaths, chiropractors, medical doctors, as well as physical and occupational therapists, use spinal manipulation, although these professionals differ in their philosophies and goals. One of the possible mechanisms of manipulative therapy is the release of entrapped tissue, such as a meniscoid impacted between facet joints—thought to cause the "acute locked back" [19]. However, manipulative therapy by clinicians can be overused and create a patient dependency. Thus, whenever possible, some self-mobilization techniques should be taught to patients [20].

TRACTION

Traction is also a physical modality in which tissues are mechanically distracted. Traction can be done either manually or through the use of equipment (Fig. 10-4). Generally, the rationale for traction includes the distraction of facet joints and mechanical distraction of vertebral bodies [13]. Overhead intermittent cervical traction, with weights of 10 to 25 pounds, can be useful in people who have cervical radiculopathy through the widening of the intervertebral foramena, especially when used in flexion. Lower weights are used for home programs on a continuous basis and can help in stretching soft tissues as well as musculature (Fig. 10-5). Traction for lumbar disc diseases is generally not very practical, as the amount of force required is very difficult to apply and tolerate by most individuals [13].

ELECTRICAL STIMULATION

The earliest historical note of the use of electricity is from the time of Caeser when patients used "torpedo" fish to treat gout and headaches. Today, transcutaneous electrical nerve stimulation (TENS) is often used for pain management [21–23].

Transcutaneous electrical nerve stimulation involves the production and transmission of electrical energy from the surface of the skin to the nervous system [10]. The rationale for the use is based on the fact that there is a mechanism of gating in the dorsal horn of the spinal

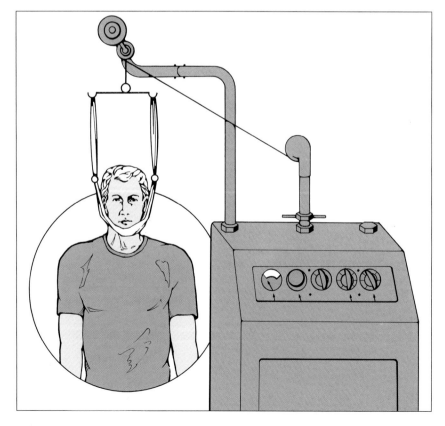

Figure 10-4 Hydraulic pressure device with automatic feedback compensation for patient movement and cable transmission. (*Adapted from* Rogoff [14]; with permission.)

cord where the small-diameter, unmyelinated C fiber's activity can be modulated by the larger-diameter myelinated A fiber's activity, thus reducing pain. The large-diameter A fibers mediate sensations of light touch and pressure. Painful sensory input is thus modulated and at times suppressed at the "gate" in the dorsal horn of the spinal cord. Usually, high-frequency, low-intensity stimulation seems to be involved through the gate control mechanism [10,11,22,23].

Research has indicated that high-intensity, low-frequency stimulation also produces pain relief, the effect of which can be reversed with naloxone, an opiate antagonist [24]. It has been postulated that there is an endogenously produced opioid-like substance acting as a mediator of

Figure 10-5 Cervical traction at home. (*Adapted from* Rogoff [14]; with permission.)

pain relief in TENS therapy. Subsequent studies identified two related pentapeptides, enkephalin and endorphin, as having potent opioid agonist activity [25]. The commonly used form of TENS (conventional TENS) based on the gate theory uses frequencies of 80 to 100 Hz. On the other hand, acupuncture-like, low-frequency, high-intensity TENS uses rates of less than 4 Hz.

The efficacy of TENS has been studied and documented, especially in cases of acute pain. In one study involving 100 patients suffering from sprains, lacerations, fractures, hematomas, and contusions, there was a statistically significant difference in pain relief found between the placebo and functioning TENS groups [26]. Subsequent randomized trials of TENS for low back pain have suggested that much of the benefit may be a result of the placebo effect [27]. The most recent randomized trial that was blinded and that used multiple electrical stimulation parameters found no significant benefit between placebo and TENS for the relief of low back pain [28] (Table 10-1). TENS has been shown to be successful in postoperative pain control [23,29].

In patients with chronic pain, TENS has been shown to be effective in treating certain conditions such as phantom pain and reflex sympathetic dystrophy syndrome [1••]. Despite the controversy, TENS provides a valuable role in the management of pain. A sound physiologic rationale exists for its use and it is a noninvasive technique that can be taught to the patient, thus increasing independence. Education about different settings, electrode placement, and proper application must be provided to patients. When used as part of a broader approach to pain management, TENS has gained acceptance in a selected group of patients with acute and chronic pain.

THERAPEUTIC EXERCISES

The natural reaction for the individual who has pain is to restrict that body part. Physicians also frequently prescribe relative rest to the body or complete bed rest. Pain itself can inhibit normal functioning of the body part, and this disuse can result in further decline in function secondary to deconditioning [2,3]. Strict bed rest can result in an up to 20% loss in strength [30].

Patients with back pain from muscular strain may be treated successfully with strict bed rest. However, 2 weeks of bed rest may result in significant weakness, and returning an individual to heavy manual labor may predispose the patient to additional injury because of the weakened state. Studies comparing recommendations of 2 days or 7 days of bed rest have indicated that functional recovery is better for those with briefer bed rest; these individuals returned to work 45% more quickly than did those who rested for 1 week [31]. Bed rest also leads to rapid muscle atrophy, cardiopulmonary deconditioning, bone mineral loss, and the risk for thromboembolism, even with bed rest of only 1 week. Deyo and coworkers [31] provide some guidelines for the use of bed rest in discussing the nonsurgical care of low back pain. They recommend that in the absence of neurologic deficits, prolonged bed rest of even 1 to 2 weeks is inadvisable. Brief bed rest for 2 to 3 days may provide symptomatic relief for some patients. Return to usual activities must be individualized [31].

Exercises are probably the most commonly applied modality in physical medicine [4,6,32]. In the rehabilitation of patients with pain, the exercise program is focused on improving the patient's physical and functional capacity, as well as quality of life, and not just on relieving pain.

Many factors are involved in the overall decrease in activity levels of patients with pain. Fear that movement will cause more damage to tissues leads to avoidance of "anticipatory pain" [32]. There is also belief by the patient,

sometimes supplemented by well-meaning health care professionals, that rest will promote the healing process, even for prolonged periods. Patients need to be informed that medically supervised and prescribed programs "will not harm them" [33]. Inactivity can lead to joint stiffness, decrease in muscle strength, and atrophy. To break the cycle of pain–stiffness–weakness–pain, a graded exercise program must be incorporated. Therapeutic exercises include range-of-motion, stretching, strengthening, general conditioning, and relaxation exercises.

Range-of-motion exercises are those that are done to maintain and increase the motion of joints and flexibility of muscles. These exercises can be done passively by the physical therapists, actively by the patient, or through a combination of active-assisted exercises in which the patient's range of motion is supplemented by the therapist's passive increase in mobility. Range-of-motion exercises increase and maintain elasticity of connective

TABLE 10-1
OUTCOMES OF THERAPY WITH TENS OR SHAM TENS (PLACEBO) AT 4-WEEK FOLLOW-UP*†

MEASURE	SHAM TENS (N = 60)	TRUE TENS (N = 65)	DIFFERENCE‡
Functional status§			
Overall modified SIP score	6.2	5.7	-0.5 (-2.2, 1.3)
Physical-dimension score	3.2	3.2	0.02 (-1.1, 1.1)
Psychosocial-dimension score	5.7	5.9	0.2 (-2.3, 2.6)
Self-rated activity level	1.7	1.7	0.01 (-0.19, 0.21)
Pain			
Self-rated improvement¶	2.9	2.9	-0.01 (0.38, 0.35)
Visual-analogue pain scale (mm)	24.0	21.7	-2.3 (-9.6, 4.9)
Visual-analogue improvement scale (mm)	41.8	47.0	5.2 (-6.6, 16.9)
Frequency of pain**	3.0	2.9	-0.1 (-0.5, 0.3)
Physical measures			
Finger-to-floor distance (cm)	8.7	8.7	0.04 (-2.5, 2.6)
Schober test (cm)	4.1	4.2	0.13 (-0.24, 0.50)
Straight-leg raising (degrees)	84	84	0.5 (-2.2, 3.2)
Use of services			
Days in hospital	0	0	0
Visits to other providers (mean no.)	0.30	0.22	-0.08 (-0.033, 0.25)
Wish to continue TENS therapy (%)	56	68	12 (-4.9, 28.9)

*From Deyo and coworkers [28]; with permission.
†Values shown are adjusted means after control for base-line values and for the main effect of exercise. None of the differences were statistically significant (P>0.3 by analysis of covariance in all cases).
‡Difference is the score with true TENS minus the score with sham TENS. Values in parentheses are 95% CI.
§SIP denotes Sickness Impact Profile. Scores range from 0 to 100, with higher scores indicating worse function. The physical-dimension and psychosocial-dimension scales are major subscales of the modified SIP, scored similarly. The self-rated activity level is scored 1 (more active than baseline), 2 (equally active), or 3 (less active).
¶Scored on a six-point scale: 1 = pain entirely gone, 4 = no change, 6 = much worse.
**Scored on a five-point scale: 1 = none, 2 = occasionally, 3 = about half the time, 4 = more than half the time, 5 = all the time.
TENS—transcutaneous electrical nerve stimulation.

tissue around joints. Stretching exercises are important, especially in muscles that cross two joints. The hamstring muscles, the gastrosoleus group of muscles, hip flexors, pectoral muscles, and paraspinal muscles are examples of muscles that frequently lapse into a shortened position, thus leading to poor posture. Stretching exercises improve body mechanics and posture. Stretching should be done slowly and steadily and the stretch should be sustained (Fig. 10-6). Jerking or bouncy ballistic movement may cause injury to tissues and may be counterproductive. Pretreatment with appropriate temperature modalities such as heat or ice may reduce the pain and facilitate range-of-motion exercises. The use of vapocoolant spray such as flourimethane can be beneficial in the stretch-and-spray technique in inactivating myofascial trigger points [1,7,12]. Range-of-motion and stretching exercises should be taught to patients and can be carried over to the home without the need for equipment; they can also be performed throughout the day.

Strengthening exercises, of which there are different types, are those done against resistance. In chronic pain, static strengthening (isometric) exercises are usually not beneficial. However, for specific muscle groups such as quadriceps and gluteal muscles, isometric strengthening can be taught to the patient and incorporated into a daily routine. Isotonic exercises include active movement as well as movement against resis-

tance. Isotonic exercises with free weights or circuit-training equipment can be advantageous in a strengthening program for patients with pain. A gradual increase in weights and repetitions provide the best results. Strengthening exercises are used to strengthen specific weak muscles and these exercises can be carried over to a home program [6].

Isokinetic exercises are done at a constant specific speed. Maximal torque can be produced with these exercises against a rate-limiting device. Isokinetic strengthening of erector spinal muscles of the back has been shown to be beneficial in decreasing chronic low back pain [34]. General conditioning exercises involve total body use and improve the physical capability of the individual. In theory, exercises raise endorphin levels and increase pain thresholds. Endurance can be improved through aerobic training followed by protocols to improve whole body conditioning and agility [35].

Mobility is dependent on the degree of flexibility of the muscles. Improved flexibility of the muscle and the surrounding soft tissue allows normal ranges of motion of the joints involved. Thus, flexibility, range-of-motion, and stretching exercises are an important and integral part of strengthening exercises [3].

A well-rounded exercise program provides not only appropriate flexibility exercises but a general conditioning program to increase cardiovascular endurance as well. Focus should also be on improving coordination

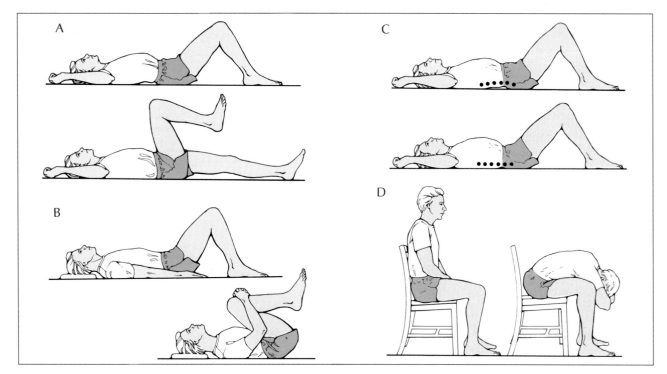

Figure 10-6 (A–D) Stretching exercises for low back pain.

through constant repetition of specific motor activity and provision of sensory cues to enhance motor performance.

In regard to specific therapeutic exercises, controversy persists about the optimal exercise regimen, especially for individuals with low back pain. Most authors agree about the benefits of aerobic fitness exercises, stretching exercises, and vigorous strengthening exercises. Randomized clinical trials suggest the efficacy of stretching exercises and vigorous extension exercises in the treatment of chronic low back pain [28,35]. Clinical trials of isometric flexion exercises have produced contradictory results, but one study has suggested that they are ineffective in patients with acute back problems [36]. Although randomized controlled trials are still required, several studies have suggested the benefits of a combined program of general endurance training, stretching, and strengthening of the back extensor, abdominal, and lower-extremity muscles [37,38].

Aerobic exercises increase cardiopulmonary capacity and fitness. These exercises are rhythmic, repetitive, dynamic activities such as running, cycling, and swimming, that involve large muscle groups. Patients with pain, especially those with chronic pain, are very deconditioned and require a program of aerobic fitness to be included in addition to muscle-strengthening and endurance-building exercise programs. The psychological benefits of aerobic exercises also play a significant role in patients with pain. Appropriate warm-up exercise and cool-down programming offers the greatest long-lasting relief from low back pain [30]. Aerobic exercise should be part of the overall fitness program in individuals with pain, especially those with chronic pain, because it can be easily incorporated into daily activities, is inexpensive, can be done independently, and can be graded with an increase in duration and intensity. Individuals who are fit seem to have less pain during activities of daily living and a greater endurance for activities [39,40].

In chronic pain, use of relaxation techniques is beneficial. These exercises are designed to relax the muscle, reduce autonomic activity, and decrease anxiety. Examples of relaxation techniques are imagery, progressive muscle relaxation, and controlled breathing. Applied relaxation, which is a coping skill approach, has been shown to be effective in decreasing chronic pain [41].

Compliance with exercise programs sometimes can be difficult, especially in patients with pain. Patients need to be educated in regard to the difference between "hurt" and "harm." Two techniques have been described that improve compliance with physical conditioning and exercise programs in patients with chronic pain [1,42,43]. An exercise "quota system" provides an achievable increase in both exercises and expectancy while decreasing worry and concern regarding overexercising. The effectiveness of exercise quota systems is related to applying reinforcement of quota achievement [42]. Goals are set for all forms of exercise, with the initial goal being lower than what the patient can perform. Early success is thus provided and the patient records daily status in order to see progress; graphs of increasing quotas are provided as signs of achievement.

Another technique is that of "group exercise" programs. Such group exercises can include and incorporate exercises for flexibility, coordination, and general conditioning, as well as strengthening and endurance building. The peer pressure, competition, and mutual support improve each individual's performance. Some of the more advanced patients can be role models for new patients and provide needed encouragement.

CONCLUSIONS

This chapter has focused on some of the physical rehabilitation approaches for patients with pain. Pain, in the normal course of events, signals the need for attention to a pathologic condition that needs to be diagnosed and appropriately treated. However, there is a significant difference between acute pain, which is usually self-limited and resolves after healing occurs, and chronic pain, in which the pain does not seem to serve a useful biologic function and can lead to significant emotional, physical, vocational, economic, and social alterations. Those programs that focus on rehabilitation approaches that use specific treatment goals and objectives that are used in chronic pain programs have been shown to be cost effective [43••].

The incorporation of physical rehabilitation approaches in a pain management program is crucial for any patient with pain. This incorporation specifically becomes important and needs emphasis in individuals who have persistent and chronic pain. Both the primary-care physician and the specialist should be knowledgeable about the rationale, physiology, and appropriate use of physical agents in pain control. In this regard, physical methods of pain control should be considered along with the appropriate pharmacologic, surgical, anesthesiologic, and psychological approaches for the management of pain.

REFERENCES AND RECOMMENDED READING

Papers of interest, published recently, have been highlighted as:
• Of special interest
•• Of outstanding interest

1.•• Vasudevan SV, Hegmann K, Moore A, *et al.*: Physical methods of pain management. In *Practical Management of Pain*. 2nd ed. Edited by Raj PP. Chicago: Yearbook Medical Publishers; 1992:669–679.

Good grounding in physical methods for pain control and their rationale. Stresses the integration of physical rehabilitation into aggressive, nonsurgical conservative treatment of acute pain and of chronic pain from musculoskeletal and neurologic disorders.

2.•• King JC, Dumitru D, Walsh NE: Rehabilitation of the pain patient: a U.S. perspective. *Pain Digest* 1992, 2:106–126.

Excellent review of some specific principles of physical rehabilitation for individuals with acute and chronic pain.

3. Mayer TG, Gatchel RJ, eds.: *Functional Restoration for Spinal Disorders; The Sports Medicine Approach*. Philadelphia: Lea & Febiger; 1988.

4. Kottke FJ, Lehmann JF, eds.: *Krusen's Handbook of Physical Medicine and Rehabilitation*. 4th ed. Philadelphia: WB Saunders; 1990.

5. Lehmann JF, deLateur BJ: Ultrasound, shortwave, microwave, superficial heat and cold in the treatment of pain. In *Textbook of Pain*. Edited by Wall PD, Melzack R. Edinburgh: Churchill Livingstone; 1984:717–774.

6. deLateur BJ, Lehmann JF: Strengthening exercise. In *Principles of Physical Medicine and Rehabilitation in Musculoskeletal Diseases*. Edited by Leek JC, Gershwin ME, Fowler WM. Orlando: Grune Stratton; 1986:25–60.

7. Lehmann JF, deLateur BJ: Diathermy, superficial heat and cold therapy. In *Handbook of Physical Medicine and Rehabilitation*. 3rd ed. Edited by Kottke FJ, Stillwell G, Lehmann JF. Philadelphia: WB Saunders; 1982:275–350.

8. Michlovitz S: *Thermal Agents in Rehabilitation*. Philadelphia: FA Davis; 1986.

9. Lehmann JF, ed.: *Therapeutic Heat and Cold*. 3rd ed. Baltimore: Williams and Wilkins; 1982.

10. Melzack R, Wall PD: Pain mechanisms: a new theory. *Science* 1965, 150:971–979.

11. Fields HL, Basbaum AL: Brain stem control of spinal pain—transmission neurons. *Ann Rev Physiol* 1978, 40:217–248.

12. Travell JG, Simons DG, eds.: *Myofascial Pain and Dysfunction—The Trigger Point Manual*. Baltimore: Williams & Wilkins; 1983.

13. Bonica JJ, ed.: *The Management of Pain*. 2nd ed, vol. 2. Philadelphia: Lea & Febiger; 1990.

14. Rogoff JB, ed.: *Manipulation, Traction and Massage*. Baltimore: Williams & Wilkins; 1980.

15. Barnes, JF: Myofascial release: questions, concepts and future. In *Progress Report No. 4*. American Physical Therapy Association, April 1988.

16. Calliet R: *Soft Tissue Pain and Disability*. Philadelphia: FA Davis; 1977.

17. Manheim CJ, Lavett DK, eds.: *The Myofascial Release Manual* Thorofare, New Jersey: Slack Inc.; 1989.

18. Maigne R: The concept of painless and opposite motion in spinal manipulation. *Ann J Phys Med* 1987, 44:55–69.

19. Bogduk N, Jull G: The theoretical etiology of acute locked back: a basis for manipulative therapy. *Man Med* 1985, 1:78–82.

20. McKenzie RA: A perspective on manipulative therapy. *Physiotherapy* 1975, 8:440–444.

21. Gersh MR, Wolf SL: Applications of transcutaneous electrical nerve stimulation in the management of patients with pain. *Phys Ther* 1985, 65:314–321.

22. Soric R, Devlin M: Transcutaneous electrical nerve stimulation: practical aspects and applications. *Postgrad Med* 1985, 78:101–107.

23. Manheimer JS: TENS: uses and effectiveness. In *Pain*. Edited by Michel TH. New York: Churchill Livingstone; 1985:73–121.

24. SJolund BH, Eriksson MB: The influence of naloxone on analgesia produced by peripheral conditioning stimulation. *Brain Res* 1979, 173:295–301.

25. Hughes GS, Lichstein PR: Response of plasma beta-endorphins to TENS in healthy subjects. *Phys Ther* 1984, 64:1062–1066.

26. Ordog GJ: TENS vs oral analgesic: a randomized double blind controlled study in acute traumatic pain. *J Emerg Med* 1987, 5:6–10.

27. Lehmann TR, Russell DW, Spratt KF, *et al.*: Efficacy of electroacupuncture and TENS in the rehabilitation of chronic low back pain patients. *Pain* 1986, 26:277–290.

28. Deyo RA, Walsh N, Martin D, *et al.*: A controlled trial of transcutaneous electrical nerve stimulation and exercise for low back pain. *N Engl J Med* 1990, 322:1627–1634.

29. Solomon FA, Viernstein MC: Reduction of postoperative pain and narcotic use by TENS. *Surgery* 1980, 87:142–146.

30. Muller EA: Influence of training and inactivity on muscle strength. *Arch Phys Med Rehabil* 1970, 51:449–463.

31. Deyo RA, Diehl AK, Rosenthal M: How many days of bed rest for acute low back pain: a randomized clinical trial. *N Engl J Med* 1986, 315:1064–1070.

32. Soric R, Devlin M: Role of physical medicine. In *Handbook of Chronic Pain Management*. Edited by Tollison CD. Baltimore: Williams & Wilkins; 1989:147–162.

33. Tollison CD, ed.: *Handbook of Chronic Pain Management*. Baltimore: Williams & Wilkins; 1989.

34. Timm K: Case studies: use of cybex trunk extension, flexion unit in the rehabilitation of back patients. *J Sports Orthop Ther* 1987, 8:578–581.

35. Nachemson AL: Advances in low back pain. *Clin Orthop* 1985, 200:266–278.

36. Gilbert JR, Taylor DW, Hildebrand A, *et al.*: Clinical trial of common treatments for low back pain in family practice. *Br Med J* 1985, 291:791–794.

37. Hazard RG, Fenwick GW, Kalisch SM, *et al.*: Functional restoration with behavioral support: a one year prospective study of patients with chronic low back pain. *Spine* 1989, 14:157–161.

38. Mayer TG, Gatchel RJ, Mayer H, *et al.*: A prospective two year study of functional restoration in industrial low back injury: an objective assessment procedure. *JAMA* 1987, 258:1763–1767.

39. Jackson C, Brown M: Analysis of current approaches and a practical guide to prescription exercise. *Clin Orthop* 1983, 179:46–53.

40. Jackson C, Brown M: Is there a role for exercise in the treatment of patients with low back pain? *Clin Orthop* 1983, 179:39–43.

41. Linton SJ, Gotestam KG: A controlled study of the effects of applied relaxation plus operant procedures in regulation of chronic pain. *Br J Chron Pract* 1983, 23:291–299.

42. Dolce JJ, Crocker MF, Molettoire C, *et al.*: Exercise quotas, anticipatory concern and self efficacy expectations in chronic pain: a preliminary report. *Pain* 1986, 24:365–372.

43.•• Vasudevan SV: Rehabilitation of the patient with chronic pain—Is it cost effective? *Pain Digest* 1992, 2:99–101.

A review of pain rehabilitation programs and their effectiveness, calling for cost-effective studies.

44. Lehmann JF, DeLateur BJ: Diathermy and superficial heat and cold therapy. In *Krusen's Handbook of Physical Medicine and Rehabilitation*. 3rd ed. Edited by Rohke FJ, Stillwell GK, Lehmann JF. Philadelphia: WB Saunders; 1982:275–350.

45. Condon RH: Conservative treatment: Part II. Modalities in the treatment of acute and chronic low back pain. In *Low Back Pain*. Edited by Finneson BE. Philadelphia: J.B. Lippincott; 1980:204–210.

46. Wood EC, Becker PD, eds.: *Bernard's Massage*. 3rd ed. Philadelphia: WB Saunders; 1981:82.

CHAPTER 11

Characteristics, Pathogenesis, and Management of Myofascial Pain Syndrome

AARON CALODNEY, JERRY SCHWARZBACH, AND TOM LORREN

The myofascial pain syndromes (MPS) are common causes of pain in patients seen in clinical practices. A study by Snootsky and coworkers [1] found that nearly one third of those patients who came to a general internal medicine practice with a chief complaint of pain met the criteria for having MPS. Despite their frequency, the MPS are likely the largest group of unrecognized, undertreated, and misunderstood medical problems in clinical medicine [2•].

CHARACTERISTICS

Myofascial pain syndrome is a regional musculoskeletal pain disorder characterized by tender trigger points in taut bands of muscle that produce pain in a characteristic reference zone [3,4]. Other clinical characteristics of MPS include tender trigger points in muscles, other associated symptoms, and the presence of contributing factors. A trigger point is a hyperirritable spot, usually within a taut band of skeletal muscle or in the muscle's fascia, that is responsible for the pain in the zone of reference and, if treated, will resolve the resulting pain [5]. The zone of reference is the area of pain referred by the trigger point.

Clinical criteria for a diagnosis of MPS have been suggested by Simons (Table 11-1) [6••]. MPS is characterized by a localized pain complaint associated with a tense muscle containing a very tender spot (trigger point) identifiable by palpation. This spot may be distant from the pain complaint but is responsible for it. Simons stresses that, unless we are aware that the symptoms are referred in a characteristic pattern, we will not be able to locate the source. The trigger point is contained in a taut band of muscle producing muscle tension and a decreased range of motion. Reproduction of the patient's pain occurs with palpation or needling of the trigger point [6••]. The ropelike band felt when rubbing the palpating fingers across the trigger point is a result of the contracture and shortening of the sarcomeres in the area of the trigger point and lengthening of the sarcomeres distant from the trigger point (Fig. 11-1) [7].

TABLE 11-1
CRITERIA FOR ESTABLISHING A CLINICAL DIAGNOSIS OF MYOFASCIAL PAIN SYNDROME*

MAJOR CRITERIA

Regional pain complaint.

Pain complaint or altered sensation in the expected distribution of referred pain from a myofascial trigger point.

Taut band palpable in an accessible muscle.

Exquisite spot tenderness at one point along the length of the taut band.

Some degree of restricted range of motion, when measurable.

MINOR CRITERIA

Reproduction of clinical pain complaint, or altered sensation, by pressure on the tender spot.

Elicitation of a local twitch response by transverse snapping.

Palpation at the tender spot or by needle insertion into the tender spot in the taut band.

Pain alleviated by elongating (stretching) the muscle or by injecting the tender spot.

*From Simons [6••]; with permission.

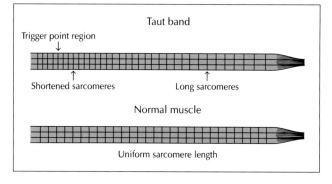

Figure 11-1 Sarcomeres that are of equal length in normal muscle fibers as compared with the likely distribution of unequal sarcomere lengths in the fibers of a palpable taut band passing through a trigger point. Shortened sarcomeres in the region of the trigger point would increase the tension in the fascicles of the taut band and restrict the stretch range of motion of the muscle.

Associated Symptoms

Several associated symptoms of MPS have been noted, including autonomic effects such as hot spots on thermography in the trigger point area and coolness in the reference zone [8,9]. Trapezius trigger points may cause pilomotor activity in the arm, and sternocleidomastoid trigger points may cause tearing of the eyes, coryza, and scleral injection. A local twitch response (LRT) is produced upon snapping or needle penetration of the trigger point. Electromyographic (EMG) recording of an LRT demonstrates an undisturbed baseline before and after the LRT.

During LRT, a burst of complex waveforms is seen. EMG recording of trigger points that did not elicit an LRT did not demonstrate any evidence of ongoing denervation or focal muscle spasm in a study done by Durette and coworkers [10•]. Deep pressure exerted on a trigger point may also evoke a jump sign in which the patient moves suddenly and verbalizes discomfort in response to hyperalgesia [11].

PATHOGENESIS

The trigger point area is in metabolic distress because of increased metabolic demand coupled with decreased oxygen and energy supply. This distress may be caused by decreased blood flow locally and produces a self-perpetuating vicious cycle (Fig. 11-2) [11]. Acute muscle strain leads to tissue damage in a localized area of muscle. Damage to the sarcoplasmic reticulum releases ionized calcium, which causes vigorous contractile activity (sarcomere shortening) which in turn increases local metabolic demand and compromises local circulation, possibly via reflex efferent sympathetic activity [12]. The result is local hypoxia and ischemia producing histologic changes of ragged red fibers and type II fiber atrophy [13,14]. The energy supply (ATP) of the sarcoplasmic reticular compartment is compromised and the calcium pump of the sarcoplasmic reticulum fails, leaving the free calcium ions available to maintain ongoing contractile activity.

Dysfunctional Myotactic Units

Functionally, the progression from wellness to MPS is complex. Rosen [15] suggests viewing MPS as an overload syndrome as opposed to an overuse syndrome. Overuse suggests rest as appropriate treatment, whereas overload suggests correction of alignment, modification of the load placed on the muscle unit, and the controlling of environmental factors. To determine where and why the primary myofascial dysfunction is occurring, Rosen views muscles in a dynamic sense—as initiators, accelerators, stabilizers, and decelerators of movement. In each area there may be a "gateway" muscle, a primary dysfunctional muscle that slowly becomes dysfunctional, creating a pattern of deteriorating function in other muscles of the myotactic unit or adjacent units. Eventually, features of pain and MPS develop.

TREATMENT

The most important aspect in the treatment of myofascial pain is an accurate diagnosis. An incorrect diagnosis can unnecessarily delay proper treatment. One must remember that, whereas myofascial pain may exist in and of itself, it can often be secondary to an underlying abnormality. Such problems can include a radiculopathy, entrapment neuropathy, peripheral neuropathy, or other neurologically based abnormalities; also, arthritis or other rheumatologic conditions or cancer can incite myofascial pain. The physician must evaluate for treatable musculoskeletal conditions such as shoulder, hip, or other joint pathology; epicondylitis; facet abnormalities; ligamentous shortening; and others. The patient should be evaluated for strength deficits and imbalances (such as quad-to-hamstring strength ratio), inflexibility, and biomechanical derangements. One must consider referred pain from a visceral source. If an underlying abnormality is present, it must be treated for there to be successful treatment of the myofascial pain.

An important concept in the treatment of myofascial pain is that of referred tenderness [16]. Myofascial foci

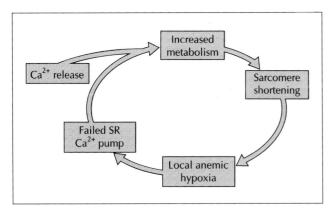

Figure 11-2 Cycle of events that could maintain sarcomere shortening. SR—sacroplasmic reticulum.

refer not only pain but also tenderness to areas remote from the primary abnormality. An example is a patient with palpable tenderness in the upper or middle trapezius muscle secondary to a cervical facet syndrome. If the primary cause of the myofascial pain is not found, the therapeutic efforts will be directed away from the true source of the dysfunction and thus the treatment outcome will be less successful.

In addition to looking diligently for inciting foci of trigger points and myofascial pain, one must look for systemic perpetuating factors of myofascial trigger points [17]. Nutritional inadequacies, including water-soluble vitamin deficiencies or mineral deficiencies, should be addressed and diet should be adjusted accordingly. Endocrine disorders, including hypothyroidism, premenstrual syndrome, menopause, hypoglycemia, gout, hyperuricemia, and crystal deposition disease can be involved. Chronic bacterial, viral, and parasitic infections must be treated if identified. Additionally, allergies, inadequate tissue oxygenation, sleep deprivation, and emotional stress [2•] can be implicated as perpetuating factors.

Other important components in the treatment of myofascial pain include evaluations for psychosocial distress and sleep deprivation. Some individuals will benefit from psychological evaluation, counseling, and stress management techniques. The use of amitriptyline and other tricyclic antidepressants is frequently effective in restoring appropriate sleep. Restoring sleep is vitally important as tenderness has been found to occur in healthy volunteers simply secondary to the deprivation of sleep [18]. Additional benefits from the use of tricyclic antidepressants are their analgesic and muscle-relaxing properties.

Antidepressants have been found useful in treating many types of chronic pain including MPS [19,20]. The heterocyclic antidepressants are most commonly used for pain management. Analgesic properties of these compounds appear to be independent of their antidepressant effects. The analgesic response occurs more rapidly and at lower doses than does the antidepressant response. Although useful properties of the antidepressants include muscle relaxation and restoration of the sleep cycle, these effects alone cannot explain their pain-relieving properties. More likely, analgesia occurs as a result of alteration of the monoamine neurotransmitters (serotonin and norepinephrine) as components in the endorphin-mediated analgesia system, the major known descending antinociceptive pathway [21]. Amitriptyline is the most commonly used antidepressant in our practice [22]. However,

minimal evidence exists to recommend the use of one drug over another for the treatment of pain. Initial dosing with amitriptyline, 25 mg 1 hour before bedtime, can be increased in 25-mg increments every other night to up to 150 mg or higher. Once a therapeutic effect has been achieved and maintained for 1 month, it is generally possible to reduce the dosage slowly. Maintenance doses of amitriptyline are often in the 10- to 150-mg range.

A general aerobic program can be helpful both in improving sleep patterns and in increasing delivery of oxygen to end tissues. Discontinuation of smoking and minimizing caffeine intake are important parts of an overall treatment program.

Physical Therapy

For the majority of patients receiving physical therapy who are seen in an orthopedic practice, soft-tissue involvement and regional myofascial pain syndromes are concurrent problems. Whether it is caused by the initial trauma or by long-term postural adaptation to chronic pain, myofascial pain is a common component of their overall pain complaints and, as such, must be dealt with in the plan of care to allow any long-term relief.

The treatment of myofascial pain from the conservative-care approach falls into two broad categories: passive treatment and active treatment, and the two are inseparable. Reliance on only one treatment type often provides only a temporary relief or, in a worst-case scenario, exacerbates the problem.

Passive Treatment

The term *passive* in this context is used to describe types of treatment concepts and techniques that do not require the patient to participate actively. These techniques are used when an external stimulus is required to elicit a specific physiologic response (modalities) or when the patient is unable to achieve the desired effect independently (soft-tissue mobilization).

Modalities

As an adjunct procedure and preparatory to many of the techniques that are used in the treatment of myofascial pain, modalities play an important role in the treatment of the soft tissue involvement and have a sound physiologic basis for their inclusion. Modalities should not be used indiscriminately or in isolation. It is important in the treatment of myofascial pain to minimize the patient's dependence and improve his or her functional abilities.

THERAPEUTIC HEAT

Heat has been widely used and is an effective agent in relieving pain. Hot packs and heat lamps, termed *superficials* because of their low penetration of the skin and surface tissues, are used to assist in the reduction of pain and stiffness, reduce muscle spasm through a decrease in gamma efferent activity [23], increase range of motion through increased tissue extensibility, and improve tissue healing by increasing the flow of blood and nutrients to the area [24]. Superficial heat elevates the surface temperature and provides the greatest effect at 0.5 cm of depth. Heating to 1 to 2 cm requires longer durations with a limiting degree of efficacy. Due to these limited depths, the thermal agents of choice in many soft-tissue dysfunctions are the deep heating agents such as ultrasound and diathermy.

Conversion is the process whereby electrical current (diathermy) and sound waves (ultrasound) are converted to heat when the energy is passed through the tissues. These deep heating agents can increase temperatures at depths of 3 to 5 cm. The ability of deep heating agents to penetrate to deep structures without unnecessary temperature increases to the overlying skin are of particular use in patients with soft-tissue dysfunction [27].

Thermal agents may also cause edema as a result of their vasodilatory effect. Caution and initial use at low levels are advised when considering how to treat the patient with acute pain. Thermal agents are ideally used at the initial phase of the treatment session and as preparation for many of the active and manual procedures that follow. Beneficial effects of heat before active or manual procedures include increased cellular metabolic rate, increased vasodilation, increased pain threshold [25], and increased extensibility in collagen (elastic properties).

COLD THERAPY

Cold and its use in the treatment of soft-tissue injuries has been extensively noted in the literature. Its physiologic effects include initial vasoconstriction followed by vasodilation (with long-term use). There is reduced inflammation and edema and decreased myospasm owing to a decrease in pain and a decrease in the sensitivity of the muscle spindle fibers to discharge [27]. Joint range of motion is increased and the connective tissue length may be maintained when cold is applied to an already stretched position.

Cold therapy is applied in the form of ice packs, direct ice massage, and cold gel packs. It is important to monitor the treatment because surface tissue can be damaged if the intensity or duration is excessive. In the initial stages of injury, ice is particularly effective because of its effect of vasoconstriction and reduction of edema. Its use in later stages should be tempered with the knowledge that hemoglobin binds tighter to oxygen with a drop in tissue temperature. In most myofascial dysfunction treatments, we are working to enhance normal physiologic function and the release of oxygen and should therefore consider this effect when choosing the appropriate modality.

ELECTRICAL STIMULATION

For therapeutic purposes, there are two types of electrical stimulation of current: direct current (galvanic) and alternating current (faradic). Faradic current provides very effective pain modulation because of its stimulation of the sensory nerves, and its stimulation of intact motor nerves, which stimulate a normal muscle contraction. When muscles are stimulated by electrical discharge, the result is the same as if the muscle was voluntarily contracted in terms of the subsequent increase in metabolism and increased waste output and evacuation.

Galvanic current can be applied by using either a positive or negative pole. If local analgesia or vasoconstriction is desired, the positive pole should be used. Use of the negative pole produces vasodilation. These properties make galvanic current very effective when treating soft tissues [26]. As with all electrical stimulation, its effectiveness is based on its intensity, duration, and wave form [27].

TRANSCUTANEOUS ELECTRICAL NERVE STIMULATION

The use of transcutaneous electrical nerve stimulation (TENS) is based on the gate theory proposed by Melzack and Wall [28] in 1965. The gate theory suggests that application of electrical stimulation is capable of interfering with the transmission of pain signals. It has also been hypothesized that TENS may act to stimulate the release of endorphins [29].

Transcutaneous electrical nerve stimulation is used extensively in the treatment of spinal dysfunction, especially in those conditions involving soft-tissue pathology. TENS may be effectively combined with myofascial release and muscle energy procedures [30]. Although TENS provides substantial pain relief in many individuals, its scientific results have been somewhat mixed. Therapists have come to realize that appropriate electrode placement is the most critical part of the TENS treatments.

Kenneth Lamm, PT, has developed a technique for optimizing TENS electrode placement for effective treatments [30]. His initial frustration with varying results in some patients led to the development and use of "spotting electrodes." Because more than 80% of acupuncture points are over trigger points, recognized motor points, and major nerve trunks, Lamm believes that the best results for TENS treatments are provided by direct stimulation of these specific sites [30]. The use of these points for stimulation provides a preferred alternative to the common practice of randomly flooding the affected area with current flow.

Lamm's technique for identifying specific optimal stimulation points involves the use of constructed spotting electrodes. The specifics of the electrode construction are detailed in his course manuals (TENS and Pain Management Seminars, 643 Wine Plum Dr., Tucson, AZ 86704).

After a detailed history is taken and examination is performed, the area of soft-tissue involvement is marked and trigger points are noted. (Note: before utilizing the following sequence, a review of TENS cautions and precautions is considered essential. Whereas there are some precautions for the use of the current itself, most of the contraindications have to do with stimulation of certain specific points that may produce adverse effects.) With the TENS unit on continuous stimulation, the wet sponges of the spotting electrodes are then placed in a bracketing position to the problem area (Fig. 11-3). The electrodes are moved slowly and separately while the patient is evaluated for changes in soft-tissue tone, pain, and mobility. Determination of the optimal placement is via patient feedback as to the extent of relief. Once the optimal sites have been determined, further investigation is necessary to fine tune the treatment. This fine tuning involves adjusting polarity, pulse width, amplitude, and modes, and rechecking after a short (5 to 10 minutes) trial at the optimal levels. Although this approach is time consuming and more complex than the characteristic "one pattern fits all" technique that is commonly used in the

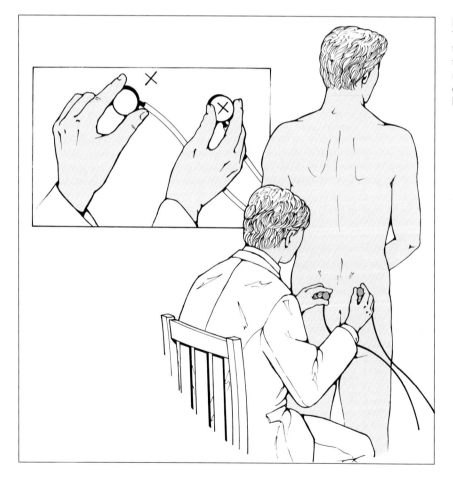

Figure 11-3 Use of spotting electrodes. The therapist moves one electrode at a time to and around areas of previously marked trigger points to determine optimal placement. Note that the transcutaneous electrical nerve stimulation output is controlled by the patient.

TENS treatment of myofascial pain, the results achieved at Restore Physical and Industrial Rehabilitation have led us to use this technique before permanent placement of the patient's electrodes. This approach may explain why many patients obtain substantial relief from TENS when it was ineffectual in a previous plan of care.

SOFT TISSUE MOBILIZATION

For the conservative-care clinician, a wide variety of soft-tissue mobilization techniques, including massage, muscle energy procedures, trigger point therapy, and myofascial release techniques, are available that are extremely useful in treating pain and dysfunction related to the myofascial system.

MASSAGE

Traditional massage was originated by the Chinese and introduced to Western medicine by the French [31]. We commonly use French terminology to describe massage strokes, including effleurage and petrissage (kneading of soft tissue). Massage is used to improve circulation and metabolic balance within the muscle and inhibit pain and reflexogenic guarding. Normally, muscle contractions during activity create a pumping action that facilitates venous blood flow. When tissue trauma is sustained, the injured area is often immobilized by the body's protective mechanisms as a result of pain. This immobilization may lead to decreased circulation and lymphatic drainage. The use of massage to provide deep stroking along the superficial veins in the direction of venous flow decreases venous pressure and increases lymphatic flow [32]. Although not as effective as normal muscular activity, massage may be used when active exercise of the affected area is still too painful.

Ischemia and subsequent pain may be caused by sustained muscle contraction as a result of reflexogenic guarding or neuromuscular tension. Massage may relieve this pain through several proposed mechanisms [33]. Pain may be modulated through increased circulation from the mechanical effect of massage on the venous and lymphatic flow. Pain may also be inhibited again through increased circulation by way of reflex vasodilation from the facilitation of cutaneous afferent nerves that mediate touch and pressure. The final theory of the massage effect on pain management is that it may alter pain through stimulation of mechanoreceptors in the tendons and fascia during the stretching and compressing strokes, which will result in inhibition of painful sustained muscle contraction.

For ligaments and tendons, deep friction massage is used instead of lighter stroking techniques. These tissues are very susceptible to breakdown through overuse because of their low metabolic rates and relatively poor vascularity. In addition, tendons and ligaments also tend to develop secondary adhesions with protective immobilization. Tissue degeneration must be addressed by decreasing stress to the tissue, increasing nutrition, or both. Cyriax and Colham [34] advocate direct manipulation at the site of the lesion (known as deep transverse friction massage) in a direction perpendicular to the normal orientation of the fibers. This technique is designed to increase interfibrous mobility and vascularity of connective tissue.

MUSCLE ENERGY PROCEDURES

Muscle energy procedures are usually contract-relax techniques used to promote muscle inhibition [35]. By inhibiting the muscle's contractibility and allowing the muscle to relax and elongate, mobility is improved. Relaxation is achieved by asking the patient to contract the limiting muscle with maximum effort. The contraction is resisted to allow no movement toward the limiting muscle. This contraction is then followed by movement away from the limiting muscle toward the position of limited movement. An example of this method would be its use in lengthening tight hamstrings. The hamstrings would first be taken to their limited end range. The patient would then contract the hamstrings against an immovable force to provide an isometric contraction. This exercise must be done against an outside object because the desired results cannot be achieved through a simple co-contraction. The patient is told to relax the hamstring and gently resist as the limb is moved into hip flexion, which immediately stretches the previously contracted hamstring, allowing elongation. Through repeated attempts, this procedure is used to achieve progressive relaxation and subsequent greater range of the antagonistic pattern [36]. This relaxation and inhibition of the antagonist during facilitation of the agonist is dependent on reciprocal inhibition [37].

TRIGGER POINT THERAPY

Simons and Travell [5,38] describe the use of trigger-point therapy as part of an overall management plan for myofascial pain syndromes. Trigger points may be active or latent. Active trigger points give rise to referred pain with sustained digital pressure, whereas latent trigger points are only locally tender to palpation.

Normal muscles do not contain active trigger points. Schriber [27] found that laborers who exercised their muscles heavily on a daily basis were less likely to develop active trigger points than were workers involved in sedentary occupations who only participated in occasional vigorous physical activity.

Active trigger points that have been identified may be treated manually in several ways. Stretch and spray [5,38–42] is a technique performed by passively stretching the muscle containing the active trigger point to its normal maximum length. The stretch is immediately followed by a stream of vapocoolant spray onto the skin overlying the muscle to inhibit pain and guarding secondary to tension on the muscle (Figs. 11-4–11-6) [43]. The essential component of this technique is the stretch applied to the muscle. Therapeutic stretching without spray, including postexercise stretching, is also important. An additional manual technique for trigger points is known as ischemic compression [38]. Direct finger pressure is applied to the active trigger point with a progressive increase in downward force as the hypersensitivity of the trigger point fades. Both techniques are directed primarily at the point where pain originates rather than at the reference zone where pain is felt [44].

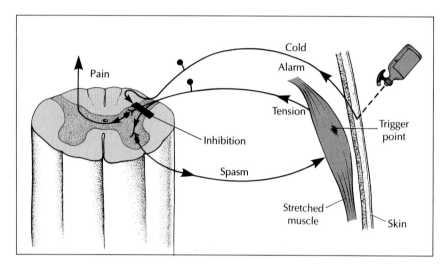

Figure 11-4 Neural pathways that can account for the effectiveness of vapocoolant applied to skin overlying an active myofascial trigger point. The sudden cold and touch stimuli of the spray inhibit the pain and reflex spasm that would otherwise prevent passive stretching of the muscle. The black bar in the dorsal horn of the spinal cord represents this inhibition.

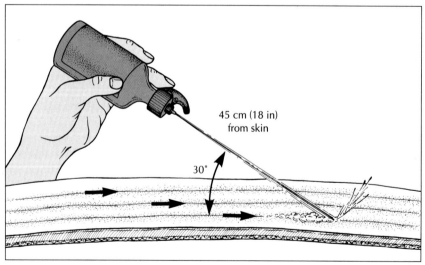

Figure 11-5 Application of the jet stream of vapocoolant. Unidirectional sweeps cover first the parallel lines of skin over those muscle fibers that are stretched the tightest, then over the rest of the muscle and its pain pattern. The lines of spray follow the direction of the muscle fibers, progressing toward the referred pain zones (stippling). The spray bottle is held at an acute angle approximately 45 cm (18 inches) from the skin as the spray sweeps over the skin at a rate of about 10 cm (4 in/sec).

TRIGGER POINT INJECTIONS

Trigger point injections are effective in the treatment of MPS (Fig. 11-7) [5,38–42]. An injection of sterile water [45], or simply dry needling the trigger point [5,46], has been shown to be effective. We recommend the use of a local anesthetic solution such as 0.5% procaine, or a 0.75% bupivacaine and 2% lidocaine mixture. It is Calodney's experience that the addition of ketorolac tromethamine, 60 mg per 20 mL of injectate, provides immediate and sustained analgesia and may eliminate the problem of injection-site pain. A 22-gauge to 25-gauge needle is used. However, the smaller the needle, the less accurate is the feel of the tissue being penetrated and the less useful the needle is in mechanically disrupting the trigger point. Obtaining a local twitch response can help confirm the presence of a trigger point. One

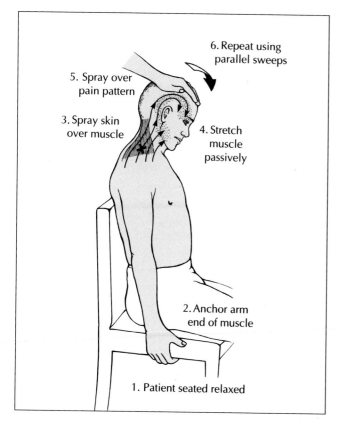

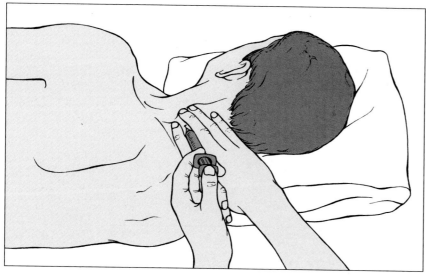

Figure 11-6 Sequence of steps when stretching and spraying any muscle for myofascial trigger points, as applied to the upper trapezius muscle. 1) Patient supported in a comfortable relaxed position; 2) one end of the muscle anchored; 3) skin sprayed with repeat parallel sweeps of the vapocoolant over the length of the muscle in the direction of pain pattern; 4) immediately after the first sweep of spray, pressure is applied to stretch the muscle and is continued as spray is applied; 5) sweeps of the spray continue to cover the referred pain pattern of that muscle; 6) steps 3, 4, and 5 are repeated only two or three times, or less if the passive range of motion becomes maximum. Hot pack and then several cycles of full active range of motion follow.

Figure 11-7 Injection of the upper trigger point in the right levator scapulae at the base of the neck where the muscle emerges from beneath the upper trapezius muscle.

must differentiate myofascial trigger points from fibromyalgia tender points (Fig. 11-8). An injection into the fibromyalgia tender points is not usually beneficial. Many reasons exist for the failure of trigger point injections (Table 11-2).

It is important that the patient be stretched after the trigger point injection. Injections without stretching are not as effective in obtaining an improved clinical response [47]. If multiple trigger points are present, a sympathetic block may be helpful in reducing them to a manageable number [48]. Blocking the spinal accessory nerve is useful in MPS involving the sternocleidomastoid and trapezius muscles; a dorsal scapular nerve block has been useful for the rhomboid and levator scapulae [49]; and a suprascapular nerve block has been used in treating myofascial syndromes of the supraspinatus and infraspinatus muscles. In patients with diffuse involvement of the cervical region, a blockade of the cervical

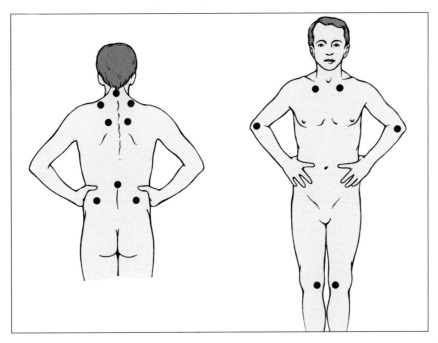

Figure 11-8 The Tender Point Map (after Smythe): 14 sites of local tenderness. The unilateral sites are at the intertransverse or interspinous ligaments of C4–C6 and the interspinous ligament at L4-L5, and the bilateral sites are at the upper borders of the trapezius, the supraspinatus origins at the medial border of the scapula, the upper outer quadrants of the buttocks, the second costochondral junctions, the lateral epicondyles, and the medial fat pads of the knees.

TABLE 11-2
REASONS FOR FAILURE OF TRIGGER-POINT INJECTION*

Injecting a latent trigger point, not the responsible active trigger point.

Injecting the area of referred pain and referred tenderness, not the trigger point. This error may provide incomplete temporary relief, or can aggravate the patient's symptoms.

Needling the vicinity of the trigger point, including needling the tense band, but missing the trigger point itself. This tends to irritate, rather than inactivate the trigger point.

Using a needle for injection that was finer than 25-gauge, which allows the tip to slide around the resistant trigger point.

Injecting a solution with an irritating or allergenic bacteriostatic preservative, such as sodium bisulfite; sodium hyposulfite is less irritating.

Inadequate hemostasis followed by irritation of the trigger point caused by local bleeding.

Overlooking other active trigger points in the myotatic unit.

Forgetting to have the patient actively move the muscle after injection so that its full range is not incorporated into daily activities.

Omitting regular passive stretch exercises at home, which would have maintained the full length of the muscle.

*From Travell and Simons [5]; with permission.

plexus has been useful. Similarly, a psoas compartment blockade has been effectively used for lumbar and lower-extremity myofascial pain. Psoas compartment blockade is best accomplished under fluoroscopic guidance using a posterior approach and relatively large volumes of injectate (40 to 60 mL). Patients with refractory myofascial syndromes and significant dysfunction may benefit from indwelling epidural catheterization and a concurrent aggressive course of physiotherapy.

Botulinum toxin has been used in the treatment of spasmodic torticollis [50•], and, more recently, in the treatment of MPS.

MYOFASCIAL RELEASE

Myofascial release is a method of soft-tissue mobilization that focuses on the fascial component of musculoskeletal pain and dysfunction. Barnes [51] defines fascia as a "three dimensional web of connective tissue surrounding and infusing every structure of our body all the way down to the cellular level." Fascia is composed of collagenous fibers coiled around elastic fibers. Collagen fibers have a plastic quality that enables them to be pliable but not specifically extensible. Fascia also contains ground substance which provides lubrication to allow gliding between muscles. Connective tissue fibers that make up fascia are interwoven rather than parallel-like tendinous fibers. This arrangement gives fascia the ability to resist tension in all directions. Fascia itself is richly innervated but poorly vascularized. Fascial trauma may lead to pain and slow healing capacity [52]. Normal fascia is slightly mobile but tends to shorten and tighten secondary to inflammation or poor posture over time [51]. The resultant fascial restrictions may generate enormous pressure on pain-sensitive structures. Prolonged shrinkage of fascial tissues may result in poor postural alignment and affect the quality of movement [53].

Myofascial release techniques involve stretching along the line of fibers of the restricted muscle until resistance to further stretch is felt. The stretch is held in the lengthened position until the soft tissue is felt to relax or "release" [54]. The slack is taken up after the initial release and a new stretch position is held. This procedure is repeated several times until the tissues are fully elongated. Myofascial release techniques may be used to elongate collagenous fibers and improve viscosity of their ground substance for the purpose of reducing pain, increasing mobility, and correcting posture.

Active Treatment

The term *active* implies activity that is essential for the body's maintenance of homeostasis. No technique or modality can replace the body's natural balancing required for optimal function. It is this component of the treatment of myofascial pain that is required if the change is to be long lasting. In our treatment of myofascial pain, the individual is always involved in an active exercise program. Care must be taken to carefully dose the activity to avoid a regression to the initial levels of pain response.

Initially, hydrotherapy allows the patient with myofascial pain to participate in light, graded exercise to establish normal muscle physiology while immersed in warm water (Fig. 11-9). This exercise creates a relaxation for the involved areas, which is essential for their treatment. The further effect of unloading allows the muscles to respond to stress levels that are subnormal in intensity, which has the effect of allowing exercise in an environment that is functionally correct but within tissue tolerance levels.

Unloading of specific tissues may be accomplished through the use of slant boards (to modify the angle of gravity) or through precise positioning. We have successfully used the ZUNI (SOMA, Austin, Texas) for this

Figure 11-9 Hydrotherapy in the initial phases helps to promote pain-free movement through the combination of heat and hydrodynamics.

purpose (Fig. 11-10) in the treatment of patients with myofascial pain. The concept of unloading is not that of traction but rather the imposing of a graded resistance to the tissues at levels of lower intensity.

Patients should be established in structured programs that emphasize controlled progressive resistance and the gradual increasing of time. The concept underlying the treatment is for the body to develop an "exercise vaccine" that will allow it to resist the development of dysfunction during occasional periods of inactivity or periods of high stress.

Equally important is the need to move the affected segment or area in the correct biomechanical sequence. Muscles that have been immobilized or incapacitated in any way will have developed movement patterns based on previous painful restrictions or on substitution patterns. The movements should not be repeated during the exercise sessions because they tend to further reinforce the abnormal movement that may have been a contributing factor to the development of myofascial pain.

In addition to active graded exercise and activity, all patients with myofascial pain must be involved in a comprehensive stretching program. The stretch may be accomplished through contract-relax techniques or may be effectively done through muscle elongation. Muscle elongation is the concept of encouraging the resistant antagonist to relax and elongate through gentle contraction of the agonist. That great "feel-good" stretch in the morning is the body's successful attempt to move and elongate tissues in preparation for normal activity.

EDUCATION

Education of the patient and his or her participation in the rehabilitation process is essential in achieving optimal outcomes. The patient's understanding of their pathology, the impending treatment process, and their role as self-care provider are important to that patient participating as an informed consumer. Correct body mechanics, protective activities of daily living, self-pain modulation, and a specific independent exercise program help the patient achieve independence and reinforce the idea of responsibility. Education for the future includes the need for a lifetime of total body fitness, stress reduction, dietary requirements for adequate nutrition, and maintenance of proper body weight. Education cannot be adequately assimilated by most individuals from a lecture setting. For education to be fully effective, it must be interactive, repetitive, and reinforced.

CONCLUSIONS

Our understanding of myofascial pain syndromes has continued to evolve. Aggressive management is recommended because the condition is very responsive to treatment as opposed to other muscle pain disorders such as fibromyalgia. Identification of active trigger points requires an understanding of referred pain patterns and of the disease process itself. Treatment involves deactivation of painful trigger points with concurrent participation in activity-based therapy programs. Patient participation is key because long-term resolution depends on lifestyle changes including postural correction, proper nutritional habits, and ongoing physical conditioning.

Figure 11-10
The ZUNI (SOMA, Austin, Texas) allows specific dosage of the patient's body weight, which allows the affected tissues to exercise with functional movements at reduced intensity.

REFERENCES AND RECOMMENDED READING

Papers of interest, published recently, have been highlighted as:
• Of special interest
•• Of outstanding interest

1. Snootsky SA, Jaeger B, Oye R: Prevalence of myofascial pain in general internal medicine practice. *West J Med* 1989, 151:157–160.

2.• Rosen NB: The myofascial pain syndromes. *Phys Med Rehabil Clin North Am* 1993, 4:41–62.
Although frequent, MPS are probably the largest group of unrecognized, undertreated, and misunderstood medical problems in clinical medicine.

3. Fricton JR: Clinical care for myofascial pain. *Dent Clin North Am* 1991, 35:1–28.

4. Calodney AK, Olsen ML, Novy D: Fibromyalgia and myofascial pain syndrome. *Pain Digest* 1992, 2:142–147.

5. Travell JG, Simons DG, eds.: *Myofascial Pain and Dysfunction: The Trigger Point Manual.* Baltimore: Williams and Wilkins; 1983:3.

6.•• Simons DG: Muscle pain syndromes. *J Man Med* 1991, 6:3–23.
In this article the author suggests the clinical criteria for the diagnosis of MPS. The trigger point, a tense muscle containing a very tender spot, is palpatted to reproduce the patient's pain.

7. Simons DG: Myofascial Pain Syndrome due to Trigger Points. International Rehabilitation Medicine Association monograph series No. 1, November, 1987.

8. Swerdlow B, Dieter JNI: An evaluation of the sensitivity and specificity of medical thermography for the documentation of myofascial trigger points. *Pain* 1992, 48:205–213.

9. Kruse RA, Christiansen JA: Thermographic imaging of myofascial trigger points: a follow up study. *Arch Phys Med Rehabil* 1992, 73:819–823.

10.• Durette MR, Rodriguez AA, Agre J, *et al.*: Needle electromyographic evaluation of patients with myofascial or fibromyalgic pain. *Am J Phys Med Rehabil* 1991, 70:154–156.
In this study, EMG recording of trigger points that did not elicit an LRT did not demonstrate any evidence of ongoing denervation or focal muscle spasm.

11. Kraft GH, Johnson EW, Laban MM: The fibrositis syndrome. *Arch Phys Med Rehabil* 1968, 49:155–162.

12. Thompson JM: Tension myalgia as a diagnosis at the Mayo Clinic and its relationship to fibrositis, fibromyalgia, and myofascial pain syndrome. *Mayo Clin Proc* 1990, 65:1237–1248.

13. Bengtsson A, Henriksson KG, Larsson J: Muscle biopsy in primary fibromyalgia. *Scand J Rhematol* 1986, 15:1–6.

14. Bengtsson A, Henriksson KG: The muscle in fibromyalgia—a review of Swedish studies. *J Rheumatol* 1989, 16(suppl 19):144–149.

15. Rosen RB: Advances in the Diagnosis, Treatment and Research of Myofascial Pain and its Related Disorders. American College of Physical Medicine and Rehabilitation Annual Course Outline, 1992.

16. Rosen NB: The Kinesiology of Myofascial Pain. Presented at The Annual Meeting of the American Academy of Physical Medicine and Rehabilitation, San Francisco, November, 1992.

17. Travell JG: The Role of Nutritional, Endocrine, and Other Systemic Factors in Perpetuating Myofascial Pain and Dysfunction. Presented at The Annual Meeting of the American Academy of Physical Medicine and Rehabilitation, San Francisco, November, 1992.

18. Moldofski H, *et al.*: Musculoskeletal symptoms and non-REM sleep disturbances in patient with "fibrositis syndrome" and healthy subjects. *Psychosomat Med* 1975, 37:341–351.

19. Monks R, Merskey H: Psychotropic drugs. In *Textbook of Pain.* 2nd ed. Edited by Wall PD, Melzack R. London: Churchill Livingstone; 1989:702–721.

20. Butler S: Present status of tricyclic antidepressants in chronic pain therapy. In *Recent Advances in the Management of Pain: Advances in Pain Research and Therapy.* 7th ed. Edited by Benedetti C, Chapman CR, Morrica G. New York: Raven Press; 1984:173–197.

21. Monks R: Psychotropic drugs. In *The Management of Pain.* Edited by Bonica JJ. Philadelphia: Lea and Febiger; 1990:1676–1689.

22. Calodney AK: Pain after spinal cord injury. *Pain Digest* 1993, 3.

23. Licht S, ed.: *Therapeutic Heat and Cold.* Baltimore: Everly Press; 1965.

24. Michlovitz S, ed.: *Thermal Agents in Rehabilitation.* Philadelphia: FA Davis; 1986.

25. Leahmann JF: Therapeutic heat and cold. *Clin Orthop* 1974, 99:207–205.

26. Sawyer M, Zbieranek C: The treatment of soft tissue after spinal injury. *Clin Sports Med* 1986, 5:2.

27. Schriber W, ed.: *A Manual of Electrotherapy.* 2nd ed. Philadelphia: Lea and Febiger; 1978.

28. Melzack R, Wall PD: Pain mechanism: a new theory. *Science* 1965, 150:971–979.

29. Kellett J: Acute soft tissue injuries—a review of the literature. *Med Sci Sports Exercise* 1986, 18:489–500.

30. Lamm KE: Optimal Placement Techniques for TENS—A Soft Tissue Approach. Course workbook for the TENS and Pain Management Seminars, 1989.

31. Tappan FM, ed.: *Healing Massage Techniques: A Study of Eastern and Western Methods.* Reston, VA: Reston Publishing; 1978.

32. Ladd MP, Kottke JF, Blanchard RS: Studies on the effect of massage on the flow of lymph from the foreleg of the dog. *Arch Phys Med* 1952, 33:604–612.

33. Jacobs M: Massage for the relief of pain: anatomical and physiological consideration. *Phys Ther Rev* 1960, 40:96–97.

34. Cyriax J, Coldham M: Treatment by massage, manipulation and injection. In *Textbook of Orthopaedic Medicine*, vol 2, 11th ed. London: Bailliere Tindall; 1984:8–12.

35. Mitchell FL, Moran PS, Pruzzo NA, eds.: *An Evaluation and Treatment Manual of Osteopathic Muscle Energy Procedures.* Valley Park, MO: Mitchell, Moran, and Pruzzo Associates; 1979.

36. Knott M, Voss DE, eds.: *Proprioceptive Neuromuscular Facilitation: Patterns and Techniques. 2nd ed.* Philadelphia: Harper and Row; 1968.

37. Kabat H: Proprioceptive facilitation in therapeutic exercise. In *Therapeutic Exercise.* 2nd ed. Edited by Licht S, III. New Haven: Licht; 1961.

38. Simons DG, Travell JG: Myofascial origins of low back pain: principles of diagnosis and treatment. *Postgrad Med* 1983, 73:66–73.

39. Travell JG, Simons DG: Myofascial origins of low back pain: part 2: torso muscles. *Low Back Pain* 1983, 73.

40. Travell JG, Simons DG: Myofascial origins of low back pain: part 3: pelvic and lower extremity muscles. *Low Back Pain* 1983, 73.

41. Rubin D: Myofascial trigger point syndrome: an approach to management. *Arch Phys Med Rehabil* 1981, 62.

42. Kraus H, Fischer AA: Diagnosis and treatment of myofascial pain. *Mount Sinai J Med* 1991, 58.

43. Travell JG: Ethylchloride spray for painful muscle spasm. *Arch Phys Med Rehabil* 1952, 33:291–298.

44. Travell JG: Myofascial trigger points: clinical view. In *Advances in Pain Research and Therapy.* vol 1. Edited by Bonica JJ, Albe-Fessard D. New York: Raven Press; 1976:419–426.

45. Byrn C, Borenstein, Linder LE: Treatment of neck and shoulder pain in whiplash syndrome patients with intracutaneous sterile water injections. *Acta Anaesthesiol Scand* 1991, 35:52–53.

46. Lewit K: The needle effect in the relief of myofascial pain. *Pain* 1979, 6:83–90.

47. Zohn BA, Mennell J: *Musculoskeletal Pain: Diagnosis and Physical Treatment.* Boston: Little Brown and Co; 1976.

48. Ramamurthy S: Nerve Block in Upper Extremity. Presented at the Meeting of the American Academy of Physical Medicine and Rehabilitation, 1989.

49. Ramamurthy S: Role of the accessory nerve block and dorsal scapular nerve block in the management of cervical pain. *Adv Anesthesiol* 1978:76–78.

50.• Anderson TJ, Rivest J, Stell R, *et al.*: Botulinum toxin treatment of spasmodic torticollis. *J R Soc Med* 1992, 85:524–529.
This study discusses the treatment of spasmodic torticouis with botulinum toxin.

51. Barnes JF: Myofascial release: questions, concepts and the future. In *Progress Report No. 4.* American Physical Therapy Association, April, 1988.

52. Calliet R, ed.: *Soft Tissue Pain and Disability.* Philadelphia: FA Davis; 1977.

53. Upledger JE, Vredevoogd JD, eds.: *Craniosacral Therapy.* Seattle: Eastland Press; 1984.

54. Manheim CJ, Lavett DK: *The Myofascial Release Manual.* Thorofare, New Jersey: Slack, Inc.; 1989.

CHAPTER 12

Cancer Pain

VITTORIO VENTAFRIDDA AND
AUGUSTO CARACENI

The treatment of pain in patients with cancer implies a knowledge of tumor pathology, specific treatments available to fight cancer, their limitations, and pain physiopathology. Yet, the phenomenon of pain is linked not only to neurophysiologic mechanisms, but also to the patient's past experiences and emotional state, which should be considered also in relation to existential, social, and environmental factors.

Hence, treatment should positively control every aspect of pain and suffering, which means that technological support and care, even the most sophisticated, cannot be separated from the assessment and control of emotional, social, and spiritual conditions [1].

Solving the problem of pain is the ultimate goal; however, therapeutic support and home care must be provided on a continuous basis until the very end. Clearly, to accomplish this task, doctors, nurses, psychologists, social workers, and spiritual assistants have to work together as a team, following the concepts of a new branch of medicine that is becoming internationally renowned—palliative care. This is a new approach that is completely changing the traditional doctor-patient and doctor-family relationships with the main objective of improving the quality of a life that is gradually deteriorating.

EPIDEMIOLOGY

It is rather difficult to outline a clear picture of cancer pain epidemiology. It is worthwhile to consider the world mortality rate for cancer, bearing in mind that pain symptoms appear more often in the advanced stages and are inevitably irreducible when patients no longer respond to specific antitumor treatments.

Data from the World Health Organization (WHO) concerning the mortality rates of different oncologic pathologies are shown in Table 12-1. Moreover, statistical data show for the future a rising mortality for oncologic pathologies (Table 12-2), which means an increase in the prevalence of pain and other related symptoms; hence the growing need for palliative care (Table 12-3) [2–5]. With regard to pain and the many important differences characterizing the oncologic population, our

TABLE 12-1
CANCER MORTALITY RATE IN 20 DEVELOPED COUNTRIES IN 1980*

SITE OR TYPE OF CANCER	MALE	FEMALE
Cervix uteri	-	33
Oral cavity	33	42
Corpus uteri	-	43
Breast	-	43
Bladder	38	45
Prostate	48	-
Larynx	50	48
Colon/rectum	59	59
Lymphoma	63	67
Ovary	-	71
Leukemia	77	77
Stomach	83	83
Liver	83	91
Esophagus	91	91
Bronchus	91	91
Pancreas	100	100
Total	67	59

*Derived from estimated regression coefficients of crude incidence and mortality [2].

TABLE 12-2
PROJECTED PERCENTAGE CHANGES IN CANCER DEATH BETWEEN 1980 AND 2000 IN FOUR COUNTRIES

COUNTRY	MALE	FEMALE
Japan	+80	+40
USA	+50	+30
France	+40	-6
United Kingdom (England and Wales only)	+20	+1

basic understanding of these aspects is still minimal. A broad review of the literature [6] highlighted that not only does medical literature in general and oncologic literature in particular show little attention for pain and its treatment, the data concerning pain prevalence are extremely variable. Fifty percent of patients (including all disease stages) and 70% of those with advanced cancer appear to have some pain symptomatology.

Just to give an idea of the magnitude of this problem, it is estimated that every year, worldwide, 3 of 5 million patients dying of cancer and 4 million of those who survive with cancer experience pain.

PHYSIOPATHOLOGY

It is useful to distinguish among pain produced directly by the disease, pain linked to the outcome of cancer therapy, and pain that is neither disease nor treatment related. Although disease-related pain is more prevalent, the latter groups of patients should not be underestimated because of their diverse therapeutic implications.

The mechanisms thought to be responsible for causing cancer pain are generally hypothetical; however, there are three recognizable categories, namely the activation of nociceptive mechanisms, neuropathic processes, and psychologic influences. Based on these

TABLE 12-3
COMMON SYMPTOMS IN PATIENTS WITH ADVANCED CANCER*

SYMPTOM	INCIDENCE ($n=100$)	MODERATE AND SEVERE, $n(\%)$
Pain	.89	77 (87)
Weight loss	58	58 (100)
Anorexia	55	45 (82)
Dyspnea	41	19 (46)
Constipation	40	24 (60)
Early satiety	40	30 (75)
Fatigue	40	28 (70)
Xerostomia	40	14 (35)
Weakness	36	24 (67)
Lack of energy	32	25 (78)
Depression	31	22 (71)
Sleep problems	28	14 (50)
Taste change	26	20 (77)
Vomiting	25	18 (72)

*From Curtis and coworkers [5]; with permission.

classifications, it is customary in clinical practice to classify pain into different types, ie, nociceptive, neuropathic, and idiopathic, when one or the other mechanism is suspected. This is a gross over-simplification because not even the difference between nociceptive and neuropathic pain is easily established in cancer pain; however, it is useful when describing the different clinical syndromes.

Nociceptive Pain

Nociceptive pain refers to pain produced by tumor stimulation or by tumor-triggered processes in the nerve pathways thought to be responsible for coding and transmitting pain messages to the brain. It is often closely related to the extent of tumor lesion and tumor progression.

Inflammation processes are believed to play a significant role in determining the characteristics of nociceptive pain. Therefore, it originates in the peripheral structures and depends on the nature and organization of pain innervation.

Somatic pain is felt as a dull, heavy, piercing, and sometimes compressive sensation. Visceral pain, however, produces cramps or colic when a hollow viscera is affected, but it is heavy and tearing when a capsule or meso is affected. Chronic stimulation due to a tumor process may lead to modifications at the various levels of the nociceptive system similar to those found in laboratory animals involving considerable plasticity of both peripheral nociceptors and of spinal cord or trigeminal nucleus cells [7]. Generally, nociceptive pain is believed to respond well to pharmacologic analgesic treatments, particularly with opioids, and also to well-targeted interventions for interrupting specific neural pain pathways.

Neuropathic Pain

This term refers to pain in which the role of peripheral receptor stimulation differs from nociceptive pain. Other mechanisms come into play as a result of a lesion to the peripheral or central nervous system, altering the normal functions of the nociceptive system [7]. In general, this coincides with a peculiar feature of pain and pain-related symptoms or signs such as dysesthesia, allodynia, hyperpathia, and changes in receptor fields. In this case, pain is often referred to as burning or lancinating.

Specific changes in nociceptors and the pathways involved in nociception have been described in some pain syndromes caused by different types of lesions of the peripheral or central nervous system (from ictus to peripheral neuropathies). However, the aim of this chapter is not to expound upon the details of such a problem, but rather to underscore that neurologic lesions, which are more often peripheral, are very frequently found in cancer pain syndromes with subjective symptoms that are significantly different from case to case. In general, these syndromes are observed in conjunction with bone lesions or lesions to other somatic structures (Fig. 12-1). For this reason as well, it is often difficult to establish to what extent, or exactly when, the neuropathic mechanism becomes a determining or dominant factor in pain pathogenesis. In fact, according to some authors, the mere presence of neurologic damage is not enough to warrant the diagnosis of neuropathic pain [8–10,11•].

Interventions involving the interruption of afferent pain pathways often lead to unpredictable if not harmful results in the case of neuropathic pain. In addition, it has been reported that this type of pain responds poorly to opioids, although it seems to benefit from other drug treatments. This statement nonetheless is quite controversial [12,13].

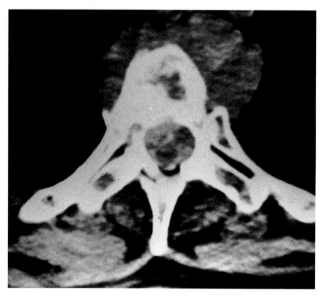

Figure 12-1 In this case (computed tomography scan) a paraspinal neoplastic lesion (sarcoma) is invading the vertebral body (D5) and the epidural space. The patient had midscapular pain with a clearcut radiculopathy, with burning and dysesthetic pain referred to a thoracic area exceeding the dermatomal distribution of the affected root that developed 3 months before the signs of spinal cord compression.

Idiopathic Pain

This term is used in the English language literature to indicate pain that is not explained by an underlying organic lesion but to which subjective psychological factors contribute significantly [11•].

THERAPEUTIC STRATEGY

The strategy for treating patients with advanced cancer pain should be aimed at achieving immediate pain relief within the framework of overall pain assessment and of a multidisciplinary approach, whereby cancer therapy and symptom control are continually intertwined and integrated, as shown in Figure 12-2. Pain assessment, constant follow-up of clinical changes, and continuing care are the most important elements of this strategy [14].

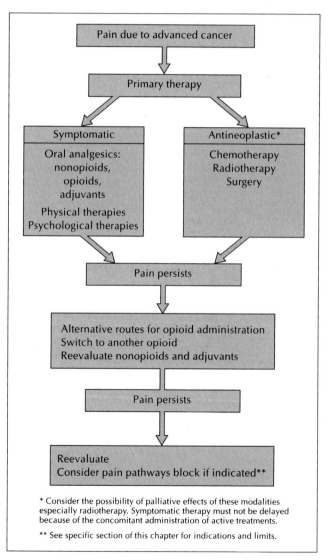

Figure 12-2 Therapeutic strategy for cancer pain relief. A multidisciplinary integrated approach is mandatory.

EVALUATION

The first step of any therapeutic strategy is always to assess pain appropriately. This evaluation should start with a physical examination, patient's medical history, and a proper quantification of pain. Several authors have shown that the subjective quantification of cancer pain is feasible and reliable and provides essential information for verifying the efficacy of drugs or treatments [15].

Several instruments have been proposed for the assessment of pain in general. Other instruments have been designed to evaluate cancer pain, specifically bearing in mind its relationship with other variables such as duration, mood, and quality of life [16–19]. Nevertheless, it is worth remembering that a simple scale from zero to 10 has proven to be the most easily comprehensible instrument to most patients presenting psychometric characteristics that overlap with more complex tests.

Furthermore, from a clinical point of view and in terms of problem understanding, one should never rely on the evaluation of pain intensity alone, but rather use integrated measurements such as pain relief, hours of nighttime sleep, or quality of life measures in reference to performance, social interaction, and emotional status [20,21] because these factors can radically influence clinical opinion which would otherwise be based on a single isolated value of pain intensity.

PHARMACOLOGIC TREATMENT

It is universally recognized that analgesic drugs are the first and most important means of controlling cancer pain. Since 1982, the WHO has placed pain relief among the top priorities of its cancer control program and, because of the suggestions of international experts, it has laid down guidelines that recommend the administration of analgesic drugs as a basic approach to cancer pain treatment. These suggestions are outlined in what has come to be widely known as the WHO analgesic ladder. This scale has been the object of validation studies involving different populations where from 70% to 90% of the patients achieved good pain control [22,23]. The administration of oral analgesic drugs is effective in most cases and should be based on an in-depth knowledge of drug pharmacokinetics and side effects.

Pain symptoms are almost always continuous in type; however, in 60% of the cases, pain may be exacerbated by breakthrough episodes [24]. Hence, pain therapy should allow for extra doses to be given to the patient, according to the concept of patient-controlled analgesia (PCA).

Nonsteroidal Anti-inflammatory Drugs

The analgesic effect of these drugs is believed to be mediated by the inhibition of cyclooxygenase, hence of prostaglandin synthesis along with that of other peripheral mediators of inflammation activating or sensitizing peripheral nociceptors. Other mechanisms have been suggested because of a lack of association between the anti-inflammatory effect and the analgesic effect of certain compounds. In a study involving more than 1200 patients, the effectiveness of nonsteroidal anti-inflammatory drugs (NSAIDs) was found to be limited over time, with an average duration of therapy of 3 weeks [22]. The main difference between NSAIDs and opioids is that the latter do not lead to a ceiling effect.

There are many classes of drugs and many molecular formulations with this kind of activity. However, differences concerning their therapeutic effect and a profile of their side effects is still lacking, and only very few studies have attempted to assess them [25].

The suggested drugs and their daily doses are shown in Table 12-4. A ceiling dose when drug therapy becomes ineffective has already been discussed; for this reason, these drugs are often indicated for slight to moderate pain. Nevertheless, NSAIDs may be effectively used for malignant bone pain, no matter how severe, and in all cases where inflammatory symptoms are prevalent.

An additional analgesic effect can be achieved by combining NSAIDs with opioids. This is very useful in treating pain syndromes of mixed etiology and may entail a reduction in the dose of opioid needed to reach analgesia [26].

The major side effects of NSAIDs are reported in Table 12-5, whereas Table 12-6 shows the interactions with other drugs [26]. Side effects may be caused by the inhibition of prostaglandin synthesis in several organs. Gastric toxicity should be duly considered, especially in patients with diagnosed gastropathies or bleeding disorders. The first 2 weeks of treatment present the highest risk, but after that gastric mucosa appears to adapt fairly well. The combination of H2-receptor antagonists is an effective way of reducing symptoms and preventing duodenal ulcer. Another symptomatic effect is achieved using antacids. More recently prostaglandins administered per os (mysoprostol, 400 to 800 μg/d) were studied and proved to be effective in preventing acute gastric lesions due to NSAIDs [27–30].

Effects on the central nervous system are still unclear, but some cases of confusion and minor cognitive impairment in the elderly were reported [31].

Renal toxicity is encountered more frequently when using indomethacin and is facilitated by the presence of congestive heart failure, chronic renal insufficiency, dehydration, and the concurrent use of diuretics. It is caused by ischemia in the absence of renal prostaglandin synthesis, which is one of the mechanisms regulating

TABLE 12-4
NONSTEROIDAL ANTI-INFLAMMATORY DRUGS

GENERIC NAME	HALF-LIFE (h)	DOSING SCHEDULE	STARTING DOSE, mg/d	MAXIMUM DOSE, mg/d	COMMENTS
Acetaminophen	2–4	q 4–6 h	1400	4000	Overdose produces hepatic toxicity. Not anti-inflammatory.
Aspirin*	3–12*	q 4–6 h	1400	6000	Higher gastrointestinal toxicity than newer nonsteroidal anti-inflammatory drugs.
Choline magnesium trisalicyclate*	8–12	q 12 h	1500 x 1 then 1000 q 12 h		Less gastrointestinal toxicity, no platelet dysfunction. May therefore be useful in some cancer patients.
Ibuprofen*	3–4	q 4–8 h	1200	4200	
Naproxen sodium*	13	q 12 h	550	1100	
Ketoprofen	2–3	q 6–8 h	150	300	
Indomethacin	4–5	q 8–12 h	75	200	
Diclofenac*	2	q 6 h	75	200	
		q 12 h*	200	200	(Slow release formulations.)
Ketorolac	4–7	q 4–6 h	30	120	Parenteral formulation available for intravenous use.
Piroxicam	45	q 24 h	20	40	High incidence of peptic ulcers.

*Starting dose should be reduced in the elderly, with multiple drugs, and in renal insufficiency.

TABLE 12-5
NONSTEROIDAL ANTI-INFLAMMATORY DRUGS SIDE EFFECTS*

GASTRO-INTESTINAL	CENTRAL NERVOUS SYSTEM	RENAL	HEPATIC	PLATELET DYSFUNCTION
Hemorrhage	Tinnitus	Hyperazotemia	(Paracetamol at high doses)	Pupura
Anorexia	Dizziness	Renal failure		Bleeding
Diarrhea	Confusion			
Abdominal pain	Sedation			
Nausea	Cognitive impairment			
Dyspepsia				

*From Stambaugh [26]; with permission.

glomerular flow. If the drugs are used following the proper precautions, it is possible that the risk-to-benefit ratio will turn out to be very favorable.

The risks of serious gastroenteric toxicity are still unclear for patients affected with advanced tumors and under treatment with steroids as well. In this patient population, the authors have not infrequently observed fatal cases of gastroenteric perforation.

Oral Opioids

The role of these drugs in treating cancer pain is fundamental. The limits imposed on their availability in certain countries and the poor knowledge of their use are the main reasons for under-medication and undue suffering of cancer patients.

The oral administration of opioids has been proven effective in the treatment of most cancer pain syndromes. The most widely used drugs are reported in Table 12-7 [32]. A solution of oral morphine administered at fixed intervals was the therapy that proved the effectiveness of opioids per os before this kind of treatment was even described in textbooks.

Oral bioavailability varies among drugs, yet to a large extent for all opioids it depends on the so-called first-pass liver metabolism. For morphine, oral bioavailability varies between 15% and 60%. This, together with other factors such as age, type and intensity of nociceptive stimulus, impaired metabolism or excretion, interaction with other drugs, and tolerance, requires that opioid doses be tailored to the individual case [32,33].

Slow-release formulations of morphine represent a safe and efficacious means of providing continuous analgesia with administration every 12 hours. Their effectiveness has been proven both in cancer and postoperative pain [34,35]. These preparations offer an improvement in that they eliminate the need for taking medication every 4 hours. The changing level of pain in cancer, however, should always be considered when extra doses or dose reductions are envisaged.

Opioid side effects are, for the most part, manageable. The main side effect, especially for the oral route, is constipation, which should be preventively and aggressively treated. It is often dose-dependent and best managed with a combination of stool softeners and stimulant laxatives. The laxative effect is also dose-dependent, therefore higher doses of laxatives are needed when opioid intake increases. In a few cases, however, this effect can require a change in therapy. Nausea and vomiting are

TABLE 12-6
DRUG INTERACTION WITH NONSTEROIDAL ANTI-INFLAMMATORY DRUGS

SITE	EFFECT	DRUGS
Central nervous system	Additive sedation	Narcotics Central nervous system depressors
Protein binding (NSAID 90%)	Displacement with increased toxicity	Methotrexate Corticosteroids Coumadin Phenytoin Oral hypoglycemics
Hepatic metabolism	Decreased NSAID metabolism	Steroids
	Increased NSAID metabolism	Phenobarbital NSAID Antihistamines
Renal excretion	Competition for tubular active transport increase in drug levels	Lithium Methotrexate

*From Stambaugh [26]; with permission.
NSAID—nonsteroidal anti-inflammatory drug.

TABLE 12-7
OPIOID DRUGS

DRUG AND ROUTE	EQUIANALGESIC DOSE, mg	PLASMA HALF-LIFE, h	EXCRETION	
			PRIMARY (% EXCRETED UNCHANGED)†	SECONDARY
Morphine		2–3.5	85% Renal	10% Biliary
Oral	60			
IM	10			
Buprenorphine		30–40		
IM	0.3			
SL	0.4			
Butorphanol		2.5–3.5	70% Renal	15% Biliary
IM	2			
IV				
Codeine		3	Renal 10% as unchanged or conjugated morphine	
Oral	200			
IM	120			
Fentanyl		3–12	75% Renal	
IV	0.5			
Heroin		0.05	Renal	
IM	5			
Oral	30			
Hydromorphone		2–3	Renal	
Oral	7.5			
IM	1.5			
Rectal	3			
Levorphanol		12–16	Renal	
Oral	4			
IM	2			
Methadone		13–50	Renal, rate increased acidic urine	Biliary
Oral	20			
IM	10			
Nalbuphine		5	Renal	
IM	10			
Oxycodone		2–3	Renal	
Oral	30			
IM	15			
Pentazocine		2–3	Renal	Biliary
Oral	180			
IM	60			
Propoxyphene		12	Renal	Biliary
Oral				
Norpropoxyphene (Metabolite)		30–40		

*Data from acute administration; 1:3 ratio more appropriate in chronic administration.
†All opioid analgesics are excreted primarily as metabolites.
IM—intramuscular; IV—intravenous; SL—sublingual.

not a constant side effect of oral opioids and are found more often in patients who already have gastrointestinal or emetic symptoms. If aggressively treated, the number of patients who do not tolerate medication can be reduced to just a few cases (Table 12-8). Preventive treatment is not necessary. Respiratory depression has never been reported after the oral administration of opioids alone. Central nervous system side effects are still unclear [36,37], and although a certain degree of sedation can be achieved with any form of opioid therapy, it is again a dose-related effect and very often analgesic doses can be reached without clinically significant sedation. Confusion or delirium has been reported in some cases [38]. However rare this effect, concomitant conditions such as metabolic dysfunction and polypharmacy should carefully be checked. Central nervous system lesions are very frequent in advanced cancer. Seizures and myoclonus have been seen with high opioid doses [39,40•,41].

The role of metabolites has only recently been studied, particularly glucuronized morphine metabolites [42••], yet much less is known about other opioid metabolites [43]. The possibility of specific metabolites triggering side effects [44] and of incomplete cross-tolerance between different drugs suggests the usefulness of switching from one opioid to another in difficult cases.

Nevertheless, when side effects limit the efficacy of an oral opioid, this is usually related to gastrointestinal complications or to sedation. In the first case, a change in the route of administration can be dramatically useful. This is also true in cases of insufficient analgesia with rather high doses of oral opioids. Parenteral administration can help to achieve a new analgesic level when oral doses prove to be impractical or cause too many gastrointestinal effects. Only when a very accurate parenteral titration (intravenous, subcutaneous, or even spinal) has been performed in the presence of insufficient analgesia and unacceptable side effects, can a pain pathway block procedure be considered.

Alternative Routes for Opioid Administration

SUBCUTANEOUS INFUSION

In the study conducted by Ventafridda and coworkers [45], it was shown that the continuous subcutaneous administration (CSCA) of morphine can be used when nausea and vomiting make oral administration impossible and also when analgesia is difficult to obtain with oral morphine or parenteral injections.

The case series by Bruera and coworkers [46] substantially confirms the indications mentioned above. In this study, the method was effective in roughly 80% of the cases. In both studies, CSCA was performed in the hospital and at home. In the Canadian case series, 94% of the patients said they preferred CSCA to previous therapies, whereas in the Italian study, 16% of the patients preferred an alternative treatment because of a psychological intolerance toward infusion devices, often because of anxiety concerning having to wear and rely on an external device. Common opioid side effects have

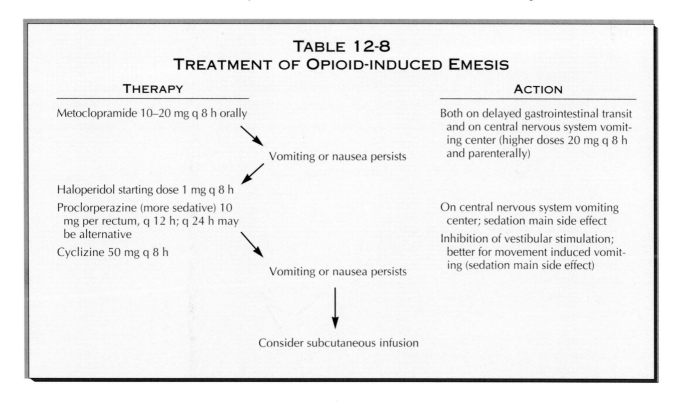

TABLE 12-8
TREATMENT OF OPIOID-INDUCED EMESIS

THERAPY	ACTION
Metoclopramide 10–20 mg q 8 h orally	Both on delayed gastrointestinal transit and on central nervous system vomiting center (higher doses 20 mg q 8 h and parenterally)
Vomiting or nausea persists	
Haloperidol starting dose 1 mg q 8 h	On central nervous system vomiting center; sedation main side effect
Proclorperazine (more sedative) 10 mg per rectum, q 12 h; q 24 h may be alternative	
Cyclizine 50 mg q 8 h	Inhibition of vestibular stimulation; better for movement induced vomiting (sedation main side effect)
Vomiting or nausea persists	
Consider subcutaneous infusion	

been found with CSCA. They are mild and only rarely hinder treatment.

Cutaneous reactions at the injection site were observed in 9% to 13% of the patients and were easily managed by changing the injection site. Bruera [47] showed that the tolerability of the subcutaneous needle is 7.3 ± 5.2 days (mean ± SD).

Continuous subcutaneous administration has been used for very long periods of time without giving rise to toxic effects. Daily doses may vary considerably from author to author as a result of patient selection and the extensive therapeutic range of opioids used in chronic therapy (Table 12-9) [45,46,48–50].

Tolerance probably develops in all forms of opioid treatment. Portenoy and coworkers [51] described three typical patterns in opioid infusion: 1) relatively stable doses with good pain control; 2) rapidly increasing doses with good analgesia; and 3) insufficient analgesia despite the fast rate of dose increase. In our view, this last case could be the result of an opioid-resistant pain syndrome [13].

Morphine doses are reported in Table 12-9, and certainly morphine is the most widely used opioid drug also in CSCA. Hydromorphone is widely used in the United States because of its high solubility (six times that of morphine) and potency (seven times that of morphine), thus permitting a reduction in the volume of infused opioid in patients who require higher doses. Diamorphine is often preferred in Great Britain because of its high solubility.

Diamorphine can help to improve local tissue compliance in cases of inflammatory reactions due to the infusion of high doses of morphine or hydromorphone. The CSCA of methadone has been associated with severe local reactions [52].

Controlled clinical trials comparing CSCA with other forms of opioid administration are very rare. It has already been reported that this method can achieve good results in cases of intolerance to morphine oral administration due to nausea and vomiting [45] and that it is feasible in patients suffering from severe side effects following the use of intramuscular or subcutaneous boli ("bolus effect") [46].

Continuous infusions can be effective in patients who obtained little benefit from repeated injections [45,53–55]. In postoperative pain therapy, it has been observed that the CSCA of morphine compares favorably with intravenous infusion [56].

A recent study using a double-blind cross-over design compared the intravenous and CSCA of hydromorphone for chronic cancer pain. No differences were reported in terms of side effects and analgesia. Plasma concentrations were also comparable between the two infusion methods. Considering the technical advantages of the subcutaneous technique, the authors suggest that intravenous opioid infusion for severe cancer pain be abandoned [57••].

Cousins and Plummer [58] stress the importance of controlled studies on the role of spinal opioid compared to CSCA that are still lacking.

PATIENT-CONTROLLED ANALGESIA

In recent years the concept of PCA gained popularity in different clinical contexts because of the wide individual variability of pain and responsiveness to analgesics. This method was successfully employed for postoperative pain often using the intravenous route; pain relief could be obtained with good patient compliance and reduced opioid consumption when compared with traditional fixed-dose treatments [59,60]. This chapter, however, will only deal with the use of this method in chronic pain treatment.

Several well-designed controlled studies were conducted to assess PCA for pain due to oral mucositis dur-

TABLE 12-9
SUBCUTANEOUS MORPHINE INFUSION DOSES

AUTHOR, YEAR	PATIENTS, n	DURATION IN DAYS		DOSE, mg/d	
		MEAN	RANGE	MEAN	RANGE
Ventafridda, 1986	60	52	(2–235)	64.8	(10–200)
Bruera, 1988*	108	31	(2–156)	310.0	(40–4024)
Kerr (PCA), 1988	18	44	(7–64)	588.0	(120–1920)
Swanson (PCA), 1989†	117	23	(1–295)	156.0	(12–360)
Drexel, 1989	36	37	(2–197)	22.1	(5–48)

*Higher doses with hydromorphone (305 mg, 80–300 mg).
†Higher doses by intravenous infusion (416 mg, 48–4320 mg).
PCA—patient-controlled analgesia.

ing high-dose chemotherapy and total-body radiotherapy. This pain syndrome is very severe and seems to respond only partially to morphine analgesia [61]. In one study patients were randomly assigned to continuous intravenous infusion regulated by the staff or to PCA. Analgesic results were comparable with a 50% or more reduction of morphine use in the PCA group. In addition, these authors hypothesized the psychological advantages of the method [62,63]. Even better results were obtained when the patients could personally control their own morphine infusion rate and plasma concentrations (pharmacokinetically based PCA). Pain relief was improved at higher morphine doses without increasing side effects [64••]. Recently, this method was used to compare alfentanyl and morphine. The two drugs gave similar analgesic effects while, interestingly enough, a relatively rapid onset of tolerance was documented for alfentanyl with respect to morphine [65].

Patient-controlled analgesia was first applied to chronic cancer pain in the 1970s [66]. Patient independence from staff intervention and close titration of analgesia to individual patient needs seem to constitute the main theoretical advantage of PCA for cancer pain management. In a preliminary study by Citron and coworkers [67], the method was found to be feasible in eight patients with intravenous morphine administration, and good analgesia with slight sedation was reported. Five patients preferred this method to previous treatments. The same authors extended their study to include the long-term treatment of outpatients with cancer pain [68]. In a cross-over study between CSCA and PCA using hydromorphone for 25 patients, pain relief was comparable between the two methods; however, all patients required extra doses (mean = 6) when treated with CSCA. At the end of the study, some patients preferred PCA while others preferred CSCA [69].

A modified application of PCA is one in which a continuous infusion of opioids is integrated with the possibility of self-administering extra boli at preestablished intervals and doses. Kerr and coworkers [48] used this approach with extra doses of 50% and 100% of the hourly infused dose and a lock-out interval of 30 to 60 minutes. The main indication for this treatment was breakthrough pain. A home care case series of 117 patients using either intravenous or subcutaneous infusion has been reported [49]. Often, different drugs were combined in the infusion (haloperidol, metoclopramide, and dexamethasone). Our experience confirms that this form of administration is practical and, in some cases, more flexible to patient needs, especially to control breakthrough pain, than continuous infusion. The psychological advantages of PCA have to be carefully assessed on a case-by-case basis. This system, in fact, is very useful for some patients, giving them a sense of self-control over pain and the overall situation. In other cases, the opposite is true; the responsibility of controlling one's pain and the fear of drug abuse can trigger anxiety and insecurity.

SPINAL ADMINISTRATIONS

The spinal administration of opioids (epidural or subarachnoid) is still one of the most widely used methods for cancer pain treatment. Though this method has been employed since the 1970s, its role and indication for chronic cancer pain are still unclear. In recent literature, it is easy to come across some contrasting statements: "Our view is that spinal opioids should be considered for opioid sensitive pain when the patient experiences intolerable side effects from systemic morphine." This is the opinion of Hanks and Justins [70]; whereas the opinion of Hassenbuch and coworkers [71] is in order for the patient to be fit for epidural infusion, he or she should "have experienced inadequate pain control by oral, rectal, and/or intravenous preparations of narcotics without significant side effects."

It is still unclear whether there are differences in the profile of side effects between spinal and systemic administrations. From a clinical standpoint, in a study by Vainio and Tigerstedt [72] comparing oral and peridural morphine, the methods gave equally effective analgesia and a lower incidence of central nervous system side effects with peridural administration, whereas Sjogren and Banning [73] did not find any difference between the central effects of oral and peridural morphine.

In general, there is a tendency for the epidural morphine success rate to be inversely related to previous systemic opiate doses [74–76]. In a recent study, Hogan and coworkers [77••] showed that of 1205 patients admitted to an oncology department, only 16 (1.24%) required spinal opioids for pain not controllable via systemic administrations. Only six of these patients had adequate analgesia with morphine alone. In the other cases, analgesia was obtained only with the addition of bupivacaine. In 11 cases, complications such as displacement and rupture of the catheter, pain upon injection, bleeding, or infection were recorded. In another study by Shetter and coworkers [76], the spinal administration of morphine was tried in patients who had pain that was no longer controlled with oral opioids or who presented unacceptable side effects. A very strict protocol of temporary epidural catheter titration was applied before a chronic system was implanted. Only 14 of 24 patients went on to chronic peridural infusion and only 10 could be considered fully successful.

Therefore, it is reasonable to conclude that when careful opioid titration is performed at adequate doses with parenteral administration, such as subcutaneous or intravenous infusions, without satisfying pain relief, it is highly unlikely that better results will be obtained with the spinal route.

A preliminary trial with a temporary catheter is always recommended before a chronic system is implanted.

The pharmacologic characteristics of spinal administrations have been well described elsewhere [78]. It is worth remembering, however, that its exclusive feature at the beginning of therapy is a prolonged analgesic effect with very low doses of the opioid drug. This is probably due to high concentrations of the drug at the receptor level. The variables that modify the clinical effect of various opioids in spinal administration are lipid solubility, rostral distribution, systemic uptake, and receptor affinity (Table 12-10) [78,79]. Larger volumes of lipid-soluble, highly-ionized compounds give shorter onset and shorter duration analgesia with less rostral spread but reveal a more pronounced systemic uptake and faster vascular clearance.

The spinal selectivity of spinal opioids, however, has to be carefully analyzed. Morphine, which is still the most widely used drug in this form of administration, has a very significant vascular uptake after peridural administration [80]; 10 mg delivered peridurally gave the same plasma levels as those achieved after intramuscular injection [81]. When intrathecal administration is preferred, plasma levels can be negligible at low doses but the cerebrospinal fluid bulk flow will lead to high supraspinal (cisterna magna) morphine concentrations—the same happens after peridural injection [82].

With regard to clinical use, no validated conversion ratio between chronic systemic administrations and spinal dose is known. Therefore, this conversion must be based on the total parenteral morphine equivalent dose and on

the data given in Table 12-10. The greatest caution should be exercised because all these considerations are, at best, hypothetical and based on wide individual variability.

The choice of the peridural versus the intrathecal route is still based more on practical and subjective considerations than on well-established guidelines; epidural catheters are considered safer and more flexible for the use of different opioids and, more importantly, for concomitant local anesthetic administration. Intrathecal catheters present fewer technical complications. Pain on injection is virtually absent, whereas it is a reported complication of epidural catheters. In addition, less technical skill is required for their placement, whereas the more expensive closed systems usually need to be employed in chronic administrations. When high doses are necessary, low capacity implantable pumps can be impractical, especially at home, and the risk of central nervous system toxicity may increase [41]. Nonetheless, technical problems are certainly the main reason warranting the need for an extremely accurate and continuous follow-up of these patients. They are also the main cause of reevaluation in most forms of spinal systems [83,77••].

The choice of continuous infusion versus intermittent boli is another issue open for discussion. Continuous infusions can prevent pain after epidural injections and have the advantage of not requiring daily nursing visits. Continuous infusion was thought to be useful for reducing side effects and tolerance and for guaranteeing more consistent analgesia. A slower development of tolerance with continuous infusion was suggested by Shetter and coworkers [76]. In a randomized trial comparing contin-

TABLE 12-10
OPIOID PHARMACOLOGIC CHARACTERISTICS RELEVANT TO SPINAL ADMINISTRATION

CHARACTERISTIC	MORPHINE	MEPEREDINE	METHADONE	FENTANYL
Molecular weight	285	247.3	309	337
% ionized pH 7.4	76	95	99	91
O/W partition coefficient*	1.42	38.8	116	995
Spinal cord receptor uptake, min†	30–60	15–30	15–30	10–15
Intravenous average effective dose, mg	10	100	10	0.1
Epidural average effective dose, mg	5–10	25–50	4–5	0.1
Onset of effect, min	20	15	10	10
Duration of action after epidural administration, h	4–24	3–10	4–15	1–4
Cerebrospinal fluid concentration	High			Low
Rostral spread	Extensive			Limited

*Oil/water partition coefficient.
†Spinal cord receptor uptake (onset of epidural analgesia, min).

uous peridural and boli administration, Gourlay and coworkers [84] found no difference in analgesia and side effects, but rather observed higher morphine consumption in the group receiving continuous infusion. Several technical devices are available for spinal treatment and are very well reviewed by Waldman and Coombs [85] who divided the systems in use into six classes. A general comment can be that technical complications are less frequent with closed and completely implanted systems and that intrathecal administration warrants closed systems with specialized nursing care for aseptic maneuvers.

OTHER ROUTES FOR OPIOID ADMINISTRATION

Intravenous infusion has been shown to be safe and useful with patients requiring very high doses, or with patients whose doses need to be increased very frequently [49,51,57••].

Morphine, as well as other opioids (ie, hydromorphone, oxycodone) can be administered rectally via aqueous solutions, suppositories, and even commercial oral preparations (slow-release tablets) [86,87]. Plasma levels may vary from one individual to another, much like oral bioavailability [88–90]. The clinical role of this form of administration is still unclear. It could be useful in cases of dysphagia or for the administration of rescue doses when other routes are impractical.

Sublingual and buccal administrations are pharmacologically feasible; however, their clinical role is doubtful (for review, Bruera and Ripamonti [90]). Instead, buprenorphine sublingual tablets are often used in Europe for treating mild to moderate pain.

Transdermal fentanyl administration is now feasible with systems designed to deliver constant fentanyl doses continuously over a 72-hour period. They are available in 25, 50, 75, and 100 µg/h doses [90]. Effective steady state concentrations are not reached before 8 to 12 hours after their initial application. Therefore, initial pain relief has to be obtained using other means. After removing the transdermal system, a slow decline in plasma concentration is observed and should be properly considered in therapy changes. A recent article reported the use of PCA with intravenous fentanyl to titrate the patient to acceptable pain relief and then shift to a transdermal patch. Relatively stable fentanyl plasma levels, as well as good pain relief, can be obtained with subcutaneous rescue doses of morphine (mean daily dose, 25 mg) for 1 week of treatment [91]. Clinical trials with these systems have to be considered as preliminary. Specific indications for this route as an alternative to subcutaneous or intravenous infusions are tentative.

Adjuvants

The term adjuvant is commonly used to define drugs that are used in combination (though not necessarily) with analgesics (ie, opioids and NSAIDs) but are not classifiable as analgesics. Also, adjuvants are believed to carry out a complementary effect in certain pain syndromes with peculiar characteristics. Some of these drugs have their own documented analgesic effect. The most widely used drugs in cancer pain treatment along with their widely accepted indications are reported in Table 12-11.

TABLE 12-11
ADJUVANT ANALGESICS

CLASS	INDICATION	PREFERRED DRUGS	DOSING SCHEDULE	STARTING DOSE, mg/d	USUAL DAILY DOSE, mg/d
Tricyclic antidepressants	Continuous neuropathic pain	Amitriptyline	1 night dose	10–25	50–100
		Imipramine	1 night dose	10–25	50–100
Anticonvulsants	Lancinating neuropathic pain	Carbamazepine	q 8 h	200	400–1600
		Phenytoin	qh	300	300
		Valproate	q 8 h	500	750–2000
		Clonazepam	q 12 h	0.5	2–5
Oral local anesthetics	Neuropathic pain	Mexiletine	q 8 h	300	450–900
Muscle relaxants	Acute musculoskeletal pain	Thiocolchicosides	q 12 h	8	8
		Orphenadrine	q 6–8 h	100	100–200
Corticosteroids	Compression of neural structures; bone pain	Dexamethasone	q 6–8–12 h	10–20 intravenous loading dose the 4 q 8 h orally	2–24

The analgesic effect of tricyclic antidepressants was shown in several controlled studies with placebo considering different pain syndromes, among which were studies of postherpetic neuralgia and diabetic neuropathy [92–96]. There are no studies to date documenting the analgesic effect of these drugs in cancer pain. It was shown that they can increase the oral bioavailability of morphine probably because of interaction at the level of liver metabolism [97]. Therefore, it is difficult to say whether the adjuvant effect is attributable to pharmacokinetics or pharmacodynamics or both. A rise in certain side effects may occur after the simultaneous administration of opioids and tricyclic antidepressants, especially central and peripheral anticholinergic effects. Acute confusional states, recovering after withholding tricyclics while continuing opioids, have been observed by the authors.

Anticonvulsants are used effectively to control essential trigeminal neuralgia, and carbamazepine is the most widely used and best-tolerated drug [98,99]. Observations support the role of these drugs as adjuvants in the treatment of cancer pain with lancinating neuropathic component [100]. According to our experience, in cases of head and neck cancer, where often lancinating pain is present with continuous pain, the addition of carbamazepine to the opioid treatment can reduce the number of lancinating episodes.

Corticosteroid administration is very frequent in advanced cancer and beneficial effects have been reported in a few controlled studies [101,102]. An acute pain-relieving effect is obtained with relatively high to very high doses of intravenous dexamethasone administered for epidural spinal cord compression [103,104]. In our experience, the same immediate effect was often observed in cases of plexi and peripheral nerve compression by the tumor and in radiculopathies.

The intravenous administration of local anesthetics has a proven effect on some forms of neuropathic pain [105•]. Recently, the efficacy of oral tocainamide and mexiletine in relieving neuropathic pain was documented, especially the burning components [106–108]. Uncontrolled experiences showed that cancer pain with neuropathic component responds to intravenous or subcutaneous lidocaine [100,109].

Clonidine has a proven analgesic effect in several animal models of acute and chronic pain [110]. The mechanism of α_2-agonist—mediated antinociception is still to be made clear [110]. In humans, clonidine showed an analgesic effect after both systemic and spinal administration [111,112]. The observation that some patients with deafferentation pain did not obtain relief with epidural morphine but were relieved by clonidine suggests the possibility of a specific role for this drug in opioid-resistant syndromes [113–116]. Side effects are mainly orthostatic hypotension and sedation. The clinical use of clonidine is preliminary.

Bisphosphonates are a relatively new class of agents that can be used in the relief of metastatic bone pain. Their action is of inhibiting osteoclast-mediated bone resorption; they have a potent hypocalcemic effect. Several uncontrolled studies showed an analgesic effect of these compounds (clodronate, etidronate, pamidronate) [117,118] that seemed to be especially evident in myeloma bone lesions [117,119,120]. The only double-blind placebo-controlled study available was conducted with clodronate (dichlomethylene bisphosphonate) at doses of 600 mg intravenous infusion/day for 7 consecutive days [121]. An advantage in terms of pain and activity was obtained in comparison with the placebo, although the magnitude of the effect was limited. The intensity-of-dose effect relationship, the kind of tumor and bone pain that are more likely to respond favorably, the differences among various bisphosphonates, and finally their very mechanism in bone pain relief all remain unresolved issues. Acute renal failure has been observed after bolus administration of clodronate but no toxicity was found after slow (4 h) intravenous infusion. Renal function should, however, be checked, together with calcemia to prevent hypocalcemic episodes.

OPIOID-RESISTANT PAIN

The issue concerning opioid-resistant pain is still widely debated. According to some authors, it is difficult to determine whether pain is unresponsive to opioid analgesics or if the dose-effect slope is so moved to the right in some cases as to make opioid treatment impractical due to the onset of undesired side effects [13]. It is true that most cases of unresponsive opioid pain can be managed by appropriate upward titration, possibly by changing the administration from oral to parenteral in cases of excessive gastrointestinal side effects at high oral doses.

Nevertheless, some pain syndromes require close evaluation, if anything, when there is an unfavorable response to opioid therapy. Neuropathic pain with a major deafferentation component is considered to be usually relatively resistant to opioids [12,122,123]. Perineal pain with rectal and vesical tenesmus and mucosal burning pain, such as in postchemoradiotherapy mucositis, are other examples [60]. Rather than initiate a theoretical discussion on the matter, a working definition might be useful in clinical practice: an opioid-resistant pain syndrome should imply either no response or an insufficient analgesic response despite an upward titration of full agonist opioids through a reliable administration route (the best choice would be intravenous infusion) to the point of unacceptable central nervous system side effects [13]. Recently, a protocol employing PCA proved useful in studying opioid responsiveness [123]. In this study, neuropathic pain showed a relative resistance to opioids, but 50% of the pain syndrome diagnosed as neuropathic did show a response. In another study, the presence of plexus or nerve involvement had no negative impact on pain relief, whereas only 6% of the patients with bone metastases were pain-free when moving [10,124,125].

The magnitude of this specific problem still awaits sound analysis and evaluation. In the previously mentioned study by Hogan and coworkers [77••], 1.24% of cancer patients were reported to be unmanageable with systemic opioids, and 75% of them with neuropathic pain required bupivacaine spinal infusion to achieve analgesia. A recent report by Du Pen and coworkers [126] presenting a case series of 375 patients covering 5 years of activity shows that 18% failed to respond to aggressive epidural opioid escalation, and 90% of the nonresponders could be managed with an admixture of morphine and bupivacaine. Chronic bupivacaine concentrations ranged from 0.1% to 0.5% with infusion rates varying from 4 to 18 mL/h. Sensory loss was present at concentrations exceeding 0.25%, while at concentrations exceeding 0.35% motor impairment was observed. Postural hypotension was observed in 9% of the cases. No central nervous system or systemic toxicity was reported. Similar results have been reported on the use of intrathecal bupivacaine and morphine with a higher incidence of urinary retention (24%) [127]. With selected patients, pain pathway blocks can be considered an alternative to continuous anesthetic blockade when nociceptive pain is implicated.

NONPHARMACOLOGIC TREATMENTS

Nerve blocking or neurolesive procedures (either anesthesiologic or surgical) have been widely used for many years. They are based on the principle of blocking pain pathways, and this can be done at the level of the I, II, or III neuron of the sensitive pathway. These procedures require the use of state-of-the-art equipment and considerable expertise. They are indicated for certain types of pain, and only a few procedures can be performed. A great many surgical or chemical lesions have been attempted, but often only case reports are available [128]. Maintaining an open stance on the subject, it is worth stressing that information is often rather limited, and a definite evaluation on the role of these procedures in the global therapeutic strategy for cancer pain treatment is still lacking [129].

The Role of Neurolesive Treatments

The most widely used techniques are percutaneous, chemical, and thermal neurolesions, provided they are: 1) accepted by the patient, 2) high-pain pathway selective, 3) not the cause of new functional deficits, or 4) not painful.

The efficacy of these treatments is very difficult to ascertain because most papers dealing with neurolytic techniques do not report appropriate follow-up. In a survey of 76 major studies on neurolytic blocks, our group observed a lack of long-term follow-up in more than 69% of the studies reported [130].

In order to obtain a better understanding of the role of these techniques, we monitored two groups of patients for over 3 months [131]. The first group was treated according to the WHO sequential pharmacologic ladder, while the second group received the same treatment supplemented by neurolesive blocks. Patients treated with neurolesive techniques in conjunction with drug therapy achieved statistically higher and faster pain relief than those treated only with drugs during the first week of treatment (Fig. 12-3). Pain relief, without any need for additional analgesic treatment, was maintained after 3 months in 25% of the patients treated with celiac plexus alcoholization, in 24% of the patients treated with percutaneous cordotomy, in 12% of the patients treated with chemical rhizotomy, and in 7% of the patients treated with Gasserian thermorhizotomy.

These results suggest that neurolesive techniques are only a complementary, albeit useful, part of a continuing care program, and they require supplementary drug analgesia. Their primary effect is to reduce the need for analgesics, thus creating a temporary pain-free period.

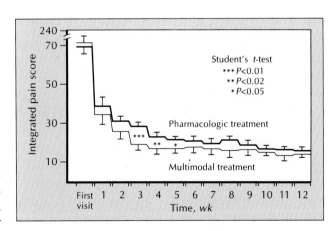

Figure 12-3 Comparison between two groups of patients (100 cases each) followed for 3 months. The pharmacologic treatment line corresponds to the pain score of the group treated according to the World Health Organization analgesic scale only; the multimodal treatment line is the score of the group where the analgesic approach was integrated with blocks. *T-bars* indicate standard deviation. (*From* Ventafridda and coworkers [131]; with permission.)

In our center the use of pharmacologic treatments and continuing care were coupled with a remarkable reduction in the use of these techniques, which are currently intended for highly selected indications (Fig. 12-4) [131].

Subarachnoid Neurolytic Blocks

The administration of chemical agents into the epidural or intrathecal space was once a very common treatment for cancer pain. In our opinion, the spinal injection of either hypobaric alcohol solution or hyperbaric phenol in glycerin has no selective action on sensitive pain fibers. There is, therefore, a high risk of disabling lesions [132].

We will limit our descriptions to the cauda-equina rhizotomy technique, as it is the only one we perform for perineal pain. With the patient in seated position, a 23-gauge needle is introduced through L5–S1 interspace into the subarachnoid space (Fig. 12-5). Once this is done the needle is withdrawn posteriorly until the cerebrospinal fluid flow is reduced to a trickle, thus avoiding the anterior roots that lie more ventrally. An 0.8 mL solution of 7.5% phenol in glycerin is then slowly injected. The patient is tilted backwards at an angle of 15° to 30° to the edge of the table. The patient is kept in this position for 30 minutes. We use chemical rhizotomy when a patient suffering from perineal pain shows signs of disease recurrence, macroscopic areas of vulvovaginal or pararectal erosion, evident "trigger points," and problems with micturition due to a preexisting bladder dysfunction. In our study, 39 patients with perineal pain were treated with chemical rhizotomy. The average duration of pain relief was 5.4 months [133]. Bladder sphincter complications were noted in 19 patients (49%). Problems concerning rectal dysfunction did not develop in our patients mainly because 79% of them had submitted to colostomy beforehand.

Celiac Plexus Block

The best indication for the celiac plexus block is celiac pain due to pancreatic involvement or to neoplastic spreading on the celiac axis after failure of analgesic drug titration. The technique currently in use has been described by Moore [134] and allows the celiac plexus region to be located percutaneously, and subsequently a neurolytic substance (phenol or alcohol) is injected. Alcohol is preferred because it is less toxic to tissues and vasal structures. The use of an image intensifier makes locating landmarks and managing alcohol diffusion more exact to the target area via the preliminary injection of a contrast medium. Moore's technique is a modification of the Kappis technique from 1919 and is generally described as retrocrural. Some modifications have been suggested to obtain better alcohol distribution at the celiac site such as the transcrural procedure, described with the aid of computed tomography scan (Fig. 12-6) [135] or fluoroscopy, and the transaortic procedure [136].

In the literature, only one work [137] has tried to evaluate the real advantage of these different technical approaches by comparing the retrocrural technique, bilateral splanchnicectomy, and the transaortic procedure in three groups of randomly distributed patients followed until their death. This study showed no real advantage in favor of any of the techniques, neither in terms of immediate pain relief nor in long-term pain relief. Moreover, the same study confirmed that duration and completeness of analgesia is unpredictable also for pain with celiac clinical characteristics. In fact, roughly 16% of the patients obtained complete pain relief until death. The course of the disease led to a gradual return of pain and almost always required combined pharmacologic treatment.

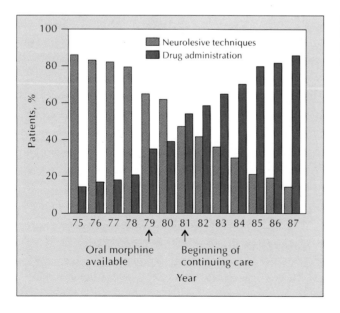

Figure 12-4 Use of pain pathway blocking procedures at the National Cancer Institute of Milan. Trend from 1975 to 1987. To date the percentage falls below 10%. (*From* Ventafridda [14]; with permission.)

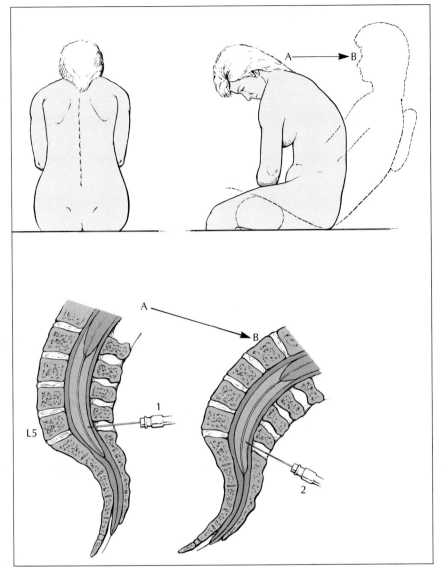

Figure 12-5 Technique for neurolytic saddle block. With the patient in seated position, a 23-gauge needle is introduced through L5–S1 interspace into the subarachnoid space (*A* and *1*). Needle is then withdrawn posteriorly until cerebrospinal fluid is reduced to a trickle (to avoid the anterior roots). An 0.8 mL solution of 7.5% phenol in glycerin is then slowly injected. Patient is filled backwards at 15° to 30° angle for 30 minutes (*B* and *2*).

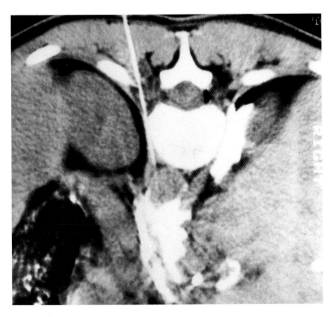

Figure 12-6 Computed tomography scan–guided technique for celiac plexus block. The contrast medium demonstrates favorable spreading via a single needle.

Additional information was obtained from another study comparing the results of analgesic administration with those of celiac block following the traditional retrocrural technique [138]. Analgesia appears to lean in favor of the celiac block during the first week of treatment, but this advantage is no longer present after the second week (Fig. 12-7). The controlled use of analgesics until the patient's death did not differ between the celiac block group and the group treated only with drugs. In a very recent article based on 20 patients with pancreatic cancer, 10 were treated with celiac plexus block and 10 with drugs: a reduction in pain and opioid use was observed in the group with celiac plexus block lasting 4 weeks [139•]. Orthostatic hypotension and transient diarrhea are the most common side effects, found in nearly 30% to 60% of the cases, and, therefore, measures should be taken to prevent or treat them. Side effects having a lesser impact on the patient are transient dysesthesia, reactive pleurisy, and transient hematuria due to renal puncture. Some rare, though serious, side effects have been described, among which are peripheral neurologic lesions (due to alcohol injections into the psoas muscle or at the lumbar plexus level) or central neurologic lesions such as paraplegia (probably due to medullary ischemia from damage to the Adamkiewicz artery) [140].

Percutaneous Cordotomy

Cordotomy was introduced as an open procedure in 1912. The technique became obsolete after the introduction of the percutaneous radiofrequency lesion by Mullan and Rosomoff [141]. Indications for this technique are restricted to monolateral chest or pelvic pain and lower limb bone fractures untreatable with orthopedic procedures. Only the most accurate correlation of unilateral symptoms with a unilateral tumor lesion via appropriate imaging will prevent the onset of contralateral pain after cordotomy. At the present time, percutaneous cordotomy is the most effective neurolesive approach. It entails interrupting the nervous structures located in the anterolateral quadrant of the spinal cord where the fibers responsible for thermal and pain sensitivity of the contralateral hemibody are found (Fig. 12-8).

Percutaneous lateral cordotomy is a procedure that can also be performed on debilitated patients and requires only a common preanesthetic sedation and local anesthesia. It can also be repeated on the same side without increasing risks for the patient. The procedure consists of a lateral approach through the C1–C2 vertebral interspace. With the patient in supine position and the head flexed backwards in order to straighten the cervical column, local anesthesia is delivered about 1 cm below the contralateral mastoid apophysis. The needle is left in place and its position controlled by radiograph. Once the C1–C2 interspace is located, a guide needle is introduced up to the subarachnoid space. Myelography is performed with a contrast medium, taking the patient's cerebrospinal fluid and air, in order to identify the anterior and posterior margin of the spinal cord and the dentate ligament (Fig. 12-9).

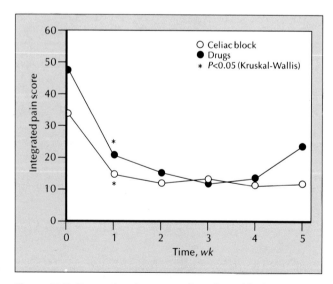

Figure 12-7 Comparison between celiac plexus block ($n = 21$ patients), and pharmacologic treatment ($n = 20$ patients) for pancreatic cancer pain. (*From* Ventafridda and coworkers [138]; with permission.)

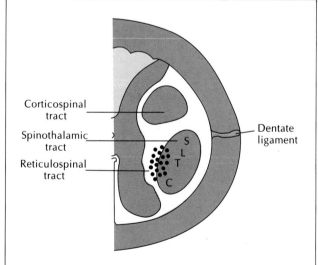

Figure 12-8 Schematic anatomy of spinothalamic tract and surrounding structures. The reticulospinal fibers are deemed important for the involuntary control of breathing. Their bilateral interruption has been related to the onset of sleep apnea syndrome. C—cervical fibers; L—lumbar fibers; S—sacral fibers; T—thoracic fibers.

The needle used for making the lesion is supplied with an electrode, which is insulated except for the tip that protrudes 2 to 3 mm from the needle. It is connected to a radiofrequency apparatus so that both the stimulation and the microlesion can be performed. This coagulates the tissues around the tip of the needle electrode.

Localization can be aided by the use of a micromanipulator ensuring the precise control of needle tip positioning. As the needle approaches the spinal cord, the variation in the resistance of the tissues can be assessed. Resistance is low in the fluid and clearly increases when the electrode penetrates the cord.

Once the needle is correctly positioned, low frequency stimulation (about 2–10 Hz) can be carried out. Stimulation must produce an ipsilateral motor response in the muscles of the neck and trapezius. Different muscle responses indicate incorrect needle positioning. Subsequently, high frequency stimulation (about 10 Hz) is carried out. This will produce a cold or warm tingling sensation. When this sensation is felt in an area closely corresponding to the side of the body where pain is localized, coagulation can be performed. If the result is positive, other coagulations can be made until analgesia is obtained throughout an area covering the side of the body where pain is located. During the whole operation, needle positioning should be checked by radiograph from both the laterolateral and posteroanterior projection.

Various case series on cordotomies performed in patients with cancer pain report different percentages of results; however, from the standpoint of follow-up, concomitant therapies to improve analgesia, overall qualitative results, and continuous pain management until the death of the patient, few of these works are useful. More accurate studies have observed that approximately 63% of the cases show the onset of contralateral pain [142,143]. Very often this occurs immediately after cordotomy when indeed monolateral lesions are not properly evaluated, or they may extend rather close to the median line (Fig. 12-10).

In another case series [142], nearly 34% of the patients still suffered from pain or developed new pain below the apparently adequate level of analgesia obtained because, according to the authors, the onset of deafferentation pain. In our study of 33 patients with Pancoast syndrome who were followed for 20 weeks after cordotomy [144], the number of patients completely pain-free dropped from 80% to 47% by the 12th week. However, 53% of the patients required less analgesics, 25% required an increase of analgesics, and 22% remained stable. Contralateral pain developed in 31% of the patients. Complications include a 0.36% mortality rate, depending on the authors, transient homolateral paresis in up to 80% of the cases, permanent paresis in 1% to 20% of the cases, and transient (20%) and permanent (5%) bladder dysfunction in some patients. Sensitivity disorders such as dysesthesia and changes in superficial sensitivity after cordotomy have received very little attention and should be seen as a direct result rather than as a side effect of the procedure.

Bilateral cordotomy was performed for bilateral pain, yet the outcome is understandably overburdened with a greater incidence of permanent side effects: mor-

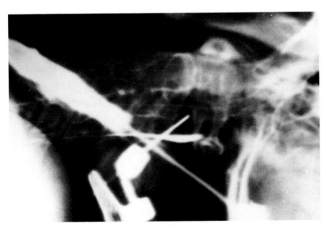

Figure 12-9 Radiograph direct image of myelogram during cordotomy. Anterior limit of spinal cord and dentate ligament are evident anteriorly and, respectively, posteriorly to the needle.

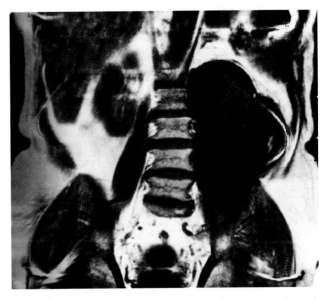

Figure 12-10 Magnetic resonance imaging shows retroperitoneal sarcoma at the level of the lumbar spine; pain was initially referred only to the left thigh and leg due to multiple root compression. Immediately after cordotomy pain was felt in the contralateral leg where it persisted, requiring further treatment.

tality (up to 10%), respiratory difficulties (20%), vesical dysfunction (up to 100%), and orthostatic hypotension (36%) [141]. It is very important to consider that lesions already present in the peripheral plexi, roots, or organs involved in micturition can facilitate the onset of a permanent deficit after cordotomy. Sexual function is hardly mentioned by authors who have performed cordotomies. According to our experience, impotence is a frequently encountered effect, possibly unacceptable to some patients.

Trigeminal Rhizotomy

The technique for this procedure may vary from the blocking of the trigeminal nerve within the foramen ovale or of its branches, to thermorhizotomy with radiofrequency at the level of the Gasserian ganglion, allowing a more selective lesion. Most of the experience gained performing these operations concerns pain due to essential trigeminal neuralgia. Some case series report their usefulness for secondary pain resulting from head or neck tumors [144]. The extension of the tumor and its spreading to nontrigeminal areas can limit the efficacy of these procedures. The introduction of the needle may sometimes be difficult because of tumor mass and changes in reference points. A 19-gauge needle with a rigid spindle is inserted under local anesthesia 2.5 cm lateral to the commissura labiorum. It is directed towards the oval space following two imaginary lines, one sagittal through the pupil, the other transverse passing along the upper margin of the ears. The length of the nonisolated portion of the needle tip is determined according to the size of the required lesion, generally 4 to 5 mm. Radiographs are then taken to confirm the correct positioning of the electrode needle. One or two stimulations are performed to ensure correct functioning. Subsequently, under ultrarapid general anesthesia, a temperature of approximately 70°C is applied for about 1 minute. Depending on the extension of the hypoalgesic area, small thermal lesions can be made at other sites. The risk of ophthalmic anesthesia and corneal ulcer and the benefits derived from using less invasive procedures should be properly weighed when choosing one of these options.

CONCLUSIONS

Treating pain is only one aspect of the therapeutic approach. It should never be separated from the control of side effects nor from the perception that various physical and psychological symptoms contribute to the patient's suffering in the advanced stages of cancer.

According to the philosophy of palliative care, all analgesic treatments should be specifically designed for the individual patient and sufficiently simple in their method of delivery that nurses, members of the family, and patients can use them. Palliative care marks a new way of supporting the terminally ill who prove to be unresponsive to specific antitumor treatments, and it is aimed at improving their quality of survival. By quality of survival, we mean the psychological, environmental, and physical conditions of the individual, which invariably deteriorate during the advanced and terminal stages of cancer. It is a multidisciplinary approach, encompassing the patient, the family, and the community in its scope. It also represents a new area of medicine aiming to counter the dehumanizing elements still present in the intensive treatments of advanced cancer patients.

ACKNOWLEDGMENT

This chapter has been made possible with the good offices of C.N.R.'s (National Council for Research) Oncology Project No. 92.02367.PF39

REFERENCES AND RECOMMENDED READING

Papers of interest, published recently, have been highlighted as:
• Of special interest
•• Of outstanding interest

1. Ventafridda V: Providing continuity of care for cancer patients. *J Psycosoc Oncol* 1988, 8:3–10.

2. Parkin DM, Laara E, Muir CS, *et al.*: Estimates of the world wide frequency of sixteen major cancers. *Int J Cancer* 1988, 41:184–197.

3. Parkin DM, Laara E, Muir CS, *et al.*: Estimates of the world-wide frequency of twelve major cancers. *WHO Bull* 1984, 622:163–182.

4. World Health Organization: cancer increases in developed countries. *Wly Epidemiol Rec* 1985, 60:125–129.

5. Curtis EB, Kretch R, Walsh TD: Common symptoms in patients with advanced cancer. *J Palliative Care* 1991, 7:25–29.

6. Bonica JJ: Treatment of cancer pain: current status and future needs. In *Advances in Pain Research and Therapy*. Edited by Fields HL. New York: Raven Press; 1985:589–615.

7. Coderre JT, Katz J, Vaccarino LA, *et al.*: Contribution of central neuroplasticity to pathological pain: review of clinical and experimental evidence. *Pain* 1993, 52:259–285.

8. Asbury AK, Fields HL: Pain due to peripheral nerve damage: an hypothesis. *Neurology (Cleveland)* 1984, 34:1587–1590.

9. Vecht CJ: Nociceptive nerve pain and neuropathic pain. *Pain* 1989, 39:243–244.

10. Ventafridda V, Caraceni A: Cancer pain classification: a controversial issue. *Pain* 1991, 46:1–2.

11.• Portenoy RK: Cancer pain: pathophysiology and syndromes. *Lancet* 1992, 339:1021–1036.
Clear update of clinical phenomology of cancer pain.

12. Arnér S, Meyerson BA: Lack of analgesic effect of opioids on neuropathic and idiopathic forms of pain. *Pain* 1988, 33:11–23.

13. Portenoy RK, Foley KM, Inturrisi CE: The nature of opioid responsiveness and its implications for neuropathic pain: new hypotheses derived from studies of opioid infusions. *Pain* 1990, 43:273–286.

14. Ventafridda V: Continuing care: a major issue in cancer pain management [editorial]. *Pain* 1989, 36:137–143.

15. Houde RW, Wallenstain SL, Beaver WT: Evaluation of analgesics in patients with cancer pain. In *International Encyclopedia of Pharmacology and Therapeutics. Clinical Pharmacology.* Edited by Lasagna L. New York: Pergamon Press; 1966:59–99.

16. Fishman B, Pasternak S, Wallenstein SL, *et al.*: The Memorial Pain Assessment Card: a valid instrument for the assessment of cancer pain. *Cancer* 1986, 60:1151–1157.

17. Daut RL, Cleeland SC, Flannery RC: Development of the Wisconsin brief pain questionnaire to assess pain in cancer and other diseases. *Pain* 1983, 17:197–210.

18. Ventafridda V, De Conno F, Di Trapani P, *et al.*: A new method of pain quantification based on a weekly self-descriptive record of the intensity and duration of pain. In *Advances in Pain Research and Therapy.* Edited by Bonica JJ, Lindblom U, Iggo A, *et al.* New York: Raven Press; 1983:892–895.

19. Ventafridda V, Tamburini M, Rosso S, *et al.*: A therapy impact questionnaire for quality-of-life assessment in advanced cancer research. *Ann Oncol* 1992, 3:565–570.

20. Ventafridda V, Caraceni A, Saita L, *et al.*: Cancer pain and mobility. In *Advances in Pain Research and Therapy.* Edited by Tiengo M, *et al.* New York: Raven Press; 1987:135–145.

21. Ventafridda V, De Conno F, Ripamonti C, *et al.*: Quality-of-life assessment during a palliative care programme. *Ann Oncol* 1990, 1:415–420.

22. Ventafridda V, Tamburini M, Caraceni A, *et al.*: A validation study of the WHO method for cancer pain relief. *Cancer* 1987, 59:850–856.

23. Grond S, Zech D, Schug SA, *et al.*: Validation of WHO guidelines for cancer pain relief during the last days and hours of life. *J Pain Symptom Manage* 1991, 6:411–422.

24. Portenoy RK, Hagen NA: Breakthrough pain: definition, prevalence and characteristics. *Pain* 1990, 41:273–281.

25. Ventafridda V, De Conno F, Panerai AE, *et al.*: Non-steroidal antiinflammatory drugs as the first step in cancer pain therapy: double-blind, within patient study comparing nine drugs. *J Int Med Res* 1990, 18:21.

26. Stambaugh JE: Role of nonsteroidal antiinflammatory drugs. In *Cancer Pain.* Edited by Patt RB. Philadelphia: Lippincott; 1993:105–117.

27. Ehsanullah RSB, Page MC, Tildesley G, *et al.*: Prevention of gastroduodenal damage by non-steroidal anti-inflammatory drugs: controlled trial of ranitidine. *B M J* 1988, 297:1017–1021.

28. Graham DY, Agrawal NM, Roth SH: Prevention of NSAID-induced gastric ulcer with misoprostol: multicenter, double-blind, placebo-controlled trial. *Lancet* 1988, 2:1277–1280.

29. Roth S, Agrawal N, Mahowald M, *et al.*: Misoprostol heals gastroduodenal injury in patients with rheumatoid arthritis receiving aspirin. *Arch Intern Med* 1989, 149:775–779.

30. Lanza F, Peace K, Gustitus L, *et al.*: A blinded endoscopy comparative study of misoprostol versus sucralfate and placebo in the prevention of aspirin induced gastric and duodenal ulceration. *Am J Gastroenterol* 1988; 83:143–146.

31. Goodwin JS, Regan M: Cognitive dysfunction associated with naproxen and ibuprofen in the elderly. *Arthritis Rheum* 1982, 25:1013–1015.

32. Inturrisi CE: Management of cancer pain: pharmacology and principles of management. *Cancer* 1989, 63:2308–2320.

33. Kaiko RF: Commentary: Equinalgesic dose ratio of intramuscular/oral morphine, 1:6 versus 1:3. In *Advances in Pain Research and Therapy. Opioid Analgesics in the Management of Clinical Pain.* Edited by Foley KM, Inturrisi CE. New York: Raven Press; 1986:87–94.

34. Kaiko RF: Clinical protocol and role of controlled release morphine in the surgical patient. In *Anesthesiology in Pain Management.* Edited by Stanley TH, Ashburn MA, Fine P. Amsterdam: Kluwer Academic Publishers; 1991:193–212.

35. Kaiko RF: Controlled-release oral morphine for cancer-related pain: the European and North American experiences. In *Advances in Pain Research and Therapy: Second International Congress on Cancer Pain.* Edited by Foley KM, Bonica JJ, Ventafridda V. New York: Raven Press; 1990: 171–189.

36. Bruera E, MacMillan K, Hanson J, *et al.*: The cognitive effects of the administration of narcotic analgesics in patients with cancer pain. *Pain* 1989, 39:13–16.

37. Sjogren P, Banning A: Pain, sedation and reaction time during long-term treatment of cancer patients with oral and epidural opioids. *Pain* 1989, 39:5–11.

38. Leipzig RM, Goodman H, Gray G, *et al.*: Reversible, narcotic-associated mental status impairment in patients with metastatic cancer. *Pharmacology* 1987, 35:47–54.

39. Frenk H, Watkins LR, Mayer DJ: Differential behavioural effects induced by intrathecal microinjection of opiates: comparison of convulsive and cataleptic effects produced by morphine, methadone and d-Ala$_2$-methionine-enkephalinamide. *Brain Res* 1984, 299:31–42.

40.• Gregory RE, Grossman S, Sheidler VR: Grand mal seizures associated with high-dose intravenous morphine infusions: incidence and possible etiology. *Pain* 1992, 51:255–258.
A rare complication with a good pathogenic discussion.

41. De Conno F, Caraceni A, Martini C, *et al.*: Hyperalgesia and myoclonus with intrathecal infusion of high-dose morphine. *Pain* 1991, 47:337–339.

42.•• Portenoy RK, Thaler HT, Inturrisi CE, *et al.*: The metabolite morphine-6-glucuronide contributes to the analgesia produced by morphine infusion in patients with pain and normal renal function. *Clin Pharmacol Ther* 1992, 51:422–431.

The authors suggest that morphine-6-glucuronide is relevant for morphine analgesia and should be considered in the evaluation of clinical and pharmacological data.

43. Babul N, Darke AC: Putative role of hydromorphone metabolites in myoclonus [letter]. *Pain* 1992, 52:260–261.

44. Hagen NA, Foley KM, Cerbone DJ, *et al.*: Chronic nausea and morphine-6-glucuronide. *J Pain Symptom Manage* 1991, 6:125–128.

45. Ventafridda V, Spoldi E, Caraceni A, *et al.*: The importance of subcutaneous morphine administration for cancer pain control. *Pain Clin* 1986, 1:47–55.

46. Bruera E, Brenneis C, Michaud M, *et al.*: Use of the subcutaneous route for the administration of narcotics in patients with cancer pain. *Cancer* 1988, 62:407–411.

47. Bruera E: Subcutaneous administration of opioids in the management of cancer pain. In *Advances in Pain Research and Therapy*. Edited by Foley KM, Bonica JJ, Ventafridda V, *et al.* New York: Raven Press; 1990:203–218.

48. Kerr IG, Sone M, De Angelis C, *et al.*: Continuous narcotic infusion with patient-controlled analgesia for chronic cancer pain in outpatients. *Ann Intern Med* 1988, 108:554–557.

49. Swanson G, Smith J, Bulich R, *et al.*: Patient controlled analgesia for chronic cancer pain in the ambulatory setting: a report of 117 patients. *J Clin Oncol* 1989, 7:1903–1908.

50. Drexel H, Dzien A, Spiegel RW, *et al.*: Treatment of severe cancer pain by low-dose continuous subcutaneous morphine. *Pain* 1989, 36:169–176.

51. Portenoy RK, Moulin DE, Rogers A, *et al.*: IV infusion of opioids for cancer pain: clinical review and guidelines for use. *Cancer Treat Rep* 1986, 70:575–581.

52. Bruera E, Fainsinger R, Moore M, *et al.*: Local toxicity with subcutaneous methadone: experience of two centres. *Pain* 1991, 45:141–143.

53. Miser AW, Davis DM, Hughes CS, *et al.*: Continuous subcutaneous infusion of morphine in children with cancer. *Am J Dis Child* 1983, 137:383–385.

54. Nahata MC, Miser AW, Miser JS, *et al.*: Analgesic plasma concentrations of morphine in children with terminal malignancy receiving a continuous subcutaneous infusion of morphine sulfate to control severe pain. *Pain* 1984, 18:109–114.

55. Miser AW, Miser JS, Clark BS: Continuous intravenous infusion of morphine sulfate for control of severe pain in children with terminal malignancy. *J Pediatr* 1980, 96:930–932.

56. Waldmann CS, Eason JR, Rambohul E, *et al.*: Serum morphine levels: a comparison of continuous subcutaneous infusion and continuous intravenous infusion in postoperative patients. *Anaesthesia* 1984, 39:768–771.

57.•• Moulin DE, Kreeft JH, Murray-Parsons N, *et al.*: Comparison of continuous subcutaneous and intravenous hydromorphone for management of cancer pain. *Lancet* 1991, 337:465–468.

A very important demonstration of subcutaneous opioid infusion and an example for the clinical pharmalogical research in cancer pain.

58. Cousins MJ, Plummer JL: Spinal opioids in acute and chronic pain. In *Advances in Pain Research and Therapy*. Edited by Max M, Portenoy R, Laska E. New York: Raven Press; 1991:457–479.

59. Bullingham RES, Jacob OLR, McQuay HJ, *et al.*: The Oxford system of patient-controlled analgesia. In *Opioid Analgesics in the Management of Clinical Pain: Advances in Pain Research and Therapy*. Edited by Foley KM, Inturrisi CE. New York: Raven Press; 1986:319–324.

60. Tamsen A, Sjoestroem S, Hartvig P: The Uppsala experience of patient-controlled analgesia. In *Opioid Analgesics in the Management of Clinical Pain: Advances in Pain Research and Therapy*. Edited by Foley KM, Inturrisi CE. New York: Raven Press; 1986:325–332.

61. Hill HF, Chapman CR, Kornekk JA, *et al.*: Self-administration of morphine in bone marrow transplant patients reduces drug requirement. *Pain* 1990, 40:121–129.

62. Hill HF, Saeger L, Bjustrom R, *et al.*: Steady state infusion of opioids in human volunteers: I. Pharmacokinetic tailoring. *Pain* 1990, 43:57–67.

63. Hill HF, Chapman CR, Saeger LS, *et al.*: Steady state infusion of opioids in humans: II. Concentration-effect relationships and therapeutic margins. *Pain* 1990, 43:69–79.

64.•• Hill HF, Mackie AM, Coda BA, *et al.*: Patient-controlled analgesic administration. A comparison of steady-state morphine infusions with bolus doses. *Cancer* 1991, 67:873–882.

This study is fundamental in showing the relationship between pharmacokinetics and pharmacodynamics in opioid analgesia.

65. Hill HF, Coda BA, Mackie AM, *et al.*: Patient-controlled analgesic infusions: alfentanil versus morphine. *Pain* 1992, 49:301–310.

66. Keeri-Szanto M, Heaman S: Demand analgesia for relief of pain problems in terminal illness. *Anesth Rev* 1976, 3:19–21.

67. Citron ML, Johnston A, Boyer M, *et al.*: Patient-controlled analgesia for severe cancer pain. *Arch Intern Med* 1986, 146:734–736.

68. Citron ML, Kalra J, Seltzer VL, Chen S, *et al.*: Patient-controlled analgesia for cancer pain: a long-term study of inpatient and outpatient use. In *Narcotic Analgesia for Cancer Pain*. Edited by Citron ML. New York: Marcel Dekker; in press.

69. Bruera E, Brenneis C, Micahud M, *et al.*: Patient-controlled subcutaneous hydromorphone versus continuous subcutaneous infusion for the treatment of cancer pain. *J Natl Cancer Inst* 1988, 80:1152–1154.

70. Hanks GW, Justins DM: Cancer pain: Management. *Lancet* 1992, 339:1031–1036.

71. Hassenbuch SJ, Pillay PK, Magdinec M, *et al.*: Constant infusion of morphine for intractable cancer pain using an implanted pump. *J Neurosurg* 1990, 73:405–409.

72. Vainio A, Tigerstedt I: Opioid treatment for radiating cancer pain: oral administration vs. epidural techniques. *Acta Anaesthesiol Scand* 1988, 32:179–180.

73. Sjogren P, Banning A: Pain, sedation and reaction time during long-term treatment of cancer patients with oral and epidural opioids. *Pain* 1989, 39:5–11.

74. Max MB, Inturrisi CE, Kaiko RF, *et al.*: Epidural and intrathecal opiates: cerebrospinal fluid and plasma profiles in patients with chronic cancer pain. *Clin Pharmacol Ther* 1985, 38:631–641.

75. Tanelian DL, Cousins JM: Failure of epidural opioid to control cancer pain in a patient previously treated with massive doses of intravenous opioid. *Pain* 1989, 36:359–362.

76. Shetter AG, Hadley MN, Wilkinson E: Administration of intraspinal morphine sulfate for the treatment of incurable cancer pain. *Neurosurgery* 1986, 18:740–747.

77.•• Hogan Q, Haddox JD, Abram S, *et al.*: Epidural opiates and local anesthetics for the management of cancer pain. *Pain* 1991, 46:271–279.
This is the first study that attempts a definition of the role of spinal opoids in cancer pain.

78. Cousins MJ, Mather LE: Intrathecal and epidural administration of opioids. *Anesthesiology* 1984, 61:276–310.

79. McQuay HJ, Sullivan AF, Smallman K, *et al.*: Intrathecal opioids, potency and lipophilicity. *Pain* 1989, 36:111–115.

80. Brose WG, Tanelian DL, Brodsky JB, *et al.*: CSF and blood pharmacokinetics of hydromorphone and morphine following lumbar epidural administration. *Pain* 1991, 45:11–15.

81. Nordberg G: Pharmacokinetic aspects for spinal morphine analgesia. *Acta Anaesthesiol Scand Suppl* 1984, 28.

82. Moulin DE, Inturrisi CE, Foley KM: Cerebrospinal fluid pharmacokinetics of intrathecal morphine sulfate and D-Ala$_2$-D-Leu$_5$-enkephalin. *Ann Neurol* 1986, 20:218–222.

83. Ventafridda V, Spoldi E, Caraceni A, *et al.*: Intraspinal morphine for cancer pain. *Acta Anaesthesiol Scand Suppl* 1987, 85:47–53.

84. Gourlay GK, Plummer JL, Cherry DA, *et al.*: Comparison of intermittent bolus with continuous infusion of epidural morphine in the treatment of severe cancer pain. *Pain* 1991, 47:135–140.

85. Waldman SD, Coombs DW: Selection of implantable narcotic delivery systems. *Anesth Analg* 1989, 68:377–384.

86. Osborne R, Joel S, Trew D, *et al.*: Morphine and metabolite behavior after different routes of morphine administration: demonstration of the importance of the active metabolite morphine-6-glucuronide. *Clin Pharmacol Ther* 1990, 47:12–19.

87. Maloney CM, Kesner RK, Klein G, *et al.*: The rectal administration of MS contin: clinical implication of use in end stage cancer. *Am J Hosp Care* 1989, 6:34–35.

88. Westerling D, Lindahl S, Anderson KE, *et al.*: Absorption and bioavailability of rectally administered morphine in woman. *Eur J Clin Pharmacol* 1982, 23:59–64.

89. Pannuti F, Rossi AP, Iafelice G, *et al.*: Control of chronic pain in very advanced cancer patients with morphine hydrochloride administered by oral, rectal and sublingual route. *Pharmacol Res Commun* 1982, 14:369–381.

90. Bruera B, Ripamonti C: Alternate routes of administration of opioids for the management of cancer pain. In *Cancer Pain*. Edited by Patt RB. Philadelphia: Lippincott 1993:161–184.

91. Zech DFJ, Grond SUA, Lynch J, *et al.*: Transdermal fentanyl and initial dose-finding with patient-controlled analgesia in cancer pain. A pilot study with 20 terminally ill cancer patients. *Pain* 1992, 50:293–301.

92. Watson CP, Evans RJ, Reed K, *et al.*: Amitriptyline versus placebo in postherpetic neuralgia. *Neurology* 1982, 32:671–673.

93. Max MB, Schafer SC, Culnane M, *et al.*: Association of pain relief with drug side effects in postherpetic neuralgia: a single-dose study of clonidine, codeine, ibuprofen and placebo. *Clin Pharmacol Ther* 1988, 43:363–371.

94. Max MB, Schafer SC, Culnane M, *et al.*: Amitriptyline, but not lorazepam, relieves postherpetic neuralgia. *Neurology* 1988, 38:1427–1432.

95. Kishore-Kuma R, Max MB, Schafer SC, *et al.*: Desipramine relieves postherpetic neuralgia. *Clin Pharmacol Ther* 1990, 47:305–312.

96. Max MB, Culnane M, Schafer SC, *et al.*: Amitriptyline relieves diabetic neuropathy pain in patients with normal or depressed mood. *Neurology* 1987, 3:589–596.

97. Ventafridda V, Ripamonti C, De Conno F, *et al.*: Antidepressants increase bioavailability of morphine in cancer patients. *Lancet* 1987, 1:1204.

98. Killian JM, Fromm GH: Carbamazepine in the treatment of neuralgia: use and side effects. *Arch Neurol* 1968, 19:129–136.

99. Swerdlow M, Cundill JG: Anticonvulsant drugs used in the treatment of lancinating pains: a comparison. *Anesthesia* 1981, 36:1129–1132.

100. Tanelian DL, Cousins MJ: Combined neurogenic and nociceptive pain in a patient with Pancoast tumour managed by epidural hydromorphone and oral carbamazepine. *Pain* 1989, 36:85–88.

101. Bruera E, Roca E, Cedaro L, *et al.*: Action of oral methylprednisolone in terminal cancer patients: A prospective randomized double-blind study. *Cancer Treat Rep* 1985, 69:751.

102. Della Cuna GR, Pellegrini A, Piazzi M: Effect of methylprednisolone sodium succinate on quality of life in preterminal cancer patients: A placebo-controlled, multicenter study. *Eur J Cancer Clin Oncol* 1989, 25:1817–1821.

103. Greenberg HS, Kim JH, Posner JB: Epidural spinal cord compression from metastatic tumor: results with a new treatment protocol. *Ann Neurol* 1980, 8:361–366.

104. Vecht ChJ, Haaxma-Reiche H, van Putten WLJ, *et al.*: Initial bolus of conventional versus high-dose dexamethazone in metastatic spinal cord compression. *Neurology* 1989, 39:1255–1257.

105.• Marchettini P, Lacerenza M, Marangoni C, *et al.*: Lidocaine test in neuralgia. *Pain* 1992 48:377–382.
A very clear and informative study on the usefulness of lidocaine infusion test in neuropathic pain.

106. Lindstom P, Lindblom U: The analgesic effect of tocainide in trigeminal neuralgia. *Pain* 1987, 28:45.

107. Dejgard A, Petersen P, Kastrup J: Mexiletine for treatment of chronic painful diabetic neuropathy. *Lancet* 1988, 1:9–11.

108. Chabal C, Jacobson L, Mariano A, *et al.*: The use of oral mexiletine for the treatment of pain after peripheral nerve injury. *Anesthesiology* 1992, 76:513–517.

109. Brose WG, Cousins MJ: Subcutaneous lidocaine for treatment of neuropathic cancer pain. *Pain* 1991, 45:145–148.

110. Kayser V, Guilbaud G, Besson JM: Potent antinociceptive effects of clonidine systemically administered in an experimental model of clinical pain, the arthritic rat. *Brain Res* 1992, 593:7–13.

111. Goldstein J: Clonidine as an analgesic. *Biol Psychiatr* 1983, 18:1339–1340.

112. Gordh T, Tamsen A: A study of the analgesic effect of clonidine in man. *Acta Anesthesiol Scand* 1983, 27:72.

113. Coombs DW, Saunders RL, Fratkin JD, *et al.*: Continuous intrathecal hydromorphone and clonidine for intractable cancer pain. *J Neurosurg* 1986, 64:890–894.

114. Coventry DM, Todd G: Epidural clonidine in lower limb deafferentation pain. *Anesth Analg* 1989, 69:424–425.

115. Glynn CJ, Jamous MA, Teddy PJ: Cerebrospinal fluid kinetics of epidural clonidine in man. *Pain* 1992, 49:361–367.

116. Petros AJ, Bowen-Wright RM: Epidural and oral clonidine in domiciliary control of deafferentation pain. *Lancet* 1987, 1:1034.

117. Attardo-Parrinello G, Merlini G, Pavesi F, *et al.*: Effects of a new aminodiphosphonate (aminohydroxybutylidene diphosphonate) in patients with osteolytic lesions from metastases and myelomatosis. *Arch Intern Med* 1987, 147:1629–1633.

118. Masud T, Slevin ML: Pamidronate to reduce bone pain in normocalcaemic patient with disseminated prostatic carcinoma. *Lancet* 1989, 1:1021–1022.

119. Merlini G, Parrinello GA: Long-term effect of parenteral dichloromethylene bisphosphonate on bone disease of myeloma patients treated with chemotherapy. *Hematol Oncol* 1990, 8:23–30.

120. Thiébaud D, Leyvraz S, von Fliedner V, *et al.*: Treatment of bone metastases from breast cancer and myeloma with pamidronate. *Eur J Cancer* 1991, 27:37–41.

121. Ernst DS, MacDonald RN, Paterson AHG, *et al.*: A double-blind crossover trial of intravenous clodronate in metastatic bone pain. *J Pain Symptom Manage* 1992, 7:4–11.

122. Rowbotham MC, Reisner-Keller L, Fields HL: Both intravenous lidocaine and morphine reduce the pain of postherpetic neuralgia. *Neurology* 1991, 41:1024–1028.

123. Jadad AR, Carroll D, Glynn CJ, *et al.*: Morphine responsiveness of chronic pain: double-blind randomised crossover study with patient-controlled analgesia. *Lancet* 1992, 339:1367–1371.

124. Banning A, Sjogren P, Henriksen H: Treatment outcome in a multidisciplinary cancer pain clinic. *Pain* 1991, 47:129–134.

125. Samuelsson H, Hedner T: Pain characterization in cancer patients and the analgetic response to epidural morphine. *Pain* 1991, 46:3–8.

126. Du Pen SL, Kharasch ED, Williams A, *et al.*: Chronic epidural bupivacaine opioid infusion in intractable cancer pain. *Pain* 1992, 49:293–300.

127. Sjoberg M, Appelgren L, Einarsson S, *et al.*: Long-term intrathecal morphine and bupivacaine in "refractory" cancer pain: I. Results from the first series of 52 patients. *Acta Anaesthesiol Scand* 1991, 35:30–43.

128. Hassenbusch SJ, Pillay PK, Barnett GH: Radiofrequency cingulotomy for intractable cancer pain using stereotaxis guided by magnetic resonance imaging. *Neurosurgery* 1990, 27:220–223.

129. Gybels JM: Indications for neurosurgical treatment of chronic pain. *Acta Neurochir* 1992, 116:171–175.

130. Sbanotto A: Revisione critica dei risultati antalgici delle tecniche neurolesive. Doctoral dissertation, University of Milan, 1984.

131. Ventafridda V, Tamburini M, De Conno F: Comprehensive treatment in cancer pain. In *Advances in Pain Research and Therapy*. Edited by Fields HL, *et al.* New York: Raven Press; 1985:617–628.

132. Ventafridda V, Martino G: Clinical evaluation of subarachnoid neurolytic blocks in intractable cancer pain. In *Advances in Pain Research and Therapy.*. Edited by Bonica JJ, Albe-Fessard D. New York: Raven Press; 1976:699–703.

133. Ventafridda V, Fochi C, Sganzerla E, *et al.*: Neurolitic blocks in perineal pain. In *Advances in Pain Research and Therapy*. Edited by Bonica JJ, Ventafridda V. New York: Raven Press; 1979:597–605.

134. Moore DC: Regional block. In *A Handbook for Use in the Clinical Practice of Medicine and Surgery, Fourth Edition*. Springfield, Illinois: C.C. Thomas; 1965:154–162.

135. Singler RC: An improved technique for alcohol neurolysis of the celiac plexus. *Anesthesiology* 1982, 56:137–141.

136. Ischia S, Luzzani A, Ischia A, *et al.*: A new approach to the neurolytic block of the coeliac plexus: the transaortic technique. *Pain* 1983, 16:333–341.

137. Ischia S, Ischia A, Polati E, *et al.*: Three posterior percutaneous celiac plexus block techniques. *Anesthesiology* 1992, 76:534–540.

138. Ventafridda GV, Caraceni AT, Sbanotto AM, *et al.*: Pain treatment in cancer of the pancreas. *Eur J Surg Oncol* 1990, 16:1–6.

139.• Mercadante S: Celiac plexus block versus analgesics in pancreatic cancer pain. *Pain* 1993, 52:187–192.

This is the first study of its kind comparing a block technique with a pharmacologic approach. The controversial nature of this field warrants a careful evaluation.

140. Van Dongen RTM, Crul BJP: Paraplegia following celiac plexus block. *Anesthesiology* 1991, 46:862–863.

141. Tasker RR: Management of nociceptive, deafferentation and central pain by surgical intervention. In *Pain Syndromes in Neurology*. Edited by Fields HL. London: Butterworth and Co.; 1990:143–200.

142. Ischia S, Luzzani A, Ischia A, *et al.*: Subarachnoid neurolytic block (L5 S1) and unilateral percutaneous cervical cordotomy in the treatment of pain secondary to pelvic malignant disease. *Pain* 1984, 20:139–149.

143. Ventafridda V, De Conno F, Fochi C: Cervical percutaneous cordotomy. In *Advances in Pain Research and Therapy*. Edited by Bonica JJ, Ventafridda V, Pagni CA. New York: Raven Press; 1982:185–198.

144. Siegfried J, Broggi G: Percutaneous thermocoagulation of the gasserian ganglion in the treatment of pain in advanced cancer. In *Advances in Pain Research and Therapy*. Edited by Bonica JJ, Ventafridda V. New York: Raven Press; 1979:463.

Mechanisms
of Neuropathic Pain

BENJAMIN W. JOHNSON
AND WINSTON C.V. PARRIS

Although neuropathic pain is frequently encountered in clinical practice, consistent success in its treatment remains elusive [1••,2•]. This chapter reviews various hypotheses regarding the mechanisms and pathogenesis of neuropathic pain and recommends appropriate therapy for this chronic pain syndrome. The role of central, sympathetic, and peripheral neurons are evaluated regarding their significance in neuropathic pain mechanisms, because involvement of the three are often inseparable in clinical practice.

The understanding that neuropathy may exist without pain and that pain may exist without evidence of nerve damage is paramount [3]. Neuropathic pain, therefore, may be defined as an unpleasant sensory or emotional experience associated with injury or dysfunction of the nervous system. Neuropathic pain differs from normal nociception in that the normal nociceptive pathways are altered by stereotypical responses to neural injury or disease processes. Thus, instead of generating an action potential initiated after sufficient summation of a receptor potential, an aberrant action potential is generated from a normally innocuous stimulus.

In the past, several attempts have been made to classify neuropathic pain into peripheral and central categories. Recent studies, however, have cast doubt on the validity of this simplistic classification. It has been proposed that neuropathic pain be divided into three pathophysiologically distinct broad categories: deafferentation pain, sympathetically mediated pain, and peripheral neuropathy [4]. The clarity of distinction between these groups of neuropathic pain is sometimes blurred by the combination of disease processes and the variations of clinical manifestations.

To effectively review current concepts of the mechanisms of neuropathic pain, the anatomy and physiology of nociception is briefly reviewed [5,6], as is the

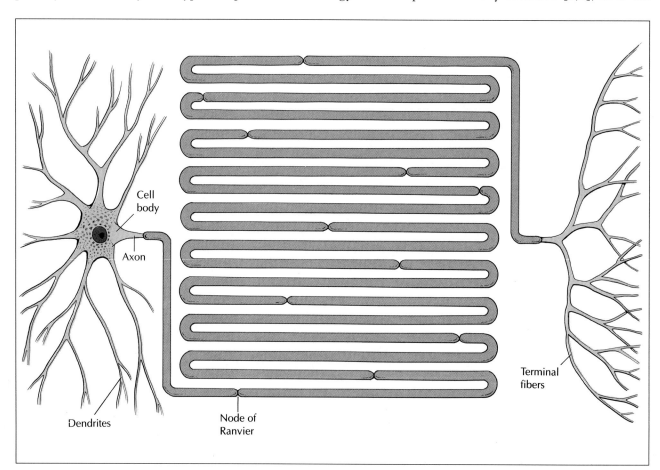

Figure 13-1 A neuron drawn to illustrate the relative extent of each region. Axons vary greatly in length and some extend for more than 1 meter. (The axon is folded for diagrammatic purposes. In addition, the caliber of the axon is distorted; most axons in the central nervous system are very thin compared with the diameter of the cell body.) Many axons are insulated by a fatty myelin sheath, which is interrupted at intervals by regions known as the nodes of Ranvier. The terminal branches of the axon form synapses with as many as 1000 other neurons. Most synapses join the axon terminals of one neuron with the dendrites or cell body of another neuron. Thus, the dendrites emerging from a neuron might receive incoming signals from hundreds or even thousands of other neurons. (*Adapted from* Stevens [59]; with permission.)

response of neural tissue to injury. Further, therapeutic options based on an understanding of nerve pathophysiology are also reviewed.

It must be emphasized that the presence of nerve pathology does not always correlate satisfactorily with a patient's report of pain; in addition, the absence of detectable neuropathology does not invalidate a patient's report of pain [7•]. Pain has been defined as "an unpleasant sensory and/or emotional experience..." and, as such, is essentially subjective. Therefore, the rationale for investigating mechanisms of neuropathic pain is to develop effective therapies designed to normalize neural function and to alleviate the resulting pain produced by neuropathic lesions.

NEURONAL ANATOMY

Peripheral Neurons

The neuron typically has four morphologically distinct regions with correspondingly distinct physiologic roles (Fig. 13-1). The soma, or cell body, is the metabolic center of the neuron and contains three major organelles: a large nucleus, the endoplasmic reticulum, and the Golgi apparatus (Fig. 13-2). The latter two organelles synthesize membrane and neurosecretory products for the neuron. The dendrites, which appear as projections from the cell body, are the chief receptive units for the neuron. The axon is the conducting unit of the neuron. Macromolecules of membrane and secretory proteins are transported from the soma to the terminal end of the neuron by axonal transport at the rate of 400 mm/d. Larger axons are covered with a fatty myelin sheath that is regularly interrupted by nodes of Ranvier. This myelin structure is vital for high-speed conduction of nerve impulses along the axon. The terminal fibers serve as transmitting elements for the neuron and often end in synapses facilitating contact with other neurons (Fig. 13-3). These synapses can be either chemical or electrical in nature.

Sympathetic Neurons

Sympathetic neurons are unique in appearance and function because of the presence of bead-like structures on the terminal fibers of the neuron called varicosities (Fig. 13-4). These varicosities function as open synapses, because their many fenestrations allow the release of norepinephrine into the surrounding extracellular fluid when the neuron is stimulated.

Central Neurons

Neurons of the central nervous system are quite similar to peripheral neurons described previously except in

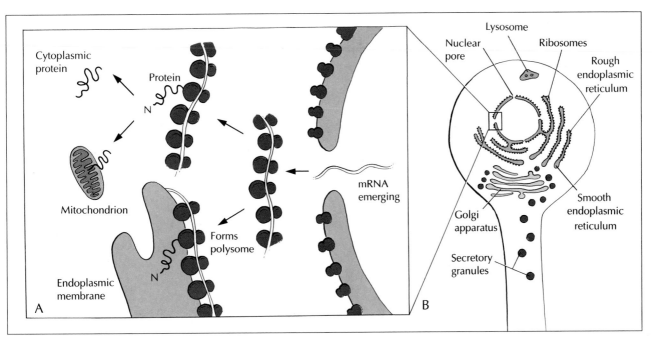

Figure 13-2 (A) Messenger RNA (mRNA) transcribed from genomic DNA in the neuron's nucleus, emerge through nuclear pores to form polysomes by attaching to ribosomes. Three classes of proteins are formed. Which class of protein depends on the fate of the particular polysome and this, in turn, is determined by information encoded in the particular mRNA. Cytosolic and some mitochondrial proteins are made on polysomes that remain free in the cytosol. Proteins destined to be inserted into membranes (for example, the membranes of secretory granules or lysosomes) or proteins that ultimately will become secretory products are synthesized by polyribosomes that attach to the membrane of the endoplasmic reticulum. (B) The organelles that are responsible for the synthesis and processing of proteins. (*From* Schwartz [65]; with permission.)

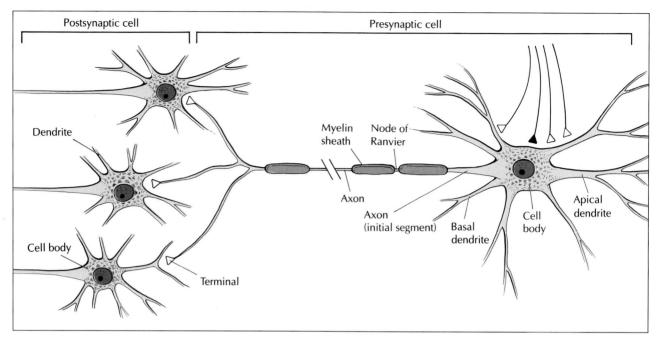

Figure 13-3 Typical neuron drawn to illustrate its various regions and its points of contact with other nerve cells. *White triangles* indicate excitatory presynaptic terminals; *black triangles,* inhibitory terminals . (*From* Kandel [60]; with permission.)

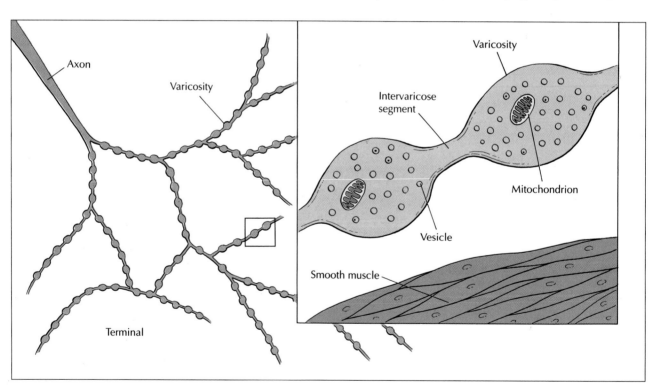

Figure 13-4 The peripheral autonomic synapse is a nondirected chemical synapse. The axon terminals are highly branched and consist of varicosities and intervaricose segments. (*From* Kandel [60]; with permission.)

their individual morphology (Fig. 13-5). The primary difference lies in the presence of glial cells that are abundant in the central nervous system (Fig. 13-6). These glial cells do not generate electrical signals as neurons do but serve a supportive role by 1) being the structural support elements of the brain; 2) scavenging cellular debris after neuronal injury or death; 3) providing myelin for the axonal sheath; 4) buffering potassium ions in the extracellular space; and 5) providing nutritive support for the neurons.

THE PHYSIOLOGY OF NORMAL NOCICEPTION

The physiology of nerve conduction involves four functional components that may transform input signals into neurotransmitter release (Fig. 13-7).

The first component is an input signal that, upon reaching an appropriate dendritic receptor at sufficient intensity, induces generation of a receptor potential, which transforms a sensory stimulus into a local electrical signal.

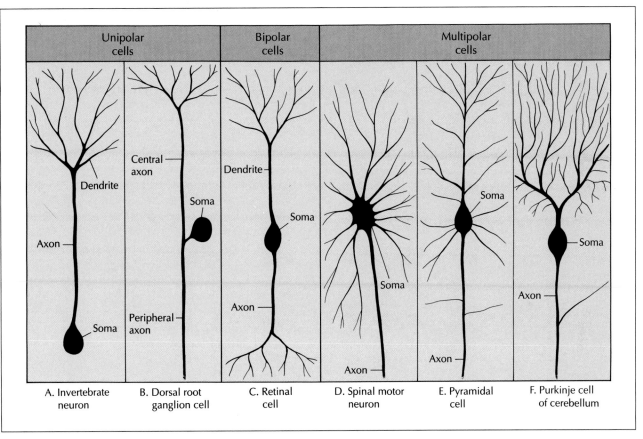

Unipolar cells		Bipolar cells	Multipolar cells		
A. Invertebrate neuron	B. Dorsal root ganglion cell	C. Retinal cell	D. Spinal motor neuron	E. Pyramidal cell	F. Purkinje cell of cerebellum

Figure 13-5 Neurons can be classified as unipolar, bipolar, or multipolar according to the number of processes that originate from the cell body. A unipolar cell has a single process leaving the soma. (A) Unipolar cells are characteristic of invertebrate nervous systems. In invertebrates, different segments of a single axonal process can serve as receptive (dendritic) surfaces or as transmitting (axonal) terminals. (*From* Kandel [60]; with permission.) (B) Neurons in the dorsal root ganglia of the spinal cord belong to a subclass of unipolar cells called pseudounipolar. In a pseudounipolar cell, the processes of the embryonic cell have apparently become fused over a short distance so that only a single process emerges from the cell body. This process then splits in a T-shaped fashion into two axons, one going peripherally to skin or muscle, the other going centrally to the spinal cord. Dorsal root ganglion cells carry information to the central nervous system from

skin, muscle, and viscera. (C) Bipolar cells have two processes: the dendrite, which carries information toward the cell; and the axon, which transmits information away from the cell. The bipolar cell shown here is found in the retina. The multipolar cell usually has dendrites emerging from all parts of the cell body and is common in the mammalian nervous system. (D) This cell is a motor neuron in the spinal cord that innervates muscle fibers. (E) A pyramidal cell is a variant of the multipolar cell. The cell body is pyramidal in shape, and dendrites emerge both from its apex (the apical dendrite) and from the base (the basilar dendrites). This pyramidal cell is from the hippocampus, a part of the brain thought to be involved in memory. Pyramidal cells are also found in the cerebral cortex. (F) A Purkinje cell of the cerebellum, another variant of a multipolar cell, is characterized by its rich and extensive dendritic tree in one plane. (*B–F adapted from* Cajal [61]; with permission.)

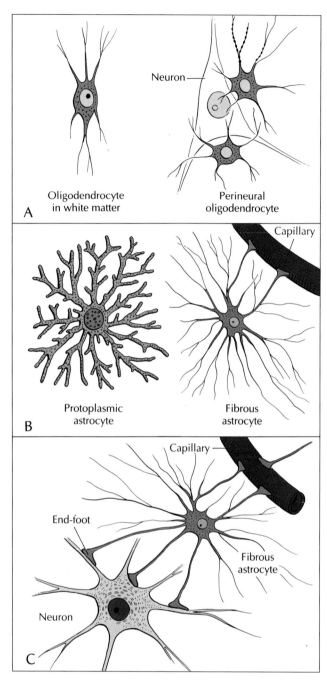

Figure 13-6 There are two principal types of macroglia in the nervous system, the oligodendrocytes and the astrocytes. (A) Oligodendrocytes have few processes, which form the myelin sheath around the central axons of nerve cells. These glial cells are small and are located in gray matter, where they surround the cell bodies of neurons, as well as in white matter. (*Adapted from* Penfield [62]; with permission.) (B) Astrocytes have many processes. They are star-shaped and may either be fibrous (found in white matter) or protoplasmic (found in gray matter). (*Adapted from* Martinez Martinez [63]; with permission.) (C) The end-feet of an astrocyte contact both capillaries and neurons, and are therefore thought to have a nutritive role. (*Adapted from* Kuffler and coworkers [64]; with permission.)

The second functional component is signal integration. Because the local receptor potential cannot of itself generate an action potential, it must be modified for further active transmission. The segment of neuronal membrane adjacent to the input component is capable of generating such an action potential; it is in this trigger zone that the first decision-making element of the neuron is located. If the receptor potentials have an integrated sum that is sufficiently excitatory, an action potential is initiated. If no action potential is generated, the input signal dissipates without any perceptible response. Therefore, the first step of nociception is encoding the input signal if the algebraic summation of the input barrage is sufficient to generate a receptor potential.

The third functional component of nerve conduction is continued propagation of the action potential to the spinal cord. The nerve axon is the anatomic component of the nervous system responsible for the propagation of the action potential and is the site of pathology in demyelinating diseases. Traumatic injury to the axon is common, because the frequently long and tortuous route to the spinal cord renders the axon vulnerable to injury.

The fourth functional component is the relaying of the stimulus to the cerebral structures of the central nervous system for further signal processing [8]. The dorsal horn is that region of the spinal cord gray matter which comprises Rexed's laminae I–VI (Fig. 13-8). Its primary purpose is to receive afferent stimuli from the periphery, modify the input according to descending influences from higher brain centers, and to relay the resultant information to the higher brain centers for continued processing [9]. The neurons in the dorsal horn project cephalad in the spinothalamic tract and the dorsal funiculus to higher brain regions, including the ventral posterolateral nucleus of the thalamus, the mesencephalon, and the reticular formation.

A customary method of classifying the neuronal population of the dorsal horn is based on the type of stimulus activating the neurons [10]. The low threshold mechanoreceptors are activated by low level stimuli, such as light touch or pressure, and are especially common in lamina IV. Thermoreceptive cells populate laminae I, III, V, and movement detection cells are located primarily in lamina VI. The nociceptor-specific (or high threshold mechanoreceptor) neurons are activated by stimuli potentially capable of causing tissue damage. The wide-dynamic-range neurons, the most common neuron of the dorsal horn, can respond to both high- and low-level stimuli such as light touch, pressure, pinch, heat, or chemicals, depending on their level of activation by higher brain centers.

The wide-dynamic-range neuron is thought to be the critical element of sensory-discriminative function for the processing of nociceptive information. Although it is considered to be a discreet cell type, there is evidence suggesting that other neurons may exhibit wide-dynamic-range characteristics when "unmasked" by light anesthesia, decerebrate states, and other pathologic conditions [11]. Thus, experimental model preparation may influence the physiology of the neuron population being analyzed [12].

The role of the wide-dynamic-range neuron is considered to be that of a general alerting mechanism for the organism as well as a modulating system of high threshold pathways. Noxious stimuli are conducted through A and C fibers and converge on nociceptive-specific neurons in lamina I [13,14]. This information is combined with non-nociceptive information that converges on wide-dynamic-range neurons in laminae I and V where the information is processed and relayed to the higher brain centers [15].

Wide-dynamic-range neuron sensitivity may be influenced by several factors.

1. Diffuse noxious inhibitory control—a phenomenon in which a patient reports less pain sensation in a given area when another area is receiving a noxious stimulus [16].

2. Local anesthetics, such as lidocaine, block the wide-dynamic-range neurons response to noxious stimuli but not to nonnoxious stimuli.

3. Sensorimotor cortex stimulation, in which descending impulses maintain the wide-dynamic neuron in an excitatory state and sensitize it to low threshold stimuli.

4. Barbiturate anesthesia has been shown to unmask wide-dynamic-range characteristics in some low threshold mechanoreceptors [11].

5. Neurotransmitters. In the cat dorsal horn, intrathecal clonidine produced suppression of noxiously induced activity of wide-dynamic neurons. This was

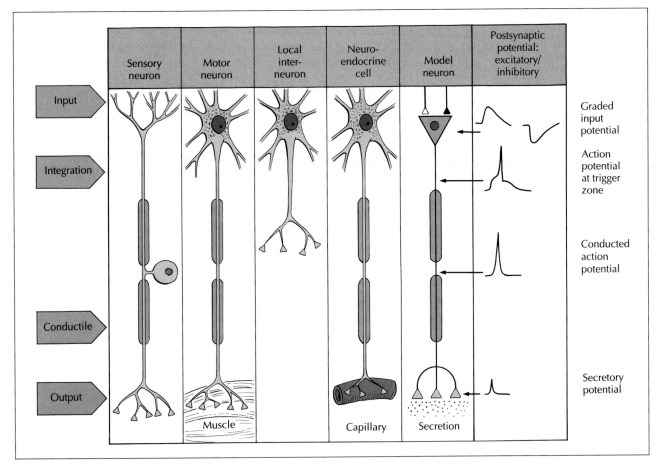

Figure 13-7 Most neurons, whether they are sensory, motor, interneuronal, or neuroendocrine, have four functional components in common: input, integrative, conductile, and output. Local interneurons often lack conductile components. On the basis of these shared features, a model neuron can be constructed that summarizes the functional organization of neurons in general. (*From* Kandel [60]; with permission.)

reversed by both yohimbine (an α_2-antagonist) and methysergide (a serotonin antagonist).

When this system operates properly, normal nociception occurs; however, when any deviation occurs, the message is distorted, inaccurate, or prolonged and has abnormal pathophysiologic consequences. This phenomenon may be described as neuropathic pain.

NEURONAL RESPONSE TO INJURY

Trauma To Peripheral Neurons

The neuron's response to trauma depends to a great degree on the severity of the injury. Seddon's nerve injury criteria use three degrees of severity: 1) neuropraxis—axon intact but nonconducting; 2) axonotmesis—some axons divided but nerve trunk intact; 3) neurotmesis—entire nerve trunk divided.

Acute injury to sensory nerve fibers provokes a brief barrage of afferent impulses described as an "injury discharge." Although lasting only a few minutes, this phenomenon is strongly correlated with the subsequent development of neuropathic pain [17••,18].

When an axon is severed (axonotmesis), the cut end of the proximal segment fuses, retracts, and begins to swell, forming a retraction bulb (Fig. 13-9). Internally, rapid axoplasmic transport ceases and axoplasmic flow decreases. Within hours of injury, the distal segment begins to degenerate because of the loss of axoplasmic transport of vital elements from the cell body. The synaptic terminal function is lost first, because no neurotransmitter or vesicles can be synthesized. After 2 or 3 days, the nucleus undergoes chromatolysis as it prepares to synthesize new cellular components for regeneration of the injured axon. After about 1 week, the entire distal axon begins to degenerate, and the myelin sheath separates from the axon and breaks apart. The axon then swells, becomes beaded, and is absorbed by the Schwann cells.

The nerve sheath remains intact, however, and provides a conduit for the regenerating axon sprouts from the cell body, which emerge from the distal tip of the injured neuronal bulb and begin to elongate. The regenerating axon must make contact with the appropriate receptor/effector organ to make the regeneration process effective and functional. If this contact does not occur,

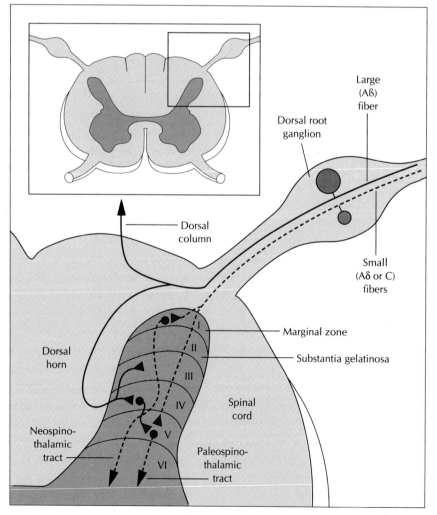

Figure 13-8 The dorsal horn of the spinal cord. The nociceptive neurons, whose axons form the ascending anterolateral system, are found in lamina I and lamina V of the dorsal horn. While neurons in the marginal layer (lamina I) receive input primarily from small A-δ and C fibers, there is greater convergence of large- and small-fiber input upon nociceptive neurons in lamina V. This difference is reflected in the electrophysiology of these cells. Many nociceptive neurons in the marginal layer do not respond to nonpainful touch stimuli, while those in the deeper layers display a wider dynamic range. (*From* Kandel [60]; with permission.)

Large (Aß) fiber

Dorsal root ganglion

Dorsal column

Small (Aδ or C) fibers

Marginal zone

Substantia gelatinosa

Dorsal horn

Spinal cord

Neospino-thalamic tract

Paleospino-thalamic tract

the opportunity for aberrant reinnervation becomes much greater. If advance of the axon sprouts is halted (*eg*, by scar tissue or wound debris), a tangled mass of neurofibrils develops in the region of the obstruction producing a "neuroma." Neuromas may form after any type of axonal interruption (partial or complete) or when the regenerating axon reaches the distal nerve sheath. Recent studies suggest that, upon reaching the intended tissue target, enzymatic action stops axonal sprout growth and prevents indefinite and uncontrolled neuroma formation.

The degeneration of a traumatized neuron is not an isolated event, in that surrounding neurons with synaptic attachments often show corresponding degenerative changes (Fig. 13-10). Neuroanatomists have depended on this phenomenon of transneuronal degeneration to facilitate the delineation of neural pathways. The path of degeneration may extend anterograde and retrograde. The anterograde changes caused by peripheral nerve injury can include sensitization of the wide-dynamic-range neurons of the dorsal horn.

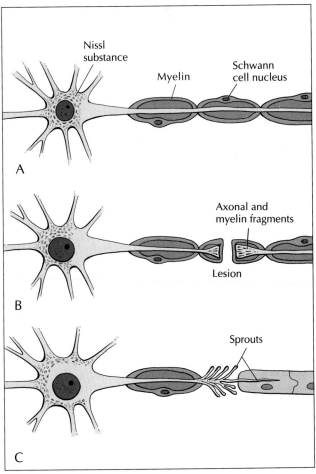

Figure 13-9 When an axon is severed there are changes in the distal axon segment and in the parent neuron after the terminal has degenerated. (A) Normal cell body and portion of axon. (The axon terminal and its changes are omitted.) (B) Retrograde cell reaction and Wallerian degeneration. About 2 to 3 days after the axon is severed, the cell body begins to swell, and the nucleus swells and migrates. About 1 week after axotomy, the myelin sheath withdraws from the axon and fragments; the axon swells and beads, and then fragments. (C) Retrograde cell reaction and axon regeneration. The cell body and nucleus continue to swell, and finally, the Nissl substance undergoes chromatolysis in preparation for regeneration of the proximal axon segment. (*From* Kandel [60]; with permission.)

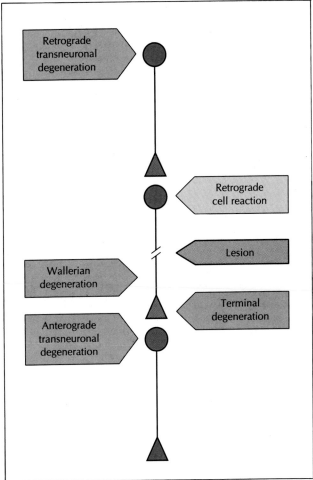

Figure 13-10 Axotomy can result in degeneration not only in the injured cell, but also in those cells with which it shares synapses. (*From* Kandel [60]; with permission.)

Trauma to Central Neurons

Traumatic injury to central nervous system neurons may produce rapid local degeneration of the axon and myelin sheath with phagocytosis of axonal debris by macrophages. Glial cells proliferate, forming a glial scar, which may prevent new axonal formation and reestablishment of central connections. In addition, glial cells absorb any remaining fragments of myelin and axonal degenerative debris. Within 1 day of injury, the nerve terminal and its mitochondria begin to swell, and within 6 or 7 days, the glial cells push the ineffective terminal away from its connections to other neurons.

After mild head injury, histologic evidence of myelin destruction may be seen, and numerous axonal retraction bulbs may be demonstrated in cerebral tissue [19•]. A spectrum of axonal damage, ranging from disruption of axoplasmic transport to delayed axonal rupture due to the internal release of putative neurotransmitters such as acetylcholine, glutamate, aspartate, and others can occur [3,19•].

Trauma to Sympathetic Neurons

Little literature exists describing the response of the sympathetic neuron to trauma or other injury [20]. Several reasons for this deficiency exist, including the size of the neurons involved, as well as the difficulty of tracing the effect of a single neuron in its tortuous and inaccessible course. In the absence of specific data, it may be assumed that sympathetic neurons undergo the same degenerative and regenerative changes described for peripheral neurons. The possible effects that these responses may have on pain perception will be addressed later.

DEMYELINATING DISEASES

Dysfunction of Peripheral Neurons

Some sensory neurons develop demyelinating disease entities that manifest the clinical phenomenon of impaired sensation caused by conduction block, slowed conduction, and impaired ability to conduct impulses at higher frequencies. The injured axon is unable to conduct action potentials at the customary rapid speed, because of damage to its myelin sheath. This produces a short-circuiting effect in that the usually high-resistance, low-capacitance sheath is changed to a low-resistance, high-capacitance region, leaving less current available to depolarize the next node of Ranvier. In addition, the demyelination unmasks the voltage-gated potassium channels in the internodal region of the injured axon, producing enhanced leakage of current out of the axon. Therefore, conduction speed and the ability to propagate an action potential are markedly reduced in the injured

section of the axon, resulting in varying conduction rates within a single axon.

The clinical effects of inconsistent conduction rates within a single axon are manifested by loss of synchrony of neural conduction. For example, functions such as tendon reflexes and vibration sense depend on a synchronous barrage of neural activity to operate properly and, therefore, may be affected by demyelinating diseases. As the demyelination process increases in severity and in intensity, conduction becomes intermittent and ultimately completely blocked. The pathophysiologic effects of central demyelination are essentially the same as for peripheral demyelination.

DISEASES OF CHEMICAL TRANSMISSION AT THE NERVE TERMINAL

Several human disease entities may be caused by pathology at the terminal synapse. The most noteworthy of these are myasthenia gravis, Eaton-Lambert syndrome, and human botulism. The pathophysiology of the latter two conditions differs from the former in that whereas myasthenia gravis is a postsynaptic disorder resulting from the production of antireceptor antibodies to the nicotinic acetylcholine receptors, both Eaton-Lambert syndrome and human botulism are presynaptic disorders resulting in impaired release of neurotransmitters.

POTENTIAL MECHANISMS OF GENERATING NEUROPATHIC PAIN

Lesions of Neuronal Encoding

As presented previously, the distal end of the afferent somatosensory neuron is a specialized transducer that encodes an appropriate stimulus into electrical impulses. Sensitization of these peripheral terminals was previously considered to be a vital component of hyperalgesia. This mechanism may be especially important in the symptoms of sympathetically mediated pain and causalgia, because sympathetic outflow seems to sensitize somatic afferent receptors. However, although sensitizing substances are known to be released into damaged tissues, it is not clear that this mechanism is important in the genesis of neuropathic pain.

Lesions of Neuronal Conduction

Injury to an axon can alter the normally passive conducting properties of the axon to that of an ectopic chemical or mechanically induced source of aberrant action potentials. Three potential axonal mechanisms of neuropathic pain are reviewed at this point [21••].

Electrical activity is a property of all neuromata and is dependent upon several factors such as age, species, and extracellular environment. It is believed that factors such as tissue ischemia, infection, inflammation, mechanical pressure, and adrenergic agonists can excite the axonal sprouts and provoke them into generating abnormal electrical activity, which may be perceived as painful [22]. Clinical evidence for the ability of neuromata to generate painful sensations exists in the alleviation of pain by excision of the neuroma [23]. Unfortunately, pain recurs with the inevitable regeneration of the neuroma. In addition, the analgesia from conduction blockade and sympathetic blockade demonstrate the effect of the extracellular milieu (eg, neurotransmitters, electrolytes, and others) on the painful neuroma.

Axons in a state of demyelination, degeneration, or regeneration also manifest spontaneous electrical activity and are exquisitely sensitive to norepinephrine in the extracellular space. This characteristic may explain the effect of sympathetic blockade on the pain of causalgia. A single action potential in an injured axon can produce multiple electrical discharges from the damaged area; this phenomenon is known as "after-discharge," and it may not only be a significant source of painful sensation, but may also modify contiguous neurons by altering ionic composition of the local extracellular milieu.

Reflected axon spikes, an abnormal type of conduction resulting from varying rates of conduction within a single axon due to alteration of axonal diameter or myelination, can result in a self-propagating circus excitation from a single stimulus. The effect of such electrical activity could result in the perception of pain from an innocuous stimulus, a phenomenon called allodynia.

Abnormal spontaneous electrical activity in dorsal root ganglia has been found to occur after peripheral nerve injury. Although this has not yet been observed in humans and its clinical relevance is presently doubtful, it does explain the presence of persistent pain after peripheral nerve lesions.

Axonal "cross-talk" has also been implicated as a possible mechanism for neuropathic pain. Recent investigations have shown the presence of electrical junctions between axons in neuromata as well as in degenerating and regenerating axonal segments. These ephaptic connections have also been observed in demyelinated axons by Raminsky [24]. If a low threshold mechanical afferent is joined to a nociceptive axon, stimulation by light touch could be interpreted clinically as pain or hyperesthesia.

Drugs inhibiting mitosis, such as vincristine, are associated with sensorimotor neuropathies such as jaw pain, burning dysesthesias of the hands and feet, and allodynia when administered to cancer patients [25]. Microtubular disruption is a proposed mechanism by which the cellular toxins vincristine and colchicine exert their desired clinical effects. Diagnostic nerve biopsy has demonstrated that inhibition of rapid axoplasmic transport by microtubular disruption is the suspected cause of the axonal degeneration. As discussed earlier, synthesized membrane components and secretory proteins are transported to the nerve terminals by anterograde axoplasmic transport. Cellular debris of synaptic transmission is then transported back to the soma by retrograde axoplasmic transport for recycling. Thus, inhibiting these processes by disabling the microtubular system prevents the neuron from engaging in synaptic transmission, creating a situation similar to deafferentation.

Lesions of Neuronal Relays

Lesions of the dorsal horn relay system include changes within the central nervous system that occur in response to peripheral or central nervous system disease or injury.

The Dorsal Horn

Recent studies suggest that peripheral nerve pathology can reduce the ability of afferent discharges reaching the dorsal horn to modify the activity of contiguous neurons, a characteristic known as the dorsal root reflex. The severity of nerve injury needed to modify the dorsal root reflex is not presently known in man [21••]. The presence of electrically silent synapses between dorsal horn cells can apparently be unmasked abruptly by axonal injury, so that when a given neuron is transected, the cell receives input from a different axon and adopts its receptive field. This event could allow for an innocuous afferent stimulus to be received by axonotomized neuron and to be interpreted as pain. One of the responses of the dorsal horn to axonal transection of peripheral nerves is the sprouting of new connections stimulated by deafferentation. Two consequences of this adaptation could be altered sensory fields or the loss of modality specificity, both of which may contribute to the phenomenon of neuropathic pain.

Another response of the dorsal horn to peripheral nerve injury as well as dorsal rhizotomy is spontaneous hyperactivity. This hyperactivity is manifested by spontaneous electrical activity as well as heightened metabolic activity in the spinal cord gray matter, as evidenced by the increased rate of metabolism of ^{14}C-2-deoxyglucose in laminae I–IX from a rat model of painful peripheral mononeuropathy [26••]. The wide-dynamic-range neuron is the principal cell type implicated in this response. These dorsal horn neurons generate ectopic signals but also increase the rate of firing in response to any stimuli from contiguous afferent input. Because of these changes, a low threshold stimulus could be interpreted as noxious. Although this phenomenon develops over several days, it seems to persist for several years. This enhanced activity is a likely factor in the development of postinjury neuropathic pain.

The most realistic description of the response of the dorsal horn to injury is that there is no fixed relationship between the input and output of individual dorsal horn neurons [27]. The variation of the response to injury may be due to the arrival of an afferent barrage to the dorsal horn, followed by the processing of the new information in the context of other inputs from the periphery as well as the brain.

HIGHER BRAIN CENTERS

The modulating effect of the higher centers of the brain on nociception is one of the most valuable contributions of Melzack and Wall's Gate Control Theory to pain medicine. The effect of the evaluative, motivational, and affective components of the brain upon neuropathic input cannot be underestimated. It is certain that the higher centers of the brain receive distorted information from damaged afferent neurons [28]. Whether or not that information is interpreted as pain is unique to each individual. In consideration of these issues, the value of a multidisciplinary approach to the neuropathic pain patient is paramount.

PAINFUL NEUROPATHIES

A useful classification of neuropathies involves the number of peripheral nerves affected by the disease process [21••,29]. Mononeuropathies involve a single peripheral nerve or nerve plexus, whereas polyneuropathies describe more generalized peripheral nerve disease processes. Only the neuropathies that are usually associated with pain are included in this presentation (Table 13-1).

THERAPEUTIC STRATEGIES FOR MANAGING NEUROPATHIC PAIN

Knowledge of the various responses of peripheral and central neurons to injury, as well as consideration for the theoretical mechanisms of neuropathic pain, presents an opportunity to plan therapeutic strategy directed toward restoring normal neural function. Devor [30] lists six treatment modalities that have been found to decrease ectopic electrogenesis *in vitro*. That list may be supplemented by added modalities known to be of benefit to man, with realization that no one

treatment has been shown to be universally effective in the relief of neuropathic pain. It is strongly urged that these modalities be used in a multidisciplinary pain management setting, so as to efficiently evaluate and comprehensively manage the varied multidimensional aspects of the patient's pain.

TABLE 13-1
CLASSIFICATION OF NEUROPATHIES USUALLY ASSOCIATED WITH PAIN

Mononeuropathies
Trauma
Entrapment syndromes
Brachial plexitis/lumbar plexitis
Connective tissue diseases
Postherpetic neuralgia
Carcinomatous neuropathy
Diabetic neuropathy
Diabetic amyotrophy
Polyneuropathies
Isoniazid neuropathy
Pellagra neuropathy
Fabry's disease
Dominantly inherited sensory neuropathy
Diabetic polyneuropathy
Amyloid neuropathy
Alcoholic neuropathy
Guillain-Barré neuropathy
Beriberi neuropathy
Strachan syndrome
Burning feet syndrome
Decompression sickness
Toxic neuropathies
   Arsenic
   Chloramphenicol
   Metronidazole
   Organophosphorus
   Thallium
   Misonidazole
   Vincristine
   Cis-platinum

Corticosteroids

Devor and coworkers [31] demonstrated that local application of corticosteroids to an experimental neuroma produced a prolonged depression of ectopic and evoked neuronal hyperexcitability. This observation may help to explain the anecdotal experience of beneficial results from the use of corticosteroid-containing local anesthetic conduction blockade of neuromas. Although the precise mechanism is not certain, membrane stabilization is a reasonable hypothesis.

Conduction Blockade

Conduction blockade of sympathetic efferents has long been the treatment of choice for sympathetic-mediated pain syndromes, including reflex sympathetic dystrophy and causalgia. A probable mechanism is the prevention of norepinephrine release from the varicosities on the sympathetic nerve fiber. Peripheral nerve blockade has been found to be effective on a temporary basis, presumably by blocking aberrant afferent discharges.

Adrenergic Modulation

α-Adrenergic modulation is an effective method of alleviating the sympathetically mediated component of neuropathic pain [32–34]. Agents such as clonidine, phentolamine, phenoxybenzamine, surgical sympathectomy, and conduction blockade of sympathetic ganglia have all been demonstrated to be effective in selected patients [35–38].

Glycerol

Burchiel and Russell [39] showed that topical application of glycerol suppresses ectopic experimental neuroma activity, while Rappaport and coworkers [40] determined that glycerol suppresses autotomy behavior. This concept has been effectively utilized in the treatment of trigeminal neuralgia by the application of glycerol to the Gasserian ganglion. The mechanism of action of glycerol is unclear.

Anticonvulsants

Sodium channel blockers such as phenytoin have been found to effectively suppress ectopic electrical activity in experimental neuromas whereas carbamazepine and other anticonvulsants have been widely used to treat such disorders as trigeminal and glossopharyngeal neuralgias [41]. Phenytoin is especially effective against high-frequency burst discharges. Calcium channel blockers may also be effective in these situations but have not been widely studied. Further studies may elucidate their possible roles in the alleviation of neuropathic pain.

Antidepressants

Both tricyclic and heterocyclic antidepressants have been reported to be beneficial in relieving neuropathic pain. The mechanism of action seems to be a direct intrinsic analgesic effect beyond the reported serotonergic and noradrenergic effects [42]. Preferential inhibitors of serotonin reuptake such as clomipramine, fluoxitine, and sertraline have been found to be beneficial in some neuropathic pain states, whereas noradrenergic reuptake inhibitors such as desipramine are useful in others. In general, tricyclic antidepressants (ie, amitriptyline, desipramine) have been noted to be more effective analgesics than the heterocyclic compounds (ie, fluoxitine, sertraline, and others) [41,43–45,46•].

Local Anesthetics

The topical application of local anesthetics have long been known to provide relief from neuropathic pain. In addition, the use of systemic and regional local anesthetic infusions has also been utilized in the treatment of painful peripheral and central neuropathies. At least two mechanisms may be operative: conduction blockade of damaged afferent axons and prevention of norepinephrine release from adjacent sympathetic fibers [47•,48•,49].

Retrograde Axoplasmic Transport

Retrograde "suicide" axoplasmic transport of cytotoxins, such as adriamycin, has been used to alleviate pain in trigeminal and intercostal neuropathic pain states [50]. The toxin is transported from the terminal fibers of the neuron to the soma where the toxic effects occur.

Axoplasmic Transport Blockers

Colchicine and vincristine have been used by Devor [51] and others to inhibit axoplasmic transport in the injured neuron and have prolonged profound suppression of neuroma hyperexcitability without conduction blockade. It must be remembered that vincristine and other cytotoxic agents have neuropathic effects themselves and must be thoroughly tested for this application before wide clinical use is approved.

Gangliosides

Gangliosides are glycosphingolipids that occur in nearly all cellular membranes, especially in nervous tissue. They have been shown to be effective in treating several diabetic and toxic neuropathies [52••]. Several possible mechanisms may help to explain their beneficial effects.

Glutamate release, triggered by nerve injury, can produce chronic changes in binding to receptor sites within the calcium channel regulated by the *N*-methyl-D-aspartate (NMDA) receptor. These changes can result in the initiation and maintenance of neuropathic pain. Gangliosides may modulate glutaminergic excitotoxicity, thus attenuating glutamine-induced neuronal injury (Table 13-2) [53,54].

Augmentative Electrostimulation

Dorsal column and peripheral nerve stimulating electrodes have demonstrated effective relief in painful neuropathic states [55,56]. Fully implantable neurostimulators have been developed and are more reliable and versatile than previously. A trial implantation of 4 or 5 days is highly recommended before considering long-term placement.

Blockade of the *N*-methyl-D-aspartate Receptor

Drugs that block NMDA receptors, such as the synthetic tetrahydro-cannabinol (THC) derivative HU211, exhibit antinociceptive activity when administered to animals with neuropathic lesions [57].

CONCLUSIONS

Neuropathic pain has been characterized as a "disease of membrane excitability regulation" [58]. Some basic aspects of normal nociception have been reviewed to contrast it to neuropathic nociception. When the normal functions of a sensory neuron are impaired or halted by disease or injury, the effects are widespread. The normally passive axon may become an active generator of aberrant discharges. This process may occur not only in adjacent neurons but also in more central neurons. These reactions are responsible for the distortion and amplification of normal aberrant communication from the periphery. In some cases, this information may be interpreted as pain. Because both the peripheral and central nervous systems are affected, an understanding of their respective roles is useful in designing a more rational therapeutic strategy for the alleviation of neuropathic pain.

TABLE 13-2
DIRECT EFFECTS ON INJURED NEURONS POSSIBLY ATTRIBUTABLE TO GANGLIOSIDE THERAPY

Enhancement of mean sprouting length

Increased number of regenerating axons

Increased conduction velocity of crushed peripheral nerves

Decreased dorsal horn metabolic rate in animal models of neuropathic disease

Inhibition of glutamate-mediated protein kinase C translocation

---

REFERENCES AND RECOMMENDED READING

Papers of interest, published recently, have been highlighted as:
• Of special interest
•• Of outstanding interest

1.•• Bowsher D: Neurogenic pain syndromes and their management. *Br Med Bull* 1991, 47:64–66.
A concise review of the diagnosis and treatment of common neuropathic pain states.

2.• Vecht CJ, Hoff AM, Kansen PJ, *et al.*: Types and causes of pain in cancer of the head and neck. *Cancer* 1992, 70:178–184.
This article stresses the importance of determining the etiology of pain states before beginning treatment of cancer-related neuropathic pain.

3. Wall PD: Neuropathic pain and injured nerve: central mechanisms. *Br Med Bull* 1991, 47:631–643.

4. Portenoy R: The neurophysiology of pain. *Neurol Clin* 1989, 7:183–231.

5. Bonica JJ: Anatomic and physiologic basis of nociception and pain. In *The Management of Pain*. Edited by Bonica JJ. Philadelphia: Lea and Febiger; 1990:28–53.

6. Williams PL, Warwick R, Dyson M, *et al.*: Further aspects of spinal organization. In *Gray's Anatomy*. London: Churchill Livingstone; 1989, 37:939–949.

7.• Baskin LS, Tanagho EA: Pelvic pain without pelvic organs. *J Urol* 1992, 147:683–686.
This article demonstrates the importance of seeking a multidisciplinary evaluation of pain before considering invasive procedures; should be helpful to our surgical colleagues.

8. Kelly JP: Anatomical basis of sensory perception and motor coordination. In *Principles of Neural Science*. Edited by Kandel ER, Schwartz JH. New York: Elsevier; 1985:223–243.

9. Janig W: Neuronal mechanisms of pain with special emphasis on visceral and deep somatic pain. *Acta Neurochir Suppl* 1987, 38:16–32.

10. Wall PD, Melzack R: The dorsal horn. In *Textbook of Pain*. 1989:102–109.

11. Collins JG, Ren K, Saito Y, *et al.*: Plasticity of some spinal dorsal horn neurons as revealed by pentobarbital-induced disinhibition. *Brain Res* 1990, 525:189–197.

12. Collins JG: A descriptive study of spinal dorsal horn neurons in the physiologically intact, awake, drug-free cat. *Brain Res* 1987, 416:34–42.

13. Price DD, Bennet GT, Rafii A: Psychophysical observations on patients with neuropathic pain relieved by sympathetic block. *Pain* 1989, 36:273–288.

14. Shir Y, Seltzer Z: A-fibers mediate mechanical hyperesthesia and allodynia and C-fibers mediate thermal hyperalgesia in a new model of causalgiform pain disorders in rats. *Neurosci Lett* 1990, 115:62–67.

15. Yezierski RP, Broton JG: Functional properties of spinomesencephalic tract (SMT) cells in the upper cervical spinal cord of a cat. *Pain* 1991, 45:187–196.

16. Talbot JD, Duncan GH, Bushnell MC: Effects of diffuse noxious inhibitory controls (DNICs) on the sensory-discriminative dimension of pain perception. *Pain* 1989, 36:231–238.

17.•• Seltzer Z, Beilin BZ, Ginzburg R, *et al.*: The role of injury discharge in the induction of neuropathic pain behavior in rats. *Pain* 1991, 46:327–336.

This article provides further evidence for the concept of preemptive analgesia for the prevention of postsurgical neuropathic pain states.

18. Dougherty PM, Garrison CJ, Carlton SM: Differential influence of local anesthetic upon two models of experimentally induced peripheral mononeuropathy in the rat. *Brain Res* 1992, 570:109–115.

19.• Evans RW: The post-concussion syndrome and sequelae of mild head injury. *Neurol Clin* 1992, 10:815–848.

An excellent comprehensive review of neuropathic pain relating to head trauma.

20. Janig W, Koltzenburg M: Sympathetic reflex activity and neuroeffector transmission change after chronic nerve lesions. *Proceedings of the VIth World Congress on Pain*. Amsterdam: Elsevier Science Publishers BV; 1991, 43:365.

21.•• Loeser JD: Peripheral nerve disorders (peripheral neuropathies). In *The Management of Pain*. 2nd ed. Edited by Bonica JJ. Philadelphia: Lea and Febiger; 1992:211–220.

An outstanding and comprehensive review of peripheral neuropathies.

22. Fried K, Govrin-Liopmann R, Rosenthal F, *et al.*: Ultrastructure of afferent axon endings in a neuroma. *J Neurocytol* 1991, 20:682–701.

23. Seltzer Z, Paran Y, Eisen A, *et al.*: Neuropathic pain behavior in rats depends on the afferent input from nerve-end neuroma including histamine-sensitive C-fibers. *Neurosci Lett* 1991, 128:203–206.

24. Rasminsky M: Ephaptic transmission between single nerve fibers in the spinal nerve roots of "dystrophic mice". *J Physiol* [London] 1980, 305:151–169.

25. Patt RB, ed: *Cancer Pain*. Philadelphia: J.B. Lippincott; 1993:41–57.

26.•• Mao J, Price DD, Coghill RC, *et al.*: Spatial patterns of spinal cord (C14) -2-deoxyglucose metabolic activity in a rat model of painful peripheral mononeuropathy. *Pain* 1992, 50:89–100.

A fascinating glimpse of postinjury spinal cord metabolic activity and its possible implications in human neuropathic pain syndromes.

27. Treede RD, Meyer RA, Raja SN, *et al.*: Peripheral and central mechanisms of cutaneous hyperalgesia. *Prog Neurobiol* 1992, 38:397–421.

28. Xu XJ, Hao JX, Aldskogius H, *et al.*: Chronic pain-related syndrome in rats after ischemic spinal cord lesions: a possible animal model for pain in patients with spinal cord injury. *Pain* 1991, 48:279–290.

29. Portenoy R: Painful polyneuropathy. *Neurol Clin* 1989, 7:265–288.

30. Devor M: Neuropathic pain and injured nerve: peripheral mechanisms. *Br Med Bull* 1991, 47:619–630.

31. Devor M, Govrin-Lippman R, Raber P: Corticosteroids suppress ectopic neuronal discharge in experimental neurons. *Pain* 1985, 22:127–137.

32. Kim SH, Chung JM: Sympathectomy alleviates mechanical allodynia in an experimental model for neuropathy in the rat. *Neurosci Lett* 1991, 134:131–134.

33. Puke MJ, Xu XJ, Wiesenfeld-Hallin Z: Intrathecal administration of clonidine suppresses autotomy, a behavioral sign of chronic pain in rats after sciatic nerve section. *Neurosci Lett* 1991, 133:199–202.

34. Zeigler D, Lynch SA, Muir J, *et al.*: Transdermal clonidine versus placebo in painful diabetic neuropathy. *Pain* 1992, 48:403–408.

35. Treede RD, Davis KD, Campbell JN, *et al.*: The plasticity of cutaneous hyperalgesia during sympathetic ganglion blockade in patients with neuropathic pain. *Brain* 1992, 115:607–621.

36. Murata K, Nakagawa I, Kumeta Y, *et al.*: Intrathecal clonidine suppresses noxiously evoked activity of spinal wide dynamic range neurons in cats. *Anesth Analg* 1989, 69:185–191.

37. Roberts WJ, Foglesong ME: Identification of afferents contributing to sympathetically evoked activity in wide-dynamic-range neurons. *Pain* 1988, 34:305–314.

38. Roberts WJ, Foglesong ME: Spinal recordings suggest that wide-dynamic-range neurons mediate sympathetically maintained pain. *Pain* 1988, 34:289–304.

39. Burchiel KJ, Russel LC: "Glycerol neurolysis" neurophysiological effects of topical glycerol application of rat saphenous nerve. *J Neurosurg* 1985, 63:784–788.

40. Rapport ZH, Seltzer Z, Zagzag D: The effect of glycerol on autonomy: an experimental model of neuralgia pain. *Pain* 1986, 26:85–91.

41. Kloke M, Hoffken K, Olbrich H, *et al.*: Anti-depressants and anti-convulsants for the treatment of neuropathic pain syndromes in cancer patients. *Onkologie* 1991, 14:40–43.

42. Nakagawa I, Omote K, Kitahata LM, *et al.*: Serotonergic mediation of spinal analgesia and its interaction with noradrenergic systems. *Anesthesiology* 1990, 73:474–478.

43. Kishore KR, Max MB, Schafer SC, *et al.*: Desipramine relieves postherpetic neuralgia. *Clin Pharmacol Ther* 1990, 47:305–312.

44. Fromm GH, Nakata M, Kondo T: Differential action of amitriptyline on neurons in the trigeminal nucleus. *Neurology* 1991, 41:1932–1936.

45. Panerai AE, Bianchi M, Sacerdote P, *et al.*: Anti-depressants in cancer pain. *J Palliat Care* 1991, 7:42–44.

46.• Sorkin LS, McAdoo DJ, Willis WD: Stimulation in the ventral posterior lateral nucleus of the primate thalamus leads release of serotonin in the lumbar spinal cord. *Brain Res* 1992, 581:307–310.

A physiologic rationale for the possible role of deep brain stimulation for the relief of intractable neuropathic pain states is presented in this treatise.

47.• Tenelian DL, MacIver MB: Analgesic concentrations of lidocaine suppress tonic A-delta and C-fiber discharges produced by acute injury. *Anesthesiology* 1991, 74:934–936.

A feasible mechanism of action for the analgesic qualities of lidocaine in neuropathic pain states.

48.• Chabal C, Jacobson L, Mariano A, *et al.*: The use of oral mexiletine for the treatment of pain after peripheral nerve injury. *Anesthesiology* 1992, 76:513–517.

This study examines the efficacy of oral mexilitine in nondiabetic patients with peripheral neuropathy, showing significant reduction in pain.

49. Sotgi ML, Lacerenza M, Marchettini P: Selective inhibition by systemic lidocaine of noxious evoked activity in rat dorsal horn neurons. *Neuroreport* 1991, 2:425–428.

50. Kato S, Otsuki T, Yamamoto T, *et al.*: Retrograde adriamycin sensory ganglionectomy: Novel approach for the treatment of intractable pain. *Stereotact Funct Neurosurg* 1990, 54–55:86–89.

51. Devor M, Govrin-Lippman R: Axoplasmic transport block reduces ectopic impulse generation in injured peripheral nerves. *Pain* 1983, 16:73–85.

52.•• Mao J, Hayes RL, Price DD, *et al.*: Post-injury treatment with GM1 ganglioside reduces nociceptive behaviors and spinal cord metabolic activity in rats with experimental peripheral mononeuropathy. *Brain Res* 1992, 584:18–27.

The critical role of gangliosides in neuronal repair and regeneration is eloquently presented here.

53. Meldrum BS: Excitatory amino acid receptors and disease. *Curr Opin Neurol Neurosurg* 1992, 5:508–513.

54. Yamamoto T, Yaksh TL: Spinal pharmacology of thermal hyperesthesia induced by constriction injury of sciatic nerve. Excitatory amino acid antagonists. *Pain* 1991, 49:121–128.

55. Winkelmuller W: Classification of trigeminal neuralgia and its effect on the results of surgical treatment. *Neurochirurgia Stuttg* 1990, 33:54–57.

56. Myerson B, Linderoth B, Lind G: Spinal cord stimulation in chronic neuropathic pain. *Lakartidningen* 1991, 88:727–732.

57. Zeltser R, Seltzer Z, Eisen A, *et al.*: Suppression of neuropathic pain behavior in rats by a non-psychotropic synthetic cannabinoid with NMDA receptor-blocking properties. *Pain* 1991, 47:95–103.

58. Devor M: The pathophysiology of damaged peripheral nerves. In *Textbook of Pain*. 2nd ed. Edited by Wall PD. 1989:63–81.

59. Stevens CF: The neuron. *Sci Am* 1979, 24:54–65.

60. Kandel ER: Nerve cells and behavior. In *Principles of Neural Science*. 2nd ed. Edited by Kandel ER, Schwartz JH. New York: Elsevier; 1985:38.

61. Cajal SR, ed.: *Histology, Tenth Edition*. Baltimore: Wood; 1933.

62. Penfield W, ed.: *Cytology and Cellular Pathology of the Nervous System, vol. 2* New York: Hoeber; 1932.

63. Martinez Martinez PFA, ed.: *Neuroanatomy: Development and Structure of the Central Nervous System*. Philadelphia: W.B. Saunders; 1982.

64. Kuffler SW, Nicholls JG, Martin AR, eds .: *From Neuron to Brain: A Cellular Approach to the Function of the Nervous System, Second Edition*. Sunderland, MA: Sinauer Associates; 1984.

65. Schwartz JH: Synthesis and distribution of neuronal protein. In *Principles of Neuronal Science*. 2nd ed. Edited by Kandel ER, Schwartz JH. New York: Elsevier; 1985:37–48.

CHAPTER 14

Diagnosis of Reflex Sympathetic Dystrophy and Therapeutic Strategies Based on Pathophysiology

DONALD C. MANNING, MARK CHURCHER, AND SRINIVASA N. RAJA

The principal function of the sympathetic nervous system is to prepare the individual to face threatening or challenging stimuli from the environment. Clinical experience during the past several decades, however, indicates that the sympathetic nervous system can be involved in the maintenance of certain chronic pain states. Reflex sympathetic dystrophy (RSD) and causalgia are two common terms used to describe chronic pain states that are dependent upon the sympathetic nervous system.

The term *reflex sympathetic dystrophy* was first used by Evans in 1946 [1] in the surgical literature; however, clinical descriptions of similar syndromes were described earlier. Early descriptions in European literature include Ambroise Pare [2] who wrote in 1634 "Charles the ninth, the French King, being sick of a fever, Monsieur Chapellan and Castellan his physicians thought it fit he should be let blood; for the performance whereof, there was called a chirurgeon wondrous famous for that business; but when as he by chance had pricked a nerve instead of a vein, the king cried out, that he felt a mighty pain in that place. Then I bid, that the ligature should straight-ways be loosed, otherwise the arm would presently be much swelled. But he going slowly about it, behold the arm began to swell with such contraction, that he could not bend it, nor put it forth, and cruel pain molested not only the pricked particle; but all the whole members besides."

The classic description of "causalgia" was first made by Wier Mitchell in 1864 during the US Civil War in soldiers following high velocity injuries to peripheral nerves [3]. RSD may follow trauma affecting the extremities with or without obvious nerve lesions. Subsequent reports have described clinical variations of the syndrome, and a wide variety of different terms have been applied to these syndromes including Sudeck's atrophy, algodystrophy, shoulder-hand syndrome, and others outlined in Table 14-1 [4]. Recent suggestions have been made to avoid some of the confusions in the terminology. This review discusses the terminology, pathophysiology, clinical manifestations, and management of chronic pain states characterized by sensory, autonomic, and motor manifestations.

TERMINOLOGY

Reflex sympathetic dystrophy has recently been defined as "a complex disorder or a group of disorders that may develop as a consequence of trauma affecting the limbs, with or without an obvious nerve lesion [5]." RSD may also develop after visceral diseases and central nervous system (CNS) lesions. On rare occasions no obvious antecedent event can be identified. The syndrome of

RSD consists of pain and related sensory abnormalities, abnormalities of blood flow and sweating, abnormalities in the motor system, and changes in structure of superficial and deep tissues (trophic changes). RSD is used in the descriptive sense and does not imply specific underlying mechanisms [5]. Such a terminology has the advantage of minimizing the confusion that is associated with the multitude of terms used for similar clinical presentations. However, because the definition does not indicate any underlying mechanism for the pain, the clinician is still left with considerable doubt as to which of these patients are likely to benefit from therapeutic maneuvers aimed at interrupting the sympathetic function to the affected region.

More recently, the terms *sympathetically dependent pain* or *sympathetically maintained pain* have been used to describe a subset of these patients in whom pain relief and reversal of associated sensory disorders is achieved by appropriate blockade of the sympathetic function in the affected region [6]. In contrast, we have used the term *sympathetically independent pain* for patients with clinical features of RSD but who fail to obtain significant relief of pain following appropriate sympathetic blockade [7].

TABLE 14-1
TERMINOLOGY OF SYMPATHETICALLY MAINTAINED PAIN SYNDROMES*

Acute bone atrophy
Algoneurodystrophy
Causalgia - minor, major, minimo
Chronic traumatic edema
Lechirche's posttraumatic pain syndrome
Minor traumatic dystrophy
Major traumatic dystrophy
Posttraumatic pain syndrome
Posttraumatic painful osteoporosis
Posttraumatic vasomotor disorder
Posttraumatic spreading neuralgia
Reflex neurovascular dystrophy
Reflex sympathetic dystrophy
Shoulder-hand syndrome
Sudeck's atrophy
Sympathalgia
Traumatic vasospasm

Adapted from O'Neill and Burchiel [4]; with permission.

The pain of RSD may be multifactorial, with components of both sympathetically mediated as well as sympathetically independent pain. Recently, Jänig [8] described a tentative classification of RSD based on the prominent clinical symptoms. Patients have been classified as having sympathetic algodystrophy, sympathetically maintained pain, and sympathetic dystrophy depending upon the preponderance of pain, hyperalgesia, autonomic and trophic changes, and response to sympathetic blockade. Whether such a subdivision of RSD is justified or will help in the management of the chronic, disabling pain syndrome will have to await further clinical studies.

PATHOPHYSIOGY OF REFLEX SYMPATHETIC DYSTROPHY

The numerous precipitating factors and the unpredictable susceptibility have contributed to the difficulties in establishing the pathophysiologic mechanisms responsible for producing RSD. In addition to alterations in the peripheral and central somatosensory mechanisms, an abnormal sympathetic efferent–somatosensory afferent linkage is established.

The role of the peripheral nervous system appears to be in the initiation and the maintenance of the pain state. RSD often follows peripheral tissue trauma but may result in a barrage of impulses along nociceptors to the central nervous system. Woolf [9] has suggested that RSD may represent a maladaptive neuronal plasticity. Neuronal plasticity refers to the capability of the adult nervous system to modify its function, structure, and chemistry in response to a variety of changing inputs [10]. Under normal circumstances, these plastic changes are adaptive, promoting repair, regeneration, and recovery of function. In some circumstances, however, these modifications may produce malfunction.

Primary Afferent Neurons

Reflex sympathetic dystrophy is often preceded by a noxious event that is likely to initiate strong nociceptive afferent inputs. The initial activation may be followed by a phase of persistent excitability or hypersensitivity to peripheral stimuli. Other plastic changes in the periphery may include sensitization of the afferent receptors and possibly recruitment of (silent) nociceptors, which are not normally activated by innoxious or noxious stimuli. Although it is clear that sensory processing primary afferents can be altered, and if persistent may produce clinical problems, the actual mechanisms responsible for this peripheral sensitization remains unclear. The initial injury may also induce alterations in the chemical contents of the primary afferents including levels of substance P and other peptides. Neuropeptides released from the central terminals of the primary afferent neurons have been shown to play an important role as modulators of neural transmission. Increased levels of these neuromodulators may play a role in the central sensitization of spinal neurons that may contribute to postinjury pain and hypersensitivity [11].

In addition, structural changes such as collateral sprouting and regenerative plasticity may occur in both the central and peripheral branches of the sensory neuron. These structural changes may have functional consequences such as widening of receptive fields and lowering of activation thresholds [12]. Thus, it is not inconceivable that primary afferent plasticity following tissue injury with or without associated nerve injury may contribute to the generation and maintenance of the RSD syndrome.

Spinal Cord

Many studies have also indicated that spinal neurons undergo multiple changes during sustained stimulation of nociceptive afferents, for example, following chronic inflammation or peripheral nerve lesions [9,13]. Several investigators have demonstrated the capacity for nociceptive primary afferents to produce prolonged changes in the spinal neurons that are likely to contribute to the mechanical hyperalgesia, a prominent feature in patients with RSD. Central sensitization processes after acute injuries are often self-limiting [9]. If central sensitization plays an important role in RSD, mechanisms to maintain the central neurons in the sensitized state are required [14••]. The most likely mechanism involved in maintaining a sustained central sensitization is persistent input from nociceptive primary afferents, for example, spontaneous activity in a neuroma or sympathetic somatic interactions resulting in ongoing activity in nociceptors.

The clinical observations in RSD, that pain often spreads beyond the area of damaged tissue or innervation of the damaged nerve and that the symptomatic region ignores traditional boundaries such as dermatomal or nerve distribution, are difficult to explain purely on peripheral abnormalities and most likely involve central changes. In addition, evidence in patients with RSD indicates that activation of large-diameter afferents by gentle stroking of the skin results in pain [7,15]. Differential blockade of the myelinated fibers results in loss of hyperalgesia to tactile stimulus [7,16]. The observation that large-diameter afferent fibers, which normally signal touch sensations, now signal pain provides strong evidence for reorganization in the central processing of somatosensory information. Increased responsiveness of dorsal horn neurons to peripheral stimuli following tissue injury has been demonstrated by several investigators. The trigger for these changes appears to be activity in unmyelinated afferent fibers excited by the injury. The extent to which central sensitization needs to be actively maintained by peripheral inputs is currently not fully known.

Sympathetic and Somatic Fiber Interactions

The pain relief from sympathetic ganglion blocks and regional depletion of catecholamines with guanethidine provides evidence for an interaction of sympathetic efferents with somatic afferents in the periphery.

Under normal physiologic conditions the sympathetic nervous system most likely has no influence on the responses of primary afferent neurons; however, an interaction between primary afferents and sympathetic efferents has been demonstrated in several animal models of nerve injury. For example, myelinated and unmyelinated afferents originating in experimental neuromas develop ongoing activity that is dramatically increased by local administration of norepinephrine or stimulation of the lumbar sympathetic chain [17]. This activation is blocked by α-adrenergic antagonists but not by β-adrenergic blockers [18]. A possible interaction of sympathetic postganglionic fibers and the nociceptors are indicated in Figure 14-1. Other possibilities include ephaptic coupling between sympathetic efferent fibers and somatic afferent fibers or an indirect mechanism involving an alteration in the micromilieu of primary afferents by changing local blood flow.

Several lines of clinical evidence point toward an α-adrenergic sensitivity developing on nociceptive fibers following trauma or tissue injury [14••]. Patients with the diagnosis of RSD have had pain relief with intravenous phentolamine (an α-adrenergic antagonist) and from topical clonidine (an α_2-adrenergic agonist acting presumably by inhibiting the release of norepinephrine from sympathetic fibers) applied at the site of injury. A reemergence of pain in the clonidine-treated region occurs with the local injection of norepinephrine or the specific α_1-agonist phenylephrine. Taken together these results point to an α_1-adrenergic receptor involvement in the pathophysiology of RSD.

Animal Models for Sympathetically Dependent Pain

Until recently, most models for the study of neurogenic pain involved sectioning of one or more peripheral nerves with the formation of neuromas. In the past 5 years, three different behavioral models of peripheral neuropathic pain have been described. One model developed by Seltzer and coworkers [19] employs a unilateral ligation of one third to one half the sciatic nerve in the rat. These animals develop hyperalgesia and spontaneous pain findings that are reversed by chemical sympathectomy with guanethidine. Another model, developed by Kim and Chung [20], is a variation of the Seltzer and

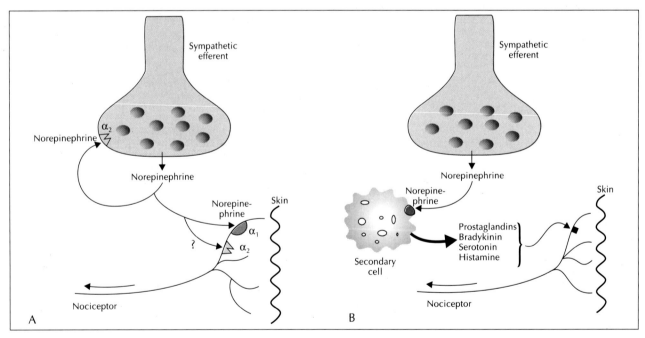

Figure 14-1 Possible mechanisms of interaction between sympathetic postganglionic fibers and nociceptors. (A) Norepinephrine released from sympathetic terminals can directly activate adrenergic receptors, possible α receptors on the nociceptor afferent fibers. While an excitatory effect on postsynaptic α receptors is suspected, actions of norepinephrine on postsynaptic inhibitory α_2 receptors cannot be ruled out. (B) Indirect mechanisms may include activation of α-adrenergic receptors on secondary cells such as mast cells, leukocytes, or platelets by norepinephrine. These cells in turn release chemical mediators such as prostaglandins, bradykinin, serotonin, and histamine that activate nociceptive afferent fibers.

coworkers [19] model and involves a tight ligature around the lumbar nerve roots. A surgical sympathectomy alleviated the mechanical hyperalgesia in these rats. A model of peripheral nerve injury neuropathic pain developed by Bennet and Xie [21] uses a loose ligature around the sciatic nerve, which produces a hyperalgesic state. Sympathetic blockade or sympathectomy, however, does not completely reverse the nociceptive behavior in this model [22]. These models provide an opportunity to study the pathophysiology and pharmacology of nerve injury–induced chronic pain states.

CLINICAL FEATURES OF REFLEX SYMPATHETIC DYSTROPHY

The hallmark of these conditions is burning pain and mechanical hyperalgesia out of proportion to the injury sustained or even in the absence of injury associated with autonomic instability. In the fully developed condition the disturbance of regional sympathetic activity presents as a cold vasoconstricted extremity, with excessive sweating and increased nail growth (Fig. 14-2). The much-touted cutaneous dystrophic changes may well be a result of disuse secondary to pain and guarding.

Typically the pain and autonomic dysfunction is not limited to the region of injury but can present diffusely starting in the distal extremity and progressing proximally at a variable rate. The pain and other features can be present in a nondermatomal or peripheral nerve distribution along the extremity. In some cases the pain, edema, and autonomic changes can spread to the contralateral extremity or further [23]. Although the most well-described sites of RSD involvement are in the extremities, RSD-like syndromes have been reported in the settings of facial pain, cervical spine injury, and penile injury.

The spontaneous pain in RSD is often described as a burning, aching sensation that is diffusely distributed over the extremity and can be the most distressing symptom. Motor dysfunction including weakness, tremor, and joint stiffness can be present [24]. All of these features could be attributed at least in part to inactivity or guarding secondary to pain. A very incapacitating and overlooked feature of RSD states is the psychologic dysfunction that can leave a patient's relationships shattered and compromise compliance with treatment plans.

The sensory disturbances include hyperalgesia to mechanical stimulation such as light brushing of the skin or even a breeze in the most sensitive cases. When there is a coexistence of nerve injury with RSD, a region of hypalgesia can be present adjacent to the hyperalgesia region. A detailed sensory examination allows the identification of a specific nerve injury. A mixed pattern of

hypalgesia with allodynia may be present in sympathetically dependent neuropathy in the absence of demonstrable nerve injury. Patients with demonstrable nerve injury may also present with a mixed response to pinprick, *ie*, areas of hypo- and hyperalgesia. While sympathetic blocks are likely to result in reversal of allodynia, the sensory deficits often persist in the latter cases. A minor degree of sensory impairment of nondermatomal distribution may be a permanent feature when treatment has been delayed.

Hyperalgesia to cold stimulation has been suggested as a sensitive but not specific diagnostic feature [25]. All patients in the study with sympathetically maintained pain had hyperalgesia to cooling stimuli, such as a drop of acetone. Only 40% of patients with sympathetically independent pain had hyperalgesia to cooling. The response to a cold stimulation typically is a delayed burning pain, which builds in intensity with duration of the stimulus and is maintained for a variable period after the cold stimulus is removed (referred to as an "afterglow").

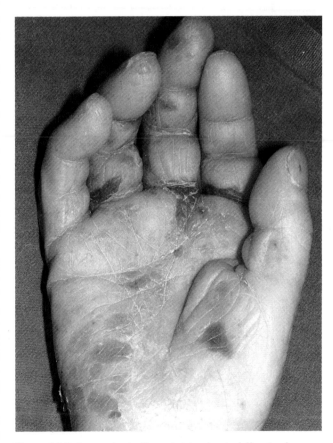

Figure 14-2 Sympathetically maintained pain following herpes zoster. A 73-year-old woman, 6 weeks after acute herpes zoster lesions in the C4, C5, and C6 dermatomes. This patient presented with intense hyperhidrosis and allodynia to mechanical stimuli. She responded well to a course of local anesthetic stellate ganglion blocks.

Stages

The clinical presentation of RSD-like syndromes can be very variable with symptoms starting anywhere from a few hours to several days or weeks after the injury. The RSD syndromes have been described as progressing in stages, each of which can last from weeks to years [24,26].

Stage I is known as the acute phase related to the original injury (if one can be identified). Patients in this phase usually describe a burning or aching quality to their pain, which is increased as the limb is made dependent with ensuing edema. Mechanical and often cold-induced hyperalgesia are reported during this stage. Emotional stimulation can exacerbate the pain as well. The extremity can be either warm or cold at this point with increased nail and hair growth restricted to the affected region. Early RSD is displayed in Figure 14-3.

Stage II or the dystrophic phase is the phase to which few patients progress; the findings in the first phase are intensified and reach a chronic level. The affected limb is usually cold and cyanotic associated with hair loss, ridged brittle nails, and brawny edema changes. The pain now assumes a more constant presence with exacerbation with physical or thermal stimulation. Diffuse osteoporosis appears in roentgenograms.

In stage III or the atrophic stage, irreversible tissue damage occurs with thinning of the skin, thickening of the fascia, which can result in contractures, and diffuse marked bony demineralization (Fig. 14-4).

The staging of RSD syndromes as outlined above remains controversial as it implies a homogeneous orderly progression to the disease process. Patients sometimes present with a several-year-history of pain and hyperalgesia with minimal dystrophic changes.

Diagnostic Considerations

Diagnostic precision assumes great importance as the condition can be progressive and debilitating and the treatment is specific to RSD. This is especially true where a surgical intervention such as a sympathectomy is contemplated.

LOCAL ANESTHETIC BLOCKS

The classic diagnostic test for RSD is the local anesthetic sympathetic ganglion block [16,27]. For a local anesthetic block, the physician must perform a careful sensory examination before and after the procedure and carefully monitor the extremity temperature to document the efficacy of the sympathetic block. An alternate and more direct method of assessment is the measurement of sympathetic reflexes such as the vascular constrictor reflex in response to a deep inspiratory gasp. The reflex assessment is performed with laser Doppler flowometry, a noninvasive measure of cutaneous blood flow [28,29].

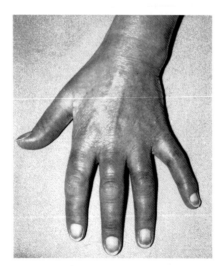

Figure 14-3 Stage I of reflex sympathetic dystrophy. Characteristic vasomotor changes associated with early or stage I reflex sympathetic dystrophy. This patient had a warm extremity with hyperalgesia to mechanical stimulation. Note the swollen edematous fingers.

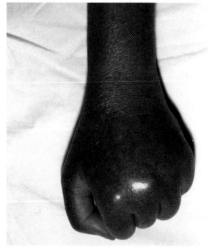

Figure 14-4 Stage III of reflex sympathetic dystrophy. A 42-year-old woman, 20 years following elbow fracture and carpal tunnel surgery for chronic ongoing pain. The patient had marked contractures of the fingers and limited movement of thumb. Tactile allodynia of the upper limb with a 50% reduction in range of movement of the shoulders was evident. This patient could be classified as Stage III. Reflex sympathetic dystrophy of long duration may result in joint stiffness and contractures.

Diagnostic blocks are usually performed using long-acting local anesthetic agents (*ie,* bupivacaine) to allow subjective and objective evaluation of alternations in the pain. Thus, following the nerve-block procedures, subjective alterations in pain and improvement in function of the blocked region should be assessed. In addition, adequacy and selectivity of sympathetic blockade should be evaluated using sensory tests and sudomotor and temperature measurements. A typical response to local anesthetic sympathetic ganglion block is displayed in Figure 14-5.

Finally, determination of the time course of blockade and associated pain relief corresponds to the duration of action of the agent employed. Significant discrepancies between adequacies of blockade and extent or duration of pain relief should be carefully assessed. This is important for determination of the presence of a placebo response, which may occur in up to 30% to 40% of patients [30]. Although placebo response is not evidence of a psychologic dysfunction, it makes interpretation of the results of local anesthetic blockade difficult. Clinical observations, however, have indicated that the duration of pain relief may far outlast the duration of local anesthetic actions in some cases. Presently, the reasons for this discrepancy are unclear.

The use of a local anesthetic sympathetic ganglion block as a diagnostic tool is fraught with several potential pitfalls. Hence, the results of the local anesthetic blocks should be interpreted with caution. The local anesthetic can easily diffuse to the dorsal nerve roots resulting in subtle small nerve fiber block that may be difficult to recognize on routine sensory testing but may have profound effects on the patient's pain. In addition, the procedures are quite involved from the patient's perspective and consequently may have strong placebo effects. Depending on the total dose of the local anesthetic used, pain relief may result from the systemic levels of the local anesthetic.

PHENTOLAMINE INFUSION

To address some of the pitfalls associated with the local anesthetic sympathetic ganglion block, an alternate test was devised employing the nonspecific α-antagonist phentolamine [31••,32]. The phentolamine can be infused via a peripheral vein with consequently little risk or discomfort to the patient. The infusion procedure also allows for a placebo period to assess the variability of the patient's pain response. A graphic depiction of the test results is presented in Figure 14-6.

In the phentolamine test, the subject is asked to rate both baseline-spontaneous and stimulation-induced pain every 5 minutes on a visual analogue scale, and the infusion of fluid is started out of sight of the patient. Once the physician observes at least 20 minutes of stable pain ratings, phentolamine is infused at a time unknown to the patient and pain ratings are continued. Phentolamine doses of 0.5 mg/kg were used initially. However, further studies are being conducted to determine the optimal dose where the reflex sympathetic vasoconstrictive activity associated with a deep gasp is abolished. The abolition of the reflex vasoconstrictor activity will provide an objective measure of adequate sympathetic blockade. Dose escalations of up to 1 mg/kg may be required in carefully monitored settings. A decrease in pain of at about 50% is used as an indication that the patient has a significant sympathetic component to their pain.

THERMOGRAPHY

The basis of thermography is the measurement of a thermal gradient by surveying the extremities involved and comparing with the corresponding sites on the contralateral, unaffected side [33,34]. Temperature changes are influenced by many factors, such as a normal regional sympathetic response to pain rather than a primary sym-

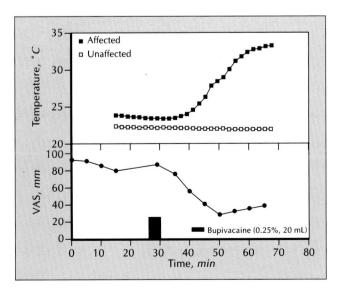

Figure 14-5 The time course of pain relief and changes in cutaneous temperature during sympathetic ganglion blockade in a patient with sympathetically maintained pain. (*Top*) Time course of temperature changes in the affected and contralateral limb following local anesthetic blockade. (*Bottom*) Changes in pain rates, both ongoing and stimulus-evoked. The decrease in pain and hyperalgesia following the sympathetic ganglion blockade is consistent with the diagnosis of sympathetically maintained pain or reflex sympathetic dystrophy.

pathetic abnormality [33]. The specificity of the thermographic changes, particularly with regard to correlation with components of RSD, is therefore controversial.

BONE SCAN

In recent years the three-phase bone scan has gained considerable popularity for the diagnosis of RSD. A positive finding is the increased periarticular uptake of radionuclide (compared with the contralateral side). Positive predictive value is increased by a duration of less than 6 months or a patient aged less than 50 years [35]. A good correlation has been reported between the response to sympathetic intervention and the presence of a positive bone scan [35,36]. The predictive value of these tests is questionable: the radiologic findings are not correlated with the severity of the pain, are not strongly correlated with the onset of the pain, and may be present before or develop well after the onset of pain.

MANAGEMENT OF REFLEX SYMPATHETIC DYSTROPHY

The principal goal of therapy should be the restoration of normal function. The wide range of treatments employed for the treatment of these conditions attests to the fact that no one treatment is uniformly successful. The difficulty in establishing treatment protocols is the lack of complete understanding of the underlying pathophysiology of these disorders. A mechanistic

rather than descriptive understanding would lead to more specific therapeutics [10].

The general strategies in the management of patients with RSD are as follows:

1. Identify the pain generator if possible and treat the cause. In early cases this may involve treatment of the precipitating injury. In others it may be treatment aimed at suppressing ectopic discharges from a neuroma.

2. Determine whether the predominant component of the pain is sympathetically mediated or sympathetically independent. In cases where the pain is predominantly sympathetically mediated, sympathetic blockade should be pursued aggressively.

3. Functional rehabilitation with aggressive, active, and passive physiotherapy.

4. Psychologic management, including behavioral modification and active treatment of the associated depression.

Pain relief can be accomplished in several ways once the diagnosis of RSD is made. Consideration should be given to safety and invasiveness in choosing the treatment. A presentation with diffuse pain without obvious neural distribution, edema, and increased sympathetic activity would argue for the early use of sympathetic blockade either via oral medications or by invasive nerve block procedures. On the other hand, if a patient presents with localized pain and signs of nerve injury or entrapment then somatic neural blockade or oral agents for neuropathic pain should be employed.

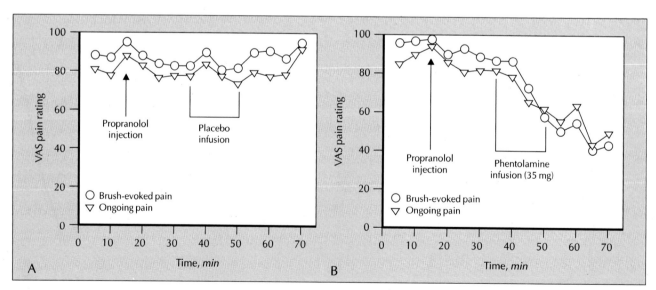

Figure 14-6 Pain relief conferred from systemic phentolamine in a patient with sympathetically dependent pain. The patient underwent two separate tests 2 days apart. (*Panel A*) Lack of change in ongoing pain as well as stimulus-evoked pain to saline infusions. (*Panel B*) In contrast, both ongoing pain and pain evoked from a cold stimulus were reduced following the intravenous administration of phentolamine. Ratings of ongoing pain and stimulus-evoked pain were made every 5 minutes and the patient was blinded to the time of drug administration. Thus, the pain was observed to decrease significantly after phentolamine but not after saline in this patient.

It should be noted that, despite years of treating sympathetically maintained pain syndromes, no treatment has been subjected to rigorous clinical trials.

Sympathetic Blocks

Once a diagnosis of RSD is made, sympathetic blockade should be initiated as soon as possible [27,37,38]. While for the purposes of diagnosis sympathetic blockade should be selective, blockade of the sympathetics to the affected region can be achieved in several ways for purposes of treatment. Thus, peripheral nerve blocks or even plexus blockade or central neuroaxial blockade such as epidural are often appropriate for the treatment of RSD. No clear-cut guidelines are available on the frequency of sympathetic blockade and whether continuous block techniques offer advantages over intermittent blocks. Often, the sympathetic blocks are done on a more frequent basis initially, and, with improvement of symptomatology, the intervals between the successive blocks are usually increased.

Whereas sympathetic block helps in alleviation of the pain for resumption of normal activity, it is important that the use and subsequent loss of normal function is to be avoided. This necessitates aggressive physiotherapy playing an important role in the management of RSD. Expert clinicians have emphasized that reliance on sympathetic blockade alone will be insufficient in achieving long-lasting cure, especially in patients who have had their symptomatology for prolonged periods [38].

LOCAL ANESTHETIC

The blockade of sympathetic plexus with injected local anesthetic provides an alternative to surgical sympathectomy. For upper extremity involvement, the stellate ganglion is blocked, and for lower extremity the paravertebral ganglia at L2-4 are blocked.

If a patient's pain is relieved by a sympathetic ganglion block, he or she can enter a therapeutic series of sympathetic blocks with the goal of achieving longer durations of pain relief as the abnormal sympathetic to somatic connection is broken. A key element to any block of this type is careful examination both before and after the block to document objectively the adequacy of blockade (*eg*, cutaneous temperature measurements). The presence of a Horner's syndrome and increased temperature of the affected arm indicates a successful stellate ganglion block, whereas the increase in temperature in the leg indicates an effective lumbar sympathetic block. With a near-complete blockade of the sympathetic nervous input, the cutaneous temperature approaches core temperature [16]. Incomplete sympathetic blockade documented by objective criteria such as temperature changes is shown in Figure 14-7 and should not be used as a diagnostic or therapeutic response. It is equally im-

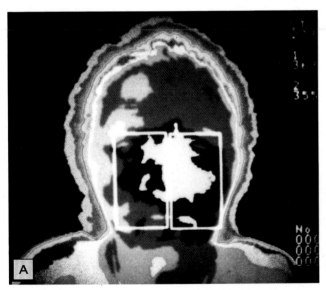
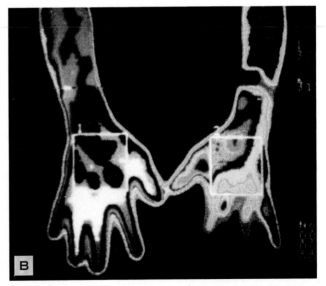

Figure 14-7 Objective evidence of sympathetic blockage is required for diagnosis. The adequacy of sympathetic ganglion blockade should be tested with objective signs of blockade in the affected region. (A) Thermogram of the face and upper chest in a patient after a left-sided, sympathetic ganglion blockade. A marked increase in cutaneous temperature is observed in the neck and facial region in the blocked left side (*light and dark areas*). (B) Thermogram of the upper extremities following the sympathetic ganglion blockade. Sympathetic fibers to the left upper extremity have not been adequately blocked as evidenced by the colder temperatures in the left limb (*dark areas*). The patient failed to achieve any significant relief of pain or hyperalgesia in the affected region. An appropriate sympathetic blockade with documented temperature changes in the distal part of the left extremity on a separate occasion resulted in significant improvement of symptomatology. Thus, this patient would have been falsely diagnosed as having sympathetically independent pain if the adequacy of sympathetic blockage was not appropriately tested.

portant to document the absence of somatic blockade if the block is to be used as a diagnostic test for potential surgical sympathectomy.

If the initial sympathetic block is technically well done, as evidenced by a loss of sympathetic function as outlined above, and the pain is unrelieved, then further blocks would not be indicated. In the same sense, if after repeated blocks the duration of pain relief does not lengthen, indicating progress, then persistence with this therapy is not indicated and surgical sympathectomy should be considered. One should be quite certain that the pain relief obtained with the sympathetic blocks is due to blockade of the sympathetic fibers only and not to the associated potential somatic blockade.

Finally and most importantly, one must have some quantitative measure of the change in pain following the block. One of the simplest ways to document this is the visual or verbal analogue scale. These tools are easy to use and can be administered repeatedly to follow the course of the therapy.

Phentolamine Infusions

As indicated in the section on diagnosis, the infusion of phentolamine to block the sympathetic nervous effects provides a specific alternative to local anesthetic blockade of the sympathetic ganglion [31••]. We have used a repeated infusion of phentolamine to treat early RSD in two patients with good long-term success.

Intravenous Regional Infusion of Local Anesthetic Agents

Bier blocks, or the infusion of sympathetically active agents, have been used to treat RSD conditions. These techniques obviously can only be applied to situations of extremity pain. Hannington-Kiff [39] has advocated the use of regional guanethidine and has reported considerable success; however, this agent is not readily available for

this indication. Other agents reported to be effective in this technique include reserpine, bretylium, and steroids.

Epidural Catheters

Several reports have claimed the benefits of epidural administration of narcotics, local anesthetics, or the combination of both [40]. Since the goal of the therapy is to improve the functional status of the patient, high concentrations of local anesthetics can only allow passive therapy to be used. Lower concentrations may allow more active rehabilitation techniques.

Oral Alpha Agents

Because of their ease of administration, several oral α-sympathetic blocking agents have been used with various degrees of success [41,42]. These agents include phenoxybenzamine, prazosin, and terazosin.

Sympathectomy

Surgical removal of the sympathetic paravertebral ganglion remains the definitive treatment for many RSD conditions once the diagnosis has been firmly established and the response to a block series remains transient [42,43]. Often the trophic changes as well as the pain can be resolved by sympathectomy as in the patient in Figure 14-8. Some controversy exists over the extent to which the sympathectomy should be carried out. Usually unilateral sympathectomy is sufficient, but in some cases, there is bilateral contribution [44]. Before committing a patient to sympathectomy, it is crucial to establish that the response to sympathetic blocks is not due to merely a somatic block from spread of the local anesthetic.

Neural Stimulation

Transcutaneous nerve stimulation (TENS) and direct neural stimulation via implanted peripheral nerve

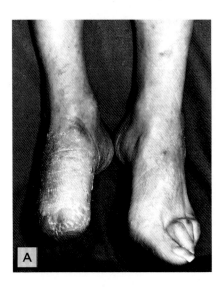 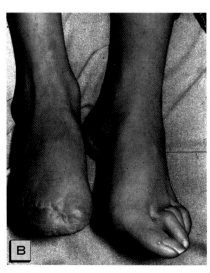

Figure 14-8 Trophic cutaneous changes can be reversed by sympathectomy. A 43-year-old man who suffered bilateral osscalsis fractures after jumping from a height. (A) Patient 3 years after initial injury, presenting with bilateral lower extremity pain with tactile allodynia and cold sensitivity. The patient's toes were amputated on right side 1 year following initial injury. Note the marked trophic changes in the foot. The patient was treated with bilateral sympathectomies. (B) Marked resolution of the trophic changes that were associated with a decrease in pain and hyperalgesia is shown 3 months after right-sided sympathectomy.

catheters or dorsal column stimulators have been reported to give pain relief in RSD for prolonged periods [45]. Large controlled studies, however, have not been available to allow definitive endorsement of these procedures.

MANAGEMENT OF CAUSALGIA

When RSD is accompanied by nerve injury (causalgia), several agents can be employed for pain control. Several tricyclic antidepressants (amitriptyline, nortriptyline, and desipramine) have been reported to have analgesic properties independent of their mood-altering properties [46–49]. Patients are typically started at a 25-mg dose by mouth at bedtime, which is increased as tolerated over several weeks to a 150-mg dose or resolution of symptoms. Carbamazepine is useful for paroxysmal pain states such as with neuromas [50,51]. One can initiate therapy at 100 to 200 mg twice a day and increase to a total dose of 800 mg/d. As therapy progresses serum levels of carbamazepine should be monitored.

The orally available local anesthetic and antiarrhythmic mexiletine can be employed as an analgesic for neuroma or other nerve injury pain [51–53]. Usually the effectiveness of mexiletine can be predicted by the patient's response to a trial of intravenous lidocaine at 5 mg/kg. If the patient's pain improves with minimal adverse effects then mexiletine can be started at 100 mg and titrated upward to approximately 10 mg/kg. Mexiletine has a narrow therapeutic window and therefore blood levels of mexiletine should be monitored at regular intervals and during dose escalation. Serum levels should be kept in the 0.75 to 2 mcg/mL range [54], which corresponds to the therapeutic range for antiarrythmic effects. Caution should be used with narcotic analgesics, as they can slow the absorption of mexiletine [55].

Clonazepam is unique among the benzodiazepines for its analgesic capabilities [50]. This is especially true in patients with an anxiety component to their syndrome complex. Clonazepam is a long half-life drug and can be started with a 0.5-mg dose at bedtime and increased over several days to 5 to 10 mg in three to four divided doses.

Aggressive Management of Pain Associated with Trauma

Clinical reports suggest that preemptive analgesia, the aggressive management of pain associated with trauma, such as the use of regional anesthetic techniques for trauma surgery, may reduce the incidence of sympathetic pain and other chronic painful sequelae. This is indicated by the reduced incidence of phantom limb and stump pain after amputation [56,57]. Thus, one can speculate that the proper management of the injury site along with relief of acute trauma-induced pain may prevent the development of RSD.

REFERENCES AND RECOMMENDED READING

Papers of interest, published recently, have been highlighted as:
• Of special interest
•• Of outstanding interest

1. Evans JA: Reflex sympathetic dystrophy. *Surg Gynecol Obstet* 1946, 82:36–43.

2. Pare A: In *The Works of that Famous Chirurgeon Ambroise Pare, Translated out of Latin, and Compared with the French by Th. Johnson.* Edited by Clark M. London: John Clark; 1678:267.

3. Mitchell SW, ed. *Injuries of Nerves and their Consequences.* New York: Dover Publications; 1865.

4. O'Neill OR, Burchiel KJ: Sympathetically maintained pain syndromes: diagnosis and surgical management. *Res Staff Physician* 1991, 41–52.

5. Jänig W, Blumberg H, Boas RA, Campbell JN: The reflex sympathetic dystrophy syndrome: consensus statement and general recommendations for diagnosis and clinical research. In *Proceedings of the VIth World Congress on Pain.* Edited by Bond MR, Charlton JE, Woolf CJ. Amsterdam: Elsevier Science; 1991:373–376.

6. Roberts WJ: A hypothesis on the physiological basis for causalgia and related pains. *Pain* 1986, 24:297–311.

7. Campbell JN, Raja SN, Meyer RA: Painful sequelae of nerve injury. In *Proceedings of the Vth World Congress on Pain.* Edited by Dubner R, Gebhart GF, Bond MR. Amsterdam: Elsevier Science Publishers BV (Biomedical Division); 1988:135–143.

8. Jänig W: The sympathetic nervous system in pain: physiology and pathophysiology. In *Pain and the Sympathetic Nervous System.* Boston: Kluwer Academic Publishers; 1989:17–89.

9. Woolf CJ: Evidence for a central component of post-injury pain hypersensitivity. *Nature* 1983, 306:686–688.

10. Charlton JE: Management of sympathetic pain. *Br Med Bull* 1991, 47:601–618.

11. Woolf CJ, King AE: Subthreshold components of the cutaneous mechanoreceptive fields of dorsal horn neurons in rat lumbar spinal cord. *J Neurophysiol* 1989, 62:907–916.

12. Woolf CJ, Shortland P, Coggeshall RE: Peripheral nerve injury triggers central sprouting of myelinated afferents. *Nature* 1992, 355:75–78.

13. Woolf CJ, King AE: Dynamic alterations in the cutaneous mechanoreceptive fields of dorsal horn neurons in the rat spinal cord. *J Neurosci* 1990, 10:2717–2726.

14. •• Campbell JN, Meyer RA, Raja SN: Is nociceptor activation by α-1 adrenoreceptors the culprit in sympathetically maintained pain? *APS Journal* 1992, 1:3–11.

This paper presents a discussion of the evidence for α-receptor mediation of sympathetically maintained pain. A good summary of the basic and clinical science of this condition.

15. Price DD, Bennett GJ, Rafii A: Psychophysical observations on patients with neuropathic pain relieved by a sympathetic block. *Pain* 1989, 36:273–288.

16. Treede R-D, Davis KD, Campbell JN, *et al.*: The plasticity of cutaneous hyperalgesia during sympathetic ganglionic blockade in patients with neuropathic pain. *Brain* 1992, 115:607–621.

17. Devor M, Jänig W: Activation of myelinated afferents ending in a neuroma by stimulation of the sympathetic supply in the rat. *Neurosci Lett* 1981, 24:43–47.

18. Scadding JW: Development of ongoing activity, mechanosensitivity and adrenaline sensitivity in severed peripheral nerve axons. *Exp Neurol* 1981, 73:345–364.

19. Seltzer Z, Dubner R, Shir Y: A novel behavioral model of neuropathic pain disorders produced in rats by partial sciatic nerve injury. *Pain* 1990, 43:205–218.

20. Kim SH, Chung JM: Sympathectomy alleviates mechanical allodynia in an experimental animal model for neuropathy in the rat. *Neurosci Lett* 1991, 134:131–134.

21. Bennett GJ, Xie Y-K: A peripheral mononeuropathy in rat that produces disorders of pain sensation like those seen in man. *Pain* 1988, 33:87–107.

22. Wakisaka S, Kajander KC, Bennett GJ: Abnormal skin temperature and abnormal sympathetic vasomotor innervation in an experimental painful peripheral neuropathy. *Pain* 1991, 46:299–313.

23. Schwartzman RJ: Reflex sympathetic dystrophy. *Curr Ther Neurol Dis-3* 1990, 66:66–69.

24. Schwartzman RJ, Kerrigan J: The movement disorder of reflex sympathetic dystrophy. *Neurology* 1990, 40:57–61.

25. Frost SA, Raja SN, Campbell JN, *et al.*: Does hyperalgesia to cooling stimuli characterize patients with sympathetically maintained pain (reflex sympathetic dystrophy)? In: *Proceedings of the Vth World Congress on Pain.* Amsterdam: Elsevier Science Publishers BV; 1988:151–156.

26. Kozin F, *et al.*: The reflex sympathetic dystrophy syndrome: I. Clinical and histological studies: evidence for bilaterality, response to corticosteroids and articular involvement. *Am J Med* 1976, 60:321–331.

27. Bonica JJ: Causalgia and other reflex sympathetic dystrophies. In *The Management of Pain.* Edited by Bonica JJ. Philadelphia: Lea and Febiger; 1990:220–256.

28. Nilsson GE, Tenland T, Oberg PA: Evaluation of a laser Doppler flowmeter for measurement of tissue blood flow. *IEEE Trans Biomed Eng* 1980, 27:597–604.

29. Valley MA, Bourke DL, Hamill MP, Raja SN: Time course of sympathetic blockade during epidural anesthesia: laser Doppler flowmetry studies of regional skin perfusion. *Anesth Analg* 1993, 76:289–294.

30. Jospe M: The laboratory study of the placebo effect in nonpatient subjects and placebos and analgesia. In *The Placebo Effect in Healing.* Edited by Jospe M. Lexington: Lexington Books; 1978:17–33.

31. •• Raja SN, Treede R-D, Davis KD, Campbell JN: Systemic α-adrenergic blockade with phentolamine: a diagnostic test for sympathetically maintained pain. *Anesthesiology* 1991, 74:691–698.

A description of the phentolamine infusion technique for diagnosis of sympathetically maintained pain. This study presents a correlation between intravenous phentolamine and sympathetic ganglion blockade.

32. Raja SN, Davis KD, Campbell JN: The adrenergic pharmacology of sympathetically maintained pain. *J Reconstr Surg* 1992, 8:63–69.

33. Hendler N, Uematesu S, Long DM: Thermographic validation of physical complaints in "psychogenic pain" patients. *Psychomatics* 1982, 23:283–287.

34. Pochaczevsky R, Wexler CE, Meyers PH, *et al.*: Liquid crystal thermography of the spine and extremities: its value in the diagnosis of spinal root syndromes. *J Neurosurg* 1982, 56:386–395.

35. Werner R, Davidoff G, Jackson MD: Factors affecting the sensitivity and specificity of the three-phase technetium bone scan in the diagnosis of reflex sympathetic dystrophy in the upper extremity. *J Hand Surg [Am]* 1989, 14:520–523.

36. Kozin F, Genant HK, Bekerman C, McCarty DJ: The reflex sympathetic dystrophy syndrome: II. Roentgenographic and scintigraphic evidence of bilaterality and of periarticular accentuation. *Am J Med* 1976, 60:332–338.

37. Charlton JE: Current views on the use of nerve blocking in the relief of chronic pain. In *The Therapy of Pain.* Edited by Swerdlow M. Lancaster: MTP Press; 1986:133–164.

38. Boas RA: *Sympathetic Nerve Blocks: Their Role in Sympathetic Pain.* Boston: Kluwer Academic Press; 1990:101–112.

39. Hannington-Kiff JG: Intravenous regional sympathetic block with guanethidine. *Lancet* 1974, 1:1019–1020.

40. Willner CL: Pain and the sympathetic nervous system: clinical considerations. In *Clinical Automonic Disorders: Evaluation and Management.* Boston: Little, Brown and Company; 1993:493–503.

41. Ghostine SY, Comair YG, Turner DM, Kassell NF, Azar CG: Phenoxybenzamine in the treatment of causalgia. *J Neurosurg* 1984, 60:1263–1268.

42. Raja SN, Hendler N: Sympathetically maintained pain. In *Current Practice in Anesthesiology.* Edited by Rogers MC. Philadelphia: BC Decker; 1992:421–425.

43. Schutzer SF, Gossling HR: The treatment of reflex sympathetic dystrophy syndrome. *J Bone Joint Surg [Am]* 1984, 66-A:625–629.

44. Nathan PW, Smith MC: The location of descending fibres to sympathetic preganglionic vasomotor and sudomotor neurons in man. *J Neuro Neurosurg Psych* 1987, 50:1253–1262.

45. Racz GB, Lewis R, Heavner JE, Scott J: Peripheral nerve stimulator implant for treatment of causalgia. In *Pain and the Sympathetic Nervous System*. Edited by Stanton-Hicks M. Boston: Kluwer Academic Publishers; 1989.

46. Kishore-Kumar R, Max MB, Schafer SC, *et al.*: Desipramine relieves postherpetic neuralgia. *Clin Pharmacol Ther* 1990, 47:305–312.

47. Tura B, Tura SM: The analgesic effect of tricyclic antidepressants. *Brain Res* 1990, 518:19–22.

48. Max MB, Kishore-Kumar R, Schafer SC, *et al.*: Clinical section: efficacy of desipramine in painful diabetic neuropathy: a placebo-controlled trial. *Pain* 1991, 45:3–9.

49. Max ME, Culnan M, Schafer SC: Amitriptyline relieves diabetic neuropathy pain in patients with normal and depressed mood. *Neurology* 1982, 2:671–673.

50. Swerdlow M, Cundill JG: Anticonvulsant drugs used in the treatment of lancinating pain: a comparison. *Anaesthesia* 1981, 36:1129–1132.

51. Tanelian DL, Brose WG: Neuropathic pain can be relieved by drugs that are use-dependent sodium channel blockers: lidocaine, carbamazepine, and mexiletine. *Anesthesiology* 1991, 74:949–951.

52. Rowbotham MC, Reisner-Keller LA, Fields HL: Both intravenous lidocaine and morphine reduce the pain of postherpetic neuralgia. *Neurology* 1991, 41:1024–1028.

53. Chabal C, Jacobson L, Marano A, Chaney E, Britell CW: The use of oral mexiletine for the treatment of pain after peripheral nerve injury. *Anesthesiology* 1992, 76:573–577.

54. Campbell RWF: Mexiletine. *N Engl J Med* 1987, 316:29–34.

55. Pottage A, Campbell RWF, Achuff SC, *et al.*: The absorption of oral mexiletine in coronary care patients. *Eur J Clin Pharmacol* 1978, 13:393–399.

56. Bach S, Noreng MF, Tjellden NU: Phantom limb pain in amputees during the first 12 months following limb amputation, after preoperative lumbar epidural blockade. *Pain* 1988, 33:297–330.

57. Wall PD: The prevention of post-operative pain. *Pain* 1988, 33:289–290.

Management of Pain Caused by Acute Herpes Zoster and Postherpetic Neuralgia

P. PRITHVI RAJ

Herpes zoster, an acute infectious disease caused by varicella virus belonging to the DNA group of viruses, primarily affects the posterior spinal root ganglion of the spinal nerves. Varicella and herpes zoster have long been recognized as manifestations of the same infectious agent, and it has been concluded that they are caused by the same virus. Antigens derived from vesicles of patients with varicella or herpes zoster react similarly, and DNA studies have confirmed biophysical similarities [1].

INCIDENCE

Herpes zoster affects approximately 125 per 100,000 persons annually, striking both sexes equally, with no apparent seasonal variation. While the incidence is only 0.5 in 1000 for children [2], it increases to five to 10 in 1000 for patients in their 80s [2]. Waning immune surveillance has been suggested for the increased incidence with age [3]. Age is also a major factor in the development of postherpetic neuralgia, which develops almost exclusively in patients older than 50 years. Incidence ranges from 15% to 70% [4,5].

Triggering factors for herpes zoster include surgery [6] or trauma; irradiation and other immunosuppressive agents; malignancies; and infections such as tuberculosis, syphilis, malaria, and acquired immunodeficiency syndrome (AIDS). Stressful life events also reactivate the latent varicella-zoster virus [7]. Secondary herpes zoster caused by inflammation, neoplasm, or direct injury to the cranial or peripheral nerve may recur more frequently, clear more rapidly, and result in less scarring and pigmentation than idiopathic zoster.

Herpes zoster is more prevalent and severe in immunosuppressed patients [8–11]. It is a major problem following radiochemotherapy and bone marrow transplantation, correlating with depressed cell-mediated immunity [12]. Patients deficient in T-lymphocyte macrophage-mediated immune defenses are more susceptible to viral spread beyond the ganglion-nerve-dermatome unit, and visceral and nervous system complications represent a major threat for these patients [13].

ACUTE HERPES ZOSTER

Herpes zoster can progress in three stages (Table 15-1). Both virus and host interact at each stage to affect the development and course.

Lesions are most often thoracic, trigeminal (mostly ophthalmic), or cervical, with < 1% bilateral (Figs. 15-1–15-3). Recurrences are experienced by approximately 1% to 8% of patients, about half the time at the site of the previous eruption.

Acute herpes zoster is associated with pain, paresthesia, and dysesthesia in the dermatomal distribution of one or more affected posterior root ganglia, sometimes accompanied by fever, malaise, headache, nausea, stiff neck, and regional or diffuse adenopathy. Pain is usually mild initially but may intensify. A vesicular eruption usually appears within 4 to 5 days, if not sooner.

Following localized erythema and swelling, red papules progress through vesicles, blebs, and pustules (Figs. 15-4 and 15-5). Lesions are usually unilateral in part of the dermatome but affect sensation of the entire segment in mild cases. More severe cases involve the entire segment, with larger blebs that tend to coalesce, in addition to continuous burning and sharp, burning pain precipitated by movement or change in skin tension.

The erythema gradually resolves; blebs dry up and wrinkle, and sharp pain recedes. Scales of encrusting blebs fall off, leaving pink scars that retract and produce pocks without pigment. Hyperesthesia and hyperalgesia gradually resolve, with the patient becoming asymptomatic.

Pathogenesis

Knowledge of the pathogenesis of varicella and herpes zoster is somewhat limited. Although varicella is exogenous and herpes zoster is endogenous, the varicella-zoster virus is present in both lesions and can serve as a source of infection to others.

Characteristically, varicella is associated with no immunity, while herpes zoster possesses partial immunity to the virus. During the course of varicella, the virus may

---

TABLE 15-1
STAGES OF HERPES ZOSTER*

Stage I   Viral replication

               Loss of immune surveillance

Stage II   Clinical syndrome (acute herpes zoster)

               Viral effect on ganglion-nerve-dermatome

               Antiviral immune response by the body

               Cytolysin from virus and host inflammatory reaction

Stage III   Sequelae of herpes zoster

               Central nervous system and visceral spread

               Antiviral immune response

*From Price [13]; with permission.

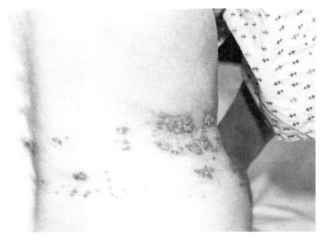

Figure 15-1 A 38-year-old woman presenting with 14-day-old acute herpes zoster in T7–T10 distribution. She was admitted to the hospital 3 weeks previously for workup with a diagnosis of renal colic prior to the appearance of the rash.

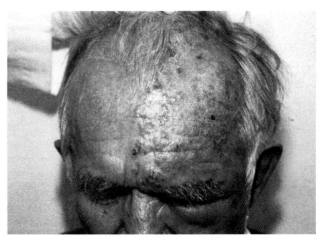

Figure 15-2 A 76-year-old man with 3-day-old acute herpes zoster in the left ophthalmic nerve distribution.

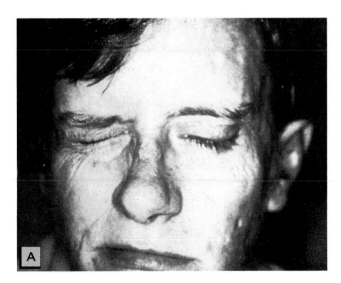

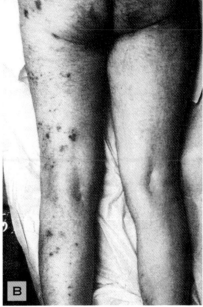

Figure 15-3
(A) A 35-year-old woman suffering from Ramsay Hunt syndrome (acute herpes zoster of geniculate ganglion). At initial examination, the patient complained of burning pain in left pinna, with deafness in left ear and weakness in left facial muscles (facial palsy).
(B) Acute herpes zoster in left sciatic nerve distribution.

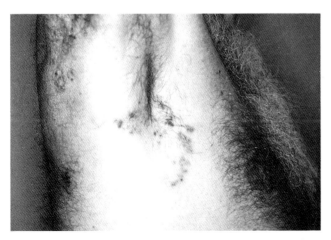

Figure 15-4 Early appearance of papules followed by vesicles in a 60-year-old man who complained of radiating pain in the T3–T4 distribution. This was confirmed as early acute herpes zoster.

pass from the sensory nerve ending up to the sensory ganglia; there it remains latent until activated and shed from the dorsal root ganglion cell, stimulating the production of antiviral antibody and other immune mechanisms. Antibodies are present only in varicella convalescent serum; however, antibody titers may be high in acute zoster and even higher in convalescent zoster, indicating an amnestic response.

If immunity falls below a critical level, the activated virus can continue to replicate within the sensory ganglion, resulting in neuronal necrosis, inflammation, and neuralgia. It is then spread antidromically to the sensory nerve endings of the skin, causing a vesicular eruption. Varicella-zoster–like particles have been seen in the ganglia of patients who died of varicella-zoster infection.

In acute zoster, hemorrhagic inflammation affects the posterior spinal ganglion, the peripheral nerve of the affected ganglion, and the dorsal spinal nerve root, spread-ing to the spinal cord and leptomeninges. De-myeliniza-tion is associated with wallerian degeneration, fibrosis, and cellular infiltration in the peripheral nerve (Figs. 15-6 and 15-7). Degeneration can reach the ipsilateral posterior spinal cord within 9 days after vesicular eruption and can last 5 to 9 months. Measurement of tissue impedance after herpes zoster indicates lower than normal impedance in affected segments [14,15].

If infection spreads along the posterior nerve root to the meninges and spinal cord, local meningitis, cere-brospinal fluid pleocytosis, and myelitis result, and spread to anterior motor roots may cause local palsies. Hematogenous dissemination can cause aberrant vesi-cles. Although the amnestic response sometimes termi-nates the infection before vesicles develop, more severe and prolonged local response and more hematogenous dissemination can occur when immune response is greatly deficient.

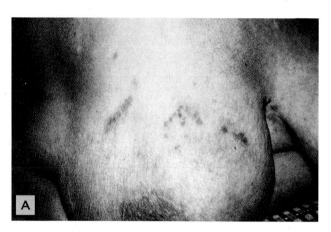

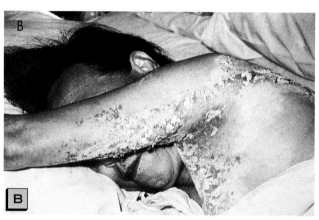

Figure 15-5 (A) A papular formation in the T3 distribution. This was confirmed as early acute herpes zoster. (B) A 3-week-old herpes zoster in the T2–T3 distribution in the crusting stage.

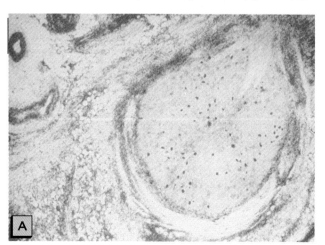

Figure 15-6 Inflammatory reaction in the geniculate ganglion due to acute herpes zoster. (A) Ganglion and satellite cells show intranuclear inclusion. There is also round cell infiltration and neu-ronal destruction. (B) The ganglion is swollen and hemorrhagic.

Immunologic Responses

The sequence of immunologic responses to varicella in patients not previously exposed has been summarized (Fig. 15-8) [16]. Mortality and severity of cell-mediated immune deficiency are directly related [9].

Status of immune response is similarly related to the occurrence of herpes zoster and its complications. Although no correlation between antibody and protection against herpes zoster has been indicated, increased antibody levels may correlate with severity and sequelae of the disease [17].

Symptomatic herpes zoster tends to occur only when cell-mediated immunity to varicella-zoster is depressed; the ability to mount a specific cellular immune response and the incidence of zoster are inversely correlated. The HLA-DR antigen is significantly expressed on T-cell sur-faces in herpes zoster, predominantly on suppressor/cytotoxic cells [18]. Lymphocyte and monocyte function is impaired, and the normal ratio of helper T cells to suppressor T cells is reversed. The infection is limited by the cell-mediated immune lymphocytic transformation [19], lymphocyte-monocyte inactivation of virus, and local host responses of interferon production and polymorphonuclear inflammatory response within the vesicle. Antibody administration also modifies the disease, perhaps altering membrane antigens and cellular cytotoxicity [20].

The association of specific IgM with acute infection suggests both reinfection with exogenous varicella virus and antigen stimulation caused by exposure to endogenous varicella zoster [21]. Repetitive asymptomatic viral activity may be important in enhancing the immunologic system.

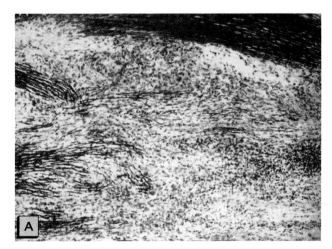

Figure 15-7 Sensory nerve showing pleomorphic, edema, and hemorrhagic appearance due to neuritis secondary to herpes zoster. (A) Round cell infiltration. (B) Edema with neuritis.

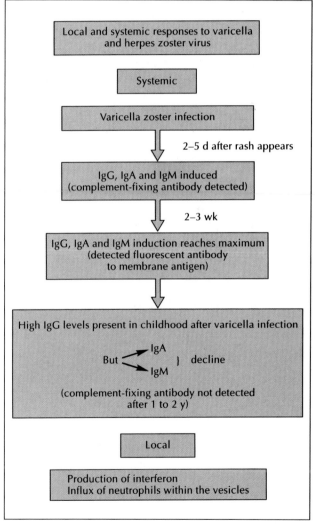

Figure 15-8 Immunologic responses to varicella- and herpes-zoster virus.

Efficacy of Measuring Immune Responses

Complement-fixing antibody is not very useful in determining immune status of a general population for herpes zoster. The fluorescent antibody to membrane antigen (FAMA) assay is earlier and more sensitive in diagnosing acute varicella-zoster virus and evaluating humoral immune states in high-risk patients with leukemia. Complement-enhanced neutralizing antibody is equivalent to FAMA for diagnosis and evaluation of humoral immunity in immunosuppressed persons, but immune adherence hemagglutination does not appear to be as sensitive. The enzyme-linked immunosorbent assay is an alternative to FAMA or complement-enhanced neutralizing antibody tests. Radioimmunoassay studies for detecting varicella-zoster, virus-specific IgG antibody show sensitivity but decreased specificity for some children.

Laboratory Diagnosis

Optimal drug treatment depends on early and accurate diagnosis. Appropriate laboratory techniques for diagnosis of acute herpes zoster are shown in Table 15-2. Rapid diagnostic tests allow earlier diagnosis.

Differential Diagnosis

Before to the eruption of lesions, herpes zoster can be mistaken for coronary disease, pleurisy, pleurodynia, costochondritis (Tietze's syndrome), pericarditis, cholecystitis, neural disease, acute and subacute abdominal conditions, appendicitis, collapsed intervertebral disk, neuropathies, and myofascial pains.

Distinguishing between herpes simplex and herpes zoster can be difficult, despite their differences [22]. Typically, herpes simplex occurs in a young woman as frequent recurrences of either Type 1 (orofacial) or Type 2 (genital) herpes simplex, whereas herpes zoster occurs as a single episode in an older man with a history of chicken pox [23,24]. Acute herpes simplex is associated with mild symptoms, few lesion sites, and limited dermatome spread, with postherpetic neuralgia uncommon; acute herpes zoster usually has severe symptoms, many lesion sites, and extensive dermatome spread, with postherpetic neuralgia a common sequela.

Pathophysiology of Nociception

The mechanisms producing pathologic changes in herpes zoster and postherpetic neuralgia are poorly under-

TABLE 15-2
LABORATORY DIAGNOSIS OF ACUTE HERPES ZOSTER*

TECHNIQUES	COMMENTS

Virus recovery from:
  Vesicles
  Blood
  Lung
  Liver
  Cerebrospinal fluid
  Oropharynx (only occasionally)
	Rapid diagnostic tests allow for early diagnosis

Scrapings from vesicles have cellular material with multinucleated giant cells	

Tzanck smear stained with:
  Hematoxylin-eosin stain
  Giemsa stain
  Papanicolaou stain
  Paragon multiple stain
	Shows acidophilic intranuclear inclusions

Punch biopsy for electron microscopy	More reliable and provides diagnosis before vesicular stage develops
Culture tests (In human epitheloids or fibroblasts) virus specifically identified in culture by intranuclear inclusions after staining and by gel precipitation techniques	Focal lesion with swollen refractile cells in 3 to 4 d
Staining of cellular material with direct fluorescent antibody of Tzanck smear	Readily identifies infected cells

*From Raj [14]; with permission.

stood. Activation of nociceptive primary afferents by direct viral attack and secondary inflammatory changes in skin, peripheral nerve, posterior root ganglion, nerve roots, leptomeninges, and the spinal cord may explain the pain in acute herpes zoster. Postherpetic neuralgia may involve both peripheral and central mechanisms (vide infra). Impairment of segmental pain-modulating systems may play a role, with diminished large-fiber function allowing increased transmission of nociceptive information through the dorsal horn of the spinal cord. Dysesthetic pain in peripheral nerve lesions may also be due to damaged or regenerating nociceptive afferent fibers, whereas aching or stabbing pain may relate to activation of nociceptive nervi nervorum [25]. Such central mechanisms may explain why proximal ablative procedures usually fail to provide sustained pain relief.

Treatment

Early resolution, and prevention of postherpetic neuralgia, are the goals of treatment for acute herpes zoster. The earlier the treatment is instituted, the less likely the development of postherpetic neuralgia [26–28]. Some data indicate that treating acute herpes zoster prevents this sequela [29]; other data suggest the opposite [30]. Because no reliable treatment for postherpetic neuralgia exists, aggressive management of acute herpes zoster is necessary for high-risk patients.

Therapy should attempt to abort segmental infection and prevent viral spread beyond the primary unit, prevent tissue injury (cytolysis), and prevent postherpetic neuralgia. Available modalities include antiviral agents, anti-inflammatory agents, systemic analgesics and adjuvant agents, nerve blocks, and miscellaneous techniques.

ANTIVIRAL THERAPIES

Considerable progress has been made with antiviral therapies [31]. For immunocompetent patients, antivirals are most beneficial early in the course of primary or initial disease or for patients with frequent or severe recurrent disease; for immunocompromised patients, antivirals are extremely beneficial [32]. The often protracted evolution and pathologically documented direct viral infection of the spinal cord in immunosuppressed patients with herpes zoster myelitis provides a rationale for using antivirals in preventing or attenuating the evolving myelopathy [33].

Acyclovir is the treatment of choice [34•,35]. Administered orally, it may prevent the ocular complications of ophthalmic zoster [35]. Chronic, disseminated herpes zoster in patients with AIDS may require prolongation of initial high-dose therapy [36]; oral dosages may need to be prescribed at a strength to produce serum concentrations similar to intravenous concentrations [37]. Whether treatment with acyclovir

decreases the incidence of postherpetic neuralgia is still controversial [30,38,39]. Stroke following herpes zoster may be treatable, and treatment with acyclovir in patients presenting with delayed contralateral hemiplegia is recommended [40]. Acyclovir and vidarabine have been shown to be equally efficacious in treating disseminated herpes zoster in the immunocompromised host [41••].

Human leukocyte interferon shortens the course of herpes zoster and protects against its complications; however, significant side effects, the necessity for parenteral administration, high cost, and limited supplies make it less attractive.

Other viral thymidine-kinase-dependent drugs including E-5-(2 bromovinyl)-2'-deoxyuridine and (2'-fluoro-5-iodi-1-β-1)arabinosylcytosine (FIAC), appear even more potent than acyclovir and are currently being investigated. Intramuscular adenosine monophosphate has effectively reduced the duration of viral shedding, pain, and healing time [42], while FIAC has decreased duration of appearance of new lesions and pain and improved and accelerated healing [43]. Although idoxuridine has been used to treat herpes zoster lesions of the conjunctiva and cornea [44,45], it is not approved for this use.

ANTI-INFLAMMATORY AGENTS

Many investigators have reported good results with anti-inflammatory agents in treating herpes zoster. Excellent pain relief and a low incidence of postherpetic neuralgia have been achieved with methylprednisolone or methylprednisolone with 0.5% lidocaine [29]. Trials of immunocompetent patients have also suggested that systemic steroids during acute zoster can prevent postherpetic neuralgia [4].

However, treatment with parenteral anti-inflammatory drugs is controversial, because the host defenses causing tissue injury may be largely inseparable from those eliminating or preventing the spread of infection. So far, dissociation of protective from harmful host responses has not been clearly demonstrated. A meta-analysis [46] indicates a significant decrease in incidence at 6 and 12 weeks but no differences at 24 weeks.

Steroids are generally administered within the first 10 days, with 60 mg/d the first week, 30 mg/d the second week, and 15 mg/d the third week. Prednisone is usually the agent of choice. Steroids have also been administered subcutaneously under affected skin and in the epidural space, on the affected ganglion, and the peripheral nerve. Inflammation and scarring are reduced with use of anti-inflammatories.

SYSTEMIC ANALGESICS AND ADJUVANT AGENTS

Analgesics are important adjuncts to antidepressants in neuropathic pain. Nonnarcotic, nonaddictive drugs are useful in controlling mild pain and have few side effects. Although moderately addictive drugs are efficacious, they may cause dependence and adverse side effects. Strongly addictive drugs may be used for a limited time, tapered off as pain decreases, and discontinued when pain is at a level controllable by nonnarcotics.

ANTIDEPRESSANTS AND TRANQUILIZERS

Antidepressants relieve both pain and depression, and centrally active antidepressants deserve a trial for any patient not obtaining pain relief. Tricyclic drugs block serotonin uptake; one of the active mechanisms in central pain states is a deficit in serotonin. Tricyclics and anxiolytics are often prescribed together, because many patients experience anxiety and severe pain; tricyclics are also sedatives and may correct sleep disturbance and frequent or early morning awakening.

VITAMINS AND MINERALS

Since the host-immune system is believed to be incompetent during an acute outbreak, vitamins, minerals, and improved general nutrition may help improve immunologic status.

NERVE BLOCKS

Repeated administration of local anesthetics at sites along the segmental pathway affected by herpes zoster is widely advocated. Local infiltration using subcutaneous injections of 0.2% triamcinolone and bupivacaine 0.25% in normal saline under areas of eruption and sites of pain and itching is simple, inexpensive, and effective (Figs. 15-9 and 15-10) [47]. Somatic nerve blocks are of limited value in acute herpes zoster. Sympathetic blockade can often dramatically alleviate pain [48•,49–52] but may [48•] or may not [53] prevent postherpetic neuralgia. Until this is determined, it is probably worthwhile to use sympathetic blocks as early as possible. Epidural blocks using local anesthetic have been successful, both alone and in combination with corticosteroids [54]. Subarachnoid blocks and neurolytic blocks are not usually indicated.

MISCELLANEOUS TECHNIQUES

Topical agents used to treat acute herpes zoster and postherpetic neuralgia include lidocaine gel (10%) [55–57], capsaicin [58,59], vincristine (via iontophoresis) [60], chloroform plus acetylsalicylic acid [54], ethyl ether plus acetylsalicylic acid [61], and benzydamine cream (3%) [62]. Several studies have investigated the usefulness of topical applications in treating postherpetic neuralgia, including chloroform-aspirin [54,55,58,59] and topical capsaicin [58,59]. Indomethacin stupe is more effective and easier to use than chloroform-aspirin [63]. When combined together and applied topically, acetylsalicylic acid and ethyl ether give excellent pain relief [61]. Ice therapy is sometimes used alone to cool the painful area. Although psychosocial therapy is not mandatory, patients with severe anxiety and fear may benefit from counseling.

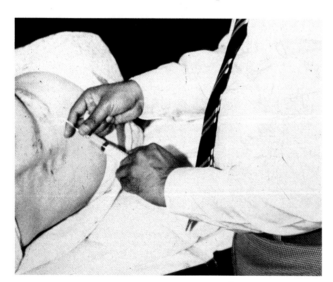

Figure 15-9 Intracutaneous infiltration of decadron with 0.125% bupivacaine in the vesicles of the acute herpes zoster, which are 3 weeks old.

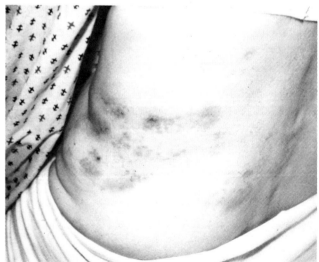

Figure 15-10 Four days after intracutaneous infiltration of decadron and bupivacaine treatment of the patient shown in Figure 15-9. Note bruising due to needle penetration, as well as flattening of vesicles and acceleration of healing.

Recommended Therapeutic Strategy

IMMUNOCOMPETENT YOUNG PATIENTS

Immunocompetent patients younger than 50 years of age who suffer no defined underlying illness have brisk reaction to the infection, enabling them to confine the rash within the initial unit. Postherpetic neuralgia is not an issue, acute morbidity is low, and healing is rapid.

Treatment should attempt to relieve intolerable pain and prevent inflammatory tissue damage. Antiviral agents administered within the first 72 hours may stop viral replication and spread of infection to peripheral nerves. Anti-inflammatory agents are very useful in decreasing tissue damage and minimizing inflammatory reaction. To decrease severe pain of neuralgia, administer sympathetic or epidural blocks within the first 3 to 4 weeks. Antidepressants are helpful adjuvants.

IMMUNOCOMPETENT OLDER PATIENTS

These patients suffer no underlying disease, but their response to varicella-zoster virus may be less vigorous, leading to slower viral clearance and a higher incidence of spread beyond the initial unit of infection. Nervous system and visceral complications occur less frequently and probably do not warrant the use of potentially toxic therapy.

The major objective is prevention of postherpetic neuralgia, and both antivirals and anti-inflammatory agents may be useful [4,50]. A reasonable approach would be to treat with a limited course of corticosteroids, 60 mg prednisone or equivalent daily for 5 days, tapering the dose over the following 2 weeks.

For pain relief, nonnarcotic analgesics combined with epidural and sympathetic blocks or local intracutaneous infiltration with bupivacaine and corticosteroids are recommended.

IMMUNOSUPPRESSED YOUNG PATIENTS

Therapy is directed at confining viral infection (Fig. 15-11). Acyclovir administered as early as possible is the treatment of choice. Hospitalization is recommended for patients at risk of developing complications, particularly those with lymphoproliferative disease or early dissemination. Pain relief should be obtained by using techniques for acute pain management. Varicella vaccine can be safely used in children with acute lymphoblastic leukemia or non-Hodgkin's lymphoma, who are undergoing chemotherapy, to effectively protect against varicella [64•].

IMMUNOSUPPRESSED OLDER PATIENTS

Therapeutic objectives include prevention of viral spread and postherpetic pain, and antiviral agents may be help-ful, especially for selected groups [11]. Acyclovir is effective in reducing infection and preventing dissemination and may reduce postherpetic pain.

However, corticosteroids are somewhat dangerous and should be used cautiously because they may impair remaining defenses beyond a critical level increasing the risk of dissemination. Whether corticosteroids in combination with potent antiviral coverage may prove safe warrants further investigation. Pain relief is best provided by nerve blocks.

Complications

Complications of herpes zoster include neuralgia, facial or oculomotor palsy, paralysis of motor nerves, myelitis [65], and meningoencephalitis. Postherpetic neuralgia seems to occur more frequently and is more protracted in the immunosuppressed patient, especially with Hodgkin's disease or other lymphomas.

Incidence of infection in the immunosuppressed patient increases markedly, often with an exaggerated and acutely disabling clinical course, with infection spreading segmentally to involve ipsilateral and occasionally contralateral dermatomes, accompanied by fever and increasing debilitation. New lesions appear while old lesions are healing, and many patients develop dissemination and visceral involvement, which may ultimately prove fatal.

Generally, patients in whom the disease remains localized for 4 to 6 days do not experience complications. Greatest morbidity and mortality usually occur with vis-

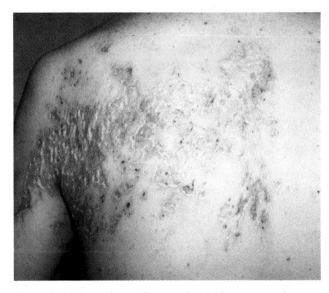

Figure 15-11 Note the confluence of vesicular response due to herpes zoster in a 30-year-old man suffering from AIDS. These aberrant vesicles can be present at multiple sites and spread with hematogenous dissemination.

ceral involvement through dissemination, especially in patients older than 40 years of age. Other complications include toxicity, fever, chills, bacterial sepsis, and, less frequently, varicella pneumonia.

Prognosis

Prompt treatment shortens the progressive course of the disease and decreases its severity. Age and response to therapy are also correlated, with patients younger than 60 generally responding better to therapy and having a lower incidence of postherpetic neuralgia.

POSTHERPETIC NEURALGIA

Postherpetic neuralgia is a sequela of acute herpes zoster. Although spontaneous resolution of herpes zoster may occur in most patients, about 10% of patients older than 40 years of age, and from 20% to 50% of patients older than 60 years of age, experience intractable pain. Some young patients experience postherpetic neuralgia for 1 to 2 weeks after herpes zoster lesions heal, with persisting hypothesia or hyperesthesia. Postherpetic neuralgia is associated with agonizing pain and suffering.

Clinical Manifestations

Unrelenting pain is often similar to that of herpes zoster neuralgia, with burning, aching, or itching accompanied by severe paroxysms of stabbing or burning pain. Many patients describe allodynia superimposed on the continuous component of the pain. Depressed affect and vegetative signs are also typically encountered.

Assessment of somatosensory perception thresholds, allodynia, and skin temperature in affected areas of acute herpes zoster and postherpetic neuralgia patients has shown significant changes in sensory threshold measurements in affected areas in postherpetic neuralgia patients [66] and a significant association between thermal threshold abnormalities in acute herpes zoster patients and the development of postherpetic neuralgia [67]. Mechanical allodynia was present in most patients; no differences were observed in skin temperature between postherpetic neuralgia patients and patients not developing postherpetic neuralgia [66]. These data indicate a deficit of sensory functions mediated by both large and small primary afferent fibers, suggesting a major central involvement in the pathophysiology.

Diagnosis

The typical postherpetic neuralgia patient has a history of previous unilateral skin eruption, sometimes with residual scarring of the skin. Hyperesthesia, dysesthesia, or anesthesia may be present. Laboratory tests to isolate antibodies specific to herpes zoster facilitate diagnosis.

Pathogenesis

The cause of intractable pain in postherpetic neuralgia is unclear. Noxious impulses may become established in centrally located, closed self-perpetuating loops, with progressive facilitation developing in these synapses, and, eventually, pain entirely unaffected by surgical section of peripheral pathways occurring spontaneously. The infection may also involve higher pathways in the cord and brain, beyond the reach of extradural and intrathecal medication, and, possibly, cordotomy.

The gate control theory postulates that pain is carried by small unmyelinated and myelinated nerve fibers to the central nervous system, where input is modified via pathways in larger myelinated nerve fibers. Since nerve impulses are transmitted faster in large myelinated than in small unmyelinated fibers, in acute herpes zoster proportionately more large fibers tend to be damaged and destroyed than small fibers. With slower regeneration than small fibers—and usually smaller diameter after regeneration—larger fibers tend to decrease in relation to smaller fibers.

Without normal modulation by large-nerve fiber stimulation, minimal small-fiber stimulation might produce pain. Because older patients have fewer large fibers and lose more because of the infection, they are more likely to feel more intense, intractable pain.

A loss of myelinated fibers and a proportional increase in nonmyelinated fibers has been reported [68], and the dysesthesia present in postherpetic neuralgia could be caused by excessive processing of the nociceptive pathway from large myelinated fibers. The pain of postherpetic neuralgia could also be caused by deafferentation and hypersensitivity in the posterior horn of the spinal cord [68].

Management Modalities

Although no modality has been specific or reliable, in many cases pain can be controlled by conservative, noninvasive therapy [69]. Drug therapy can provide analgesia, reduce depression and anxiety, and decrease insomnia. Hypnotics, tranquilizers, antidepressants, and anticonvulsants have frequently been used.

To decrease the possibility of noncompliance, it is important to warn the patient of potential adverse effects. However, because an average of 35% of patients significantly benefit from the placebo effect, it is equally important to be positive and enthusiastic.

PHARMACOLOGIC

Antivirals are generally inappropriate in treating postherpetic neuralgia; however, when given before treatment such as chemotherapy or radiation therapy that is likely to reactivate the virus, they may be useful in patients such as those with Hodgkin's disease.

Narcotics may temporarily relieve extreme pain [70•]; they should however, be used with extreme caution, if at all, because of attendant side effects.

Antidepressants and tranquilizers are frequently used in conjunction with analgesics. Tricyclic antidepressants are the most effective single drug for management of postherpetic neuralgia. Drugs should be given in appropriate dose levels, and several different drugs should be tried if necessary.

Tricyclics and anxiolytics are usually prescribed together. Many patients unable to obtain relief with tricyclics alone can benefit from the addition of phenothiazine [71]. Amitriptyline hydrochloride 50 to 75 mg/d and fluphenazine hydrochloride 1 mg three or four times daily is usually recommended, to be continued throughout life for lasting pain relief (Fig. 15-12).

Excellent pain relief has also been achieved with chlorprothixene 50 mg every 6 hours for 5 days; however, this requires hospitalization and may cause intolerable side effects and only temporary analgesia.

Anticonvulsants may be useful when other medications have failed, although side effects tend to limit their use. Phenytoin 100 mg three to four times a day or carbamazepine 500 to 1000 mg daily in three to four divided doses can be used to relieve sharp pain.

Sodium valproate 200 mg twice a day and amitriptyline 10 to 15 mg twice a day have also been used successfully [72•], with dosage of the former increased to 200 mg twice a day for relief of resistant stabbing pain and dosage of the latter increased for relief of resistant burning and hyperesthesia. Infiltration of the scar with local anesthetic and steroids or transcutaneous electrical nerve stimulation may be used to treat the persistent dull ache component of pain.

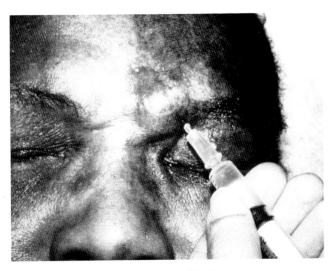

Figure 15-12 Supraorbital neurolytic block (6% phenol) in a 75-year-old woman suffering from posttherpetic neuralgia.

NERVE BLOCKS

Analgesic blocks can be used prognostically, therapeutically, and prophylactically to help predict effects of prolonged interruption of nerve pathways through injection of neurolytic agents or surgery, to interrupt pain pathways to influence autonomic response to noxious stimulation and breaking the vicious cycle of the disease, and to relieve severe intractable pain.

Subcutaneous infiltration of steroids is effective, with daily injections of 0.2% solution of triamcinolone in normal saline and subcutaneous infiltration of 0.25% bupivacaine and 0.2% triamcinolone alone or in conjunction with medication and sympathetic blockade [47]. There are no significant complications, and the technique is simple and inexpensive.

Sensory nerve blocks are used in early attempts to relieve pain, with limited success; for diagnosis; and as a prognostic block before neurolytic block. Steroids injected around the dorsal horn have had unpredictable and limited success.

Good temporary results have been achieved with paravertebral somatic sympathetic blocks using 0.2% procaine at 4-day intervals, with best results obtained in postherpetic neuralgia of less than a 2-month duration and no effect on postherpetic neuralgia of 2-year duration [49].

A comparison of the effects of somatic and sympathetic blockades on relief of pain and tactile allodynia in long-standing ophthalmic or high cervical postherpetic neuralgia in a small group of patients indicated the former were more efficacious [73].

In a series of three epidural steroid injections given 1 week apart, patients had progressively decreased pain with methylprednisolone 80 mg used for single-root involvement, 60 mg/root for two-root involvement, and 40 mg/root for three-root involvement, and the total dose of any one visit not exceeding 120 mg. Patients were kept in a lateral position for 30 minutes and discharged 6 hours later; however, a significantly different technique has been unsuccessful [14].

Neurolytic blocks may be considered when other blocks have failed; however, they should only be performed after a prognostic block has demonstrated that effective block is possible. Ethyl alcohol (50% to 90% in aqueous solution) or phenol (6% to 10%) can be used for prolonged destruction of nerves. The former is associated with a higher incidence of neuritis. Duration of effects usually ranges from 2 to 6 months but may vary. Good results have been achieved with thoracic or lumbar blocks using alcohol, in combination with antidepressants and antianxiety drugs [74].

Peripheral nerve block can also be achieved with ammonium compounds, using a solution of 10% ammonium sulfate in 1% lidocaine or 15% ammonium chloride. Duration of action ranges from 4 to 24 weeks. Neuritis does not occur, but the resulting numbness can be annoying.

PSYCHOSOCIAL THERAPY

It is especially important to treat the whole patient, and counseling by a psychologist or clinical social worker experienced in pain management is recommended. Training in stress management may allow some control of pain.

Anxiety and stress can exacerbate and prolong pain, and the pain-tension-anxiety cycle can convert acute pain symptoms into a chronic condition. Individuals susceptible to chfonicity include tense, hard-driving, conscientious perfectionists, and dependent individuals with repressed anger and hostility. Positive reinforcement of responses to pain may lead to chronic pain behavior.

Patients should be enlightened as to the relationship between the psyche and pain and relieved of the fear of organic disease. Family and friends should be taught to provide effective emotional support. Appropriate social service agencies should be contacted to assist elderly patients living alone.

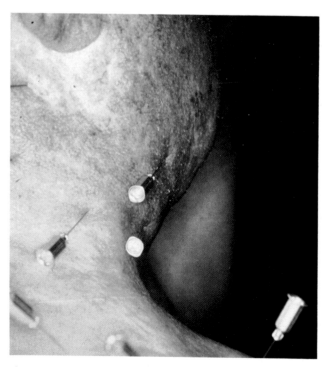

Figure 15-13 In a patient with postherpetic neuralgia, acupuncture in progress for pain relief.

MISCELLANEOUS THERAPIES

When all else fails, the following techniques may be used to manage residual pain. Transcutaneous electrical nerve stimulation has a low success rate but provides sufficient relief to permit a return to normal activity without analgesic therapy [75]. Ice and other cold therapies have also been used, applied to the skin for 2 to 3 minutes several times a day, starting with the least sensitive and approaching the most sensitive area. A vibrator is then used in the same manner, in conjunction with psychotropic drugs. Ethyl chloride or other cold sprays are used by themselves, sprayed over the painful area beginning at the upper area and working down, repeated twice at 1-minute intervals until the skin is thoroughly cooled. If response is satisfactory, pain can be relieved by two or three sets of sprays per day. Good-to-excellent pain relief can be maintained using cryocautery with a stick of solid carbon dioxide (dry ice) applied directly to the hyperesthetic skin areas of cutaneous scars [76]. Other techniques include acupuncture [77] (Fig. 15-13), hypnosis, capsaicin [78], and dimethylsulfoxide, although the latter is of unknown therapeutic value.

Surgery is the last resort, but is not always successful. Surgery is usually done at the sites of the pain pathway in progressively higher stages. Wide excision, skin grafting, rhizotomy of the somatic afferents and sensory root ganglia, and sympathectomy have poor results.

COMPLICATIONS

Complications are primarily emotional, including depression and possible suicidal tendencies. Destruction of lifestyle may affect the long-term patient, with physical function further impaired by extended immobility.

PROGNOSIS

Prompt treatment shortens the course of postherpetic neuralgia and decreases its severity. Age and response to therapy appear to be correlated, with young patients generally responding better and, even untreated, having a lower incidence of the disease. Postherpetic neuralgia lesions in the ophthalmic division of the trigeminal nerve are difficult to treat successfully. Psychological make-up of the individual patient is always important in therapeutic efficacy. One fifth of patients with neoplasms who have had herpes zoster will have at least one recurrence.

REFERENCES AND RECOMMENDED READING

Papers of interest, published recently, have been highlighted as:
• Of special interest
•• Of outstanding interest

1. Human RW: Structure and function of the varicella-zoster virus genome. In *The Human Herpesviruses: An Interdisciplinary Perspective.* Edited by Nahmias AJ, Dowdle WR, Schinazi RF. New York: Elsevier Science Publishing; 1981:27–35.

2. Loeser JD: Review article–Herpes zoster and postherpetic neuralgia. *Pain* 1986, 25:149–164.

3. Berger R, Florent G, Just M: Decrease of the lymphoproliferative response to varicella-zoster virus antigen in the aged. *Infect Immun* 1981, 32:24–27.

4. Eaglstein WH, Katz R, Brown JA: The effect of early corticosteroid therapy on skin eruption and pain of herpes zoster. *JAMA* 1970, 211:1681–1683.

5. Keczkes K, Basheer AM: Do corticosteroids prevent postherpetic neuralgia? *Br J Dermatol* 1980, 102:551-555.

6. Dirbas FM, Swain JA: Disseminated cutaneous herpes zoster following cardiac surgery. *J Cardiovasc Surg* 1990, 31:531–532.

7. Schmader K, Studenski S, MacMillan J, *et al.*: Are stressful life events risk factors for herpes zoster? *J Am Geriatr Soc* 1990, 38:1188–1194.

8. Arvin AM, Pollard RB, Rasmussen LE, *et al.*: Cellular and humoral immunity in the pathogenesis of recurrent herpes viral infections in patients with lymphoma. *J Clin Invest* 1980, 65:869–878.

9. Gershon AA, Steinberg SP: Antibody responses to varicella-zoster virus and the role of antibody in host defenses. *Am J Med Sci* 1981, 282:12–17.

10. Miyagawa Y, Miyazaki M, Inutsuka S, *et al.*: Herpes zoster in patients with sarcoidosis. *Respiration* 1992, 59:94–96.

11. Rusthoven JJ, Ahlgren P, Elhakim T, *et al.*: Risk factors for varicella zoster disseminated infection among adult cancer patients with localized zoster. *Cancer* 1988, 62:1641–1646.

12. Atkinson K, Meyers JD, Storb R, *et al.*: Varicella-zoster virus infection after marrow transplantation for aplasma anemia or leukemia. *Transplantation* 1980, 29:47–50.

13. Price RW: Herpes zoster: an approach to systemic therapy. *Med Clin North Am* 1982, 66:1105–1117.

14. Raj PP ed.: *Practical Management of Pain.* 2nd ed. St. Louis: Mosby-Year Book; 1992:517–545.

15. Chen H-J: Measurement of tissue impedance in dorsal root entry zone surgery for pain after brachial plexus avulsion and herpes zoster. *Clin J Pain* 1991, 7:323–329.

16. Steele RW: Immunology of varicella-zoster virus. In *Immunology of Human Infection Part II. Viruses and Parasites: Immunodiagnosis and Prevention of Infectious Diseases.* Edited by Nahmias AJ, O'Reilly RJ. New York: Plenum Publishing; 1982.

17. Higa K, Kenjiro D, Haruhiko M, *et al.*: Factors influencing the duration of treatment of acute herpetic pain with sympathetic nerve block: importance of severity of herpes zoster assessed by the maximum antibody titers to varicella-zoster virus in otherwise healthy patients. *Pain* 1988, 32:147–157.

18. Yoshiike T, Aikawa Y, Wonghwaisayawan H *et al.*: HLA-DR antigen expression on peripheral T-cell subsets in pityriasiorosea and herpes zoster. *Dermatologica* 1991, 182:160–163.

19. Zanolli MD, Powell BL, McCalmont T, *et al.*: Granuloma annulare and disseminated herpes zoster. *Int J Dermatol* 1992, 31:55–57.

20. Gershon AA, Steinberg SP: Inactivation of varicella zoster virus in vitro: effect of leukocytes and specific antibody. *Infect Immun* 1981, 33:507–511.

21. Gershon AA, Steinberg SP, Borkowsky W, *et al.*: IgM to varicella-zoster virus: demonstration in patients without clinical zoster. *Pediatr Infect Dis* 1982, 1:164–167.

22. Straus SE: Clinical and biological differences between herpes simplex virus and varicella-zoster virus infections. *JAMA* 1989, 262:3455–3458.

23. Straus SE, Ostrove JM, Inchauspe G, *et al.*: Varicella-zoster virus infections. *Ann Intern Med* 1988, 108:221–237.

24. Ragozzino MJ, Melton LJ III, Kurland LT, *et al.*: Population-based study of herpes zoster and its sequelae. *Medicine (Baltimore)* 1982, 61:310–316.

25. Watson CPN, Morshead C, Van der Kooy D, *et al.*: Postherpetic neuralgia: post-mortem analysis of a case. *Pain* 1988, 34:129–138.

26. Rutgers MJ, Dirksen R: The prevention of postherpetic neuralgia: a retrospective view of patients treated in the acute phase of herpes zoster. *Br J Clin Pract* 1988, 42:412–414.

27. Raj PP: Herpes zoster: preventing postherpetic pain. *Consultant* 1981:71–76.

28. Li WH, Ming ZL, Chen Q, *et al.*: The prevention of postherpetic neuralgia: a retrospective view of patients treated in the acute phase of herpes zoster. *Clin Med J Engl* 1989, 102:395–399.

29. Pernak JM, Biemans JCH: The treatment of acute herpes zoster in trigeminal nerve for the prevention of postherpetic neuralgia. In *The Pain Clinic.* vol. 1. Edited by Edmann W, Oyama T, Pernak MJ. Utrecht, The Netherlands: VNU Science Press; 1985.

30. Benoldi D, Irizzi S, Zucchi A, *et al.*: Prevention of postherpetic neuralgia: evaluation of treatment with oral prednisone, oral acyclovir, and radiotherapy. *Int J Dermatol* 1991, 30:288–290.

31. Hirsch MS, Swartz MN: Antiviral agents. *N Engl J Med* 1980, 302:903–907.

32. Bautner KR: Rational use of acyclovir in the treatment of mucocutaneous herpes simplex virus and varicella zoster infections. *Semin Dermatol* 1992, 11:256–260.

33. Devinsky O, Cho ES, Petito CK, *et al.*: Herpes zoster myelitis. *Brain* 1991, 114:1181–1196.

34. • Keating MR: Antiviral agents. *Mayo Clin Proc* 1992, 67:160–178.

Review of antivirals in current use that differentiates between agents and their optimal uses for different types of patients.

35. Peterslund NA: Management of varicella zoster infections in immunocompetent hosts. *Am J Med* 1988, 85:74–78.

36. Hoppenjans WB, Bibler MR, Orme RL, *et al.*: Prolonged cutaneous herpes zoster in acquired immunodeficiency syndrome. *Arch Dermatol* 1990, 126:1048–1050.

37. Dellamonica P, Carles M, Lokiec F, *et al.*: Preventing recurrent varicella and herpes zoster with oral acyclovir in HIV-seropositive patients. *Clin Pharmacol* 1991, 10:301–302.

38. Neumann M, Chung D: Intravenous acyclovir for the reduction of postherpetic neuralgia. *Pain* 1990, (suppl 5):S57.

39. Hirschel R: Antiviral drugs—1988. *Schweiz Med Wochenschr* 1988, 118:1830–1837.

40. Rawlinson WD, Cunningham AL: Contralateral hemiplegia following thoracic herpes zoster. *Med J Aust* 1991, 155:344–346.

41. •• Whitley RJ, Gnann JW Jr, Hinthorn D, *et al.*: Disseminated herpes zoster in the immunocompromised host: a comparative trial of acyclovir and vidarabine. The NIAID Collaborative Antiviral Study Group. *J Infect Dis* 1992, 165:450–455.

Double-blind, controlled trial comparing the efficacy of acyclovir and vidarabine in immunocompromised patients with disseminated herpes zoster. There were no differences in rates of cutaneous healing, resolution of acute neuritis, frequency of postherpetic neuralgia, or adverse clinical and laboratory events between groups; however, acyclovir recipients had shorter hospital stays than vidarabine recipients.

42. Sklar SH, Blue WT, Alexander EJ, *et al.*: The treatment and prevention of neuralgia with adenosine monophosphate. *JAMA* 1985, 253:1427–1430.

43. Leyland-Jones B, Donnelly H, Groshen S, *et al.*: 2'Fluoro'5-iodoarabinosyl-cytosine, a new potent antiviral agent: efficacy in immunosuppressed individuals with herpes zoster. *J Infect Dis* 1986, 154:430–436.

44. Burton JW, Gould PW, Hursthouse MW, *et al.*: A multicentre trial of Zostrum (5 percent idoxecridine in dimethyl sulphoxide) in herpes zoster. *N Z Med J* 1981, 94:384–386.

45. Esmann V, Wildenhoff KE: Idoxuridine for herpes zoster. *Lancet* 1980, 2:474.

46. Lycka BA: Postherpetic neuralgia and systemic corticosteroid therapy—efficacy and safety. *Int J Dermatol* 1990, 29:523–527.

47. Epstein E: Treatment of herpes zoster and post zoster neuralgia by subcutaneous injection of triamcinolone. *Int J Dermatol* 1981, 20:65–68.

48. • Currey TA, Dalsania J: Treatment for herpes zoster ophthalmicus: stellate ganglion block as a treatment for acute pain and prevention of postherpetic neuralgia. *Ann Ophthalmol* 1991, 23:188–189.

Reports efficacious use of stellate ganglion nerve blocks in the treatment of zoster ophthalmicus in 19 patients, which resulted in relief of pain for all patients.

49. Riopelle JM, Maraghi M, Gursch KP: Chronic neuralgia incidence following local anesthetic therapy for herpes zoster. *Arch Dermatol* 1984, 120:747–750.

50. Toyama N: Sympathetic ganglion block therapy for herpes zoster. *J Dermatol* (Japanese) 1982, 9:59–62.

51. Lipton JR, Marding SP, Wells JCD: The effect of early stellate ganglion block on post-herpetic neuralgia in herpes zoster ophthalmicus. *The Pain Clinic* 1987, 1:247–251.

52. Tenicela R, Lovasik D, Eaglstein W: Treatment of herpes zoster with sympathetic blocks. *Clin J Pain* 1985, 1:63–67.

53. Brookshire GL, Cook J, Sklar H: Sympathetic blockade vs. adenoise monophosphate for the prevention and treatment of postherpetic neuralgia. *Anesthesiology* 1987, 67(3A):8247.

54. Berger JJ, Perkins HM: Comparison of epidural methylprednisolone alone or combined with lidocaine for relieving postherpetic neuralgia. *Pain* 1990, (suppl 5):S60.

55. Rowbotham MC, Fields HL: Clinical note: topical lidocaine reduces pain in post-herpetic neuralgia. *Pain* 1989, 38:297–301.

56. Kissin I, McDanal J, Xavier AV: Topical lidocaine for relief of superficial pain in post-herpetic neuralgia. *Neurology* 1989, 39:1132–1133.

57. Stow PJ, Glynn CJ, Minor B: EMLA cream in the treatment of post-herpetic neuralgia: efficacy and pharmacokinetic profile. *Pain* 1989, 29:301–305.

58. Drake HF, Harries AJ, Gamester RE, *et al.*: Randomised double-blind study of topical capsaicin for treatment of postherpetic neuralgia. *Pain* 1990, (suppl 5):58.

59. Bernstein JE, Korman N-J, Bickers DR: Topical capsaicin treatment of chronic post-herpetic neuralgia. *J Am Acad Dermatol* 1989, 21:263–270.

60. Layman PR, Argyras E, Glynn CJ: Iontophoresis of vincristine versus saline in post-herpetic neuralgia: a controlled trial. *Pain* 1986, 25:165–170.

61. DeBenedittis G, Lorenzetta A, Besana F: A new topical treatment for acute herpetic neuralgia and postherpetic neuralgia. *Pain* 1990, (suppl 5):57.

62. McQuay HJ, Carroll D, Moxon A, *et al.*: Benzydamine cream for the treatment of post-herpetic neuralgia: minimum duration of treatment periods in a cross-over trial. *Pain* 1990, 40:131–135.

63. Morimoto M, Inamori K, Hyodo M: The effect of indomethacin stupe for postherpetic neuralgia: particularly in comparison with chloroform-aspirin solution. *Pain* 1990, (suppl 5):S59.

64. • Yeung C-Y, Liang D-C: Varicella vaccine in children with acute lymphoblastic leukemia and non-Hodgkin lymphoma. *Pediatr Hematol Oncol* 1992, 9:29–34.

Controlled study investigating the safety and efficacy of varicella vaccine in immunocompromised children receiving chemotherapy for acute lymphoblastic leukemia or non-Hodgkin's lymphoma. Vaccinated children had a significantly lower incidence of varicella.

65. Rosenfeld T, Price MA: Paralysis in herpes zoster. *Aust N Z J Med* 1985, 15:712–716.

66. Marmikko T, Bowsher D: Somatosensory findings in postherpetic neuralgia. *J Neurol Nerosurg Psychiatry* 1990, 53:135–141.

67. Nurmikko TJ, Rasanen A, Hakkinen VL: Clinical and neurophysiological observations on acute herpes zoster. *Clin J Pain* 1990, 6:284–290.

68. Watson CPN, Deck JH, Morshead C, *et al.*: Post-herpetic neuralgia: further postmortem studies of cases with and without pain. *Pain* 1991, 44:105–117.

69. Niv D, Ben-Ari S, Rappaport A, *et al.*: Postherpetic neuralgia: clinical experience with a conservative treatment. *Clin J Pain* 1989, 5:295–300.

70. • Rowbotham MC, Reisner-Keller LA, Fields HL: Both intravenous lidocaine and morphine reduce the pain of postherpetic neuralgia. *Neurology* 1991, 41:1024–1028.
Randomized, double-blind, placebo-controlled trial evaluating the analgesic efficacy of intravenous infusion of lidocaine and morphine in adults with well-established postherpetic neuralgia. Both lidocaine and morphine reduced pain intensity, with a majority of patients who achieved pain relief also reporting disappearance of allodynia.

71. Kramer PW: The management of postherpetic neuralgia with chlorprothixene. *Surg Neurol* 1981, 15:102–104.

72. • Watson CPN, Chipman M, Reed K, *et al.*: Amitriptyline versus maprotiline in postherpetic neuralgia: a randomized, double-blind crossover trial. *Pain* 1992, 48:29–36.
Randomized, double-blind, crossover trial that found amitriptyline to be more effective than maprotiline.

73. Nurmikko T, Wells C, Bowsher D: Pain and allodynia in postherpetic neuralgia: role of somatic and sympathetic nervous systems. *Acta Neurol Scand* 1991, 84:146–152.

74. Kageshima K, Wakasugi B, Shiotaniu M, *et al.*: Thoracic and lumbar sympathetic ganglion block for postherpetic neuralgia. *Masui* 1992, 41:106–110.

75. Winnie AP: The patient with herpetic neuralgia. In *Postgraduate Seminar in Anesthesiology*. Program syllabus. Edited by Moya F, Gion H. Miami Beach; 1983:165–170.

76. Suzuki H, Ogawa S, Nakagawa H, *et al.*: Cryocautery of sensitized skin areas for the relief of pain due to postherpetic neuralgia. *Pain* 1980, 9:355–362.

77. Lewith GT, Field J: Acupuncture and postherpetic neuralgia [letter]. *BMJ* 1980, 77:622.

78. Peikert A, Hentrich M, Ochs G: Topical 0.025% capsaicin in chronic post-herpetic neuralgia: efficacy predictors of response and long-term course. *J Neurol* 1991, 238:452–456.

INTRODUCTION

Phantom pain has frequently been referred to as phantom "limb" pain; this term is inappropriate, however, because phantom pain may occur after other tissue has been removed as well (eg, breast [1,2], penis [2], nose [3], even viscera [2]). For simplification, the term extremity will be used in this chapter. Phantom pain is pain that occurs beyond the stump or site of removal. Stump pain is sometimes present, but it is a separate problem, associated with postsurgical, myofascial, and sometimes ischemic pain sources. Nevertheless, it is not uncommon for phantom and stump pain to coexist in the same patient.

The clinical profile of phantom pain varies a great deal from patient to patient, and often in the same patient over time. The patient may complain of pain in the entire extremity, in a general region of the extremity (eg, the hand after entire arm amputation), along the distribution of one or more specific nerves, or pain in some combination of these areas. The pain may be constant, intermittent, or, more frequently, constant with intermittent exacerbations or lancinating pain. Consistent with other neuralgic pain problems, the descriptors for the pain are varied and often unusual (Fig. 16-1).

MECHANISMS

There are several etiologic theories for how phantom pain develops and none of them alone fit characteristics of all patients. Several peripheral theories exist. One theory holds that hyperexcitable nerves, along with spontaneous firing of pain fibers, may play a role [5]. Neuromas occur as a source for these problems, but only in approximately 20% of patients [6]. Some evidence indicates that poor blood flow with ischemia may cause phantom pain with a "burning" quality and that residual-area muscle spasms may cause "cramping" pain [7]. Whether the sympathetic nervous system is causative or a potentiator is unknown, but some patients get relief from sympathetic blocks or ablation [8,9]. Central theories include loss of inhibition at the spinal cord from peripheral input, with changes in wide dynamic neuron function [10], or a central pattern–generating mechanism associated with multiple levels of the brain and spinal cord [2,11]. Concluding from an association of these theories with clinical presentations, perhaps patients with pain in the distribution of a specific nerve are more likely to have that nerve as the source of pain with or without a neuroma; regional or entire limb pain would more likely come from a central source.

There may be preamputation factors that cause phantom pain to occur or persist. Pain before amputation may [12] or may not [13] play a role, and patients with rigid, compulsive, and self-reliant personalities may be more likely to have pain or simply be more likely to report it [4]. Another confusing feature involves the occasional onset or exacerbation of phantom pain when spinal or epidural local anesthetics are administered [15–17]; these same blocks have been known to also relieve or reduce phantom pain. Clearly, multiple etiologic features are responsible, probably at multiple levels.

TREATMENT

Patients with phantom pain should be treated according to whether they have acute or chronic pain. In particular, calcitonin may be very effective when administered close to the onset of pain [18•], although its effectiveness in patients with chronic pain is less studied and apparently less long term [19]. The administration of preamputation epidural analgesia in patients with preoperative pain may reduce the incidence of phantom pain [20], but less effectively than with post-onset calcitonin. I am aware of patients with phantom pain who have achieved long-term relief or reduction in pain when postoperative epidural analgesia was administered

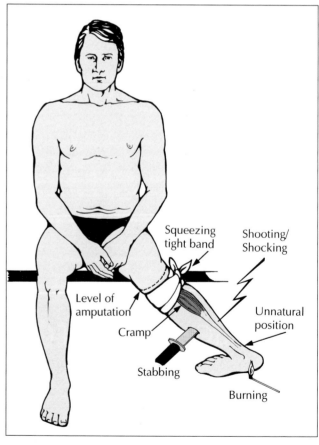

Figure 16-1 Phantom limb pain: some of the typical feelings of pain that seem to stem from the missing limb. (*From* Sherman [4]; with permission.)

close to the onset of their pain, although only a few cases have been reported in the literature [21]. Some of this relief may be from sympathetic blockade; one study concluded that sympathetic blocks are effective in patients with acute onset [8]. Physical therapy may be effective if used early because patients who have not been active with a prosthesis have a higher incidence of phantom pain [22]. Direct studies of physical therapy have not shown much effectiveness over time [9,23], although these studies have not focused on patients with acute-onset pain.

Patients with chronic pain have not received consistent, long-term benefits through the use of any one treatment. For each patient, the physician should examine the description of pain distribution, stated severity of pain, previous trials, psychological condition, and ability to withstand failure or complications, including increased pain. The treatments cited are intended to be in increasing order of invasiveness or potential damage, and probably should be tried in some semblance of that order, with many patients not receiving the most invasive approaches, even if they still have some pain.

There are several "nonphysician" treatments worth mentioning. Transcutaneous electrical nerve stimulation (TENS) has given relief to a varying percentage of patients when the electrodes are placed either near the site of removal or contralateral to the phantom extremity [24–26]. Unfortunately, TENS relief in general tends to diminish over time. Acupuncture may give some relief, but also shows decreasing effectiveness over time [27]. Physical therapy techniques (exercises, warm baths, massage, ultrasound) have been reported to give some short-term relief [8], but scant long-term information is available. Psychological treatments (relaxation training, biofeedback, and hypnosis) have demonstrated some effectiveness in reducing pain [9,23], perhaps specifically for complaints of burning or cramping pain [7]. Cognitive behavioral therapy can decrease some of the distress and suffering from chronic pain and loss of the extremity; these issues exacerbate but do not cause the pain.

The use of medications has demonstrated some benefit for patients with phantom pain. Although the role of calcitonin for the long-term relief of chronic phantom pain is currently unknown, this hormone does give short-term relief in many patients [19].

Many medications are used to treat chronic pain in general or neuralgic pain in particular. The response rates for any one of them in treating central pain problems are less than 50% (in a probable range of 5%–20%), but no controlled studies are available regarding phantom pain. There are anecdotal reports of relief from carbamazepine [28], chlorpromazine [29], tricyclic

antidepressants with opioids [30], beta blockers [31], and even "subhallucinogenic" doses of lysergic acid diethylamide [30,32,33]. The textbook *The Management of Pain* has an excellent review of "neuralgic" medications and the evidence for their use [34••]. A reasonable approach to the use of these drugs takes into account their efficacy (including quality of investigation) and potential side effects and complications. Table 16-1 lists the general classes of agents in the order in which I have given trials most frequently.

Tricyclic antidepressants have been the mainstay in the treatment of chronic pain, selected for sedation if needed or in an effort to minimize side effects. At present, the serotonin-specific antidepressants have not yet been proven effective, but my experience has shown them to be a reasonable replacement for tricyclic antidepressants when sedation or other side effects are not tolerated.

Phenothiazines and some related medications can be used, and probably show best results when used in combination with antidepressants. Doses are generally one tenth to one fourth the dose necessary for the treatment of psychosis, and the incidence of dyskinesia is rare.

Depending on pain description and concern for complications, several anticonvulsant agents can be tried before or after the administration of baclofen and mexiletine. These anticonvulsants (Table 16-1) may be most effective for lancinating pain but can be effective for more constant pain as well. Each of these drugs carries a significant incidence of medical complications, however. Baclofen has a better documentation of efficacy than does mexiletine and is generally tried first.

The medications mentioned previously are often effective in combination rather than singly, so medications that are safe and tolerated should be maintained as subsequent ones are tested. The next two medications or classes of medications both carry a risk for dependence and, perhaps, tolerance and should be tried with caution only after the previously mentioned medications have been tried and then only after significant discussion with the patient regarding these issues.

Clonazepam has demonstrated some efficacy in relieving neuralgia and is probably the best choice of the benzodiazepines. As mentioned previously, opioids can be effective for some patients, although doses required are often fairly high and side effects may be significant. Many physicians involved in pain management believe that opioid use in patients with benign pain is inappropriate and frequently ineffective in treating patients with neuropathic pain [35]. Nevertheless, a trial of opioids should be considered before performing some of the ablative or other invasive treatments listed further on.

Nerve blocks are touted by those who perform them as very effective for the phantom pain, but surveys of patients' responses have not been so positive [23,36]. Trigger-point or "neuroma" injection with local anesthetics and corticosteroids or with neurolytic agents [34] may help some patients and is more effective for stump pain.

Sympathetic blocks can give short-term relief for some patients with chronic phantom pain, but even when studied in a series they have rarely been shown to achieve long-term relief. It may help determine the maximum benefits of a neurolytic sympathetic block or surgical sympathectomy, but even these procedures generally lose their benefit over a few weeks or months [23]. Plexus blocks, epidural blocks, and intrathecal blocks have been tried, with minimal long-term relief, although there are a few case reports of prolonged relief with the use of an epidural block of meperidine [37]. Short-term relief brings the consideration of long-term infusions by epidural or intrathecal catheters, but this approach is more invasive, with more problems and complications. Neurolytic blocks at these progressively more central sites are not reported to be successful over time and have serious potential complications, including increased pain.

Surgical approaches can be classified as repairs, ablations, or augmentations. Stump revisions or repairs may alleviate stump pain if ischemia or infection are present but are rarely effective for phantom pain, even in the presence of neuromas [6]. Neuroablative techniques range from neuromal excision, through plexus, spinal root, and dorsal-root-entry-zone (DREZ) lesions, cordotomy, midbrain, and thalamic lesions, to prefrontal and parietal lobectomies or tractotomies (also cingulate on postcentral gyrus ablation) [9,23]. Each of these procedures has their "champions," but the effectiveness of neuroablation techniques in general is often lost after 12 months. Perhaps DREZ lesions are helpful for phantom pain with no stump pain [38], but five of six good responders also had root avulsion along with traumatic amputation, and DREZ lesions are known to have good results in patients with root avulsion. The pain of root avulsion can mimic phantom pain as well and may have been the cause of those patients' pain.

The lack of relief achieved from the use of these techniques, along with new pain complaints from these procedures, is postulated to occur from the "neuromatrix" or pattern-generating mechanism, with changes in stimulatory and inhibitory input at higher centers. This process

TABLE 16-1
NEURALGIC PAIN MEDICATIONS

MEDICATIONS	COMMENTS	SIDE EFFECTS
Antidepressants, *eg*, amitriptyline, imipramine, nortriptyline, desipramine, doxepin, fluoxetine*	Best documentation of efficacy; many are effective; dose usually less than for depression	Sedation/confusion, constipation, dry mouth, urine retention, tachycardia, weight gain/fluid retention
Neuroleptics, *eg*, fluphenazine, perphenazine, haloperidol, chlorpromazine, methotrimeprazine†	Usually used in combination with antidepressants	Alpha blockade/orthostatic hypotension, sedation/confusion, acute extrapyramidal reaction, tardive dyskinesia
Anticonvulsants, *eg*, carbamazepine, valproic acid/sodium valproate, dilantin	Best for intermittent, sharp, "shooting" neuralgia but can be effective for constant pain	Sedation/confusion, gastrointestinal distress, bone marrow suppression, hepatic toxicity, gingival hyperplasia (dilantin)
Baclofen	Combination with carbamazepine optimal for tic douloureux; usually used in combination with other neuralgic medications	Sedation/confusion, gastrointestinal distress/intolerance, central nervous system withdrawal symptoms with abrupt discontinuation
Mexiletine	Perhaps more useful for diffuse neuralgia (*eg*, diabetes)	Sedation/confusion/"lightheaded," gastrointestinal intolerance, tremor
Clonazepam	—	Dependence, sedation/confusion, withdrawal symptoms with abrupt discontinuation

*Different side effect profile; see text.
†Intramuscular preparation only; has been used sublingually.

has led to the concept of neuroaugmentation, with no destruction, and electrical stimulation of inhibitory systems or administration of neurotransmitter analogues. Stimulation of peripheral nerves, spinal cord, and deep brain (usually thalamus) have been described, with most information available on spinal cord stimulation (SCS). Unfortunately, there is a significant loss of response with SCS over time, with at best 65% of patients responding initially [39] and only one third of those responders achieving 50% relief in a 5-year follow-up [40]. There is no literature on peripheral nerve stimulation for phantom pain, but this procedure would only be reasonable for a single nerve source of pain without prolonged response to blocks at the excision site or the excision of neuromas, if present. The use of deep brain stimulation also has been shown to decrease from 80% significant relief to 20% over time [41]; it would therefore seem that stimulation holds no significant advantage over ablation techniques regarding results over time, although side effects and complications should be less. There is no information on the long-term use of opioids, local anesthetics, or other medications by epidural or intrathecal catheter for the treatment of phantom pain, although opioids alone are generally not effective for patients with neuropathic pain.

I believe that patients should receive a trial of oral opioids before one of a spinal opioid.

CONCLUSIONS

Best results appear to be achieved with the early use of aggressive management. Perioperative analgesia, including sympathetic block (*eg*, epidural local anesthetics) can help reduce long-term phantom pain. Patients should be questioned early as to the presence of phantom pain and be reassured that many patients feel it. Calcitonin should be administered early if phantom pain occurs. Physical therapy, TENS, and psychological techniques should be provided if calcitonin use is ineffective; if specific nerves seem involved, trigger-point or excision-site nerve blocks may help.

Chronic phantom pain is much more difficult to treat, with nonmedical and noninvasive treatment as effective as or more effective than invasive treatment. Careful consideration of a patient's psychological condition and ability to withstand failure, complications, or worsened pain should be made by a psychologist or psychiatrist before potentially damaging procedures are performed. "Above all, do no harm."

REFERENCES AND RECOMMENDED READING

Papers of interest, published recently, have been highlighted as:
• Of special interest
•• Of outstanding interest

1. Jamison K, Wellisch DK, Katz RL, *et al.*: Phantom breast syndrome. *Arch Surg* 1979, 114:93–95.

2. Melzack R: Phantom limbs and the concept of a neuromatrix. *Trends Neurosci* 1990, 13:88–92.

3. Riddoch G: Phantom limbs and body shape. *Brain* 1941, 64:197–222.

4. Sherman RA: Stump and phantom limb pain. *Neurol Clin* 1989, 7:250.

5. Nyström B, Hagbarth K-E: Microelectrode recordings from transected nerves in amputees with phantom limb pain. *Neurosci Lett* 1981, 27:211–216.

6. Bailey AA, Moersch FP: Phantom limb. *Can Med Assoc J* 1941, 45:37–42.

7. Sherman RA, Arena JG, Sherman CJ, *et al.*: The mystery of phantom pain: growing evidence for psychophysiological mechanisms. *Biofeedback Self Regul* 1989, 14:267–280.

8. Blankenbaker WL: The care of patients with phantom limb pain in a pain clinic. *Anesth Analg* 1977, 56:842–846.

9. Sherman RA: Published treatments of phantom limb pain. *Am J Phys Med* 1980, 59:232–241.

10. Omer GE Jr: Nerve, neuroma, and pain problems related to upper limb amputations. *Orthop Clin North Am* 1981, 12:751–762.

11. Melzack R, Loeser JD: Phantom body pain in paraplegics: evidence for a central "pattern generating mechanism" for pain. *Pain* 1978, 195–210.

12. Jensen TS, Borge K, Nielsen J, *et al.*: Immediate and long-term phantom limb pain in amputees: incidence, clinical characteristics and relationship to pre-amputation limb pain. *Pain* 1985, 21:267–278.

13. Wall R, Novotny-Joseph P, MacNamara TE: Does preamputation pain influence phantom limb pain in cancer patients? *South Med J* 1985, 78:34–36.

14. Parkes CM: Factors determining the persistence of phantom pain in the amputee. *J Psychosom Res* 1973, 17:97–108.

15. Sellick BC: Phantom limb pain and spinal anesthesia. *Anesthesiology* 1985, 62:801–802.

16. Mackenzie N: Phantom limb pain during spinal anaesthesia: recurrence in amputees. *Anaesthesia* 1983, 38:886–887.

17. Mihic DN, Pinkert E: Phantom limb pain during peridural anaesthesia. *Pain* 1981, 11:269–272.

18.• Jaeger H, Maier C: Calcitonin in phantom limb pain: a double-blind study. *Pain* 1992, 48:21–27.

This study found that calcitonin may be very effective when administered close to the onset of pain.

19. Kessel C, Wörz R: Clinical note: immediate response of phantom limb pain to calcitonin. *Pain* 1987, 30:79–87.

20. Bach S, Noreng MF, Tjéllden NU: Phantom limb pain in amputees during the first 12 months following limb amputation, after preoperative lumbar epidural blockade. *Pain* 1988, 33:297–301.

21. Rosenblatt RM: Phantom limb pain. In *Practical Management of Pain*. Edited by Raj PP. Chicago: Mosby-Year Book Medical; 1986.

22. Sherman RA, Sherman CJ: Prevalence and characteristics of chronic phantom limb pain among American veterans: results of a trial survey. *Am J Phys Med* 1983, 62:227–238.

23. Sherman RA, Sherman CA, Call NG: A survey of current phantom limb pain treatment in the United States. *Pain* 1980, 8:85–99.

24. Shealy CN: Transcutaneous electrical stimulation for control of pain. *Clin Neurosurg* 1974, 21:269–277.

25. Long DM: Cutaneous afferent stimulation for relief of chronic pain. *Clin Neurosurg* 1974, 21:257–268.

26. Carabelli RA, Kellerman WC: Phantom limb pain: relief by application of TENS to contralateral extremity. *Arch Phys Med Rehabil* 1985, 66:466–467.

27. Levine JD, Gormley J, Fields HL: Observations on the analgesic effects of needle puncture (acupuncture). *Pain* 1976, 2:149–159.

28. Patterson JF: Carbamazepine in the treatment of phantom limb pain. *South Med J* 1988, 81:1100–1102.

29. Logan TP: Persistent phantom limb pain: dramatic response to chlorpromazine. *South Med J* 1983, 76:1585.

30. Urban BJ, France RD, Steinberger EK, *et al.*: Long-term use of narcotic/antidepressant medication in the management of phantom limb pain. *Pain* 1986, 24:191–196.

31. Marsland AR, Weeks JW, Atkinson RL, *et al.*: Phantom limb pain: a case for beta blockers? *Pain* 1982, 12:295–297.

32. Fanciullacci M, Bene ED, Francchi G, *et al.*: Phantom limb pain: sub-hallucinogenic treatment with lysergic acid diethylamide (LSD-25). *Headache* 1977, 17:118–119.

33. Monks R: Psychotropic drugs. In *The Management of Pain*. Edited by Bonica J. Philadelphia: Lea & Febiger; 1990.

34.•• Hord A: Phantom Pain. In *The Practical Management of Pain, Second Edition*. Edited by Raj PP. St. Louis: Mosby-Year Book; 1992.

An excellent review of neuralgic medications and evidence for their use. Trigger-point or neuroma injection with local anesthetic and corticosteroids or with neuralytic agents may help some patients.

35. Arner S, Meyerson BA: Lack of analgesic effect of opioids on neuropathic and idiopathic forms of pain. *Pain* 1988, 33:11–23.

36. Sherman RA, Sherman CJ, Parker L: Chronic phantom and stump pain among American veterans: results of a survey. *Pain* 1984, 18:83–95.

37. Gorski DW, Chinthagada M, Rao TLK, *et al.*: Epidural meperidine for phantom limb pain. *Reg Anaesth* 1982, 7:39–41.

38. Saris SC, Iacono RP, Nashold BS, Jr: Successful treatment of phantom pain with dorsal root entry zone coagulation. *Appl Neurophysiol* 1988, 51:188–197.

39. Krainick JU, Thoden U, Riechert T: Spinal cord stimulation in post-amputation pain. *Surg Neurol* 1975, 4:167–170.

40. Krainick JU, Thoden U, Riechert T: Pain reduction in amputees by long-term spinal cord stimulation: long-term follow-up study over 5 years. *J Neurosurg* 1980, 52:346–350.

41. Levy RM, Lamb S, Adams JE: Treatment of chronic pain by deep brain stimulation: long-term follow-up and review of the literature. *Neurosurgery* 1987, 21:885–893.

CHAPTER 17

Management of Chronic Headaches

SEYMOUR DIAMOND

The impact of chronic pain, particularly chronic headache, on the economy is staggering. Expenditures for pain relief have been estimated at over 10 billion dollars worldwide. This fiscal maelstrom should give impetus to continued research into newer methods of treating chronic headache.

Epidemiologic studies of the incidence of all types of headache have increased during the past decade. Estimates have set the number of US citizens experiencing headache at approximately 60 to 70 million. The National Institutes of Health has supported population surveys in Washington County, Maryland. Linet's group [1] conducted a survey of 15,000 households, to which a self-administered questionnaire was forwarded. The first mailing generated responses from 20,468 subjects (63.4% response rate). The final data compilation involved 10,169 residents, aged 12 through 29 years. A headache occurring in the previous 4 weeks was reported by 57.1% of the males and 76.5% of the females. A chronic pattern of four or more headaches in the prior month was reported by 6.1% of the males and 14.0% of the females. If these numbers are representative of most communities, headache is indeed one of the most prevalent disorders in the world.

These numbers also exhort the medical professions to continue aggressive research into the pathogenesis of chronic headaches and the development of newer, effective therapies. As with other forms of chronic pain, two complications can be observed in patients with chronic headache—depression and dependency on analgesics, tranquilizers, and sedatives. Determining the correct diagnosis and selecting appropriate therapy may prevent these two scenarios.

CHRONIC CLUSTER HEADACHES
Diagnosis

The clinical presentation of chronic cluster headache is similar to that of the episodic cluster headache. Cluster headache gained its name because of the periodicity of its occurrence, that is in series or "cluster periods." These clusters are separated by periods of remission lasting several months to years. However, some unfortunate patients will experience these headaches without any periods of remission, or with remission periods of less than 15 days [2].

Cluster headache is noted for its unilateral appearance, usually localized behind or around one eye (Fig. 17-1). The acute pain is very severe, and may be depicted as a burning sensation or as a "knife-like pain" in the eye. The severity is so intense that patients have considered suicide during a cluster series. Acute cluster headache is identified by its short duration, usually lasting from 30 minutes to 4 hours. In contrast to migraine (Fig. 17-2), in which the patient prefers to be quiet and lying down, the pain is of such severity that the patient prefers standing or walking.

Nausea and vomiting rarely occur during an acute cluster attack. Cluster attacks are associated with partial Horner's syndrome, ptosis and miosis, flushing or blanching of the face, conjunctival injection, nasal congestion or rhinorrhea, and ipsilateral lacrimation. The associated symptoms are always unilateral, and the side of the headache usually remains the same during a cluster series.

In addition to the absence of the remission periods, chronic cluster headaches characteristically are refractory to conventional forms of prophylactic therapy. Approximately 50% of patients with this type of cluster headache have never experienced a remission from the attacks.

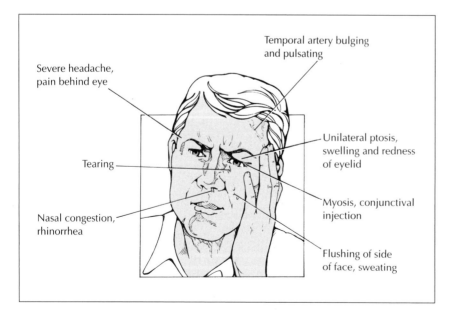

Temporal artery bulging and pulsating

Severe headache, pain behind eye

Unilateral ptosis, swelling and redness of eyelid

Tearing

Myosis, conjunctival injection

Nasal congestion, rhinorrhea

Flushing of side of face, sweating

Figure 17-1 Common clinical manifestations of a cluster headache. (*Adapted from* Netter, CIBA Pharmaceutical Company; with permission.)

Pharmacologic Therapy

Acute attacks are difficult to treat because of their short duration. Parenteral analgesics are often precluded as the headache may have disappeared by the time the patient has arrived at the physician's office or emergency room. Therapies used in the abortive therapy for episodic cluster may be considered in the treatment of acute pain in chronic cluster headaches. Administering 100% oxygen inhalation by face mask at 7 liters per minute for 10 to 15 minutes has been used successfully for aborting the acute cluster headache [3].

Ergotamine preparations may also be used at the onset of the acute attack. Patients may be taught the self-injection of dihydroergotamine, to be used at the first signs of an acute cluster headache. The intranasal application of lidocaine [4] or cocaine [5] has also demonstrated efficacy in treating the acute headaches. The solutions are applied to the sphenopalatine fossa region for 15 seconds to 3 minutes. Dependency problems have not been demonstrated with these therapies. Investigations are ongoing into the use of sumatriptan in acute cluster headaches [6••]. Patients are taught self-injection of sumatriptan, used subcutaneously at the onset of acute pain [7].

Prophylactic therapies prescribed in patients with episodic cluster are not indicated in chronic cluster headaches because of the prolonged nature of these headaches. Methysergide and the corticosteroids are the agents of choice in episodic cluster headaches but are precluded in chronic cluster because of the risks associated with long-term therapy [8••].

Ekbom [9] has reported on the successful use of lithium carbonate in chronic cluster headache. The method of action of lithium carbonate is not fully understood, but it has been suggested that lithium alters the electrical conductivity in the central nervous system. Lithium inhibits the action of the antidiuretic hormone, thereby affecting the metabolism of sodium, calcium, and magnesium, and reduces the REM stage of sleep. Serum lithium levels must be obtained at regular intervals and should be maintained between 0.7 to 1.2 mEq/L to prevent toxicity. Transient effects may occur such as thirst, polyuria, fatigue, and tremor. Persistent nausea and vomiting as well as blurred vision and fasciculation may occur, and could progress to movement disorders and convulsions. Some diuretics, as well as indomethacin and diclofenac, impede lithium elimination.

The calcium channel blockers have also been used for the prophylaxis of chronic cluster headaches. The effect of these agents in cluster is probably not attributable to vascular dilation. The probable mechanism is blockade of the release of the pain-inducing neurotransmitters, such as substance P, which is considered a factor in the pathogenesis of cluster. Substance P is dependent on calcium for its release. Verapamil [10] and nimodipine have demonstrated efficacy in some cases of chronic cluster headaches [11].

Histamine desensitization in cluster headaches was introduced by Horton [12] in 1939 but has never gained widespread use for cluster prophylaxis. Patients receive intravenous infusions of a solution of histamine phosphate, 2.75 mg in 250 mL of normal saline or D_5W, and

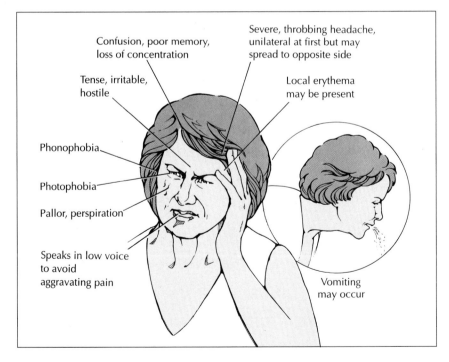

Figure 17-2 Common clinical manifestations of a migraine attack. (*Adapted from Netter, CIBA Pharmaceutical Company; with permission.*)

5.5 mg in 500 mL of the same solution on successive days. This therapy is best undertaken in an inpatient setting where the patient can be closely monitored for reactions during treatment. Patients whose headaches were refractory to other forms of therapy have experienced beneficial responses to intravenous histamine desensitization [13]; however, this procedure should only be considered for headaches refractory to conventional agents.

Surgical intervention should only be considered for chronic cluster headache that has been refractory to all other forms of treatment [14]. Some surgical procedures used for chronic cluster headaches have been discarded, including resection of the greater superficial petrosal nerve, section of the nervous intermedius, and ablation of the sphenopalatine ganglion. The surgical procedures now considered for chronic cluster headaches focus on the trigeminal region. These methods include partial trigeminal root section through a posterior approach, percutaneous radiofrequency gangliorhizolysis, posterior fossa trigeminal sensory rhizotomy, glycerol injections of the trigeminal cistern, and thermal trigeminal rhizotomy.

TENSION-TYPE HEADACHES

Diagnosis

The origins of tension-type headaches are considered to be manifestations in response to stress, depression, anxiety, emotional conflict, fatigue, repressed hostility, or simply the creation of an environment too overwhelming for the patient to handle. Episodic tension-type headaches are experienced by almost everyone. These headaches occur infrequently and are easily managed by over-the-counter analgesics. Patients with episodic tension-type headaches will rarely consult a physician unless the acute headache is not responding to routine analgesics or the severity of the headache is severely affecting functioning.

The distinguishing feature between episodic and chronic tension-type headache is the continuous, daily, or almost daily pattern of occurrence. Its frequency has been established as at least 15 days a month. These headaches are more inclined to occur during adulthood when the patient is more susceptible to frustration over daily stress. The sex distribution of chronic tension-type headaches demonstrates a female dominance.

Most patients note that the pain location is variable, presenting at the forehead and temples, or at the back of the head and neck. In contrast to migraine, these headaches are usually bilateral, involving the frontal, temporal, occipital, or parietal regions, or any combination of these sites. Despite the variations in sites and degrees of severity, patients with prolonged headache histories may note that the pain has remained localized in one region, with varying intensity, for weeks, months, or even years.

The pain of these headaches is often depicted as a steady, nonpulsatile ache. Patients may also describe the acute pain as viselike pressure, drawing, soreness, tightness at the temporal or occipital areas, and band-like sensations about the head that may be termed a "hatband" effect. Combing or brushing the hair, or putting on a hat may exacerbate the pain (Fig. 17-3). These headaches characteristically are continuous, although the pain may increase in intensity at times.

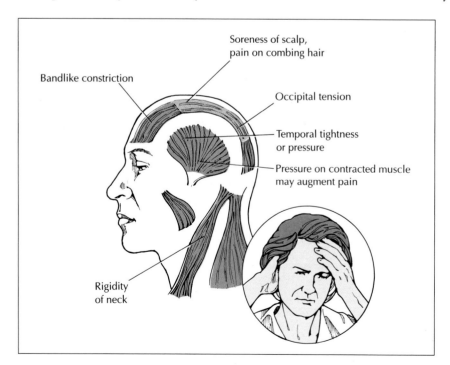

Figure 17-3 Common clinical manifestations of a tension-type headache. (*Adapted from* Netter, CIBA Pharmaceutical Company; with permission.)

Soreness of scalp, pain on combing hair

Bandlike constriction

Occipital tension

Temporal tightness or pressure

Pressure on contracted muscle may augment pain

Rigidity of neck

Sharply localized "nodules" may be palpated during physical examination of the neck, head, and upper back. Applying pressure on contracted, tender muscles may increase the severity of the headache. Also, this technique may trigger tinnitus, vertigo, and lacrimation, and may cause the pain to radiate to other parts of the head. The headaches may also be aggravated by shivering from exposure to the cold.

In diagnosing chronic tension-type headaches, the physician should be cognizant that these headaches may obscure a serious emotional disorder, such as anxiety or depression. Many patients are convinced that their headaches are caused by an organic disorder. Also, the headaches are more socially acceptable than are symptoms of anxiety or depression.

As part of the initial evaluation, the physician should attempt to obtain a detailed psychological inventory. Because many patients are uncomfortable relating these intimate details, the interview process may require several visits before completion. The inventory should include questions regarding the patient's marital relations, occupation, social relationships, life stresses, personality traits, habits, methods of coping with stressful situations, and sexual difficulties.

HEADACHES CAUSED BY ANXIETY

Diagnosis
The patient with tension-type headache caused by an underlying anxiety can be differentiated from the patient with depression by the type of sleep disturbance the patient is experiencing. Unlike the depressed patient, the patient with anxiety will complain of difficulty falling asleep. These patients will present with a daily and persistent headache, which is not disabling but may be described as annoying. Associated symptoms, such as nausea and vomiting, are not identified with this type of headache. During the interview, the patient with anxiety will implicate job complaints, general anxiety, or being overwhelmed with too many tasks as the cause of the headaches.

Therapy
The treatment of patients with chronic tension-type headaches resulting from anxiety is multifaceted. The physician will need to reassure the patient that the headaches are not a result of an organic disease or severe psychiatric disorder [15•]. By listening attentively and demonstrating an interested attitude during the initial interview, the physician can establish the rapport needed for successful treatment. Many patients with chronic headaches caused by anxiety do not need to be referred to a headache specialist because they can be easily managed by the primary physician. Some patients may require a psychiatric referral.

Owing to the chronic nature of the headaches, it is essential that the physician avoid prescribing habituating analgesics or sedatives. The long-term use of benzodiazepines is precluded in these patients because of the potential for dependency problems. Nonhabituating anxiolytic agents may be considered if stress or anxiety factors affect the headache problem. For example, the patient may benefit greatly from buspirone, which is a $5HT_1A$ serotonin receptor-partial agonist. Buspirone has a low potential for sedation, estimated at 10%, whereas placebo has demonstrated this effect at 9%. Prolonged therapy with buspirone has not demonstrated dependency problems.

HEADACHES CAUSED BY DEPRESSION

Diagnosis
Chronic tension-type headaches resulting from depression are often misdiagnosed and frequently treated inappropriately. Patients with these headaches do not present as classically depressed patients with the characteristic sad look, slow speech and movement, and absent affect.

During the initial interview, the physician should be aware of other signs of depression. Emotional complaints include feeling "blue," anxiety, and rumination over the past, present, and future. Patients may provide long lists of physical complaints in addition to the headache, such as sleep disturbances, severe insomnia and early awakening, appetite changes, and anorexia and rapid weight loss. A decrease in sexual activity may occur, ranging at times to impotence in males and amenorrhea or frigidity in females. Psychic complaints may be vague, with the patient noting that "morning is the worst time of the day." The patient may have considered suicide.

The headache associated with depression is usually described as a steady, nonpulsatile ache, often distributed in a band-like pattern around the head. Patients may depict the pain as viselike, a steady pressure, a weight, soreness, or a distinct cramp-like sensation. The depression headache is usually dull and generalized, characteristically worse in the morning and in the evening. This diurnal variation provides the most distinctive characteristic of the headache and has aided in establishing a correct diagnosis of severe depression when other features have been obscure. To further impede identifying the diagnosis, these headaches follow no definite pattern in regard to location, although pain is often noted at the occiput. Typically, the headache is described as continuous and as lasting for several years. Some patients will note that they do not remember a time when they did not have headaches.

The patient will relate that the headaches usually appear at regular intervals, occurring on weekends,

Sundays, or holidays, and on the first days of vacation or after examinations. Tension-type headaches most often occur from 4:00 PM to 8:00 PM and from 4:00 AM to 8:00 AM, usually the periods of the greatest and sometimes the most silent family crises. It is not unusual for the headaches to occur early in the morning, when the depressed patient awakens and fantasies of conflict with family members or at work are manifested. The headaches often occur when the patient leaves the relatively quiet atmosphere of the office for a weekend at home. Certain interpersonal situations may greatly affect the occurrence of the headache. The sufferer may feel compelled to appear comfortable, relaxed, and agreeable while struggling to repress resentment toward someone he or she is expected to love and respect.

The physical complaints often eclipse the situation and the underlying depression may be overlooked. These patients often manifest their depression in bodily symptoms and, conversely, people with painful organic diseases have a tendency to become depressed.

During the initial interview, the physician should determine if the patient has a prior history of depression or if a similar pattern has occurred in the family. The patient may relate obscure symptoms that are actually depressive equivalents. Also, the patient may relate the onset of the headaches to a particular event. These events may be remembered as traumatic or felt as a personal loss. The event may be viewed disproportionately to the severity of the resultant depression. The symptoms may be related to some form of bodily injury, an illness, an injection, surgery, or a diagnostic examination. The incident that precipitated the headache or other depressive equivalents would not be compatible with the illness or be as overwhelming as perceived.

The patient may also relate the headaches to a change in personal role, position, or socioeconomic status. Depression may be identified with the loss of a loved one, an event that may trigger a malignant depression beyond the scope of the loss. This loss may have a peculiar significance and be a very important facet within the personal scope of the individual.

In my clinical experience, the majority of depressed patients indicated that headache was one of their complaints or their only complaint [16]. Sleep disturbances may manifest as hypersomnia, insomnia, early awakening, or disturbing dreams. In depressed patients, the most common sleep disturbance is early awakening. Older patients experience more difficulty with sleep.

Therapy

Treatment for the patient with chronic tension-type headaches caused by depression focuses on antidepressant therapy. These agents are selected for both their antidepressant effects and their analgesic action [17].

The pain-control action of the antidepressants is attributed to their effects on the synthesis and metabolism of serotonin (5-hydroxytryptamine) and norepinephrine. The analgesia system of the brain consists of neurons found to contain serotonin and norepinephrine [18••]. Investigations by pain researchers have focused on identifying a descending serotonin pathway in the dorsal spinal cord, originating in the raphe nucleus, and an interlacing of norepinephrine and opioid neurons in the locus ceruleus [16]. Almost all antidepressants can alter the synthesis or uptake of serotonin or norepinephrine and would be expected to play a role in the brain's regulation of pain. Both opiate- and stimulation-induced analgesia are believed influenced by serotonin antagonists [19]. The tricyclic antidepressants produce analgesia directly or through potentiation of opiates [20].

The most popular biologic theories of depression hold that the disorder is associated with depletion of brain monoamine neurotransmitters such as serotonin and norepinephrine [21,22]. The discovery of endogenous, opiate-like substances in the brain, the endorphins and enkephalins, has significantly advanced our understanding of pain [23]. Recent findings suggest that pain transmission in the central nervous system is controlled by an endorphin-mediated analgesia system [24••]. This system can be activated by several exogenous actions, including opioid substances, electrical stimulation, acupuncture, and even placebo [25].

Tricyclic antidepressants are usually the drugs of choice in the treatment of chronic tension-type headaches caused by depression [26]. The choice of tricyclic agent is not simple because each drug has unique characteristics [27]. Table 17-1 reviews the various effects of the antidepressants and, in particular, the sedative effect of each of these drugs [28]. The presence of a sleep disturbance is a determining factor.

In headache prophylaxis, the most widely used tricyclic antidepressant is amitriptyline. Other tricyclic agents frequently used in headache therapy include doxepin, protriptyline, nortriptyline, trimipramine, and desipramine. Amitriptyline, doxepin, or nortriptyline in large, bedtime doses may be effective for those patients with early or frequent awakening. If the patient does not present with a sleep disturbance, desipramine or protriptyline should be considered. Protriptyline is the least sedating of this class of drugs, and the majority of the dose should be administered early in the morning.

Newer antidepressants are also available, such as trazodone. Trazodone has a very low profile for cardiovascular and anticholinergic effects, and drowsiness is the most commonly cited side effect. Persistent priapism has occasionally been reported with trazodone therapy [29]. A bicyclic antidepressant, fluoxetine, is much slower in action than the tricyclic antidepressants [30•]. However, it is associated with less adverse effects than are the tricyclic agents [31]. Maprotiline, another bicyclic, has effects similar to amitriptyline, doxepin, and nortriptyline. Bupropion hydrochloride is not related to the tricyclic agents [32•]. Amoxapine is an antidepressant of the dibenzoxazepine class with marked dopamine effects. It is not indicated in the treatment of chronic tension-type headaches because of its reported adverse effects, tardive dyskinesia, and neuroleptic malignant syndrome. We have found that two new antidepressants, sertraline and paroxetine, which have potent serotonin inhibition, demonstrated promising results in the therapy for these headaches.

The second line of drugs for depression are the monoamine oxidase inhibitors (MAOIs). These agents are not considered as effective as the tricyclic antidepressants. Their use is associated with more frequent drug interactions. It is essential that a patient receiving an MAOI is instructed regarding the tyramine-free diet that must be strictly followed (Table 17-2). Patients must also be cautioned about those drugs that cause potentially serious reactions with the MAOIs, including certain opiates and drugs with pressor agents.

The MAOIs block the oxidative deamination of numerous monoamines, including epinephrine, norepinephrine, serotonin, and dopamine. These substances are believed to be increased in the brain and other tissues. The use of the MAOIs relieves the depression caused by the deficiency of these substances. Because of the potential for serious drug interactions [33], the MAOIs should only be used in those patients refractory to conventional agents [34]. In studies comparing tricyclic agents and MAOIs, the MAOIs tended to exert a stronger antianxiety action, whereas the tricyclic agents were more effective in reversing weight loss and improving sleep [35].

Previously, the prescription of combination therapy with a tricyclic antidepressant and MAOI was not considered because of reports of fatalities caused by drug interactions. The two drugs were never given in combination. In 1971, Schuckit and coworkers [36] reviewed the 25 reported cases of morbidity secondary to combination therapy. Their results indicated that the risks of combination therapy had been greatly exaggerated, as many of the fatalities could be attributed to drug overdose. Other symptoms could be related to the concomitant use of other drugs that act on the central nervous system. In the remaining cases, the tricyclic agent involved was imipramine and the MAOIs included iproniazid, tranylcypromine, isocarboxazid, pargyline, and phenelzine.

Phenelzine is the most commonly used MAOI [37]. Isocarboxazid may also be used in these patients. It is essential that combined therapy with an MAOI and a tricyclic antidepressant only be attempted by physicians experienced with this therapy.

TABLE 17-1
EFFECTS OF ANTIDEPRESSANTS

DRUG	SEROTONIN INHIBITION	NOREPINEPHRINE INHIBITION	DOPAMINE INHIBITION	SEDATIVE EFFECTS	ANTICHOLINERGIC EFFECTS
Amitriptyline	Moderate	Weak	Inactive	Strong	Strong
Desipramine	Weak	Potent	Inactive	Mild	Moderate
Doxepin	Moderate	Moderate	Inactive	Strong	Strong
Imipramine	Fairly potent	Moderate	Inactive	Moderate	Strong
Nortriptyline	Weak	Fairly potent	Inactive	Mild	Moderate
Protriptyline	Weak	Fairly potent	Inactive	None	Strong
Trimipramine	Weak	Weak	Inactive	Moderate	Moderate
Amoxapine	Weak	Potent	Moderate	Mild	Mild
Trazodone	Fairly potent	Weak	Inactive	Strong	Mild
Fluoxetine	Potent	Weak	Inactive	None	Mild to none
Bupropion HCL	Weak	Weak	Weak	None	None
Maprotiline	Weak	Moderate	Inactive	Moderate	Moderate
Sertaline HCL	Potent	Weak	Weak	None	None
Paroxetine HCL	Potent	Weak	Weak	None	None

COEXISTING MIGRAINE AND TENSION-TYPE HEADACHES

Diagnosis

The patient with chronic headache most frequently seen by the headache specialist experiences coexisting migraine and tension-type headaches. Patients with these headaches will relate a history of the following symptoms: 1) daily, continuous headache; 2) a hard or sick headache (migraine) occurring one to 10 times monthly; and 3) easy susceptibility to habituation of over-the-counter or prescribed analgesics and to ergotamine tartrate [38].

TABLE 17-2
DIET FOR THE PATIENT WITH HEADACHE TAKING
MONOAMINE OXIDASE INHIBITORS

	FOODS ALLOWED	FOODS TO AVOID
Beverage	Decaffeinated coffee, fruit juice, club soda, noncola soda (*eg*, ginger ale); limit caffeine sources to 2 cups/d (coffee, tea, cola)	Chocolate, cocoa, alcoholic beverages, buttermilk
Meat, fish, poultry	Fresh or frozen: turkey, chicken, fish, beef, lamb, veal, pork; egg as meat substitute (limit 3 eggs/wk); tuna or tuna salad	Aged, canned, cured, or processed meat, including ham or game; pickled herring, salad, and dried fish; chicken livers, bologna, fermented sausage; any food prepared with meat tenderizer, soy sauce, or brewer's yeast; any food containing nitrates, nitrites, or tyramine
Dairy products	Milk: homogenized, 2%, or skim; cheese: american, cottage, farmer, ricotta, cream, processed cheese product; yogurt (limit 1/2 cup per day)	Cultured dairy products (buttermilk, sour cream); chocolate milk; cheese: bleu, Boursault, brick, Brie types, Camembert types, cheddar, Gouda, Stilton, Swiss, Roquefort, mozzarella, parmesan, provolone, romano
Bread, cereal	Commercial bread, English muffins, melba toast crackers, bagel; all hot and dry cereals	Hot fresh homemade yeast bread, bread or crackers containing cheese; fresh yeast coffee cake, doughnuts, sourdough bread; any product containing chocolate or nuts
Potato or substitute	White potato, sweet potato, rice, macaroni, spaghetti, noodles	None
Vegetable	Any except those to avoid	Beans such as pole, broad, lima, Italian, fava, navy, pinto, garbanzo; snow peas, pea pods, sauerkraut, onions (except for flavoring), olives, pickles
Fruit	Any except those to avoid; limit citrus fruits to 1/2 cup per day; limit banana to 1/2 per day	Avocados, figs, raisins, papaya, passion fruit, red plums
Soup	Cream soups made from foods allowed in diet; homemade broths	Canned soup, soup or bouillon cubes, soup base with autolytic yeast or monosodium glutamate (*read labels*)
Dessert	Fruit allowed in diet; any cake, pudding, cookies, or ice cream without chocolate or nuts; no yeast items; jello	Chocolate ice cream, pudding, cookies, cake, or pies; mincemeat pie, nuts, peanut butter
Sweets	Sugar, jelly, jam, honey, hard candy	Chocolate candy or syrup, carob
Miscellaneous	Salt in moderation, lemon juice, butter or margarine, cooking oil, whipped cream, white vinegar, and commercial salad dressings in small amounts	Pizza, cheese sauce, monosodium glutamate in excessive amounts, yeast, yeast extract, meat tenderizer, seasoned salt, mixed dishes (macaroni and cheese, beef stroganoff, cheese blintzes, lasagna), frozen TV dinners, marinated dishes

Therapy

It is vital that the diagnosis of this syndrome be established. As with other forms of chronic headache, the use of sedatives, tranquilizers, habituating analgesics, and narcotics must be strictly avoided to prevent dependency problems that thereby perpetuate the headache. Frequent use of the ergotamine preparations, without a 4-day hiatus between days of use, will result in the rebound phenomenon [39]. The use of ergotamine must be strictly restricted to relief of the hard or sick headache; it must never be used on a daily basis. Caffeine-containing analgesics, over-the-counter and prescribed, should be limited along with the patient's consumption of caffeine-containing beverages. When discontinuing the caffeine-containing agent, the patient may experience severe caffeine-withdrawal headaches.

If the patient is able to distinguish the acute migraine attacks from the daily headaches, the use of sumatriptan administered subcutaneously may be considered. Sumatriptan is a novel selective agent of 5-hydroxytryptamine–like receptors, which are theorized to be membranal "trigger" proteins with which 5-HT must interact to produce its various actions [40••]. The actions of 5-HT include dilation of certain cranial arteries or arteriovenous anastomoses by neurogenic dural plasma extravasation. Both of these mechanisms can trigger a migraine attack. Sumatriptan has been demonstrated to be a highly effective, rapid-acting, and well-tolerated abortive therapy for acute migraine attacks. This therapy should not be considered for patients experiencing more than eight acute migraine or "hard headaches" per month.

The nonsteroidal anti-inflammatory agents (NSAIDs) may be beneficial in relieving the daily headaches. The NSAIDs, such as ibuprofen, fenoprofen, naproxen sodium, diflunisal, and ketoprofen, have been used successfully in many patients with this syndrome.

The tricyclic agents or the MAOIs are the drugs of choice in the prophylactic treatment of coexisting migraine and tension-type headaches [41]. Combination therapy consisting of a tricyclic antidepressant and an MAOI may be indicated in the recidivist patient [42]. Ideally, this therapy should be initiated in an inpatient setting, and propranolol may be added to the regimen [43]. The long-acting form, in once-daily dosages, may enhance patient compliance, and the addition of an NSAID to the therapeutic regimen may be helpful.

The patient with coexisting migraine and tension-type headache may require a copharmacologic approach with several agents. Again, this therapy should only be initiated in an inpatient setting at which a patient can be carefully monitored. Continuity of care is essential in these patients.

CONCLUSION

The impact of chronic headaches on a patient's life, including work and family relationships, is startling. It is essential that the diagnosis be established to initiate appropriate therapy. Because of the chronicity of these headaches, any medication with a potential for habituation should be avoided. Many of these patients have consulted numerous physicians and have been tried on numerous therapies, with minimal or no response. Continuity of care is an integral part of the successful treatment of any form of chronic headache.

REFERENCES AND RECOMMENDED READING

Papers of interest, published recently, have been highlighted as:
• Of special interest
•• Of outstanding interest

1. Linet MS, Stewart WF, Celentano DD, *et al.*: An epidemiologic study of headache among adolescents and young adults. *JAMA* 1989, 261:221–226.

2. Olesen J: Classification and diagnostic criteria for headache disorders, cranial neuralgias and facial pain. *Cephalalgia* 1988, 8(suppl 7):1–96.

3. Kudrow L: Cluster headache: diagnosis, management, and treatment. In *Wolff's Headache and Other Head Pain, Fifth Edition.* Edited by Dalessio DJ. New York: Oxford University Press; 1987:112–130.

4. Kitrelle JP, Grouse DS, Seybold ME: Cluster headache, local anesthetic abortive agents. *Arch Neurol* 1985, 42:496–498.

5. Barre F: Cocaine as an abortive agent in cluster headache. *Headache* 1982, 22:69–73.

6.•• Ekbom K: Subcutaneous sumatriptan in acute cluster headache. [editorial]. *Headache Quart* 1992, 3:260–261.

In a concise manner, Ekbom reviews recent European studies on the use of sumatriptan in acute headache. He observes that sumatriptan, administered subcutaneously in an auto-injector preparation, should be considered for acute attacks of cluster headache. Ekbom edited the article by the Sumatriptan Cluster Headache Study Group (1991) which details the multicenter investigations of this agent in the indication of cluster headache.

7. Sumatriptan Cluster Headache Study Group: treatment of acute cluster headache with sumatriptan. *N Engl J Med* 1991, 325:322–326.

8.•• Diamond S, Dalessio DJ: Cluster headaches. In *The Practicing Physician's Approach to the Headache Patient.* Edited by Diamond S, Dalessio DJ. Baltimore: Williams & Wilkins; 1992:80–92.

This latest edition of an internationally recognized textbook on headache contains updated information on classification, diagnostic procedures, and treatments. The newest agents available for cluster headache therapy are detailed.

9. Ekbom K: Litium vid kroniska symptom av cluster headache. *Preliminart Meddelande Pousc Med* 1974, 19:148–156.

10. Gabai IJ, Spierings ELH: Prophylactic treatment of cluster headache with verapamil. *Headache* 1989, 29:167–168.

11. Ekbom K: Treatment of cluster headache in Europe. *Headache Quart* 1990, 1:65–70.

12. Horton BT, Maclean AR, Craig W McK: A new syndrome of vascular headache: Results of treatment with histamine: preliminary report. *Proc Staff Meeting Mayo Clin* 1939, 14:257–260.

13. Diamond S, Freitag FG, Prager J, *et al.*: Treatment of intractable cluster. *Headache* 1986, 26:42–46.

14. Sweet WH: Surgical treatment of chronic cluster headache. *Headache* 1988, 28:669–670.

15.• Glass DE: Tension headache and some psychiatric aspects. *Headache Quart* 1992, 3:280.

The focus of this review is the psychiatric aspect to tension-type headache, and the impact of these factors on treatment. Various characterizations are offered to facilitate an understanding of these features.

16. Diamond S: Migraine and depression. In *New Advances in Headache Research.* Edited by Rose FC. London: Smith-Gordon; 1989:291–300.

17. Fields HL: Pain II: new approaches to management. *Ann Neurol* 1981, 9:101–106.

18.•• Kantor TG: Pharmacology and mechanisms of some pain relieving drugs. *Headache Quart* 1993, 4:57–62.

This review article provides exceptional descriptions of the various NSAIDs used in chronic pain therapy. The individual NSAID groups are delineated and will facilitate prescribing these agents.

19. Messing RB, Lytle LD: Serotonin-containing neurons: their possible role in pain and analgesia. *Pain* 1977, 4:1–21.

20. Malseed RT, Goldstein FJ: Enhancement of morphine analgesia by tricyclic antidepressants. *Neuropharmacology* 1979, 18:827–829.

21. Maas JW, Kocsis JH, Bowden CD, *et al.*: Pretreatment neurotransmitter metabolites and response to imipramine or amitriptyline treatment. *Psychol Med* 1982, 12:37–41.

22. Roy A, Picker D, DeJong J, *et al.*: Norepinephrine and its metabolites in cerebrospinal fluid, plasma, and urine. *Arch Gen Psychiatr* 1988, 45:849–857.

23. Basbaum AI, Fields HL: Endogenous pain control mechanisms: review and hypothesis. *Ann Neurol* 1992, 4:451–462.

24.•• Yazici O, Ariciohlu F, Gürvit G, *et al.*: Noradrenergic and serotoninergic depression? *J Affective Disorders* 1993, 27:123–129.

The latest research and developments into chronic depression are presented. This article enhances our understanding of depression and will assist the physician in selecting appropriate therapies.

25. Mayer DJ, Price DD: Central nervous system mechanisms of analgesia. *Pain* 1976, 3:1.

26. Feighner JP: Pharmacological management of depression. *Fam Pract Recert* 1982, 4(suppl 1):13–24.

27. Cobbin DM, Requin-Blow B, Williams LR, *et al.*: Urinary MHPG levels and tricyclic antidepressant drug selection. *Arch Gen Psychiatr* 1979, 36:1111–1115.

28. Saarnivaara L, Mattila MJ: Comparison of tricyclic antidepressants in rabbits: antinociception and potentiation of the noradrenalin pressor responses. *Psychopharmacologia* 1974, 35:221–236.

29. Scher M, Krieger JN, Juergens S: Trazodone and priapism. *Am J Psychiatr* 1983, 140:1362–1363.

30.• Bittman B, Emanuele S: Fluoxetine: side effects and efficacy in a headache population. *Headache Quart* 1992, 3:82–85.

The authors provide a historical and media review of fluoxetine, in the light of the poor press it has received in recent years. They also describe their investigation into its use in headache patients. The results of their study suggest that fluoxetine can be safely used in patients with chronic headache.

31. Diamond S: The use of fluoxetine in the treatment of headache. [letter]. *Clin J Pain* 1989, 5:200–201.

32.• Goodnick PJ, Sandoval R, Brickman A, *et al.*: Bupropion treatment of fluoxetine-resistant chronic fatigue syndrome. *Biol Psychiatr* 1992, 32:834–838.

These authors examine the use of a new antidepressant, bupropion, for an indication other than headache. However, their findings may impact on the use of this agent in chronic pain states, including headache.

33. Gelenberg AJ: Adverse reactions to MAO inhibitors. *Biol Ther Psychiatr* 1985, 8:1–4.

34. Diamond S, Freitag FG: The long-term use of monoamine oxidase inhibitors in the management of headache. In *New Advances in Headache Research.* Edited by Rose FC. London: Smith-Gordon; 1989:301–304.

35. Ravaris C, Ravaris CL, Robinson DS, *et al.*: Phenelzine and amitriptyline in treatment of depression: a comparison of present and past studies. *Arch Gen Psychiatr* 1980, 37:1057–1080.

36. Schuckit M, Robins E, Feighner J, *et al.*: Tricyclic antidepressants and monoamine oxidase inhibitors. *Arch Gen Psychiatr* 1971, 24:509–514.

37. Robinson DS, Nies A, Ravaris CL, *et al.*: The monoamine oxidase inhibitor, phenelzine, in the treatment of depressive-anxiety states: a controlled clinic trial. *Arch Gen Psychiatr* 1973, 29:407–413.

38. Diamond S, Freitag FG: The mixed headache syndrome: a review. *Clin J Pain* 1988, 4:67–74.

39. Klapper JA: Rebound headache: definition, symptomatology, treatment, and prevention. *Headache Quart* 1992, 3:398–403.

40.•• Cady RK, Wendt JK, Kirchner JR, *et al.*: Treatment of acute migraine with subcutaneous sumatriptan. *JAMA* 1991, 265:2831–2835.
This article serves as an excellent resource on the use of sumatriptan in acute attacks of migraine. It provides insight into the appropriate doses and the potential for side effects. Any physician starting to administer sumatriptan via subcutaneous injection should review this citation.

41. Freitag FG, Diamond S, Solomon GD: Antidepressants in the treatment of mixed headache: MAO inhibitors and combined use of MAO inhibitors and tricyclic antidepressants in the recidivist headache patient. In *Advances in Headache Research*. Edited by Rose FC. London: John Libbey; 1987:271–275.

42. Sandyk R, Iacono RP: Phenelzine and migraine headaches. *Int J Neurosci* 1987, 35:243.

43. Pfaffenrath V, Kellhamer U, Pollman W: Combination headache: practical experience with a combination of a beta-blocker and an antidepressive. *Cephalalgia* 1986, 1 (suppl 5):25–32.

INDEX

Acetaminophen, 80–81, 81f
  in cancer, 160t
  in pediatric patients, 96
Acetylcholine, in nociception modulation, 21
Acetylsalicylic acid, in herpes zoster, 216
Acupuncture
  in phantom pain, 227
  in postherpetic neuralgia, 220, 220f
Acute pain
  analgesia in *see* Analgesia
  anger in, 26
  anxiety in, 26
  assessment of *see* Assessment
  cardiac function in, 23, 30–31
  characteristics of, 18
  vs. chronic pain, 39, 39t
  classification of, 24
  definition of, 18
  depression in, 26
  frustration in, 26
  irritability in, 26
  management of, 48–60
    brachial plexus block in, 49–50, 49f–50f
    chronic pain prevention in, 62–65, 64f
    delivery techniques for, 53–54, 54f
    epidural analgesia in, 51–52, 55–56
    intercostal nerve block in, 48, 48f
    interpleural analgesia in, 48–49, 48f
    intraspinal opioids in, 52–54, 52t, 53f–54f, 56–57
    intrathecal analgesia in, 51–52, 56–57
    lower extremity block in, 50–51, 50f–51f
    outcome studies of, 55–57
    peripheral nerve blocks in, 57
    preemptive analgesia in, 54
  neuroendocrine responses in, 21
  neuropathic, 24–25, 25f
  nociception in, 24
    initiation of, 18–19, 18f
    modulation of, 20–21, 22f
    propagation of, 19–21, 19f
  pathophysiology of, 18–22, 18f–19f, 22f–23f
  in pediatric patients, 94–102
    assessment of, 94–95, 95t
    behavioral treatment of, 95–96
    nonopioid drugs in, 96
    opioids in, 96–98, 97t
    physiologic cost of, 94
    regional analgesia in, 98–100, 99f, 100t
    treatment of, 95–100, 97t, 99f, 100t
  peripheral vascular system function in, 24
  psychogenic, 25–26
  pulmonary function in, 23–24, 23f, 31, 31f
  vital organs affected by, 23–24, 23f
Acyclovir, in herpes zoster, 62, 215, 217
Adenosine, receptors for, in nociception modulation, 21, 22f

Adenosine monophosphate, in herpes zoster, 215
Adjuvants, analgesic, 81–82, 167–168, 167t
Adrenergic receptors, in nociception modulation, 20–21
Adrenergic sensitization, in neuropathic pain, 7
Adriamycin, in neuropathic pain, 191
Aerobic exercise, 138
Afferent neurons
  activation of, 18–20, 18f–19f
  in after-responses, 4–6, 4f
  alterations of, in reflex sympathetic dystrophy, 197
After-responses, in painful stimulation, 4–6, 4f–5f
Alcohol, in neurolytic block, 65
  celiac plexus, 170
  intrathecal, 66, 69, 69f
  in postherpetic neuralgia, 219
  subarachnoid, 170, 171f
Alfentanil, liposome encapsulated, 89
Algoneurodystrophy *see* Reflex sympathetic dystrophy
Alizapride, in opioid-induced emesis, 163t
Allodynia
  definition of, 25
  mechanical, 8–9
  mechanisms of, 6, 8–9
  in postherpetic neuralgia, 218
  in reflex sympathetic dystrophy, 199, 199f
Alpha-adrenergic agents
  in neuropathic pain, 191
  in reflex sympathetic dystrophy, 204
Alpha-adrenergic agonists, as adjuvant analgesics, 82
Amino acids, excitatory, in nociception, 20
Amitriptyline
  as adjuvant analgesic, 167t
  in cancer, 167t
  in causalgia, 205
  in depression, 236, 237t
  in myofascial pain syndrome, 144
  in postherpetic neuralgia, 219
Ammonium compounds, in nerve block, in postherpetic neuralgia, 219–220
Amoxapine, in depression, 237, 237t
Amputation, phantom pain after, 226–229, 226f, 228t
Analgesia
  absorption of, 85
  in acute vs. chronic pain, 88–89
  adjuvants with, 81–82, 167–168, 167t
  administration routes for, 82–88, 83f–84f
    inhalational, 87
    intramuscular, 85
    intravenous, 86–87, 86f, 167
    oral, 85
    rectal, 88, 167
    subcutaneous, 85–86, 163–164, 164t
    transdermal, 87, 87t, 167
    transmucosal, 88, 167
  in benign vs. cancer pain, 89

Analgesia, *continued*
  bioavailability of, 85
  brachial plexus, postoperative, 49–50, 49f–50f
  in cancer pain
      vs. benign pain, 89
      see also Cancer pain, treatment of
  in chronic vs. acute pain, 88–89
  clinical applications of, 88–89
  combined agents for, 30, 30f, 80–81, 81f
  epidural *see* Epidural analgesia
  in herpes zoster, 215–216
  interpleural, 48–49, 48f
  intrathecal *see* Intrathecal analgesia
  iontophoresis in, 87
  local, systemic use of, 82
  nerve block in *see* Nerve block
  for neuroma, 57
  parent-controlled, in pediatric patients, 98
  patient-controlled *see* Patient-controlled analgesia
  pharmacokinetics in, 84–85
  postoperative, vs. preoperative, 89
  subarachnoid, 56–57, 165–167, 166t
  targeted delivery of, 89–90
  therapeutic window in, 83–84
  see also Nonsteroidal anti-inflammatory drugs; Opioids;
      specific drugs
Analogue chromatic continuous scale, in pain assessment, 94
Anesthesia
  epidural, thoracic, cardiopulmonary effects of, 30–31
  local
      as adjuvant analgesic, 167t, 168
      in cancer, 167t, 168
      in neuropathic pain, 191
      in reflex sympathetic dystrophy, 200–201, 201f, 203–204, 203f
      systemic use of, 82
  in postherpetic neuralgia, 218
  regional
      pulmonary effects of, 31
      in reflex sympathetic dystrophy, 204
Anesthesia dolorosa, in retrogasserian rhizotomy, 111
Anger
  perioperative, 26
  psychogenic pain in, 26
Antacids, with NSAIDs, 159
Anticipatory pain, in exercise, 136
Anticonvulsants
  as adjuvant analgesics, 82, 167t, 168
  in cancer, 167t, 168
  in neuropathic pain, 191
  in phantom pain, 227, 228t
  in postherpetic neuralgia, 219
Antidepressants
  as adjuvant analgesics, 81–82, 167t, 168
  in cancer, 167t, 168
  in causalgia, 205
  in headache, 236–237, 237t, 239
  in herpes zoster, 216
  in myofascial pain syndrome, 144
  in neuropathic pain, 191

Antidepressants, *continued*
  in phantom pain, 227, 228t
  in postherpetic neuralgia, 219
Antihistamines, as adjuvant analgesics, 82
Antiviral agents, in herpes zoster, 215
Anxiety
  headache in, 235
  perioperative, 26
  in postherpetic neuralgia, 220
  psychogenic pain in, 26
Anxiolytics, in postherpetic neuralgia, 219
Arachidonic acid metabolites, in nociception, 19
Aspartate, in nociception, 20
Aspirin, 80
  in cancer, 160t
Assessment, pain, 26–30
  analogue chromatic continuous scale in, 94
  behavioral scales in, 95
  body outlines in, 29, 30f
  in cancer, 159
  in children, 29–30, 29f–30f
  Faces Rating Scale in, 29, 29f, 94
  importance of, 26, 43
  inaccuracy in, 26
  McGill Pain Questionnaire in, 28–29, 28f, 45
  numerical rating score in, 29
  objective pain scale in, 95, 95t
  Oucher Scale in, 29, 29f, 94
  pain slide rule in, 94
  patient evaluation in, 44–45
  in pediatric patients, 94–95, 95t
  physiologic data in, 44
  physiologic scales in, 95
  poker chip tool in, 94
  psychologic data in, 44
  verbal pain scales in, 27–28
  Visual Analogue Scale in, 26–27, 27f, 29, 44–45, 94
Astrocytes, 184f
Atelectasis, postoperative, 23
Autonomic nervous system
  activity of, in myofascial pain syndrome, 143
  see also Reflex sympathetic dystrophy; Sympathetic
      nervous system
Axillary catheter, in brachial plexus block, 49–50, 49f
Axon(s), 180f, 181
  injury of, neuropathic pain in, 188–189
  regeneration of, 186–187, 187f
Axonotmesis, neuron response in, 186, 187f
Axoplasmic transport, in neuropathic pain, 191

B ack pain
  bed rest in, 135–136
  exercises for, 138
  intractable, neurosurgical procedures in, 105t, 107–110, 108f–109f,
      110t–111t
Baclofen, in phantom pain, 227, 228t
Balloon microcompression, in trigeminal neuralgia, 112–113
Bed rest, adverse effects of, 135–136

Behavioral scales, in pain assessment, 95
Behavioral treatments, in pain, in pediatric patients, 95–96
Benign pain, vs. cancer pain, analgesia in, 89
Benzamides, in opioid-induced emesis, 163t
Benzodiazepines, in phantom pain, 227
Beta blockers, in phantom pain, 227
Biofeedback, 119–121, 120f, 121t
    in phantom pain, 227
    vs. relaxation training, 120, 120f
    with relaxation training, 121, 121t, 122f
Biphosphonates
    as adjuvant analgesics, 168
    in cancer, 168
Bipolar neurons, 183f
Blebs, in herpes zoster, 210
Blood flow, postoperative pain effects on, 21–22, 23f
Body outlines method, in pain assessment, 29, 30f
Bombesin, in nociception, 20
Bone, atrophy of, acute see Reflex sympathetic dystrophy
Bone pain
    biphosphonates in, 168
    NSAIDs in, 159
    opioid resistance in, 169
Bone scan, in reflex sympathetic dystrophy, 202
Botulinum toxin, in myofascial pain syndrome, 151
Brachial plexus block, postoperative, 49–50, 49f–50f
Bradykinin, in nociception, 18–19
Brain
    electrical stimulation of
        in cancer pain, 106, 106f
        in failed back surgery syndrome, 108
        in phantom pain, 229
        in trigeminal neuralgia, 111
    neurons of, 181, 183, 183f–184f
    in neuropathic pain modulation, 190
Bretylium, in sympathetically mediated pain, 63
E-5-(2-Bromovinyl)-2'-deoxyuridine, in herpes zoster, 215
Buccal administration, of opioids, 167
Bupivacaine
    in cancer, 169
    in epidural analgesia, in pediatric patients, 100, 100t
    in fascia iliaca block, 99
    in herpes zoster, 216, 216f
    in interpleural analgesia, 48–49
    in intrathecal analgesia, 169
    in lower extremity block, 51
    in postherpetic neuralgia, 219
    in trigger point injection, 149
Buprenorphine
    in cancer, sublingual administration of, 167
    equianalgesic dose of, 162t
    pharmacokinetics of, 162t
    transmucosal administration of, 88
Bupropion, in depression, 237, 237t
Burning/lancinating pain
    in cancer, 157–158, 158f
    mechanisms of, 8–9, 9f
Buspirone, in headache, anxiety-induced, 235
Butorphanol, 162t

Caffeine withdrawal, headache in, 239
C-afferent neurons, in after-responses, 4–6, 4f–5f
Calcitonin, in phantom pain, 226–227
Calcitonin gene-related peptide, in nociception, 18f, 19–20
Calcium channel blockers
    in cluster headache, 233
    in neuropathic pain, 191
Cancer
    advanced, symptoms of, 157t
    mortality rate in, vs. site, 156t
Cancer pain, 156–178
    vs. benign pain, 89
    cancer-caused, 39
    classification of, 39–40
    epidemiology of, 156–157, 156t–157t
    idiopathic, 158
    neuropathic, 157–158, 158f
    nociceptive, 157
    physiopathology of, 157–158, 158f
    somatic, 157
    treatment of
        adjuvants in, 167–168, 167t
        analgesia in, vs. benign pain, 89
        assessment of, 159
        celiac plexus block in, 170, 171f–172f, 172
        cordotomy in, 172–174, 172f–173f
        intrathecal neurolytic block in, 66–68, 67f–69f
        neurolesive, 169–170, 169f–170f
        neurosurgical procedures in, 105–107, 105t, 106f–107f
        nonpharmacologic, 169–174, 169f–173f
        NSAIDs in, 159, 160t–161t, 161
        opioid resistance in, 168–169
        opioids in, 161–167, 162t–166t
        pharmacologic, 159–169, 160t–167t
        strategy for, 158, 158f
        subarachnoid neurolytic block in, 170, 171f
        trigeminal rhizotomy in, 174
    treatment-related, 39
    visceral, 157
Capsaicin
    in herpes zoster, 216
    in postherpetic neuralgia, 220
Carbamazepine
    as adjuvant analgesic, 82, 167t, 168
    in cancer, 167t, 168
    in causalgia, 205
    in neuropathic pain, 191
    in phantom pain, 227
    in postherpetic neuralgia, 219
Catabolism, postoperative, 21
Catheter
    axillary, 49–50, 49f
    in brachial plexus block, 49–50, 49f–50f
    in epidural analgesia
        in cancer pain, 105
        in pediatric patients, 99–100, 100t
    in femoral nerve block, 51
    infraclavicular, 49–50, 50f
    intercostal, 48, 48f

Catheter, *continued*
    interpleural, 48–49, 48f
    in intrathecal drug administration, 56–57
    in sciatic nerve block, 50–51, 50f
Caudal approach, in epidural analgesia, 99, 100t
Caudal block, in pediatric patients, 98
Causalgia
    with reflex sympathetic dystrophy, 205
    see also Reflex sympathetic dystrophy
Celiac plexus block
    in cancer, 170, 171f–172f, 172
    technique for, 69–71, 69f–71f
Central nervous system
    NSAID effects on, 159, 160t
    opioid effects on, 163
    see also Brain; Spinal cord
Central neurons
    anatomy of, 181, 183, 183f–184f
    response to injury, 188
Central pain, 24
Cervical traction, in pain management, 134, 135f
Chemical dorsal rhizotomy, 66–68, 67f–69f
Chemotherapy, neuropathic pain in, 189
Chloroform-aspirin, in herpes zoster, 216
Chlorpromazine
    in opioid-induced vomiting, 56
    in phantom pain, 227
Chlorprothixene, in postherpetic neuralgia, 219
Choline magnesium trisalicylate, in cancer, 160t
Chronic constrictive nerve injury, pain mechanisms in, 11–12, 12f
Chronic pain
    vs. acute pain, 39, 39t
    analgesia in *see* Analgesia
    in cancer, taxonomic classification of, 39–40
    coping with, cognitive approaches in, 123–124, 123f, 124t
    definition of, 38, 40
    description of, 38–39
    disability in, 40
    functional limitation in, 40
    headache *see* Headache
    impairment in, 40
    management of, 62–77
        acute pain treatment in, 62–65, 64f
        biofeedback in, 119–121, 120f, 121t, 122f, 227
        celiac plexus block in, 69–71, 69f–71f
        cognitive approaches in, 123–124, 123f, 124t
        differential nerve block in, 62
        epidural neurolytic block in, 68–69
        ganglion impar block in, 72–73, 73f
        group therapy in, 125
        hypnosis in, 122–123
        intrathecal neurolytic block in, 66–68, 67f–69f
        lumbar sympathetic block in, 75, 75f–76f
        neurolytic block in, 65–73, 65f–73f
        neurolytic solutions for, 65–66, 65f–66f
        neurosurgery in *see* Neurosurgical procedures
        operant approaches in, 125, 125f
        peripheral neurolytic block in, 66
        relaxation training in *see* Relaxation training

Chronic pain, management of, *continued*
        stellate ganglion block in, 73–75, 74f
        superior hypogastric plexus block in, 72, 72f–73f
    in phantom tissue *see* Phantom pain
    taxonomic classification of, 38, 40
        in cancer, 39–40
        multi-axis, 40, 41t–42t, 43
Clodronate
    as adjuvant analgesic, 168
    in cancer, 168
Clonazepam
    as adjuvant analgesic, 82, 167t
    in cancer, 167t
    in causalgia, 205
    in phantom pain, 227, 228t
Clonidine
    as adjuvant analgesic, 82, 168
    in cancer, 168
    in reflex sympathetic dystrophy, 198
    transdermal administration of, 87
Cluster headache, 232–234, 232f–233f
Cocaine, in cluster headache, 233
Codeine
    equianalgesic dose of, 162t
    pharmacokinetics of, 162t
Cognitive approaches, in pain management, 123–124, 123f, 124t
Colchicine, in neuropathic pain, 191
Cold, response to, in reflex sympathetic dystrophy, 199
Cold therapy, 132–133, 132f
    in herpes zoster, 216
    in myofascial pain syndrome, 145
    in postherpetic neuralgia, 220
    in trigger point treatment, 148, 148f–149f
Collagen, heat effects on, 131
Complement-enhanced neutralizing antibody assay, in herpes zoster, 214
Computed tomography
    in celiac plexus block, 71, 71f
    in hypogastric plexus block, 72, 72f–73f
Conduction blockade, in neuropathic pain, 191
Conjunctiva, cluster headache effects on, 232
Constipation, in opioid therapy, 161
Contraction, muscular, in myofascial pain syndrome, 143, 143f
Contraction-relaxation procedures, in myofascial pain syndrome, 147
Coping, with chronic pain, cognitive approaches in, 123–124, 123f, 124t
Cordotomy, in cancer pain, 106–107, 172–174, 172f–173f
Corticosteroids
    as adjuvant analgesics, 82, 167t, 168
    in cancer, 167t, 168, 167t, 168
    in cluster headache, 233
    in disk herniation, 65
    in herpes zoster, 215, 217
    in neuropathic pain, 191
    in postherpetic neuralgia, 219
Counterirritant theory, in cold therapy, 132
Cryocautery, in postherpetic neuralgia, 220
Cyclizine, in opioid-induced emesis, 163t
Cysapride, in opioid-induced emesis, 163t

Deafferentation pain
    dorsal-root-entry-zone lesion removal in, 107, 107f
    subtypes of, 24
Decadron, in herpes zoster, 216, 216f
Deep venous thrombosis, postoperative, 24
Demyelination
    neuronal dysfunction in, 188
    in postherpetic neuralgia, 218
Dendrites, 180f, 181
Depolarization, in slow temporal summation, 6
Depression
    coping strategies for, 124
    headache in, 235–237, 237t–238t
    perioperative, 26
    psychogenic pain in, 26
Desipramine
    in causalgia, 205
    in depression, 236, 237t
Dexamethasone
    as adjuvant analgesic, 167t, 168
    in cancer, 167t, 168
Dexmedetomidine, as adjuvant analgesic, 82
Dextropropoxyphene, with NSAIDs, 81, 81f
Diamorphine, in cancer, 164
Diathermy, 131–132, 131f
    in myofascial pain syndrome, 145
Diclofenac, 80
    in cancer, 160t
Diet, with monoamine oxidase inhibitors, 237, 238t
Dihydroergotamine, in cluster headache, 233
Dimethylsulfoxide, in postherpetic neuralgia, 220
Diphenhydramine, in opioid-induced pruritus, 56
Disability, in chronic pain, 40
Disk, intervertebral, herniation of, treatment of, 64–65
Distraction, in pediatric patients, 95–96
Dorsal horn, response to injury, neuropathic pain in, 189–190
Dorsal root ganglionectomy, in failed back surgery syndrome, 109–110
Dorsal root reflex, neuropathic pain in, 189
Dorsal-root-entry-zone lesion removal
    in cancer pain, 107, 107f
    in phantom pain, 228
Double pain phenomenon, 4–6, 4f–5f
Doxepin, in depression, 236, 237t
Dynorphins, 20
Dysesthesia
    definition of, 25
    description of, 24
    in herpes zoster, 210
    postcordotomy, 107
    in postherpetic neuralgia, 218
Dysesthetic pain, description of, 24

Edema
    chronic traumatic *see* Reflex sympathetic dystrophy
    pain and, 19
Education, on myofascial pain syndrome, 152
Electrical stimulation, 134–135, 136t

Electrical stimulation, *continued*
    in cancer pain, 106, 106f
    in failed back surgery syndrome, 107–108, 108f–109f
    in myofascial pain syndrome, 145–147, 146f
    in neuropathic pain, 192
    in phantom pain, 227, 229
    in trigeminal neuralgia, 111
    see also Transcutaneous electrical nerve stimulation
Electrodes, for TENS, 146, 146f
Electroencephalogram biofeedback, 119
Electromyography
    in biofeedback, 119–121, 120f, 121t, 227
    in myofascial pain syndrome, 143
Endorphins, in depression, 236
Enkephalins, 20
Enzyme-linked immunosorbent assay, in herpes zoster, 214
Ephapses, in neuropathic pain, 8
Epidural analgesia
    in cancer pain, 105–106, 165–167, 166t
    caudal approach to, 99, 100t
    in failed back surgery syndrome, 108
    lumbar approach to, 99, 100t
    patient-controlled, 87
    in pediatric patients, 99–100, 100t
    in phantom pain, 226–228
    postoperative, 51–54
        continuous infusion of, 54, 54f
        delivery techniques for, 53–54, 54f
        drugs for, 51–53, 52t, 53f
        efficacy of, 51–52
        outcome studies of, 55–56
        risks of, 55–56
    in reflex sympathetic dystrophy, 204
    thoracic approach to, 99–100, 100t
Epidural anesthesia, thoracic, cardiopulmonary effects of, 30–31
Epidural neurolytic block, 68–69, 170, 171f
Epinephrine, postoperative release of, 21
Ergotamine, in headache, 233, 239
Ethyl chloride, in postherpetic neuralgia, 220
Ethyl ether, in herpes zoster, 216
Etidronate
    as adjuvant analgesic, 168
    in cancer, 168
Evoked pain, 25
Exercise, 135–138, 137f
    in myofascial pain syndrome, 151–152, 151f–152f

Faces Rating Scale, in pain assessment, 29, 29f, 94
Failed back surgery syndrome, neurosurgical procedures in, 105t, 107–110, 108f–109f, 110t–111t
Faradic current stimulation, in myofascial pain syndrome, 145
Fascia, release of, 133–134
    in myofascial pain syndrome, 151
Fascia iliaca block, 98–99, 99f
Femoral cutaneous nerve block, 98–99, 99f
Femoral nerve block, 51, 98–99, 99f
Fentanyl in cancer

Fentanyl in cancer, *continued*
    spinal administration of, 166t
    transdermal administration of, 167
  in epidural analgesia
    in pediatric patients, 100, 100t
    postoperative, 52–54, 52t, 53f
  equianalgesic dose of, 162t
  inhalational administration of, 87
  pharmacokinetics of, 162t
  transdermal administration of, 87
  transmucosal administration of, 88
Flecainide, systemic use of, 82
Flexibility exercises, 137–138
Fluidotherapy, 131–132
Flunitrazepam, preoperative, 89
Fluorescent antibody to membrane antigen assay, in herpes zoster, 214
(2'-Fluoro-5-iodi-1-a-1)arabinosylcytosine, in herpes zoster, 215
Fluoroscopy, in celiac plexus block, 70–71, 71f
Fluoxetine, in depression, 236–237, 237t
Fluphenazine, in postherpetic neuralgia, 219
Flushing, in cluster headache, 232
Forced expiratory volume in 1 second, postoperative, 23, 23f
Friction massage, 133
Frustration
  perioperative, 26
  psychogenic pain in, 26
Functional limitation, in chronic pain, 40
Functional residual capacity, postoperative, 23, 23f

Galvanic current stimulation, in myofascial pain syndrome, 145
Gamma-aminobutyric acid receptors, in nociception modulation, 20
Ganglion, herpes zoster infection of, 212, 212f
Ganglion impar block, 72–73, 73f
Ganglionectomy, dorsal root, in failed back surgery syndrome, 109–110
Gangliosides, in neuropathic pain, 191–192, 192t
Gastrointestinal system
  epidural analgesia effects on, 31
  NSAID effects on, 159, 160t, 161
Gate control theory, in postherpetic neuralgia, 218
Geniculate ganglion, herpes zoster of, 212f
Glial cells, 183, 183f–184f
  injury of, 188
Glutamate
  antagonists to, in neuropathic pain, 11–12
  in nociception, 20
  in slow temporal summation, 6
Glycerol
  in neuropathic pain, 191
  in rhizolysis, 112, 112t–113t
GM1 ganglioside, in neuropathic pain, 11, 11f
Group therapy, in pain management, 125
Guanethidine
  in reflex sympathetic dystrophy, 204
  in sympathetically mediated pain, 63
Guided imagery, in pediatric patients, 95–96

Haloperidol, in opioid-induced emesis, 163t
Headache
  caffeine withdrawal, 239
  chronic, 232–241
    anxiety-induced, 235
    cluster, 232–234, 232f–233f
    depression-induced, 235–237, 237t–238t
    epidemiology of, 232
    tension-type, 234–235, 234f, 238–239
  migraine
    vs. cluster headache, 232, 233f
    with tension-type headache, 238–239
Heart, postoperative pain and, 21–23, 23f, 30–31
Heat therapy, 130–132, 131f
  in myofascial pain syndrome, 145
Herniation, intervertebral disk, treatment of, 64–65
Heroin
  equianalgesic dose of, 162t
  pharmacokinetics of, 162t
Herpes simplex virus infection, vs. herpes zoster, 214
Herpes zoster, 210–223
  clinical manifestations of, 210, 210t, 211f–212f
  complications of, 217–218
  differential diagnosis of, 214
  fatal, 217–218
  hematogenous dissemination of, 212
  immune response in, 213–214, 213f
  incidence of, 210
  laboratory diagnosis of, 214, 214t
  pathogenesis of, 210, 212, 212f
  pathophysiology of, 214–215
  postherpetic neuralgia in, 218–220, 219f–220f
  stages of, 210, 210t
  treatment of, 62, 215–217, 216f–217f
    with postherpetic neuralgia, 218–221, 219f–220f
  triggering factors in, 210
Histamine, in nociception, 18–19
Histamine desensitization, in cluster headache, 233–234
History, in pain assessment, 44–45
Horner's syndrome, in cluster headache, 232
Human immunodeficiency virus infection, herpes zoster in, 215, 217, 217f
Hydrocollator pack, 131
Hydromorphone
  in cancer, 164–165, 167
  in epidural analgesia, in pediatric patients, 100, 100t
  equianalgesic dose of, 162t
  pharmacokinetics of, 162t
Hydrotherapy, 132, 151, 151f
Hypalgesia, in reflex sympathetic dystrophy, 199
Hyperalgesia
  definition of, 25
  heat-induced, 8
  mechanisms of, 8
  primary, 5–7, 6f
  in reflex sympathetic dystrophy, 199, 200f
  secondary, 5–7, 6f
  thermal, treatment of, 11–12, 11f–12f
Hyperbaric technique, for intrathecal neurolytic block, 66, 69, 69f

Hyperesthesia
    definition of, 25
    in postherpetic neuralgia, 218
Hyperhidrosis, in reflex sympathetic dystrophy, 199, 199f
Hyperpathia, definition of, 25
Hypertension, postoperative, 21–22, 23f
Hypnosis, 121–123, 123t
    in phantom pain, 227
    in postherpetic neuralgia, 220
Hypobaric technique, for intrathecal neurolytic block, 66–68, 67f
Hypogastric plexus block, superior, 72, 72f–73f
Hypoxia, in myofascial pain syndrome, 143, 143f

Ibuprofen
    in cancer, 160t
    in pediatric patients, 96
Ice therapy, 132–133, 132f, 145
Idiopathic pain, in cancer, 158
Idoxuridine, in herpes zoster, 215
Iliohypogastric nerve block, 98
Ilioinguinal nerve block, 98
Imipramine
    as adjuvant analgesic, 167t
    in cancer, 167t
    in depression, 237, 237t
Immune response, in herpes zoster, 213–214, 213f
Immunodeficiency, herpes zoster in, 210, 213, 217, 217f
Immunoglobulin M, in herpes zoster, 213
Impairment, in chronic pain, 40
Implantable pump, for analgesia delivery, in cancer pain, 105–106
Impotence, in cordotomy, 174
Indomethacin
    in cancer, 160t
    in herpes zoster, 216
    in pediatric patients, 96
Infants see Pediatric patients
Inflammation
    in cancer pain, 157
    mediators of, 5–6
    of nerve roots, in disk herniation, 64–65
    pain in, vs. neuropathic pain, 8
Infraclavicular catheter, in brachial plexus block, 49–50, 50f
Inhalational administration, of analgesia, 87
Injection
    glycerol, in trigeminal neuralgia, 112, 112t–113t
    for nerve block see Nerve block; Neurolytic block
    of trigger points
        in myofascial pain syndrome, 149–151, 149f–150f, 150t
        in phantom pain, 227–228
Intercostal nerve block, postoperative, 48, 48f
Interferons, in herpes zoster, 215
International Association for the Study of Pain
    pain definition of, 38
    pain taxonomic classification of, 40, 41t–42t, 43
Interpleural analgesia, postoperative, 48–49, 48f
Intervertebral disk, herniation of, treatment of, 64–65
Intractable pain, neurosurgery in see Neurosurgical procedures
Intrathecal analgesia, postoperative, 51–54

Intrathecal analgesia, continued
    delivery techniques for, 53–54, 54f
    drugs for, 51–53, 52t, 53f
    efficacy of, 51–52
    outcome studies of, 55–57
    risks of, 55–56
Intrathecal neurolytic block, 66–68, 67f–69f, 170, 171f
Iontophoresis, in analgesia administration, 87
Irritability
    perioperative, 26
    psychogenic pain in, 26
Ischemia
    myocardial, postoperative, 22–23
    in myofascial pain syndrome, 143, 143f
    phantom pain in, 226
Ischemic compression technique, in trigger point treatment, 148
Isocarboxazid, in depression, 237
Isokinetic exercises, 137

Ketamine, as N-methyl-D-aspartate antagonist, 6
Ketoprofen, in cancer, 160t
Ketorolac, 80–81, 80f
    in cancer, 160t
    intramuscular administration of, 85
    in pediatric patients, 96
    preoperative, 89
    in sympathetically mediated pain, 63–64
    in trigger point injection, 149
Kidney
    NSAID effects on, 159, 160t, 161
    postoperative hypoperfusion of, 22
Kneading massage, 133
Knee, analgesia for, 51, 51f

Laboratory tests, in pain assessment, 45
Lacrimation, cluster headache effects on, 232
Lamm technique, for TENS, 146, 146f
Lancinating/burning pain
    in cancer, 8–9, 9f, 157–158, 158f
    mechanisms of, 8–9, 9f
Lechirche's posttraumatic pain syndrome see Reflex sympathetic dystrophy
Leukotrienes, in nociception, 19
Levator scapulae muscle, trigger point in, treatment of, 149f
Levorphanol, 162t
Lidocaine
    in cluster headache, 233
    in sympathetically mediated pain, 63
    systemic use of, 82
    topical gel, in herpes zoster, 216
    in trigger point injection, 149
Limb, phantom pain in see Phantom pain
Liposome encapsulation, in drug delivery, 89
Lithium carbonate, in cluster headache, 233
Liver, NSAID effects on, 160t
Local twitch response, in myofascial pain syndrome, 143
Loss of resistance technique

Loss of resistance technique, *continued*
    in intercostal block, 48, 48f
    in interpleural analgesia, 48, 48f
Lower extremity block, postoperative, 50–51, 50f–51f
LSD (lysergic acid diethylamide), in phantom pain, 227
Lumbar approach, in epidural analgesia, 99, 100t
Lumbar sympathetic block, 75, 75f–76f
Lung, postoperative pain effects on, 23–24, 23f
Lysergic acid diethylamide, in phantom pain, 227

M

McGill Pain Questionnaire, 28–29, 28f, 45
Macroglial cells, 184f
Manipulation, 134
Maprotiline, in depression, 237, 237t
Massage, 133, 133f
    ice, 132, 132f
    in myofascial pain syndrome, 147
Meperidine
    in cancer, 166t
    epidural
        in phantom pain, 228
        postoperative, 52, 52t
    preoperative, 89
Mesencephalotomy, in cancer pain, 106
Metabolism, postoperative, 21
Metastasis, to spine, neurosurgical procedures in, 105–107, 106f–107f
Metenkephalins, 20
Methadone
    in cancer, 164, 166t
    in epidural analgesia, postoperative, 52t
    equianalgesic dose of, 162t
    in pediatric patients, 96–97, 97t
    pharmacokinetics of, 162t
N-Methyl-D-aspartate, receptors for
    activation of, 6
    antagonists to, 5–6, 11–12, 11f–12f
    in neuropathic pain, 192
Methylprednisolone
    in herpes zoster, 215
    in postherpetic neuralgia, 219
Methysergide, in cluster headache, 233
Metoclopramide, in opioid-induced emesis, 163t
Mexiletine
    as adjuvant analgesic, 167t
    in cancer, 167t
    in causalgia, 205
    in phantom pain, 227, 228t
    systemic use of, 82
Microvascular decompression, in trigeminal neuralgia, 111
Microwave diathermy, 131–132
Midazolam, nasal administration of, 88
Midline myelotomy, in cancer pain, 106
Migraine headache
    vs. cluster headache, 232, 233f
    with tension-type headache, 238–239
Mineral supplements, in herpes zoster, 216
Miosis, in cluster headache, 232
MK-801, as N-methyl-D-aspartate antagonist, 7, 11, 11f

Monoamine oxidase inhibitors
    in coexisting migraine-tension headaches, 239
    in depression, 237, 238t
Moore technique, for celiac plexus block, 170, 171f–172f, 172
Morphine, 81
    in cancer
        oral, 161
        patient-controlled administration of, 164–165
        rectal administration of, 167
        spinal administration of, 165–167, 166t
        subcutaneous infusion of, 163–164, 164t
    in epidural analgesia
        in pediatric patients, 100, 100t
        postoperative, 51–52, 52t, 55–56
    equianalgesic dose of, 162t
    inhalational administration of, 87
    lipophilic derivatives of, 89
    mechanism of action of, 7, 20
    metabolism of, 85, 161, 163
    in pediatric patients, 96–97
    pharmacokinetics of, 162t
    slow/sustained-release, 85, 161
    subcutaneous infusion of, 85–86
    targeted delivery of, 89–90
Motor dysfunction, in reflex sympathetic dystrophy, 199
Mouth, analgesic absorption in, 88
Mucosal membranes, analgesia administration through, 88, 167
Mullan-Rosomoff technique, for cordotomy, 172–174, 172f–173f
Multiaxial Assessment of Pain taxonomy, 43
Multipolar neurons, 183f
Muscle(s), contraction of, in myofascial pain syndrome, 143, 143f
Muscle energy procedures, in myofascial pain syndrome, 147
Muscle relaxants
    as adjuvant analgesics, 167t, 168
    in cancer, 167t, 168
Myelography, in cordotomy, 172–173, 173f
Myelotomy, in cancer pain, 106
Myocardium, oxygen consumption of, postoperative, 22–23
Myofascial pain syndrome, 142–154
    clinical characteristics of, 142–143, 142f, 142t
    cold therapy in, 145
    diagnosis of, 142–143, 142t
    disorders associated with, 143–144
    education on, 152
    electrical stimulation in, 145–147, 146f
    exercise in, 151–152, 151f–152f
    heat therapy in, 145
    incidence of, 142
    massage in, 147
    muscle energy procedures in, 147
    myofascial release in, 151
    pathogenesis of, 143, 143f
    psychosocial aspects of, 144
    referred tenderness in, 143–144
    sleep disorders in, 144
    soft tissue mobilization in, 147–151, 148f–150f, 150t
    treatment of, 143–152
        active, 151–152, 151f–152f
        physical therapy in, 144–151, 146f, 148f–150f, 150t

Myofascial pain syndrome, *continued*
    trigger point therapy in, 147–151, 148f–150f, 150t
Myofascial release, 133–134, 151
Myotactic units, dysfunction of, in myofascial pain syndrome, 143
Mysoprostol, with NSAIDs, 159

Nail growth, excessive, in reflex sympathetic dystrophy, 199
Nalbuphine, 162t
Naloxone, in opioid-induced respiratory depression, 56
Naproxen, 80, 160t
Narcotics *see* Opioids
Nausea and vomiting
    in opioid therapy, 56, 161, 163, 163t
Nerve(s), injury of
    classification of, 186–187, 187f
    neuropathic pain in *see* Neuropathic pain
Nerve block
    caudal, 98
    fascia iliaca, 98–99, 99f
    femoral, 98–99, 99f
    femoral cutaneous, 98–99, 99f
    in herpes zoster, 216, 216f
    iliohypogastric, 98
    ilioinguinal, 98
    intercostal, 48, 48f
    in neuropathic pain, 191
    obturator, 98–99, 99f
    in pediatric patients, 98–100, 99f, 100t
    penile, 98
    in phantom pain, 227–228
    in postherpetic neuralgia, 219–220
    in reflex sympathetic dystrophy, 200–201, 201f
    in trigger point treatment, 150–151
Nerve roots
    anatomy of, 68f
    avulsion of, phantom pain in, 228
    inflammation of, in disk herniation, 64–65
    trigeminal, decompression of, 110–111
Neuralgia
    postherpetic, 215, 218–220, 219f–220f
        prevention of, 62
    posttraumatic spreading *see* Reflex sympathetic dystrophy
    trigeminal, neurosurgical procedures in, 105t, 110–113, 112t–113t
Neuroablation techniques, in phantom pain, 228
Neuroaugmentation, in phantom pain, 228–229
Neuroendocrine responses
    in acute pain, 21
    in postoperative pain, 21
Neurokinins
    in nociception, 18f, 19
    receptors for, activation of, 6
Neuroleptics, in phantom pain, 228t
Neurolytic block
    in cancer, 169–172, 169f–172f
    celiac plexus, 69–71, 69f–71f, 170, 171f–172f, 172
    dermatomes and, 65–66, 65f–66f
    epidural, 68–69
    ganglion impar, 72–73, 73f

Neurolytic block, *continued*
    intrathecal, 66–68, 67f–69f
    lumbar sympathetic, 75, 75f–76f
    peripheral, 66
    in postherpetic neuralgia, 219, 219f
    solutions for, 65–66, 65f–66f
    stellate ganglion, 73–75, 74f
    subarachnoid, 170, 171f
    superior hypogastric plexus, 72, 72f–73f
    temporary, before permanent block, 66
    test dose in, 70
Neuroma
    excision of, analgesia for, 57
    formation of, 187
    pain mechanisms in, 188–189
    phantom pain and, 226, 228
    sensitivity of, 7–8
Neurons
    afferent
        activation of, 18–20, 18f–19f
        in after-responses, 4–6, 4f
        alterations of, in reflex sympathetic dystrophy, 197
    anatomy of, 180f–184f, 181, 183
    C-afferent, in after-responses, 4–6, 4f–5f
    central, 181, 183, 183f–184f
        response to injury, 188
    classification of, 183, 183f
    conduction disorders of, neuropathic pain in, 188–189
    degeneration of, 187, 187f
    encoding disorders of, neuropathic pain in, 188
    functional components of, 183–186, 185f
    nociceptive
        in neuropathic pain, 7–9, 9f
        ongoing impulse discharge of, 9–11, 10f
        wide-dynamic-range, 2–4, 3f–4f, 9–11, 10f, 185–186
    peripheral, 180f–181f, 181
        in demyelinating diseases, 188
        response to injury, 186–187, 187f
    relay system lesions of, neuropathic pain in, 189
    response to injury, 186–188, 187f
    sympathetic, 181, 182f, 188
    wide-dynamic-range
        function of, 185–186
        in neuropathic pain, 9–11, 10f
        in pain radiation, 2–4, 3f–4f
Neuropathic pain, 180–194
    animal models of, 8, 10–11
    in cancer, 157–158, 158f
    characteristics of, 24–25
    in chemotherapy, 189
    classification of, 180
    definition of, 180
    demyelinating diseases and, 188
    dorsal horn circuitry deficiency in, 9–11, 10f
    higher brain centers and, 190
    vs. inflammatory pain, 8
    mechanisms of, 7–11, 9f–10f, 188–190
        neuronal response to injury in, 186–188, 187f
    modulation of, brain in, 190

Neuropathic pain, *continued*
    neuronal anatomy and, 180f–184f, 181, 183
    neuropathies associated with, 190, 190t
    neurotransmitter disorders and, 188
    nociceptive afferent impulse discharge in, 9–11, 10f
    vs. normal nociception, 183–186, 185f–186f
    opioid resistance in, 168–169
    postoperative, 24–25, 25f
    treatment of, 11–12, 11f–12f, 190–192, 192t
    types of, 24–25, 25f
Neuropathy, classification of, 190, 190t
Neurosurgical procedures, 104–115
    ablative, 104, 104t–105t
    anatomic, 104, 104t–105t
    augmentative, 104, 104t–105t
    in cancer pain, 105–107, 105t, 106f–107f
    dorsal-root-entry-zone lesion removal
        in cancer pain, 107, 107f
        in phantom pain, 228
    in failed back surgery syndrome, 105t, 107–110, 108f–109f, 110t–111t
    indications for, 104, 105t
    percutaneous cordotomy, in cancer, 172–174, 172f–173f
    in phantom pain, 228–229
    in trigeminal neuralgia, 105t, 110–113, 112t–113t
    types of, 104, 104t
    see also Neurolytic block; Rhizotomy; Sympathectomy
Neurotensin, in nociception modulation, 21
Neurotransmitters
    antidepressant drug effects on, 236
    disorders of, 188
    excitatory, 18–20, 18f
Nimodipine, in cluster headache, 233
Nociception
    in acute pain
        initiation of, 18–19, 18f
        modulation of, 20–21, 22f
        propagation of, 19–21, 19f
    in cancer pain, 157
    pathophysiology of, in herpes zoster, 214–215
    physiology of, 183–186, 185f–186f
    in postoperative pain, 24
        initiation of, 18–19, 18f
        modulation of, 20–21, 22f
        propagation of, 19–21, 19f
Nociceptive neurons
    in neuropathic pain, 7–9, 9f
    ongoing impulse discharge of, 9–11, 10f
    wide-dynamic-range, 2–4, 3f–4f, 9–11, 10f, 185–186
Nociceptors, interaction with sympathetic nervous system, in reflex sympathetic dystrophy, 198, 198f
Node of Ranvier, 180f–181f, 181
Nonsteroidal anti-inflammatory drugs, 80–81, 80f–81f
    in cancer, 159, 160t–161t, 161
    drug interactions of, 161t
    in headache, 239
    mechanism of action of, 159
    with opioids, 159
    in pediatric patients, 96

Nonsteroidal anti-inflammatory drugs, *continued*
    preoperative, 89
    side effects of, 159, 160t, 161
Norepinephrine
    antidepressant drug effects on, 236
    interaction with sympathetic nervous system, in reflex sympathetic dystrophy, 198, 198f
    release of
        in guanethidine therapy, 63
        postoperative, 21
    sensitivity to, in neuropathic pain, 7
Norpropoxyphene, 162t
Nortriptyline
    in causalgia, 205
    in depression, 236, 237t
Nose, analgesic absorption in, 88
NSAIDs *see* Nonsteroidal anti-inflammatory drugs
Nucleus pulposus, herniation of, treatment of, 64–65
Numerical rating score, in pain assessment, 29
Nutrition, in herpes zoster, 216

Objective pain scale, in pain assessment, 95, 95t
Obturator nerve block, 98–99, 99f
Odanterisin, in opioid-induced vomiting, 56
Oligodendrocytes, 184f
Operant approaches, in pain management, 125, 125f
Ophthalmic nerve, herpes zoster of, 211f
Opioids, 81
    bioavailability of, 161
    in cancer, 89, 161–167
        buccal administration of, 167
        intravenous administration of, 167
        with NSAIDs, 159
        oral, 161, 162t, 163, 163t
        patient-controlled administration of, 164–165
        rectal administration of, 167
        spinal administration of, 165–167, 166t
        subcutaneous infusion, 163–164, 164t
        sublingual administration of, 167
        transdermal administration of, 167
    continuous infusions of, 97, 97t
    endogenous, 20
        in TENS, 135
    in epidural analgesia, 165–167, 166t
        in pediatric patients, 100, 100t
    equianalgesic dose of, 162t
    excretion of, 162t
    half-life of, 162t
    intermittent boluses of, 96–97
    with interpleural analgesia, 49
    with NSAIDs, 81, 81f
    pain resistant to, 168–169
    in pediatric patients, 96–98, 97t
        patient-controlled administration of, 97–98
    in phantom pain, 227
    pharmacology of, in pediatric patients, 96
    in postherpetic neuralgia, 219
    postoperative

Opioids, postoperative, *continued*
    delivery techniques for, 53–54, 54f
    drugs for, 51–53, 52t, 53f
    efficacy of, 51–52
    epidural administration of, 51–57, 52t, 53f–54f
    outcome studies of, 55–57
  preoperative, 89
  receptors for, in nociception modulation, 20
  side effects of, 55–56, 161, 163, 163t
  targeted delivery of, 89–90
  tolerance to, 164
  see also specific drug eg, Morphine
Oral administration
  of analgesics, 85
  of opioids, 161, 162t, 163, 163t
Organelles, of neuron, 181, 181f
Orphenadrine
  as adjuvant analgesic, 167t
  in cancer, 167t
Osteoporosis, posttraumatic painful *see* Reflex sympathetic dystrophy
Oucher Scale, in pain assessment, 29, 29f, 94
Oxycodone
  in cancer, rectal administration of, 167
  equianalgesic dose of, 162t
  pharmacokinetics of, 162t
Oxygen therapy, in cluster headache, 233

Pain
  assessment of *see* Assessment
  definition of, 38
    taxonomic classification based on, 39
  mechanisms of, normal, 2–7, 3f–6f
  taxonomy of *see* Taxonomic classification
  see also Nociception
Pain intensity index, in McGill Pain Questionnaire, 28f, 29
Pain rating index, in McGill Pain Questionnaire, 28
Pain slide rule, in pain assessment, 94
Pain threshold, factors affecting, 38
Pamidronate
  as adjuvant analgesic, 168
  in cancer, 168
Pancreatic cancer, pain in, celiac plexus block in, 170, 171f–172f, 172
Paraffin wax bath, 131
Paravertebral ganglion, procedures on, in reflex sympathetic
  dystrophy, 203–204, 204f
Parent-controlled analgesia, in pediatric patients, 98
Paresthesia, in herpes zoster, 210
Paroxetine, in depression, 237, 237t
Patient-controlled analgesia, 85–87, 86f
  in cancer, 164–165
  epidural, 87
  as pain assessment tool, 26
  in pediatric patients, 96–98
  postoperative, 54
Pediatric patients, 94–102
  monitoring of, in drug treatment, 100
  pain in
    assessment of, 29–30, 29f–30f, 94–95, 95t

Pediatric patients, pain in, *continued*
    behavioral treatment of, 95–96
    epidural analgesia in, 99–100, 100t
    nonopioid drugs in, 96
    opioids in, 96–98, 97t
    patient-controlled analgesia in, 96–98
    physiologic cost of, 94
    regional analgesia in, 98–100, 99f, 100t
    treatment of, 95–100, 97t, 99f, 100t
Pelvic pain, superior hypogastric plexus block in, 72, 72f–73f
Penile block, 98
Pentazocine, 162t
Percutaneous cordotomy, in cancer pain, 106, 172–174, 172f–173f
Percutaneous radiofrequency facet denervation, in failed back
  surgery syndrome, 110, 110t–111t
Periaqueductal/periventricular gray stimulation, in cancer pain,
  106, 106f
Perineal pain
  ganglion impar block in, 72–73, 73f
  opioid resistance in, 168–169
  subarachnoid neurolytic block in, 170, 171f
Peripheral nerves
  neurolytic block of, 66
  stimulation of, in phantom pain, 229
Peripheral neurons
  anatomy of, 180f–181f, 181
  in demyelinating diseases, 188
  response to injury, 186–187, 187f
Phantom pain, 226–230
  clinical manifestations of, 226, 226f
  mechanisms of, 226
  treatment of, 50, 226–229, 228t
Phenelzine, in depression, 237
Phenol, in neurolytic block, 65
  celiac plexus, 70–71, 170
  epidural, 68–69
  intrathecal, 66, 69, 69f
  in postherpetic neuralgia, 219f
  subarachnoid, 170, 171f
Phenothiazines, in phantom pain, 227
Phenoxybenzamine, in reflex sympathetic dystrophy, 204
Phentolamine, in reflex sympathetic dystrophy, 198, 201, 202f, 204
Phenytoin
  as adjuvant analgesic, 167t
  in cancer, 167t
  in neuropathic pain, 191
  in postherpetic neuralgia, 219
Physical examination, in pain assessment, 45
Physical rehabilitation, 130–140
  approaches to, 130
  cold therapy in *see* Cold therapy
  diathermy in, 131–132, 131f, 145
  electrical stimulation in *see* Electrical stimulation; Transcutaneous
    electrical nerve stimulation
  exercise in, 135–138, 137f, 151–152, 151f–152f
  fluidotherapy in, 131–132
  goals of, 130
  heat therapy in, 130–132, 131f, 145
  hydrotherapy in, 132, 151, 151f

Physical rehabilitation, *continued*
    manipulation in, 134
    massage in, 133, 133f, 147
    in myofascial pain syndrome, 144–151, 146f, 148f–150f, 150t
    in phantom pain, 227
    rationale for, 130
    soft tissue mobilization in, 133–134, 147–151, 148f–150f, 150t
    traction in, 134, 134f–135f
    ultrasound in, 131–132, 145
Physiologic scales, in pain assessment, 95
Piroxicam, in cancer, 160t
Pleural space, analgesia infiltration in, 48–49, 48f
Pneumonia, postoperative, 23
Pneumothorax, in interpleural analgesia, 49
Poker chip tool, in pain assessment, 94
Postherpetic neuralgia, 215, 218–220, 219f–220f
    prevention of, 62
Postoperative pain, 18–35
    anger in, 26
    anxiety in, 26
    assessment of, 26–30, 27f, 28f
        in children, 29–30, 29f–30f
    cardiac function in, 23, 30–31
    characteristics of, 18
    classification of, 24
    depression in, 26
    frustration in, 26
    irritability in, 26
    management of, 30–32, 31f, 48–60, 89
        brachial plexus block in, 49–50, 49f–50f
        combined agents for, 30, 30f
        delivery techniques for, 53–54, 54f
        epidural analgesia in, 51–56, 52t, 53f–54f
        intercostal nerve block in, 48, 48f
        interpleural analgesia in, 48–49, 48f
    traspinal opioids in, 52–54, 52t, 53f–54f, 56–57
        intrathecal analgesia in, 51–57, 52t, 53f–54f
        lower extremity block in, 50–51, 50f–51f
        outcome studies of, 55–57
        peripheral nerve blocks in, 57
        preemptive analgesia in, 54
        premedication in, 89
    neuroendocrine responses in, 21
    neuropathic pain in, 24–25, 25f
    nociception in, 24
        initiation of, 18–19, 18f
        modulation of, 20–21, 22f
        propagation of, 19–21, 19f
    peripheral vascular system function in, 24
    psychogenic pain in, 25–26
    pulmonary function in, 23–24, 23f, 31, 31f
    sympathoadrenal responses in, 21–22, 23f
    vital organs affected by, 23–24, 23f
Posttraumatic pain syndrome *see* Reflex sympathetic dystrophy
Prazosin, in reflex sympathetic dystrophy, 204
Prednisone, in herpes zoster, 215, 217
Preemptive analgesia, postoperative, 54
Premedication, for postoperative pain, 89
Procaine, in postherpetic neuralgia, 219

Procaine, *continued*
    in trigger point injection, 149
Proclorperazine, in opioid-induced emesis, 163t
Propoxyphene, 162t
Propranolol, in coexisting migraine-tension headaches, 239
Propriospinal connections, in pain radiation, 2–3, 3f
Prostaglandins, in nociception, 19
Protein C kinase inhibitors, in neuropathic pain, 11–12, 12f
Protriptyline, in depression, 236, 237t
Pruritus, from opioids, 56
Psoas compartment block, in trigger point treatment, 151
Psychogenic pain, postoperative, 25–26
Psychological aspects
    of headache
        anxiety-induced, 235
        depression-induced, 235–236
        tension-type, 235
    of myofascial pain syndrome, 144
    of reflex sympathetic dystrophy, 199
Psychological data, in pain assessment, 44
Psychological techniques, 118–127
    biofeedback, 119–121, 120f, 121t
        in phantom pain, 227
    cognitive approaches, 123–124, 123f, 124t
    group therapy, 125
    hypnosis, 121–123, 123t
        in phantom pain, 227
        in postherpetic neuralgia, 220
    operant approaches, 125, 125f
        in phantom pain, 227
        in postherpetic neuralgia, 220
    relaxation training, 119–121, 120f, 121t, 138
        heat therapy in, 131
        in phantom pain, 227
    types of, 118, 118t
Psychosocial factors, in pain assessment, 45
Ptosis, in cluster headache, 232
Pulmonary embolism, postoperative, 24
Pulmonary function, postoperative pain and, 23–24, 23f, 31, 31f
Pulvinar, selective lesioning of, in cancer pain, 106–107
Pump, implantable, for analgesia delivery, in cancer pain, 105–106

Questionnaires, in pain assessment, 44–45

Racz technique, for stellate ganglion block, 74f, 75
Radiation, of pain, 2–4, 3f–4f
Radicular pain
    in disk herniation, 64–65
    electrical stimulation in, 108, 108f–109f
Radiofrequency cordotomy, percutaneous, in cancer pain, 106
Radiofrequency facet denervation, in failed back surgery syndrome, 110, 110t–111t
Radiofrequency retrogasserian rhizotomy, in trigeminal neuralgia, 111–112
Radioimmunoassay, in herpes zoster, 214
Ramsay-Hunt syndrome, 211f
Range-of-motion exercises, 136–137

Ranvier, node of, 180f–181f, 181
Receptive fields, expansion of, 5
Receptors
    adenosine, in nociception modulation, 21, 22f
    adrenergic, in nociception modulation, 20–21
    gamma-aminobutyric acid, in nociception modulation, 20
    N-methyl-D-aspartate
        activation of, 6
        antagonists to, 5–6
        in neuropathic pain, 11–12, 11f–12f, 192
    neurokinin, activation of, 6
    opioid, in nociception modulation, 20
Rectal administration
    of analgesia, 88, 167
    of opioids, 167
Referred pain
    in myofascial pain syndrome, 143–144
    from viscera, 24
Reflex sympathetic dystrophy, 196–207
    acute phase of, 200, 200f
    animal models for, 198–199
    atrophic phase of, 200, 200f
    causalgia with, 205
    classification of, 197
    clinical features of, 199–200, 199f
    definition of, 196
    diagnosis of, 200–202, 201f–202f
    dystrophic phase of, 200
    historical perspective of, 196
    management of, 62–64, 54f, 202–205, 203f–204f
        brachial plexus block in, 50
        lumbar sympathetic block in, 75, 75f–76f
        stellate ganglion block in, 73–75, 74f
    onset of, after injury, 200
    pain mechanisms in, 8–9
    pathophysiology of, 197–199, 198f
    stages of, 200, 200f
    vs. sympathetically independent pain, 196
    synonyms for, 196, 196t
    terminology of, 196–197
Regional analgesia
    in pediatric patients, 98–100, 99f, 100t
    see also Epidural analgesia; Nerve block
Regional anesthesia
    pulmonary effects of, 31
    in reflex sympathetic dystrophy, 204
Rehabilitation, physical see Physical rehabilitation
Relaxation training, 119–120, 138
    vs. biofeedback, 120, 120f
    with biofeedback, protocol for, 121, 121t, 122f
    heat therapy in, 131
    in phantom pain, 227
Relaxation-contraction procedures, in myofascial pain
    syndrome, 147
Respiration, monitoring of, in pain management, 100
Respiratory depression, from opioids, 55–56
Retrocrural celiac plexus block, 170, 171f–172f, 172
Retrogasserian rhizotomy, in trigeminal neuralgia, 111–112

Retrograde axoplasmic transport, in neuropathic pain, 191
Rhinorrhea, cluster headache effects on, 232
Rhizotomy
    in cancer pain, 106–107, 170, 171f
    chemical, 66–68, 67f–69f, 170, 171f
    in failed back surgery syndrome, 109
    in postherpetic neuralgia, 220
    retrogasserian, in trigeminal neuralgia, 111–112
    trigeminal
        in cancer, 174
        in cluster headache, 234
        in neuralgia, 111

Sarcomeres, shortening of, in myofascial pain syndrome,
    143, 143f
Savedra body outlines method, in pain assessment, 29, 30f
Sciatic nerve, herpes zoster of, 211f
Sciatic nerve block, postoperative, 50–51, 50f
Sciatica, in disk herniation, 64–65
Scopolamine, in opioid-induced vomiting, 56
Second pain, in painful stimulation, 4–6, 4f–5f
Serotonin
    antidepressant drug effects on, 236
    in nociception, 18, 21
Sertraline, in depression, 237, 237t
Sexual dysfunction, in cordotomy, 174
Shingles see Herpes zoster
Short-wave diathermy, 131–132, 131f
Shoulder-hand syndrome see Reflex sympathetic dystrophy
Skin lesions, in herpes zoster, 210, 211f–212f, 216f, 217–218
Skin temperature biofeedback, 119, 121, 122f
Slant board, in myofascial pain syndrome, 151–152, 152f
Sleep disorders
    in depression, 236
    in myofascial pain syndrome, 144
Slow temporal summation, in painful stimulation, 4–6, 5f, 8–9, 9f
Soft tissue mobilization, 133–134
    in myofascial pain syndrome, 147–151, 148f–150f, 150t
Soma, of neuron, 181, 181f
Somatic fibers, interaction with sympathetic nervous system, in reflex
    sympathetic dystrophy, 198, 198f
Somatic pain
    in cancer, 157
    postoperative, 24
Somatostatin, in nociception, 20, 21
Spinal administration, of opioids, 165–167, 166t
Spinal cord
    alterations of
        in cancer pain, 106–107
        in reflex sympathetic dystrophy, 197–198
    analgesia toxicity to, 57
    dorsal horn circuitry deficiency in, 9–11, 10f
    electrical stimulation of, in failed back surgery syndrome, 107–108,
        108f–109f
    neurons of, 181, 183–184, 183f–184f
    nociceptive pathways in, 184, 186f
    opioid receptors in, 20

Spinal cord, *continued*
    pain pathways in
        interruption of, in cancer, 172–174, 172f–173f
        spatial dispersion and, 2–4, 3f–4f
    stimulation of, in phantom pain, 229
Spine
    metastasis to, neurosurgical procedures in, 105–107, 106f–107f
    traction on, in pain management, 134, 134f–135f
Spotting electrodes, in TENS, 146, 146f
Spray, vapocoolant, 133, 148, 148f–149f
Stellate ganglion block, 73–75, 74f
    in reflex sympathetic dystrophy, 203–204, 203f
Stereotactic surgery, in cancer pain
    mesencephalotomy, 106
    thalamotomy, 106–107
Stomach, NSAID effects on, 159
Strengthening exercises, 137
Stress, in postherpetic neuralgia, 220
Stretch and spray technique, in trigger point treatment, 148, 148f–149f
Stretching exercises, 137, 127f
    in myofascial pain syndrome, 151
Stroking massage, 133, 133f
Stump pain *see* Phantom pain
Subarachnoid analgesia
    in cancer, 165–167, 166t
    postoperative, 56–57
Subarachnoid neurolytic block, in cancer, 170, 171f
Subcutaneous infusion
    of analgesia, 85–86
    of morphine, 163–164, 164t
Sublingual administration, of opioids, 167
Substance P
    inhibition of
        adrenergic agonists in, 21
        gamma-aminobutyric acid in, 20
        opioids in, 20
    in nociception, 18f, 19–20
    in slow temporal summation, 6
Sudeck's atrophy *see* Reflex sympathetic dystrophy
Sufentanil
    in epidural analgesia, 52t, 53
    nasal administration of, 88
Sumatriptan, in headache, 233, 239
Superior hypogastric plexus block, 72, 72f–73f
Sweating, increased, in reflex sympathetic dystrophy, 199, 199f
Swimming pool therapy, 132
Sympathalgia *see* Reflex sympathetic dystrophy
Sympathectomy
    in phantom pain, 228
    in reflex sympathetic dystrophy, 204–205, 204f
Sympathetic block
    in herpes zoster, 62
    in phantom pain, 227, 229
    in postherpetic neuralgia, 219
    in reflex sympathetic dystrophy, 200–201, 201f, 203–205, 203f–204f
    in sympathetically mediated pain, 62–63
Sympathetic nervous system, interaction with somatic fibers, in reflex sympathetic dystrophy, 198, 198f

Sympathetic neurons
    anatomy of, 181, 182f
    response to injury, 188
Sympathetically independent pain, vs. reflex sympathetic dystrophy, 196
Sympathetically maintained pain, 24, 25f
Sympathetically mediated pain
    mechanism of, 64, 64f
    treatment of, 62–64, 64f
Sympathoadrenal responses
    in acute pain, 21–22, 23f
    in postoperative pain, 21–22, 23f

T lymphocytes, in herpes zoster, 213
Taxonomic classification, of pain, 38
    in cancer, 39–40
    cause-based, 42t
    definition-based, 39
    intensity-based, 42t
    multi-axis, 40, 41t–42t, 43
    postoperative, 24–26, 25f
    region-based, 41t
    system-based, 41t
    temporal characteristic-based, 42t
Tender Point Map, 150, 150f
Tenderness, referred, in myofascial pain syndrome, 143–144
TENS *see* Transcutaneous electrical nerve stimulation
Tension-type headache, 234–235, 234f, 238–239
    with migraine, 238–239
Terazosin, in reflex sympathetic dystrophy, 204
Thalamotomy, in cancer pain, 106–107
Therapeutic window, 83–84
Thermography, in reflex sympathetic dystrophy, 201–202, 203f
Thiocholchicosides
    as adjuvant analgesic, 167t
    in cancer, 167t
Thoracic epidural analgesia, 99–100, 100t
Thoracic epidural anesthesia, cardiopulmonary effects of, 30–31
Thrombosis, deep venous, postoperative, 24
Tocainamide
    as adjuvant analgesic, 168
    in cancer, 168
Traction, in pain management, 134, 134f–135f
Tramadol, 81
Tranquilizers, in herpes zoster, 216
Transcutaneous electrical nerve stimulation, 134–135, 136t
    in myofascial pain syndrome, 145–147, 146f
    in phantom pain, 227
    in postherpetic neuralgia, 220
    in reflex sympathetic dystrophy, 204–205
Transdermal administration
    of analgesia, 87, 87t, 167
    of opioids, 167
Transmucosal administration, of analgesia, 88, 167
Trapezius muscle, trigger point in, treatment of, 149f
Trauma
    neuronal response to, 186–188, 187f
    pain management in, 205

Traumatic dystrophy, major and minor *see* Reflex
   sympathetic dystrophy
Traumatic edema, chronic *see* Reflex sympathetic dystrophy
Traumatic vasospasm *see* Reflex sympathetic dystrophy
Trazodone, in depression, 236, 237t
Triamcinolone
   in herpes zoster, 216
   in postherpetic neuralgia, 219
Tricyclic antidepressants
   as adjuvant analgesics, 167t, 168
   in cancer, 167t, 168
   in causalgia, 205
   in headache, 236–237, 237t, 239
   in herpes zoster, 216
   in myofascial pain syndrome, 144
   in neuropathic pain, 191
   in phantom pain, 227
   in postherpetic neuralgia, 219
Triflupromazine, preoperative, 89
Trigeminal ganglion, procedures on, in cluster headache, 234
Trigeminal nerve, neurolysis of, in trigeminal neuralgia, 111–112
Trigeminal nerve root, resection of, in cluster headache, 234
Trigeminal neuralgia, neurosurgical procedures in, 105t, 110–113,
   112t–113t
Trigeminal rhizotomy, in cancer, 174
Trigger points
   active, 148
   definition of, 142
   electrical stimulation of, 146–147, 146f
   injection of
      in myofascial pain syndrome, 149–151, 149f–150f, 150t
      in phantom pain, 227–228
   multiple, 150
   palpation of, 142, 142f
   pathophysiology of, 143, 143f
   physical therapy for, 147–148, 148f–149f
Trimipramine, in depression, 236, 237t

Ultrasound, 131–132
   in myofascial pain syndrome, 145
Unipolar neurons, 183f
Urinary retention, from opioids, 56

Valproate
   as adjuvant analgesic, 82, 167t
   in cancer, 167t
   in postherpetic neuralgia, 219
Vapocoolant spray, 133
   in trigger point treatment, 148, 148f–149f
Varicella, herpes zoster and, 210, 212–213
Varicosities, of sympathetic neurons, 181, 182f
Vascular resistance, postoperative, 22
Vascular system, postoperative pain effects on, 24
Vasomotor disorder, posttraumatic *see* Reflex sympathetic dystrophy
Vasospasm, traumatic *see* Reflex sympathetic dystrophy
Verapamil, in cluster headache, 233
Verbal pain scales, in pain assessment, 27–28
Vesicles, in herpes zoster, 210, 211f
Vibration therapy, in postherpetic neuralgia, 220
Vidarabine, in herpes zoster, 215
Vincristine, in neuropathic pain, 191
Virchow's triad, postoperative, 24
Visceral pain
   in cancer, 157
   postoperative, 24
   referral of, 24
Visual Analogue Scale, in pain assessment, 26–27, 27f, 29,
   44–45, 94
Vital capacity, postoperative, 23–24, 23f
Vital signs, in pain assessment, 44
Vitamins, in herpes zoster, 216

Wallerian degeneration, 187f
Ways of Coping Scale, 124
Whirlpool bath, 132
Wide-dynamic-range neurons
   function of, 185–186
   in neuropathic pain, 9–11, 10f
   in pain radiation, 2–4, 3f–4f

ZUNI slant board, in myofascial pain syndrome, 151–152, 152f